INTIMATE RELATIONSHIPS, MARRIAGE, AND FAMILY

SECOND
EDITION

INTIMATE RELATIONSHIPS, MARRIAGE, AND FAMILY

James C. Coleman

Professor Emeritus
University of California, Los Angeles

Macmillan Publishing Company
New York

Macmillan Publishing Company
866 Third Avenue, New York, New York 10022

Collier Macmillan Canada, Inc.

Library of Congress Cataloging-in-Publication Data

Coleman, James C. (James Covington)
    Intimate relationships, marriage, and family.

    Bibliography: p.
    Includes index.
    1. Marriage.   2. Family.   3. Intimacy (Psychology)
I. Title.
HQ734.C596 1988   306.8′1   87-24007
ISBN 0-02-323530-6

Printing: 6 7   Year: 1 2 3 4

Photo research and permissions: PAR/NYC, John Schultz.

ISBN 0-02-323530-6

Dedication

This text is dedicated with the greatest respect and appreciation to Joseph A. Gengerelli—Professor of Psychology Emeritus at UCLA—whose scholarship, wisdom, and dedication "made a difference" for the better in the lives of four generations of students, including that of the author.

PREFACE

It seems only a short time since 1984, when the first edition of this book was published. But during these years, rapid and accelerating technological and social change have continued to erode the traditional values and patterns that formerly guided our lives. As a result, our marital, family, and other intimate relationships are engulfed in a tidal wave of change. Value conflicts and confusion seem to be the order of the day as we try to sort things out and achieve a meaningful way of life.

Amid this conflict and confusion, however, a new trend has emerged. This is the increasing emphasis on intimate relationships. During the early 1980s, this new orientation began to make its presence felt. By the mid-1980s, it was a clear-cut trend as people turned to intimate relationships as the primary source of personal happiness and a refuge from the impersonal, often hostile, world surrounding them. As a consequence, the 1980s have been called the We Decade —in contrast to the Me Decade of the 1970s, when people mainly pursued their personal desires and goals. Certainly, a key theme of the 1980s is the "search for intimacy."

CONTENT SELECTION AND PRESENTATION

In both writing and revising a text in the complex and changing field of marriage and intimate relationships, I have faced the task of selecting content that is relevant to the needs of today's students and will stand the test of time. In the first edition, the scarcity of research findings made this difficult. In this edition, the abundance of new information made selection perhaps more difficult in the sheer number of articles to be evaluated. You might say that this revision took me from "rags to riches" in terms of available research studies. Even so, I still found many topics— such as romantic love—underrepresented and that many research findings raised more questions than they answered—a not uncommon event in science. In any event, many relevant studies had to be omitted because the space in our book is inadequate to include them.

A second task I faced was to present content in a way that made it meaningful and useful to students—who represent a heterogeneous group in terms of age, experience, and life goals. To accomplish this, I have used such special aids as clinical case material, enduring issues that are intended to be both informative and thought provoking, and quotes from literature and drama that provide poignant examples of love, despair, and other experiences that are truly meaningful— especially to those of us who have "been there."

Throughout, I have placed strong emphasis on "getting to where the student is," on student involvement in the learning process, and on encouraging students to extend and enrich their learning. The following objectives also receive special attention:

1. Helping students to realize that sociology and psychology provide scientific information that goes far beyond the popular beliefs—often erroneous—that many people rely on in choosing a mate and building intimate relationships.

2. Helping students to learn more about intimate relationships and to clarify their own views and values as a basis for deciding on the type of marriage or other intimate relationships best suited to them.

3. Helping students to improve their interpersonal competence in such areas as communication, self-disclosure, and conflict resolution that are essential for building and maintaining intimate relationships.

4. Helping students to develop awareness—a realistic view of themselves, their partners, and their relationships—and to prepare for transitions and "booby traps" likely to be encountered in marriage and other intimate relationships.

5. Helping students to distinguish between opinions, value judgments, and scientific findings, and to realize that the latter provide the soundest basis for both theory and practical applications.

Overall, this new edition focuses on the concepts and methods involved in initiating, building, maintaining, and enriching intimate relationships, as well as terminating relationships and building new ones if it should become necessary to do so. Strong emphasis has also been placed on social-exchange theory, symbolic-interaction theory, and general-systems theory in conceptualizing and dealing with problems in intimate relationships.

CHANGES

This second edition of *Intimate Relationships, Marriage, and Family* has been shortened from 17 to 14 chapters. No relevant material is omitted, but the content of three original chapters is now integrated with that in other chapters.

Specifically, the material on single-parent families is combined with the chapter on separation and divorce to form a new chapter entitled "Separation, Divorce, and Single-Parent Families." The material on stepfamilies is combined with the chapter on rebuilding and remarriage to form a new chapter entitled "Rebuilding, Remarriage, and Stepfamilies." The chapter on passages has been combined with the chapter on marital conflicts to create a new chapter entitled "Marital Conflict, Coping, and Change," which still covers such topics as the midlife crisis, the retirement marriage, and bereavement and remarriage. Finally, the relevant material on sex-roles has been integrated in Chapter 1, where it receives greater emphasis as a key factor underlying the nature and quality of man–woman relationships and serves as an important reference point for the chapters that follow.

All chapters have been extensively updated and rewritten. Of particular importance here are the chapters that focus on the difficult transformation from an industrial age to an information age that constitutes the social setting in which contemporary marriages in our society form and function: the chapter on brief encounters that can, for a few minutes or hours, enrich our lives and provide the raw materials out of which intimate relationships are built; the chapter on sexual values and behavior, which emphasizes informed and fulfilling sexuality as well as sexually transmitted diseases (STDs), including AIDS; and the chapter on love, which addresses the crucial question of whether romantic love is an illusion or a higher realm of human experience that can endure under certain conditions.

Major changes also appear in the chapters on dual-career marriages; the challenge of children; divorce and single-parent families; and rebuilding, remarriage, and stepfamilies. The incidence and importance of these topics require that each receive intensive coverage. Although it is risky to deal with the future in a rapidly changing society such as ours, the final chapter on marriage and intimate relationships in the early 21st century attempts to broaden our perspective concerning the options and choices with which most of us will probably be faced.

The preceding changes provide for better integration of text material, more intensive coverage of specific topics, and greater interest and readability. A comprehensive glossary—literally a minidictionary—has also been included to assist the student and to clarify and enrich the material in this new edition.

ORGANIZATION

The organization of material in five parts remains the same as in the first edition.

Part I contains the introduction and focuses on changing sex-roles and man–woman relationships, the transition in marriage and family patterns, and the methods of social-science research. Part II deals with the course of events as we progress from encounters to intimate relationships. Included here are such topics as communication, self-disclosure, ground rules, conflict resolution, awareness, caring, trust, and commitment. The final section also contains chapters on the challenging topics of sexual values and behavior and of love and romance.

Part III covers marriage and alternative patterns, such as singlehood and cohabitation. The material on marriage includes mate selection, the transition from singlehood to marriage, marital relationships and enrichment, dual-career marriages, the challenge of children, marital conflicts, and typical changes in marital relationships over time. Part IV focuses on the termination of marriage and intimate relationships and on starting over. Part V delineates several possible scenarios concerning marriage and intimate relationships in the early 21st century.

Finally, the Appendices add substantially to the content coverage. Appendix A describes the anatomy and physiology of the sexual response; Appendix B deals with prenatal development and childbirth; and Appendix C, revised by Professor Molly Weiss of Arizona State University, covers the common problems associated with finances and the family.

SPECIAL ACKNOWLEDGMENTS

As in the first edition, I have been greatly helped in this new edition by the many scientists whose research findings and writings provide the essential basis for a book such as this. I would like to thank my colleagues, who used and evaluated the first edition of this text and offered comments and suggestions for improving this second edition. In particular, I would like to thank Morris L. Medley, Professor of Sociology at Indiana State University, for many constructive criticisms and suggestions that have added so much to this new edition.

On a more general level, I would like to thank the many pioneers in the social sciences who have influenced my thinking and research as well as the direction of my writing. Included here are Jesse Bernard, Harold Kelley, David Mace, Margaret Mead, Karl Menninger, Lois Murphy, Carl Rogers, B. F. Skinner, and Virginia Satir. There are, of course, many others who have contributed to our hard-won advances in psychology, sociology, and related fields of science.

My personal thanks go to Dr. Milton Mohr, president of Quotron Systems, whose enduring friendship and stimulating discussions of computer technology and world events have contributed so much to the author; to Edward Cornish, president of the World Future Society, to whom the author is indebted for encouragement and creative ideas; to John Heiken, M.D., and Donna Rozella, R.N., of the Malibu Medical Group for sharing insights into the medical aspects of marriage and divorce; to my nephew, Ronald James Kinsling, for sharing with me, as an attorney, his extensive knowledge concerning the legal consequences of divorce; to Professor Andrew Comrey of UCLA and Barbara Comrey, both marriage and divorce therapists, for their friendship, encouragement, and thought-provoking ideas; and to the many students who have taken the time to read and comment on this new addition. My personal thanks also go to Murray Curtin for his friendship, assistance, and wise counseling; and to D. Anthony English, Editor-in-Chief of the Macmillan Publishing Company, for his continued support and personal guidance of this revision at each stage of the publishing process. In addition, my thanks go to Janice Marie Johnson for her efficiency and patience as Production Supervisor, and to the other members of the Macmillan team.

Finally, my special thanks and deepest gratitude go to my wife, Azalea, who has contributed so much to the successful completion of this second edition.

CONCLUSION

In concluding this preface, it seems appropriate to paraphrase a statement by John F. Kennedy, former President of the United States.

> Our country will not be judged by the riches it has accumulated, the technological advances it has achieved, or the wars it has won, but by its contribution to the human spirit.

Translated into the realm of marriage and intimate relationships, it might be said that a marriage will not be judged by the affluence of a dual-career couple; by the state-of-the-art computers, hi-fi equipment, or other gadgets the couple has accumulated; or by the number of conflicts they have or have not resolved; but by the personal growth, happiness, and spiritual fulfillment achieved in their marital relationship. Just as a country is a reflection of the inner life of its inhabitants, so a marital relationship is a reflection of the inner life of its marital partners.

J. C. C.

BRIEF CONTENTS

IV

V

DETAILED CONTENTS

I

II

III

MARRIAGE AND ALTERNATIVE PATTERNS 173

IV

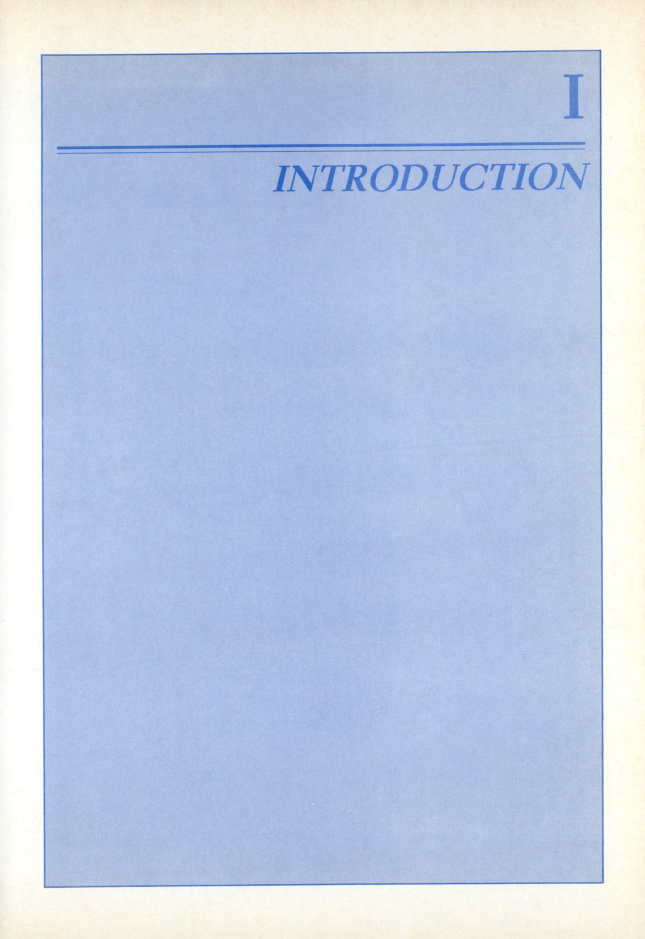

I

INTRODUCTION

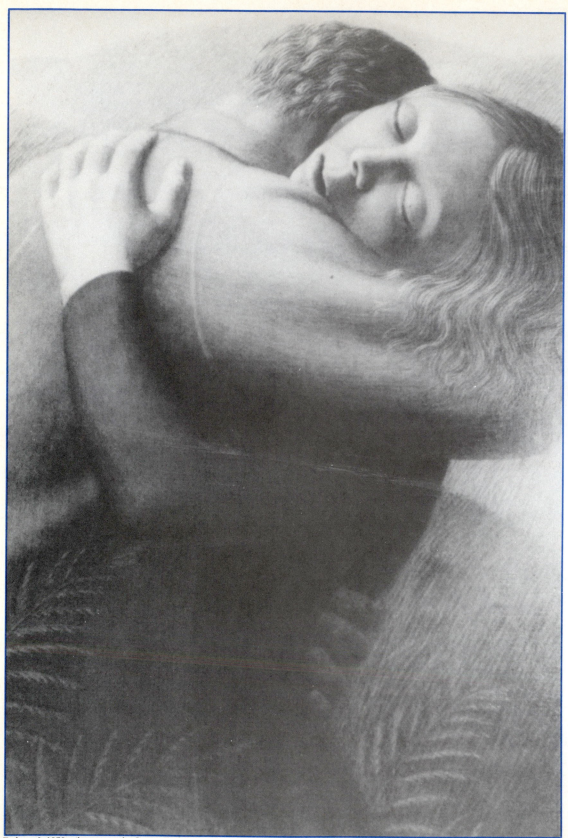

Embrace I, 1979, oil on canvas by George Tooker. Reproduced by kind permission of the artist and Marisa del Rey Gallery, New York

MARRIAGE AND FAMILY AS WE APPROACH THE 21ST CENTURY

The future is not some place we are going, but one we are creating. The paths to it are not found but made, and the activity of making them changes both the maker and the destination.

—Schaar (1974, p. 1)

———————————— ⌒ ————————————

*E*ven though marriage and family patterns vary from one society to another and from one historical period to another, these two institutions have been the basic units of society throughout recorded history. In fact, it has been suggested that no society can survive the deterioration of marriage and family life.

Today, however, we are faced with drastic changes in marriage and family relationships, changes with which most of us are ill-prepared to cope. Although we place great value on marriage and family—more than 90 percent of Americans will marry at some time in their lives and most married couples will have at least one child—we have the highest divorce rate of any country in the world. No other major enterprise is entered into with such high hopes and yet fails so regularly. This failure leaves emotional scars on parents and children alike.

Our marital failures are ironically occurring at a time of increasing emphasis on intimate relationships. In the 1950s, young people expected to find happiness by fulfilling their role in society (for example, by being an excellent lawyer or secretary). But happiness eluded them, and, in the 1960s, many of these young people rebelled against the "Establishment." In the 1970s—the "Me Decade"—they shifted their emphasis to achieving personally defined goals. Again they failed to find happiness. In the 1980s—the "We Decade"— they have shifted their emphasis to intimate relationships. But happiness is still proving elusive, in large part because of the lack of needed information and interpersonal skills.

Consequently, this text is directed toward helping readers learn more about marriage and family relationships, become aware of the "booby traps" that may lie in wait for them, improve their communication and other interpersonal skills, and think about what they value and want in their marriage and other intimate relationships. Achieving these objectives will, in turn, foster personal growth and help readers to analyze and improve on their current relationships or to build new and fulfilling ones.

Initially in this chapter, we shall comment on the social setting of contemporary married and family life. Then we shall note some of the profound changes taking place in marriage and the family and question whether these institutions are disintegrating. Finally, we shall summarize scientific approaches to studying marriage and intimate relationships and elaborate briefly on the orientation of this text.

THE SOCIAL CONTEXT: A CHANGING AND TROUBLED WORLD

Marriages and families do not exist in a vacuum. They are strongly influenced by the social context in which they function. In describing this social context, our

Tom Kelly

discussion will be both brief and limited. And, for present purposes, our focus will be on rapid and accelerating technological and social change.

In 1970, Alvin Toffler proposed the term **future shock** to describe the effects of social change that had become too fast for many people to assimilate. In essence, the future had arrived too soon. In 1980, he pursued this theme in an interesting book entitled *The Third Wave*. The following exerpt is from this book:

> Until now, the human race has undergone two great waves of change, each one largely obliterating earlier cultures or civilizations and replacing them with ways of life inconceivable to those who came before. The First Wave of change—the

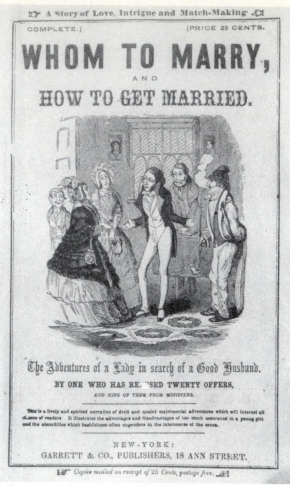

Smithsonian Institution Archive Center/Business Americana Collection

agricultural revolution—took thousands of years to play itself out. The Second Wave —the rise of industrial civilization—took a mere 300 years. Today history is even more accelerative, and it is likely that the Third Wave will sweep across history and complete itself in a few decades. We, who happen to share the planet at this explosive moment, will therefore feel the full impact of the Third Wave in our lifetimes. . . . Tearing our families apart, rocking our economy, paralyzing our political system, shattering our values, the Third Wave affects everyone. (p. 26)

What is the **Third Wave?** It represents the transformation of our society from an industrial age to an information age that relies on computers, robots, and other technological advances to replace our present energy sources, methods of production, and life styles. It is fueled by the ever-increasing information pouring out of the world's research laboratories. As described in Box 1–1, it has also led to some curious paradoxes.

Perceiving this transformation from a broad perspective, Edward Cornish (1987) has described it this way:

BOX 1-1 / PARADOXES OF OUR TIME

1. *The Paradox of Technology.* While modern technology has enabled us to land people on the Moon and return them safely to Earth, it has not enabled us to solve many critical problems on Earth, some of which—such as nuclear wastes—have been caused or aggravated by technology.

2. *The Paradox of Speed.* Our high-speed automobiles are slowed to a crawl during many hours of the day on crowded urban freeways, and high-speed jet travel that involves crossing many time zones tends to upset our bodies' rhythms. In addition, it may take longer to get to and from the airport than to our destination.

3. *The Paradox of Communication.* Via communications satellites and mass media, we have developed highly advanced communication facilities and techniques, yet "communication gaps" prevent or distort our understanding of each other's ideas, feelings, and motives.

4. *The Paradox of Equality.* In a society based on the principles of freedom, equality, and justice for all, we find widespread group prejudice and discrimination, with limited opportunities and unequal justice for many of our citizens.

5. *The Paradox of Affluence.* The United States is the richest nation the world has ever known. Yet, in 1986, over 30 million Americans lived below the government-set poverty line—including one in four children under 5 years of age. We spend more money on alcohol, drugs, and gambling than we do on our children's education.

6. *The Paradox of Values.* In a society founded on principles that have brought unprecedented opportunity and well-being to the majority of its citizens, many youth feel alienated and many others appear to base their lives on the assumption that "the person with the most toys when he dies, wins."

7. *The Paradox of Defense.* The security our costly military system should provide is offset by the proliferation of nuclear weapons, the spiraling arms race, and the assumption that peace between the "superpowers" can only be assured by "mutual terror." Ironically, global atomic war would probably doom not only the superpowers but also humankind.

8. *The Paradox of Intimacy.* Few paradoxes in our society are as tragic as the search for warm, loving, and enduring intimate relationships—and the inability of so many of us to achieve them. Thus, we have the highest divorce rate in the world with the broken dreams and emotional hurt that accompany it.

Something big is happening to the human race—something that could be called the Great Transformation. This Transformation consists of all the changes that are occurring in human life due to advancing technology.

Nobody knows what all these changes really will mean in the long run. But this mysterious Transformation is the biggest story of all time. It is the story of the human race itself. (p. 2)

Whatever the ultimate outcome, we are living in an age of unprecedented progress and unprecedented problems. We can point with pride to our tremendous and continuing achievements in space, genetics, biotechnology, computers, artificial intelligence, and many other scientific areas. Whether we like it or not, our technological advances are making us masters of the Earth and the plant and animal life on it. And, having placed men on the Moon and returned them safely to Earth, we are reaching toward Mars and the unfathomable universe beyond.

On the other hand, we are living in a period when rapid social change has played havoc with our established customs and values, when economic fluctuations have taken a heavy toll in terms of employment and financial security, and when violent crime and drug abuse have taken the lives of many and eroded the quality of life for all. It is a period when advances in communication and transportation have reduced the "size" of the world and made our interdependence with other peoples abundantly clear, when grinding poverty and discrimination exist side by side with affluence and privilege, and when widespread pollution of air, water, and soil poses a threat to the health and lives of millions of people. Finally, it is a period when we are confronted by a new Black Plague in the form of AIDS (Acquired Immune Deficiency Syndrome), and when the "cold war" between the superpowers could erupt into a global conflict that would doom most if not all who travel on Spaceship Earth.

While this transformation from an industrial age to an information age does hold the promise of a better life, this new life will not come about without profound dislocations, conflict, and change. And for many people the increasing rate of change has already become so fast, the forces of society so powerful and encompassing, and the future so uncertain that they feel alienated, stress-ridden,

Don Smetzer/Click/Chicago

United States Department of Housing and Urban Development

and incapable of controlling the direction of their lives or of making their lives count for something (Harris, 1987).

This is the social context in which we live and function as we try to find our way in an increasingly complex and impersonal mass society. It is the setting in which we learn, play, work, marry, raise children, and retire. It is the setting that influences our expectations, values, and behaviors as well as the quality and duration of the intimate relationships we form and the satisfaction we derive from them. Ultimately, it is the setting that will determine the structure, functioning, and survival of our entire society.

MARRIAGE AND FAMILY IN TRANSITION

Living in the latter part of the 20th century in the midst of accelerating technological and social change, it is difficult to realize how much our views of marriage and the family have changed, even in the last decade. But change they have, and these changes affect all aspects of our lives.

Now, as we focus on the transition taking place in marriage and the family, we shall extend our view of the social context to include three interrelated assumptions: (1) that America is going through a difficult transition from an industrial society to an information society; (2) that when environments change, institutions and people also change as they attempt to adapt; and (3) that these changes—in the environment, institutions, and people—interact in shaping the future. Only in this broad context can we understand the profound changes taking place in contemporary marriage and intimate relationships.

Changing Sex-Roles and Man–Woman Relationships

> Since the latter half of the twentieth century . . . the world has been engaged in an ongoing battle: not between armies, but between the traditional masculine and feminine value systems. (p. 134)
>
> —*William Farrell (1984)*

Smithsonian Institution Archive Center/Business Americana Collection

By way of clarification, our masculinity or femininity has three components: the biological, psychological, and social. Biologically, our **sex**—male or female—is determined by our chromosomes. Psychologically, our **gender identity** is our subjective feeling of being male or female. Socially, our masculinity or femininity is defined by **sex-roles**—society's expectations of how a male or female should behave. Here our focus will be on sex-roles.

"Is it a boy or a girl?" has traditionally been the first question asked after the birth of a baby. Baby boys are usually treated and expected to behave differently from baby girls. From this early point, the combined forces of family, peer group, and mass media ensure that children learn and engage in behavior considered appropriate in terms of their age and sex. Although the forces of socialization are comparable from one society to another, there are cultural differences—as described in Box 1–2—in what are considered appropriate sex roles.

Traditional versus Egalitarian Sex-Roles.   In our own society, the effects of sex-roles are clearly illustrated by the differences between traditional and contemporary sex role expectations and behaviors.

Traditional masculine behavior consists of a constellation of **instrumental,** or goal-oriented, **characteristics**—such as competitive, aggressive, self-reliant, and assertive. The expression of anger is acceptable but not the expression of fear or other feelings which reflect weakness. On the other hand, traditional feminine traits consist of a constellation of **expressive characteristics**—such as nuturant, compassionate, affectionate, and sensitive to the needs of others. Box 1–3 contains a list of traits scored as masculine or feminine on the Bem Sex Role Inventory.

Translated into the intimate relationship of marriage, the man traditionally played the role of "breadwinner" and the woman that of "homemaker." The husband had the authority. He made the decisions concerning money and other important matters. And he had the power to enforce his decisions with respect to his wife and his children. The wife's primary responsibilities were housekeeping, child-rearing, and providing comfort and sex for her husband.

All this has changed. In a 1981 survey of a large cross-section of Americans conducted by the Connecticut Life Insurance Company, it was found that the traditional sex-roles of husband and wife were largely things of the past. They had given way to the new marital ideal of egalitarian sex-roles in marriage and intimate relationships. This egalitarian approach involves husband and wife cooperating in financial support, homemaking, and child rearing. It provides women with equality in terms of sexual beahvior and gratification as well as family decision making.

Despite the trend toward greater equality between the sexes, some people are more comfortable conforming to traditional sex-roles in marriage and intimate relationships. But these people have become a distinct minority in our society (Norton & Moorman, 1987).

One major result of this shift has been that both men and women are freer to follow their own interests without feeling the pressure to conform to stereotyped sex-role expectations. For example, the "new husbands" can share and perhaps even enjoy the concerns of housekeeping and child-rearing without fearing a loss of masculinity. Conversely, the "new wives" can pursue such careers as business executive, lawyer, or even military officer without fearing a loss of femininity.

This change toward greater sex-role equality affects premarital as well as marital relationships. It is now acceptable for a woman to ask a man for a date, to take the initiative in sexual behavior, to participate as an equal in decision making, and to

BOX 1-2 / CULTURAL DIFFERENCES IN SEX-ROLES

Our traditional views of masculine and feminine characteristics are not found in every culture. In her early studies of three New Guinea tribes, for example, the noted anthropologist Margaret Mead (1939) described the strikingly different sex-roles that characterized each tribe.

1. *The Arapesh*. In this tribe, both sexes showed characteristics and behavior that would be considered feminine in our own society. Both men and women were encouraged to be unaggressive, mild, cooperative, and responsive to the needs of others. Neither sex took an aggressive role in courtship. The ideal marriage was a mild, responsive man married to a mild, responsive woman.

2. *The Mundungumor*. In this tribe, both sexes would be characterized as masculine by our traditional standards. Both men and women were encouraged to be aggressive, violent, and ruthless; gentleness and tender behavior were at a minimum. The ideal marriage was that of a violent, aggressive male married to a violent, aggressive female.

3. *The Tchambuli*. While neither the Arapesh nor the Mundungumor had clearly defined roles which distinguished the behavior of the sexes, the Tchambuli did have such roles. But . . . they were reversed by our standards. The women were characteristically dominant, impersonal, and businesslike and took the initiative in courtship and sexual behavior. By contrast, the men were irresponsible, emotionally dependent on the women, relatively passive, concerned about their physical appearance, and interested in arts and home activities.

In this study, then, we see three societies in which sex roles differ considerably from our own. In two, the roles are social rather than specifically sexual; there is very little distinction between the norms for the two sexes but a striking difference between the norms of the two societies. In the third, there is a reversal of sex roles as compared with ours.

More recently, social psychologist Susan Basow (1984) reported a lack of strong sex-role typing in the South Pacific nation of Fiji. Both Fijian high-school males and females scored high in nuturant, expressive characteristics. Child-care and other nuturant activities were viewed as part of the male role.

Cross-cultural studies show, however, that most cultures do distinguish between male and female sex-roles. Independence, aggressiveness, and achievement are emphasized for males and nuturance, expressiveness, and responsibility for females. Presumably such differences in sex-roles are the result of socialization rather than innate biological differences and are related to the responsibilities assigned to each sex. For example, girls are trained to have and rear children, while boys are trained to protect the family and provide for its basic needs.

The most common sex-role difference found in cross-cultural studies is the pattern of aggression by males—presumably resulting from the male's biological predisposition. But it is apparent that such a predisposition toward aggression and violence—if it exists—can be modified by sex-role socialization.

propose marriage. The man not only has the same rights as before, but he is now free to express his feelings and share his fears, hurts, and frustrations.

Masculinity and Femininity in Transition. However, matters are not as cut and dried as the previous discussion may imply. Full equality between the sexes is

BOX 1–3 / TRAITS SCORED AS MASCULINE OR FEMININE ON THE BEM SEX-ROLE INVENTORY

MASCULINE

Defend my own beliefs
Independent
Assertive
Strong personality
Forceful
Have leadership abilities
Willing to take risks
Dominant
Aggressive
Competitive
Self-reliant

FEMININE

Affectionate
Nurturant
Sympathetic
Sensitive to needs of others
Understanding
Compassionate
Eager to soothe hurt feelings
Warm
Tender
Love children
Gentle

Subjects are asked to rate each characteristic on a scale of 1–7 in terms of how well it describes them. Seven refers to "always" or "almost always" true, while 1 refers to "never" or "almost never" true.

John Running

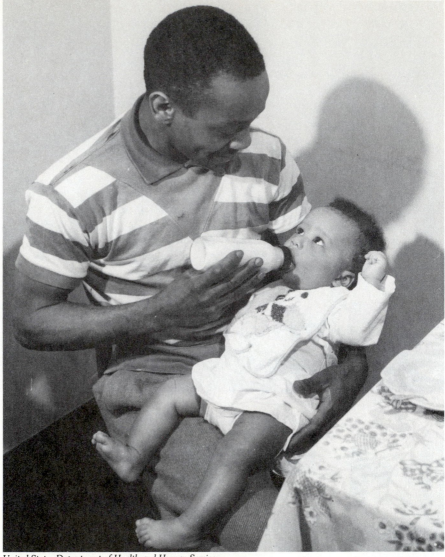

United States Department of Health and Human Services

still to be achieved, and sex-roles are still in transition. Consider the following exchange:

"Why don't you act like a real man?"
"I'm looking for a real woman."

What images do the terms "real man" and "real woman" bring to mind? Do most people share similar images? Probably not to the extent that traditional concepts of masculine and feminine were shared—as in the "good provider" and "good homemaker" roles.

To complicate matters, both men and women are receiving contradictory messages. Women are encouraged to be more like men—to be career-oriented, competent, competitive, and aggressive. But if they achieve high-level career success in our male-dominated world, they are likely to be labeled "unfeminine."

At the same time, men are encouraged to be more like women—particularly in terms of being more nurturing, emotionally expressive, and sensitive to the feelings of others. But if they go very far in this direction, they are likely to be labeled "Wimps." This confusion in sex roles appears to be detrimental to many intimate man–woman relationships. In a controversial study of 4,500 American women, for example, Shere Hite (1987) found that most of them were dominated and even abused by the men in their lives. As a result these women were disillusioned with and wanted to make basic changes in their love relationships. We shall pursue this topic in Chapter 8 dealing with marital relationships, happiness, and enrichment.

Where this transition in sex-roles will take us remains to be seen. But it seems likely that the first step in developing acceptable sex-roles will require achieving true equality between the sexes in educational, occupational, political, and interpersonal areas. Perhaps such equality will be based in large part on the recognition that we are first and foremost human beings, then males or females.

In the meantime, femininity seems to be making a return on its own terms, in the sense that women are no longer letting men and social custom define what is or is not feminine but are defining it for themselves. And men, too, are redefining the traditional "macho" stereotype. In short, fewer men and women are letting

---

BOX 1–4 / SOME KEY EFFECTS OF SEX ROLES

1. *Personal Effects*
   Self identity—your sense of "who you are"
   Goals and aspirations
   Self-ideal—view of who you should be
   Self-esteem—feelings of adequacy and worth
   Attitudes—views of reality and value

2. *Relationship Effects*
   Marital expectations and goals
   Choice of a mate
   Marital relationship
   Duration of marriage
   Marital satisfaction

3. *Social Effects*
   Power and Control—men dominate occupational, political, legal, and interpersonal areas
   Aggression—male socialization involves more combative activities, e.g., "masculine" sports
   Prejudice against women—found in occupational and all other important areas of society

In dealing with gender and sex roles, we view males and females as "equals but different."

traditional sex-roles dictate the course of their lives. But, in the short-term, at least, the result of these trends is not free of conflict—either for males and females personally or for their intimate relationships.

Sociologist Richard Sennett (1987) has described the situation quite succinctly:

> Men and women today are moving in opposite directions: women are trying to prove themselves and are discovering that it can be a treadmill; men are trying to sort out what it means to no longer play the invulnerable male. . . . Women have to learn what difference having more power makes, men what having less means. (p. 363)

Until full equality between the sexes has been achieved and both men and women are comfortable in their new roles, it would apear that what has been called "the longest war" is likely to continue, often at the expense of achieving compatibility and harmony in marriage and intimate relationships.

Changing Marital Expectations and Patterns

In addition to changing sex-roles in marriage and intimate relationships, there have been major changes in marital expectations and patterns.

Rising Expectations.

Even as recently as the 1950s, marriage in American society was highly traditional. Marriages were formed primarily for three purposes: meeting sexual needs, rearing children, and providing for economic needs. Sexual needs referred primarily to those of men because women were not supposed to experience sexual desire or pleasure.

Today, young people expect far more of marriage than they did in the past. Rather than marrying primarily for sexual, economic, and child-rearing reasons, they are marrying to meet psychological needs—companionship, emotional support, friendship, and most of all an intimate and romantic love relationship in which to share all aspects of their lives and achieve happiness.

In addition, more and more young people look to marriage as a means for personal growth and fulfillment. It is not enough to have a warm, supportive, and dependable partner with whom life is comfortable and with whom one has a secure "home base." Rather, people are increasingly seeking a relationship that offers the opportunity to fulfill their potential as unique human beings, to grow as individuals as well as marital partners.

These rising expectations have been made possible by the increasing equality between the sexes, the economic independence of young career women, and the changed view of the potentialities and alternatives that contemporary marriage can offer.

Dual-Career Marriages.

Prior to World War II and the influx of women into the work force to assist the war effort, most women did not work outside the home. It was a source of pride among industrial workers and white-collar workers to make sufficient money to provide for their wives and children. For a wife to work outside the family, even in a professional position such as a doctor or lawyer, tended to undermine the husband's "good provider" role and his self-concept as an adequate male.

Not surprisingly, more-egalitarian sex-roles ended this situation. In a poll conducted in 1981, Daniel Yankelovich found that norms concerning whether wives should work outside the home had been reversed within a single generation. Probably no other change in marital norms has been more significant in our culture. During the same period, a comprehensive study of the nation's families by George Masnick and Mary Jo Bane (1980)—of the Joint Center for Urban Studies of M.I.T. and Harvard University—led to the prediction that, by 1990, the great majority of American households would consist of dual-career (worker) couples. The following are some of the anticipated repercussions of this trend:

1. Dual-career marriages will lead to more-egalitarian sex-roles and man–woman relationships.
2. Marital sex will be adversely affected because couples will have less time together and less energy when they are together.
3. Parents will have children at a later age and fewer of them, if any.
4. Parents will have less time to devote to child rearing, and child-care facilities—regulated by the government—will be increasingly used.
5. The increased income of dual-career couples will become essential for maintaining a middle-class life style. Single-earner families will be in danger of becoming an economic underclass.
6. Changes in the work place, such as "flextime" and "family leave," will be increasingly demanded and provided.
7. The divorce rate will increase because of greater stress imposed on dual-career couples.

United States Department of Health and Human Services

A wealth of more-recent research findings support the accuracy of these predictions. For example, in 1985, the majority of mothers with children under 5 years of age—including many with infants—were in the labor force (White House Task Force Report on the Family, 1986). In addition, there were over four million **"latchkey" children,** children who arrive home after school before either parent returns from work. We will elaborate on dual-career marriages in Chapter 9.

Increasing Incidence of Divorce.   As Edward Cornish (1979) has pointed out:

Until the twentieth century, divorces were exceptional occurrences. Marriages were supposed to last 'until death do us part'—and most did, partly because death came much sooner than it does today. A nineteenth-century marriage lasted an average of only 12 years before one or the other of the partners died. (pp. 46–47)

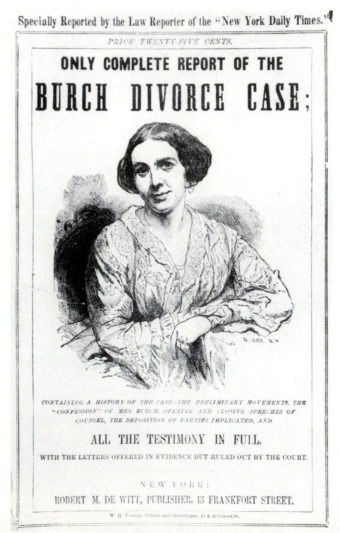

Smithsonian Institution Archive Center/Business Americana Collection

The divorce rate has increased markedly since the early 1900s. In 1920, one out of seven marriages ended in divorce. By 1950, the divorce rate had increased to about one in five marriages, and, by 1985, to approximately one divorce in two marriages (White House Task Force Report on the Family, 1986). In terms of numbers, there were 2,425,000 marriages in 1985, and 1,187,000 divorces, representing a slight decrease in marriages and increase in divorces from 1984 (National Center for Health Statistics, 1986). Recent figures indicate that the divorce rate will likely level off in the late 1980s to about one divorce in every two marriages and remain that way through the 1990s. In any event, the U.S. divorce rate is the highest the world has ever known. It is having a major impact on our marital and family relationships and traditional way of life. Marriage and divorce statistics in our society are shown in Figures 1–1 and 1–2.

This high rate results in large part from the change in our attitudes toward divorce. The social stigma once attached to divorce has greatly diminished or disappeared. Divorce is not only socially acceptable, it is also relatively easy to obtain. In 1970, California passed a revolutionary piece of legislation called the Family Law Act. This abolished the concept of only one partner being at fault in divorce and substituted the concept of "no-fault" divorce—an approach adopted in all but one state by 1985 (National Center for Health Statistics, 1986). Under the no-fault doctrine, to obtain a divorce, it is only necessary to show that "irreconcilable differences leading to the irremediable breakdown of the marriage" have occurred. In Chapter 12, we shall deal with the emotional trauma behind these impersonal divorce statistics.

Overall, it is apparent that, although internal demands and pressures on marriage have increased, the external social barriers to divorce have largely crumbled. Thus, it is hardly surprising that our traditional view of marriage as a life-long commitment is in serious trouble.

Remarriage.   In the early 1900s, the incidence of remarriage was low in the United States, and most remarriages were of widowed persons. As the divorce rate

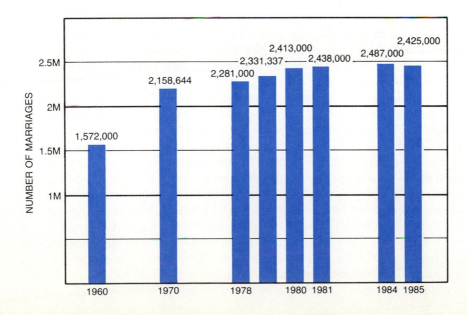

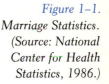

Figure 1–1.
Marriage Statistics.
(Source: National
Center for Health
Statistics, 1986.)

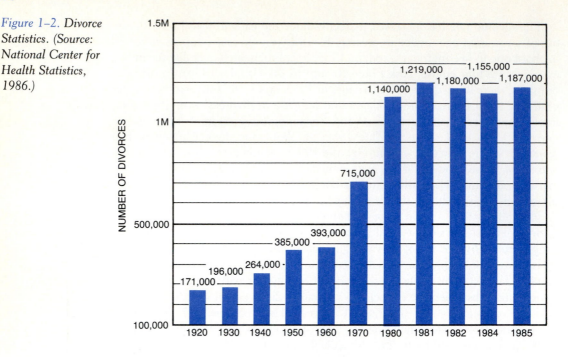

Figure 1–2. Divorce Statistics. (Source: National Center for Health Statistics, 1986.)

climbed, however, there was a swelling tide of remarriages in which one or both partners had been previously married and divorced. By 1985, over 40 percent of all marriages involved such "repeat performances" (Glick, 1985; Glick & Lin, 1986; Norton & Moorman, 1987). As in the case of divorce, the increasing incidence of remarriage—about five out of six divorced men and four out of five divorced women remarry—is having a major impact on our way of life.

In 1986, as many as 35 million families in the United States included a step-parent, and their numbers were increasing at almost 1,500 a day. Unfortunately, more than half of these remarriages will break up, and the cycle of marriage, divorce, and remarriage will continue.

In place of the traditional vow, "Till death do us part," we have entered a new era of "serial monogamy." If a person's present marriage isn't working out, the trend is to start over with a new marital partner. And, although people may lose faith in a particular marital relationship, they still seem to have confidence in the institution of marriage itself.

In addition to the trends we have just enumerated, there are many other changes that have been occurring in traditional marital patterns. For example, people stay single longer before marriage, have more sexual experiences prior to marriage, marry less, divorce more, remarry more, and live together more often as unmarried couples (McBee, 1985). Furthermore, couples have been able to separate the ideas of marriage and child-bearing. Thus, many wait until their late 30s or early 40s to have children or to opt for the child-free alternative. In addition, singlehood has become an acceptable way of life; some single women even choose to have children without benefit of marriage. Also, there are an increasing number of marriages across racial, religious, and economic boundaries.

Finally, AIDS—the lethal sexually transmitted disease—is changing dating, marital, and extramarital relationships in our society. While AIDS is not likely to reverse the so-called "sexual revolution," it is leading to more-conservative atti-

UPI/Bettmann Newsphotos

tudes toward sexual morality, including decreased tolerance for casual sex and extramarital affairs. In advising adult Americans that the best insurance against AIDS is monogamy, the Surgeon General of the United States, C. Everett Koop (1987), stated in his usual direct manner, "If you have a monogamous relationship keep it. If you don't have one, get it" (p. 13).

Changing Family Forms and Functions

Because marriage and family are so closely interwoven, it is not surprising that the changes we have noted for marriage have also affected traditional family patterns. In addition, there are a number of important changes in family life associated with the advent of children—the transition from a married couple to a family.

Let us go back in time for a moment. The Kiplinger Washington Letter of December 23, 1949, contains the following description of an "average family man" in the United States:

> There's such a thing as an "average family man" . . . statistically. He is a composite of all the men of all ages who are heads of families.
> Here's the dope on him: He is 45 years of age. His wife is 43. She is the same woman he married originally. They have three children. Two at home. The other is old enough to be away at school or working.
> Family's income is about $3300 a year. They live in a house, not an apartment. They 'own' it . . . or have an equity . . . also a mortgage. They live in a city of about 25,000. The husband is a skilled workman, or semi-skilled. He is not of the "professional class." His schooling, one year of high school. (p. 4)

While this sketch is limited—that is, it does not mention the fact that the wife was a homemaker and did not work in the labor force—it does indicate how much the "nuclear family" has changed. Formerly, the typical, or nuclear, American family consisted of a husband, wife, and two to four children. Today, the nuclear family, as we know it, is in a distinct minority. It has been replaced by a variety of other family forms.

There are many marriages with "full-time" or "live-in" children from the wife's or husband's former marriage, or from both. There are marriages with no children and no intent to have any. There are marriages with "part-time" children (noncustodial parents) from a prior marriage and full-time children from the present marriage. And increasingly there are marriages complicated by children from several prior marriages of the wife or husband or both. As a consequence, the traditional nuclear family represents less than 10 percent of American families today.

This is a useful perspective to keep in mind as we describe some other major changes taking place in the American family.

Family Planning and Fewer, If Any, Children.   In the early part of this century, the average family included four children. By 1970, the number decreased to three, and, by the mid-1980s, it decreased to about two. But, although young people today plan to have fewer children than previous generations, most do plan to have at least one child.

Such family planning has been made possible by the development of effective contraceptives and the widespread dissemination of information concerning the advantages of keeping population growth to a minimum. Undoubtedly, both personal and social considerations enter into family planning. For example, a sizeable number of young people—some 20 percent or more—in our society do not wish to have children. There are many reasons for this decision, including the decreased marital satisfaction that children tend to bring, the possible disruption of careers, and the long-range time and expenses associated with child-rearing. In any event, the child-free alternative has become acceptable in our society. If present trends continue, by the mid-1990s, there will be an estimated 60 million American households with no children under age 15.

Reduced Role of Parents in Child-Rearing.   As an increasing number of mothers enter the work force, parents in dual-worker marriages must inevitably depend on day-care facilities or other social support systems to assist them in raising their children. When both parents work full-time, the time spent with children may be more limited in comparison to parent–child interactions in more-traditional families.

The children of working mothers who come home from school to an empty house or apartment and are unsupervised by parents several hours each day are referred to as "latchkey" children. There are an estimated four million or more such children in our society (Landers, 1986). Many live solitary and sometimes fearful lives after school—often with the TV set acting as babysitter in the home —until one or both parents return. In single-parent households in which the parent works, the problem is particularly difficult.

As the number of working mothers increases, so will the number of latchkey children unless society provides the necessary facilities for dealing with the problem. Unfortunately, the provision of high-quality day-care programs can be a both costly and controversial matter (White House Task Force Report on the Family, 1986).

Yankelovich (1981) found in his survey of contemporary Americans that parents "expect to make fewer sacrifices for their children than did parents in the past" (p. 72). However, this does not mean that Americans have stopped loving or being concerned about the well-being of their children. Rather, as William Watts

(1981) has expressed it, "Parents may no longer regard children as wards whose future lives they must plan and orchestrate" (p. 47). Nevertheless, in the latter 1980s over 20 percent of working mothers took time off to raise their first child. This often involves considerable financial and career sacrifice, but it does permit mothers to have greater influence over the early years of their children's development. Usually, the mother plans to return to her career when the child enters nursery school or kindergarten.

Another effect of reduced parental involvement in child-rearing appears to be the emergence of the peer group as an increasingly powerful influence in children's lives. Peer pressure is something to be reckoned with. Even as recently as 20 years ago, young people rated parents as the primary influence in their lives, but children's beliefs and values are now more influenced by friends and peer group members than by parents (Johnson, 1981). The significance of this trend over the long run is difficult to determine and is a matter of interest to many social scientists.

Single-Parent Families.   In 1980, one in every five children under 18 lived with only one parent (U.S. Bureau of the Census, 1980). If trends in the 1980s continue, about half of all children born in the mid- to late 1980s will live with only one parent at some time before they reach age 18 (Visher & Visher, 1986). Although an increasing number of fathers are being granted sole custody or joint custody of their children, it is still the mother who ordinarily heads the single-parent household. As a result of court-granted custody of children, about 90 percent of households are headed by women and 10 percent by men.

Stephen Shames/Visions

Single-parent households headed by divorced women are likely to encounter severe financial problems, even though the mother may work and do her best. This situation has led to increasing criticism of "no-fault" divorce, particularly by women (Weitzman, 1985; Goldfarb & Libby, 1984). In addiition, the overall situation has been referred to as "the feminization of poverty."

Stepfamilies.   As we noted earlier, over 40 percent of all marriages each year are remarriages in which one or both parents have been married and divorced before. In 60 percent or more of these families, children from a previous marriage are part of the package. This means that some 35 million American families now include a step-parent. Unfortunately, there are few guidelines for helping such **stepfamilies** to function effectively; more than half of these marriages eventually break up (Norton & Moorman, 1987). The primary cause: children.

In any event, stepfamilies—also referred to as "blended," "remarried," and "reconstituted" families—are increasing in number and represent a major change in family life. Children must adjust to new parents and new siblings; couples must adjust to an entire constellation of new problems and family members in addition to adjusting to each other. To further complicate matters, ex-spouses must be considered, especially if they see the children regularly. These are some of the many conditions that set stepfamilies apart from traditional families.

Family Mobility: The New Nomads.   Most families in the United States move about once every 5 years. This means that about 15 million families, including children, are confronted with saying goodbye to friends and familiar places and adjusting to new surroundings. In addition, the sheer logistics of moving tend to make it a highly stressful situation.

Alvin Toffler (1980) has gone so far as to suggest that we are "breeding a new race of nomads" in the United States, and that few of us are aware of how massive these migrations are. In the early 1980s, for example, a large number of families in the Midwest moved to the Sunbelt states as unemployment plagued the so-called "smokestack" industries. Moving can be an especially difficult problem for dual-career couples when one partner wants to remain in his or her present position.

Some researchers, including Paul Glick of the U.S. Census Bureau, have concluded that mobility will not be as great among families in the 1990s. But this fails to consider adequately the massive immigration of people from other countries and their moving about within our society as they try to make a life for themselves (Sheils et al., 1983). And, of course, some families move as a result of the influx of particular ethnic groups into the area where they live.

In addition, about one-fourth of the U.S. work force is making or planning to make a change in occupation each year (Hawes, 1984; Porter, 1986). Such occupational change is likely to accelerate along with the pace of new technology, and this change may necessitate moving to a new locale. Thus, it would appear that a high degree of family mobility will continue during the 1990s, if not longer. Even if the pace of family mobility slows, we can still expect major changes as the American family attempts to adapt to accelerating social change.

Are the Institutions of Marriage and Family Disintegrating?

The traditional fabric of American society is under seige. The extended family, once so significant in the development of the American family, is almost a museum

BOX 1-4 / PROBLEMS IN DEFINING THE TERM "FAMILY"

The United States Census (1980) defines a family as "a group of two persons or more related by birth, marriage, or adoption and residing together." However, the generally accepted and most often cited definition of "family" has been that of George Murdock (1949):

The family is a social group characterized by common residence, economic cooperation and reproduction. It includes adults of both sexes, at least two of whom maintain a socially approved sexual relationship, and one or more children, own or adopted, of the sexually cohabiting adults. (p. 1)

Included in Murdock's definition are: (1) the **nuclear** family—consisting of husband, wife, and offspring, and (2) the **extended family**—consisting of one or more nuclear families living with additional relatives (two or more) in a household joined together by multiple marriage.

In our society, there are derivatives of the nuclear and extended families, including the single-parent and remarried families. However, the problem of including cohabiting couples in long-term relationships as well as long-term homosexual relationships as families has not been resolved. In both of the preceding relationships, children of one or both partners or adopted children may be involved as well as additional relatives. In addition, many investigators extend the definition of a nuclear family to include a married couple—whether or not they have children—and also any persons related by blood or marriage who cooperate economically and live together in the same household. Thus, the problem of defining the family—except in a preliminary way—has yet to be resolved (Bohannan, 1985; Skolnick, 1981; Hudson & Harrison, 1986).

But as Arlene Skolnick (1981) has pointed out, "Defining the family is not just an academic exercise; how one defines it determines which kinds of families will be considered normal and which deviant, and what rights and obligations will be recognized by legal and other social institutions" (p. 43).

piece. The nuclear family, bombarded by divorce, inflation, and drug abuse, is in danger of atomizing. (p. 148)

—*Ludmila and Herbert Hoffman (1985)*

A number of investigators have concluded that contemporary marriage and family are deteriorating if not downright distintegrating. For example, the respected sociologist David Mace (1986) has pointed to the present tendency to treat divorce as a simple matter of personal choice without regard for the long-range effects on the family and society. Similarly, the White House Task Force Report on the Family (1986) uses such phrases as "family life has been frayed" and the "continuing deterioration of American families." Curiously enough, assessing the present condition of the family is complicated by problems in defining the meaning of "family." This problem is described in Box 1–4.

Some social scientists, including members of the White House Task Force on the Family, seem to long for a return to the "good old days" of the extended family in America. Without in any way minimizing concern with contemporary marriage and family patterns, it may be emphasized that our folklore image contains a high degree of illusion. As we have noted, in the 19th century, most parents did not live long enough to end their days living with their children and grandchildren. Not until recent times has it become common to find families with three and four generations alive at the same time.

Tamara Hareven (1980) has pointed out other characteristics of families in the past that conflict with our common image. For example, she noted that single-parent families were common due to the early death of one parent, that being orphaned at an early age was common, and that orphanages were a familiar part of the American landscape. The shorter life expectancy also tended to prevent the formation of a significant number of extended families. Thus, as the saying goes, "Things aren't like they used to be and never were."

But were things really that bad in the past? It depended on the historical period and the social class, but no doubt marriage and family life offered many rewards, just as they do today. Our forebears were human beings just like us, and they fell in love, had happy or unhappy marriages, and had harmonious or conflict-filled families. Probably the bottom line is that marriage and family life in the past were no better and quite possibly worse than they are today.

Nevertheless, Hareven and other social scientists are concerned that idealized images of an imaginary "golden age" of marriage and the family have led many to overstate the alleged deterioration of these institutions in contemporary America. Admittedly, marriage and the family are going through a difficult transition period, but they have proven to be resilient and flexible insitutions, and it appears highly unlikely that they will become extinct in the near future. As Arlene Skolnick (1981) has so succinctly summarized the situation:

> Yet, however grim the present moment may appear, there is no point in giving in to the lure of nostalgia. There is no "golden age" of the family to long for, nor even some past pattern of behavior and belief which would guarantee us harmony and stability if only we had the will to return to it. Family life is bound up with the social,

Joel Gordon

economic, and ideological circumstances of particular times and places. We are no longer peasants, Puritans, pioneers, or even suburbanites circa 1955. We face conditions unknown to our ancestors, and we must find ways to cope with them. (p. 47)

THE SCIENTIFIC STUDY OF MARRIAGE AND FAMILY

Science is concerned with providing new and useful information—information that can be verified by other qualified researchers who make similar observations. Individual research studies focus on describing and understanding limited aspects of a subject, such as the nature and types of marital conflict. As increasing amounts of data are collected, researchers then try to organize the information into a unified body, in the form of models or theories. In this section, we shall describe some of the main techniques used in studying marriage and the family and some of the theories that have been developed to acccount for research results.

Methods of Social-Science Research

The first step in science is gathering basic information. In the social sciences, four major methods are used: the experimental method, the observational method, the survey method, and existing sources.

The **experimental method** often involves laboratory research in an effort to control the collection of data precisely and to define cause-and-effect relationships. Thus, subjects may go to a university laboratory to perform various tasks under strictly controlled conditions. For example, a study may be designed to see what happens to subjects who must perform a task at faster and faster speeds until they can no longer complete it. This type of study might be helpful in learning about the effects of "overload" on people—for example, dual-career and single-parent mothers.

The **observational method** typically involves observing how a person or group of people behave in their natural environment—for example, men and women hanging out in a singles bar. However, the observational method may also be used in the laboratory, as Masters and Johnson did with their studies of human sexual response (Chapter 4).

The **survey method** is frequently used in social-science research for gathering facts or exploring the relationship between facts. For example, questionnaires or interviews may be used for gathering information about the opinions of college students concerning premarital sex, the degree of happiness experienced in marriage, or attitudes regarding mothers working outside the home. The population or group of people in which the researcher is interested may vary from a specific group, such as young married women, to a random sampling of the United States population as a whole.

Use of **existing sources** involves systematically analyzing relevant data that have already been collected, such as Census Bureau statistics. These statistics can be analyzed to determine trends in marriage, divorce, number of children in

BOX 1–5 / SOME DIFFICULTIES IN SOCIAL SCIENCE RESEARCH

Ian Robertson (1977) has delineated five difficulties that seem particularly characteristic of sociological and social science research:

1. *The mere act of investigating social behavior may alter the very behavior that is being investigated.* When people know they are being studied, they may not behave as they normally would do. Suppose, for example, that a sociologist who is studying family interaction patterns visits your home: would your family behave in exactly the same way as usual?

2. *People—unlike bacteria or hydrogen atoms—have emotions, motives, and other highly individual personality characteristics.* They may give false information deliberately, to put themselves in a better light, or unintentionally, because they misinterpret a question or do not understand the reasons for their own behavior or attitudes.

3. *The origins of social behavior are almost always extremely complex, involving many social, psychological, historical, and other factors.* It is usually much more difficult for the sociologist than for the natural scientist to sort out cause and effect because so many more variables tend to be involved.

4. *It is not possible, for ethical reasons, to perform certain kinds of experiments on human beings.* The natural scientist has no moral qualms about experimenting with rays of light and often few qualms about experimenting with animals. But the dignity and privacy of human beings must be respected.

5. *The sociologist, unlike the natural scientist, is part of the very subject he or she is studying.* It is therefore much more difficult to maintain a detached attitude, and objectivity becomes harder to achieve. All sociologists recognize these problems, but not all are agreed on how to deal with them. Some focus on refining statistical techniques, modeling their methodology as closely as possible after the example of the natural sciences. They aim to make sociology as exact and precise a science as possible. Others protest that a dependence on these methods produces mounds of figures but very little understanding. Debate among the overzealous advocates of each approach has at times become heated (pages 33–34).

We have attempted to avoid some of these pitfalls in this text by avoiding the indiscriminate mixing of fact, opinion, and value judgment. We have also tried to distinguish between the use of the objective approach of the natural sciences and the interpretive, subjective approach designed to deal more effectively with certain types of subject matter, such as love and loneliness, that are studied frequently in the social sciences.

families, and so on. Existing sociological research studies may also be reevaluated and reinterpreted in light of new findings.

A distinction is often made between cross-sectional and logitudinal research studies. A **cross-sectional study** measures a particular sample at a given point in time. For example, a researcher might study the percentage of marriages rated as happy by doing a cross-sectional survey of couples who have been married for 5 years. A **longitudinal study,** on the other hand, measures the same subjects at

BOX 1-6 / COMMON SOURCES OF ERROR IN SOCIAL SCIENCE RESEARCH

Among the more common sources of error leading to invalid generalizations in social science research are:

1. *Overgeneralizing from a limited and nonrepresentative sampling.* The attitudes of young people toward premarital sex cannot be ascertained simply by surveying a sample of college students. A researcher cannot validly generalize from a limited sample to the total population.

2. *Mistaking correlation for causation.* Although two variables may show a statistical correlation, that does not mean that one causes the other. A cause-effect relationship may indeed be involved, but then again it may not, or a third variable may be the cause of both. For example, there is a strong correlation between personal maladjustment and divorce, but this does not necessarily mean that maladjustment leads to divorce. Maladjusted people tend to earn less money, so it may actually be financial problems that lead to the divorce.

3. *Regression toward the mean.* Generalizations made on the basis of one incident may prove inaccurate; gathering data on many different incidents of the same kind allows the researcher to discount unusually high or low results for a particular incident and focus on the mean or average of data for all incidents.

4. *Confusing fact, opinion, and value judgment.* Often social scientists become emotionally involved in their research and tend to let their cherished opinions influence the way in which they interpret and generalize from their findings.

5. *Slanting the findings.* A few researchers feel compelled to slant their findings to make them appear more significant than they actually are. They seem to obey the dictum that if the facts don't fit the theory, the facts must be modified. Fortunately, however, scientific ethics are stringent with respect to such "doctoring" practices.

As we noted in Box 1-5, subjects may give false information in answer to questions in order to conceal what they really think or to try to portray themselves in a favorable light. Often, too, they tend to supply answers they think the researcher wants. Such false information is another common source of error in social science research.

two or more points in time. Thus, a researcher might give a questionnaire to 100 couples and then follow up the same couples 5 years later to see if their ratings of marital happiness have changed.

Social science research is not without its problems. Box 1-5 describes some of the major difficulties in conducting social science research and Box 1-6 lists some common sources of error.

Theoretical Views of Marriage and Intimate Relationships

The second step in social-science research is organizing research findings into a unified body of information. For this purpose, models and theories are heavily relied on.

BOX 1–7 / OTHER THEORETICAL PERSPECTIVES

In addition to symbolic interaction theory, social exchange theory, and general systems theory, there are several other perspectives that can help us better to understand marriage, family, and other intimate relationships. The following are prominent among them:

1. *Role Theory*. The term **role** has been borrowed from the theater. The words and actions of a role are designated by the "script" and remain essentially the same regardless of who plays the role. Society prescribes roles for its members that are designed o facilitate interpersonal interactions and relationships as well as the overall functioning of the group. In this book, we shall have occasion to refer to many aspects of roles in our society, particularly sex-roles.

2. *Developmental Theory*. This approach focuses on understanding the growth and development of both individuals and families. Developmental theorists think of the life cycle of the individual and the family in terms of specific stages. The stages follow an orderly sequence that is the same for almost everyone, but within each stage people vary greatly in their psychological reactions. But even on the psychological level, each stage builds on the one preceding it. Thus, we shall find it useful to examine the developmental tasks that must be mastered at each stage of the life cycle. For example, a developmental task in middle age is to re-establish a warm and loving relationship with one's spouse after the children have left home.

3. *Conflict Theory*. Conflict theorists assume that relationships are in a constant state of conflict and change. Emphasis is on the competing needs of marital partners and on disagreements over goals and values. It is assumed that the things most people want are in short supply and that in order to meet their needs and protect their own interests, people must compete and fight for what they want. Conflict theorists do not perceive marital or other interpersonal conflict as necessarily destructive. Rather, they consider it a catalyst that brings disagreements and conflicts of interest out in the open, where they can be dealt with constructively by means of negotiation and compromise. Thus, they perceive conflict as having the potential for promoting personal and family growth.

4. *Functional Theory*. Functional theory emphasizes the resources that the individual brings to the relationship and the functions that he or she performs in the relationship. Thus, in attempting to explain certain aspects of marriage, we may ask what functions each person performs that enable the marital relationship to continue. This theory also provides for explanations of "dysfunctional" behavior that is detrimental to the relationship.

5. *Cognitive Theory*. The cognitive perspective emphasizes the ways in which an individual's beliefs and expectations can influence his or her perceptions, emotional reactions, and behavior in intimate relationships. Thus, a woman who erroneously assumes that what she wants is also what her husband wants is likely to generate conflict in her marriage unless or until she modifies this assumption. From a practical viewpoint, this theory paves the way for analyzing and modifying self-defeating ways of thinking and feeling that can impair intimate relationships. Cognitive theory is also capable of encompassing **self-theory.** The latter assumes that each of

(continued)

> **BOX 1–7** (*continued*)
>
> us exists in a private world of experi- ence of which the "I," "me," or "self" is the center. As new situations arise, they are perceived, thought about, and acted on in ways that are consistent with our view of ourselves. Often the term **phenomenology** is used to refer to the unique way in which each indi- vidual perceives a given situation and reacts to it. By understanding the per- son's view of himself or herself and of the world, we have another key to un- derstanding how a person behaves and relates to others in given situations.

Models are essentially analogies that help scientists order their findings and see important relationships among them. The computer model of the brain, for example, has made it commonplace to use the metaphors of input, information processing, and feedback in describing human thought processes. Even though there are many ways in which the brain is not like a computer, the model can be helpful in organizing and interpreting masses of data that might otherwise prove meaningless and unwieldly.

Theories are more comprehensive than models and have a more clearly for- mulated and agreed-on structure. Although they try to account for all the relevant data, theories must occasionally be modified to accommodate new evidence. It is this "self-correcting" ability of science that makes it such a powerful tool for pursuing objective truth.

Social scientists who study marriage and the family have found three theories particularly useful in explaining how people interact with and relate to each other. These are symbolic interaction theory, social exchange theory, and general sys- tems theory. Five other theoretical perspectives have also proven helpful. The latter are summarized in Box 1–7.

Symbolic interaction theory focuses on the interaction between people in terms of symbols, such as signs, gestures, language, shared rules, and social roles. As Ian Robertson (1977) has summarized it:

> The crucial point is that people do not respond to the world directly; they place a social meaning on it and respond to that meaning. The words of this book, the red light of a traffic signal, or a wolf whistle in the street have no meaning in themselves. People learn to attach symbolic meaning to these things, and they order their lives on the basis of these meanings. (p. 21)

In essence, we live not only in a physical world but also in a symbolic world, and people behave largely on the basis of the meanings they attach to various symbols, for example, wedding rings.

The concept of **socialization** plays a key role in symbolic interaction theory. People must understand and share the meaning of given symbols if they are to interact with and relate to each other in orderly and predictable ways. Socialization is the means by which they acquire the meanings of the symbols of their society. For example, a wedding ring would be useless as a symbol of the marriage union between two people if this were not an agreed-on and shared symbol in our society. And, in fact, when a couple come from disparate ethnic and social-class backgrounds, they soon discover that symbols can have different meanings, which may lead to difficulties in their relationship.

Symbolic interaction theory has been widely used in couple research, especially in the study of interpersonal attraction, mate selection, and marital relationships.

Social exchange theory is based on the idea that interpersonal relationships are formed for the purpose of meeting each individual's needs. Each person in the relationship wants something from the other, and the exchange that results is governed by economic principles. Thus, intimate relationships are seen as trading or bargaining situations, in which "costs" are balanced against "rewards" as each person decides whether the relationship is worth establishing or continuing. The person enters into and remains in the relationship only as long as the perceived cost reward ratio is satisfactory.

Another aspect of social exchange theory is the idea of equity. According to **equity theory,** most people are uncomfortable in a relationship if they think they are getting less or more than they deserve. They are most comfortable when they perceive the relationship as a fair one in which they are getting exactly what they deserve.

A second offshoot of social exchange theory is referred to as **resource theory.** This focuses on what resources each person brings to the relationship in terms of money, physical attractiveness, emotional warmth, and so on. Resource theory fits together with equity theory in that it essentially deals with the value of what each person contributes to the relationship. Of course, one person may place a greater value than the other person on a specific resource—such as physical beauty.

In sum, social exchange theory applies economic principles to the interpersonal marketplace. It is considered highly useful in explaining interpersonal attraction, establishment and maintenance of intimate relationships, and termination of such relationships when they are perceived as unsatisfactory by one or both partners. We shall examine this theory in more detail in Chapter 2.

General systems theory is a comprehensive approach to understanding the behavior of living systems—from individuals and marital dyads to organizations and nations. The focus is on the structural, functional, and field properties or characteristics of the system being studied.

In terms of a marital couple, for example, we would be concerned with such structural properties as the personality makeup of each partner, the roles each plays, the common goals and interests, and the methods of communicating and resolving conflicts. In terms of functional properties, we would be concerned with the effectiveness of their communication and problem-solving methods, their success or failure in achieving agreed-on goals, and the quality and stability of their marital relationship—in short, with their performance as a married couple. In terms of field properties, we would be concerned with the nature and effects of the environment in which their relationship occurs.

The general systems approach provides us with a tool that is equally useful whether the "system" we are considering is a disturbed individual, a failing marriage, a pathological family, or a community or national problem. In each case, we look for the structural and functional properties of the system under study as well as the properties of and transactions with the field in which the system is imbedded. Only with such a broad perspective are we likely to identify the interacting causal factors that may be involved and undertake a "treatment" program broad enough to be effective. Thus, it is not surprising that an increasing number of social scientists have found it helpful to view individuals, couples, and families in the context of general systems theory.

Throughout this book, we shall have occasion to refer to one or more of these theoretical approaches—the three main theories as well as the theories summarized in Box 1–7— in attempting to describe, understand, predict, and perhaps modify the development and outcome of specific relationships.

THE ORIENTATION OF THIS BOOK

There is an old saying: "Understanding economics may not keep you out of the poorhouse, but it will help you understand how you got there." Translated for sociology, we might say that understanding marriage and family relationships may not keep you out of the divorce court, but it may help you understand how you got there. We hope, however, that this will not be the normal outcome.

Admittedly, there are obstacles to understanding this field. For one thing, people ofen feel that studying marriage and the family is a waste of time because they already know so much about it from personal experience. But personal experiences may not be a broad-enough basis for making generalizations, and many commonsense notions about marriage and the family are inaccurate. In addition, the area of marriage and the family is charged with emotion and saturated with moral values. It is often difficult to be objective or to see the realities involved with any degree of clarity.

Thus, instead of using the information that sociology and its allied sciences have made available, many of us "muddle through" our intimate relationships. We worry along and solve our problems after a fashion, but we are essentially traveling in the dark and making many needless and costly mistakes as we stumble along. We choose incompatible mates, bring up children in the naïve hope that good intentions will be sufficient, and stagger from one disastrous relationship to another. But behind the façade of confidence we may present o the world are apt to lie deep-seated feelings of bewilderment, inadequacy, and unhappiness, for the price of muddling through is usually a high one. At best, this mode of running our lives is likely to lead to a serious waste of opportunities, time, and resources. More commonly, it takes a high toll in unnecessary failures, missed satisfactions, and emotional wear and tear. And a curious facet of our nature tends to make us highly aware of our losses—of what might have been.

A Scientific and Experiential Approach

Today, the findings of the social sciences can be of tremendous help. Although it is still a young science, sociology has acquired a substantial body of knowledge about intimate relationships; communication; self-disclosure; sex-roles; power and decision making; conflict resolution; mate selection; marital relationships; and the family, including single-parent families and stepfamilies.

Yet it has become apparent that we cannot expect sociology or any other science to give us all of the answers. In fact, science often presents us with new and difficult problems rather than answers. For example, science can predict the consequences of using contraceptives on both individual and group levels, but it cannot say whether the use of contraceptives is desirable or undesirable. This is a value judgment that individuals and societies must make. So, in this text we will use scientific findings to analyze the present and think about the future, but we will not expect the impossible of them. And, while we will view the social sciences as dependable sources of information about human beings and intimate relationships, we will use information from other sources as well.

Despite remarkable advances in recent years, there are still many important problems in intimate relationships about which the social sciences have little to say. We know very little, for example, about romantic love, trust, hope, loneliness, courage, and despair. Human beings alone of all animals can recount their experiences, describe their feelings, and compare them with each other. In literature, art, religion, philosophy, drama, and autobiographical accounts, we often find poignant and authentic renditions of experiences that are meaningful to all of us. In fact, over the centuries we have accumulated a vast store of nonscientific information about the nature, behavior, mistakes, and grandeur of human relationships. To ignore such a wealth of experience and insight would be to run the risk of dehumanizing ourselves. No description and explanation of human behavior would be complete if it did not encompass the intimate experiences and relationships that characterize our existence.

Consequently, in this book we shall not hesitate to draw on the humanities as well as the social sciences for insights into our intimate relationships. While we shall attempt to be scholarly and comprehensive in our coverage, we shall also offer practical information and suggestions that readers may find useful in evaluating and coping with their own intimate relationships.

Toward Personal Growth and Fulfilling Relationships

We do not propose that personal growth and satisfying intimate relationships can be achieved simply by reading a book. Nor does exposure to research findings about human behavior and relationships ensure that people can or will use this information in their own lives. Modern social science can provide dependable information about intimate relationships, marriage, and the family, but the mastery and effective use of this knowledge is up to the individual. However, a key finding of modern psychology is that most people, given the opportunity, do show good potential for personal growth and responsible self-direction—and hence for achieving satisfying intimate relationships and fulfilling lives.

The following are among the many reasons for studying marriage and the family:

1. To improve communication, conflict-resolving, and other interpersonal skills.
2. To understand change in marriage and the family and its significance for ourselves.
3. To develop a realistic view of ourselves, our partners, and our relationships.
4. To clarify our values as a basis for making sounder choices.
5. To prepare for and achieve satisfying and fulfilling marital and family relationships.

Throughout this text, we shall emphasize these objectives and suggest practical means for achieving them. If we are successful, the results will contribute to personal growth and fulfilling relationships.

This book is only a rough map of the road we hope to travel. But the route and destination will become clearer as the reader applies his or her own knowledge, values, and experience to the information presented here. Admittedly, no single student, instructor, or textbook can clear up the gaps in our understanding of marriage and intimate relationships. But, together, we can make a start, and it is difficult to imagine a more-crucial endeavor in our time.

SUMMARY—Chapter 1

1. Our society is going through a transformation from an industrial age to an information age characterized by rapid technological and social change, conflict, and stress. It is in this setting that intimate relationships, marriage, and family form and function.

2. Sex roles have changed. The traditional marriage and family in which the husband's role was that of "breadwinner" and the wife's role that of "homemaker" has given way to dual-career marriages and more egalitarian sex roles. However, sex roles are still in transition as are concepts of masculinity and femininity.

3. Major changes in marriage include rising expectations, more egalitarian sex roles, increasing dual-career marriages, and a high incidence of divorce and remarriage—which have become socially acceptable. Although couples may lose faith in a given relationship, they still have confidence in marriage.

4. Important changes in family life include a child-free alternative, a decrease in number of children per couple, a reduced role of parents in child-rearing, more family mobility, and an increase in single parent and stepfamilies. Although changing, the family as an institution is not disintegrating.

5. Many people think of families of the past as strong, stable, extended families. But it is doubtful that many such idealized families existed due to low life expectancy that led to short marriages, a sizeable number of single parent families due to the death of one spouse, and many orphanages.

6. In gathering information about marriage and intimate relationships, social scientists rely on the experimental, observational, survey, and existing information methods. In organizing research data, the three most important theories are symbolic interaction, social exchange, and general systems.

7. This text takes a scientific and experiential approach to marriage and intimate relationships. Science provides objective data; the humanities provide insights into areas where scientific data are scarce. The overall objective is to foster personal growth and fulfilling relationships.

II

FROM ENCOUNTERS TO INTIMATE RELATIONSHIPS

Dance at Bougival, 1883, by Pierre Auguste Renoir, French, 1841–1919. Oil on Canvas, 181.8 × 98.1 cm (71⅝ × 38⅝ in.) Picture Fund. 37.375. Courtesy Museum of Fine Arts, Boston

ENCOUNTERS: MEETING PEOPLE, GETTING ACQUAINTED

Some fortuitous encounters touch only lightly, others leave more lasting effects, and still others branch people into new trajectories of life.
—Albert Bandura (1982, p. 747)

John meets Melissa at a party. In the course of small talk, they discover that they both like blues singers, artichokes, and historical novels and have similar views on nuclear power and capital punishment. Before leaving the party, John asks Melissa for a date.

Luis and Carmen are sitting next to each other on a cross-country flight. They strike up a conversation to pass the time. Luis talks about his work as a public-relations officer for an industrial firm in the Midwest. Carmen describes her problems looking for housing near campus at the university where she will begin classes soon. They discuss airline food and the high cost of flying. At their destination, they go their separate ways.

Sheila and Herb meet at a popular nightclub. They dance and seem to hit it off quite well. Herb sees Sheila home, asks for her number, and says he'll call. Sheila can't wait to see him again, but he never calls.

These are but a few examples of the sorts of encounters people have with each other on a daily basis. Some encounters add a touch of excitement and help to enrich our lives; others can change our lives dramatically. And, of course, it is out of such chance encounters that many intimate relationships are built.

In this chapter, we shall examine the nature of encounters—how they are initiated, the tasks to be performed during initial encounters, and their potential value. In the course of this examination, we shall note how we form impressions of others, the kinds of errors we often make in "sizing up" other people, and what makes other people attractive to us. Next, we shall look at self-presentation—how we present ourselves in encounters. Finally, we shall see what factors are involved in determining whether an encounter will be terminated or upgraded to a beginning relationship, and we shall see how social exchange theory—which interprets social interactions in terms of costs, rewards, and related factors—can help us to understand better the nature and course of encounters.

THE NATURE OF ENCOUNTERS

Most of us find meeting and getting to know another person an interesting prospect, particularly if we perceive the other person to be attractive as well as accepting of us. True, not all encounters are pleasant, and some have unhappy endings. But, despite the potential risks, most of us do seek to meet and get to know others, especially if we are looking for someone with whom to establish an intimate relationship. But how do we go about meeting people, and, once we meet someone interesting, how do we check that person out?

Charles Harbutt/Archive Pictures, Inc.

Initiating an Encounter

Unfortunately, it is not easy to meet or get acquainted with other people in our society. In fact, we have been described as a "nation of strangers." Brief interactions with others are usually governed by social rituals, such as "How are you?" "I'm fine, thank you. How are you?" "Nice seeing you." "Take it easy." "Have a nice day."

We tend to distrust strangers, and there appears to be an unwritten rule that we do not strike up conversations with strangers in public places. For example, elevator etiquette dictates that we stand toward the back, avoid eye contact and touching, and keep conversation to a minimum. While it is sometimes possible to strike up a meaningful conversation in a supermarket, it is not easy and usually requires considerable social skill if we are not to be labeled as overly aggressive or weird. Such rule breaking requires the willingness to expose ourselves to possible ridicule and rejection. Society does not make room for certain exceptions, however, as in the case of social gatherings and travel situations.

Whatever the nature of the situation, an encounter usually begins with some communicative act that invites a response from another person. Such an act may be a formal introduction, or it may simply involve eye contact, a smile, or a pleasant remark. If the other person responds positively, the encounter is underway.

At the beginning of an encounter, both people are often hesitant and uncertain about what to say or how to behave. As the encounter progresses, however, each person learns about the other's life situation, status, interests, beliefs, and other characteristics. Thus, the initial uncertainty tends to diminish as both persons become more relaxed and better able to concentrate on really getting acquainted with each other.

This early interaction does not ordinarily involve the sharing of deep personal secrets. In fact, revealing a great deal about ourselves during an initial encounter is likely to be interpreted as self-centeredness, maladjustment, or both. This is particularly true for men who reveal too much too soon. Rather, the interaction usually focuses on an exchange of information about personal goals, interests, backgrounds, competencies, and values. A high level of self-disclosure, however, may sometimes prove desirable. We have to consider the personality of the self-discloser as well as that of the person eliciting the information (Miller et al., 1983). But, as Edelmann (1985) has pointed out, misjudging the type or degree of self-disclosure expected in an initial encounter can cause embarrassment for both of the persons involved. Thus, caution is desirable.

Tasks To Be Performed During the Initial Encounter

Interaction during initial encounters serves as a screening device—we use this encounter to "size up" or evaluate the other person and to determine whether we have enough in common to justify continuing the encounter. Bernard Murstein (1980) has summarized several tasks to be performed during this initial encounter:

1. Determine whether the other person possesses the **qualifiers,** or characteristics, that make it worthwhile to engage in an encounter.
2. Determine whether the other person is **cleared for** an encounter or possible relationship—is not "taken" or committed to someone else.
3. Find an **opener** that engages the other person's attention and an **integrating topic** that interests both parties and keeps the interaction going.
4. Project a **come-on** or rewarding self, rather than an aloof or distant one, that induces the other person to continue the initial encounter and be receptive to possible future ones.
5. If the person passes this screening, schedule a **second meeting** in order to continue the encounter.

IF the charming young Lady, who on Tuesday Evening was observed by a Gentleman walking up Cheapside, and from thence to the Temple Gardens, will be so obliging as to inform the said Gentleman, by a Line directed to F. G. at the Chancery Coffee-House, Chancery-Lane, where he may have the Happiness of an Interview, it will lay him under the greatest Obligation, as his Intentions are strictly honourable, and too serious to be trifled with. He hopes no other Person will trouble him with Letters, as Regard will be paid to none, unless their Companion (at that Time) is described, or some Circumstance, that he may be certain it comes from the agreeable Lady, who was dress'd in a Cloth-Colour Lustring Gown, with Silk and Bugle Fringe Trimming to the Sleeves, a black Gawfe Shade with red Flowers, and a black Hat with Pink Ribbons. It is imagined she lives in Westminster, as they went into the Park.

Smithsonian Institution Archive Center/Business Americana Collection

1754

IF any Lady of the Years of Twenty or Thirty-five, that is willing to join a young Gentleman of Birth and Family, whose Temper and Person can be no ways disagreeable to any Lady of Reason or Understanding, let them send a Line directed to C. D. to be left at St. Paul's Coffee-House near St. Paul's Church untill call'd for, they may depend upon meeting a Man of Honour and Honesty, whose Character will bear the strictest Enquiry. He has seen all the Gaety of Life, and has kept the best Company in the Kingdom; his Fortune is but small, therefore if any Lady of Honour can be contented with his small Fortune, she may depend upon it that her Want of Fortune will not debar him of having of her, provided she be a Lady of good Sense, and well-natur'd. It is to be hoped that no Person will answer this except those that can and will be sincere to him. He is no more than twenty-five Years of Age. He will wait with the greatest Impatience unless he has the Happiness of receiving a Letter from the agreeable Fair One, whom he intends to be happy with for Life.

Smithsonian Institution Archive Center/Business Americana Collection

These tasks are primarily aimed at encouraging an initial encounter and establishing conditions necessary for pursuing it and perhaps moving toward a relationship. Obviously, in certain types of encounters (such as enjoying a stranger's company for a few minutes while waiting in line at an airline-ticket counter) these tasks may not be relevant.

The Value of Brief Encounters

Although we value long-term relationships rather than brief encounters in our society, such encounters often make a marked impression on our lives. They allow us to compare notes about life with another person. And as we share our feelings and experiences, we often find that we have many things in common as human beings. For a little while, we are less alone in what often seems to be a cold and hostile world. In some instances, we may experience an unusual degree of mutual understanding, acceptance, and affinity. Most of us can remember brief encounters that touched us very deeply and permanently enriched our lives, encounters that we perhaps wished had grown into intimate relationships.

In addition, brief encounters can serve as important learning experiences. They help us to size up people more realistically, to understand our own needs and values, and to improve our communication and other interpersonal skills—skills that can later be used to nurture and enliven long-term relationships (see Box 2–1). Usually over time we also learn to be more discriminating and effective in our encounters, and we learn to deal with the problem of when and how to terminate an encounter or upgrade it to a relationship. And brief encounters can help us learn to cope with the ever-increasing "people turnover" in our lives that seems to be an inevitable part of our mobile and changing society (Coleman & Edwards, 1979; Cornish, 1987). Finally, as we have noted, encounters are the starting point for building intimate relationships.

BOX 2–1 / DEVELOPING CONVERSATIONAL SKILLS

Many people have difficulty opening a conversation in an encounter. And even if they do manage to open the conversation, they can't think of anything more to say. As a result, the conversation often consists of a few comments interspersed with gaps of silence that are uncomfortable for both persons.

Being able to sustain a conversation consists of three key skills: (1) using effective **openers**—ways of initiating a conversation; (2) using **follow-up openers,** which are aimed at finding some topic of common interest to pursue; and (3) using appropriate **closers**—knowing when and how to terminate a conversation or encounter.

Openers. Psychologist Chris Kleinke (1981) asked several hundred male college students to suggest opening lines they might use with female strangers in various situations—at bars, supermarkets, beaches, and so on. He then sorted the answers into three categories: direct, innocuous, and cute lip. For example, in general situations a direct approach might be, "I feel embarrassed, but I would like to meet you." An innocuous approach at the beach might be, "The water is beautiful today, isn't it?" A cute lip approach at the supermarket might be, "Do you really eat that junk food?"

In rating these approaches, both men and women stated that they preferred the direct and innocuous approaches to the cute lip. Kleinke also reported that men underestimated the extent to which women were put off by the cute lip approach. Whatever the case, in meeting strangers, most people learn to use approaches that are comfortable for them and that seem to be effective.

Follow-Up Openers. Even a simple opener—such as "This is sure some rain, isn't it?"—may backfire if the other person simply says "Yes." Thus, it is recommended that a person have two or three back-up remarks ready for following up openers. For example, the above opener might be followed by, "Do you recall it raining this hard so early in the year?" or "Is this unusual weather for this part of the country?" or "Do you remember last year when we had 6 inches of rain in 12 hours?"

Follow-up openers are useful in maintaining a conversation long enough to determine whether the other person wants to continue the encounter. Curt yes and no answers accompanied by looking away are a good indication that the other person has no interest in an encounter. On the other hand, more-informative answers tend not only to indicate interest but also to provide needed information for asking additional questions to keep the conversation going. Such questions may vary considerably, from those that are primarily factual and impersonal to those involving feelings and personal data. A factual question might be something along the lines of "Did the Redskins beat the Cowboys yesterday?" If the other person doesn't follow football, it may be followed up with a question about the other person's interests in sports. A somewhat more personal but still factual question would be something like, "Do you live here in San Diego?" An example of a primarily personal question would be "Do you feel that a college education is really worthwhile?" In general, personal questions focus on the person's feelings, beliefs, and values.

The most effective questions tend to be those that are not too personal but that encourage people to talk about themselves. A question such as "You seem to know a lot about art—are you an artist?" may come to mind. If the answer is "No, I'm a lawyer," the way is paved for such questions as "What field of law do you specialize in?"

It is important to keep the questions focused on the other person's interests and areas of expertise. Of course, some give

(continued)

BOX 2–1 (*continued*)

and take is necessary, and, in replying to the other person's questions or elaborating on his or her answers, it can be helpful to provide some information about yourself so the other person will have fuel for additional questions to keep the conversation going. However, you must take care to avoid focusing the conversation solely on yourself and dominating the discussion.

When a topic seems to have been exhausted, you can rescue the conversation by changing quickly to a new one. One procedure is to return to an earlier topic: "Incidentally, you made a statement earlier that intrigued me . . ." or "Okay, but to get back to the mundane world of reality. . . ." Sometimes it is possible to relate the new topic to the one that has reached a dead end. In any event, such shifts are often essential in keeping the conversation going.

Many people think a good conversationalist is one who does most of the talking—who says something entertaining or profound and is interesting to listen to. Although some good conversationalists may fit this pattern, most do not. Rather, they are good listeners who take a sincere interest in others and encourage them to talk about subjects of personal interest. Of course, the conversation should not be one-sided. But two key rules to being a good listener are to give the other person your full attention and to avoid interrupting unless the other person is unusually long-winded and dull or offensive.

Closers: Terminating the Conversation. Time is usually limited during initial encounters. Thus, after a brief conversation, the other person may stand, move away, excuse himself or herself, or provide other cues that it's time to end the conversation. Such cues may include breaking eye contact, glancing around the room looking for acquaintances, or looking at an empty glass in hand and acting uncomfortable.

While it may be tempting to get in a few last comments or questions, conversational etiquette dictates that you not challenge their reasons for leaving and not detain them. At this point, a polite comment such as "It was nice talking to you" may be in order. If you wish to continue the encounter at a later date, however, it is important to express an interest in seeing the person again and to obtain the needed information. Thus, a closer such as "I enjoyed talking to you" might be followed by "May I call you some time?"

If the person does not wish to continue the encounter, it need not be considered a rejection. The other person may be busy or preoccupied with personal problems. At another time and place, the encounter might have been continued.

HOW WE PERCEIVE OTHERS

One of the most important and challenging tasks we face in meeting new people is evaluating them as persons. Psychologists call such "people watching" **person perception.** Some of us are better people watchers than others, and some people are easier to size up than others. But, because people play such important roles in our lives and inaccuracies in evaluating others can be both unfortunate and hurtful, it is a serious game in which we do the best we can.

Forming an Impression

A girl stood before him, alone and still, gazing out to sea. Her long slender bare legs were delicate as a crane's. Her long fair hair was girlish; and girlish and touched with the wonder of mortal beauty, her face. When she felt his presence and the worship of his eyes her eyes turned to him in quiet sufferance of his gaze. Her image had passed into his soul forever.

James Joyce
A Portrait of the Artist as a Young Man

Interestingly enough, our first impressions of others are formed quite rapidly—often within a matter of seconds (Bersheid & Graziano, 1979). It seems that we each have a sort of mental rating sheet, and when we meet a new person, we automatically rate him or her according to the categories on that sheet. For example, we may give a person a high, medium, or low rating in physical attractiveness, manners, and friendliness. Thus, when forming an impression of others, we tend to use a small amount of information in a brief period of time to develop an overall picture. We use this picture to determine whether we wish to initiate or continue an encounter.

In making our mental ratings, we tend to focus on three key factors: physical appearance, behavior, and interactional possibilities. When it comes to **physical appearance,** we are particularly concerned with whether the person is male or female, young or old, attractive or unattractive. Although these categories may seem simple enough, they help us to integrate our perceptions. For when we register this information, we immediately assign the person to a category based on our previous experience. The categories "male, young, unattractive" and "female, middle-aged, attractive," for example, yield a wealth of information from prior experiences that we tend to apply to the person we are evaluating. Of course, many of these categories are subjective. A middle-aged person might be assigned to the "old" category by a teenager and to the "young" category by an octogenarian.

When we focus on another person's **behavior,** we are concerned with readily observed behavior, such as whether he or she is friendly or aloof, is outgoing or shy, maintains or avoids eye contact, or speaks fluently or hesitantly. In forming impressions of behavior, we need to determine whether the behavior results from **internal** dispositional factors of the person or from **external** situational factors. This takes us into the realm of **attribution**—of attempting to answer the question, "What caused the behavior?" For example, the person who is aloof and unsmiling at a party and who seems to ignore you may actually be looking for his teenage daughter who is supposed to meet him and is inexplicably late. You may at first judge this person unfavorably, attributing his behavior to an undesirable personality, but, informed of his situation, you may see him in a quite different light.

In terms of **interactional possibilities,** we are concerned with ways in which the person can affect us. For example, does the person have the characteristics we value in a potential friend, lover, or spouse? Is he or she in a position to hurt us or help us? Do we have needs that we perceive the person being able to fulfill? Again, seemingly simple cues may have far-reaching implications. For example, a woman may view the same man quite differently depending on whether she is looking for a lover, a bridge partner, an employee, or a husband. Ellen Berscheid and William Graziano (1979) suggest that we are likely to ignore or be indifferent to people we perceive as having no power to meet our needs or influence our welfare. On the other hand, we are likely to expend great effort in initiating an encounter with a person we perceive as important in meeting our needs—especially if we have strong needs. Thus, interactional possibilities may prove highly important in determining the way we evaluate others and react to them.

Person perception is a complex process. Ultimately, it depends not only on the characteristics of the person being perceived but also on the characteristics of the

Drawing by Frascino, © 1981 The New Yorker Magazine, Inc.

perceiver and the situation. As an encounter continues, the perceiver becomes able to focus on deeper and less readily observable characteristics of the other person—such as intelligence, honesty, and concern for others—and to make needed adjustments in his or her initial impression. Nevertheless, that first impression, whether accurate or inaccurate, can color further interactions. There is plenty of room for error in person perception, as we shall now see.

Common Sources of Error in Sizing Up People

Our initial evaluation of another person is subject to several sources of error. Because we typically form impressions based on brief and limited interactions, we almost inevitably **overgeneralize.** That is, we arrive at a "global evaluation" of the person without adequate information. This global evaluation may alter our perception of the person's specific attributes. For example, if we like someone, we may perceive him or her as more attractive than if we dislike that person. We shall pursue this point a bit further in a moment, but first let us examine some other common and interrelated sources of error in person perception.

Implicit Personality Theory.   We rely on our own experience and assumptions about human nature and behavior—on our own **implicit personality theory**—when evaluating others. If our learning and experience lead us to believe that people are basically friendly and honest, we will judge new people quite differently

Peter Arnold, Inc., © Erika Stone, 1978

than if we assume human beings are basically predatory and deceitful. Similarly, we may view a talkative person differently depending on whether we assume that talkative people are self-centered and superficial or intelligent and knowledgeable. Thus, our evaluations may be more or less accurate depending on the assumptions we have built into our theory and on how well they apply to the person in question. When our implicit personality theory is biased or inaccurate, it becomes a potent source of error in evaluating others.

Assumed Similarity.   Closely related to our implicit personality theory is our tendency to use ourselves as a reference point and to assume that other people are pretty much like we are in terms of feelings, beliefs, and values. When people come from backgrounds similar to our own, this assumption of similarity works pretty well—or at least is not unduly misleading. But when people come from backgrounds different from our own, assumed similarity may lead to serious errors in evaluation. Arabs, for example, like to stand very close in order to have a conversation and to stare directly into each other's eyes—they are very good readers of the silent language of pupillary response (Hall, 1979). Americans who engage in conversations with Arabs may interpret this close contact as arrogant, intense, and pushy. Yet the Arabs are just behaving in their normal manner of trying to learn all they can about the person with whom they are conversing.

In any event, we tend to be more accurate in evaluating people who are like us in background than those who are unlike us.

Stereotypes.   A **stereotype** is an overly simplified but widely shared belief about some group of people that is applied to all members of the group without considering the differences among them. For example, we tend to view Germans as methodical, Quakers as peace loving, Irish as heavy drinkers, and college professors as absentminded and unworldly. Thus, stereotypes may be racial, ethnic, economic, or occupational.

Stereotypes are often perpetuated by the so-called "germ of truth." That is, some members of the group do fit the stereotype. We are usually quick to spot such "confirming evidence" and to feel justified in applying the stereotype to a stranger whom we perceive as belonging to that group. Of course, if the person doesn't fit the stereotype, we see him or her as "the exception that proves the rule." Thus, stereotypes tend to be self-perpetuating.

Stereotypes may also represent a type of prejudice, in which someone is prejudged as good or bad based on insufficient evidence. Unfortunately, such prejudice is rarely checked against reality or modified by information that contradicts the rigid image. In general, we tend to be prejudiced favorably toward people we view as similar to us and negatively toward people we view as dissimilar. In this way, we may negatively assess a person belonging to some stigmatized group without ever getting to know that person in his or her own right.

The Halo Effect. First impressions may be distorted because we focus on a single characteristic that we particularly like or dislike. If the trait is a desirable one, such as beauty, we tend to form a positive impression of the person and to attribute all sorts of other favorable characteristics to him or her. On the other hand, if we focus on a negative trait, such as arrogance, we form a negative impression of the person and attribute other negative characteristics to him or her.

This "**halo effect**" has been well illustrated by Nisbett and Wilson (1977), who presented videotaped interviews to a group of subjects. One group of subjects saw a tape in which a college instructor who spoke English with a European accent acted warm and friendly. A second group of subjects saw a tape featuring the same instructor, but this time he acted cold and distant. When the subjects were asked to rate the man's appearance, mannerisms, and actions, those who saw the "warm" version rated these characteristics as being appealing, while those who saw the "cold" version were more likely to rate these attributes as irritating. These subjects were apparently unaware of how their impressions of the instructor's warmth or coolness had influenced their ratings of his specific characteristics.

Fundamental Attribution Error. Another common source of error in person perception is our tendency to assume that people's behaviors arise from dispositional factors rather than situational factors. This is called the **fundamental attribution error** because it involves attributing behaviors to internal as opposed to external causes. For example, if a young woman spills coffee on you at a social gathering and doesn't apologize, you may consider her inconsiderate and rude. But if you realized that she was bumped and in the confusion didn't notice that she had spilled her coffee, you would consider her and her behavior differently.

The fundamental attribution error tends to work in reverse in evaluating our own behavior: When things go wrong, we tend to attribute the cause to situational factors rather than to our own personal characteristics (Jellison & Greene, 1981; Mehlman & Snyder, 1985). Thus, we tend to operate on a causal "double standard," depending on whether we are dealing with another person's behavior or our own.

BOX 2-2 / COMMON SOURCES OF ERROR IN PERSON PERCEPTION

Source	Error	Source	Error
Inadequate information	The tendency to form a "global impression" based on limited information about a person.	Fundamental attribution error	The tendency to underestimate situational influences on behavior and to attribute behavior to internal personal characteristics.
Implicit personality theory	Relying solely on our own experience and assumptions about human nature and behavior.	Social role	Assuming that persons possess characteristics associated with their roles in society.
Stereotyping	Applying a generalized belief about some group of people to individuals belonging to that group, without considering differences among group members.	Logical error	Assuming that because a person has one characteristic he or she will have other characteristics that "go with" it.
Assumed similarity	Using ourselves as reference points and assuming that other people are pretty much like us.	Wishful thinking	Seeing others as we would like them to be rather than as they are.
Halo effect	The tendency to let some positive or negative characteristic bias our overall impression.	Leniency effect	The tendency to give people "the benefit of the doubt" and to evaluate them positively unless some negative characteristic stands out.

Other Common Errors. Sometimes we are deceived by the "good front" people erect to impress us. Or we may be misled by wishful thinking into seeing another person as we would like him or her to be rather than as he or she is. Often, too, we assume that people possess the characteristics associated with the social roles they play. Thus, we may assume that a member of the clergy is pious, circumspect, and highly moral, which may or may not be true. Closely related is the so-called **logical error,** in which we make a connection between one important bit of information about a person and other traits that we assume go along with it. For example, if a woman has written a highly successful book on sex and love, we may assume that she is a great lover, which she may or may not be. Finally, we are subject to the **leniency effect**—unless negative characteristics stand out, we tend to give other people the benefit of the doubt and evaluate them positively. Box 2-2 summarizes these common sources of error in forming impressions of people.

Because we meet new people all the time, using stereotypes and other learned guidelines can be useful and timesaving in day-to-day encounters. As we have seen, however, these guidelines are subject to error. Fortunately, when encounters continue, the snap judgments of first impressions can be replaced by clearer and more-accurate perceptions of the person's characteristics as a unique human being.

What Attracts Us to Others?

When we encounter someone and form a favorable impression, we may or may not feel attracted to that person. Why is it that we are attracted to one person and not to another? Research findings indicate that certain desirable personal traits certainly play a part in interpersonal attraction. These traits include physical attractiveness, personal warmth, sincerity, a sense of humor, superior intelligence, and communicative understanding—the ability to understand others and make ourselves understood. It comes as no surprise that we are attracted to persons who possess these traits. But there are other factors that also play an important role in attraction, including similarity, complementarity, mutual liking, and competence.

Physical Attractiveness.   Most of us are attracted to members of the opposite sex who are physically attractive. In a pioneering study, Elaine Walster and her associates (1966) matched student subjects randomly for blind dates at a dance. These researchers found that physically attractive subjects were much more likely to like each other and to want to make another date. In fact, physical attractiveness was more-strongly related to the desire to date a person again than any other measure, including personality, similarity of interests, and intelligence. Similarly, Dion, Berscheid, and Walster (1972) found that students judged to be highly attractive were also rated as having more-desirable personalities, a greater chance of achieving success, a greater likelihood of being good husbands and wives, and a greater chance of leading happier lives. And these judgments were based solely on looking at pictures of the students. The more-attractive ones in the study were also rated as being more sensitive, kind, poised, strong, honest, and sexually warm than the less-attractive students. The researchers summarized their findings in the title of the article: "What Is Beautiful Is Good." To any astute observer of American mass media, it would often seem that way.

More-recent research findings, as well as everyday observations, strongly attest to the importance of beauty in our society (Cunningham, 1986; Hatfield & Sprecher, 1986). For example, the latter researchers cited the comments of one young female subject to the effect that:

> She had been introduced to various influential people, had been offered jobs, and had been granted extra privileges solely as a result of her looks. As she pointed out, these opportunities and privileges were denied to equally qualified people who lacked her attractive appearance.

In the development of relationships, however, it is also apparent that there is more to attractiveness than beauty alone. As Judith Jobin (1979) has pointed out, "Few men go for a pretty face until they hear what comes out of her mouth" (p. 77). We could paraphrase the preceding statement with "Few women go for a

Tom Kelly

handsome face until they hear what comes out of his mouth." Physical beauty without other desirable characteristics—such as intelligence, warmth, and sensitivity—is not likely to maintain its initial attractiveness very long. In addition, physical attractiveness can be largely negated by undesirable characteristics such as self-centeredness, deceitfulness, and stupidity.

Finally, it may be emphasized that physical beauty appears to be far more important in initial encounters and sexual attraction than it is in the formation of enduring relationships (Nevid, 1985; Mall, 1986).

Of course, most of us would probably like to date and marry breathtakingly beautiful people who are also intelligent, witty, kind, and so on. But we usually pair up with persons of about equal physical attractiveness as ourselves. In fact, Elaine Walster and G. William Walster (1978) have cited evidence to show that we feel uncomfortable if we perceive our partner to be more attractive than we are—perhaps because of fear of competition and rejection. As we get to know people better, positive personality traits, such as warmth, sincerity, and intelligence, become increasingly more important in our evaluation of a person's overall attractiveness. In short, a person doesn't have to be beautiful to be attractive, although admittedly it does help.

Similarity.   Not only do people select partners who are similar in physical attractiveness, but also they are attracted to those with a similar level of intelligence, dependability, warmth, honesty, and mental health. Mentally healthy persons, for example, tend to end up with partners who are also mentally healthy, whereas maladjusted persons tend to pair up with other maladjusted persons (Walster, Walster, & Bersheid, 1978).

Similarity is also reflected in our attraction to individuals who share our basic beliefs, interests, values, and social background. The more important the shared beliefs and values are to us, the more we tend to be attracted. For example, Joseph Grush and Janet Yehl (1979) have shown that similarity in sex-role orientation— that is, traditional versus egalitarian—is an important factor in interpersonal attraction.

Perhaps we like people who agree with our beliefs and values because they reinforce our feeling that we are "correct" in our views, which bolsters our feelings of adequacy and self-esteem. Common interests and values also tend to be part and parcel of a common purpose—to strive together toward agreed-on goals. If two people find that their goals are in conflict, they are less likely to pursue an encounter.

In short, when others disagree with our beliefs, goals, and values, it is easy to like them. When they disagree, it is difficult to like them and easy to dislike them.

Complementarity.   While the rule is "like attracts like," in some instances "opposites attract," depending on the nature of the differences. Differences in interests, beliefs, and values are likely to prove disturbing over time. On the other hand, differences in which one person's resources compensate for the other person's lack of resources may lead to mutual attraction. In social-exchange terms, there is a tradeoff in personal resources.

Probably the best-documented and most widespread tradeoff in our society is between beauty and money. Traditionally, in our society, men have been valued for their economic success and women for their beauty. Thus, a complementary match might involve a beautiful younger woman and a rich older man. On a different level, an outgoing person and a shy person may hit it off quite well. In essence, if each person has some characteristic that the other needs but lacks, the way is paved for mutual attraction—at least in terms of these characteristics. This situation is referred to as **need complementarity.** We shall further examine the concept of complementarity in Chapter 7.

Mutual Liking.   We tend to be attracted to persons who like us and who reward us with expressions of approval. In fact, we tend to disclose more about ourselves and take a more-positive attitude toward people we think like us (Curtis & Miller, 1986). Although it helps to feel that the other person is sincere in his or her approval, flattery also tends to work. After reviewing available research, Berscheid and Walster (1978) concluded that the "flatterer—who goes too far in shouting our praises—may lose a few points but not many" (p. 56). Flattery is especially likely to succeed when a person has suffered a setback in self-esteem and needs emotional support. In such instances, a person is not likely to be too critical of the flatterer or of his or her motivation. Nevertheless, it is useful to remember that people may react negatively to compliments, even sincere ones, if they feel that they are being set up to do something they don't want to do.

Studies have shown that we tend to be more attracted to people who do not appear to like us initially—or who appear neutral—but who like us more over time (Aronson, 1980). Perhaps we feel that their growing to like us represents discrimination and sincerity on their part. Conversely, if a person likes us initially but

Joan Liftin/Archive Pictures, Inc.

comes to dislike us, we tend to be more hurt than if he or she had disliked us from the start.

Why is being liked by others so important to us? It may be that feeling understood and appreciated helps to alleviate feelings of self-doubt and to reinforce our feelings of worth and self-esteem. The other person "rewards" us by making us feel good about ourselves. It is difficult not to like such a person.

Competence and Other Characteristics.   We tend to be attracted to persons who seem at least moderately competent. This competency may take the form of special abilities or skills or of being a self-confident person who seems capable of dealing effectively with the problems of living. However, people who are vastly superior to us in a number of areas tend to turn us off. Perhaps they make us feel inferior by comparison, or we may feel that they would be disappointed in us.

A number of other personality traits regarded as socially desirable are usually associated with interpersonal attractiveness. As we noted, such traits include superior intelligence, a good sense of humor, and communicative understanding. In addition, we tend to be attracted to people who are pleasant to be around. Desirable characteristics contribute to a couple being compatible, to getting along well together. Conversely, negative traits and marked differences in ethnic background and personality characteristics may contribute to incompatibility. However, as they do with person perception, people differ in the traits they consider to be positive or negative. In some instances, it may be difficult to account for a couple's compatibility. We may even refer to them as the "odd couple."

In general, the various factors involved in interpersonal attraction can be seen as fitting into a pattern of mutual reward. If an encounter is perceived as likely to be unrewarding to one or both persons, it is usually terminated. But if the encounter is perceived as likely to be rewarding, it is usually continued. In essence, people tend to like each other because each offers things the other considers of value. We will look further at this reward approach to interpersonal attraction later in this chapter.

SELF-PRESENTATION IN ENCOUNTERS

Most of us want to be approved of and liked. Consequently, we try to make a good impression when meeting people. As sociologist Erving Goffman (1959) has pointed out, we behave like actors trying to maintain behavior appropriate to the situation and to present ourselves in the best possible light. Thus, most of us have a repertoire of facial expressions, body postures, voice inflections, and conversational approaches that we use in trying to make a favorable impression on others. For, whether we like it or not, first impressions can be difficult to modify (Gollwitzer & Wicklund, 1985). If we are attracted to someone and wish to get acquainted, it is a distinct advantage to get off on "the right foot." In this section, we shall examine several factors that can influence our self-presentation—or, as social psychologists call it, **impression management**—and the initial impression we make on others.

BOX 2–3 / ITEMS FROM SNYDER'S SELF-MONITORING SCALE

The following statements concern personal reactions to a number of different situations. No two statements are exactly alike, so consider each statement carefully before answering. If a statement is true, or mostly true as applied to you, circle the T. If a statement is false, or not usually true as applied to you, circle the F.

1. I find it hard to imitate the behavior of other people.   T F

2. I guess I put on a show to impress or entertain people.   T F

3. I would probably make a good actor.   T F

4. I sometimes appear to others to be experiencing deeper emotions than I actually am.   T F

5. In a group of people, I am rarely the center of attention.   T F

6. In different situations with different people, I often act like very different persons.   T F

7. I can only argue for ideas I already believe.   T F

8. In order to get along and be liked, I tend to be what people expect me to be rather than anything else.   T F

9. I may deceive people by being friendly when I really dislike them.   T F

10. I'm not always the person I appear to be.   T F

Scoring: Give yourself one point for each of questions 1, 5, and 7 that you answered F. Give yourself one point for each of the remaining questions that you answered T. Add up your points. If you are a good judge of yourself and scored 7 or above, you are probably a low self-monitoring individual.

Self-Monitoring (Self-Presentation)

Psychologist Mark Snyder has found that people differ markedly in the extent to which they can control their self-presentations. In order to examine these differences, he developed what he calls a "**self-monitoring scale,**" which is shown in Box 2–3. He uses this scale to separate what he calls "high" self-monitors and "low" self-monitors. According to Snyder (1980), high self-monitors

Oh wad we had the giftie to see oursels as others see us.
Robert Burns

have developed the ability to carefully monitor their own performances when signals from others tell them that they are not having the desired effect . . . low self-monitoring individuals are not so concerned about taking in such information; instead, they tend to express what they feel, rather than mold and tailor their behavior to fit the situation. (p. 33)

The available research does indicate that persons who score high on the self-monitoring scale are superior at impression management (Snyder, 1980; Snyder & Gangestad, 1982; Synder & Simpson, 1984; Synder et al., 1985; Rother et al., 1986). Typically, they are able to make better initial impressions on others than are persons with low scores. Whether or not this advantage is maintained over the long run from initial encounters to intimate relationships remains to be clarified. Interestingly enough, high self-monitors are also more adept at detecting impression management by others—at seeing behind the mask. They are also keenly aware of the motives and intentions of others. Low self-monitors, on the other hand, tend to accept other people's behavior at face value. Finally, high self-monitors place greater emphasis on the physical appearance of the other person and low self-monitors place greater emphasis on "interior" personality characteristics such as intelligence and a sense of humor.

While skill in self-monitoring may have advantages in initial encounters, it also has inherent dangers. Wearing masks and playing roles in order to disguise our real selves and impress others tends to kill spontaneity. We have to remain on guard and not express our true feelings or act in certain ways. In addition, most of us can only play ourselves well. While we may be able to maintain a convincing façade during an initial encounter, we are likely to be "unmasked" as others get to know us better. And the outcome may be the opposite of what we had hoped for—they may distrust and dislike us for being a phony.

Nevertheless, self-monitoring can serve an important purpose. Individuals who tend to make unfavorable impressions in social situations—such as by talking too much, appearing aloof, acting gloomy, or even trying too hard to please—may simply be acting out of nervousness and not truly reflecting their typical behavior. Given a chance to improve on their self-monitoring skills, they can learn to project a more favorable and valid self-image and facilitate initial encounters.

The Toll of a Negative Self-Concept (Self-Evaluation)

Our self-evaluation is based on experience and largely determined by the way other people view us, by observation of our own behavior, and by the extent to which we measure up to social norms in terms of appearance, behavior, and achievement. As a result of this input, we may have a positive self-image, accompanied by feelings of self-esteem, adequacy, and worth, or a negative one, accompanied by feelings of inferiority, inadequacy, and worthlessness.

What happens if we have a negative self-evaluation? For one thing, other people are likely to accept our evaluation at face value. If we do not like or respect ourselves, they probably won't like or respect us either. Also, when we concentrate on our liabilities, we tend to limit our initiative—what we are willing to try. As a result, we may avoid opportunities to meet and interact with people, opportunities that could be enjoyable and growth producing. When we do interact with others, we are likely to feel ill at ease and defensive. In fact, we may even attempt to don a mask to hide our true selves. And, probably not being good at impression management, we are likely to come across as phony. We only play ourselves well (see Boxes 2–4; 2–5).

In contrast, a positive self-evaluation tends to be associated with self-confidence, competence, and a more-positive attitude toward others. Research has shown that it is difficult to appreciate others when we do not like or approve of ourselves (Bower & Bower, 1976; Rogers, 1985). On the other hand, when we feel comfortable with and good about ourselves, we tend to relate to others in a positive and enjoyable way. And just as people are inclined to accept a person's

No one can make you feel inferior without your own consent.
Eleanor Roosevelt

BOX 2–4 / DO WE NEED OUR MASKS?

All the world's a stage
And all the men and women merely players.
                                              —Shakespeare

Most of us learn to wear masks to hide our true feelings, to disguise our real selves, or to portray our desired self. Like ancient Greek actors who held stylized masks before their faces to denote the character they were playing and the emotion they were portraying, we also are mask-wearers.

Does wearing a mask mean that we are phonies? Not necessarily. For one thing, we are complicated people and have many selves —even though these selves may be integrated into an overall and consistent self-identity. But a given situation may elicit a given self. In addition, we are confronted with the necessity of some role-playing as a means of facilitating social interactions, of behaving in ways that seem understandable, appropriate, and predictable to others.

However, to the extent that people don masks to disguise or conceal their "real selves" or to pass themselves off as someone other than who they are, they can be called phonies. Often people hide behind the masks they wear, however, because they are afraid that if they revealed their true selves, others would reject them. Only in intimate relationships are people likely to remove their masks and say "This is the real me, flaws and all."

The American poet Ralph Waldo Emerson once wrote, "Insist on yourself." But to do so requires a high degree of self-esteem—placing a high value on yourself—and the courage to face the very real possibility of rejection. Do we need our masks? The answer is probably "Yes"—at least to some extent. But it is useful to remember that we play only one person well—ourselves.

---

negative self-evaluation at face value, they are likely to accept a positive one. Admittedly, of course, it takes more than a positive self-concept to make the most of encounters. But it is helpful in making ourselves attractive to others and facilitating interaction with them. And, as with self-monitoring and self-presentation, a person can improve his or her self-evaluation.

BOX 2–5 / SOME QUESTIONS ABOUT OURSELVES

Are you genuine?
Or merely an actor?
A representative?
Or that which is represented?
In the end perhaps you are merely a copy of an actor.

Are you one who looks on?
Or one who lends a hand?
Or one who looks away and walks off?

Do you want to walk along?
Or walk ahead?
Or walk by yourself?
*One must know **what** one wants and **that** one wants.*
                                              —Nietzsche

BOX 2–6 / PEOPLE CAN BE THEIR OWN WORST DOWNERS

"Self-downing," or "sabotaging oneself," is ideally suited to developing and maintaining a negative self-concept. Why then do people sabotage themselves? Several reasons have been suggested.

1. "*I can't do it, so why try?*" This self-downing attitude serves as an excuse for not exerting the effort necessary for achievement. If we accept ourselves as incapable, there is no need to try.

2. "*I don't want to disappoint others.*" This self-downing approach is designed to cue others to set low expectations for us. In this way, we are less likely to disappoint them or feel that we have let them or ourselves down.

3. "*My beliefs are not self-defeating.*" This approach causes us to refuse to examine and change our self-defeating beliefs—such as "I must do everything well," or "It's terribly important that everyone like me." Such beliefs guarantee failure and a negative self-image.

4. "*Defensive pessimism.*" This self-downing approach prevents the fear of failure from immobilizing us. Because we anticipate the worst anyway, failure will be less painful.

5. "*It was my fault.*" When something goes wrong, we automatically blame the failure on some defect on our part. For example, a date didn't work out "because nobody likes me."

Unless we take constructive measures for changing such self-defeating behavior, our negative self-image is likely to be supported by lack of achievement and failure. We shall not attempt to describe ways of modifying such behavior, but it may be useful to note that (1) in encounters, we have only 50 percent of the responsibility (If an encounter doesn't work out, it may be the other person was not receptive for reasons of their own—reasons that may have little or nothing to do with you); (2) the field of therapy known as Rational-Emotive Therapy (RET) is designed to pinpoint and modify self-defeating beliefs and behaviors; and (3) even "defensive pessimism" can be a constructive attitude providing "you prepare for the worst and then hope for the best."

Perhaps the bottom line is contained in a statement made by Eleanor Roosevelt, "No one can make you feel inferior without your own consent."

In addition, a person's self-evaluation may be at considerable variance with the facts. A highly capable and talented person may suffer from deep-seated feelings of inadequacy and inferiority and a person with inferior capabilities may be convinced of his superiority. Of course, with time, our social interactions tend to correct discrepancies between self-evaluation and reality. But, in the case of negative self-evaluations, these corrections are rarely made quickly or easily. When such negative feelings have deep roots, even positive experiences will probably not entirely correct them. Some examples of negative thinking are in Box 2–6.

Being a Rewarding Person

Our attractiveness to another person depends not only on our appearance and other characteristics but also on whether we accept and approve of him or her. We

Ellis Herwig/The Picture Cube

can be extremely sensitive to others' reactions and are easily turned off by rejection. On the other hand, it is difficult not to like someone who obviously likes and approves of us—who rewards us by trying to understand and appreciate us without analyzing or judging our behavior.

To those of us who knew the pain of Valentines that never came and those whose names were never called when choosing sides for basketball It was long ago, and far away The world was younger than today and dreams were all they gave for free to ugly duckling girls like me.

Janis Ian "At Seventeen"

Approval is likely to have its greatest impact when it is sincere and the other person has gone a long time without receiving approval or has been rejected recently. It is easy to see why some people fall in love "on the rebound"; after feeling unworthy and rejected, they are highly receptive to someone who seems to understand, approve, and appreciate them. But even if someone is accustomed to receiving approval, rewarding him or her still helps to facilitate an initial encounter.

People who approve of and accept us help to lower our defenses and express our thoughts and feelings without fear of rejection. Conversely, people who are critical of or who accept us with obvious reservations make us feel defensive and ill at ease. Such "unrewarding" individuals may be highly competitive in their social interactions, trying to prove their superiority, or they may be quick to criticize and judge rather than understand. Unrewarding people may also express their views in such a dogmatic way that they make others feel their own views are of no importance. Others may be too proud to apologize when an apology is required.

In these and other ways, unrewarding persons can cause potentially enjoyable encounters and possibly good relationships to be aborted before they have a chance to get off the ground.

Most people, of course, can dispense social approval. However, using it effectively requires practice and skill. During the initial phase of an encounter, for example, it is often more effective to use approval sparingly and to increase its use as the encounter progresses. While adherence to social expectations and conventions can be overdone, sensitivity to what is appropriate in given situations can be helpful, for using good manners and behaving appropriately can make us more-attractive and rewarding persons to be around. In short, being a rewarding person usually involves considerable competence in interpersonal or social skills—and these skills can be learned and improved.

FROM ENCOUNTERS TO RELATIONSHIPS

As we have noted, an encounter can consist of one meeting that may last from a few minutes to several hours. If the encounter is pursued, additional meetings are arranged, and the encounter may last for days, weeks, or even months. But eventually it is either terminated or upgraded to a beginning relationship.

Pursuing an Encounter

Let us assume that two people have met, feel attracted to each other, and wish to get better acquainted. What do they do next? The most common way of pursuing an initial encounter is to agree on an informal get-together, such as for coffee or perhaps lunch. The basic idea is to pursue the encounter with no strings attached. In this way, if the next meeting proves disappointing, neither person is obligated, and the encounter can be terminated with a minimum of hurt to either party.

Most people who meet for the first time are not absolutely sure that they want to pursue the encounter. Braiker and Kelley (1979) note, for example, that after encounters people rarely report that they have fallen in love or feel part of a union or partnership. Rather, the encounters simply serve as screening devices for learning more about a person without getting involved.

How many encounters usually continue beyond the first meeting? Probably very few. Take, for example, two people who meet on a cross-country flight. They may be attracted to each other, spend a few pleasant hours together, exchange phone numbers, and go their separate ways when the plane reaches its destination. Yet, it is likely that they will never see each other again. However, this does not necessarily devalue the enjoyable and perhaps growth-producing encounter they had. Despite the fact that so few encounters continue beyond the first meeting or so, it is out of the encounters that *are* pursued that intimate relationships are eventually built.

Terminating an Encounter

Encounters may end for a variety of reasons, including lack of attraction, competition from others, and adverse environmental conditions. As George Levinger

(1979) has pointed out, most encounters terminate after an initial impression and a shallow degree of interaction and require little or nothing in the way of termination procedures.

In the case of an encounter that has continued through one or more casual meetings, the termination is usually accompanied by a sort of ritualistic role enactment. That is, each person assures the other that the encounter will be resumed ("I'll call you") even though one or both know it has come to an end. Presumably, this ritual is intended to prevent either person from feeling rejected or devalued. However, when one person sincerely believes the encounter will be resumed and is looking forward to building a relationship (such as Sheila in the example at the beginning of this chapter), the later realization that the encounter has been terminated may be disappointing and hurtful.

In a limited but interesting study of the "I'll-call-you-again" syndrome, Christine Wills (1981) found it to be tied in with the old double standard in which the male dominates the course of the encounter. However, she also found that some women wanted the man to say he'd call even if he didn't mean it. Presumably this was considered less hurtful than some statement such as "I don't think we have enough in common to justify seeing each other again."

Psychologist Fritz Perls (1969) stated that, because we are all unique individuals, our ability to establish intimate relationships with others either works or it doesn't. He also pointed out that we have no obligation to pursue an encounter in order to make another person happy. In such situations, it is usually preferable to be honest and lay the cards on the table, as it were, even if it does cause some disappointment and pain for the other person. The longer the relationship is permitted to continue, the greater the hurt is likely to be.

People can be terribly brutal with themselves. Out of the whole animal kingdom, only humans are endowed with this capacity to make themselves miserable.

S. A. Bower and Gordon G. Bower

While it is important not to terminate prematurely a potentially good relationship, it is time to terminate an encounter when it becomes apparent that it is not going anywhere or is headed in an undesirable direction, such as when one person begins to feel "used" or the other person reveals previously unknown and disturbing personality characteristics (Synder et al., 1985). If one person is much more attracted to the other, it puts the latter in a position to dominate the encounter and to exploit the other sexually, financially, or in other ways. This is commonly referred to as the "principle of least interest." When one realizes this principle is in effect, it is time to evaluate and quite possibly terminate the encounter. The other person will not only survive the loss but also prosper.

Upgrading an Encounter to a Relationship

From the time two persons begin an encounter, they enter into a process of interaction in which each person receives certain rewards and pays certain costs. And, in the process of interacting, they decide whether the encounter is worth pursuing and possibly upgrading to a relationship.

Upgrading an encounter to a beginning relationship is essentially a continuation of this interaction process. It does require, however, that the parties enter into an agreement that stipulates the "ground rules" of the proposed relationship—what each person will contribute to the relationship and what each will receive from it. Such agreements may or may not be verbalized, and they may be clear or unclear, fair or unfair. In most cases, these ground rules are not discussed and simply consist of what happens in the course of the interaction. In these instances, an implicit agreement does emerge, but its terms are likely to be far from clear. When an agreement is unclear, it is easy for one person to resent the other for not living up to "what was promised"—that is, what one person thinks the other promised.

When upgrading an encounter to a relationship, it is also vitally important that each person be "aware"—that each have a realistic view of himself or herself, of the other person, and of the relationship each hopes to achieve. We shall elaborate on awareness and other building blocks of intimate relationships in Chapter 3.

ENCOUNTERS AND RELATIONSHIPS: A SOCIAL EXCHANGE VIEW

According to **social exchange theory,** encounters are initiated and relationships formed to meet the needs of the persons involved. Each person in the relationship receives certain rewards from the other and also pays certain costs. The resulting exchange is governed by economic principles—that is, whether the rewards received are sufficient to justify the costs incurred. In this final section, we shall briefly review the social exchange principles that largely determine the nature, course, and outcome of encounters and relationships.

Rewards and Costs

Rewards are any positively valued consequences that a person gains from an encounter or relationship. Rewards vary from obvious benefits such as money or sex to more-complex ones such as approval and emotional support. Of course, what may be highly rewarding for one person may have little or no reward value for another. And, as might be expected, the value of a reward may change with time.

Costs are any negatively valued consequences incurred by a person in an encounter or relationship. Costs may also take obvious forms such as time, effort, and money, as well as more-subtle forms such as conflict, insecurity, and self-devaluation. Costs are conditions stemming from the interaction that deplete the person's resources or have other adverse consequences. Like rewards, specific costs may be evaluated differently over time. And what may be considered a high cost by one person may be viewed quite differently by another.

Outcomes: Profits and Losses

When the rewards outweigh the costs, the outcome is a gain, or **profit.** Conversely, when the costs outweigh the rewards, the outcome is a liability, or **loss.** This does not mean that the main goal in an encounter or relationship is to make the largest profit at the least cost. Rather, the participants expect to receive something of value that is roughly equivalent to what is given. When a loss seems excessive to one or both parties, the encounter or relationship is likely to be terminated.

Thus, in a fair or equitable exchange, the participants do not receive far less than they give, nor do they take what they don't deserve. Rather, they should strive to "balance the books." As Walster and Walster (1978) have pointed out:

> People feel most comfortable when they're getting exactly what they feel they deserve in a relationship. *Everyone* in an inequitable relationship feels uneasy. While it's not surprising that deprived partners (who are getting less than they deserve) feel resentful and angry about their inequitable treatment, it's perhaps not so obvious why their *over*benefited mates (who are getting more than they deserve) feel uneasy. But they do. They feel guilty and fearful of losing their favored position. (p. 135)

Market Value and Comparison Level

Underlying the idea of costs, rewards, and outcomes are the concepts of social desirability, or market value, and standards of evaluation, or comparison level. Our **market value** is what we have to offer to others in the interpersonal marketplace. If our market value is high, it is likely to pay off in terms of more-attractive friends, lovers, and mates. Of course, some people overestimate their market value and end up paying a high price in disappointment and rejection. Others underestimate their market value and settle for less-attractive merchandise than they could actually obtain. With time and experience, however, most of us develop a fairly realistic view of our market value. We know when someone is out of our league or when we can do better. This view influences our goals and expectations. Of course, our value in the marketplace is not fixed or frozen. It may fluctuate with changes in age, status, income, and health. Furthermore, different prospective "buyers" may have different needs and preferences that influence our value in their eyes.

Comparison level refers to the standards against which we evaluate our present encounters and relationships. There are two kinds of standards: (1) those based on experience, in which we evaluate our present encounters and relationships in light of past ones of a similar type, and (2) those based on alternatives we perceive as open to us—especially alternatives that may provide more-favorable outcomes. The second type is often influenced by our appraisal of our market value or social desirability and by our observation of the payoffs that other persons seem to be obtaining in comparable relationships.

Comparison level helps to explain why many seemingly satisfying encounters and relationships break up: One person or the other sees an alternative relationship that promises to provide greater rewards or that is available at a lower cost. Conversely, many unsatisfactory encounters and relationships continue because the participants fail to perceive more-promising alternatives. Here it becomes apparent that competition—as in economic theory—is something with which to be reckoned. We compete for friends, lovers, and mates in the interpersonal marketplace.

While social exchange theory emphasizes an equitable or fair exchange in the marketplace, it by no means guarantees one. Sometimes we settle for faulty or mislabeled merchandise; that is, we are deceived, exploited, and hurt by others. As in the world of business, the motto "Let the buyer beware" applies here. Of course, most of us do learn to examine the merchandise pretty carefully before entering into intimate relationships. But sometimes we rush matters, make costly

Joel Gordon

miscalculations, and have to start over. Usually, however, what seems to emerge in the course of bargaining is a compromise between fantasy and reality, between what we would like and for what we are willing to settle. As Leonard Berkowitz (1980) has pointed out, most people have a pretty good idea of their market value and are realistic in their aspirations.

As we have noted, people tend to feel more comfortable in a relationship when they feel they are getting what they perceive as an equitable deal—not less or more than they deserve. Many years ago, sociologist Erving Goffman (1952) expressed this view rather unromantically with respect to marriage when he observed, "A proposal of marriage in our society tends to be a way in which a man sums up his special attributes and suggests to a woman that hers are not so much better as to preclude a merger or a partnership in those matters."

We shall find social exchange theory useful in future chapters, when we discuss building, maintaining, and enriching intimate relationships. We must emphasize, however, that this theory is simply a convenient analogy. People are more than "merchandise" whose "value" is determined by existing conditions in the interpersonal "marketplace." And personal encounters and relationships are more than business transactions. There are many dimensions to human experience and behavior—such as love, hope, and despair—that go far beyond social exchange theory.

SUMMARY—Chapter 2

1. Brief encounters may touch us only lightly or change our lives. Most of us enjoy meeting and getting acquainted with others. But it is not easy to make new acquaintances in "a nation of strangers."

2. An initial encounter provides the opportunity to screen the other person. According to Bernard Murstein, there are five key tasks to be performed during an initial encounter: (a) to decide whether the other person attracts us, (b) to determine whether the other person is open to a new acquaintance and possi-

ble relationship, (c) to find an appropriate opening remark and topic of conversation, (d) to project a friendly and rewarding personality, and (e) to schedule a second meeting if the person passes this initial screening.

3. Our first impressions of others are formed very rapidly and tend to focus on their physical appearance, their behavior, and possibilities of interaction with them.

4. Errors in person perception commonly arise from generalizing on the basis of inadequate information, relying on our assumptions about human nature and behavior, assuming others are like we are, using stereotypes, and attributing the other person's behavior to his or her disposition rather than to situational factors.

5. Attributes that attract us to others include physical attractiveness, their similarity to us, need complementarity, competence, and mutual liking. Often we like people who are outright flatterers.

6. We can influence the impression we make on others by monitoring our behavior, having a positive view of ourselves, and being a rewarding person—showing that we like and approve of others.

7. Encounters may be pursued by arranging another meeting—although few are, they may be terminated, or they may be upgraded to relationships.

8. According to social exchange theory, encounters follow basic economic principles. We weigh the costs against the rewards to determine whether the interaction provides us with a profit, a loss, or an equitable balance. We may also compare it with our past experiences and with alternatives available in the interpersonal marketplace. These principles apply to relationships as well as encounters.

FOUNDATIONS OF INTIMATE RELATIONSHIPS

The biggest problem confronting young people coming into adulthood now is the problem of achieving intimacy with other people.
—John Conger (1981, p. 1)

Despite the importance of achieving intimate relationships in our lives—and the disappointment, hurt, and self-devaluation that accompany failure in such relationships—little research has focused on the problem. Aside from the fact that the word **intimacy** comes from the Latin **intimus,** which means innermost and deepest, there is no generally agreed-on definition of what we mean by **intimate relationship.** Nor do we adequately understand the principles involved in building such relationships. Nevertheless, some promising attempts have been made to describe the nature of such relationships and to establish guidelines for achieving them.

As a starting point, psychologists George Levinger and H. L. Rausch (1977) have suggested that intimate relationships have three essential ingredients: a strong feeling of interdependence, a heavy emotional involvement, and a definitive structure. Pursuing the concept of intimacy a step further, social exchange theorists Ted Huston and Robert Burgess (1979) noted that, as partners grow closer, or more intimate, the following key changes take place in their relationship:

1. Interaction occurs more often, for longer periods of time, in a wider range of settings.
2. When separated, the partners attempt to restore proximity and feel more comfortable when it is regained.
3. Partners disclose secrets, share physical intimacies, and are more open in criticizing and praising each other.
4. The partners develop agreed-on goals, efficient means of communication, and stable patterns of interaction.
5. Investment in the relationship increases, enhancing its importance in the couple's lives and the feeling that their personal interests are tied in with the well-being of the relationship.

Huston and Burgess also pointed out that as partners grow closer, intimacy may take somewhat different forms. For example, a couple may achieve physical and intellectual closeness but remain strangers emotionally (see Box 3–1). Relationships may also vary markedly in quality of communication, intensity of emotional involvement, and degree of trust and commitment. In addition, intimate relationships change over time, reflecting the ebb and flow of the partner's intellectual, emotional, and physical closeness. There will be times when the relationship is a joyous one, and other times when it is filled with conflict and pain. In building and maintaining intimate relationships, one of the most difficult tasks is to get close and remain close to another person.

In this chapter, we shall examine the key factors that are essential for increasing all aspects of intimacy in a relationship. These "building blocks" of closeness include effective communication, mutual self-disclosure, appropriate "ground

BOX 3-1 / ASSESSMENT OF INTIMACY IN CLOSE RELATIONSHIPS

There is a saying in science that "If you can't measure it, you can't talk about it." True to this dictum, researchers have developed methods for measuring just about every facet of human behavior and interaction, from love and trust to sexual satisfaction. One instrument that has been developed to measure human intimacy in marital and other close relationships is the PAIR (Personal Assessment of Intimacy in Relationships) Inventory.

This inventory, devised by Mark Schaefer and David Olson (1981), measures intimacy in five areas.

Area	Sample Items		Area	Sample Items	
1. Emotional Intimacy	"My partner listens to me when I need someone to talk to."	"I often feel distant from my partner."	4. Intellectual Intimacy	"My partner helps me clarify my thoughts."	"I feel 'put down' in a serious conversation with my partner."
2. Social Intimacy	"We enjoy spending time with other couples."	"We usually keep to ourselves."	5. Recreational Intimacy	"We enjoy the same recreational activities."	"I share in very few of my partner's interests."
3. Sexual Intimacy	"I am satisfied with our sex life."	"I feel our sexual activity is just routine."			

Among the key objectives of the PAIR Inventory is to help marital counselors assess various kinds of intimacy in their clients' relationships and to reveal any discrepancies between expected and experienced levels of intimacy in relationships.

rules," effective methods of conflict resolution, and such components of long-term relationships as acceptance, caring, commitment, and awareness.

EFFECTIVE COMMUNICATION

For a beginning relationship to develop toward intimacy, it is essential that the partners communicate effectively with each other. Communications involve two kinds of information: **cognitive** information, which is concerned primarily with facts about each other and the surrounding world, and **affective** information, which is concerned primarily with emotions—with how a couple feel about each

BOX 3-2 / INFORMATION DERIVED FROM NONVERBAL COMMUNICATION

By such means as gestures, voice inflections, and facial expressions, nonverbal communication can impart various kinds of information that supplement what is being communicated on a verbal level.

1. The nonverbal can emphasize the meaning of the verbal message. (I say I don't like you and my voice, gestures, and facial expression say so too.)
2. The nonverbal can anticipate future verbal content. (Even before I tell the punch line, I start to laugh.)
3. The nonverbal can contradict the verbal message. (I say I like you, but I'm backing away.)
4. The nonverbal can be delayed, under-

mining what has already been expressed. (I tell you something in seeming seriousness, and then, after a moment's delay, I explode with laughter.)

5. The nonverbal can modify the overall interaction. (I call you a bad name, but I am smiling).
6. The nonverbal can be a substitute for a word or phrase in a verbal message. (I shrug my shoulders, meaning "Who cares?")
7. The nonverbal can fill or explain silences or changes of topic. (I stop talking and indicate with my eyes that the person we have been talking about is approaching.)

other, their experiences, and the world around them. Both facts and feelings are usually involved in specific communications.

Verbal and Nonverbal Messages

In general, verbal statements are used primarily to communicate cognitive information, whereas **nonverbal messages** are used primarily to communicate affective information (Dellinger & Deane, 1980). Nonverbal messages are conveyed by facial expression, gestures, eye contact, voice inflection, pauses, odors, dress, touch, bodily movements, posture, and other types of **body language.** Ways in which nonverbal communication can supplement verbal communication are described in Box 3-2.

When verbal and nonverbal messages conflict, the speaker's voice, posture, and facial expression may be a more-reliable guide to his or her feelings that what is said. For example, in the early stages of a relationship, a man asks his partner if she would like to see a performance of "Swan Lake" by a touring world-famous ballet company. She replies, "Great, I just love classical ballet." But she answers in a dull voice, with a facial grimace and a notable lack of enthusiasm. It is apparent that going to the ballet is probably not one of her favorite pastimes.

Women are slightly better than men in decoding nonverbal cues including emotions—except in recognizing anger, where men appear more accurate (Hall, 1978; Gaelick et al., 1985; Wagner et al., 1986; Gallois & Callan, 1986). Unfortunately, however, neither sex is particularly adept at interpreting body language. Yet, in close relationships, it is crucial that the partners understand each other, feel understood, and communicate effectively on verbal and nonverbal levels. When partners are unable to express their thoughts and feelings clearly or to communicate about common problems effectively, difficulties are bound to arise.

Sending and Receiving

Meaningful communication does not take place automatically. In order for communication to be effective, the communicator must be a good "sender," and the listener must be a good "receiver." What are the characteristics of good sending and receiving?

Sending: Getting Through to the Other Person.

As a sender, you have to know what you are trying to communicate and how to "code" your message so that your receiver will interpret it accurately. If you are unclear about the message or if you fail to code the message meaningfully, the other person is likely to misunderstand it. You may find yourself saying, "That's not what I meant" or "I didn't say *that*." After such misunderstandings, you might ask yourself, "What could I have said?" "What did I do wrong?" "How could I have conveyed the message more accurately?"

If you want to make sure that your partner understands your message, you may find the following guidelines helpful:

1. *Be specific: Get to the point.* If you talk around the point and your message is not explicit, you are not likely to get your message across.
2. *Express feelings and perceptions—don't issue facts.* It is hard for the other person to take offense or argue when you express your views in terms of your own perceptions and emotions. It is much easier to communicate about a problem if, for example, you say, "I feel very upset because you didn't call me last night" rather than if you say, "You're an inconsiderate creep for not calling me." Putting your listener on the defensive will not make him or her open to what you have to say.
3. *Check your body language.* Does your body language help you get your message across, or does it interfere with your communication? Sloppy diction, such as mumbling and mispronunciation of words, may be distracting and produce "sloppy listening" on the part of the receiver. Similarly, using a bored tone of voice or speaking in a monotone can make your listener lose interest in what you have to say. If you don't seem interested, why should your listener be? In addition, avoiding eye contact or using meaningless, repetitive, or nervous gestures can distract from the message you are trying to send. In short, your body language can be appropriate to and emphasize the point you are making or it can de-emphasize or even negate your message.
4. *Allow for the other person's perspective.* Not only is it important for you to express your own perceptions and feelings, but also it is important to consider the perspective of the other person. It is in the context of this perspective that your message will be interpreted. An understanding of the person's needs, goals, interests, beliefs, values, and knowledge about a given topic can help you code your message more clearly and appropri-

"Alone," said Eliza with the old suspicion. "Where are you going?" "Ah," he said, "You were not looking, were you? I've gone."

Thomas Wolfe
Look Homeward, Angel

Ulrike Welsch

BOX 3-3 / TEN COMMON POSTURE EXPRESSIONS

1. Hanging your head.
2. Turning your back.
3. Crossing your arms.
4. Tapping your forehead with your hand.
5. Covering your ears.
6. Holding your nose.
7. Crossing your fingers.
8. Covering your mouth with your hand.
9. Shaking your fist.
10. Bowing your head.

ately. For this reason, it is often helpful to ask the other person how he or she feels about a given subject before expressing your own views.

5. *Use feedback.* One way you can tell whether your message is getting through is from the type of **feedback,** or response, that you get from the receiver. You probably have had the experience of trying to communicate with someone who is not really tuning you in—someone who is too busy to listen, does not want to hear what you have to say, or is impatiently waiting for a chance to have his or her own say. Usually, however, your listener responds in some way, letting you know not only *that* your message is being received but also *how* it is being received—favorably or unfavorably, accurately or inaccurately. Observing the person's postural expressions can be helpful (see Box 3–3).

Sometimes the feedback you get from your partner is anger or defensiveness. In such situations, you need to make some adjustment in your message or method of communicating it. It may be time to shut up and ask yourself a few questions. Are you talking too much? Focusing on negative communications? Sending conflicting messages? Unintentionally putting the other person down? Belaboring a particular point? Failing to give the other person "equal time"—making sure the other person has an opportunity to express his or her own beliefs and feelings? In fact, willingness to listen to the other person may be the most important part of communicating.

In short, is there a better way to communicate with this person?

Receiving: Tuning the Other Person In.   Although being a good sender is essential to effective communication, it is just as important to be a good receiver. Being a good receiver requires developing specific skills that help you to interpret accurately what the other person is trying to say. The following are among the most important of these skills:

1. *Paying attention.* Basic to being a good receiver is giving your total attention to the other person. Paying attention involves maintaining eye contact but not staring, avoiding distractions while the other person is talking, and restraining yourself from interrupting. In effect you are saying, "I want to hear what you have to say," "I want to understand your viewpoint," and "I value what you have to say." In fact, *really* listening is one of the greatest compliments you can pay to another

person and is crucial in building and maintaining an intimate relationship (Kern, 1981).

You can show the other person that you are paying attention by your posture, by nodding approval and agreement, and by responding in other ways that let the speaker know you are interested in what he or she has to say. If the person has undergone a traumatic experience, has been emotionally hurt, or is experiencing severe pressures at work or in school, he or she may need to talk about the situation to relieve emotional tension and pain. It is important to be sensitive to this need to "talk it out" and to take the time to listen.

2. *Reading body language.*   Because most messages are sent at both the verbal and the nonverbal levels, being a good listener involves the ability to read body language as well as the ability to understand spoken communications. In fact, Dane Archer and Robin Akert (1977) have found that nonverbal cues often carry more meaning than verbal cues. Furthermore, as we have mentioned, the verbal message may or may not agree with the nonverbal one. The ability to make this distinction is important, because receivers are often called on to interpret the real meanings of messages.

3. *Uncovering hidden meanings.*   Words can be used to obscure true feelings, thoughts, and meanings. For example, in the early 1980s, the federal government substituted the term "tax enhancement" for "tax increase," presumably in the hope of lessening the pain for the taxpayer. Similarly, individuals communicating with each other use certain words and phrases that hint at meanings and fish for responses without coming right out and saying what they mean. Gerald Smith (1975) found, for example, that there are many hidden meanings in common communications between lovers. Such statements as "Tell me that you love me," "Would you like to kiss me?" and "I hate you!" seem straight-forward enough, but this is not necessarily the case. You can probably think of some hidden meanings in each of them. For example, the question "Will you always love me?" may mean "I'm feeling insecure right now" or "I'm thinking about marrying you."

If the message is to be interpreted accurately and responded to appropriately, the underlying meaning must be uncovered. Relationships can be eroded by communications in which meanings continue to be hidden and by feelings and desires left unheeded because words fail to convey the meaning or fail to produce a response that the sender needs and wants.

4. *Asking for clarification.*   While being alert to body language can help to detect hidden feelings and meanings, this approach is not always sufficient. You may need to ask for direct clarification—a technique referred to as reflective, or facilitative, listening. This technique may involve asking the sender questions about feelings rather than thoughts: "Are you saying that you feel . . . ?" A related approach is to mirror or reflect the feelings that the sender seems to be expressing. For example:

Sender: "My boss is impossible to work with."
Receiver: "Your boss makes you angry."
Sender: "Not really angry. It's just that he keeps changing his mind."

There is only one way to make people talk more than they care to. Listen. Listen with hungry earnest attention to every word. In the intensity of your attention, make little nods of agreement, little sounds of approval. You can't fake it. You have to really listen. In a posture of gratitude. And it is such a rare and startling experience for them, such a boon to ego, such a gratification of self, to find a genuine listener, that they want to prolong the experience. And the only way to do that is to keep talking. A good listener is far more rare than an adequate lover.

Travis McGee *in John MacDonald's* "Nightmare in Pink"

Receiver: "You feel frustrated at your boss's behavior."
Sender: "Yes. I feel really frustrated working for him."

As this example shows, reflective listening is not simply a matter of parroting the other person's words; rather, it involves providing feedback indicating that you are trying to understand the sender's feelings and meanings. It also provides a sort of mirror for the sender so that he or she can gain a clearer picture of his or her own feelings, and it makes the sender feel that these feelings do matter.

A common mistake in trying to use this technique is interrupting the sender before he or she is finished speaking. A second mistake is assuming that you already know what the other person's feelings are so that there is no need for clarification. But, as our example shows, the receiver's first assumption—that the sender was angry—was not accurate. In fact, a common complaint in faulty communication is "You always assume that you know what I feel" or "You're always telling me how I feel." In short, don't try to be a mindreader.

5. *Maintaining an accepting attitude.* Finally, being a good receiver means encouraging the sender to communicate his or her thoughts openly, without fear of ridicule or rejection. An accepting attitude seems particularly important when it is most difficult to maintain—when the person is saying something you strongly disagree with, is critical about you or your behavior, or is perhaps afraid to level with you (Lister, 1982). But if open channels of communications are to be maintained and personal differences and misunderstandings to be worked out, each person must be willing to really listen to what the other person is saying or would like to feel free to say. And really listening often requires being silent, for silence combined with reassuring body language tends to draw people out.

Ultimately, being a good receiver in an intimate relationship involves hearing what your partner is *not* saying and perhaps will never be able to say. Our deepest feelings often defy expression by the spoken word. The challenge is to be a sensitive and empathic listener who can put himself or herself in his or her partner's position and perceive and feel much as he or she does (Clark, 1980).

Evaluating Communication Patterns

The overtones are lost, and what is left are conversations which, in their poverty, cannot hide the lack of real contact. We glide past each other. But why? Why—?

—*Dag Hammarskjöld (1974, p. 40)*

One approach to improving communication is to analyze **metacommunication,** your typical patterns of communicating with each other. Metacommunication involves such factors as (1) the amount of relevant information communicated versus "noise," (2) the typical emotional climate created by talking about problems, (3) whether one partner does most of the talking and the other most of the listening, (4) whether certain topics or problems create difficulties in under-

BOX 3-4 / COMMON COMMUNICATION ERRORS IN PERSONAL RELATIONSHIPS

1. Dwelling too much on the past.
2. Talking too much about one subject, repeating yourself.
3. Thinking about what you are going to say instead of listening.
4. Focusing excessively on problems.
5. Being critical about something that can't be undone.
6. Getting emotional—losing your temper.
7. Sending conflicting messages.
8. Bad timing—choosing the wrong time to discuss a "hot" issue.
9. Failure to consider the other person's perspective.
10. Distorting or disqualifying the other person's message.
11. Not leveling with the other person; telling lies.
12. Mindreading—telling your partner what he or she thinks or feels.
13. Failing to take advantage of feedback.
14. Insensitivity to the feelings behind words.
15. Revealing impatience, irritation, hostility, or fear at an inappropriate time.
16. Interpreting your partner's statements in terms of what you want them to mean rather than in the way they were intended.

standing and reaching agreements, and (5) whether communications are predominantly rewarding or aversive. Such information can help each partner better understand his or her own ways of communicating as well as how both partners communicate as a couple. It can also be used as a basis for making needed corrections and improvements in communication patterns. Some common communication errors in relationships are listed in Box 3-4.

When messages are both personal and positive—such as when you tell your partner you think he or she is a truly wonderful person—they are **rewarding**. Conversely, when messages are personal and negative—such as when you tell your partner he or she is an idiot—they are **aversive**. During encounters and beginning relationships, communications are usually rewarding. As the relationship progresses, however, more negative content may creep in. Often these negative messages are conveyed during "lovers' quarrels." But the accent is usually on the positive because a disproprionate amount of negative content makes the other person aversive rather than rewarding to be around. Even in long-term relationships, aversive communications are likely to be hurtful and destructive. With the growth of intimacy, the partners become progressively more emotionally vulnerable to each other. Thus, an aversive comment from a stranger may be brushed aside, but the same comment from someone we love and respect is another matter entirely.

In short, positive and effective communications are important at every stage in building intimate relationships. Deteriorating relationships and patterns of communication go hand in hand. In fact, one indication of a failing relationship is the inability of the partners to talk about their problems with any degree of objectivity or mutual understanding. Eventually, the breakdown of communication may reach a point of almost total silence. Each partner has given up trying to "get through" to the other.

We are living in a world saturated with communication, on the verge of perishing for lack of it; a world smothered with words, hungry for one meaningful word; a world bombarded with data, rarely capable of sorting out the truth; and a world in which we can flash messages across the ocean by way of space, but one in which we find it difficult to get through to each other face to face.

Roger Schinn

Harriet Gans/The Image Works

MUTUAL SELF-DISCLOSURE

The road to intimacy is paved with self-disclosure.

—*Larry Losoncy (1985)*

The building of intimate relationships depends not only on effective communication but also on mutual **self-disclosure**—on each person revealing personal information to the other. But self-disclosure is not a simple matter. It can destroy a beginning relationship as well as make an essential contribution to trust and intimacy.

Nature and Course of Self-Disclosure

At the beginning of an encounter, it is conventional to maintain a cheerful "mask" and to avoid embarrassing topics and intimate disclosures. In answer to a direct question such as "Are you married?" a simple yes or no may suffice. If it seems appropriate, the person may supply factual data such as "I was married for 5 years and have a 4-year-old daughter."

Ulrike Welsch

At first, people tend to avoid unnecessary disclosures and to disclose information about themselves that they think will enhance their attractiveness to others. In fact, John Johnson (1981) has commented that initial self-disclosures may serve as a means of self-presentation and of instructing others about how one should be regarded.

If an encounter progresses to a beginning relationship, there still seems to be no need to rush the disclosure of intimate details. However, it is important to supply information that seems appropriate to the other person and to the situation. Low self-disclosers—those who reveal little or nothing about themselves—are likely to block or slow down the growth of closeness. On the other hand, as we noted earlier, high self-disclosers—those who go almost immediately into the intimate details of their lives—are likely to be perceived as self-centered and maladjusted (Strassberg, et al., 1977; Coleman, et al., 1987). The other person may wonder, "Why is he or she burdening me with all this?" Thus, moderate self-disclosure is usually most effective during beginning relationships and tends to be interpreted as indicating both truthfulness and a desire to move toward increasing intimacy.

Interestingly, high self-disclosers tend to reveal not only more information but also more-accurate information about themselves. Low self-disclosers, on the other hand, tend to mask or gild information and to resort to outright falsification in order to conceal personal information and present themselves in a favorable light. And, when they do deceive others, they often come to believe their own false disclosures, perhaps because their stories represent aspects of themselves that they would like to believe are true (Gitter & Black, 1976).

As a relationship progresses, the amount and intimacy of self-disclosure usually increase in a step-by-step progression as one person's disclosure is responded to in kind by the other's. Thus, when one person reveals some aspect of himself or herself, the other is expected to reply with an equally personal revelation; this is a process referred to as **reciprocity.** Mutual self-disclosure seems to follow the same principle of exchange as that of other commodities in the interpersonal market-place: One must expect to give in order to receive.

Secrets: To Tell or Not To Tell?

> If I revealed myself without worrying about how others will respond, then some will care, though others may not. But who can love me, if no one knows me? I must risk it or live alone.
>
> —*Sheldon Kopp (1972)*

Whether to tell or not to tell secrets about ourselves is often a far from simple matter, for there are powerful forces operating both toward and against intimate self-disclosures.

In close relationships, we usually want to share our experiences and feelings to gain self-affirmation and to obtain emotional support. Disclosing our concerns to a

M. Kagan/Monkmeyer Press Photo Service

BOX 3–5 / TABOO TOPICS IN BUILDING INTIMATE RELATIONSHIPS

Reciprocal self-disclosure and open channels of communication are usually emphasized in relationship development. However, most of us have learned that certain topics are better avoided, even in intimate relationships.

The latter point is supported by the findings of Leslie Baxter and William Wilmot (1985). These researchers conducted in-depth interviews with 90 undergraduate men and women—12 in platonic relationships, 25 in the "romantic potential" relationships, and 53 in romantic relationships. Only three subjects reported that no topics were off-limits. The remaining subjects admitted that some topics were better avoided.

Taboo Topic	Percentage Reporting	Taboo Topic	Percentage Reporting
State of the relationship—current or future	68	Relationship norms—rules of behavior in the relationship	25
Extra-relationship activity	31	Conflict-inducing topics	22
Prior relationships with members of the opposite sex	25	Unpleasant or damaging self-disclosures	17

Of particular interest is "talking about the present or future status of the relationship," which headed the list of taboo topics. This was so important because subjects felt that the relationship would suffer if different degrees of involvement or commitment were revealed. Couples in "romantic potential" relationships were most likely to avoid this topic—88 percent—as compared with 58 percent in romantic and 50 percent in platonic relationships. Partners who were more committed feared that revealing this would scare the other person away, and partners who were less committed feared that revealing this would put unwanted pressure on their partner.

partner whom we respect and trust can help us clarify our feelings, see situations more objectively, and resolve inner conflicts and hurts. In fact, talking about painful experiences has been referred to as a "built-in damage repair mechanism" that can be highly therapeutic in dealing with such problems. Self-disclosure has other rewards as well. In disclosing acutely embarrassing experiences, a person often gains relief from loss of face and self-devaluation. And, as we have said, mutual self-disclosure helps to build trust and intimacy (Middlebrook, 1980; Milholland & Avery, 1982).

Self-disclosures, however, almost inevitably entail some measure of risk; and the more information that is disclosed, the greater the risk. A person who reveals something of his or her "real" self may be rejected, especially if the revelation is highly negative. In addition, revealing such information may enable your partner to put you in an inferior position, make excessive demands on you, or continually confront you with questions about the episode you disclosed. Hence, it is not surprising that the greatest obstacle to self-disclosure is fear of being judged and being found wanting (Levinger & Raush, 1977; Hatfield, 1985). As Elaine Hat-

BOX 3–6 / WHEN YOUR PARTNER REVEALS SOMETHING PERSONAL, DON'T BE A . . .

Moralist. Don't make statements like, "You should have done this instead of that." The moralist preaches at his or her partner.

Know-it-all. Don't give advice to your partner based on your extensive knowledge of such matters. The know-it-all tries to show his or her superiority.

Judge. Don't pronounce your partner guilty of some "immoral" act without giving him or her benefit of counsel or trial. The judge is interested in proving that he or she is right and the partner wrong.

Psychologist. Don't interrogate your partner in order to get all the details as a basis for making a diagnosis and treating your partner's problem.

Consoler. Don't hold back from getting involved. The consoler treats his or her partner's feelings lightly by providing a pat on the back, giving simple reassurance, and pretending that all is well when it isn't.

Commander-in-chief. Don't issue orders, commands, and threats in order to keep the upper hand and to keep your partner under control. The commander-in-chief makes it clear that he or she expects the partner to "shape up."

In each of these roles, one partner takes a superior attitude instead of really listening to and trying to understand the feelings and needs of the other. He or she is both unwilling and unable to empathize with the partner and provide appropriate emotional support.

field expressed it "How intimate dare I be?" If a disclosure is highly upsetting to one's partner, it may damage the relationship or lead to its termination. Again caution appears to be advisable. Boxes 3–5 and 3–6 elaborate on this point.

Because serious risks are involved, most of us learn to be wary of disclosing information about ourselves, especially negative information. We are usually content with an enormous amount of small talk, with self-disclosures arising naturally as the needs of the situation dictate. But when disclosures do occur, it is usually important to anticipate—as much as possible—their effect on the other person and on the relationship. In essence, we weigh the risks against the values of openness and honesty. As a relationship becomes more intimate, the problem becomes more complex, and the issue of what to keep secret and what to disclose assumes increasing importance.

It has been suggested that "then" secrets of the past are often best not disclosed, whereas few "now" secrets should be kept in an intimate relationship. Yet, as a relationship progresses, partners are likely to be curious about each other's past. People are rarely content to know only bits and pieces about someone with whom they want to build an intimate relationship. At this stage, the question of whether to tell becomes a most difficult one. Do we owe it to our partner to reveal past sexual experiences? A criminal record? A suicide attempt? An abortion? A prior marital experience? And if we don't reveal such information, what is the risk of exposure by a third party at some later time?

Of course, self-disclosures may differ markedly depending on the persons involved and the nature of their relationship. But, in general, the amount and the

Ulrike Welsch

Smithsonian Institution Archive Center/Business Americana Collection

intimacy of self-disclosures do increase over time. However, it may be noted that Cozby (1973) found that highly intimate levels of self-disclosure tend to be rewarding at first, but that eventually the costs outweigh the rewards. The most apparent cost is anxiety about upsetting the other person, demeaning ourself in the other person's eyes, and damaging the relationship. In addition, the motivation for revealing highly intimate and potentially damaging information becomes suspect, as when feelings of guilt lead a person to confess his or her "sins" in the hope of being forgiven. For example, confessing an extramarital affair may alleviate a person's guilt but may be devastating to the unsuspecting husband or wife. Of course, some people are easily upset by their partner's disclosures of faults or mistakes, while others seem to take them in stride.

Do We Ever Really Know Another Person?

In close relationships, we may reveal a great deal about our private self—our desires, hopes, fears, angers, triumphs, and failures. In return, we may learn a great deal about our partner's private self. But do we ever really know that person, even in a long-term intimate relationship? Perhaps, but it is doubtful.

Even though we allow our partner to cross the boundary into our own private world—into the inner space where we are most ourselves and most vulnerable—we do not give our permission lightly, and some of our private world may still be off limits. Some observers have expressed concern about a growing trend toward the "tyranny of openness," in which people deny themselves privacy and perhaps "mystery" because they believe that full self-disclosure is demanded in personal encounters and beginning relationships, not to mention in long-term intimate relationships. However, resistance to such excessive demands is common, as evidenced by the finding that lying occurs more commonly with intimate information than with more superficial disclosures (Gitter & Black, 1976; Ludwig & Franco, 1986; Miller et al., 1986).

To what does all this add up? Perhaps all we can say is that the building of intimacy requires the lowering of defenses and the dropping of masks by each partner, together with the willingness to share beliefs, hopes, feelings, values, achievements, and disappointments. This does not mean that partners must "bare their souls" to each other, but it does mean building trust and intimacy by being more open and coming to know each other more fully. Still, human beings are complex and mysterious. Because there are usually aspects of ourselves, both past and present, that we prefer not to reveal, it seems unlikely that another person can ever really know the "whole truth" about us or that we can ever "really know" the other person.

ESTABLISHING "GROUND RULES"

As an encounter develops into a relationship, the process of establishing **ground rules,** or structuring the relationship, begins. For a number of reasons, structuring a relationship is a complex process. Often the structure develops from expectations of which the individual may not be clearly aware. For example, a man may expect his partner to be like his mother, although he does not realize it. Furthermore, in their eagerness to build close relationships, people often agree to unrealistic rules that they won't be able to follow. A related problem is the tendency to overestimate the extent of mutual understanding and agreement on rules. One partner may say, "You understand what I mean, don't you?" and the other will agree, yet they may be far apart in their interpretations of what they've agreed on. If ground rules are not structured by mutual agreement, they will be structured by what actually happens in the interaction between the partners, and this is likely to prove unsatisfactory to one or both.

Ground rules apply to three main areas: (1) goals (what the couple want from the relationship), (2) roles and responsibilities (the behavior each partner will enact in order to achieve the goals), and (3) norms (acceptable and expected patterns of behavior considered right or appropriate to their situation) (Braiker & Kelley, 1979; Robertson, 1981).

Goals: What Do You Want from the Relationship?

Through intimate relationships, people try to meet various personal needs—for love and affection, self-esteem and worth, emotional support and security, and the sharing of common interests and activities. But, when a relationship meets one person's needs and fails to meet the other person's, it is likely to be difficult to maintain. It, therefore, becomes essential that the persons involved agree on common goals so that their interaction will be harmonious and satisfying to both.

The importance of such common goals can be illustrated in many ways. For example, if one person wants to get married and have children and the other does not, the relationship may have difficulty getting off the ground. Similarly, an intimate relationship may fall apart if the goals of one or both partners change over time. The couple may suddenly awaken to the realization that they have nothing left in common—at least not enough to maintain the relationship.

In working out common goals, it is important for the partners to share their thoughts, feelings, and fantasies about the kind of relationship they hope to build together and what they want from it. It is also important that they make clear what they *don't* want from the relationship. This sharing helps to ensure mutual understanding and agreement on relationship goals. Otherwise, the partners are likely to work at cross purposes, each undercutting what is important to the other.

Of course, emotions play a significant role in interpersonal relationships. People rarely take the time to establish ground rules and goals before they get involved with each other. Many ultimate goals become important only after the relationship has developed. Nevertheless, before the relationship proceeds too far, the couple should try to discuss salient points in an open and rational manner.

Roles and Power

Once goals have been agreed on, the question arises as to who is going to do what in order to achieve these goals. This brings us to the matter of roles and responsibilities. The term **role** is borrowed from the theater, where it refers to a specified part in a play. The words and actions of the role are designated by the **script**, the set of directions the actors follow in order to convey the playwright's story. Society, too, prescribes for its members roles that are designed to facilitate functioning of the group. Although each individual lends his or her own interpretation to a role, there are limits to the "script" beyond which the individual is not permitted to go. Thus, a role carries with it specific **role expectations,** whether that role is priest, construction worker, nurse, or general. It can readily be seen, for example, that a priest who tells people he does not believe in God would not be enacting his expected role behavior.

As in society as a whole, in intimate relationships each person is expected to play certain roles and carry out the responsibilities associated with these roles. In some instances, the partners have **complementary roles**—that is, each partner enacts the role and carries out the responsibilities not covered by the other. In traditional marriage, for example, the husband enacts the "breadwinner" role and the wife takes on the "homemaker" role. In other instances, roles develop as a result of the partners' interactions and are **reciprocal roles**—that is, they involve mutual give and take.

Closely related to roles and responsibilities are power and decision making. Power is important because it conveys the right to make decisions and, hence, to exert some control over the partner's behavior. In building intimate relationships today, most decisions that affect the two partners are made together. Of course, one partner may defer to the other if the latter has greater expertise in a given area. Often the partners may take turns or make other compromises to assure an equitable distribution of decision-making power.

Unless expected roles and responsibilities are made clear and agreed on, difficulties are likely to arise. For example, a conflict may arise if one partner expects to play a traditional male or female sex-role and the other expects and demands an equitable relationship. Similarly, conflicts can arise if the power of each partner to make decisions that affect the other is not discussed and shared. Thus, roles, responsibilities, and decision making are important components in establishing ground rules and building intimate relationships.

Standards of Satisfaction

When watching a movie on TV, you expect it to meet certain standards of plot, character portrayal, and photography. If it does not, you are likely to switch to another program. Similarly, you establish **standards of satisfaction** with respect to intimate relationships, in terms of both the overall relationship and specific interactions. Partners' standards may be based on those perpetuated by the mass media, on prior experiences with other partners, or on their present relationship. If one or both partners fail to provide the expected standard of satisfaction, difficulties are likely to develop. In social exchange terms, we might say that the costs outweigh the rewards and that the comparison level is unfavorable.

Admittedly, standards of satisfaction may be realistic or unrealistic, may vary markedly from one person to another, and may change over time. But if these standards are not met and the person's needs are not satisfied, the result is likely to be frustration and conflict.

Now that we have examined the basic components of ground rules, we should point out that such rules are more likely to be effective when (1) the couple have similar backgrounds, goals, beliefs, and values; (2) the rules have been discussed, understood, and agreed on by both partners; (3) the rules are realistic and comfortable for both; and (4) the rules are periodically reviewed and updated.

Of course, not all couples actively establish ground rules in their relationships. Nevertheless, relationships do take on structure with time. If partners do not take active measures to structure their relationship in terms of the goals they hope to achieve, the responsibilities each is to assume, and so on, the structure will be established by what takes place, whether or not this structure is satisfactory to the persons involved. Once the structure has been established, it becomes increasingly difficult to change. For example, a woman who takes on house-cleaning chores at her boyfriend's apartment in order to help him out when he is busy may find that he expects her to handle these chores from now on. Unfortunately, most of us are relatively naïve in the matter of establishing ground rules that are appropriate to the situation and persons involved.

RESOLVING CONFLICTS

Almost inevitably, disagreements and conflicts arise in the course of building intimate relationships. Here we shall comment briefly on some common sources of conflict and ways of dealing with and constructive uses of conflict. We explore conflicts and conflict resolution in greater detail in Chapter 11.

Common Sources of Conflict

Many conflicts arise from unclear, uncomfortable, or unrealistic ground rules. Differences in partners' ideas about goals, roles, and norms tend to be masked during the initial phase of a relationship, when interaction is usually rather superficial and focuses on the positive. But, as the relationship progresses, such underlying differences begin to emerge. Common areas of conflict include sex-roles (traditional versus egalitarian), money, sex, power and decision making, jealousy and possessiveness, sexual exclusivity, and unmet needs and expectations.

These and other conflicts can be intensified by ineffective communication. Similarly, differences in cultural background, education, and values may not only lead to misunderstandings but make it more difficult to resolve them.

Ways of Coping with Conflict

Methods of coping with conflict can be effective or ineffective. On the negative side, coping may take the form of bitter and destructive quarrels, one-sided concessions, or emotional withdrawal and refusal to talk (see Box 3–7). More commonly, however, conflict resolution occurs through negotiations aimed at changing the ground rules so they are mutually acceptable. These negotiations usually involve compromise and concessions. One person may make concessions in one area in exchange for the partner's concessions in another area. Or the partners may agree to a "middle ground" that seems a reasonable way of resolving the issue. As a result, the relationship may go through a continual structuring and restructuring as the partners attempt to deal with disagreements and conflicts.

In some cases, the partners may end "agreeing to disagree." Often a statement

H. Armstrong Roberts

such as "I understand and respect your feelings even though I disagree with you" is helpful. However, if the matter in question is considered crucial by one of the partners—as is often the case with sexual exclusivity—failure to reach an agreement may lead to deterioration and termination of the relationship. Some relationships do continue despite disagreement and conflict, perhaps because the costs of terminating the relationship are high and neither partner sees a better alternative. So they simply let matters drift along.

Timing is an important consideration in dealing with conflicts. For example, it is usually better to postpone discussion when there is inadequate time to pinpoint and examine the issue or when the issue is a "hot" one and one or both partners are angry. Although people often find it difficult to live with unresolved conflicts, especially if the issue is important, it is usually unwise to force a resolution if the timing is inappropriate.

Effects of Conflicts

Researchers Harriet Braiker and Harold Kelley (1979) have concluded that conflicts tend to have negative effects on developing relationships unless (1) the frequency and intensity of the conflicts are low, (2) there is a background of

BOX 3-7 / "DETOURS": DIVERSIONARY TACTICS IN DEALING WITH CONFLICTS

Sharon and Gordon Bower (1976) have delineated a number of defensive detours that people use to avoid facing and dealing with disagreement or conflict. Here are some of the more common ones:

Detours	Examples	Detours	Examples
Put-off detours	"Not now, I'm too tired"; "Some other time, I'm busy."	Psychoanalytic detours	"You're saying that because you're a castrating female."
Distracting detours	"You look beautiful when you're angry"; "That's a big word you're throwing around."	"Poor me" detours	"Your remarks are so mean, I just can't cope with them (sob)."
Denying detours	"That's not true"; "Where did you get that dumb idea?"	Apologizing detours	"I've been a complete idiot. I promise I won't do it again. It's unforgiveable, but if you could find it in your heart . . . How can I make it up to you."
Blaming detours	"If you hadn't kept nagging me, I wouldn't have done it."		
Verbal abusing detours	"Stop dumping your garbage on me"; "You ought to see a therapist."	Threatening detours	"If you keep talking to me this way, I'll leave you."
Joking detours	"Well *excuse* me!"	Debating detours	"That's one way to look at it, but . . ."
Reinterpreting detours	"I wasn't being sarcastic, I was being humorous."	Procrastinating detours	"Interesting. Let me think about it."
		Non-negotiating detours	"That's unacceptable."

In their book *Asserting Yourself*, the Bowers make suggestions for countering each of these barriers to resolving conflicts. These suggestions involve learning to stand up for your rights and learning negotiation skills. The overall objective is to develop a more-positive self-concept based in part on the knowledge that you can assert yourself in solving relationship problems.

Bower & Bower, *Asserting Yourself*, © 1976, Addison-Wesley Publishing Company, Inc., Reading, Massachusetts. Chapter 8 (excerpts). Reprinted with permission.

positive interaction between the partners, and (3) the couple are superior in conflict-coping capabilities. In addition, Braiker and Kelley have pointed out that continual conflict can itself become a source of conflict.

According to the social exchange model of relationships, couples maintain their relationships only when they perceive them to be equitable and when the cost/reward ratio and comparison level are favorable. It seems that couples tend to focus on the cost/reward and comparison level most often during the formative stages of the relationships and during crisis periods when serious conflicts arise. Thus, in building intimate relationships, the outcome depends heavily on the severity of the conflicts the couples experience and on the effectiveness with which they resolve the conflicts.

Although conflict is usually thought of as a destructive force, it can also play a constructive role in relationships. Conflict can be constructive if it helps the couple to develop skills in resolving disagreements, so that they find conflict resolution easier as their relationship progresses. Often, too, conflicts help the partners to better understand each other and their relationship and to avoid unnecessary future conflicts. Furthermore, openly communicating about and resolving conflicts can promote a spirit of trust and mutuality that fosters increased intimacy.

GROWING SEPARATELY AND GROWING TOGETHER

Our intimate relationships have a profound influence on us, whether for better or for worse. They can diminish us or help us grow and actualize our potentials as human beings. In this final section, we shall focus on those conditions in close relationships that help us grow as separate persons as well as grow together as a couple. These conditions include such elusive concepts as acceptance and caring, trust and commitment, and awareness.

Acceptance and Caring

Acceptance means that neither person takes a judgmental attitude toward the other. This does not mean that each has to agree with everything the other believes in or does, but it does mean that, when disagreements occur, the partners do not reject each other as persons, making each other feel inadequate, unworthy of love, or devalued. Personal criticism produces pain and defensiveness and makes disagreements much more difficult to deal with constructively. In some instances, acceptance means granting the other person's right to entertain his or her own convictions while retaining the same freedom for ourself.

Acceptance is essential if each person is to feel free to share his or her private world with the other. A judgmental attitude almost inevitably forces the other person to conceal certain experiences, ideas, or feelings. In turn, such holding back blocks further sharing—at least in certain areas—and, hence, mutual understanding, and it blocks the possibility that, by revealing and discussing such beliefs and experiences, each person will be better able to understand himself or herself and thus grow as a person. Conversely, acceptance makes it possible for each person to share his or her private world with the other. Rogers (1969) has described this as the feeling that "at last someone understands how it feels and seems to be *me* without wanting to analyze me or judge me. Now I can blossom and grow and learn" (pp. 11–12).

Caring means many things, but perhaps its central theme is concern for the well-being of another person. As Kelley (1979) has defined it, caring means giving up personal benefits or enduring costs out of consideration for the needs of one's partner. In essence, each partner is no longer solely focused on his or her immediate concerns but on helping the other and building the relationship. Knowing there is someone who truly cares and on whom we can count for support—"who will pick you up if you fall"—is vital emotional nourishment.

Caring in an adult relationship is helping each other grow by receiving and not denying each other's authentic feelings. . . . Caring thus is encouraging someone to do something he wants to do, not what you want him to do— encouraging him to act the way he feels, not the way you think he should feel.

Nena and George O'Neill

Caring may be expressed in words, or it may be expressed in actions ranging from simple courtesy to emotional and financial support in times of stress. In close relationships, caring involves respect for the rights and autonomy of the other person. When one person infringes on the rights of the other—dominates, manipulates, or uses him or her—a constructive relationship is not likely to develop (Marietta, 1982). Caring also means maintaining a balance between separateness and togetherness, building mutuality and union while simultaneously giving each other the freedom to grow as a person.

Finally, the importance of friendship in intimate relationships is often overlooked. Yet, friendship is based on caring, on being concerned about meeting our partner's needs as well as our own. When we trust our partner to be sincerely concerned about and attentive to our own needs, we are more free to relax and be concerned about meeting our partner's needs.

Trust and Commitment: They Make a Difference

O what a tangled web we weave, When once we practice to deceive.
Sir Walter Scott

Building an intimate and enduring relationship is not a guaranteed venture. It involves risk and the potential for severe emotional hurt. In the face of an uncertain future, the willingness to take the risks involved requires faith and **trust** in the other person. To believe in the relationship and give it our best requires what John Rempel and his associates (1985) call a "leap of faith." As they have noted:

> It is a curious paradox that, whereas trust is slow and difficult to build up, it appears notoriously easy to break down. Furthermore, it seems that once trust has been betrayed it is doubly difficult to reestablish. (p. 111)

Thus, trust is considered essential for commitment and the building of intimate relationships. Box 3–8 deals with the measurement of interpersonal trust.

Commitment refers to the avowed or inferred intent of each partner to maintain the relationship (Rosenblatt, 1977; Lund, 1985). Thus, commitment serves as a stabilizing influence in the relationship and tends to restrain the types of behaviors in which the partners engage. In the past, commitment was implied in the marriage vow—to love, honor, cherish, and obey, "till death us do part." Because divorce was rare and life expectancy was short, the form if not the spirit of the vow was usually followed. A partner might not love, honor, cherish, or obey his or her spouse, but the marriage usually lasted. As Kanter (1972) has pointed out, commitment may not only result from personal dedication but also from external pressures.

Today, however, commitment is more a matter of choice than of obligation. Current attitudes toward personal freedom, sexual fidelity, and divorce often make the promise of permanent commitment seem unrealistic—or perhaps even undesirable. Of course, there are some husbands and wives who maintain their marriage commitment "despite everything," perhaps because it is important for them to be married. There are others who feel committed to each other but want an "open marriage" that does not include sexual fidelity. There are also those who are committed to the institution of marriage rather than to the individuals they marry (Walters, 1982). At the other extreme are those who feel they can be totally committed to a partner without going through the formality of marriage.

Given the flexibility of commitment in today's society, how can we measure it? Marcia Lasswell and Norma Lobsenz (1978) offer three basic standards: duration,

BOX 3-8 / THE SPECIFIC INTERPERSONAL TRUST SCALE

This scale has only been validated for use with persons of the same sex. In determining your general level of trust for same-sex individuals, think of a person of the same sex in whom you have a great deal of trust. Then put that person's name in each of the blanks in the relevant items. As you think about an item, answer it on the following scale:

Strongly disagree   1   2   3   4   5   6   7   8   9   Strongly agree

Make sure you use the appropriate scale for your sex. Males should use the first set of twenty-one items; females should use the second set of thirteen items.

THE SIT SCALE FOR MALES

Overall Trust

1. If _____ gave me a compliment I would question if _____ really meant what was said.
2. If we decided to meet somewhere for lunch, I would be certain _____ would be there.
3. I would go hiking with _____ in unfamiliar territory if _____ assured me he/she knew the area.
4. I wouldn't want to buy a piece of used furniture from _____ because I wouldn't believe his/her estimate of its worth.
5. I would expect _____ to play fair.
6. I could rely on _____ to mail an important letter for me if I couldn't get to the post office.
7. I would be able to confide in _____ and know that he/she would want to listen.
8. I could expect _____ to tell me the truth.
9. If I had to catch an airplane, I could not be sure _____ would get me to the airport on time.

Emotional Trust

10. If _____ unexpectedly laughed at something I did or said, I would wonder if he/she was being critical and unkind.
11. I could talk freely to _____ and know that _____ would want to listen.
12. _____ would never intentionally misrepresent my point of view to others.
13. If _____ knew what kinds of things hurt my feelings, I would never worry that he/she would use them against me, even if our relationship changed.
14. I would be able to confide in _____ and know that he/she would want to listen.
15. If _____ didn't think I had handled a certain situation very well, he/she would not criticize me in front of other people.
16. If I told _____ what things I worry about, he/she would not think my concerns were silly.

(continued)

BOX 3-8 (*continued*)

Reliableness

17. If my alarm clock was broken and I asked ____ to call me at a certain time, I could count on receiving the call.

18. If ____ couldn't get together with me as we planned, I would believe his/her excuse that something important had come up.

19. If ____ promised to do me a favor, he/she would follow through.

20. If ____ were going to give me a ride somewhere and didn't arrive on time, I would guess there was a good reason for the delay.

21. If we decided to meet somewhere for lunch, I would be certain he/she would be there.

THE SIT SCALE FOR FEMALES

Reliableness

1. If I were injured or hurt, I could depend on ____ to do what was best for me.

2. If ____ borrowed something of value and returned it broken, ____ would offer to pay for the repairs.

3. If my alarm clock was broken and I asked ____ to call me at a certain time, I could count on receiving the call.

4. If ____ agreed to feed my pet while I was away, I wouldn't worry about the kind of care it would receive.

5. If ____ promised to do me a favor, he/she would follow through.

6. If ____ were going to give me a ride somewhere and didn't arrive on time, I would guess there was a good reason for the delay.

7. I would be willing to lend ____ almost any amount of money, because he/she would pay me back as soon as he/she could.

Emotional Trust

8. If ____ couldn't get together with me as we had planned, I would believe his/her excuse that something important had come up.

9. I could talk freely to ____ and know that he/she would want to listen.

10. ____ would never intentionally misrepresent my point of view to others.

11. If ____ knew what kinds of things hurt my feelings, I would never worry that he/she would use them against me, even if our relationship changed.

12. I would be able to confide in ____ and know that he/she would not discuss my concerns with others.

13. I could expect ____ to tell me the truth.

(continued)

BOX 3-8 (*continued*)

For males only: For items 1, 4, 9, and 10, reverse your scores: change 1s to 9; 2s to 8; 3s to 7; 4s to 6; 5s stay the same; 6s to 4; 7s to 3; 8s to 2; 9s to 1.

	Males	Females
Overall	54–84	—
Emotional	37–63	41–57
Reliableness	28–44	46–66

For males and females to determine your scores: For each factor (Overall, Emotional, and Reliableness for males; Reliableness and Emotional for females), add together your score for each item under that factor. You can then compare your scores with the following average scores for the several hundred college students studied by Johnson-George and Swap (see right column).

You can also use this scale to see different levels of trust you might have for different people. After going through the scale the first time, go through it again, thinking of another person. You can then compare the two people on each factor.

Johnson-George, C., and W. Swap. (1982). Measurement of specific interpersonal trust: Construction and validation of a scale to assess trust in a specific order. *Journal of Personality and Social Psychology* 43:1306–1317. Copyright 1982 by the American Psychological Association. Reprinted by permission of the author.

intensity, and priority. **Duration** refers to how long a person is willing to give unreserved love and support to another. Some people think duration is the most important sign of commitment, yet this dimension is perhaps overemphasized. Time span may have little to do with the quality of a relationship. **Intensity** refers to the strength of feeling and depth of concern for the partner. Just as enduring relationships may be shallow, brief encounters may be intense. The third standard is the **priority** given to the relationship—the extent to which it takes precedence over other matters, such as work, hobbies, family, and other relationships. In essence, commitment can be measured by the value placed on the relationship and the willingness to take the responsibility for maintaining it.

Often the partners are not equally committed to building the relationship. This is congruent to what Willard Waller (1951) has referred to as "the principle of least interest"—pointing out that the person with the least interest in the relationship is more likely to exploit the other. The person with the least commitment may dictate and manipulate the development of the relationship because he or she will not be so badly hurt if the relationship ends (Duck & Gilmour, 1981; Michaels et al., 1986). This unequal commitment poses a trap for the unwary who venture into intimate relationships. But having just roughly equal degrees of commitment is not enough: Relationships require a *high* degree of commitment from each partner; otherwise neither person is likely to devote the time and effort needed to sustain the relationship.

Awareness: Seeing Things the Way They Are

A Realistic View of Yourself.   For a relationship to survive and thrive, the individuals involved must have a realistic view of themselves, of each other, and of the relationship. Seeing yourself realistically includes having an accurate evaluation of your assets and liabilities, your motives and goals, your beliefs and values, your aspirations for personal growth and achievement, and your "market value."

It is also important for you to have an accurate view of your "stimulus value." For example, you may see yourself as affectionate and flexible, while your partner may see you as cold and rigid. While the other person's view may be inaccurate, it nevertheless is an important source of feedback, and differences in perceptions need to be checked out and resolved.

In gaining a realistic view of yourself, it is often helpful to keep in mind three key questions: (1) *Who am I?* The need for a clear sense of self-identity has become crucial in modern life, where people often feel themselves to be puppets in the hands of a vast, impersonal bureaucracy with little ability to direct and control their own lives. (2) *Where am I going?* This involves clarifying your life plans, the skills you need to develop for attaining them, and the hazards you are likely to encounter along the way. (3) *Why?* This question refers to values, what you consider desirable and undesirable. From among the alternatives available, you must choose those most likely to lead to a meaningful and fulfilling life. While there is no easy answer to these questions, they can provide a useful perspective in helping you to cope with your world.

A Realistic View of the Other Person.   Being realistic about your partner means having an accurate view of his or her assets and liabilities, goals and motives, beliefs and values, aspirations for growth and achievement, and "market value." Of course, when you are involved in an intimate relationship, it is often easy to engage in wishful thinking—to see your partner as you would like him or her to be, not as he or she really is. Also, the accuracy of your view depends on the openness and honesty of your partner. Consequently, it is important to check out any discrepancies between the image your partner projects and his or her actual behavior. These are key questions to ask: here: Who are *you?* Where are *you* going? *Why?*

An Accurate View of the Relationship.   Both you and your partner must develop a realistic view of the relationship you now have as well as the relationship you hope to achieve. It is also important to clarify what each partner does *not* want in the relationship, understand what the relationship will require of each partner, and be reasonably sure that each partner is willing and able to do his or her share. Do you both have realistic and similar views of your mutual goals, roles and responsibilities, ways of communicating and resolving conflicts, standards of satisfaction, and degrees of commitment? These are relevant questions here: Who are *we?* Where are *we* going? *Why?*

In this context, it is important to note that each close relationship has its own "climate," which may vary from positive and constructive to aversive and destructive. As Hazel Markus and Paula Nurius (1986) have pointed out, such a relationship climate may foster what the individual would like to become or what they are afraid of becoming. Along the same vein, Steve Duck (1984) has noted that relationships can repair and heal the people in them and contribute to personal and relationship growth, or they can be highly detrimental and destructive to both the persons and the relationship. In essence, close relationships can launch the partners as well as the relationship in constructive or destructive trajectories (Neimeyer & Neimeyer, 1985).

In the course of building a relationship, all the factors we have discussed in this chapter—self-disclosure, communication, ground rules, caring, and so on—will, of course, undergo change. Each partner will change and the relationship will change as it evolves. If the partners remain aware, however, they can usually make reasonably accurate evaluations of what is happening and can anticipate and adjust to such changes.

Unfortunately, many relationships that were once satisfying are allowed to deteriorate and perhaps terminate simply because the partners have failed to realize that vigilance and effort are a necessary part of ensuring the continuation of a rewarding relationship.

SUMMARY—Chapter 3

1. We have little scientific information concerning the nature of intimate relationships or the principles involved in building and maintaining them. However, social scientists have suggested three essential ingredients: a strong emotional involvement, strong feelings of interdependence, and a definite structure.

2. The key factors in building intimate relationships are effective communication, mutual self-disclosure, appropriate ground rules, effective methods of resolving conflicts, and such components as acceptance, caring, trust, commitment, and awareness.

3. Communication involves cognitive or factual information and affective information about feelings and emotions. Factual information is usually conveyed verbally and affective information nonverbally—by means of body language. Effective communication involves being a good sender and a good receiver. These are skills which can be acquired and cultivated.

4. The effectiveness of a couple's communication can be assessed by examining metacommunication: their typical patterns of communicating with each other. These patterns can be improved.

5. Self-disclosure involves revealing personal information to each other. As a relationship progresses, more intimate details are revealed. Mutual self-disclosure helps to build trust and closeness; but even in long-term relationships, some secrets may best be kept to oneself. One major risk of self-disclosure is rejection by one's partner.

6. Appropriate ground rules include clarifying common goals, agreeing on individual roles and responsibilities, sharing or allocating power and decision making, and establishing norms or standards. Ground rules provide structure for the relationship.

7. Differences in goals, roles, power and decision making, and norms can lead to conflicts. Conflicts can have both positive and negative effects on a relationship. Unresolved conflicts can destroy a relationship.

8. The best intimate relationships encourage a couple to grow as persons and to grow together as a couple. To build and maintain an intimate relationship, it is necessary to be aware—to have a realistic view of oneself, of one's partner, and of the relationship. And it is essential to keep this view updated as the relationship changes over time.

SEXUAL VALUES AND BEHAVIOR

Every person has sexual feelings, attitudes, and beliefs, but everyone's experience of sexuality is unique because it is processed through an intensely personal perspective.

—Masters, Johnson, & Kolodny (1985, p. 3)

———————————————————— ❮ ————————————————————

*E*ach society approves of certain sexual behaviors and disapproves of others. Such a **sexual-values system** is formed in response to the religious, economic, political, and ethical beliefs that predominate in the society. Because approved behaviors vary from one society to another, the members of one society may have radically different sexual views from the members of another. Sexual behavior affects human interactions and the size and health of the population, so all societies attempt to regulate the sexual behavior of their members.

In developing a personal sexual-values system, each of us is influenced by the society in which we are born, by the family group in which we grow up, and by those with whom we share the discovery and demands of sexuality—our peer group. What John Gagnon (1977) has called our **sexual script,** then, depends on our culture, on our personal relationships, and on our experience with sex in the context of these first two. We may not consciously express or even be aware of our sexual values, but they are reflected in our opinions about sex and the sexuality of others, our emotional responses to certain sexual situations, and our own sexual behavior.

Even though sexual behaviors tend to conform to established social norms, there is room for variation. This is particularly true when a society is in a state of transition regarding sexual values—as our own society has been from the 1950s until today. As a result, both individuals and couples have far greater freedom to choose the sexual life styles that seem right for them. Like all freedoms, however, sexual freedom may exact a high toll in terms of choice and responsibility. The lack of clear-cut sexual norms leaves many of us confused about what is really best for us. Is it better to engage in premarital sex or wait until marriage? Is it better to have a succession of sexual partners or limit the number to one or two? Is casual sex something to be enjoyed for its own sake or is it an emotional booby trap? Adding to the confusion has been the appearance of new "epidemics" of sexually transmitted diseases (STDs)—genital herpes in the late 1970s and AIDS in the early 1980s. A summary of sexually transmitted diseases is given in Box 4–4; the critical problem of AIDS is discussed in Box 4–5.

In this chapter, we shall explore sexual values and look at how and why they are changing. We shall then describe several sexual-behavior patterns to see how our values are expressed in action. Next, we shall review the sexual-response sequence and some common sexual problems and dysfunctions. Finally, we shall deal with the problem of achieving informed, responsible, and fulfilling sexuality. In the latter context, we shall also deal with the problem of sexually transmitted diseases, with difficulties in communicating about sex with one's partner, and with the role of sex in building intimate relationships.

THE SEXUAL REVOLUTION IN AMERICA

Probably never before have so many people been affected so much in such a short time by a change in society's view of sexuality. Previous sexual revolutions tended to affect primarily a small upper-class segment of the population. It would take quite a while for new beliefs to filter through to the rest of society. Now our high literacy rate and mass media ensure that changes happen quickly and involve millions of people. In the past thirty years, we have had the world's first truly *democratic* sexual revolution.

—*Sharon Brehm (1985, p. 117)*

A broad distinction can be made between societies that are moralistic in orientation toward sex and those that are naturalistic. **Moralistic societies** view sex as basically evil and are highly restrictive in regulating the limits of sexual behavior. Sex is considered for procreation only, and sex for pleasure is forbidden, especially for women. Women are likely to have no sexual rights and are presumed, conveniently, to lack desire. Men are seen as lustful creatures whose needs must be met.

An example of a moralistic society is found on the island of Inis Beag, off the coast of Ireland. The residents (about 350) are taught a highly repressive sexual script (Messenger, 1971). Both before and after marriage, the sexes are sharply segregated. Any discussion of sexual topics is taboo; both children and adults are ignorant of the most rudimentary aspects of sexual physiology and response. Petting and premarital sex are virtually unknown, as is the female orgasm. Nudity is considered evil, and breast-feeding of children is out of the question. Even the visibility of an animal's sex organs can arouse anxiety. Sexual intercourse takes place at night and is for procreating only: The husband and wife open their night clothes under the blankets and perform the act as quickly as possible.

Naturalistic societies, on the other hand, view sex as a normal activity to be cultivated and enjoyed. Such societies are far more permissive and are more likely to regard males and females as equals in sexual rights and desires. The Trobriand Islanders, for example, allow the sexual impulse almost free rein prior to marriage. There is a strong sexual element in childhood romances, and older boys and girls live together in a dormitory community called **bukumatula,** a shelter for sleeping and making love (Henriques, 1959). In the bukumatula, couples can come together and part at will. There are no rights, duties, or obligations, and these young people continue to eat their meals and keep their belongings in their parents' homes. The bukumatula is for making love—a more serious commitment would be to have a meal together!

Despite these disparate sexual values systems, the islanders of Inis Beag and Trobriand do share two sexual norms that appear to be common to all societies. The first is the **incest taboo,** which forbids relatives from being sexual partners. The second is the requirement that sexual intercourse eventually fall within the confines of marriage. Presumably, such norms are necessary to ensure the society's capacity to reproduce itself in an orderly way and to provide a stable family setting in which to socialize new members.

Most societies fall somewhere along a continuum between moralistic and naturalistic, and many fluctuate in regard to particular values. In our society, for

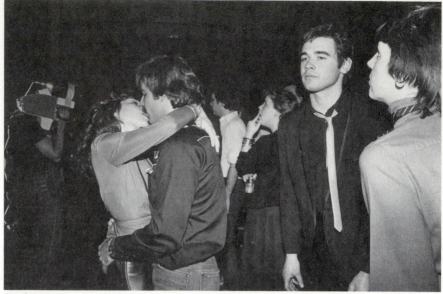

Hazel Hankin

example, a moralistic heritage dominated sexual activities from the colonial period until quite recently. However, our society also has a tradition of individual freedom to choose. There has always been tension between certain religious-values systems and this freedom of choice, and we see this conflict currently in such controversial areas as abortion, homosexuality, and sex education. These issues arouse strong emotions on both sides.

In the 1960s and 1970s, our society went through what has been called a **sexual revolution,** in which a more-naturalistic attitude toward sex emerged. This new permissiveness in sexuality has given us the freedom to do research on sexual behavior, talk about sex openly, and choose our own sexual-value system. But it has also caused conflict with some traditional moral and religious assumptions about sexuality that have prevailed for centuries.

What are some of the specific value changes that have occurred, and why have they occurred?

Major Changes in Sexual Values

There are many areas in which changes in sexual values have occurred. Included here are discussions of the double standard, sex for pleasure rather than simply for procreation, premarital sex, sex with successive partners, and casual sex.

Decline of the Double Standard.   Since medieval times, a **double standard** has dominated sexual relationships in Western society. That is, it is considered acceptable for men to enjoy sex and engage in premarital and extramarital affairs, but it is not appropriate for women to do so. With the double standard, women are expected to be virgins when they marry, but men are not. Women are expected to be faithful after they marry; men are not. In times and societies in which women were considered the property of men, virginity and fidelity on the part of women were strongly emphasized because the man did not want "his" property despoiled before or after marriage—he wanted to be sure that the children his wife bore were really his.

Since the 1960s, the women's movement has called for an end to the inequality between men and women in the sexual, as well as the social, sphere. Women sought the right to reach for the same goals as men and to decide their own sexual needs and pleasures. But long-standing traditions are not easily eradicated. Ira L. Reiss (1981) has pointed out that although the double standard is declining in our society, it has not been completely eliminated. Certainly, men and women have made great strides in reducing the unfairness of the double standard, but various researchers have continued to find evidence of the double standard (or at least modern variations of it) in our society, especially on college campuses (Robinson & Jedlicka, 1982; Jacoby & Williams, 1985).

Sex for Pleasure.   Our changing sexual standards have made sex for pleasure not only socially acceptable but also highly desirable, especially as an aspect of intimate relationships. With the separation of sex from reproduction, sexual activity has come to be seen as a pleasurable end in and of itself. In addition to more-egalitarian sex-roles and more-effective birth-control methods, major contributions to this attitude have come from the work of sex researchers and from the proliferation of sex-education materials for both adults and children. Sex therapists, such as Masters and Johnson, have developed methods for helping couples improve their sex lives, while popular works such as Alex Comfort's *The Joy of Sex*, erotic novels, and X-rated movies have helped open the pleasure chest of sexuality. Some examples of sexual fantasies are in Box 4–1.

As we know, however, the availability of these materials causes concern as well as enlightenment. There are those who question whether sex-education materials should be available to children and those who wonder about the possible connections between sexually explicit literature and sex crimes. Some see the availability of sexual publications and films as a sign of declining moral standards in our society. These are important issues, and a considerable amount of research is being directed toward them.

Nevertheless, the work of social scientists, medical professionals, and other experts has enabled us to talk more openly about sex and alerted us to the capabilities of both men and women to experience sexual pleasure and fulfillment. But the idea of sex for pleasure does not mean going to an extreme in a frantic search for new partners or techniques as a means of maintaining a "sexual high." Rather, it encompasses the human potential for pleasurable and meaningful sexual experiences within the context of intimate relationships.

Acceptance of Premarital Sex.   Our moralistic tradition has frowned on sexual relations prior to marriage, especially for women. One of the reasons for this "rule" was the problem of unwed pregnancy. Today, however, young people not only have better access to birth control (although several studies show that they do not always take advantage of this availability) but they have two other options as well. Because single parenthood carries less social stigma today than it did in the past, one option is to have a child and raise him or her alone or with the help of family or friends. The other option is abortion, which has always been an option but today is relatively safe and legal. Abortion is discussed later in Box 4–8.

We may also note that the term **premarital sex** does not necessarily mean having sexual intercourse. Many young people are sexually active prior to mar-

One new value is the very notion that sexual pleasure is right pleasure—that it can be widely enjoyed in a variety of circumstances and perhaps with a variety of partners. Even for those who still believe that sexual contact should be restricted to the married, marital sex now represents a delight instead of a duty, and even a form of play.

J. Gagnon

BOX 4-1 / SEXUAL FANTASIES

Everyone makes love but everyone is thinking something different when they do.

—*Richard von Kraft-Ebing*

A **sexual fantasy** is a reverie or dream with an elaborate script that is sexually stimulating. Only in recent years have research studies penetrated the veil of secrecy surrounding male and female sexual fantasies. Most men and women have such fantasies, which can vary from the mundane to the exotic. Sexual fantasies can occur during daydreams or night dreams, as an accompaniment to masturbation, or during sexual encounters with a partner.

In general, women fantasize about sex with men with whom they are involved or with whom they are familiar, such as their employers or their husbands' best friends. Other female fantasies tend to fall into one of the following categories: being overpowered and forced to have sex; having sex with more than one partner at a time; performing oral sex; and performing sexual acts the woman would never engage in in real life. Many of these fantasies may involve faceless strangers. In her *Cosmo Report*, Linda Wolfe (1981) related the fantasies of several female subjects:

I'm with my husband, but there's another man in bed with us, too, and while my husband is entering my vagina, the second man explores other parts of my body. (p. 263)

I'm a librarian. A married librarian with three kids. But in my fantasies, I'm always a prostitute, and I have a pimp who says if I don't make love with one customer after another, he'll beat me black and blue. I always do what he says. (p. 263)

I usually have sex fantasies about my boss. Sometimes he and I are in bed together, but sometimes we're in the office. I'm sitting at my desk stark naked, typing away, and he's just standing at the door, watching me. Or we go to lunch, and I take off my panties in the ladies'

room and come back to the table, take his hand, and slip it under my skirt. Then we sit there talking insurance rates. (p. 263)

Male fantasies tend to follow a similar pattern, with intercourse with a loved or desired person being the predominant fantasy. Other fantasies include being overpowered or raped by a powerful and aggressive woman; having sex with several people at the same time; seducing some willing woman or using force if she resists; and sex with other men.

In general, men would rather be dominated by, rather than dominate, women in their fantasies. And, unlike women, men are more likely to have fantasies that involve specific individuals rather than faceless strangers. Neither men nor women want to hurt others or be hurt in their fantasies. Many men's fantasies can involve unusual twists, as the following examples (from the author's files) indicate:

It really excites me when I think about my wife having sex with her previous husband. I imagine him taking her clothes off and seducing her—with all the details included.

When I have intercourse with [my girlfriend, who had formerly had a lesbian relationship], I keep imagining her kissing the woman's breasts, sucking her nipples, having oral-genital contact, and having an orgasm with that woman. It really adds to my sexual enjoyment.

I visualize this beautiful woman I know refusing to take no for an answer. She keeps after me and eventually overpowers me and forces me to have sex with her. It is really great.

Both men and women use fantasy to increase the performance or pleasure of sex, whether they are alone or with a partner. In fact, some men and women report that they cannot achieve orgasm with their mates unless they use fantasy to add to the excitement and

(continued)

BOX 4-1 (*continued*)

variety. As a result, some sex therapists have suggested that certain clients use specific fantasy themes when having sexual encounters (Eisenman, 1982).

In addition, some researchers have suggested exploring the specific content of sexual fantasies in connection with the personality makeup or nature of the relationship in which the fantasy occurs. For example, do women who are not physically attracted to their sexual partner tend to have specific types of sexual fantasies during intercourse (Arndt, Foehl, & Good, 1985)?

riage without having coital experience, for example, by means of petting or oral–genital sex. However, in our present discussion we shall use terms such as premarital sex, casual sex, and sex with successive partners to include sexual intercourse. Of course, in this context we are not dealing with homosexual experiences, which may involve a variety of sexual techniques but preclude sexual intercourse.

In any event, the expectation of virginity at marriage appears to be a thing of the past. In his study of *Sexual Behavior in the Human Female*, Alfred Kinsey (1953) reported that about one-third of 21- to 25-year-old women had premarital intercourse. By the early 1980s, the corresponding figure was about 80 percent and still rising with each passing year (Reiss, 1981; Horn & Tanfer, 1985; *California Magazine*, 1986). In addition, the age of first premarital intercourse for women was also dropping. For example, David Gelman and his associates (1980) estimated that in the 15- to 19-year-old age group, about half of the females—and a much higher percentage of the males—had premarital intercourse. In 1986, a Harris Poll funded by the Planned Parenthood Federation of America reported that almost one-third (and possibly a considerably higher number) of 12- to 17-year-old teenagers had had sexual intercourse. The primary reason was peer pressure. Because available statistics over the years have shown the majority of males to have engaged in premarital intercourse, the major change appears to have been made by young women.

What these statistics do not reveal, however, is how young people feel about premarital sex. A number of early studies have indicated that more women than men require emotional intimacy to justify sexual intimacy. Thus, premarital sex may pose a problem for young women who feel pressured by their partners or peer-group members to engage in casual sex. And in many cases, young women feel "used" by men who insist on having sex but have no intention of establishing a close relationship (Wolfe, 1981; Delamater & MacCorquodale, 1979; Masters et al., 1985). Because premarital sex is part of the traditional male role, problems of guilt and being used by aggressive women are minimal, although they do occur.

In general, it would appear that premarital sex has become an acceptable and established pattern in our society. This is especially true when the sex takes place in intimate relationships such as serious dating, engagement, and cohabitation.

Sex with Successive Partners.   Not only is premarital sex acceptable, but also for many young people it involves successive partners. Rubenstein and Tavris (1987) reported that 23 percent of the women in the *Redbook* survey had just 1 lover before marriage, whereas 32 percent of the women had 6 or more lovers. In a

Hazel Hankin

similar 1976 *Redbook* survey, comparable figures were 51 percent and 15 percent. In another survey of over 600 students attending various California colleges and universities, *California Magazine* (1986) asked a variety of questions. In answer to the question "How many sexual partners have you had?" the replies revealed that 12 percent of the students had had two partners, while 42 percent had had three or more partners. In short, more than half of the students questioned reported having had two or more sexual partners.

The relationship between the number of sexual partners and one's desirability as a mate among unmarried college students was studied by Joseph Istvan and William Griffitt (1980). At least when this study was made, it appears that many college students did place limits on the number of sexual partners they considered acceptable on the part of a person they would choose as a mate. Of course, their stated preferences might not carry much weight if the "right person" came along. And some men and women would actually prefer not to know the details if they suspected the person they were planning to marry had an extensive background of sexual experience with numerous partners.

Utilizing a sample of 200 never-married students in introductory sociology classes at a large Midwestern university, Jacoby and Williams (1985) attempted to extend the earlier findings of Istvan and Griffitt. Several of their conclusions are of particular interest.

1. Virgins were consistently desired as partners in terms of dating and mating—and this preference was expressed as frequently by females as by males. The second preference for both sexes was for partners with moderate sexual experience.

2. No relationship was found between the sexual experience of the person doing the rating and that of the person being rated. In other words, the same preference was expressed whether the rater had a great deal of or very little sexual experience.

3. Subjects who had had their sexual experience in an intimate relationship were rated less highly as potential dates and mates than those who had had sexual experience in a more-casual setting.

In commenting on their findings, these researchers noted the striking similarity between males and females in their responses. In addition, it appeared more important for young people to be their partner's "first love" than to be their partner's first sexual partner, although they would prefer to have it both ways.

So far, we have been discussing never-married singles. In addition, during any given year there are 13 million or more American men and women who are single as a result of divorce. Because the great majority of these divorced persons will remarry, they will obviously have included more than one sex partner in their lives. And this says nothing of extramarital sex, which adds to the number of sexual partners for a sizable number of men and women (Wolfe, 1981; Spanier & Margolis, 1983; Masters & Johnson, 1985).

Casual Sex.   Widely differing degrees of affection and intimacy may be involved in sexual encounters. Single or divorced people may engage in sex simply because they enjoy it or for reasons other than emotional closeness. A man may seduce a woman to prove his sexual prowess or gratify his physical sexual needs. A woman may seduce a man to demonstrate her attractiveness or satisfy her sexual desires. In fact, sex can be an important component in helping restore confidence after an unhappy love affair or marriage.

Despite the prevalence of **casual sex,** it by no means meets with unanimous approval. Although many people feel that the desire for and pleasure of sex do not need to be restricted to love relationships, this situation remains a moral issue for many. In a report on a survey of *Cosmopolitan* readers, Linda Wolfe (1981) has found that the majority of women had had two to ten sexual partners, and many had had far more:

> But sexual discontent was still rife among them. This discontent made itself apparent in many ways other than the mere answer to a multiple-choice question. The women wrote about it repeatedly, and even admirers of the sexual revolution expressed it. Many complained that they often went to bed with men on first dates not out of choice but necessity: a man would not ask to see them again if they did not have sex the first time. Many explained that they had had numerous lovers not because sexual variety appealed to them but because they couldn't find men willing to form steady relationships, which they emphatically preferred. . . . No wonder, then, that so many of the *Cosmo* women were disillusioned with sexual freedom. (p. 25)

Of course, women who read *Cosmopolitan* and respond to surveys are not representative of our society at large, probably because they are more sexually sophisticated and earn their own livings (although a few were homemakers and students). In addition, their willingness to respond to the survey indicates a concern with sexual matters. Nevertheless, their answers and comments do tell us something about how many women in our society feel about casual sex.

From a practical viewpoint, Masters and Johnson (1985) have pointed out that matters are likely to be simpler if the individual engages in casual sex simply because he or she enjoys it and expects nothing more from the encounter. Of course, the person also has to be willing to risk contracting a sexually transmitted disease. In such instances, the person is less likely to feel used and to be disappointed by a lack of further contact. However, as we shall see in our discussion of singlehood in Chapter 6, "date rape" is a common occurrence and may add to the danger of contracting some STDs.

It seems apparent that the widespread challenging of traditional sexual values and the sexual revolution have led to a great deal of confusing viewpoints regarding casual sex and other aspects of sexual behavior. Within the broad outlines laid down by society, each person is expected to work out sexual values and behaviors that he or she deems appropriate. And this is by no means an easy task.

Why Sexual Values Have Changed

In reviewing the value changes that have characterized the sexual revolution, we have alluded to some of the many factors that have led to these changes, which include the following:

1. Greater equality in sex-roles and sexual behavior—brought about in large part by the women's movement—and leading, among other things, to the demise of the double standard.
2. The disengagement of sex from procreation—made possible by the development of the birth-control pill and other modern contraceptives—and leading to the expectation of sex for pleasure.
3. The disengagement of sex from marriage, resulting in premarital sex becoming an accepted part of the courtship ritual in our society.
4. The increasing ease of obtaining divorce and its social acceptance, leading to successive sexual partners as persons marry, divorce, and remarry.
5. Major changes in the overall values and life styles of Americans, which in turn affect sexual values and behavior. Such changes include the explicit portrayal of sexual behavior—even previously taboo topics—by the mass media.

Finally, our sexual values and behavior have been greatly affected by scientific research in this area. At the turn of the century, Sigmund Freud was the first scientist to emphasize the role of sexual factors in human behavior, thus helping to bring sex out into the open where it could be discussed and studied. However, it was the pioneering research of Alfred Kinsey and his associates (1948, 1953) that documented what people actually did sexually. These mid-century surveys of the American male and the American female showed us that we practiced more sex and more sexual variations than we thought we did—or than we thought the rest of us did.

The early studies of Kinsey and his associates were followed by those of William Masters and Virginia Johnson (1966, 1970), a physician and a behavioral scientist, who were interested in the physiology, psychology, and sociology of sex. These and other major studies are summarized in Box 4–2. In general, these studies have had a tremendous impact on our sexual values by making available accurate information about sexual behavior. It has become apparent, for example, that some sexual patterns once considered deviant and undesirable, such as masturbation and oral sex, are widely practiced and can be considered normal from a

BOX 4-2 / SEX RESEARCH: METHODS AND PROBLEMS

Studying the sexual behaviors and attitudes of human beings poses a number of problems for researchers. Most fundamentally, sex is a highly personal and private experience that does not readily lend itself to research study. Thus, traditional research methods—such as direct observation of behavior and experimental studies in the laboratory—are difficult to apply. Instead, most sex researchers have had to rely on interviews and questionnaires in order to compile **surveys** on sexual behaviors and activities. Unfortunately, the survey method brings with it several problems that can influence the results.

The first and perhaps the most famous of sex researchers was Alfred Kinsey. He and his associates interviewed 5,300 men and 5,940 women in the late 1940s and early 1950s to put together a profile of the sexual patterns of Americans. Although the study was carefully designed and very comprehensive, the great majority of subjects tended to be young, urban, and educated, so it did not really provide a typical cross-section of Americans.

No large scale survey was attempted again until the Playboy Foundation funded a study reported by Morton Hunt (1974). Although the survey provided information about a broad range of sexual behaviors, it was based on a telephone survey of only 1,044 women and 982 men. Shortly thereafter, *Redbook* magazine published the results of a questionnaire survey involving 75,000 women readers (Tavris and Jayaratne, 1976). Another landmark was a questionnaire survey by *Cosmopolitan* magazine based on 106,000 of its women readers (Wolfe, 1981).

These early studies led to later magazine surveys utilizing large numbers of subjects—for example *New Woman* (1986) with 60,000 women subjects and *Redbook* (1987) with 36,000 subjects. However, these surveys lacked representative samples of American women, relying on their readers as subjects.

Striking out pretty much on her own, Shere Hite published the results of her studies of female (1976) and male (1981) sexuality. In a later study of women and love, she utilized a sample of 4,500 subjects. However, her subjects were not randomly chosen—she selected many of them herself—and probably were not representative of American men and women. In addition, she appears to have injected her own attitudes into the interpretation of her results.

These later surveys view sex as simply one factor in the broader context of marriage and man–woman relationships. Most later studies have also concluded that marriage is not as important or central in the lives of women today as it was formerly (*Cosmopolitan*, 1985; Hite, 1987, *New Woman*, 1986; *Redbook*, 1987; Glen and Weaver, 1988). The latter study was based on 15 years of survey data compiled by the National Opinion Research Center.

Surveys are also often conducted with smaller samples of selected groups to ascertain their attitudes and/or behavior regarding specific topics. For example, researchers may wish to ascertain the attitudes and practices of surgeons with respect to AIDS patients.

In addition to the problem of finding a representative sample of respondents, researchers who conduct surveys must take into account the fact that people who are willing to respond to questionnaires may differ in their sexual attitudes and behaviors from those who are not willing to respond. Furthermore, answers given on a questionnaire may not be an accurate reflection of actual attitudes and behaviors.

Some sex researchers have been able to study aspects of sexual behavior without

(continued)

BOX 4–2 (*continued*)

using the survey method. Masters and Johnson were able to use direct observation by setting up conditions for studying human sexual response in a laboratory setting. This method has the advantage of providing objective data rather than relying on subjective reports of past behaviors. However, for practical reasons the number of subjects is limited, and obviously only certain types of people are willing to participate in such research.

Two other limited methods that have been used in sex research are case studies and experimental studies. **Case studies** are in-depth explorations of the sexual attitudes and behaviors of individuals. In contrast to surveys, this approach obtains a great deal of data on a very small sample of persons. This approach is often used in studying sex offenders. In **experimental studies,** subjects are exposed to specific sexual stim-

uli—such as erotic pictures—under controlled conditions and their physiological reactions are measured by instruments. Again, this method is limited to relatively small samples of subjects.

As yet, a truly representative study of the sexual behavior of men and women in our society has still to be made. Such a study would (1) have to distinguish between stated sexual values and actual behavior, (2) need to be longitudinal as well as cross-sectional in design, and (3) require due consideration of the subjects' rights to privacy and confidentiality. It would also require trained research personnel and a great deal of research time and money. This is a tall order. For the foreseeable future, it would appear that we have to make the best possible use of available findings, even though these findings have limitations.

statistical point of view. As a result, many people have been relieved of unnecessary guilt about their sexual practices. In addition, people have become freer to experiment with sexual behaviors other than traditional intercourse, re-evaluate their attitudes toward premarital sex and other sexual patterns, and develop more-meaningful values for guiding their own sexual behavior.

AIDS and the New Sexual Restraint

At various points in our discussion, we have referred to two new sexual epidemics: genital herpes, which made its appearance in the early 1970s, and AIDS, which made its appearance in the early 1980s.

Genital herpes made the "big-time" in **sexually transmitted diseases (STDs)** in August 1982, when *Time* magazine ran a cover story on it entitled "The New Scarlet Letter." This article led to a bandwagon of publicity on genital herpes, and it soon became the "terror" of the single's world (Halpern, 1986). This terror gradually subsided, however, as additional facts became available. First, it was not a "new epidemic" because it had a history dating back over 2,000 years. Second, it was not life threatening, although it could have serious side effects, particularly for infants born to infected mothers. Third, it was not much different from the familiar sun blisters and cold sores that occasionally break out around the mouth of about 90 percent of the American population.

Even though there is no cure for genital herpes, there is no need to press the panic button. People can live relatively normal sexual lives providing they inform their sexual partners when the herpes virus makes its appearance in genital blisters and is contagious—usually about three to four times a year lasting about a week each time. Additional information on genital herpes is contained in Box 4–3.

Ironically, the most common STD, one that can cause pelvic inflammatory disease and sterility in women, is rarely mentioned. It's medical name is *Chlamydia trachomatis*, and it infects some 5 million new victims each year. Fortunately, it can be treated with antibiotics (see Box 4–3).

As far as is known, AIDS is a "new epidemic"—at least in the United States —and it is life threatening and spreading rapidly in our population. We shall comment on it briefly here and in greater detail in Box 4–4. According to the federal Centers for Disease Control (1986), about 1.5 million Americans have been exposed to the AIDS virus, or viruses. It is predicted that, by 1991, about 145,000 cases a year will require medical care. Of these, 54,000 will die of the virus.

Formerly, it was thought that AIDS was restricted to homosexuals, drug abusers using contaminated needles, and occasional people receiving blood transfusions with infected blood. The latter problem has been corrected. But, more important, it is now known that the AIDS virus infects heterosexuals as well as homosexuals, women as well as men, and children as well as adults. It qualifies as a "new epidemic" that could spread to millions of Americans and cause enormous casualties in the 1990s, unless the public observes certain precautions or science comes up with effective methods of prevention and treatment. It is encouraging to note that scientists throughout the world are working on this problem.

The preceding data raise the question of how sexually active singles—or married persons planning to engage in extramarital affairs—can protect themselves. There is no sure way, except perhaps to say "No" to new sexual partners unless they are cleared for AIDS. This is part of the new sexual restraint. An additional and crucially important part in controlling AIDS is observing the precautions outlined by C. Everett Koop (1986), the Surgeon General of the United States:

> AIDS is preventable. It can be controlled by changes in personal behavior. It is the responsibility of every citizen to be informed about AIDS and to exercise the appropriate preventive measures. This report will tell you how. (1986, p. 2)

It is quite possible, as the Surgeon General has pointed out, that AIDS may bring an end to the free-wheeling sexual life style that has been called the sexual revolution. If and when AIDS is conquered—and the probabilities are that it will be—the question of whether we as a society will return to our former sexual life style cannot be answered with certainty. However, ours is a highly sexualized society and it seems unlikely that sexual restraint based on fear is likely to survive once that fear is removed. Nevertheless, we may exercise greater precautions than we have in the past to prevent contacting other types of STDs.

As we noted in Chapter 1, the AIDS epidemic is having repercussions throughout our society in terms of dating, marriage, and other intimate relationships in which sex plays a role. Because available research does not yet reflect the impact of AIDS on our behavior and life styles, it is necessary for the reader to interpret various research findings with AIDS in mind as part of our present social setting. However, this challenge may help to foster a better understanding of intimate relationships and have a positive, rather than a negative, effect on our thinking in this area.

BOX 4-3 / SEXUALLY TRANSMITTED DISEASES

There are over 20 types of non–life-threatening sexually transmitted diseases (STDs), of which gonorrhea, syphilis, and genital herpes are perhaps the best known. The incidence of these diseases has shown a great worldwide increase in recent years, particularly among young people. There are an estimated 30 million or more cases of STDs in the United States, with some 7,000 new cases per day (which comes to about 5 cases per second). Over half of the reported victims are between the ages of 15 and 24. In fact, an estimated one out of three high-school students in large cities will contract an STD before graduating.

In this box, we shall briefly examine four of the most widespread STDs. Because of its tremendous impact on the contemporary scene, we shall deal with AIDS separately in Box 4-4.

Gonorrhea.   Although only about 1 million cases of gonorrhea are officially reported each year, experts estimate that there are actually two to three times as many actual cases. The causitive agent is a bacterium that is transmitted exclusively by sexual contact. The early symptoms in males include a discharge from the penis and a burning sensation during urination. The symptoms in women are often so mild that they do not even know they have the disease. Early signs, if detectable, are usually a mild vaginal discharge, which may irritate vulvar tissue.

Later complications in males include prostate, bladder, and kidney infection. In some cases, gonorrhea may lead to sterility in men. In females, the possible complications include pelvic inflammatory disease, abdominal adhesions, and sterility. Penicillin is effective in treating most cases, and alternative antibiotics are available for those allergic to penicillin. However, having gonorrhea does not confer future immunity; a person can contract the disease again if exposed to it.

Syphilis.   There are an estimated 1 million or more Americans with untreated syphilis, and some 100,000 new cases occur each year. The disease is caused by a corkscrew bacterium, or spirochete, called *Treponema pallidum*. Because, like the gonorrhea bacterium, it is highly vulnerable to dryness and heat, the syphilis spirochete is rarely transmitted by any means other than sexual contact. In exceptional cases, however, it may be acquired through direct contact with open syphilitic sores or lesions. If the disease is transmitted from mother to child during fetal development, the baby will be born with syphilis.

When untreated, syphilis typically progresses through four stages:

1. The primary stage is characterized by a sore called a **chancre,** which appears at the point of infection some 20 days after the spirochete has entered the body.
2. The secondary stage is characterized by a copper-colored skin rash that appears some 3–4 weeks after the chancre.
3. The third stage is a latent period—a period of several years during which overt symptoms disappear and the person may mistakenly think he or she is cured. Actually, the spirochetes have gone "underground" into the bloodstream, where they spread through the body, attacking various internal organs.
4. In the tertiary period, some 10 or more years later, the accumulated damage of the latent period becomes apparent in the form of cardiovascular disease, blindness, liver damage, paralysis, or severe brain damage. In fact, syphilis has been called the "great imitator" because of the wide range of disease symptoms it can produce.

(continued)

BOX 4-3 (continued)

Syphilis can be treated by penicillin at any stage. The outcome depends on the extent of bodily damage accomplished prior to treatment. Unfortunately, in many cases treatment is not undertaken until the disease has already caused extensive and irreparable damage to one or more body organs.

Genital Herpes.   There are more than 20 million Americans with genital herpes and an estimated 400,000 new cases are reported each year.

The virus implicated in this disease is herpes simplex type 2. The virus is usually transmitted by contact between infected and noninfected skin surfaces, so it can be communicated by kissing and other contact as well as by sexual relations. Typically, about 2–8 days after infection, small red bumps appear on the genitals. These bumps then develop into tiny but painful blisters that contain millions of infectious virus particles. The victim may become feverish and urination may be painful, especially for women. The body attacks the blisters with white blood cells, and the tiny blisters develop into painful open sores with a surrounding red ring. After about 3 weeks, the sores heal. Unfortunately, however, the virus is not gone. Rather, it has retreated up nerve fibers to the spinal cord, where it may remain dormant. In about one-third of cases, the virus flares up again periodically, during which time the person is contagious.

Herpes is rarely dangerous to otherwise healthy patients, although it may increase the probability of cervical cancer in women and can be transmitted to babies at the time of delivery. Even though there is as yet no cure for herpes, medication has been developed to reduce the pain and the spread and length of the viral attack. Persons who do have recurrent attacks of herpes should avoid sexual relationships during the period of the attack, which usually means a period of 2–3 weeks per year of abstinence.

While genital herpes is not good news, it is not life threatening and need not interfere with relationships. But it is important to tell one's partner when having an attack and to avoid sexual contacts during this period. In short, the so-called "herpes hysteria" has largely abated.

Chlamydia.   Currently, chlamydia appears to be the most common sexually transmitted disease in the United States. There are an estimated 5 million new cases each year.

Symptoms in men include painful urination and a watery discharge. The symptoms in women include genital itching, dull pelvic pain, and purulent cervical discharge. However, in an estimated 70 percent of the women it infects, chlamydia is asymptomatic—that is, it is not painful and the preceding symptoms do not occur. Typically, it infects women in their 20s.

Chlamydia itself is considered a relatively minor infection that can usually be prevented by the use of spermicides and effectively treated by antibiotics if it does occur. However, chlamydia presents a potentially major health risk for women. Because it is asymptomatic in the majority of cases, it can cause infertility before it is diagnosed. In addition, it can lead to the development of pelvic inflammatory disease —which hospitalizes some 300,000 women each year—and can have a variety of undesirable effects.

The American Medical Association recommends that women be tested for chlamydia bacteria at least once a year to ensure its early detection. Women under 24 years of age who have changed sex partners within the last 2 months are considered high-risk cases and should also undergo diagnostic tests.

BOX 4-4 / AIDS

There is a global epidemic of AIDS that
leaves no country untouched. We can't stop
AIDS anywhere until we stop it everywhere.
—Dr. Jonathan Mann, Director of the World
Health Organization's AIDS Program (1987)

AIDS (Acquired Immune Deficiency Syndrome) is a newcomer to the list of STDs.
Although the AIDS virus was identified somewhat earlier, the first case of AIDS in the
United States was reported in 1981. However,
it was not until the mid-1980s that the potential dimensions of the AIDS epidemic were
recognized, by either the health authorities or
the general public. Earlier, it was considered
an isolated problem confined primarily to homosexual males, intravenous drug abusers, and
immigrants from Haiti. Even in 1987, 66 percent of new cases involved gays and another 17
percent involved drug abusers. However, the
killer virus was rapidly closing in on heterosexuals. By 1991, it is predicted that 1 in 10 new
cases of AIDS will involve heterosexuals.

AIDS, a complex and fatal disease, is receiving a great deal of national and international research attention. In the present context, we cannot explore this topic in great
detail. Rather, we shall attempt to present a
summary of this deadly and rapidly spreading
disease.

Incidence.   AIDS is an "equal opportunity"
disease. Although the incidence is higher in
some countries than others, there are no geographically "safe zones." AIDS does not respect age, sex, or religion. However, it is more
common among the poor and women die of
AIDS much faster than men do.

In our society, every state now reports
AIDS cases—with the highest incidence in
California on the West coast, New York and
Florida on the East coast, and Texas in the
Southwest. In terms of cities, the highest rates
are found in San Francisco and New York
City. As we noted earlier, most cases involve
gay males and intravenous drug abusers. But

from 1982–1986, the proportion of heterosexuals having AIDS increased from about 1 to 5
percent. In our society, the incidence of AIDS
is disproportionately high among blacks, His-
panics, and the poor—regardless of sexual
preference.

Since the first reported case of AIDS in
1981, the incidence of AIDS in the United
States has reached epidemic proportions. In
1986, there were an estimated 1.5 million
Americans infected with the AIDS virus. Of
these, from one-fourth to one-half are expected to develop the lethal AIDS syndrome
—most within 5 years. By the end of 1986, the
cumulative total of AIDS cases numbered
about 30,000—of whom some 17,000 had
died. By June, 1987, the number of cases
diagnosed as having AIDS had increased to
about 36,000 cases—and the number of
deaths was approaching 20,000 cases.

By 1991, it has been estimated that between
5 and 10 million Americans will be infected
with the AIDS virus; there will be 270,000
cumulative diagnosed AIDS cases (all cases
since 1981); and the death toll will rise to
54,000 cases per year.

On an international level, the incidence of
AIDS is difficult, if not impossible, to ascertain. Some countries do not report their number of AIDS cases to the World Health Organization (WHO), and others send in greatly
reduced incidence figures, usually for fear of
the effect on tourism. At the Third International Conference on AIDS in June 1987,
however, the head of WHO's program ha-
zarded the estimate that some 10 million people worldwide are infected with the AIDS
virus. By 1991, this figure is expected to exceed 100 million.

Nature and Symptoms.   By way of introduction, it is important to note that when we talk
about AIDS, we are talking about three interrelated conditions.

1. Infection with the AIDS virus.   When a
   person contracts the AIDS virus, he or she

(continued)

BOX 4-4 (continued)

is said to be infected. Although the person is contagious and can spread the AIDS virus—through sexual contact—there are no overt symptoms and the person is unaware of the infection and the danger to sexual partners. Exceptions to this lack of awareness of infection are persons who undergo testing for the AIDS virus.

As emphasized in the Surgeon General's report, the AIDS virus is not transmitted by casual social, workplace, or school contacts. Rather, it is transmitted by body fluids—particularly semen, vaginal secretions, and blood. Prior to March 1985, the AIDS virus was occasionally transmitted by blood transfusions. Since that time, blood used for transfusions is screened and the risk of receiving a contaminated unit is estimated at 1 in 80,000. In short, blood transfusions are relatively, but not entirely, safe. Currently, the main route of infection is sexual contact. Bringing up a distant second is the exchange of contaminated needles or syringes by intravenous drug abusers.

2. *AIDS-Related Complex (ARC).* Once a person has been infected by the AIDS virus, there are several possibilities. Some people remain well, although they can infect others. Other infected persons develop a disease referred to as AIDS-Related Complex, or ARC.

Symptoms here may include weight loss, fever, night sweats, skin rashes, diarrhea, chronic tiredness, and lowered resistance to infections. Because these symptoms may also occur in other diseases, a medical diagnosis is essential to determine whether or not the person is infected with the AIDS virus.

The symptoms of ARC are less severe than those of AIDS. Although the exact ratio is not known, the group of persons with ARC is estimated to be about 10 times the size of the group diagnosed as AIDS victims. Over time, however, ARC may progress to the classic AIDS syndrome.

3. *AIDS.* This syndrome results from the natural progress of the AIDS virus, which attacks and destroys the body's immune (defense) system. As a result, the person becomes susceptible to "opportunistic" infections and diseases that would not ordinarily get through the body's defenses.

Symptoms of these infections and diseases include a persistent cough, fever, shortness of breath, and difficulty breathing—which may be the initial symptoms of pneumocystis pneumonia. In addition, multiple purplish blotches and bumps on the skin may indicate Kaposi's sarcoma—a particularly malignant form of cancer. The AIDS virus may also attack the nervous system and damage the brain. The resulting symptoms may include memory loss; severe depression; and dementia, a severe form of mental disorder involving impairment of mental ability.

While these opportunistic diseases may differ somewhat from one patient to another, they are lethal. Within 2 years after the AIDS syndrome makes its appearance, the majority of patients die. Death is imminent for the remainder.

New drugs may prolong a patient's life by a matter of weeks, months, or even a year or longer. As yet, however, there is no preventive vaccine or cure for AIDS.

Testing. After a person has been infected with the AIDS virus, it takes about 6 weeks for the body to produce antibodies against the virus. Because the AIDS test is for antibodies, this means that someone could be tested shortly after infection with the virus and still come up negative. After a period of 12 weeks, however, a negative result virtually guarantees that the person is not infected with the AIDS virus. It is important to note, though, that during the initial 6-week period, an infected person can still transmit the virus to others. This problem can be minimized when a method is developed that tests directly for the AIDS virus.

Currently, it is impossible to test everyone. Thus, the question "Who should be tested?"

(continued)

BOX 4-4 (continued)

has arisen. There seems to be general agreement that persons planning to get married, women planning to get pregnant, and persons starting a new sexual relationship should be tested. In fact, Utah passed a law in 1987 prohibiting anyone diagnosed as having the AIDS virus from getting married. In addition, a number of states were considering laws requiring the testing of persons in high-risk groups—gay males, intravenous drug abusers, prostitutes, and bisexuals. The issue of required testing is a highly controversial one.

Another major issue in testing is confidentiality. In most states, a physician or testing center will release information only to the person tested. But many people feel that if a person tests positive, others have a right to know —particularly their spouses or recent sexual partners. In 1987, an increasing number of lawsuits were being brought against sexual partners who had AIDS and knowingly or unknowingly exposed the person to the AIDS virus.

Closely related to the issue of confidentiality is that of "contact tracing." This involves the time-consuming detective work of finding and informing people who have had sex with the infected person. Although contact tracing is common for persons with syphilis and several other STDs, only a few states have made much of an effort in this direction with respect to AIDS.

Treatment and Prevention.   In late 1987, there was as yet no cure for AIDS. Preliminary efforts to develop an AIDS vaccine appeared promising, and it was hoped that such a vaccine would be developed by the early 1990s or before—but there was no guarantee. Nevertheless, AIDS patients require medical treatment and usually hospitalization if their lives are to be prolonged and the terminal phase of the disease made as tolerable as possible.

The cost of such treatment can only be described as staggering—$50,000 to $150,000 per patient. Thus, if the estimated increase in AIDS patients does occur, our health-care system will face a burden of unprecedented proportions. As the Surgeon General has pointed out, "Although AIDS may never touch you personally, the social impact will."

Preventive measures can be taken on the personal as well as the social level. The individual can avoid sexual contact with high-risk persons—including people who have had a large number of sexual contacts in the last 10 years—have a potential mate or sexual partner take tests for the AIDS virus, and maintain a monogamous relationship. Ultimately, of course, there is no substitute for knowing and trusting one's sexual partner. In case of doubt, the wisest course is either to practice safe sex or to abstain. If one does have sex under such circumstances, the use of a latex condom can greatly—but not entirely—reduce the risk.

On a social level, the importance of education and other preventive measures have been well described by the Surgeon General. It may be noted, however, that the introduction of AIDS-education programs into school systems is a matter of considerable controversy. Also controversial is the amount of money and effort that should be devoted to AIDS research. In any event, the specter of AIDS is not being taken lightly by the American people. It has already had a marked influence on our sexual attitudes and behaviors.

Finally, it may be emphasized that, by informing ourselves about AIDS and using available preventive measures, we can contain the AIDS epidemic until medical science can deal effectively with the problem. In the meantime, it is useful to remember that the AIDS virus is spread by people who appear healthy and are usually unaware that they are infected. It is also useful to remember that "When you are having sex, you are not only having sex with your partner but with everyone your partner has had sex with in the last 10 years."

(continued)

BOX 4-4 (*continued*)

Some additional information which may be useful in extending your knowledge of AIDS.

FACTUAL DATA

1. There are an estimated 30 to 50 persons infected with the AIDS virus for each person diagnosed as having AIDS.
2. The estimated mean survival time after a diagnosis of AIDS is 12 months.
3. Once the lethal AIDS syndrome makes its appearance, women die much more rapidly than men.
4. "High-risk" groups for AIDS include gay males, bisexuals, intravenous illegal drug users, prostitutes and their clients, persons who have had a large number of sexual partners during the last 10 years, and male inmates of state and Federal prisons. In New York area prisons, the death rate for male inmates is 100 times that in the general population.
5. An estimated 20 percent or more of the residents in cities and along truck routes in Equatorial Africa are infected with the AIDS virus.
6. If the AIDS epidemic continues, it will have a major impact on life styles in the United States as well as in the global community.
7. Unless the AIDS epidemic is checked, it could result in the death of one-fourth or more of the world's population—more than 1 billion people; or AIDS could run its course after killing tens of millions of people.

AIDS AND THE "BLACK DEATH"

AIDS has been compared to the Black Death which swept through Europe during the period from 1347 to 1350 killing some 30 million people out of a total population of about 70 million. The potential death rate for AIDS may be about the same, but it spreads more slowly than the Black Death did.

ARE VICTIMS OF AIDS THE "NEW LEPERS"?

In the Middle Ages, people who showed the telltale symptoms of leprosy—e.g., white scaly scabs—were shunned and isolated into leper colonies. Could this happen to the victims of AIDS today?

The following incident is based on a report in the October 12th, 1987 issue of *U.S. News & World Report*.

Steve, an American youth, received a diagnosis of AIDS in a large city clinic. He decided to return to his small home town in another state for refuge.

However, family and friends shunned him, vandals shot out the windows of his car, and the public swimming pool was drained and scrubbed after he used it. In short, it was made clear that he was not wanted.

On the day Steve left town, he stopped to get gas. As he was about to leave, his aunt Phyllis pulled in behind his car and approached him. Through the shattered window of his car, she told him that she loved him and was sorry for her behavior.

"I guess I am afraid" she finished with tears in her eyes. Steve turned the key in the ignition, trying to hold back his own tears.

"I understand," he replied softly. "Because I am too."

Based in part on Koop, 1986; Cornish, 1987; Bezold, Peck, and Olson, 1987; Platt, 1987; Rosellini and Goode, 1987.

SEXUAL-BEHAVIOR PATTERNS

As with sexual values, sexual behaviors differ enormously across cultures. The classic example is the missionary position for sexual intercourse, in which the woman lies on her back and the man lies on top of her. This common Western position got its name from the Trobriand Islanders, whose habits and behaviors were being studied by British and American anthropologists. These Westerners did something the Islanders found hilarious: having sex with the man on top. Because they had no name for such an activity in their own language, they picked a word from the language their visitors spoke, and it stuck. Although the ancient Egyptians, the Chinese, and the Hindus were among those cultures who had never used this position, it was the Christian church that banned use of any other position and encouraged its use in the modern Western world. We do not know why the church banned the other positions, unless the reason had something to do with believing pregnancy to be more likely with the man on top (Wolfe, 1981).

Wolfe found that the missionary position has received bad press in recent years, as feminists have attacked it as a symbol of men's power over women. Besides, sex researchers have found that many women are unable to reach orgasm in this position. In fact, women are more likely to reach orgasm when *they* are on top, because they are able to move freely in ways most likely to stimulate the clitoris. But Wolfe also found that most women in the survey preferred to have the man on top, even when it meant they would not reach orgasm themselves. They said they enjoyed the "feeling of protection" from being enveloped by a man in this way and liked the "pressure of his body on top of me." These findings must be evaluated in light of the possibility, however, that the "Cosmo girl" may be more interested in pleasing men than some other women might be.

In this section, we shall look at the most common sexual behaviors—what they are, who engages in them, and how people feel about them.

Abstinence and Masturbation

In the present context, **abstinence** refers to the act of voluntarily doing without sex. Of course, abstinence has long been practiced by certain religious orders as well as by young women (virgins) who refrain from sex prior to marriage. As part of a mandatory education program for grades 7–12, the California State Legislature voted in early 1987 to recommend abstinence as the primary method of preventing the spread of AIDS by unmarried teenagers. Condoms were not considered 100 percent effective. Unless religious convictions dictate otherwise, abstinence would not necessarily preclude masturbation.

Masturbation—self-stimulation for sexual gratification—is now considered a normal, healthy primary or secondary source of sexual expression. Nevertheless, this behavior has traditionally been condemned on religious and moral grounds. Because the Judeo–Christian tradition considers any sexual behavior that is not procreative to be sinful, masturbation has for centuries been treated as an immoral behavior. Furthermore, self-stimulation has been condemned for its alleged harmful physical effects; everything from physical weakness to impotence, mental deterioration, and insanity has been attributed to it. At one time, mental-hospital administrators maintained separate wards for patients whose insanity was presumably due to this practice.

The idea of "self-abuse" being physically harmful apparently arose among physicians in the 18th century. Their views influenced medical and scientific thought in the 19th century as well as the early part of this century. In 1879, a distinguished American physician, J. H. Kellog, wrote in his book *Plain Facts for Young and Old* that masturbation "uses up the vital forces, and finally leaves the poor victim a most utterly ruined and loathsome object." Some of the more "enlightened" medical authorities of the period even recommended surgical removal of the testicles (or clitoris in women) in addition to a range of other measures, including punishment and handcuffing.

Even today, many young people are taught that masturbation is a vile habit that can be prevented with a little self-control. As a result, many individuals fight against masturbating, promising themselves never to do it again. When they do give in, they subject themselves to feelings of guilt and self-devaluation. Although we now know that no evil per se comes of masturbating and that hands that masturbate do not turn hairy or fall off, phrases such as "jerking off" to describe wasting time persist in devaluing what is a useful and pleasurable sexual outlet for many.

Masturbation is a continuing part of sexual expression throughout the life cycle for married and unmarried individuals. It may be used, for example, as a primary outlet during periods of separation from a mate or following the end of a marriage or relationship. It may also be used as a secondary outlet to help partners equalize their sexual drives. Sex therapists often advocate masturbation for women who have never had an orgasm, in order to help them learn their own sexual capabilities. Masturbation can also be enjoyed with a partner as an adjunct to intercourse or as an act in itself.

Petting

Although young people may no longer call it "petting," "necking," or "making out," the activities associated with these terms remain an important form of sexual behavior. Essentially, **petting** refers to the erotic caressing of another person, sometimes to the point of orgasm. It is distinguished from **foreplay,** which is a similar activity that serves as a prelude to intercourse rather than being an end in itself.

Before the development of effective contraceptives, petting was a practical means of sexual expression prior to marriage. It greatly reduced the probability of unwanted pregnancy while permitting a relatively high degree of pleasure and tension reduction. Although it was sometimes rushed and furtive, it had the potential to serve as a means of expressing mutual affection and of teaching young people about their own bodily and emotional reactions to sexual stimulation.

Today, many young people—and not-so-young people—rush through or even skip the "petting stage" in relationships and go directly to sexual intercourse. Our more-permissive sexual attitudes, combined with the development of contraceptives that are more accessible and easier to use, have made petting seem passé. Yet many sex researchers and therapists feel that this stage is important in people's sex education, helping them acquire and appreciate pleasure-giving skills. As if in recognition of this vanishing part of sexual education, Masters and Johnson (1985) have devised a series of exercises, called **sensate focusing,** designed to provide partners with the opportunity to concentrate on tender and pleasurable touching and caressing as a means of developing needed skills and more-intimate

Touch is an end in itself. It is a primary form of communication, a silent voice that avoids the pitfalls of words while expressing the feelings of the moment.

Masters and Johnson

feelings. In sensate focusing, couples are encouraged to use petting as an end in itself rather than as an avenue to intercourse.

Intercourse

Here we shall restrict the term **sexual intercourse** to refer to vaginal intercourse between heterosexuals. It is the means by which we perpetuate our species. But with the separation of sex from procreation through use of contraceptive methods, intercourse has also come to play other roles in our lives. For most, it is a source of pleasure and of sharing intimacy with a loved one. But intercourse can also be used to demonstrate one's masculinity or femininity, express anger or hostility, escape from boredom or loneliness, flaunt parental authority and values, or serve other purposes. Of course, the reasons for engaging in intercourse vary not only from person to person but also within the same person from occasion to occasion. In this section, we shall look at what is known about first-time intercourse and at the most common sexual positions. In Chapter 8, we shall explore the role of sexual intercourse in marriage.

First-Time Intercourse.   Women today are losing their virginity earlier than men, according to the Playboy Survey reported in 1982. Although *Playboy* readers are not a random sample of the population, this statistic is based on the responses of both male and female readers and thus provides a fair basis for comparison within the population. Of the women under age 21 answering the survey, 58 percent said they had had their first sexual experience before age 16, as compared to only 38 percent of the men in the same age group. Among the "Playboy generation," the average age for sexual initiation was 17.5 for women and 17.8 for men. This is in contrast to earlier studies, which consistently found the situation reversed, with men losing their virginity at around age 16 and women at age 17 (Zelnick & Kanter, 1980; DeLamater & MacCorquodale, 1979; Guttmacher Institute, 1981).

Back in 1953, Kinsey found that about half of the women had waited until marriage to have their first intercourse. But even though more women are now having their first intercourse before marriage, most do so in the context of a close relationship. Wolfe (1981) has reported that 64 percent of the women in *The Cosmo Report* had their first sexual experience with a steady boyfriend. Another 11 percent lost their virginity to a fiancé or husband, and only 16 percent lost it to a casual acquaintance. Comparable data are not available for men, although the work of Peplau, Rubin, and Hill (1977) suggests that men were more likely than women to have first sexual intercourse with a casual acquaintance. Of course, AIDS is likely to make casual acquaintances as sexual partners now "out of bounds" for both men and women.

This rite of passage, which appears to occur for most people in high school or in the early years of college, is often less than satisfying. Robert Sorenson (1973) has reported that reactions vary from excited, afraid, and happy at one extreme to foolish, used, and disappointed at the other. In general, about 50 percent of the men reported being excited, 33 percent said they were satisfied, and 7 percent felt used. In contrast, about 25 percent of the women said they were excited, only 20 percent said they were satisfied, and 16 percent felt used. In her survey, Wolfe (1981) has found that only 18 percent of the women considered their first intercourse "thrilling," while 17 percent said it was painful or upsetting. For the rest, the experience ranged from mildly pleasant to no reaction or disagreeable. In other words, first intercourse is a variable experience for both men and women.

As Richard Jessor and his associates (1983) have pointed out, however:

> Making the transition from virginity to nonvirginity is a developmental milestone of major personal and social significance. Variation in the timing of this change in status is obviously affected by both physical maturation and the vagaries of social opportunity. However, a psychosocial act of such salience as engaging in sexual intercourse for the first time is unlikely to be completely determined by biology or completely capricious socially. Its timing ought to reflect, instead, a more general psychosocial readiness for such an experience. . . . (p. 608)

In our society, it appears that little systematic effort has been directed toward the psychological preparation of young men and women for their first sexual intercourse. In a study of sexual decision making for first intercourse, F. Scott Christopher and Rodney Cate (1985) found that three influences appeared to be of crucial importance: a physical arousal factor, a relationship factor, and a circumstance factor. In line with earlier research, they found that the relationship factor—for example, casual dating versus serious dating—was considered more important for females than for males, in decision making. However, an unexpected finding was a lack of sex differences in the influence of physical arousal. The latter played a significant and equally important role for men and for women. These researchers suggested that this finding may have reflected "the growing trend of equality in sexual fulfillment for both men and women in our society" (p. 269).

But in the Christopher and Cate study, neither sex had received systematic instruction pertaining to first intercourse. The personal and social ramifications of this lack of preparation remain to be explored.

Positions During Intercourse.   People can have sex in many ways, but Hunt (1974) found that the most commonly used position for all age groups is the missionary position, followed by the lateral position (side-by-side), rear-entry position, and sitting position. The women in the *The Cosmo Report* cited the woman on top, lateral, and rear-entry positions as highly satisfying, and some mentioned enjoying sitting and even standing positions (Wolfe, 1981).

Of course, sexual partners are not limited to just one position. Over time, however, a couple usually settles down to one or two favorite positions. The desirability of a particular position depends on the age, health, weight, physique, and other factors of the partners. Sex therapists often recommend the side-by-side/facing-each-other position for couples who have difficulty reaching orgasm during intercourse. In this position, neither partner has to bear all the weight and the genitals of both are available for extra stimulation.

Oral–Genital Sex

Oral stimulation of the genitals may be used to produce arousal and pleasure as well as orgasm. It can be done individually by male to female and vice versa, or it can be done simultaneously, in the so-called "69" position. Oral stimulation of the female is called **cunnilingus;** oral stimulation of the male is called **fellatio.** In some instances, one partner may enjoy receiving cunnilingus or fellatio but may be unwilling to reciprocate.

The incidence of **oral–genital sex** appears to be quite high. Even in the late 1940s and early 1950s, Kinsey and his associates found that 60 percent of college-educated, 20 percent of high-school–educated, and 10 percent of grade-school–educated couples had engaged in oral–genital stimulation as part of their marital sexual behavior. Kinsey also noted that women were less likely to give stimulation than to receive it. By the early 1970s, Hunt (1974) reported that 90 percent of married couples under 25 in a Playboy Foundation study had engaged in oral–genital sex. In the more recent *Redbook* magazine survey of 26,000 women, Rubenstein and Tavris (1987) reported that women were "both giving and receiving oral sex even more often than women were in 1976" (p. 149). Many women who could not achieve orgasm by means of intercourse did so with oral sex. These findings are consistent with those of The Cosmo Report (Wolfe, 1981). Similarly, in her studies of male and female sexuality, Shere Hite (1976, 1981) reported that women frequently and men almost always considered oral sex highly enjoyable.

Despite the reported prevalence of oral–genital sex, many people still have reservations about it. One common reservation is based on the idea that oral sex is unsanitary, although the facts indicate that it is no more unsanitary than intercourse. Apparently, this reservation is related to the older view of the sex organs as being "dirty." For example, Hite (1976) noted that many women are concerned about "smelling bad down there" and are fearful of alienating their partners. A second reservation stems from the traditional moralistic view that any sexual behavior other than intercourse for procreation is evil. A final reservation is that many people consider oral–genital sex to be a homosexual act. But, as Masters and Johnson (1985) have pointed out:

> While many homosexuals engage in oral-genital sex, so do a majority of heterosexual couples. The activity itself is neither homosexual nor heterosexual. (p. 314)

Homosexuality and Bisexuality

In his classic research, Alfred Kinsey found that about one-third of all men and one-fifth of all women subjects had had at least one homosexual experience involving orgasm. As a result of his studies, Kinsey designed a continuum with exclusively heterosexual persons at one extreme and exclusively homosexual persons at the other. On this continuum, only a small minority—about 4 percent of men and 2–3 percent of women—considered themselves to be exclusively **homosexual;** that is, they preferred to have sexual relations only with members of the same sex. By way of contrast, about 80 percent considered themselves to be exclusively heterosexual. The remaining 16–17 percent fell along the continuum, having various gradations of involvement with members of the same sex. Kinsey considered those people who fell halfway on the continuum, who were equally attracted to males and females, as **bisexuals.** Currently, an estimated 15 percent of males and 10 percent of females are bisexual.

People who are exclusively heterosexual are often curious about gay sexual behavior. But homosexuals do about the same things that heterosexuals do, with the exception of vaginal intercourse. In terms of petting and foreplay, about the only difference is that homosexuals tend to proceed at a more leisurely pace than heterosexuals. In the past, homosexual males have been much more likely than

Joel Gordon

heterosexual males to engage in anal intercourse. It would appear, however, that AIDS has markedly reduced the use of this sexual pattern. Female homosexuals, or **lesbians,** also commonly engage in tribalism, in which one lies on top of the other and they move in such a way as to stimulate each other's genitals. In terms of oral–genital sex, there are no reliable figures contrasting its use among homosexuals and heterosexuals. However, one curious difference is that lesbians are more likely than heterosexual females to be multiorgasmic (Masters & Johnson, 1985). Letitia Anne Peplau (1981) also found that gay males were considered more promiscuous than heterosexual males. It would appear that AIDS has also resulted in a marked decrease in promiscuous sexual behavior among gay males, as well as most other people.

Homosexuality has existed throughout recorded history; it was condemned in some societies and accepted, and even expected, in others. In our own society, there are many people who strongly disapprove of homosexual behavior, often considering it a form of moral degeneracy or mental disorder. However, most mental health personnel—as well as homosexuals—prefer to think of it as an alternative life style. Ironically, the trustees of the American Psychiatric Association, which had formerly classified homosexuality as a form of mental disorder, voted on December 14, 1973, to drop homosexuality from its official list of psychiatric disorders. In effect, millions of gay men and women in our society underwent an "instant cure."

Despite a great deal of research, we still do not understand the causes of homosexuality (Masters & Johnson, 1985). But it does not appear, whatever our personal views, that our society is in any danger of being "done in" by rampant homosexuality.

There are, of course, a number of other sexual practices that are considered deviant and socially unacceptable. One of these practices—anal sex—is described briefly in Box 4–5.

BOX 4–5 / ANAL SEX

The anus is well supplied with nerve endings, and anal stimulation—by manually inserting a finger or by anal intercourse—can be highly sexually arousing and lead to orgasm in males or females (Masters & Johnson, 1970, 1979; Masters, Johnson, & Kolodny, 1985). It may be noted that anal intercourse is also called sodomy. Although anal stimulation can be the primary form of sexual activity, it is usually an accompaniment of other types of sexual behavior.

Anal sex is considered to be much higher in incidence among homosexuals, but a sizable number of heterosexual couples—some 10–20 percent—may use anal stimulation occasionally for additional arousal and variation (Rubenstein & Tavris,

1987; Masters, Johnson, & Kolodny, 1985). However, many people find this form of sexual behavior distasteful. And, like vaginal sex, it does increase the chance of spreading disease—including AIDS—unless proper hygiene is observed.

In 1986, a divided U.S. Supreme Court ruled 5–4 that individual states may make oral and anal sex between consenting homosexual adults a criminal offense. At the time, over 20 states had laws, usually of long standing, making sodomy a criminal offense. But these laws were rarely enforced against homosexuals and almost never against heterosexuals. However, the specter of AIDS now complicates the overall picture.

THE SEXUAL-RESPONSE SEQUENCE

Human sexual response is a complex physiological and psychological process that may involve a variety of motives, feelings, verbal and nonverbal communications, fantasies, and physiological changes. Our knowledge of the physical aspects of the sexual response was greatly advanced by the work of Masters and Johnson (1966), who studied more than 10,000 sexual-response cycles under controlled conditions. As a result of their research, they determined that men and women proceed through four phases of physiological response, whether the stimulation is masturbation, fantasy, oral sex, intercourse, or another source. They also found that orgasm is the same physiologically in men and women, with the exceptions that men ejaculate and that orgasm may last longer in women.

Masters and Johnson have labeled the four stages of human sexual response as (1) excitement, (2) plateau, (3) orgasm, and (4) resolution. We shall describe the main physiological events at each stage and attempt to describe the subjective experiencing of these events.

Excitement Stage

The first phase of the sexual-response cycle is arousal in response to physical contact or exposure to erotic sights, sounds, or other stimuli. Excitement is accompanied by a number of common physiological changes, including an increase in muscle tension, heart rate, and blood pressure. Perhaps the most significant changes are penile erection in the male and clitoris enlargement and vaginal lubrication in the female. Other changes include nipple erection in both sexes, dilation of the vagina in the female, and enlargement of the testes in the male.

Most young men have erections quickly and easily, and many continue to have

UPI/Bettmann Newsphotos

erections well into old age. Most women also become sexually aroused quite easily under favorable circumstances.

The excitement phase may vary greatly in duration, from less than a minute to several hours. This depends on the length of **foreplay.** For many people, the kissing, touching, hugging, and caressing prior to intercourse are an essential part of its enjoyment, and many women find it impossible to reach orgasm unless they have received such stimulation. Most women indicate that they prefer from 15–30 minutes of foreplay, and many say that they prefer even more (Kando, 1978; Wolfe, 1981). In her study of male sexuality, Hite (1981) found that men also tended to place a high value on foreplay.

Plateau Stage

Foreplay continues and sexual arousal increases in intensity during the plateau phase, until it reaches the extreme level that precipitates orgasm. Unlike the excitement phase, the **plateau** does not have a clear sign to indicate onset. Rather, a number of physiological changes continue to increase. Breathing grows faster, heart rate and blood pressure continue to rise, the breasts swell, and a **sex flush** (red rash over the abdomen, chest, and neck) and genital coloration become more pronounced. Among women, the plateau phase is also characterized by what Masters and Johnson term the **orgasmic platform,** the marked thickening and swelling of the outer third of the vagina.

The plateau stage is typically brief, lasting from a few seconds to a few minutes. However, many people find that maintaining a high plateau level for a sustained period before having orgasm is highly pleasurable and increases the pleasure of the orgasm. As one woman reported:

> When I get up there, almost on the verge of coming, I try to hang in as long as possible. If my partner cooperates, stopping or slowing when necessary, I can stay right on the edge for several minutes, sometimes even longer. I know that all it would take is one more stroke and I'm over the top. Sometimes my whole body gets to shaking and quivering and I can feel incredible sensations shooting through me

like electric charges. The longer I can make this supercharged period last, the better the orgasm. (Crooks & Baur, 1980, p. 120)

Men who wish to delay orgasm have to fine-tune their performances, often by withdrawal or by interruption of stimulation. In some instances, when a man uses this procedure several times during the same plateau period, he seems to gain more control and staying power. That is, he can maintain a high plateau level of arousal without proceeding to orgasm:

When I first approach orgasm, it is essential to slow down or stop if I don't want to finish quickly. This is relatively easy during masturbation, but somewhat harder during intercourse. I may have to use this slow-down tactic several times in a short period. However, something then happens to me which is difficult to explain. It's almost like I pass a crisis point where, if I don't come, my staying power gets better. (Crooks & Baur, 1980, p. 121)

Whether the procedure of consciously entering and leaving the intense plateau level of stimulation results in a more-pleasurable orgasm is difficult to say, although many persons report this to be the case. In any event, it does prolong the period of intense pleasure prior to orgasm.

Orgasmic Stage

With continued stimulation, the plateau stage gives way to a sudden intense sensation known as **orgasm**, climax, or "coming." In the male, involuntary rhythmic contractions of the urethra and muscles at the base of the penis cause the expulsion of semen in two or three intense spurts at about .8 second intervals. These are followed by several weaker and slower contractions. In the female, there are three to fifteen rhythmic contractions of the vagina, uterus, abdomen, and rectum; other body musculature may be involved to a lesser extent. The first three to six contractions are intense, occurring, as in the male, at .8 second intervals. The contractions that follow are slower and weaker.

Orgasm is usually the most intensely pleasurable phase of the sexual cycle, yet it is relatively brief, lasting only a few seconds (although it may last considerably longer in women than in men). One common misconception that has stemmed from traditional sex-roles is that orgasms are not important for women and are usually less pleasurable for them. However, Shere Hite (1976) quotes one woman who disagrees: "Whoever said orgasm wasn't important for women was undoubtedly a man. Good sex expresses love, relaxation, and letting go, plus pure bodily pleasure" (p. 58). Supporting Shere Hite's conclusion is the finding of Waterman and Chiauzzi (1982) that consistency of orgasm is significantly related to sexual satisfaction in females but not in males. In short, women appear to be more frustrated than men when they don't have orgasms. This appears to be particularly true when the man has an orgasm and rolls over and goes to sleep, leaving the woman frustrated and unsatisfied.

In any event, available evidence indicates that, for both men and women, the subjective experience of orgasm is very similar (Vance & Wagner, 1981; Wiest, 1977; Masters, Johnson, & Kolodny, 1985).

Aside from the similarities in orgasmic experiences, there can be marked variations in how individuals describe their orgasms. Of course, the experience can be less positive—and even negative—under certain conditions, depending on the

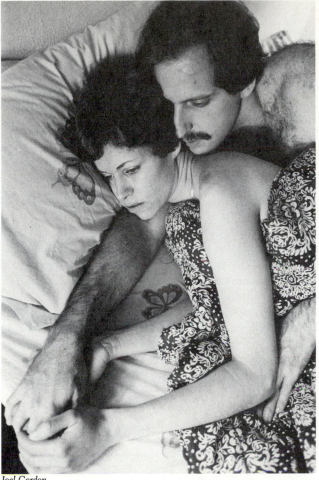

Joel Gordon

person's background, motives, and feelings toward the partner. In some cases, orgasm can even be physically painful. But, normally, it is a unique and highly pleasurable experience for men and women alike. As one person described it:

> An orgasm to me is like heaven. All my tensions and anxieties are released. You get to the point of no return, and it's like an uncontrollable desire that makes things start happening. I think that sex and orgasm are one of the great phenomenons that we have today. It's a great sharing experience for me. (Crooks & Baur, 1980, p. 123)

Is the speaker a male or a female? It could be either, but these are the remarks of a woman.

A complicating factor at this stage of sexual cycle is faking orgasm—pretending to experience it. This seems to occur relatively frequently in women. In fact, Hite (1976) reported that more than half of the women in her study had faked orgasms at one time or another and many still did. Helping one's partner to feel he is performing adequately seems to be a common motive. As one woman expressed it, "Yes, I always fake orgasms. It just seems polite. Why be rude?" (p. 156). While men may fake orgasms, it is relatively rare. Faking orgasm tends to create a vicious circle. Because the partners are not communicating honestly with each other, they are not likely to make needed corrections for achieving a more-satisfying sex life.

Resolution Stage

During the final phase of the sexual-response cycle, the person returns to normal levels of physiological functioning. Heart rate, blood pressure, breathing, and muscle tension revert to their pre-excitement states, the penis returns to its normally flaccid condition, and the clitoris and vagina resume their unstimulated size. Often the duration of the resolution stage is influenced by the length of the arousal period prior to orgasm—the longer the period of arousal, the longer it takes to return to normal physiological functioning.

There is one major difference in the resolution stage between men and women: receptivity to further stimulation. Men may require a considerable time after an orgasm before they can have another climax. This time period increases with age. Some women, on the other hand, are able to have multiple orgasms—several orgasms within a short period of time.

How do the partners feel after orgasm? Do they feel satisfied and fulfilled? Do they feel relaxed and ready for sleep? Do they experience an afterglow in which they find peace and joy lying together in a state of mutual appreciation and intimacy? The answers depend greatly on the persons involved and on the quality of the relationship. Of course, if one partner immediately rolls over and goes to sleep, signaling the end of the sexual encounter, the other partner is not likely to be pleased. Many couples do, however, experience warm feelings of tenderness, love, and wanting to be close. In caring relationships, the few minutes after sex are often enriched by caressing, cuddling, and "pillow talk," which give meaning to the passion just experienced and reaffirm affection, friendship, and love.

SEXUAL DYSFUNCTIONS

Sometimes the journey through the stages of the sexual-response cycle is bumpy or incomplete. Such interference with the sexual cycle is referred to as **sexual dysfunction** (American Psychiatric Association, 1980). According to available research studies, about half of all married couples experience sexual problems severe enough to impair the marriage. In this section, we shall summarize some common sexual dysfunctions, the causes of such disorders, and the methods used to treat them.

Male Sexual Dysfunctions

The main types of sexual dysfunctions that commonly affect men are inhibited sexual excitement, premature ejaculation, and inhibited male orgasm.

Formerly referred to as "**impotence**" or erectile insufficiency, male **inhibited sexual excitement** (ISE) involves the inability to achieve or maintain an erection sufficient to accomplish intercourse. Some men are never able to achieve sufficient erection, but this condition is relatively rare. More commonly, the man has succeeded at intercourse at least once and usually on a number of occasions prior to the first experience of erectile failure. In some instances, this problem occurs only with a specific partner. Such situational dysfunction is relatively common and has been experienced—at least on a short-term basis—by half or more of the male population. In both types of male inhibited sexual excitement, the disorder is usually psychological in origin, although factors such as illness, extreme fatigue, and drug use may be involved. It has been estimated that more than 10 million men in our society experience ISE (Impotence Information Center, 1986).

In **premature ejaculation,** the male is unable to control ejaculation long enough for his partner to achieve sexual satisfaction. A more-precise definition is difficult because some women require longer periods of intercourse and greater clitoral stimulation than others in order to achieve orgasm. Premature ejaculation is probably the most common form of male sexual dysfunction, especially among young males.

In **inhibited male orgasm,** the male is either unable to trigger an ejaculation or has extreme difficulty doing so. Also referred to as ejaculatory incompetence or retarded ejaculation, this disorder may be accompanied by inhibited sexual excitement. Sometimes this problem can be helped by using fantasy or manual or oral stimulation to bring the man to orgasm.

Female Sexual Dysfunctions

The most common sexual dysfunctions among women are inhibited sexual excitement, inhibited female orgasm, and vaginismus.

Female **inhibited sexual excitement** (formerly called "**frigidity**") is in many ways the female counterpart to male ISE. The woman reports little or no responsiveness to sexual stimulation and often fails to achieve and maintain lubrication and swelling of the vaginal cavity during intercourse. As with men, some women may have never experienced sexual responsiveness, but more commonly it is an occasional or situational problem.

Inhibited female orgasm following a normal excitement phase during sexual activity is the most common female dysfunction. Some women have never had an orgasm and are unable to achieve orgasm by any method. This condition is called primary orgasmic dysfunction. Many such women have sexual desire, feel sexual arousal, and enjoy sex, but others find sex disappointing and upsetting. Women with secondary or situational orgasmic dysfunction can have orgasms, but not during intercourse or without manual stimulation. This pattern is so common, however, that the label of sexual dysfunction hardly seems appropriate. As Helen Singer Kaplan (1974) has pointed out, "There are millions of women who are sexually responsive, and often multiply orgasmic, but who cannot have an orgasm during intercourse unless they receive simultaneous clitoral stimulation" (p. 397). Situational orgasmic dysfunction may also involve special conditions other than low clitoral stimulation. For example, a woman may have no difficulty reaching orgasm with her lover but may be unable to do so with her husband, or she may reach orgasm only in the back seat of a car or while on vacation.

A much less-common female dysfunction is **vaginismus,** in which involuntary spasms of the musculature of the outer third of the vagina prevent coitus. In some instances, women who suffer from vaginismus also have arousal difficulties—possibly as a result of conditioned fears associated with rape or some other traumatic experience. In other cases, however, women afflicted with the disorder are otherwise sexually responsive. Another rare form of sexual dysfunction is **dyspareunia,** or painful intercourse. Dyspareunia is often physical in origin and can also occur in males.

Lack of Sexual Desire

Recently, lack of sexual desire has become a major concern in our society. In fact, "I'm just too tired to have sex" has a familiar ring to it for many people. In a recent survey, 38 percent of the men and 40 percent of the women reported that lack of sexual desire impaired their sexuality (Rubenstein and Tavris, 1987). Adams (1980) found that as many as 50 percent of all couples seeking sex therapy complain of this problem.

Lack of sexual desire may have many causes, ranging from fatigue and worry to lack of emotional closeness to the sexual partner. Rubenstein (1983) has found lack of love or romantic feelings toward the sexual partner to be the primary cause. Florence Schumer (1983) does not consider infrequent sexual interest to be a disorder unless the person is distressed by the lack of desire. She notes that many married couples seem to settle into a routine in which one partner is not turned on by the other but may still be responsive to someone else. In a minority of cases, men and women who have had aversive experiences with sex may simply focus their energies on their work or other life activities and keep their sex lives to a minimum. However, when insufficient sexual desire is distressing and persistent, it may represent underlying depression or other conditions that do merit therapy.

In some instances, too much rather than too little sexual desire may be a problem. For example, Maggie Scarf (1980) has pointed out that the promiscuous female and the "Don Juan" male are engaged in a similar desperate search for a person who will cherish, nourish, and care for them. These promiscuous individuals often feel an abiding rage at having lost or never having had such a caring person in their lives, so they go through endless partners, treating them as objects and often harboring feelings of contempt for them. These persons give their bodies but withhold themselves, possibly as a defense against being hurt. Promiscuity may also be a means of defending against strong underlying feelings of depression or loneliness. Thus, rather than being driven by an insatiable desire for sexual satisfaction, this type of promiscuous behavior is governed by a variety of nonsexual motives.

Causes and Consequences of Sexual Dysfunctions

Both sexual desire and sexual functioning are affected by a wide variety of organic conditions, including genital injury, disease, fatigue, and drugs. In general, however, the following psychosocial factors are among those most commonly found with sexual dysfunctions:

1. *Faulty information.* Although we emphasize the importance of sex in our society, the learning of sexual values and behaviors is left largely to chance. The resulting faulty knowledge combined with highly emotional attitudes about sexual matters leads to misconceptions, unrealistic expectations, and lack of performance skills. Box 4–6 lists a number of common myths concerning sexual behavior.

2. *Aversive conditioning.* Many women, and a lesser number of men, have been subjected to early training in which they are indoctrinated with the idea that sex is dirty and evil—something that they have to put up with or get through quickly. The attitudes and inhibitions established by such early training can lead to a great deal of later conflict and guilt in sexual behavior, both in and out of marriage. And people who have been

BOX 4–6 / COMMON MYTHS ABOUT SEXUAL BEHAVIOR

1. Women want a man with a large penis.
2. If a woman doesn't have an orgasm during intercourse, she should fake one.
3. Sexual intercourse tends to overstimulate a woman's clitoris.
4. Most men are turned off by women who take the initiative in sex.
5. Most sexual fantasies of men and women involve sadistic practices.
6. Women rarely masturbate.
7. During sex, women rarely fantasize, whereas men often do so.
8. Women are less easily aroused and less erotic than men.
9. Sexual practices that depart from usual male–female sexual intercourse are abnormal.
10. Simultaneous orgasm is indicative of a truly fulfilling sex life.
11. If a woman needs stimulation before intercourse, she lacks sexual desire.
12. Normal women almost always have orgasms during intercourse.
13. Women cannot enjoy intercourse during menstruation.
14. Most people over 60 are incapable of enjoying sex.
15. Variety is the best way to keep sexual desire and pleasure alive.
16. If a man doesn't take the sexual initiative, he is not masculine.
17. Men enjoy adultery much more than women do.
18. Oral sex is a perversion.
19. Men are ready for sex any time.
20. Homosexuals are sick and should be hospitalized for treatment.

subjected to rape, incest, or other traumatic experiences are likely to be impaired in their later sexual functioning and satisfaction.

3. *Performance anxiety.*   David Barlow (1986) has studied individual differences in the ability to respond to sexual situations when the person is anxious. While some perform well, others do not. Similarly, Masters and Johnson (1985) have concluded that most sexual dysfunctions are based on inhibitions, fears, and unhealthy attitudes toward sex. Some of these emotions and attitudes come from the person's cultural or religious background and some come from experience. For example, a woman who is unable to get aroused in one love-making situation may be unable to become aroused on the next occasion because of thoughts about her previous difficulty. Similarly, a man who has had difficulty getting an erection in the past may continue to have problems simply because he expects to. Thus, once a person experiences a situational sexual problem, anxieties can lead to its recurrence. Such worry over how (or whether) we will perform in a sexual situation is often referred to as "**performance anxiety.**"

4. *Relationship problems.*   Lack of emotional closeness to our sexual partner can also lead to sexual dysfunction. The individual may be in love with someone else, may find his or her partner unattractive, or may have hostile feelings toward the partner. Inability to communicate about sex can exacerbate the situation. The result may be sexual dysfunctions

The sexual realm remains for most men and women . . . a world through which they move warily, cautiously, and self-protectively, not a home but an alien land.

Peter Marin

as well as apathy and loss of desire. In short, a close relationship is often essential for satisfactory sex.

5. *Changing sex-roles.*   Although the "liberated woman" seems to turn some men on, she seems to threaten others who have an image of themselves as the "dominant" partner who takes control of sex. On the other hand, times are changing. Shere Hite (1981) has found that many men wish women would be *more* assertive and resent being cast in the role of having to initiate and orchestrate sexual behavior.

Finally, a person may experience difficulties in a sexual relationship because he or she is more attracted to members of their own sex. Although many persons who are homosexual in their sexual preference are able to function bisexually, others are not.

In general, sexual dysfunction is a highly traumatic experience for men. As Masters, Johnson, and Kolodny (1985) have pointed out "For most men in most societies, sexual adequacy is considered a yardstick for measuring personal adequacy" (p. 462). The man who fails to "measure up" sexually is likely to feel humiliated, confused, and devalued as a person. These feelings create anxiety on his next sexual encounter which tends to perpetuate the dysfunction. Thus a "vicious circle" is set up.

Until recent times, sexual dysfunction was not considered a problem for women, since they were not supposed to experience sexual desire or pleasure anyway. With more egalitarian sex roles, however, women too are faced with performance pressure. And they are likely to feel frustrated and devalued by a failure to experience pleasure and orgasm in sexual relations. In essence, sexual dysfunction is traumatic for both men and women.

In addition, sexual dysfunction may have negative consequences for the partner as well. The following comments are typical of those made by partners of dysfunctional husbands or wives.

American Psychological Association

Gosh, I just can't satisfy her. I guess if I could last longer, if I could make her relax, if I were a better lover, if I had a bigger penis . . . I just don't know what to do. I really care about her and I want her to like me but she never will if I can't make things happen for her. I wonder what I'm doing wrong.

I wonder if I am unattractive to him. Is there some way I could be more sexually attractive? Is there something about me that turns him off? Does he expect me to take the initiative? Would that make a difference? I have tried before, but nothing seems to work. Sometimes I feel that if I can't get sex in this relationship, I will try another one.

As a result of sexual dysfunction, the person may try to avoid sexual situations —anticipating failure—or slip into a "spectator role" which reduces spontaneity and intimacy. Unless the problem is faced and the couple seek therapy, the result is likely to be a continuing unsatisfactory sex life or a deteriorating marital relationship.

Sex Therapy

The pioneering contribution in the field of sex therapy was the publication in 1970 of Masters and Johnson's *Human Sexual Inadequacy*, which represented the culmination of an 11-year program to develop effective treatment procedures for common sexual dysfunctions. Masters and Johnson see such dysfunctions as belonging to the **relationship** rather than to the individual. Thus, they ask couples to focus on making changes in their relationship rather than on blaming or accusing each other.

The following steps are basic to Masters and Johnson's sex therapy program: (1) a thorough medical examination to rule out organic causes; (2) sensate focusing—learning to explore each other's body and experience pleasure caressing each other while temporarily abstaining from intercourse; and (3) prescribed sexual experiences and therapy sessions under the supervision of qualified sex therapists. Since Masters and Johnson developed this program, a number of new techniques have been introduced. Consequently, the specific formats employed by sex therapists may vary, but these basic principles tend to provide a central theme.

Psychiatrist Helen Kaplan (1974, 1975) has also pioneered a widely used approach to sex therapy. Her approach is based on the view that the sexual response is **triphasic,** consisting of three interlocking phases: desire, arousal, and orgasm. Each of these phases can lead to various types of sexual dysfunction. She considers desire-phase disorders most difficult to treat because they may be associated with deep-seated personality problems and relationship problems.

Masters and Johnson claim high success rates with an almost 100 percent "cure" rate for premature ejaculation and vaginismus and about 80 percent for inhibited sexual desire. Lower cure rates are reported for other dysfunctions depending on the type and severity of the problem, the quality of the relationship, and the couple's commitment to therapy. Similar success rates have been reported by Kaplan.

Various approaches used in the treatment of sexual dysfunctions and their effectiveness have been summarized by Joseph LoPiccolo and Wendy E. Stock (1986). As these authors have pointed out, many people have been helped by sex therapy even though they do not become fully adequate sexually. At least the therapy helps them to better understand their problem and to communicate more openly with their sex partners about their needs and feelings.

TOWARD INFORMED, RESPONSIBLE, AND FULFILLING SEXUALITY

When it comes to sex, many of use are not entirely certain about our feelings and values. Often we operate in terms of a confusing mixture of moralistic and naturalistic attitudes combined with a fear of sexually transmitted diseases. Indeed, it is not uncommon to discover that our real sexual desires, preferences, and values are not exactly what we thought they were. And our behavior may not always match our values. This leaves us feeling betrayed and unhappy about our sex lives.

Yet in this society we can be responsible for determining our own sexual scripts. There are opportunities to explore and learn about our sexual selves. Thus, in this final section it seems appropriate to address an important question: How does one achieve informed, responsible, and fulfilling sexuality? Obviously, there are no easy answers to this question. Here we shall attempt to clarify some of the key factors involved and to point the direction a solution is likely to take. Admittedly, however, our focus will be on questions rather than answers, for the latter are in short supply. Figure 4–1 contains a basic model for decision making.

Being Informed and Taking Responsibility

Being informed requires obtaining accurate information. This includes information about alternative sexual values, behavior patterns, and response sequences. In writing our sexual script, this information has to be sorted out, including the effects of given values and behavior on relationships, life styles, and fulfillment as a person. The need for accurate information also applies to a wide range of related topics, including the use of contraceptives (see Box 4–7), abortion (see Box 4–8), infertility, and sexually transmitted diseases.

In our present social setting, people need to familiarize themselves with the various STDs (see Boxes 4–3 and 4–4), the risks involved, and the preventive measures that may be used to reduce such risks. Confronted with the menace of AIDS, this information can literally be a matter of life and death. In the context of AIDS, Kathleen McAulifee and others (1987) have pointed out that when you have sex with a new partner, you are not only having sex with that person, "You are having sex with everybody your partner has had sex with for the past decade or more" (p. 62). Of course, this would include spouses who engage in extramarital affairs.

Informed and responsible sex also requires making decisions based on your sexual values. One problem that commonly arises is deciding when and if sex is appropriate in a developing relationship. Unfortunately, there are no conclusive answers to this question. But, in addition to your sexual values, other key considerations include the importance you attach to building an intimate relationship with this person, the affect that sex is likely to have on the relationship, a realistic evaluation of the risk of AIDS or other STDs, and your ability to communicate about sex with each other.

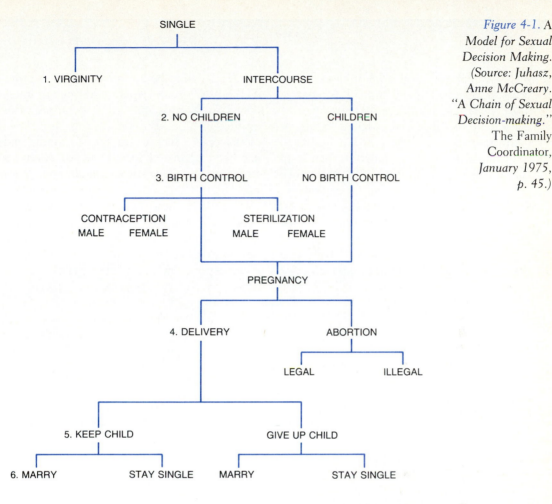

Figure 4-1. A *Model for Sexual Decision Making. (Source: Juhasz, Anne McCreary.* "A Chain of Sexual Decision-making." The Family Coordinator, January 1975, *p. 45.)*

Communicating About Sex

Even in warm, caring relationships, couples are often unwilling or unable to communicate about sex, so that neither person really understands or is sure about the other's needs, preferences, and expectations. There are many reasons why sexual communication is so difficult. One is our moralistic heritage about sexual matters—we have been taught that sex is something you do but not something you talk about. A second reason is reluctance to communicate sexual needs and preferences for fear of revealing too much and opening ourselves to criticism or rejection. Hite (1981) found, for example, that many men would welcome more caressing and foreplay from their partners but are reluctant to express such "unmanly" desires.

Noting that some of their sex therapy clients did not know how to talk to a potential sex partner, Zilbergeld and Ellison (1979) developed a social-skills training program as an adjunct to their human sexuality therapy groups. Because almost all of the clients said that fear of rejection was their biggest obstacle, the participants were encouraged to talk about their experiences with and feelings about rejection. Time was also spent discussing the making and receiving of sexual advances and the sexual pressures that many people feel. Clients eventually

BOX 4-7 / COMPARISON OF CONTRACEPTIVE METHODS

In 1985, an estimated 16.5 million Americans—42 percent male and 58 percent female—had had contraceptive surgery other than abortion. Married women who formerly used birth-control pills are turning to sterilization—especially older women—apparently due to advances in surgical procedures. About half of female operations are done on an outpatient basis, and about two-thirds of vasectomies are done in doctors' offices.

While some major forms of contraception—for example, the intrauterine device, or IUD—are being phased out, other methods of contraception are being introduced in Europe and other countries. For example, Depo-Provera is an injectable contraceptive that works for 3 months and has been approved for use in 90 countries including Sweden, Switzerland, and West Germany (Population Crisis Committee, 1986). It is anticipated that several of these new methods will become available in the United States. But, at the moment, sterilization is the number-one choice of contraceptives in the United States.

Method	How It Works	Percent Chance of Pregnancy	Cost Per Year	Disadvantages
Vasectomy	Barrier to sperm	0–1	$240 (one time)	Usually irreversible
Tubal sterilization	Barrier to sperm	0–1	$1,180	Usually irreversible
Birth-control pill	Prevents ovulation	2.4	$175	Daily use; side effects
Intrauterine device (IUD)	Prevents implantation of fertilized ovum	5	$130	Unreliable; medical problems
Condom	Barrier to sperm	10	$30	Reduced sensation
Sponge and spermicide	Destruction of sperm	9–15	$100	Unreliable
Spermicides	Destruction of sperm	18	$50	Unreliable
Diaphragm with spermicides	Destruction of sperm (barrier)	19	$210	Unreliable
Withdrawal	External ejaculation	23	$0	Reduces sexual pleasure; unreliable
Rhythm (natural family planning)	Periodic abstinence	24	$0	Requires periods of abstinence
Douching	Removal of sperm		$30	Unreliable
No method of contraception		90% (Theoretical)	$0	Ineffective

BOX 4–8 / ABORTION

Abortion is one of the oldest methods of fertility control used by human beings. The first recorded abortion was in 3000 B.C. in China, and abortion has been widely practiced throughout the world since then—and probably even before. Although abortion continues to be a volatile issue in the United States, attitudes toward this practice have varied widely over different time periods and in different cultures.

Abortion became illegal in the United States around the turn of the century, but the various state laws usually allowed for exceptions. Despite the illegality, however, the number of abortions skyrocketed, and, during the 1950s, an estimated 1 million or more abortions were performed annually—accompanied by a high rate of bleeding, infection, and death (Masters, Johnson, & Kolodny, 1985). However, in January 1973, the U.S. Supreme Court found the state laws restricting abortion to be unconstitutional, and, in effect, established the legal right of women to choose or not choose to have an abortion. By 1980, the number of abortions in the United States had increased to over 1.5 million, with few medical complications (Gest, 1983).

Again in 1986, the Supreme Court upheld abortion rights. By this time, the number of abortions approximated 2 million per year. The problem was particularly acute among teenagers, with an estimated 1 million or more pregnancies and over 400,000 abortions reported (National Research Council, 1986). However, with more-effective educational and contraceptive measures, the number of abortions is expected to decline in the late 1980s and early 1990s.

In a broader perspective, an estimated 40–60 million abortions are performed worldwide each year—of which, about 33 million are performed illegally (Henshaw et al., 1986). In Islamic countries, Latin America, and many so-called Catholic countries, abortion is only legal to save the life of the mother. However, about three-fourths of the world's people can obtain a legal abortion, at least for health reasons. But, whether legal or illegal, abortion is still a common practice throughout the world. Interestingly, the Soviet Union and Rumania report far more abortions, and Canada and West Germany far fewer abortions, than the United States.

Since the 1800s in the United States, a heated debate has raged between the pro-abortion/pro-choice groups and the anti-abortion/pro-life groups. The debate focuses around several questions, but one of the most fundamental is "When does life begin?" The pro-choice people say life does not begin until the fetus is viable or able to live outside the mother's womb; the pro-life people believe that life begins at the moment of conception. However, the question has proved impossible—at least so far—to answer to anyone's satisfaction. Thus, the debate now focuses on several other questions.

Who has the right to decide? The pro-life people believe that only God can take or give a life, whereas the pro-choice people argue that a woman has control over her own body and is the one who must decide whether or not to have an abortion. Who should pay for abortions? Many of the pro-choice lobbyists say that the government should fund abortions for poor women, while pro-life advocates maintain that their tax money should not go to an operation they feel is immoral. What will happen if abortions are outlawed? The pro-life people say we will be better for it, while the pro-choice people predict a rise in illegal, unsafe abortions.

In general, it appears that people who

(continued)

BOX 4–8 (continued)

are against abortion tend to have strong religious and moral convictions and feel that violating these convictions will lead to punishment. It would also appear that women's attitudes toward abortion are more complex than men's (Finlay, 1981; Mall, 1986). This does not mean that men lack feelings about abortion. But women, because of the responsibility for child-rearing placed on them by society, have more to think about. For example, a pregnant woman may face not only the moral issues involved in abortion but also the affect of the child on her life plans and the burden that unwanted children tend to place on society. Often fathers—particularly teenage fathers—appear unconcerned and either encourage the abortion or place the responsibility solely on the woman. But, later, they usually have to deal with feelings of anger and guilt.

Although abortion is legal in the United States, it is by no means a simple solution to the problem of unwanted pregnancies.

learned that other people would accept their feelings and respect their preferences if they just expressed them. Participants indicated that as a result of their involvement in these social-skills training groups they felt more confident and less anxious about sex.

The problem for most people is how to start talking about sex. Crooks and Baur (1980) have made a number of suggestions for ways to get started and to continue the conversation. The following are some of these suggestions:

1. *Sharing sexual histories.*   This means telling each other about parental attitudes toward sex, sexual learning in school, reactions to initial sexual experiences, and so on.

2. *Taking turns at self-disclosure.*   Direct questioning can put one's partner on the spot, but offering information about one's own sexual feelings can encourage one's partner to reciprocate with similar information. Partners can compare notes about masturbation, oral sex, and other practices by first sharing their own feelings: "I like having the lights on while making love—how about you?"

3. *Sharing fantasies.*   One way of avoiding possible negative reactions from one's partner is simply to share fantasies about desired sexual experiences.

4. *Learning to make requests.*   No matter how close a couple becomes, the partners cannot expect each other to be mindreaders. Thus, it often helps to express a desire to see how one's partner reacts: "I would like you to spend more time caressing me before we have intercourse. Would you like that, too?"

To choose to ask questions and learn the truth about sex is a personal choice. To evaluate answers is a personal necessity. To be comfortable with what one learns and to utilize what one knows in the establishment of an enduring sexual relationship is a lifelong quest.

Masters and Johnson

Along the way, partners can be supportive and sensitive to each other by making such remarks as, "I find your ears/toes/breasts exciting" and "Do you like to have me touch you here? Here?" In addition, nonverbal combined with verbal feedback is often of key importance. For example, moving our partner's hand and saying "Oh, that's wonderful" can convey a wealth of information. Or questions such as "Am I being gentle enough?" "Is this the way you like to be touched?" and "Is there something I could do to improve?" might be appropriate.

Given two unique individuals with different sexual values, different body clocks, different work schedules, different levels of desire, and different sexual preferences, it seems inevitable that difficulties in sexual adjustment will arise. Being able to communicate about such differences is the first step in building a successful sexual relationship.

Awareness in a Loving Relationship

One additional prerequisite appears to be necessary for responsible, informed, and fulfilling sexuality: awareness in a loving relationship. By "awareness" we mean sexual sensitivity—being in touch with and comfortable with our own sexuality; understanding the needs, expectations, and desires of our partner; and addressing the effects of given values and behaviors on the relationship. We dealt with the importance of awareness in Chapter 3 and need not elaborate here. Awareness is fundamental to all aspects of a relationship, including the sexual. It also means being comfortable with the awareness of one's own sexuality because if a person feels uncomfortable with his or her sexuality, that person is not likely to deal coherently with sexual values and behaviors.

Because sexual activities usually take place in the context of an ongoing relationship, the partners' attitudes and feelings toward each other are highly important. If, for example, a relationship is torn by quarrels and dominated by negative emotions, the couple's sex life is not likely to be fulfilling. On the other hand, sexual pleasure and bonding can foster intimacy in a close relationship. Awareness thus becomes an extension of our responsibility to ourselves and to loved ones. As

Joel Gordon

we will see in the next chapter, love can greatly enhance sexual relationships and vice versa.

The 1960s and 1970s were years when our sexual values underwent a sexual revolution. This revolution achieved some spectacular changes, including the decline of the double standard and far greater equality in man–woman relationships. It was also a revolution that included some highly questionable changes including the acceptance and spread of casual sex. As the revolution continued into the 1980s, our society became overtly preoccupied with sex—mass produced, slickly marketed, performance oriented, and dehumanizing. And, in the 1980s, at least in part due to the sexual revolution, we came face to face with the reality of sexually transmitted diseases, including the deadly AIDS.

The late 1980s and the 1990s will be a period when our sexual values are likely to be subjected to increasing scrutiny, when we base our value choices concerning sex on more-accurate information, and when we really learn to communicate. It is also likely to be a period when the fear of AIDS will lead to more-conservative sexual behavior, including a marked reduction in casual sex. We can hope that the 1990s will also be a decade when the menace of AIDS and other STDs will be brought under control, and when we more fully appreciate the ways in which intimate relationships and sex can interact in enhancing sexual pleasure, intimacy, and self-fulfillment.

SUMMARY—Chapter 4

1. Approved sexual behaviors vary from one society to another. In societies which take a moralistic view, sex is for procreation only; in societies which take a naturalistic view, sex is considered natural and enjoyable. All societies, however, prohibit incest and place other controls on sexual behavior.

2. Since the 1960s, our society has undergone a sexual revolution, resulting in a movement toward more naturalistic and permissive views of sexual behavior. With the rise of the women's movement, the double standard declined; with advances in birth control, sex for pleasure became acceptable as did premarital sex and sex with successive partners. Casual sex also became common but with the threat of AIDS has declined.

3. Sexual behavior varies from abstinence to sexual intercourse. Either abstinence or monogamous relationships are recommended as the best safeguard against AIDS. Abstinence includes masturbation which was once considered immoral and self-damaging but is now considered a normal form of sex expression. The new restraint in sexual behavior is expected to continue at least until AIDS is conquered.

4. The age at which young people first have sexual intercourse is declining, especially among women. However, women are less likely than men to find first intercourse exciting or satisfying. Surveys indicate that few young people of either sex are adequately informed about sexual behavior including the danger of AIDS and other STDs.

5. The positions used by partners in sexual intercourse vary. The missionary position or man-on-top is the most common position, although it may not be conducive to female orgasm. Most people engage in oral-genital sex, although a sizeable number consider it immoral or find it unpleasant.

6. The great majority of people consider themselves exclusively heterosexual, although Kinsey found that a substantial number had had at least one homosexual experience to the point of orgasm. A distinct minority of people— some 2 to 3 per cent—consider themselves exclusively homosexual. In between are a sizeable group of bisexuals—about 15 per cent of the adult population. Until the early 1970s, homosexuality was considered a psychiatric disorder but is now considered an alternative sexual lifestyle. The nature and incidence of homosexual behavior has been limited by the fear of AIDS.

7. Masters and Johnson have identified four stages of the human sexual response: excitement, plateau, orgasm, and resolution. About half of all marriages are impaired by sexual dysfunctions. Most common among men are impotence and premature ejaculation. Inhibited sexual excitement and inability to experience orgasm are most common among women. Lack of sexual desire is widespread among both sexes.

8. Sexual dysfunction may have physical or psychosocial causes. The most important psychosocial causes are faulty information, aversive conditioning by prior sexual experiences, anxiety about performance, and lack of emotional closeness to one's sexual partner.

9. The approaches to sex therapy of Masters and Johnson and Helen Singer Kaplan have helped many people. Although some sex experts express doubts about the effectiveness of sex therapy, it does bring the problem out in the open where it can be dealt with and often resolved.

10. Informed, responsible, and fulfilling sexuality requires being informed about sex including your own sexual values, taking the responsibility about whether and when to engage in sex, and learning to communicate in intimate relationships about your sexual needs and preferences. It also requires being aware of and comfortable with your own sexuality as well as sensitive to that of your partner's.

LOVE AND ROMANCE

Although sexuality has never been unimportant in any culture, romantic love in our society has come to be regarded not only as a source of special pleasure but as an experience of great beauty and a major source of self-enhancement. Americans treat love as an uniquely intimate, spiritual experience in a world perceived as isolated, impersonal, and amoral.

—*Jerome Kagan, 1985, p. 29*

Of all the goals we seek in life, romantic love must be the most longed for, dreamed of, sung about, cursed at, and cried over. The search for enduring romantic love is also the most difficult quest many of us are likely to undertake. Some of us have found romantic love and have lost it, suffering crushing disappointment and pain. The more fortunate ones among us have found romantic love and have been able to maintain it. But, whatever our immediate status, most of us are deeply concerned about our ability to establish and maintain romantic love relationships.

This concern appears to stem in large part from a lack of needed information about romantic love—what it is, how it develops, what it requires of us, what we can expect in return, and why it sometimes flourishes but more often withers and dies. This lack of information is not confined to individuals; social scientists have only begun to explore the nature of love relationships in recent years, and there is much yet to be learned. In this chapter, we shall present some of what they *have* learned. We shall also consider, among other things, a brief history of romantic love, ways of viewing romantic love, social and other conditions that appear to foster romantic love, and the question of whether or not romantic love can endure.

ROMANTIC LOVE: AN HISTORICAL PERSPECTIVE

There are many types of love—such as parental love, brotherly love, love of country, self-love, and love of God. However, it is the love involved in intimate man–woman relationships that is the primary focus of this chapter.

We recognize that love is a private experience and it may differ considerably depending on the persons involved. Furthermore, we know that such love relationships may change over time.

A Brief History of Romantic Love

In a review of romantic love in history, Kurland (1953) and Hunt (1959) found instances of such love in ancient Greece, Rome, Carthage, Egypt, and other early civilizations. Dido, the founder and queen of Carthage, has the distinction of being the first person in recorded history to kill herself over unrequited romantic love.

The ancient Greeks considered romantic love and marriage to be quite distinct experiences. In fact, romantic love was considered a form of madness that fortunately was "cured" by marriage. Although there were occasional instances of loving marriages in Greek literature, such as that of Odysseus and Penelope, these were the exceptions and not the rule. The Greeks also contributed the idea of **platonic love**—usually involving two men—as a transcendental or spiritual form of love in which ecstasy was achieved by the nonsexual adoration of the loved one.

The Romans also considered romantic love to be a form of torment and madness that occurred, if at all, outside of marriage. However, the Romans added a new ingredient—the view that romantic love was a "game." While lovers were expected to play the game with skill and persistance, it wasn't to be taken seriously. In addition, the Romans added a new twist to marriage; they established divorce as an acceptable procedure. Thus, Gathorne-Hardy (1981) refers to "a raging epidemic of divorces" during the later years of the Roman Empire.

With the fall of the Roman Empire in the 5th century, there began a period in Europe called the Middle Ages, which was to last almost 1,000 years. In medieval times, marriage was based on economic and political considerations; love had nothing to do with it. For love, the aristocracy of Europe turned to partners outside of marriage. However, during the 12th century in the south of France, a new form of romantic love, called courtly love, emerged. The concept of courtly love was quite different from the Greek concept of love as a disastrous madness or the Roman concept of romantic love as a game. Rather, courtly love required knights—who enlisted in the Court of Love around Eleanor of Aquitaine—to pay homage to their lady loves by performing courageous and virtuous deeds on their behalf. The knights were extremely serious in their devotion, but their lady loves were often married, and—in any event—they were considered too pure to be sex objects. Although romantic love was idealistic and, in theory at least, nonsexual, it was meant to be enjoyed. The troubadors of that period sang the praises of love and romance much as many of our popular singers do today.

The next 500 years was a transition period during which feudalism (the economic, political, and social system in medieval Europe) gradually gave way to the industrial age. It was a period characterized by the rebirth of the humanities and arts, advances in science, and the emergence of a middle class. It was also a period of wars, famines, and plagues. More relevant, it was a period accompanied by the loosening of sexual restrictions and the relegation of courtly love to a treasured tradition of the past. During the 17th and 18th centuries, the English and other Europeans began to consider love as a basis for marriage and to believe that romantic passion might not be a catastrophic madness after all but may lead to a "happy ending."

Our American Ideal of Romantic Love

Most historians trace our American ideal of romantic love back to the courtly love of the Middle Ages. This ideal may be summarized as follows:

1. *"Love at first sight."*   The lover immediately recognizes the "object of his or her affections."
2. *"Love is blind."*   The lover idealizes his or her beloved and is oblivious to any faults (see Box 5–1).

I have sought love, first, because it brings ecstasy— ecstasy so great that I often would have sacrificed all the rest of life for a few

BOX 5-1 / THE ILLUSIONLESS MAN

"You are a great and good man," she said.

"I'm petty and self-absorbed," he said.

"You're terribly unhappy."

"I'm morose . . . probably like it that way."

"You have suffered a great deal," she said. "I see it in your face."

"I've been diligent only in self-pity," he said, "have turned away from everything difficult, and what you see is the scars of old acne shining through my beard; I could never give up chocolate and nuts."

"You're very wise," she said.

"No, but intelligent."

They talked about love, beauty, feeling, value, love, life, work, death—and always she came back to love. They argued about everything, differed on everything, agreed on nothing, and so she fell in love with him. "This partakes of the infinite," she said.

But he, being an illusionless man, was only fond of her. "It partaketh mainly," he said, "of body chemistry," and passed his hand over her roundest curve. (1966, pp. 5-6)

Allen Wheelis' fantasy of *The Illusionless Man* illustrates the "madness"—and "blindness"—of romantic love.

---

hours of this joy. I have sought it, next, because it relieves loneliness—that terrible loneliness in which one shivering consciousness looks over the rim of the world into the cold unfathomable abyss. I have sought it, finally, because in the union of love I have seen, in a mystic miniature, the prefiguring vision of the heaven that saints and poets have imagined. This is what I sought, and though it might seem too good for human life, this is what—at last—I have found.

Bertrand Russell

3. *"Love conquers all."* Love is such a powerful force that it will overcome all obstacles.

4. *"Love is both ecstasy and agony."* The person in love alternates between joy and despair, depending on how the romance is faring.

5. *"Love is passionate."* Love is characterized by an intense desire for sexual union with the beloved.

The mass media—including movies, television, magazines, novels, and popular music—have tended to perpetuate this idealistic view of romantic love in our society. We are quite familiar with the old script of "Boy meets girl; boy and girl overcome seemingly insurmountable obstacles; boy and girl get married and live happily ever after." If only it were so simple.

In completing our brief history of romantic love, it may be pointed out that dramatists, poets, and songwriters have been trying for centuries to capture the essence of romantic love. Romeo and Juliet, for example, remain a symbol of romantic love and a treasured part of our cultural heritage. But, despite vivid and often poignant descriptions of the ecstasies, anxieties, and traumas of being in love—and of the feelings and relationships between lovers—this illusive emotion has largely remained a mystery. Even Shakespeare, in *Twelfth Night*, felt compelled to ask "What is love?" Perhaps Edna St. Vincent Millay (1945) has best expressed the illusiveness and mystery of love:

I cannot say what loves have come and gone,
I only know that summer sang in me
A little while, that in me sings no more.

"What lips my lips have kissed, and where, and why" by Edna St. Vincent Millay. From *Collected Poems*, Harper & Row. Copyright © 1923, 1951 by Edna St. Vincent Millay and Norma Millay Ellis. Reprinted by permission.

You may read in your Books, of love stories — but no
I declare you shall never have me for a beau!

Smithsonian Institution Archive Center/Business Americana Collection

DEVELOPMENT OF SCIENTIFIC VIEWS OF ROMANTIC LOVE

Scientists have not fared much better than dramatists and poets. But they have come to recognize that romantic love is a private experience and may differ considerably depending on the person involved. Furthermore, we do know that romantic-love experiences and relationships may change considerably over time, usually in an unfavorable direction. Although we have not yet come up with a generally agreed-on definition of romantic love, we do realize that people—including scientists—know when they are experiencing romantic love and usually whether or not their love is being returned. Finally, we do realize that some things have to be experienced to be believed. Romantic love appears to be one of them.

Of course, a hard-headed scientist would likely counter with the statement that "If you can't define it in objective terms, you don't know what you're talking about." Perhaps not, but we are accumulating an increasing amount of scientific information about romantic love. In the remainder of this chapter, we shall review this information and some issues it raises concerning the quality of our lives.

BOX 5-2 / CONFLICTING ASSUMPTIONS ABOUT ROMANTIC LOVE

Based on intuition, personal experience, and uncontrolled observation, it has been claimed:

1. That romantic love inevitably leads to disillusionment and is the principal cause of our high divorce rate—and also that romantic love mitigates the stresses of monogamous marriage, preventing its disintegration as a social institution.

2. That romantic love is blind and irrational—and also that romantic love involves a sharpening of perception so that the other person is seen realistically but loved despite his or her limitations.

3. That adequate sexual relationships stem from and can be found only in the context of romantic love—and also that adequate sexual relationships often pave the way for the later development of love.

4. That finding the right person is the most important ingredient in romantic love—and also that our capacity to give and receive love is the most important determinant.

5. That each successive love relationship is a unique and distinctive experience—and also that we love as we have loved before so that there is a continuity in our love relationships and we will keep making the same mistakes.

6. That true romantic love leads to harmony and bliss—and also that the "path of true love never does run smooth," that the intensity of feeling in romantic love will inevitably lead to conflict and anxiety.

7. That it is possible in romantic love to lower our defenses and let our faults be freely seen by the partner—and also that we must be lovable to be loved and hence must always keep our best foot forward in appearances and behavior.

8. That romantic love can be felt for only one love object at a time—and also that the individual may be in love with more than one person simultaneously.

Romantic Love

What is **romantic love?** In a pioneering attempt to answer this question, Zick Rubin (1970, 1973) developed a questionnaire to measure the nature, depth, and intensity of romantic love. He found three basic components essential to romantic love: (1) attachment—a need for the physical presence and emotional support of the other person; (2) caring—a feeling of concern and responsibility for the other person; and (3) intimacy—a close bond manifested in part by confidential communications. It may be noted here that Rubin did not find passion to be an essential component of romantic love. For some assumptions about love see Box 5-2.

In their book A *New Look at Love*, psychologists Elaine Hatfield and G. William Walster (1978) defined romantic love—they preferred the term **passionate love**—as a wildly emotional state associated with strong physiological arousal, confused feelings, intense absorption with and longing for the loved one, and strong desires for fulfillment through this person. This definition emphasizes the intense emotional state of romantic love—a state characterized by a profusion of feelings including tenderness and sexual desire, ecstasy and pain, altruism and selfishness, and vulnerability and jealousy.

Dorothy Tennov (1979) calls this intense passionate state **limerence.** In her studies of people who have experienced limerence, she found the following characteristics of this type of love:

1. Intrusive thinking about the loved one crowds all other interests and concerns into the background.
2. The person experiences a deep and acute longing for the loved one to return these feelings.
3. The person experiences mood swings dependent on the actions—or an interpretation of the actions—of the loved one. He or she experiences feelings of buoyancy or "walking on air" when love is returned and of "heartache" when the loved one's sentiments are uncertain.
4. The person is shy and clumsy in the presence of the loved one, crippled by fear of rejection.
5. The person is unable to have such intense feelings for more than one person at a time.

Passion is a fragile essence. It provides joy, excitement, delirium, and fulfillment—along with anxiety, suffering, and despair—for a short time. Companionate love is a heartier flower. It can provide gentle friendship for life.
Walster and Walster

Smithsonian Institution Archive Center/Business Americana Collection

6. The person emphasizes the loved one's positive points and overlooks or minimizes faults.
7. The person has a strong sexual attraction to the loved one.

Tennov also found that the moment of falling in love is often an intense one—ignited by a "biochemical spark" and involving a magical, intoxicating feeling of being "in love." Because of the magical feeling that many experience on falling in love, it is not surprising that up until recent times romantic love was thought to result from the intervention of supernatural powers, such as a dart from Cupid's arrow, a love potion, or a sorcerer's spell.

Companionate Love

Walster and Walster (1978) suggest that romantic or passionate love eventually comes to an end or else ripens into **companionate love.** Companionate love is a lower-keyed emotion. It involves deep attachment to and friendly affection for the loved person, which is not to say that sexual attraction is completely excluded. Companionate love often seems to result from two people being together over long periods, sharing hurts and triumphs, learning to trust and rely on each other, developing feelings of caring and concern, and forming a strong attachment that may serve in part as a defense against loneliness. In fact, Weiss (1975) considers attachment to have a strong bonding effect that helps partners to feel comfortable with each other and to hold relationships together even when they are far from optimal.

While most people are in search of romantic love, companionate love may prove just as fulfilling and meaningful. In fact, Tennov (1979) has suggested that an enduring companionate love relationship may be far more important than a short-lived romantic one. In essence, there appear to be advantages to both types of love. Romantic love provides excitement and joy, although it is often accompanied by anxiety and suffering. Companionate love isn't as exciting, but it provides friendship, caring, and trust. And although romantic love tends to fade, companionate love does not.

Perhaps a combination of romantic and companionate love offers the greatest potential for happiness and fulfillment. Romantic love can inject passion and excitement into the relationship and companionate love can provide the trust and commitment essential for the relationship to endure. In short, complete love, or "true" love—as Sternberg (1986) has suggested—may involve a combination of passion, intimacy, and commitment.

Liking and Loving

What is the difference between liking someone and loving someone? In the course of his research on love, Rubin (1970) developed two scales, one to measure liking and one to measure loving. Representative items from these scales are provided in Box 5–3. While he found the basic components of romantic love to be attachment, caring, and intimacy, he found the basic components of liking to be affection and respect. Liking based on affection is experienced as emotional

BOX 5–3 / ITEMS FROM RUBIN'S LIKING SCALE AND LOVE SCALE

Here are some of the items in Zick Rubin's Liking Scale and Love Scale:

I.

LIKING SCALE

I have great confidence in _____'s good judgment.

Most people would react favorably to _____ after a brief acquaintance.

I would highly recommend _____ for a responsible job.

II.

LOVE SCALE

I feel that I can confide in _____ about virtually anything.

If I could never be with _____ , I would feel miserable.

If _____ were feeling bad, my first duty would be to cheer him/her up.

The person rates each item from a scale of 1–9. Number 1 means "not at all true/disagree" and number 9 means "definitely true/agree completely."

The Love Scale was found to tap the components of attachment, caring, and intimacy, while the items on the Liking Scale evaluated such dimensions as adjustment, maturity, intelligence, and similarity to oneself.

warmth and closeness; liking based on respect is experienced as admiration. Both components are usually found in friendship.

Rubin concluded that a moderate amount of liking is probably a prerequisite for establishing a love relationship. He noted that, although liking and loving have much in common, he would hesitate to equate the two: "People often express liking for a person whom they would not claim to love in the least. In other instances, they may declare their love for someone whom they cannot reasonably be said to like very well" (1973, p. 215). Thus, while Rubin considered liking and loving to be related, he nevertheless saw them as distinctly different attitudes.

This distinction between liking and loving becomes important when we try to figure out how we "really" feel about another person—whether we are dealing with liking, with companionate love, with romantic love, or with some combination. Many couples are often concerned about whether they are still in love with each other or have simply just become "good friends." Are they "in like" or "in love"? We shall explore this question further when we get to some of the enduring questions about romantic love.

Love and friendship are the warp and woof of the social fabric. They not only bind society together but provide essential emotional sustenance, buffering us against stress and preserving physical and mental health.

Keith E. Davis
(1985, p. 22)

Styles of Loving

Canadian sociologist John Lee (1974, 1977) has suggested that people have different **styles of loving**—that they can love in different ways. Just as all colors can be derived from three primary ones, he has concluded that there are several types of love that can be derived from these three primary ones:

1. **Eros**—This style is characterized by strong sexual desire and intense emotional attachment. It is a passionate type of love emphasizing physical attraction and love at first sight. Common interests and attitudes may help to sustain the relationship.
2. **Storge**—This style, comparable to what Walster and Walster call companionate love, is a slow to develop, affectionate, and comfortable form of love emphasizing friendship. It is characterized by interdependency and mutual need fulfillment. Although sex is involved, it is based on affection and familiarity rather than intense sexual attraction and desire.
3. **Ludus**—This term means "game" in Latin and refers to love as play or fun, including playful sexuality. It is a nonpossessive type of love that does not typically lead to marriage or long-term commitment. The focus is more on enjoying a number of sexual partners.

By mixing varying degrees of these three styles, Lee derived three secondary styles of loving:

. . . some people do not seek or want traditional romantic love . . . some people do not experience romantic love.

Keith E. Davis
(1985, p. 28)

4. **Mania**—This is an obsessive, jealous, possessive, and dependent style of loving. It is highly stressful and characterized by alternative peaks of excitement and depths of depression. In many ways it is similar to Tennov's "limerence."
5. **Pragma**—This style is characterized by keen awareness of one's market value and comparison level. Love is maintained for practical reasons and is terminated when these reasons no longer exist.
6. **Agape**—This altruistic style of loving focuses on unselfish concern for the loved one. Love is freely given without expecting anything in return.

Lee emphasized that these six styles are ideal constructs and that a person rarely is a "pure" type who fits into a given category. Other researchers, such as Laswell and Lobenz (1980) and Hendrick and Hendrick (1986), have attempted to check on and extend Lee's basic findings. Both studies supported Lee's six types of love. These researchers also suggest that difficulties are likely to arise when two people who fall in love differ markedly in styles of loving. Each expects the other to love and behave in ways similar to his or her own. This situation may be complicated further if neither partner is aware of his or her style of loving. Thus, each partner simply perceives the other as not responding in ways he or she wanted and expected.

Of course, one or both partners may adapt their views of love and styles of loving to fit the situation. But the outcome is still likely to be far from optimal in terms of marital happiness.

A Triangular Theory of Love: An Encompassing View

Probably the most encompassing view of love is the triangular theory developed by Robert Sternberg (1986) (see Figure 5–1). This researcher starts with three basic components of love—intimacy, passion, and commitment. In various combinations, these components give rise to seven types of love. Sternberg also included

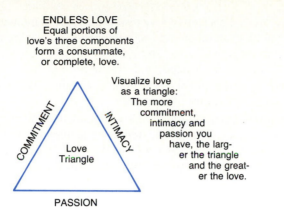

ENDLESS LOVE
Equal portions of
love's three components
form a consummate,
or complete, love.

Visualize love
as a triangle:
The more
commitment,
intimacy and
passion you
have, the larg-
er the triangle
and the great-
er the love.

COMMITMENT

INTIMACY

Love
Triangle

PASSION

*Figure 5–1.
Sternberg's Triangle
of Love. (Source:
Trotter, Robert J.
"The three faces of
love." Psychology
Today, September
1986, pp. 46–50;
54.)*

an eighth kind of love, in which all three components are missing. He calls this "nonlove."

The kinds of love in the triangular theory may be summarized as follows:

1. *Nonlove.*   This refers to the absence of all three components of love. Casual interactions that constitute the large majority of our personal relationships fit this category because they do not involve love at all.

2. *Liking.*   This is when a person experiences only the intimacy component of love, and passion and commitment are missing. This type of love is more than nonlove and characterizes friendships. Friends experience feelings of closeness, bondedness, and warmth toward each other but not intense passion or long-term commitment.

3. *Infatuation.*   This is "love at first sight" and consists of passionate arousal without intimacy or commitment. Often it is difficult for the individual to distinguish between feelings of infatuation and true romantic love. Of course, it is usually easy enough to make the diagnosis once the infatuation has worn off. Infatuated love applies to some triangles in which an affair may be dominated by passion and evidence little intimacy or commitment.

4. *Empty love.*   This type of love involves the decision that one person loves another and is committed to that love, but both intimacy and passion are missing. This type of love may be seen in marriages that have endured but are stagnant. Earlier in the relationship, the couple confided in each other and evidenced passion, but now they have lapsed into silence, the passion is dead, and all that remains is commitment to remain with the partner. In arranged marriages, which characterize many societies, empty love may precede the development of intimacy and possibly passion as well.

5. *Romantic love.*   This kind of love involves intimacy and passion components but not commitment. It appears similar to the love found in classic works of literature, such as *Romeo and Juliet* and *Tristan and Isolde.* This type of love may be found in a summer romance, in which the lovers meet while on vacation, fall romantically in love, and then part when their vacations are over.

*A walk in the valley
I came in from the
night.
I was lonely
Your light was on,
You were there.
Thanks.
A Friend*

Robert Cummings

6. *Fatuous love.* This kind of love results from the combination of passion and commitment components but lacks the intimacy component. It is the kind of love sometimes associated with "whirlwind courtships," in which a couple meet, get engaged, and are married all within a few weeks. Fatuous love is at high risk for termination of the relationship, especially in the case of "shot-gun" marriages.

7. *Companionate love.* Here there is a combination of intimacy and commitment components, but passionate love is missing. Sternberg likens it to a "long-term committed friendship, the kind that frequently occurs in marriages in which the physical attraction (a major source of passion) has died down" (p. 124). This definition of companionate love is essentially the same as the one used by Hatfield and Walster (1978) and Berscheid and Walster (1978).

8. *Consummate love.* Sternberg considers this kind of love to be complete—to result "from the full combination of the three components" (p. 124).

Figure 5–2.

Sternberg's Triangle of Love (Continued). (Source: Trotter, Robert J. "The Three Faces of Love." Psychology Today, *September 1986, pp. 46–50; 54.)*

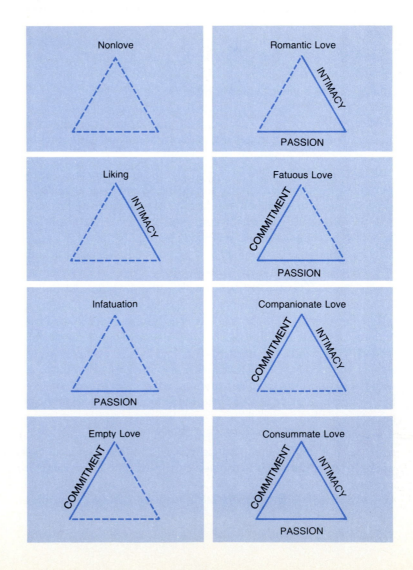

It is a kind of love toward which many of us strive, especially in romantic relationships . . . [but]. . . . Reaching the goal is often easier than maintaining it. The attainment of consummate love is no guarantee that it will last. . . . One is often not aware of the loss of the goal until it is far gone. (p. 124)

Situational factors are also considered to play a key role in the development and maintenance of consummate love. This kind of love is possible only in very special relationships.

The specific strength of each component—passion, intimacy, commitment—gives rise to the intensity of love. The strength of each component relative to the other two determines the kind of love we experience. For example, infatuated love is based on only the component of passion; intimacy and commitment are missing. When each component is about equal in strength to the other two, we find consummate love. Romantic love, on the other hand, shows strength in the components of passion and intimacy but lacks long-term commitment. Figure 5–2 demonstrates the relation of components in each of the eight categories of love.

Sternberg (1986) also stresses the importance of "action" in his triangular theory of love; that is, the actions of one partner affect the feelings and actions of the other. When one partner expresses his or her feelings in positive action—such as touching, hugging, or simply saying "I love you"—the partner is more likely to reciprocate in kind. As Sternberg concluded: "Without expression, even the greatest of loves can die" (p. 132).

Perhaps the bottom line is that love is a highly complex subject with many interacting dimensions. At the risk of some oversimplification, Sternberg has tried to present us with a coherent picture of love and love relationships. As the triangular theory is tested in the laboratory of real-life relationships, its strengths and limitations will become apparent. However, it may well help us to answer the baffling question, "What is love?"

PARADOXES OF ROMANTIC LOVE

Love relationships bring many seeming paradoxes—problems that convey a sense of both conflict and irony, such as the high vulnerability to emotional hurt that accompanies the ecstasy and joy of romantic love. In dealing with these paradoxes, perhaps we can gain some further insights into the nature of romantic love.

Separateness and Togetherness

One of the basic paradoxes of romantic love is that of being part of a romantic union and simultaneously retaining our own separate identity and freedom to grow as a person. As Robert Solomon (1981) has expressed it:

Love is . . . the taut line of opposed desires between the ideal of an eternal merger of souls and our cultivated urge to prove ourselves as free and autonomous individuals. No matter how much we are in love, there is always a large and nonnegotiable part of ourselves which is not defined by the loveworld, nor do we want it to be. (p. 147)

Eastcott/Momatiuk/The Image Works

Romantic love does not give one person ownership of the other. Yet some lovers make exorbitant demands on their partners' time, attention, and effort. They want their partners to drop all outside interests and focus their lives on them. In essence, they want to possess their partners. Often, of course, lovers feel that their great love for their partners justifies these demands. Unfortunately, however, such engulfing love is not great but little. The demanding partner does not really care that much about the well-being of the other; rather, he or she is concerned primarily with meeting his or her own dependency or other needs. This is what Lee calls the manic or obsessive style of loving. The target of this great love is likely to feel a sense of suffocation at being so "lovingly" possessed.

Nathaniel Branden (1980) suggests that people in clinging, dependent relationships will see their love die, whereas those in relationships in which both partners are autonomous are better able to keep their love alive. According to Branden, autonomy indicates a secure sense of self-esteem, so that the person's feelings are not easily hurt over minor conflicts. Immature, dependent individuals tend to translate such minor incidents into evidence of rejection. Between autonomous persons, both the partners and the love relationship can grow, while between dependent partners love often dies of suffocation.

Of course, we may readily agree in principle that each partner should be free to realize his or her full potential and not be trapped in a "loving" relationship. But when we are actually "in love," such a seemingly simple answer to the paradox of separateness versus togetherness may prove far from adequate. In short, the problem of "becoming one and remaining two" is often difficult to resolve in romantic relationships.

Ecstasy and Despair

Tennov noted that people in love often interpret their partner's actions as stop or go signals. When they interpret a behavior positively, they feel elation and joy, but when they think they've received a negative message, they feel doubt and despair. It is ironic that the ecstasy and happiness that romantic love brings can only be attained at the cost of increased vulnerability to emotional hurt. In fact, it has been pointed out that only those we love can really subject us to severe emotional damage. As Willard Gaylin (1978) puts it, "We can be touched—and delighted —by an unexpected kindness or courtesy from strangers. When we are 'hurt,' it is invariably by those we love" (p. 117). Perhaps it is the great vulnerability of partners in love that accounts for the saying that "you always hurt the one you love."

If we could be sure there is no risk in a relationship, our vulnerability would be of little or no consequence. Unfortunately, falling in love involves a high degree of risk. Although most people are sure their romantic love relationship will last, the odds are against it. The person we love may take advantage of our feelings and use us. He or she may sincerely love us at first, but stop returning our love and later leave us. Or the person may die, causing the greatest pain of all. In actual love relationships, Rubin and others (1978) found that only 15 percent ended by mutual agreement. Usually one partner pulled out of the relationship while the other was still in love, producing a terribly hurtful situation for the partner in love.

This raises two questions: Why get involved? Why subject ourselves to the possibility of such hurt and pain? After all, many love relationships are not all that rewarding and may in fact be psychologically damaging as well as emotionally painful. Nevertheless, most people seem to feel that if they don't take the risk and make themselves vulnerable, they will never really live—they will have shut themselves off from the most rewarding experience in human existence.

Jealousy and Trust

We tend to be sensitive to anything we perceive as a threat to our love relationship—anything that could expose us to the risk of being hurt (Salovey & Rodin, 1985; 1986). In this regard, jealousy serves a legitimate function in alerting us to threats to our relationship—to our security and well-being. The more insecure we feel, the more jealous we get.

There are two somewhat distinct types of **jealousy.** The first involves feelings of being left out of some activity in our partner's life—something that takes his or her attention away from us and directs it toward another person or an absorbing interest. We can be jealous of our partner's work or hobbies. The second and more-serious kind of jealousy arises from fear of losing love. This may be fear of losing our partner to another person or fear that our partner's love will fade and

BOX 5-4 / THE DYADIC TRUST SCALE

Larzelere and Huston (1980) have developed the following eight-item questionnaire to assess the amount of trust in a relationship. Answers that indicate a high level of trust are listed to the right.

1. My partner is primarily interested in his (her) own welfare. No

2. There are times when my partner cannot be trusted. No

3. My partner is perfectly honest and truthful with me. Yes

4. I feel that I can trust my partner completely. Yes

5. My partner is truly sincere in his (her) promises. Yes

6. I feel that my partner does not show me enough consideration. No

7. My partner treats me fairly and justly. Yes

8. I feel that my partner can be counted on to help me. Yes

Researchers have found that couples who score high on this scale also score high on love scales and that there is a strong association between trust and mutual self-disclosure. It has also been found that mutual trust increases with commitment and decreases when relationships are falling apart—which is no surprise, of course.

Jealousy is not a barometer by which the depth of love may be read. It merely records the degree of the lover's insecurity. It is a negative, miserable state of feelings, having its origin in a sense of insecurity and inferiority.

Margaret Mead

die. It is not surprising that people with low self-esteem or with experiences of rejection are particularly prone to jealousy. They often tend to perceive threats to their relationships where none exists. Their imaginations may work overtime with agonizing fantasies of betrayal in which they picture their loved one in the arms of another.

Although it is important to understand the extent to which jealousy can be attributed to past experiences, the ultimate answer to jealousy lies in learning to trust each other. For many people, developing such trust is not easy because it involves lowering our guard and making ourselves more vulnerable. But, as we noted in Chapter 3, trust is essential to the development and continuation of an intimate relationship (see Box 5–4).

"I Love You, But I'm Not in Love with You"

When we are in love, there are few situations more frustrating and painful than to hear our partner say, "I love you, but I'm no longer *in love* with you." This statement represents perhaps the ultimate paradox in romantic love: the longing for permanence and the ever-present danger of change.

This statement can mean one of two things. It may mean that the excitement, ecstasy, and sexual desire are no longer there. Romantic love has faded, but friendship and caring remain. A second possible meaning is opposite to the first: The sexual attraction and excitement endure, but respect and friendship have faded. In essence, the person is still "in love"—at least in the sense of being sexually attracted—but is not "in like." As one college student said of his lover,

"She is exciting as a date and fantastic sexually, but I wouldn't want to marry her or have her as a friend."

Regardless of how the statement "I love you, but I'm not *in love* with you" is interpreted, it is still likely to present a bewildering and painful problem for the person at the receiving end. If the biochemical spark and excitement of romantic love have faded, it is usually impossible to rekindle them. And if the partner is no longer "in like," the possibility of maintaining anything but a temporary sexual relationship is remote. Either way, continuation of the romantic love relationship appears doomed.

CONDITIONS FAVORABLE TO ROMANTIC LOVE

Now that we have examined the nature of romantic love and some of the paradoxes associated with it, let us focus briefly on certain key conditions that, are definitely favorable to, if not essential for, establishing romantic relationships.

Social Conditions

To most of us, particularly to those who are in love, romantic love seems to be the most natural thing in the world, but sociological analysis shows that it is a purely cultural product, arising in certain societies for specific reasons. In a different time or in a different society, you might never fall in love, nor would you expect to.

—Ian Robertson (1981)

Columbia Pictures Industries, Inc. from Movie Still Archives, Santa Fe, New Mexico

Human beings appear to have the potential for romantic love, but this potential is only realized under favorable social and cultural conditions. For example, in Tahiti, Samoa, and the Marquesas, romantic love is completely unknown (Wilkinson, 1978). As Walster and Walster (1978) have noted, "When one anthropologist asked the Tahitians to describe their passionate feelings, they were incredulous. They never heard of anyone feeling like that. Was such a person, they wondered, mad?" (p. 27).

Wouldn't it be wonderful to have surprise Valentine Days all during the year—days when we tell someone we love them, send notes, or flowers, or candy. (p. 5)

Buscaglia & Welles

Although romantic love is found in most industrialized countries, it appears to have reached its zenith in the United States. Our society not only places great value on romantic love but also provides a climate highly favorable for its development. Admittedly, our schools usually ignore or neglect this topic, but our mass media more than make up for this deficit, particularly in perpetuating stereotyped ideas about romantic love and the romantic love ideal. Love is the theme of most popular music, books and magazines, and films, and many TV shows, especially soap operas.

Our society expects us to fall in love, and most of us do. By their late teens, more than 90 percent of American men and women have fallen in love—often more than once (Walster & Walster, 1978). For most of us, love is a prerequisite to marriage.

Personal Characteristics

A number of personal characteristics are considered helpful in building romantic love relationships. Among the most important are the ability to love and accept love—including "love readiness"—a positive self-concept, and being a rewarding person. Because we dealt with the importance of a positive self-concept and being a rewarding person in Chapter 2, we shall simply add a few comments here.

People differ greatly in their ability to fall in love and to build a loving relationship. At one end of the continuum are those who are essentially insulated from intimate love relationships and are unable to experience love on the most superficial level. At the other extreme are those who are capable of loving deeply and of forming durable love relationships.

The ability to give and receive love depends on a number of factors, including the amount of love the person received as a child and his or her personal maturity and adjustment. In an evaluation of the most important ingredients of happiness, Jack Horn (1976) has reported the research of Robert Gordon. Gordon found a high correlation between love and happiness but not between money and happiness. In relating love to childhood background, he found that adults who grew up in "love poor" families typically placed less value on love and more on material goods than those who had received a lot of love during childhood. This finding held regardless of whether the children's families were materially poor or well off. Similarly, in a study of over 500 subjects between the ages of 15 and 52, Mary Ainsworth (1985) found that about half fit into a secure style of romantic love. The remainder were almost evenly split between anxious clingers and persons who tended to avoid romantic ties. She found that the clingers and avoiders—in contrast to those who readily formed love relationships—had experienced insecurity in their relationships with parents during infancy and early childhood.

Individuals who are immature and maladjusted also have trouble in love relationships. They bring their problems with them and inevitably complicate or destroy the relationship. Similarly, persons who lack "love readiness" may not yet be ready to enter into a committed love relationship. Rather than viewing romantic love as desirable and rewarding, they may view it as infringing on their personal freedom or as interfering with their careers. In addition, there are persons "rebuilding" from prior love relationships. Until their wounds are healed, they too lack "love readiness." Of course, some of the latter persons do get involved on the "rebound," but the consequences are likely to be undesirable.

Finally, persons who are low in self-esteem often consider themselves unworthy of love and find it difficult or impossible to believe that someone can accept and love them. They may even try to "prove" they are unlovable by sabotaging any developing relationship. However, even long-held patterns of insulation and low self-esteem can sometimes be dissipated by the experience of being genuinely loved by another human being—and by learning to love in return. Curiously enough, it is often when a person seems least worthy of love and acceptance that he or she needs it the most. It usually takes a rewarding person—a person who communicates an attitude of love, attraction, acceptance, appreciation, encouragement, and commitment—to break through the defense of an "unlovable" person and bring out the best in him or her. Unfortunately, such efforts do frequently fail.

Relationship Factors

The various conditions that foster the growth of intimate relationships—effective communication, mutual self-disclosure, and conflict-resolution skills—also foster romantic relationships. In romantic love, open and effective communication is not easily achieved. Love focuses heavily on the communication of feelings, and our inner feelings often involve a mixture of emotions that are difficult to sort out and communicate. Thus, even though persons in love do tend to work out their own unique ways of communicating feelings, the danger of miscommunication is very real. The results are unnecessary misunderstandings, disagreements, and conflicts.

Self-disclosure (which is also the third component in Rubin's definition of love) is essential in building romantic relationships. Couples in love do tend to reveal a great deal about themselves to each other. As we noted in Chapter 3, such disclosures greatly increase vulnerability to hurt, although they help couples to become closer and understand each other better. Even in romantic relationships, a certain amount of discretion in content and appropriate timing are called for.

Conflicts between persons in love are often referred to as "lovers' quarrels," and such quarrels are bound to occur from time to time in any relationship. They represent a warning that some problems need to be resolved if the relationship is to remain healthy. As Braiker and Kelley (1979) have pointed out, the turbulent emotions involved in romantic relationships can make such quarrels difficult to handle. Thus, the communication and conflict-resolving skills of the partners can be of crucial importance in maintaining and fostering the love relationship.

Realistic Romanticism

Is love an art? Then it requires knowledge and effort. Or is love a pleasant sensation which to experience is a matter of chance, something that one "falls" into if one is lucky?

—*Erich Fromm (1956, p. 1)*

The fact that two human beings love each other does not guarantee they will be able to create a joyful and rewarding relationship. Their love does not ensure their maturity or wisdom; yet without these qualities their love is in jeopardy. Their love does not automatically teach them communication skills or effective methods of conflict resolution, or the art of integrating their love into the rest of their existence. Their love does not produce self-esteem;

In his book *The Art of Loving*, Erich Fromm concluded that while people think romantic love is extremely important, few think there is anything to be learned about it. If love is a matter of chance, Fromm says, then it simply involves finding the "right" person rather than understanding the nature of love. But if love is an art, then it must be learned as one would learn any other art, such as painting or gourmet cooking.

Echoing Fromm's notion that love is indeed an art, many of today's social scientists advocate the idea that there are certain understandings and behaviors that people can apply to help love flourish and grow, once it has been born. One important understanding is to realize that we cannot hang on to an idealized view of our partner or our relationship—we must have realistic views of them and of ourselves. From such realistic perceptions, we can develop realistic expectations for the relationship.

Another way to pursue the art of love is to cultivate communications, conflict-resolving, and other interpersonal skills. We need to find ways to show our partner that we appreciate him or her—that we do not take our partner for granted. By working at love, we show our partner that we consider the relationship worth the effort. Building a love relationship requires continual work and commitment; it is not a product that we buy once and for all with a lifetime guaranty. Although falling in love can be more or less instantaneous, building a meaningful relationship takes time and keeping it alive takes effort.

SOME ENDURING QUESTIONS

it may reinforce it but it cannot create it; still without self-esteem love cannot survive.

Nathaniel Branden

In this chapter, we have dealt with some of the important concepts and findings about the elusive concept of romantic love. There are a number of interesting and important questions, however, that remain essentially unanswered. Here we shall raise some of these questions and provide provisional answers based on the little research and theorizing that has been done.

How Important Is Romantic Love?

> Although sexuality has never been unimportant in any culture, romantic love in our society has come to be regarded not only as a source of special pleasure but as an experience of great beauty and a major source of self-enhancement. Americans treat love as an uniquely intimate, spiritual experience in a world perceived as isolated, impersonal, and amoral.
>
> —*Jerome Kagan (1985, p. 29)*

Although people differ on the value they place on love, most Americans consider romantic love a prerequisite for marriage and true happiness (see Box 5–5). In a questionnaire study of some 400 college students, Jack Horn (1976) reported that love was considered their major source of happiness—far ahead of money, possessions, sex, and other considerations. In a more-recent survey of slightly over 1,000 adults conducted by the Roper Organization (1987), the question "How enduring is love in marriage?" was asked. More than 90 percent of males and females replied that it either lasts through a long marriage or turns into "a deeper kind of

BOX 5-5 / LOVE QUIZ

Based on your experience with love, can you determine whether the following statements are true or false?

1. Love at first sight is typical of romantic love.
2. Men and women have different needs in romantic love.
3. A man usually falls in love with someone who reminds him of his mother; for a woman, it is someone who reminds her of her father.
4. Well-adjusted persons can only be happy when they are in love.
5. True love only happens once in a lifetime.
6. It is impossible to hate someone you love.
7. Love is all you need to keep a relationship going.
8. Beautiful women and handsome men rarely have problems in romantic love.
9. It is impossible to be in love with more than one person at a time.
10. Parental objections or disapproval usually destroy romantic love.

Answers: All the statements are false.

love." Conversely, Tennov (1979) found that problems in love—the inability to find love, unrequited love, and unsatisfactory love relationships—were the major source of *un*happiness among college students.

Are love and romance only for the young and beautiful people?

Often our culture gives us the message, particularly via TV, that love is only for beautiful young women and handsome young men, and that older people are no longer interested in, or suitable for, romance and passion.

Abigail Heyman/Archive Pictures, Inc.

Enrico Ferorelli/DOT

Not content to accept this cultural message at face value, Bulcroft and O'Connor-Roden studied a group of older single men and women ranging in age from 60–92; the average age was 68. A key question asked by these researchers was "What is the age of love?" The answer given by a 64-year-old woman seemed to reflect best the feelings of these older people:

> I suppose that hope does spring eternal in the human breast as far as love is concerned. People are always looking for the ultimate, perfect relationship. No matter how old they are, they are looking for this thing called "love." (p. 69)

Thus, romantic love appears to be important to young and old alike. As David Heller (1987) has summarized it, "the quest for love speaks to all of us" (p. 75).

Perhaps it speaks loudest to those of us who feel alone and insignificant in an impersonal and often cruel world. For when we love and are loved in return, we can share our feelings and experiences, establish truly intimate relationships, and help each other grow and build constructive and fulfilling lives. From a broader perspective, psychoanalyst Willard Gaylin (1986), in his book *Rediscovering Love*, contends that we are rapidly creating a world without love. And he considers love to be absolutely essential for human survival. The latter conclusion cannot be proven, at least as yet. But it seems doubtful that it will elicit a lot of flack from social scientists.

But suppose our love relationship does not last. It can be terribly hurtful, but we can try to understand why it faded and what we might have done differently. If we are fortunate enough to find love again, perhaps this time we will be better equipped to ensure its success.

So how important is love? In the last line of their comprehensive study of love, Clyde and Susan Hendrick (1986) provide a very succinct answer: "What is more important than love" (p. 402).

Are There Sex Differences in Romantic Love?

The traditional stereotype in our society is that women are the romantics and men are the pragmatic breadwinners. Women presumably live for love, whereas men live for their work. However, more-recent research findings, such as those of Rubin, and others (1978), Rubenstein (1983) and Hendrick and Hendrick (1986), have cast doubt on these traditional views. In general, this research indicates that, in contrast to men, women are less "romantic" and more cautious about entering into romantic relationships, are less likely to believe in romantic myths about love—such as love conquering all—are more inclined to merge love and friendship, and are less happy in love relationships. Women are also more likely to end a relationship that appears to be ill-fated and are better able to cope with the breakup—to "fall out of love." Thus, sociologists characterize the pattern for men as FILO—"first in, last out"—and the pattern for women as LIFO—"last in, first out."

Smithsonian Institution Archive Center/Business Americana Collection

How can these findings be explained? One explanation is that there are deep personality and emotional differences between men and women, but the evidence for such an explanation is slim. A second explanation is that in Western society women have to be more cautious, realistic, and practical in mate selection for economic and social reasons. With greater equality of the sexes, however, this argument will no longer carry much weight. A third explanation, emphasized by Rubin, Peplau, and Hill (1978), is that women are more capable of understanding and dealing with their emotions, so they are less likely to enter blindly into romantic relationships, are more aware and critical of the relationships they do enter, and are better able to get over the breakup than men, who have been socially conditioned to avoid dealing with their emotions.

In considering these various explanations, it appears that males and females in our society have somewhat different "scripts" for love and romance. Such scripts are part of our social learning and sex-roles. For example, the traditional script for males calls for marrying a "good homemaker"; the script for women calls for marrying a "good provider." As our sex-roles have changed, so have the scripts we follow. As a result, there appears to be an increasing overlap between the sexes in contemporary love scripts. Of course, there are those persons who have rather unique scripts based on their unique experiences.

As intriguing as these findings and explanations are, they are strictly tentative. Subjects in research studies have been primarily college students—an unrepresentative sample of the total population—and there is a great deal of overlap between men and women in the differences we have described. Nevertheless, the subject of sex differences in romantic love is both interesting and important; if available findings and speculations serve to stimulate further research, they will have served a useful purpose.

Is Romantic Love Simply a Matter of Social Exchange?

In Chapter 2, we introduced the social exchange view, the idea that relationships are based primarily on cost reward analyses and social comparison. Fromm (1956) expresses this approach rather succinctly:

> Two persons thus fall in love when they feel they have found the best object available on the market, considering the limitations of their own exchange values. Often, as in buying real estate, the hidden potentialities which can be developed play a considerable role in this bargain. (pp. 3–4)

Ironically, Fromm does not agree with the social exchange view because he feels that it reduces human beings to commodities whose value is subject to existing conditions in the interpersonal marketplace. There are many other social scientists who, like Fromm, feel that romantic relationships, with their magical aura, transcend social exchange principles.

So what are we to conclude? Is romantic love a matter of mutual exchange, in which costs and rewards are balanced, or is it a matter of giving freely of ourselves without expecting anything in return? Perhaps in our society we are dealing with a mixture of both, depending to a large extent on the individuals involved. In his view of love as going beyond social exchange theory, Zick Rubin (1973) comes to this conclusion: "In close relationships one becomes decreasingly concerned with

Erika Stone/Peter Arnold, Inc.

what he can get *from* the other person and increasingly concerned with what he can do *for* the other. But even in the closest relationships, the principles of the inter-personal marketplace are never entirely repealed" (pp. 86–87).

In this context, it may be helpful to review Box 5–6 which summarizes various "models" of love.

Can Romantic Love Endure?

> Sometimes when we think about the challenges of romantic love, think about all the hurdles that have to be met and crossed, it is difficult not to feel sadness—sadness for every couple who have ever fallen in love, and then helplessly watched while love slipped away and they did not know how to stop it, did not know what happened or why.
>
> —*Nathaniel Branden (1980, p. 160)*

Lasting love is hard to find. Typically, romantic love relationships have been found to last from about 6 months to 3 years (Tennov, 1979; Hatfield & Walster, 1978; Sternberg, 1986). In essence, romantic love is not expected to endure, which may be one reason why it doesn't.

Perhaps the most common reason for the fading of romantic love is idealization of one's partner. In the excitement and joy of falling in love, most lovers idealize their partners and then later become disillusioned when limitations and faults become apparent. On the other hand, some lovers see their partners quite realistically and still love them passionately. Certainly couples in romantic relationships that endure for months or years are not likely to remain completely "blind" to each other's weaknesses.

Love may also fade because the love relationship itself does not live up to one or both partners' idealized vision of it. If not all the elements of stereotypical "true

BOX 5-6 / MODELS OF LOVE

Each of the following models contributes some measure of understanding of romantic love. But neither singly nor collectively do they adequately encompass the phenomenon of romantic love as we experience it in our lives.

1. *Love as a fair exchange.* This model is based on the social exchange view in which intimate relationships are formed for the purpose of meeting each other's needs. In an equitable exchange, each person presumably receives what he or she deserves in terms of what he or she contributes to the relationship (in terms of approval, sex, companionship, money, and so on). Here the individual is keenly aware of his or her market value and comparison level in terms of available alternatives. The love relationship is maintained as long as the bargain is a fair one or a better alternative is not perceived.

   While the social exchange model may explain some of the motives for establishing and maintaining a love relationship, it tends to ignore the experience and "we" of love—the joy and despair, and the intellectual, emotional, and spiritual union of two persons.

2. *Love as communication.* For many years, it was popular to emphasize the role of communication in romantic love—particularly reciprocal self-disclosure. Each partner accepts the risks of baring his or her innermost self to the other and is left essentially "naked" in terms of masks, charades, defenses, and "security forces" to protect feelings of self-esteem and worth. This requires a great deal of courage because his or her greatest fear is possible rejection by the partner as a result of such self-disclosures. But, by trusting and sharing his or her most private feelings and experi-

ences with another person, the path is opened for two human beings to meet and form a unique union that can be achieved in no other way. In fully exposing ourselves and finding we can still be loved, accepted, and affirmed as a worthy person, we are, for a brief period at least, as one with another human being.

   This model is hard to fault. It helps to explain the development of intimacy and union—two essential ingredients of romantic love. It emphasizes the taut line between togetherness and autonomy—a line that must be drawn and respected if the partners are to grow individually and together. So where does this model falter? Perhaps in emphasizing talk and "heavy discussion" as if these were the essence of love itself. While mutual self-disclosure and communication are essential, they are not in and of themselves romantic love.

3. *Love as work.* This goes back to the old Puritan ethic that whatever is truly worthwhile requires work, and love is no exception. After the initial biochemical spark, the work begins—the partners must "work at it" if they are to maintain their love. Heavy emphasis is placed on standing together against an unfeeling and often hostile world. The partners provide each other with companionship, emotional support, and a defense against loneliness. Caring, sacrifice, commitment, and "working at it" become key words. The person we marry is minimized in this approach. The point is that love can be made to work with any number of people if we are capable of loving and working at a relationship.

   This model strikes a familiar chord in terms of our traditional views of marriage and has much to recommend

(continued)

BOX 5–6 (continued)

it. But somehow it seems to lack excitement and to be an economic unit formed for survival and procreation in a hard and hostile environment.

4. *Love as drama.* Here romantic love is a play in which each partner is a leading actor. It is a play involving excitement, great expectations, emotional "highs," the intriguing role of lover, and the games that lovers play. Certainly it makes romantic love a matter of high drama and adventure—not to mention excitement and fun. It is an experience to be savored and enjoyed, an experience that transcends all other emotional "highs."

Again this model of love also has much to recommend it in emphasizing the potential for adventure and joy in romantic love. But somehow it seems—as the theater often does—to lack substance and reality. If the actor doesn't fit the role, he or she can be replaced. And if our mate is disappointing or is no longer exciting, it is time to terminate the relationship and find someone who can inject new excitement into the relationship—who can play the lover's role so that our emotional "high" is restored.

5. *Love as biology.* This model focuses on the biological aspects of love such as the so-called "biochemical spark," sexual desire, feelings of excitement and ecstasy, and a "broken" heart if love is not returned. In this context, love has been referred to as an "addiction." Here one partner becomes so dependent on the other that they are both in essence addicted. In the partner's absence, the person becomes anxious and even panic stricken. The loss of the partner can trigger depression and despair. The person suffers "withdrawal symptoms" in the form of yearning for and desiring the presence of the other. Over time, the person may go through a withdrawal syndrome involving a severe grief reaction after which the person is presumably "cured" of his or her addiction.

This model seems limiting when we consider that a favorite metaphor used in the social sciences in talking about intimate relationships is the medical or disease model. The individual whose love addiction is not assuaged by a dosage of his or her loved one becomes "sick." The other side of the medical metaphor is to view love as a cure for disease. Thus, it may be prescribed as a cure for loneliness or low self-esteem. Although the biology of love still remains an intriguing and important problem, its solution does not appear to represent the entire answer to the mystery of romantic love.

Perhaps it is apparent as we review these models that love may occur in various forms and relationships. Yet the essence of true love eludes us. Romantic love is a relationship involving physical attraction, pleasurable desire, communication, intimacy, friendship, mutuality, and a transcendent union between two human beings.

love" are present, one person may drop out of the relationship and move on in his or her search for something closer to this fictional ideal.

Time itself may contribute to the fading of love. Time is necessary for lovers to get to know each other and to grow closer, but time can also reveal differences in goals, values, and interests that can create conflicts and cause the lovers to grow apart. Furthermore, people change over time. Their needs and desires at the beginning of a love relationship—the needs fulfilled by this particular loved one—can shift, so that they are no longer being met later in the relationship. As Sternberg (1986) has summarized the situation, "The factors that count change, people change, relationships change" (p. 133).

Although unrealistic views of love and change over time can be identified as "killers" of love, we really do not know all the reasons why love withers and dies. But it does die or fade for a great many couples. The longer a couple is married, for example, the lower they tend to score on various measures of love, suggesting how fragile and poorly understood romantic love really is.

Although romantic love usually loses its fight against time, companionate love does not. Instead of terminating a relationship when love fades, a couple could do worse than settle for a companionate love relationship. This is a choice partners often have, and indeed it is one often made, in the sense that most marriages that endure are based on companionate rather than on romantic love. After all, companionate love is usually more relaxing and harmonious than romantic love, and many older couples find it more appropriate. But companionate love may also have risks. Retirement from passion may lead to a tranquil but dull relationship. And there is always the risk that one partner may meet someone new, fall in love, and abandon the "comfortable" love relationship in favor of the more-exciting one. Certainly for most people who have experienced romantic love, settling for companionate love—however practical and tranquil it may be—is second best.

Because romantic and companionate love have somewhat different strengths and weaknesses, some social scientists have suggested that couples try to achieve a combination of both. As we mentioned earlier, the challenge is to keep romantic love—with its physical attraction and passion—alive, while developing the shared experiences, caring, trust, and friendship of companionate love. This is not an easy task. It requires a great deal of effort as well as deep commitment to our partner and the relationship.

In view of the importance of romantic love, Nathaniel Brandon (1987) has suggested that we need to rethink our view of love—of what it is, what experiences it provides, what human needs it meets, what conditions it requires, and what its ultimate promise is. This rethinking will require considerable research time and money, but many social scientists do not consider the topic worth such expenditures. Some view romantic love primarily as a biological mechanism designed to ensure sexual attraction and perpetuation of the species. Others view romantic love as an illusion, perpetuated by the mass media, that leads to unrealistic expectations in marriage and a high divorce rate. However, social scientists such as Dorothy Tennov and Robert Sternberg consider romantic love to be a unique and valuable experience that helps us to understand our potential as human beings.

Certainly those of us who have experienced romantic love—and perhaps lost it—would hesitate to shut the door on possibly the most meaningful aspect of human existence before we have fully explored its potential for human happiness and fulfillment.

SUMMARY—Chapter 5

1. In ancient times, romantic love existed as an experience separate from marriage. Usually, it was considered a form of madness that could be cured by marriage. Not until the 17th century was love considered a basis for marriage.

2. The American tradition of romantic love, which arose out of the medieval ideal of courtly love, is characterized by five main beliefs: love occurs at first sight, love is blind, love is both ecstasy and agony, love is passionate, and love conquers all.

3. Pioneers in the scientific study of romantic love, Elaine Walster and G. William Walster described romantic love as a wildly emotional state associated with strong physiological arousal (passion), a confusion of feelings, intense absorption with and longing for the loved one, and a strong desire for fulfillment through this person.

4. Companionate love is a lower-keyed emotion than romantic love. It involves deep attachment, caring, concern, and commitment but lacks the peaks and valleys of romantic love. Whereas romantic love usually fades with time, companionate love endures. Ideal or complete love may be a combination of romantic and companionate love.

5. Zick Rubin identified the basic components of romantic love as attachment, caring, and intimacy. He distinguished it from liking, the basic components of which are liking and respect. At least a moderate amount of liking is probably necessary for establishing an enduring love relationship.

6. John Lee distinguished three basically different styles of loving: **eros** or passionate love; **storge** or companionate love; and **ludus** or love as play. He also identified three secondary styles of loving: **mania** or obsessive love; **pragma** or practical love; and **agape** or unselfish love.

7. Recently, Robert Sternberg has derived seven types of love from three basic components—intimacy, passion, and commitment. Their equal and "full combination" results in consummate or complete love; the other types reflect the dominance of one of the three components. An eighth type, from which all three components are absent, he called "nonlove."

8. Romantic love is paradoxical: involving autonomy within a union; the experience of extremes of ecstasy and despair; the need for trust despite jealousy; and the idea that we can love someone without being **in love** with that person.

9. Romantic love is a cultural phenomenon, unknown in some societies and highly valued in others. Important personal characteristics in achieving romantic love relationships are the ability to love and to accept love, a positive self-concept, and being a rewarding person. Women appear to be more cautious than men about embarking on romances. They are also more likely to terminate an unsatisfactory relationship.

10. Most people in our society, both young and old, consider romantic love a prerequisite to marriage and happiness. Since romantic love usually fades over time, the challenge seems to be keeping romantic love alive while developing companionate love—no easy task.

III

MARRIAGE
AND
ALTERNATIVE
PATTERNS

The Boating Party, 1893/1894 by Marry Cassatt (1845–1926), oil on canvas, 0.902 × 1.171 m. (35½ × 46⅛). Chester Dale Collection, National Gallery of Art, Washington, D.C.

6

SINGLEHOOD AND COHABITATION

Singlehood and cohabitation are usually looked on as way stations to marriage. For many people, however, they serve as alternatives to marriage. How satisfactory these alternatives are is an open question.

—Anonymous

Couples still fall in love, go through traditional wedding ceremonies, and confidently expect to live "happily ever after." In fact, if present trends continue, over 90 percent of American men and women will enter into legally sanctioned marriages at some time in their lives. Although this basic pattern has remained much the same, traditional man–woman relationships have not. The relationships most men and women establish today are significantly different from those their parents established. These differences include today's more-egalitarian sex-roles, a longer period of singlehood prior to marriage, and a trend toward substituting cohabitation for traditional courtship and sometimes for marriage.

Of course, singlehood is far more complex than merely being a stage before marriage, and cohabitation is far more complex than merely serving as a substitute for dating or marriage. In this chapter, we shall provide a perspective on both these phenomena and on their role in changing man–woman relationships in our society. Based on the limited amount of research on these topics, we shall examine the myths and realities of the singles life style, the nature of cohabiting relationships, and the pros and cons of both these potential alternatives to traditional marriage.

RISE OF THE SINGLES

In the past, being "single" meant "not yet married." People in their late 20s or older who remained unmarried were often thought of as losers in the matrimonial marketplace, as the "leftovers" whom no one wanted. The men were called "bachelors" and the women were referred to as "spinsters" or "old maids"—not exactly positive images. People who became single because of divorce or death were not looked at in the same light; they were "divorcées," "widows," and "widowers." However, as the number of unmarried persons has increased dramatically and the status of being unmarried has become more socially acceptable, people in these various categories are now all grouped together as "singles."

The rise of the singles in America has involved much more than simply an increase in the number of unmarried persons or the improvement of their status. Today, being single often means being a member of a special subculture—a subculture in which individuals are allowed a great deal of freedom to experiment, grow, and construct their own life styles.

Who Are the Singles?

In the mid-1980s, approximately 80 million Americans aged 18 and older were classified as **singles** (U.S. Census Bureau, 1986). Who are these people?

Smithsonian Institution Archive Center/Business Americana Collection

Never-Married Singles.   By far the largest number of singles are people who have never married. In 1985, there were more than 20 million women and 25 million men aged 18 and over in this category (U.S. Census Bureau, 1986). These figures represent a dramatic increase in recent years in the number of young men and women who remain single during their early and mid-20s.

Apparently, young people today feel less pressure to rush into marriage. This is partly because they are spending more years in college, women are enjoying greater employment opportunities, and the single life is receiving greater acceptance as an alternative life style.

Separated and Divorced Singles.   We tend to think of singles as people who have never married, but, in 1985, there were over 18 million American men and women who were single again as a result of separation or divorce (U.S. Census Bureau, 1986). As shown in Figure 6–1, there were more than twice as many divorced as separated singles. In the latter case, the person is married but the spouse is absent. Presumably the separation is not for a trial period but precedes the granting of a divorce.

The median age of divorce was about 34 for men and 31 for women, and about half the divorces occurred within the first 7 years of marriage. Approximately four out of five divorced people remarry—usually within about 3 years of their divorce—but some remain single either because they can't find a suitable mate or because they choose single living. Thus, at any given time, separated and divorced singles represent a sizable segment of the American population.

Widowed Singles.   In 1987, there were more than 13 million widowed persons in the United States, forced into singlehood by the death of a spouse. Of these widowed persons, women outnumbered men by more than five to one—approximately 11.3 million to 2.1 million. The median age of remarriage for the widowed was approximately 60 for men and 53 for women. However, widowed singles are much less likely to remarry than divorced singles. Even in the 45–54 age range, the divorced were almost twice as likely to remarry as the widowed (Glick, 1980; 1985).

Often singlehood—especially for widowed women—is not a choice but the result of age and the decreased pool of potential spouses. Women in our society tend to outlive men by about 8 years. Thus, there are about five times as many widows as widowers. Furthermore, men tend to marry women who are younger than themselves. As a result, many older widows are forced to remain single simply because there are not enough men to go around.

It is estimated that, in 1982, the three types of singles—never-married, divorced, and widowed—headed nearly as many American households (about 31 million) as were headed by married couples (U.S. Bureau of the Census, 1982). These three groups are a significant portion of our population. However, it must

Figure 6–1.
(Source: U.S.
Census Bureau.
InfoGraphics ©
News America
Syndicate, 1986.)

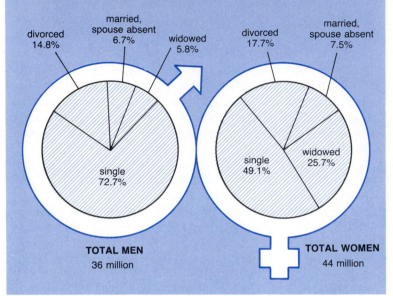

U.S. SINGLES POPULATION

Today nearly 22 million U.S. adults live alone - four times as many as in 1940 - and a further 58 million are single but do not live by themselves. Figures for 1985 show more single women than men - 44 million as compared to 36 million - mainly because women live longer than men. There are around five times as many widows as widowers.

U.S. singles population, 1985
Marital status of single adults, in percent:

divorced
14.8%

married,
spouse absent
6.7%

widowed
5.8%

single
72.7%

divorced
17.7%

married,
spouse absent
7.5%

widowed
25.7%

single
49.1%

TOTAL MEN
36 million

TOTAL WOMEN
44 million

Joel Gordon

Frederick Lewis

be realized that we are dealing with three groups that, although similar in some respects, are different in many ways. For example, because most young people get married in their early to mid-20s and divorce in their early 30s, there is a considerable age difference between most never-married singles and most divorced singles. As we have noted, widowed singles tend to be in an even older age group. In addition, divorced singles are more likely to evidence a sense of failure, low self-esteem, doubt, and uncertainty when compared with singles in the other two groups.

Because of the differences between these groups, we shall tend to focus in this chapter on the never-married singles. We shall deal with widowed singles in Chapter 11 and with separated and divorced singles in Chapter 12. Where applicable, however, we shall also refer to these groups in this chapter.

The New Singles Subculture

The new singles subculture consists primarily of organizations, groups, facilities, and other social supports that help provide a network for unmarrieds and that offer greater opportunities for people to enjoy—or at least tolerate—a singles life style. There are three basic components to the singles subculture: (1) organizations, facilities, and activities for making the single life more rewarding; (2) marriage-broker-type services with information about eligible persons for dating or marriage; and (3) opportunities for improving communication and other social skills helpful in understanding ourselves, others, and relationships. As we shall see, however, the singles subculture is a selective one designed primarily for relatively well-educated singles with adequate incomes and not for the educationally or occupationally disadvantaged.

Organizations, Facilities, and Activities.   Singles clubs, singles bars, singles apartments, singles magazines, and packaged singles vacations have become big business. For example, a singles apartment complex is likely to come complete with swimming pool, sauna, recreation room, coed gym, and planned leisure activities such as weekly parties and get-togethers.

In addition to businesses that cater to the singles market, the singles themselves have also generated their own organizations and activities that make a contribution to their overall subculture. Most major cities abound with singles-organized social clubs and workshops designed to help singles cope with an unmarried life style. In addition, singles now have their own national organization, the American Singles Club.

These specialized groups and facilities enhance the image of the singles scene as well as contribute to the desires and pleasures of their members. More important, these resources help provide young never-married singles with a social-support system and a sense of identity and belonging.

Matchmaking Services.   Not only is business involved in making life more enjoyable for single persons, but also it is involved in matchmaking—trying to help singles find dates and mates. Peter Stein (1978) summarized this function of the singles subculture quite realistically:

> The profit-making sector has been supplying other goods and services to the "singles market," a constantly expanding one consisting of a relatively affluent population with substantial amounts of discretionary income. This market consists primarily of singles who expect to marry and are more or less actively seeking groups of eligible potential mates. The singles facilities made available to them are oriented to ending that state. . . . As far as the "singles industry" is concerned, singles are for coupling. (p. 10)

Stein is referring primarily to young never-married singles as well as to relatively young divorced persons, usually under 40. The facilities available to these singles include videotape and video-phone dating services, newspaper and magazine ads, singles magazines that provide matching services, and social clubs with planned activities—such as ski trips, dances and discussion groups—where singles can meet, get acquainted, and pair off.

Building Social Skills.   A third and very important segment of the singles subculture is devoted to building social skills. This may involve attendance at professionally led workshops or ongoing encounter groups. Many of these formal groups focus primarily on divorced single persons who are trying to make the transition from married life to singlehood. The objectives are to improve the interpersonal skills of the persons, to help them in building social-support networks of friends and intimates, and to increase their life style options.

BOX 6-1 / HOMOSEXUAL SINGLEHOOD AND COHABITATION

Contrary to the popular stereotype, most male homosexuals are not effeminate in behavior and interests, nor are female homosexuals masculine in appearance and behavior. In a roomful of people, homosexuals are not conspicuously different from heterosexuals and, except in rare instances, cannot be detected or identified. Even when such an identification may seem obvious, it may be in error. Just as a masculine-appearing professional football player may be homosexual, an effeminate-appearing hairdresser may be heterosexual.

In a general way, homosexuals make up a fourth group of singles—in addition to the never-marrieds, divorced, and bereaved singles. Of course, homosexual singles may formerly have been married and divorced or bereaved, and have changed sexual orientation. In any event, homosexual singles have developed their own singles subculture, largely as a response to the tendency of the "straight" world to stigmatize homosexuals who display overt sexual interest in members of their own sex. In larger cities, this includes bars, clubs, and "singles weekends" in resorts that cater to homosexuals. And, of course, there are more extended "love boat"–type cruises and other travel events. Thus, much as there is a new singles subculture for heterosexuals, there is a somewhat parallel one for gays.

Although the singles subculture does provide facilities that have led to the "swinging singles" image, it also provides facilities for personal growth and eventually for "coupling," via cohabitation or marriage. Although singles bars (or "body shops," as they are sometimes called) and other highly publicized singles activities may not appeal to some singles, it is not our intent to evaluate these various components of the singles subculture. As summarized in Box 6–1, however, there is also a parallel gay singles subculture in our society.

Stereotypes: Swingers and Lonely Losers

In mass-media advertising for cosmetics, travel, sportswear, and so on, highly attractive models are employed, giving the impression that the advertised product is what makes the individual so attractive. The models in these ads are obviously unmarrieds and presumably lead a highly exciting and adventurous life as "swinging singles." Stein (1976) described this stereotype in the mid-1970s, and it apparently hasn't changed much since then. According to this stereotype, singles are the beautiful people, having the time of their lives—one long round of parties, barbecues around the condo pool, and meals in expensive restaurants. On vacations, they stay at expensive resort hotels in Hawaii or the Caribbean. During the winter, they may be seen in Aspen or other popular ski resorts, where they meet in the evening around the fireplace at their lodge. The atmosphere is one of continual gaiety and excitement. Sex is taken for granted and involves no commitments. Singles never have bad complexions, they are never overweight, and they are never poor.

While most swinging singles plan to marry eventually, they are in no hurry. They want to live life to the hilt and learn about themselves and their world before

BOX 6-2 / STATEMENTS ABOUT SINGLES: TRUE OR FALSE?

1. Most singles are more selfish than married people.
2. Most singles are better off financially than married people.
3. Singles who lead an active social life are rarely lonely.
4. Most singles are happier than married people.
5. Most married people wish they were single.

6. Most singles in their 30s and 40s would rather cohabit than marry.
7. Most singles currently avoid sex because of the specter of AIDS.
8. Most singles consider sexual variety to be "the spice of life."

Answer: All of these statements are false.

they settle down, and they are not willing to settle for just an ordinary marriage like that of their parents. They expect something more—much more (see Box 6–2).

The opposite stereotype is the "lonely loser." According to this stereotype, singles are unhappy, depressed individuals who desperately pursue their quests for sex, relationships, and mates despite one rejection after another. They frequent singles bars and join singles clubs, but somehow they just don't make it. No one seems to want to make contact with them. They live alone, often drink excessively, and eat no end of frozen TV dinners. They are manipulated, used, and often sexually exploited. They feel inadequate, have low self-esteem, and lack a sense of control over their lives. Although lonely and discouraged, they doggedly continue in the hope that their single status is simply an unpleasant way station on the road to matrimony.

As one 27-year-old woman expressed it:

> I go to all these singles events but they always turn out to be disasters. Occasionally I meet some predatory male bastard who would go to bed with anyone —but that's all he wants. I end up feeling used, and even more discouraged than before. I want to build a meaningful relationship with someone. Is that too much to ask for? I even take self-improvement courses, but maybe I'm a hopeless case. Anyway, nothing ever comes of them. Sometimes I feel like killing myself and getting it over with. But then the pendulum swings back to hope. I guess hope is what I exist on—what gets me through the long lonely nights. I hope I don't run out of hope—but sometimes I sure do feel down.

Thus, the stereotype of the lonely loser is to some extent based on fact—there are indeed lonely people among America's singles. But to a large extent the stereotype of the lonely loser is based on the notion that being single in our couples-oriented society *must* entail loneliness. Research does show that singles as a group are lonelier than marrieds (Gargan, 1981; Gargan & Melko, 1982; Jong-Gierveld & Aalberts, 1980; Cockrum & White, 1985). Being lonely, in turn, presumably leads the single person to enter the singles scene in hopes of meeting someone, even though it may only be for one evening of casual sex. In essence, anything is better than staying home and drinking alone night after night.

Enrico Ferorelli/DOT

If a person is successful in the singles scene, he or she is seen as a "swinger"; if a person is unable to connect with others, he or she is presumed to be a "lonely loser." Yet these closely related stereotypes, however well they fit a few singles, fail to portray adequately the majority of unmarried men and women in our society.

Reality: Widely Differing Life Styles

Real life is much more complex than our two basic singles stereotypes indicate. For example, Leonard Gargan (1981) has concluded that "the loneliness stereotype is not a general feeling for all singles or even most singles," (p. 384). In order to understand the complexity involved in trying to pinpoint the "typical single," it is helpful to look at the situation of the current generation of unmarried young people in this country. These individuals belong to the first generation to focus on personal growth and career advancement before or while searching for a mate and to place unrealistically high expectations on marriage while being wary of tradi-

"Remember, total honesty between us was your idea. I hate it."
Drawing by Wm. Hamilton; © 1982 The New Yorker Magazine, Inc.

tional marriage. They are also the first generation to live in a social climate in which singlehood is an acceptable alternate life style and social supports are being provided to cater to their needs. Thus, today's singles have many more options than any previous generation of singles.

One of the most important aspects of the singles scene today is the freedom it gives a person to explore, evaluate, and develop a life style that seems appropriate at this time in his or her life. Such life styles may vary markedly from one single person to another. To give some examples for comparison, we'll mention a few of the singles we know:

Chuck is a twenty-six-year-old musician who likes to camp in the desert, go to rock concerts, and grow plants in the small hothouse he built in his back yard. He rarely dates but has several friends with whom to socialize.

Patty is a thirty-two-year-old magazine editor who enjoys traveling and "partying." She shares her small apartment with her cat and has a boyfriend she sees regularly.

Vickie is a thirty-five-year-old sales manager for a printing company. She owns her own home and enjoys decorating it and doing gardening and landscaping. Although she has a busy social life, she is particularly devoted to activities with her parents and four sisters.

Forty-year-old George has a number of advanced science degrees from major universities and is an expert on paleontology. He earns a living by compiling data, but he spends most of his time corresponding with paleontologists and cataloging his various collections of books and magazines. When he takes his girlfriend out, she rides on the back of his motorcycle.

As you can see, none of these people really fits either of the common singles stereotypes. In fact, Jacqueline Simenauer and David Carrol (1981) referred to the singles at that time as the "New Americans." The name still seems to fit today.

SEX AND THE SINGLE PERSON

Until recently, the typical scenario called for a young man and woman to meet at a singles bar, go to his or her apartment and spend the night together, and separate the next morning—often without remembering each other's names. Even before the appearance of AIDS on the scene, the preceding scenario was greatly exaggerated, at least in terms of the number of singles who followed it. In addition, the singles who did follow this or a similar script usually reported unsatisfactory sex lives.

Sex with Successive Partners

Here we may recall that in the *Cosmopolitan* survey, Linda Wolfe (1981) found that the majority of single women had had two to ten sexual partners, and a sizable number had far more. However, she concluded that sexual discontent was rife among them and that most *Cosmo* women were disillusioned with sexual freedom. Similarly, in her comprehensive survey of male sexuality, Sheri Hite (1981) reported that most men still placed a high value on feelings of intimacy and closeness in their sexual relationships. As one man expressed it, "I've been picked up by women who just wanted sex, and afterward just rolled over and went to sleep—I don't like it any more than a woman does."

Another study shedding light on the number of sex partners among singles was conducted by Gargan (1981) in the Dayton, Ohio, area. His 400 subjects consisted of never-married, first-married, divorced, and remarried individuals. Of the never-married, 25 percent claimed that they presently had no sexual partners at all, even though all were over age 18. About 67 percent claimed they had had three or fewer partners in their sexual history, and 15 percent claimed that they had had eleven or more partners. In contrast, 33 percent of the divorced had had eleven or more partners. Gargan concluded that only about 20 percent of the singles fit the "swinger" stereotype and they were more likely to be divorced than never-married. He also noted that singles did not seem to enjoy their sexual freedom and were significantly less satisfied with their sex lives than marrieds.

Sex without Intimacy

Gargan (1981) found that half of the singles in his study did not consider love a prerequisite to sex. On the other hand, he did not interpret this finding as an indication of "a morally abandoned sexuality" because three-fourths would not engage in sexual relationships as the price of a date. But, even though attitudes have changed and sex is now viewed as a legitimate source of pleasure for both women and men, the problem of sex without intimacy seems to be a very real one for singles of both sexes.

Like the never-marrieds, divorced singles also encounter this problem. Many divorced men, for example, look forward to a swinging singles life but then find it disillusioning. Both men and women report that they want an enduring and meaningful relationship, not a swinging post-divorce existence. Casual sex and lack of intimacy may be a problem for divorced singles because they have had the experience of intimacy in marriage. It would appear that many never-marrieds are also troubled about casual sex and are searching for guidelines to make sex more meaningful as well as safer—in the context of the singles life style.

After reviewing the threat of AIDS and the available research on casual sex, Masters and others (1985) summarized the situation very succinctly:

> To be sure, people won't simply be frightened [by STDs] into restricting their sexual activity largely to long-term relationships. There are other, more compelling, reasons why this pattern will become widespread. Chief among them is the fundamental fact that more people find greater personal comfort and satisfaction with sex in the context of an intimate, caring relationship than find these qualities in the relatively impersonal context of sex without commitment or caring. (pp. 562–563)

Booby Traps on the Sexual Hunting Ground

Increasingly, single women—especially career-oriented women in their 30s and 40s—are settling for relationships with married men. This "married-man gambit" often seems to pay off, but in the long run it is likely to prove hurtful.

A. C. Chenault

In addition to the problem of lack of intimacy, singles pursuing an active sex life encounter a number of "booby traps" in the sexual hunting ground. Among these are social pressures to have sex, "date rape," the "married-man gambit," self-devaluation and loneliness, and the dangers of contracting sexually transmitted diseases.

The sexual hunting ground is inhabited by both male and female predators looking for lonely singles on whom to prey. Many single women report being pressured into having sex with their dates when they really don't want to. Many submit for fear their date will not ask them out again; others submit because they feel it is the expected and socially acceptable thing to do. Usually it is the woman who is pressured by her date, but in a substantial number of cases men report being pressured into having sex by seductive and aggressive female dates. Many men apparently feel that it is necessary to "perform sexually" in order to prove their masculinity and live up to their "macho" image. It would appear that recently divorced men and women are particularly vulnerable to sexual exploitation—possibly because they desire to prove their sexual desirability or to re-establish a satisfying sex life (Brehm, 1985).

Unfortunately, many men do not stop with social pressure but use force in order to obtain sex with their dates; this is referred to as "**date rape.**" In a study of undergraduate students at a large Midwestern university, Tom Jackson (1985) found that over 20 percent of the 247 women interviewed in his study stated they had been physically forced to have sexual relations on a date. And in a questionnaire study of violence, dating, and sex at a large Northwestern university, Katherine Lane and Patricia Gwartney-Gibbs (1985) found that almost 25 percent of female respondents reported submitting to sex as a result of the threatened, or actual, use of force. In a minority of cases, the sexual aggressors were females and the victims were males. Alcohol and drugs played a prominent role in perpetuating sexual aggression. Because the latter researchers defined sex as "kissing, fondling, or sexual intercourse," a direct comparison with the Jackson study is not possible.

Finally, in a comprehensive study of men and women students at 32 higher-education institutions across the country, Mary Koss (1987) and her colleagues reported that almost 28 percent of college women had experienced rape or attempted rape—often involving incidents in which alcohol or drugs were used. A unique finding of this study was that almost 8 percent of the men admitted performing actual or attempted rape.

Some singles who engage in "one-night stands" are really searching for that one special person or at least a more-fulfilling and enduring relationship. It is these individuals who often find the sexual hunting ground a damaging place. As Maxine Schnall (1979) put it:

> People who see casual sex as just a physical release won't be devasted by it. But those who are looking for something more may find that instead of filling up the void they feel inside, meaningless sex heightens the feeling of emptiness. If a woman has casual sex with someone in the hope that it will lead to a more personally fulfilling relationship that never materializes, she may feel let down, and the brief encounter is likely to reinforce her loneliness, self-doubt, and depression. (pp. 60, 62)

Perhaps a key problem of the singles scene is that people have sex before they become friends or even before they get acquainted on more than a superficial level. As a result, they may have sex with persons they would not dream of having as friends. In addition, many singles events and activities are simply exercises in group loneliness and futility and tend to breed distrust and hostility between the sexes. For those who are sophisticated at game-playing and who accept the rules of organized singles activities or facilities, the outcome may be a series of more or less satisfying sexual encounters. But, even so, emphasis on performance and lack of intimacy can prove anxiety-arousing and devaluing for the less-sophisticated partner.

Finally, a deadly new threat—AIDS—is changing the rules on the sexual hunting ground (Kantrowitz et al., 1986). The danger of AIDS, as well as other STDs, is inherent in sexual encounters with strangers or casual acquaintances. Even singles who try to pursue a minimum sex life are faced with the delicate task of quizzing potential sex partners about these diseases. Even the best-educated and most-respectable members of the singles subculture can contact and spread AIDS without being aware that they carry the virus and are highly contagious in terms of sexual encounters. As a consequence, an increasing number of singles are practicing abstinence—at least until they know their partner well enough to feel secure about the risk involved—or are using condoms and other precautionary measures. Gay men were the first to receive and heed warnings about "safe sex," but now straight men and women are rewriting their own sexual scripts.

Of course, the changeover in rules is still in transition. There are still many singles who, feeling that "It won't happen to me," engage in casual sex despite the risks—in some cases without even taking routine precautionary measures. But, in general, it would appear that there is an increasing emphasis on intimate relationships that involve commitment and sexual exclusivity. Although it is premature to predict the affect AIDS will have on singles who plan to defer marriage for career or other reasons, there is a popular saying that "Marriage never looked so good." It seems unlikely that cohabitation will suffer either.

SINGLEHOOD AS A STAGE AND AS A LIFE STYLE

For young never-married singles as well as the newly divorced, singlehood is usually a stage on the way to marriage or remarriage. But, for a minority, it becomes—with some variations—a permanent life style. What are the differences between these two attitudes toward singlehood?

Singlehood as a Stage of Development

In the lives of those who plan to marry eventually, singlehood offers a number of advantages:

1. *Freedom.* Singlehood frees the individual from the constraints and responsibilities of marriage and family life. The person is free to travel, have encounters with different people, and change sexual partners. Within limits, such persons are free to do what they want when they want, thus permitting a wide range of exploratory behaviors and experiences.

2. *Career advancement.* Singlehood enables individuals to devote more time, energy, and financial resources to pursuing their careers. Many young women in our society are career-oriented and financially independent and enjoy the opportunity to advance their careers much as men do. In fact, involvement in their career plays an important role for many young people in adjusting to being single.

3. *Personal growth.* Many graduates find that college has added little to their self-understanding or emotional development. Singlehood provides them with the opportunity to learn about themselves, about other people, and about relationships in the real world. It also provides a chance to evaluate different life styles and to assess beliefs, goals, and values—and change them, if necessary. Finally, it provides the opportunity to develop or improve social skills that enable the person to relate more easily and effectively to others.

4. *Preparation for marriage.* Young people today are seeing the effects of marriage on their parents and others around them, and many are becoming wary of traditional marriage. Singlehood gives them time to reflect on what they want and can really expect in marriage and on what they have to contribute to achieve a good marriage. The person is able to delay marriage until he or she feels ready for the responsibilities and commitment involved and has had time to find the "right" person to marry.

In these ways, singlehood today enables young people to establish a rewarding life style *now*—not at some hoped-for date in the future when they finally meet Mr. or Ms. Right and get married. In essence, making constructive use of the present instead of waiting for the future enables young people to prepare themselves better for making their dreams of a romantic and happy marriage come true.

Singlehood as a Permanent Life Style

As we have noted, singlehood has become an acceptable alternative to marriage in our society. It is possible that an increasing number of young people will not only delay marriage but will find the singles life style rewarding and choose it rather than marriage.

Researchers' reactions to singlehood based on free choice vary from pessimistic to optimistic. In a study of singles in the Netherlands, Jong-Giervald and Aalberts

(1980) found both "creative singles," who apparently adjusted well to singlehood, and "lonely singles," who adjusted more precariously. James Lynch (1977) takes a pessimistic view of singlehood, citing statistics that show a relationship between singlehood and decreased life expectancy, not to mention increased vulnerability to a wide range of physical and mental disorders. On the other hand, Donna Anderson and Rita Braito (1981) have discovered data that led them to question the long-held belief that the never-married are less mentally healthy than the married.

Roger Libby (1977) has expressed optimism, emphasizing the creative aspects of singlehood:

> A creatively single person is not emotionally, sexually, or financially dependent on one person; psychological and social autonomy are necessary to be defined as single. A single person does not make an exclusive commitment which precludes other emotional and sexual experiences. Singlehood is a state of availability. This definition rules out those who are totally or mostly dependent on a relationship which demands conformity to the monogamous model. . . . Singlehood is beginning to emerge as a positive option to marriage and other couple images. Social and ideological support for singlehood as a choice, rather than as a residual category for the unchosen and the lonely, has come from the women's liberation movement, from the alternative lifestyle and human potential movement, and from several other groups. (pp. 38, 40)

Singlehood represents a distinctive life style with its own unique characteristics separate from the norms that regulate the thinking and behavior of married persons. In other words, for many, singlehood is a chosen and enjoyed way of life. We may note here, however, that Libby is referring primarily to upper-middle-class college graduates, who are educationally, occupationally, and financially in a position to take advantage of the options available to them. Libby's statement was also written before AIDS made its menacing appearance on the singles scene.

There is some evidence to suggest that marriage is not as important to women as it once was.

Shere Hite

Of course, for older divorced and widowed persons, singlehood as a permanent life style may be another matter. In many cases, this life style may be imposed rather than chosen. These people are unable to find a new mate from the dwindling pool of eligibles. In other cases, people may choose to remain single because of such personal reasons as a negative self-image, distrust of the opposite sex, or fear of being hurt in a new relationship after being traumatized by a divorce or a spouse's death. Some individuals may be haunted by the fear that intimacy is only an interlude between single states and they are not sure that the reward justifies the risk. Thus, it would appear that some reasons for choosing the singles alternative may be more rewarding than others.

Is Singlehood a Satisfactory Alternative to Marriage?

It is possible that an increasing number of young people will not only delay marriage until a later age but will find the singles life style so appealing that they will choose it in preference to marriage. But this option appears limited in the main to those individuals who do not wish to be restricted by marital bonds, who are not interested in having children, and who have successful careers and can afford an independent life style without needing the combined income of a two-paycheck marriage (Nadelson & Notman, 1981; Cockrum & White, 1985).

Thus, it would seem that the number of people choosing a permanent singles life style will be limited by economic factors, if by nothing else.

For most young people, singlehood is a stage of development that has both advantages and disadvantages. By no means the least of the disadvantages is the risk factor involved in maintaining a sexual life as a single. Here, of course, we are referring primarily to AIDS, although other STDs also present serious dangers. Most if not all singles experience some degree of loneliness, in that it is often difficult to cope with the realization that we are on our own. Because of such loneliness, it is unlikely that the great majority of singles will opt for maintaining their status. Rather, they are likely to seek the intimacy, companionship, and commitment of marriage when the opportunity presents itself. In short, for most young people, singlehood is not—nor does it appear likely to become—an acceptable alternative to marriage. One alternative that many unmarried people *are* choosing, however, is cohabitation.

COHABITATION: LIVING TOGETHER

I don't know of many people who think [that] two people living together ought to be a crime.

Massachusetts Governor Michael Dukakis, signing a measure in 1987 repealing a 200-year-old state law banning cohabitation.

For our purposes, we shall use the term **cohabitation** to refer to heterosexual couples living together without benefit of a marriage contract. While this definition may include a wide range of adults in terms of age and prior marital status, we shall focus primarily on college students here because most studies on cohabitation have been limited to college couples. In fact, cohabitation came into the limelight in 1968 as a result of a widely publicized story about a Barnard College coed who admitted to having lived off campus for 2 years with a young man. This was a violation of college rules, and charges were brought against her. Although she responded that the regulation was unjust, she was nevertheless suspended. Apparently, however, she represented a sizable number of students in other colleges, because cohabitation has now become a well-established alternative to more-conventional living arrangements in the college community.

Studies of cohabitation on college campuses indicate that some 25–35 percent of students are living together with a person of the opposite sex at any given time (Macklin, 1978; Newcomb, 1979; Newcomb & Bentler, 1980a). Of course, cohabitation is not limited to college students. In 1970, there were an estimated 500,000 cohabiting couples in the United States. By 1986, this number had increased to 2.2 million (U.S. Census Bureau, 1986). This means that about 3 percent of American households are made up of unmarried persons living together. Although most couples are under age 35, a significant number are beyond that age. The majority of cohabitants have never been married, but about 35 percent have been divorced. Almost 30 percent have one or more children living with them. Most cohabitors plan to marry eventually, but not necessarily to marry the person with whom they are living.

Court rulings and other indicators point to an increasing social acceptance of cohabitation. Most researchers predict an increase in cohabitation in the 1990s and beyond. Whether the United States will reach the much higher incidence figures for cohabitation in Norway and Sweden, however, remains to be seen (Blanc, 1987). But the trend is definitely in that direction, particularly for both never-married and divorced singles.

Ulrike Welsch

It does not seem possible that is was only the late 1960s when college students were able to make headlines by admitting that they lived together without being married. Although we do not know the full extent of changing attitudes and behaviors, it is apparent that American views of appropriate sexual behavior and couple relationships have undergone a major change in a very brief period of time.

Ways of Viewing Cohabitation

Cohabitation can be viewed solely in economic terms, or it can be viewed sociologically as a replacement for traditional courtship, as a trial marriage, or as an alternative to marriage. Curiously, each of these sociological interpretations lacks an appropriate word for introducing one's live-in-partner—see Box 6–3.

Replacement of Traditional Courtship.   In a study of cohabitation at the University of Washington, Barbara Risman and her colleagues (1981) concluded that among students, living together is a form of "going steady" and is not as different from traditional courtship as popular articles would have us believe. However, the couples cohabiting reported that they were more intimate—in terms of feelings of closeness, love, self-disclosure, and sex—than couples who were "going together." Risman and her associates also noted that living together

BOX 6-3 / NEEDED: USABLE WORD FOR LIVING TOGETHER

When a married person introduces his or her spouse, the introduction usually takes the form of "I'd like you to meet my wife" or "This is my husband." But how do unmarried persons living together introduce their partners?

Most people would probably find it uncomfortable to introduce their partner as "my live-in lover" or "my cohabitor." Trying to be helpful, the Census Bureau came up with the acronym POSSLQ to denote "persons of the opposite sex sharing living quarters." A more-humanized version uses the pronunciation "posselque," but this term is hardly an icebreaker over martinis. Psychology's entry, "This is my significant other," is another conversation stopper.

A few years ago, Emily Post concluded that etiquette permits a two-pronged approach. For peers, the introduction might take the form of "This is the person I live with." For elders, she suggested "This is my friend." Other people have come up with "This is my intimate," "This is my LT (living-together) friend," or simply "This is Peter" or "This is Marianne."

As David Behrens (1981) has pointed out, however, when an unknown couple enters a party, the unspoken question raised is: Are you married, are you living and sleeping together, or did you simply meet in the elevator coming up?

often generates a feeling of commitment, so that couples eventually reach a point where marriage is the next logical step. Thus, these and other investigators (Newcomb & Bentler, 1980; Brehm, 1985; Abernathy, 1981; Gwartnew-Gibbs, 1986) view cohabitation as a developmental stage between singlehood and marriage.

Of course, among older, divorced people cohabitation may not serve as a replacement for courtship the way it does for many college students.

Trial Marriage.   The relatively high incidence of premarital cohabitation is taken as evidence of a sort of **trial-marriage** approach on the part of many couples. Some couples are committed to getting married if things work out but consider it silly to promise to spend the rest of their lives with someone they've never lived with. In essence, they view their relationship as a trial marriage in which they try to determine whether they are compatible before making a life-long commitment. Certainly, many of the problems they have to deal with in living together—money, communication, sex, rules and roles, and conflict resolution— are similar to those they will later face in marriage. In fact, Patricia Gwartney-Gibbs (1986) found that cohabitation is often considered a trial marriage by the couples involved, especially by couples with dissimilar characteristics—such as a marked difference in age, educational background, or financial status.

Of course, for many participants cohabitation is not viewed as a trial marriage, but rather as a relationship alternative that suits their present life situation.

Alternative to Marriage.   For young college students, the idea of cohabitating as a long-term alternative to marriage seems untenable. Thus, Cherlin and Fursten-berg (1983) refer to cohabitation as a precursor of, rather than an alternative to, marriage. Most of these students plan to marry when they feel ready and when

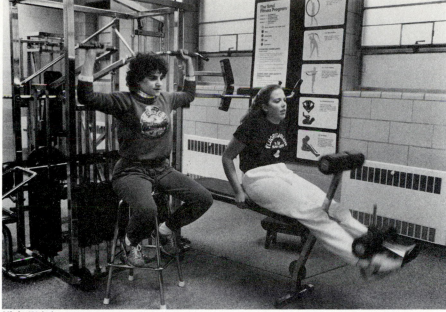

Ulrike Welsch

they have found the right person; they do not feel that living with someone implies a life-long commitment. Although many young cohabiting couples do periodically discuss marriage, such discussions may be a means of maintaining the equilibrium of the present relationship—for example, by reassuring the partner who is deeply committed to the relationship—rather than sincere attempts to decide about marriage.

However, cohabitation may be seen as a suitable alternative to marriage by many divorced persons who are wary of the possible emotional and legal hassles involved in marriage. Also, many divorced cohabitors may fear a loss of individuality and freedom in marriage. For these divorced persons, cohabitation may have a quite different meaning than it does for young college students. The following comments of a 26-year-old divorced teacher provide a rather extreme example of this view:

> I was never psychologically married. I always felt strained by attempts that coupled me into a marital unit. I was just never comfortable as "Mrs." I never got used to my last name. I never wanted it. The day after my marriage was probably the most depressed day of my life, because I had lost my singularity. The difference between marriage and a deep relationship, living together, is that you have this ritual, and you achieve a very definite status, and it was that that produced my reactions— because I became in the eyes of the world, a man's wife. And I was never comfortable and happy with it. It didn't make any difference who the man was." (quoted in Vaughan, 1979, p. 420)

Types of Cohabiting Relationships

Closely related to ways of viewing cohabitation are the types of cohabiting relationships that are formed. These relationships may have positive or negative consequences, depending on the persons involved, their motives for entering into such an arrangement, and the type of relationship they build together.

In an attempt to delineate common types of cohabiting relationships, Carl Ridley and his associates (1978) came up with the following classifications:

1. *"Linus blanket."*   In this type of relationship, one person enters the arrangement because of an overwhelming need to be involved with someone—almost anyone. Typically, the person agrees to whatever the partner wants for fear of the relationship being terminated. As a result, the individual is likely to gain little if any practice in resolving disagreements and conflicts; is in the position of clinging to the relationship; and usually feels rejected, devalued, and deeply hurt when the relationship is terminated.

2. *Emancipation.*   In this situation, the person enters into a cohabiting arrangement primarily as a means of achieving symbolic independence from parents and as a means of rebelling against authority and tradition. In this type of relationship, the individual often develops feelings of guilt and eventually withdraws from the situation. Again, this relationship is not likely to produce much in the way of personal growth, unless the individual is able to work through ambivalent feelings toward parents, who may be disapproving of the relationship. In essence, the person has problems that are unlikely to be solved by cohabitation; thus, the consequences are likely to be negative or at best minimally positive.

3. *Convenience.*   This type of relationship is presumably based on mutual convenience in terms of finances, sex, companionship, and other considerations. Unfortunately, however, one partner—usually the man—does not carry his share of the responsibility. Rather, he falls back into the traditional male role, while the woman ends up doing all the household tasks in addition to working or going to school. The arrangement often turns out to be exploitive rather than reciprocal.

4. *Testing.*   This type of relationship may be entered into for a number of "testing" reasons: to see whether the person is ready for a close relationship or perhaps marriage; to see whether the couple are compatible prior to entering into a marriage contract; to test and improve communication and other interpersonal skills prior to entering a more enduring relationship with this or other partners. In general, the consequences of a testing-type arrangement are likely to be more favorable than those of the other three types. However, many of the women who enter into testing-type arrangements are actually settling for less than what they want, which is marriage.

Common Problems of Cohabitation

The problems found in living together are both similar to and different from those found in marriage. Problems such as communicating, resolving problems, and agreeing on roles and responsibilities are common to both. On the other hand, conflicts that arise between cohabitants are usually less intense than those between married partners because the cohabiting relationship usually involves less commitment, is more temporary, and can be more-readily terminated.

The following are among the most common problems faced by cohabiting couples:

1. *Parental disapproval.*   Despite permissive attitudes toward premarital sex in our society, some parents do disapprove of their son or daughter entering into a cohabitating relationship. Students who continue to accept their parents' financial support seem especially likely to conceal their cohabiting arrangement from their parents. Women have been found to be more fearful of parental disapproval than men and may go to considerable lengths to make sure their parents don't find out.

2. *Lack of common purpose.*   Available research indicates that most cohabitors do not intend to marry each other and, in fact, do not marry each other (Newcomb, 1979; Newcomb & Bentler, 1980a; Risman et al., 1981). However, it appears that women are more likely to think they will marry their current partners than men are. Thus, men tend to take the relationship more casually, accepting sex and other advantages without making much of an investment—financially or emotionally. Because the possibility of marriage seems to loom much larger for women, they are more subject to exploitation in such relationships.

3. *Sex-roles and division of labor.*   Although we might expect to find egalitarian sex-role relationships among cohabiting couples, this is not necessarily the case. Although cohabiting couples typically see themselves as independent, sexually liberated, and mature, Risman and others (1981) found that their relationships tend to drift toward traditional male–female patterns of behavior. This finding is not unexpected because many wives in dual-career marriages complain that their husbands do not assume a share of household responsibilities.

4. *Money.*   Although cohabiting couples usually agree to split expenses 50-50, it appears that, in general, women contribute more money to the relationship than men. Regardless of who contributes what, money is considered a major source of disagreement as well as a major concern. Because many students simply do not have sufficient funds to pay for adequate living quarters and other necessities, they have to cope with a shortage of money and with deciding how available funds are to be used.

5. *Incompatibility.*   Students entering into cohabiting relationships may find that they lack common interests, goals, and values with their partners. And, of course, sexual incompatibility and dissatisfaction are not solely the province of married couples. As a result, some individuals feel trapped in a relationship that they did not expect and do not really want. Infidelity, especially on the part of men, also appears to be a common source of jealousy and conflict. A related problem in cases where cohabiting partners do not get married is how a future spouse will view his or her partner's previous live-in relationship.

Often it is prudent to consult an attorney and draw up a contract concerning areas of particular concern—for example, pregnancy, child custody, and finances—in order to minimize conflicts when the relationship terminates. This seems especially relevant for couples in which one partner works in order to finance the education of the other.

Terminating Cohabiting Relationships

Most cohabiting couples seem to "drift into" the arrangement, usually by saying something to the effect that "since you're over at my place all the time anyway, why not just move in?" Often couples are unable to remember who suggested the live-in arrangement. Usually the relationship involves couples who have known each other for 6 months to a year, so deciding to cohabit is not the same as "falling in love" and getting married almost immediately thereafter.

The duration of cohabitation among college students varies from a few weeks to several years, although the majority appear to live together for about 6–18 months (Macklin, 1978b; Newcomb & Bentler, 1980a; Kotkin, 1985). Obviously, during this period, two people who are sharing living space, responsibilities, sexual relations, and leisure pursuits are likely to grow either closer together or further apart. Although lack of commitment is commonly cited as characteristic of live-in arrangements, some partners do become committed to the relationship. In some instances, there is considerable commitment even before the couple agree to cohabit. However, if commitment fails to develop, decreases over time, or is unequal, the relationship is likely to end. In cases in which one partner is committed to the relationship and the other is not, terminating the arrangement is not likely to be the easy matter it is commonly depicted to be. In fact, it has been pointed out that the dissolution of a live-in arrangement often differs little from the termination of a marriage, with the usual sequence of grief over the loss, anger

Hazel Hankin

BOX 6-4 / POSSIBLE LEGAL COMPLICATIONS OF COHABITATION

Until recently, couples living together without benefit of marriage could dissolve their relationship without legal complications. However, in 1976, the much-publicized case of *Marvin vs. Marvin* changed this situation. Actor Lee Marvin and Michelle Triola had lived together from 1964–1970. She adopted his last name and called herself Michelle Marvin. After they separated, the actor supported her for 2 years. But, after the support ceased, Michelle Marvin sued on the grounds that Lee Marvin had promised to share his earnings with her and support her for life if she would live with him and drop her career as an entertainer—which she did.

Lacking legal tradition and guidelines for cohabitation such as those that exist for marriage, the California Supreme Court made a landmark decision by defining the value of Michelle Marvin's services in the relationship for purposes of property settlement. Eventually, in 1979, she was awarded $104,000. This essentially represented compensation for the lost years of her career as well as a fund to help her re-establish herself.

However, neither a share of the actor's earnings nor lifetime support was awarded. Nevertheless, Michelle Marvin was the first unmarried woman to obtain "equitable relief" comparable in a general sense to alimony. As a result, the term **palimony** was coined to describe such awards.

As a result of the *Marvin vs. Marvin* case and related considerations, couples who plan to cohabit are being advised by lawyers to draw up an agreement concerning how they will share property, earnings, and possible child custody and support should the relationship end. In one type of agreement, called contract cohabitation, one partner essentially hires the other as a live-in companion. The contract specifies each partner's rights and obligations. For middle-aged people who are financially well off, this is often considered a useful arrangement, particularly because the agreement can be cancelled at any time. In short, the "employer" is protected from having to pay palimony and from dividing up his or her property, as might be the case without such a contract.

and depression, and eventual rebuilding (see Box 6–4 for an example of the legal complications of this dissolution). In fact, after reviewing the available evidence, Kando (1978) has concluded, "When an unmarried couple splits up, the pain and trauma are identical with those of divorce" (p. 382). This statement may be an exaggeration, but it does serve to emphasize the emotional trauma that may be associated with terminating a cohabitation relationship—especially when the relationship has been highly beneficial to each partner and there is considerable depth of emotional involvement.

EVALUATING COHABITATION

What are the consequences of living together? How does this relationship affect the individuals involved? Does it have any value as a preparation for marriage? These are some of the questions to be addressed in evaluating cohabitation among young couples.

Advantages

In her study of cohabitation at Cornell University, Eleanor Macklin (1974) reported that 90 percent of the cohabiting couples reported their experience of living together as pleasurable, maturing, and successful. In fact, many people who have cohabited prior to marriage say that they would not consider getting married without first cohabiting.

More specifically, cohabiting students have reported:

1. Greater sexual satisfaction, more self-disclosure, and more-intense feelings of intimacy than couples "going together."
2. A greater opportunity to understand themselves, their partners, and close relationships. Many feel that cohabitation avoids the "phoniness" often characteristic of conventional dating and courtship.
3. An opportunity to ascertain compatability and see how their partners respond in a wide variety of situations.
4. Increased interpersonal skills and confidence in building close relationships.
5. A higher standard of living, resulting from the pooling of economic resources.

Risman and others (1981) also reported that both men and women, when compared with traditional dating couples, were more likely to express overall satisfaction with their cohabiting relationships. Mark Kotkin (1985) reported that 95 percent of young married couples in his study—had prepared them for marriage. Also couples entering a **second** marriage report more satisfying and stable marriages, if they lived together first (Lauer & Lauer, 1987).

Disadvantages

Although cohabiting relationships have many advantages over traditional courtship procedures, they are also subject to disadvantages. These include the following:

1. *Premature limiting of the dating experience.* While most students who enter a cohabiting relationship do so after a considerable amount of dating experience, a minority cohabit with little prior dating. In fact, difficulty in getting dates may make some students more amenable to a live-in arrangement because cohabitation tends to assure companionship, sex, and the other advantages previously mentioned. But it may also handicap the individual in future dealings with members of the opposite sex.
2. *Perpetuation of the traditional wife role.* A particular disadvantage for women is that they may end up playing the traditional wife role in the relationship, doing housework, shopping, laundry, and so on. In addition, some women may give up pursuing their educations and future careers in order to work and support their partners. Thus, as we have noted, the

Erika Stone/Peter Arnold, Inc.

overall picture is often one in which the man benefits but the woman is exploited.

3. *Unequal emotional involvement.* One partner may become more-seriously involved in the relationship than originally intended, which eventually leads to conflict and hurt.

4. *Change in social life and reduction in friends.* Living as a couple often changes each person's relationships with friends and acquaintances. Cohabiting couples tend to associate with other such couples or with married people and to give up former friendships. This reduces each person's social-support network in times of stress.

5. *Legal complications.* As we have mentioned, the possible legal complications associated with cohabitation are considerably greater than those associated with more-conventional types of courtship. In addition, many states have laws that make it illegal for unmarried persons to cohabit. Although these laws are not usually enforced, they do provide for fines and imprisonment.

Despite these and other disadvantages, cohabitors tend to evaluate the rewards of their relationship as outweighing the costs.

The Issue of Commitment

While commitment in cohabitation may be minimal, proponents of cohabitation point out that commitment isn't all that great in modern marriage either. In fact, the lack of commitment and other frailties of modern marriage are commonly used to justify cohabitation as a way for a couple to demonstrate their love and share their lives.

However, this argument is valid only for those couples who choose cohabitation as an alternative to marriage. What about the role of commitment in relationships between college students who use cohabitation primarily as an alternative to traditional courtship? Recent research comparing the commitment of cohabiting students with students who are going together is incomplete and somewhat contradictory. As we have noted, however, commitment seems to be greater on the part of women than on the part of men.

Barbara Risman and her associates (1981) have assessed commitment by seeing which college couples broke up and which ones married during the course of their 2-year study. They concluded that "there was no statistically significant association between cohabitation and relationship outcome by the end of the study. Couples who lived together were not less likely to have married, nor were they more likely to have broken up . . ." (p. 80). In essence, they found that cohabiting couples were no less or more committed than noncohabiting couples. But these researchers admitted that differences might have shown up if the study had lasted longer.

These investigators also explored commitment in terms of attitudes toward long-term relationships. While the vast majority thought they would eventually marry, "those who were cohabiting were somewhat less likely to think so than those not cohabiting. . . . When asked to estimate the probability that they would marry their current dating partners, there were no significant differences in the reports of cohabiting versus noncohabiting men. But cohabiting women tended to think that the probability of marrying their partners was higher than did noncohabiting women" (p. 80). The couples in the study had been together for a median period of about 18 months when they were first contacted. By the end of the 2-year study, 18.6 percent of the 231 couples were married, 32 percent were still either going together or cohabiting, and 44.6 percent had broken up.

We can conclude very little about cohabitation and commitment. Among undergraduate college students, the degree of commitment appears to depend heavily on the persons involved, their motives for entering the relationship, and the type of relationship they build. This generalization also appears to apply to middle-aged divorced persons and other persons who choose cohabitation as an alternative to marriage. We need additional research before we can be more definitive in our conclusions.

Does Cohabitation Lead to Better Marriages?

It would be unfortunate to conclude that cohabitation is inherently good or bad preparation for marriage, but rather it should be viewed as having the potential for both, with the characteristics of the individuals and the relationship being of critical importance in determining the long-range effects of cohabitation.

—*Carl Ridley, Dan Peterman, and Arthur Avery (1978, p. 136)*

The question of whether cohabitation leads to better marriages is a difficult one to answer. For some persons, cohabitation may prove to be better preparation for marriage; for others, more-conventional courtships may be more suitable. But without more specific details as to what makes cohabitation preferable for one person and courtship for another, this information is of little value. Perhaps we can come up with an answer to our question by addressing some more specific questions related to this issue.

1. *Are participants in cohabiting relationships more likely to marry each other than persons who are going together?* The percentage of cohabitants who eventually marry each other is not known. However, recall that Risman (1981) found no differences in rates of marriage or break up between couples living together and those going together. If we may assume that the findings of this study are typical, then the answer to this question is no.

2. *Are students who cohabit likely to marry sooner than couples going together?* Risman (1981) found that cohabitation appeared to speed up the rate of relationship development. For example, they found that the cohabiting couples exhibited greater intimacy than the couples going together, even though none of the couples in either group had known each other longer than those in the other. Perhaps of more importance, "Among those who married, those who had cohabited had decided to marry sooner than those who had not cohabited" (pp. 82–83). As we noted, the time elapsing between first date and time of marriage was 22.8 months for cohabitors versus 35.8 months for noncohabitors. In attempting to explain these findings, the researchers stated:

> On the one hand this faster rate of development may be the result of cohabitation. Living together provides greater opportunities to interact, and disapproval of cohabitation by parents and others may put pressure on cohabiting couples to decide sooner whether to marry or break up. On the other hand, it may be that couples whose relationships are developing rapidly are more likely to be the ones who cohabit. (p. 83)

However, cohabitation may serve to delay marriage for young people who do not as yet want to assume the responsibilities and commitment of marriage (Gwartney-Gibbs, 1986). But for young people as a group, the answer to our second question would appear to be yes.

3. *Do couples who have cohabited prior to marriage have happier marriages than those who have not cohabited?* Newcomb and Bentler (1980b), in a study of 68 marriages of 4-year duration, found no reliable difference in marital satisfaction between couples who had cohabited and those who had not. Nor were there reliable differences in divorce rates. However, these researchers did find that cohabitors differed from noncohabitors in terms of the numbers and types of problems that led to marital conflict; that is, cohabitors tended to bicker less but reported more conflicts over adultery, alcohol, drugs, and autonomy than couples who had not cohabited. Cohabitors who divorced reported less emotional distress than noncohabitors who divorced. The latter may help to explain Paul Newcomb's (1979) finding that prior cohabitors had more amicable divorces than noncohabitors.

It is usual to point out that the registered marriage differs from cohabitation because it represents a deeper personal and social commitment. That was certainly true in the past, as long as the marriage bond was, with rare exceptions, binding for life. But today, the strength of the commitment has been severely eroded by the ease with which divorce can now be obtained, and by the consequent collapse of most of the legal and religious restraints which formerly prevented it. Now, the only vows that are really valid are those which the man and woman make personally to each other and which they make together to God.

David and Vera Mace

BOX 6–5 / WHY DO PEOPLE COHABIT INSTEAD OF MARRYING?

There are several reasons why a person may prefer cohabitation to marriage.

1. The person may not feel ready for marriage.
2. The person may not want to marry this particular person—at least not until they know him or her much better.
3. The person may consider cohabitation as a better means than engagement as a test of marital compatibility. However, the intent may ultimately be marriage if things work out.
4. The person may have experienced an unhappy marriage and a traumatic divorce, and, as long as cohabitation is working, sees no reason to get married again.
5. The person may not want to live alone but also may not want ever to get married.

Most studies of cohabitation have taken place in the United States, where it is considered another stage in the courtship process rather than as an alternative to marriage. In a study of cohabitation in Australia, Siew-Ean Khoo (1987) found that about 5 percent of all couples living together were cohabiting. As in the United States, it was considered a stage of courtship rather than an alternative to marriage. In Sweden, however, David Popenoe (1987) found that marriage was being replaced by nonmarital cohabitation. We shall comment further on this finding in Chapter 14, which deals with the future of marriage and family.

Jacques and Chason (1979) studied 584 randomly selected married students at two universities and found that those persons who engaged in premarital cohabitation did not describe their marriage any differently than those who had not cohabited. As a result, these researchers concluded that premarital cohabitation may not provide learning experiences likely to alter a person's success in marriage. In a longitudinal study of high school graduates, Michael Newcomb (1986) found a higher rate of divorce among both men and women who had cohabited prior to marriage than among noncohabitors. It would appear, as Carin Rubenstein (1981) has expressed it, that "Practice marriages don't make perfect" (p. 19).

To summarize, the answer to our original question of whether cohabitation leads to a happier marriage appears to be no. This answer takes on added significance when we note that persons who have participated in premarital cohabitation appear more likely to be "trigger happy" when it comes to divorce. As Frank Furstenberg (1980) has pointed out, "Cohabitation has provided training not only for entering relationships but also for exiting them" (p. 446).

Is Cohabitation a Satisfactory Alternative to Marriage?

Some couples—especially those in their 30s and older—choose cohabitation as an alternative to marriage (see Box 6–5). For some, the relationship becomes a type of "common-law marriage" that endures over time. For others, it is a variation on the choice of singlehood but in the form of a more-intimate and enduring relationship that is similar to marriage.

In many instances, one or both partners have been married before and the marriage was so disastrous that they are wary of a second marriage. Consequently, they may approach a new relationship cautiously, and use cohabitation as a trial run before making a marital commitment. If the cohabiting relationship is a happy one, the couple may decide not to alter a good thing with the more formal restrictions and commitment of marriage. As one person expressed it, "We were both married before and were miserable. Now we are living together and are really happy. Why not leave well enough alone?"

But most couples do not seem willing to leave well enough alone. Even in European countries such as Sweden where cohabitation has become an acceptable substitute for marriage, many cohabitors intend to get married eventually—even after years of living together (Eckclaar & Katz, 1980; Trost, 1981; Popenoe, 1987). Bo Lewin (1982) considers the rituals of marriage, with their commitment and bonding effects, to be very important in this decision. Apparently, there is something about the quality of intimacy and long-term commitment in marriage that is difficult or impossible to duplicate in cohabitation.

Although living together may pose a threat to traditional patterns of courtship, it does not appear to represent a satisfactory alternative to marriage. As the census data show, even though people in our society are tending to stay single longer and to try living-together arrangements, marriage is still number one, and it appears likely to remain that way.

SUMMARY—Chapter 6

1. There are more than 80 million single adults in the United States. Of these, more than half are individuals who have never been married—a group that has increased dramatically in recent years. The remainder are divorced and widowed singles. Most of the widowed are women, a result of their longer life expectancy.

2. The new singles subculture consists of social organizations and facilities—including housing as well as clubs, matchmaking services, and courses and encounter groups designed to improve social skills. However, many singles who are educationally, occupationally, or financially disadvantaged tend to be excluded.

3. Singles are often stereotyped as "swingers" or "lonely losers," but in reality they vary greatly and have a wide range of lifestyles.

4. Although half of the singles do not consider love a prerequisite to sex, most value intimacy and seek an enduring and significant relationship. Their alleged sexual freedom is seriously curtailed by the threat of AIDS.

5. Among the perils and traps that singles face are social pressures to have sex, "date rape," and loneliness. As a result of AIDS, an increasing number of singles are taking time to learn about potential sexual partners before engaging in sex.

6. Postponing marriage offers singles a number of advantages: personal freedom, opportunities to advance their careers, and more time to prepare for marriage. Remaining single permanently, however, is advantageous mainly for the minority who have superior personal, occupational, and financial resources.

7. More than 2 million households in the United States consist of unmarried persons who are living together, and their number is growing. Sociologically, cohabitation can be viewed as a replacement for traditional courtship, as trial marriage, or as an alternative to marriage.

8. Cohabitating relationships have been classified as "Linus Blanket"—in which one person clings to the other out of need; as a form of emancipation from parents and tradition; as a convenience; and as a testing of the couple's relationship.

9. Cohabitation has a number of advantages over dating, including greater sexual satisfaction, greater closeness, better opportunities to assess compatibility, increased interpersonal skills, and a higher standard of living. Among the disadvantages are premature limiting of the dating experience, perpetuation of the traditional wife role, unequal emotional involvement, changes in social life, and legal complications.

10. In general, couples who live together are neither more nor less committed to each other than couples who live apart. Some couples combine engagement with cohabitation. When cohabiting relationships break up, it is usually traumatic for at least one of the partners.

11. Except for divorcees considering remarriage, there is no evidence that cohabitation provides better preparation for marriage than conventional courtship. Nevertheless, most cohabiting couples believe the rewards outweigh the costs.

12. Although cohabitation may prove to be a viable alternative to traditional patterns of courtship, it is not a satisfactory alternative to marriage for most people in our society.

MATE SELECTION AND MARRIAGE

MATE SELECTION TODAY

THE SEARCH FOR A MATE
Where Do People Meet Their "Match"?
Similarity, Complementarity, and Compatibility
The Shopping List: "Must" Items and "Luxuries"
The Marriage Market

PAIRING OFF
Traditional Dating: Functions and Problems
"Getting Together" and Casual Dating
From Casual to Serious Dating
Engagement and/or Cohabitation

GETTING MARRIED
The Wedding
The Honeymoon
Marriage Contracts
Marriage as a Commitment and a Transition

SOME ENDURING QUESTIONS AND ISSUES
Is There a "One and Only"?
Can Marital Success Be Predicted?
How Effective Is Premarital Counseling?
Is Marriage for a Lifetime Obsolete?

SUMMARY

The land of marriage has this peculiarity, that strangers are desirious of inhabiting it, whilst its natural inhabitants would willingly be banished from thence.

—Montaigne (1533–1592)
French Essayist

For most of us, marriage is a major goal of life, marking maturity and adulthood as well as personal achievement and fulfillment. Some 90 percent or more Americans will marry at least once in the hope of experiencing the benefits, challenges, and excitement of marital intimacy. Most people who are divorced or widowed will marry again. Marriage—rather than singlehood—is the dominant choice for Americans today.

The selection of a mate is one of the most important decisions we will ever make. At stake is our happiness or misery, the heredity and rearing of our children, and the disposition of our property. In many societies, the decision of whom to marry is considered too important to be made by the young people involved, so the parents or family—sometimes with the aid of a marriage broker—make the choice for them. However, we live in a society that emphasizes free choice. Thus, aside from a few restrictions pertaining to age and kinship, the selection of a mate is up to us.

In this chapter, then, we shall examine the factors that enter into the choice of a mate, the nature of courtship and getting married, and some enduring questions about modern marriage.

MATE SELECTION TODAY

Although patterns vary from culture to culture, marriage is a universal institution. Its traditional purpose has been to regulate sexual behavior, provide a social unit for bearing and rearing children, and serve as a basic economic unit. Today, our society still relies on marriage as the basic unit for regulating sexual relations and socializing the young, but the traditional reasons for marrying no longer exert the force they formerly did. Sexual gratification can be obtained without being married; having children is no longer a fundamental purpose in many people's lives; and, as increasing numbers of women enter the work force, the economic justification for marriage is no longer dominant.

Both the reasons for marrying and the expectations for marriage have changed, as we noted in Chapter 1. With more-egalitarian sex-roles, women have acquired a new sense of themselves as equal partners in marriage. As a consequence, their expectations have changed dramatically. No longer are they content with the dependent role of homemaker and sexual servant. Today, they expect love, companionship, emotional support, respect, friendship, sexual satisfaction, freedom to pursue a career or other interests, and—most of all—an intimate relationship in which to share all aspects of their lives and achieve happiness and fulfillment. For men, these changes have removed some of the burden of their traditional role in marriage, of having to take primary responsibility for supporting a family and resolving economic problems, for making most major decisions, and for putting up a "macho" front and hiding tender feelings and hurts.

In essence, traditional marriage has given way to a new form of marriage involving genuine intimacy, companionship, and equality. Perhaps the term **egalitarian marriage** best describes this new concept. For the first time in human history, men and women have the option of not only selecting mates but also of building marital relationships best suited to their needs and desires—of creating their own marital world. In this new context for marriage, there seems to be three primary reasons people marry: for love, for companionship, and for self-fulfillment.

In most other parts of the world, romantic love is viewed as a nuisance that may get in the way of more-rational processes of mate selection. In our society, however, romantic love and marriage "go together like a horse and carriage" in the minds of most people. When asked why they are planning to marry, most

Smithsonian Institution Archive Center/Business Americana Collection

BOX 7-1 / MIRAGES OF MARRIAGE

As might be expected, there are a number of common misconceptions concerning the emotionally involved topic of marriage. The following are among them:

1. Love usually guarantees a happy marriage.
2. Most married partners are romantically in love with each other.
3. Children tend to stabilize an unhappy marriage.
4. Loneliness is ordinarily "cured" by marriage.
5. Wives who are strongly religious usually experience less sexual satisfaction in marriage.
6. Interfaith and interracial marriages are rarely successful.
7. People in traditional marriages are much less happy than those in egalitarian marital relationships.
8. Arranged marriages are much less happy than those based on romantic love.
9. Marriages among younger people are usually happier than those among older people.
10. If people had it to do over again, the great majority would remarry the same person.

engaged couples reply, "Because we're in love." In fact, if a person says he or she is marrying for reasons other than love, such as financial security, we are likely to be disapproving.

In analyzing the replies of 75,000 married women to a *Redbook* questionnaire on marriage, Carol Tavris and Toby Jayaratne (1976) reported that, although love was given as the main reason for marrying, companionship ranked just behind love. Undoubtedly this term has somewhat different meanings for different people. In the simplest possible terms, companionship in marriage means having someone to be with, to share and do things with, and to come home to—in short, a friend.

Finally, fulfillment as a person ranks close behind love and companionship as a primary reason for marrying. Again, personal fulfillment may mean different things to different people, depending on their abilities, values, and life situations. For some, it may mean political success and power; for others, it may mean artistic or athletic achievement; and, for still others, it may mean a happy family life. In a basic sense, however, personal fulfillment refers to meeting our physical and psychological needs, mastering needed competencies, and growing personally—actualizing our potential as a human being. And, for many, this includes the achievement of a loving, happy, and enduring marital relationship.

She feared being trapped in a frustrating and unhappy marriage like that of her parents.

Anonymous

Of course, there are many other reasons people give for getting married, including sexual compatibility, refuge from loneliness, peer pressure, financial security, escape from parental restraints, and pregnancy. There are also many reasons people give for *not* marrying, such as wariness of traditional marriage, distrust of the opposite sex, and fear of intimacy.

By the time a person has decided to marry, many reasons—both pros and cons—have probably blended together to produce a highly complex pattern of motives. Many of these reasons may be misconceptions or "wrong" reasons for getting married, which would seem to doom the relationship from the start (see

BOX 7-2 / FILTERING MODEL OF MATE SELECTION

In our society, each successive filter screens out potential mates until the field is narrowed to a few from which the person chooses.

Proximity Filter—Potential Mates to Which Exposed

Similarity–Complementarity Filter

Personal-Attractiveness Filter

Compatibility Filter

Choice Filter

Married Couple

Box 7–1). However, there are couples who seem to marry for all the wrong reasons and still achieve happy marriages. Perhaps a happy marriage is not a destination but a mode of travel that requires continual effort and commitment. Although romantic love and companionship seem well suited to this mode of travel, there seem to be other ways of moving forward as well.

THE SEARCH FOR A MATE

How do people go about finding and identifying the "perfect" mate? Many factors are involved, including opportunities for interaction, similarity of background and interests, need complementarity, and various "market" costs and rewards. As shown in Box 7–2, mate selection is essentially a filtering process in which the field of "eligibles" is successively narrowed until a choice is made. Let us look more closely at some of the factors involved.

Where Do People Meet Their "Match"?

Traditionally, the principle of **propinquity,** or proximity, tended to operate in meeting and marrying. That is, people were most likely to marry the boy or girl next door, or at least someone in the same neighborhood or at the same school. In today's highly mobile society, this principle is more applicable to small communities than to large cities.

The impersonal isolation of modern life makes it particularly difficult for many people, especially in large cities, to meet eligible mates. While there seem to be "wall-to-wall" people in our society, how do you meet them and get acquainted? And how do you increase your chances of finding someone who is right for you?

Two pioneers in the field of mate selection—Walster and Walster (1978)—have suggested that you associate with a variety of eligible persons on a fairly regular basis. They consider it unfortunate that so many unmarried Americans subscribe to the myth that our true love will somehow happen along if we just sit and wait. People are often reluctant to admit that they are searching for a mate and they do not even know how to undertake such a search. But the Walsters conclude that if we are going to find eligible partners, it is necessary to get involved in social activities—a little theater group, a ski club, a crafts class—in which we are personally interested. In short, we should make a point of exposing ourselves to a wide range of interesting people rather than pinning all our hopes on one person, and we should maintain the exposure on a regular basis because people tend to respond more positively as they get to know each other. Most people end up with someone they see on a day-to-day basis, a factor referred to as **differential association.**

Sociologist Julia Erickson (1981), in a study to find out how married couples first met, questioned a representative sample of 1,800 people in Philadelphia. She found that a surprising 22 percent fell into the category she called "marital pickups." Very few of these pickups had occurred in singles bars or similar places designed for romantic encounters. Rather, all of the pickups had been unplanned and had happened in such diverse places as buses, restaurants, stores, and even elevators. Nevertheless, a much larger portion of the sampling—40 percent—had met their spouses in college or at work, while 13 percent had grown up with their future spouses—they had married "the boy or girl next door." Interestingly

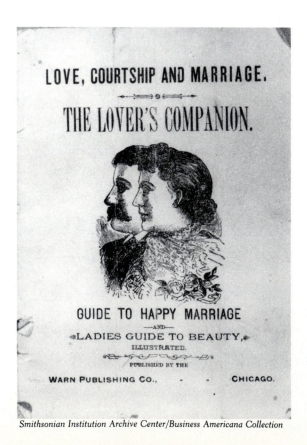

Smithsonian Institution Archive Center/Business Americana Collection

enough, couples who had met in college, at work, or in that magical chance encounter had approximately equal divorce rates—all high—whereas the 13 percent who married their childhood sweethearts showed the lowest divorce rate.

In Chapter 6, we noted that one recent innovation in meeting people and matchmaking is the use of videotapes as a go-between. Here it is possible to view the tapes of people who seem to fit the qualifications that you are looking for in a mate, and the ones that interest you are invited to view your tape. If one of them returns your interest, names and phone numbers are exchanged, and you take it from there. In addition, video-phones, which enable the persons talking to see each other, are coming into use. Such approaches enable people living in different parts of the country—or even in different countries—to interact and set up later face-to-face encounters. In short, new technology now provides us with the potential to make "global matchmaking" a reality, a far cry from "the boy- or girl-next-door" approach to mate selection.

People who have used computer-dating services, however, often feel that computer matchmaking is unable to capture the biochemical spark that seems to occur in more-spontaneous meetings. Thus, the old concept of proximity still operates in the sense that eventually two people have to meet, interact, and fall in love before marrying. But, in our contemporary world, the pool of eligibles is far bigger than it once was.

Similarity, Complementarity, and Compatibility

There are two old sayings about coupling: "Birds of a feather flock together" and "Opposites attract." While each of these sayings has elements of truth, both have been amplified by modern observations. In addition, both have been used in developing a third component in mate selection, called **compatibility** (Kelly & Conley, 1987).

It has been assumed that the most significant factor in mate selection is the **similarity** of the two people involved. In more-formal terms, this is referred to as the theory of **homogamy:** people are attracted to, become involved with, and marry those who are similar to them in age, race, religion, social class, and other characteristics. Common interests, beliefs, goals, and values are also conducive to the development of a close relationship that can, in turn, lead to marriage.

Because of greater social mobility in our society, as well as the lessening of parental influence and the changing of cultural norms, young people are finding greater freedom to marry across racial, ethnic, religious, and social-class lines, and such marriages are likely to become more frequent in the years ahead (Murstein, 1980; Labov & Jacobs, 1986). In general, however, differences in race, ethnic background, social class, and religion—as well as in such characteristics as sex-role expectations, interests, and values—add to the problems that the marital partners are likely to encounter. As Tavris and Jayaratne (1976) conclude in their survey analysis, "One lesson this survey shows is that like should marry like" (p. 92). Ultimately, of course, the outcome depends on the persons involved.

The sociological term for the idea that opposites attract is **complementarity**. This concept essentially refers to a couple's having complementary needs, needs that fit together. To put it more bluntly, each person makes up for the other's deficiencies. As Robert Winch (1971) expressed it, "Within the field of eligibles, persons whose need patterns provide mutual gratification will tend to choose each

Smithsonian Institution Archive Center/Business Americana Collection

other as marriage partners" (p. 507). Thus, a person with a strong need to dominate might choose a submissive partner.

Although a couple may differ in ways that tend to complement each other's weaknesses, they are not usually "opposite" in terms of personality characteristics such as interests, beliefs, and goals. Rather, complementarity refers to the meshing of the resources that each person brings to the marriage and, hence, to mutual need gratification. As we noted in Chapter 2, the best documented and most widespread example of "complementarity fit" would involve a beautiful young woman and a rich older man. However, today it could easily involve a handsome young man and a highly successful older career woman. Although complementarity is important in mate selection, similarity appears to be more important.

Now that we know the roles that proximity, similarity, and complementarity play in marital selection, can we use this information to predict whether two people will appeal to each other as marriage partners? Unfortunately, there is no way that we can predict the occurrence of that biochemical spark of physical attraction that usually paves the way to romantic love. Without this physical attraction, similarity and complementarity are likely to be irrelevant. Furthermore, we are unable to predict how two people will get along, or "fit," in terms of personality makeup. When two people seem to have everything going for them but somehow lack personality fit or compatibility, the situation is called **interactive disqualification**. Admittedly, Cupid's arrow does not strike at random, but we still cannot predict where and when it will strike. Romantic love and mate selection remain intriguing mysteries—as perhaps they should be.

"That's my Caroline. She's one of a kind."
Drawing by Charles Saxon; © 1987, *The New Yorker Magazine, Inc.*

The Shopping List: "Must" Items and "Luxuries"

Most people have rather definite ideas about what they are looking for in a mate, about what categories of persons are "eligible" or "ineligible." They exclude certain potential partners based on such **disqualifiers** as age, education, race, appearance, and social background. Such disqualifiers lead to the screening of dating partners and potential mates. Often they are referred to as **mate-selection filters.**

Of course, people may differ markedly in the characteristics they view as disqualifiers, as well as in the characteristics they are looking for in a mate. Zev Wanderer and Erika Fabian (1979) have suggested a way for us to formulate ideas about what we want in a mate by making up a "shopping list" of the characteristics we would like in an "ideal" mate. As they point out, "At first it may seem silly, knowing that no such perfect person exists, but don't worry. Keep on writing" (p. 29). This shopping list should contain items relating to

1. Personal appearance—such as height, hair, eye color, and so on.
2. Personality traits—such as intelligence, dependability, good sense of humor, and so on.
3. Economic potential or worth—such as career potential or attainment, future prospects.
4. Beliefs and values—such as attitudes toward sex-roles, religious beliefs, and the values that guide the individual's behavior.
5. Special interests and abilities—such as bridge playing, skiing, classical music, or whatever.
6. Your secret hopes and desires—such as for a fantastic lover.

When we have completed our shopping list, it's time to get down to earth by taking a new page and dividing it into two columns: must items and luxuries. The "must" items include those characteristics that we consider absolutely essential, on which we are unwilling to compromise. The remaining items on our original shopping list become the "luxuries," the characteristics we would like to have in a prospective mate but could do without.

As we mentally take this list when we go "shopping" for a partner, remember that, although it may be possible to change some of another person's characteristics to conform to our must list or even to our luxuries list, it is usually difficult, if not impossible—unless he or she understands the changes, considers them desirable, and is motivated to make them. In general, it is unwise to count on being able to change the characteristics of a potential mate who lacks some of our crucial must items. In fact, if we have found someone we really care about who doesn't quite meet our qualifications, perhaps we should re-evaluate our shopping list.

The Marriage Market

Although we usually prefer not to talk about it in our society, mate selection takes place in a "**marriage market.**" The merchandise consists of eligible males and females who can be "exchanged" for a given price. The currency used in the marriage market consists of the socially valued characteristics of the persons involved, such as age, physical appearance, and economic status. In our free-choice system of mate selection, we typically try to get as much in return for our social attributes as we can. To settle for less would be a "bad exchange."

Today wives are older than husbands in more than 20 percent of all marriages.

Jane Seskin

This market orientation to mate selection is much more apparent in societies in which marriage is arranged by the parents. Because the "merchandise" bears a price tag, the task of the parents is to find a suitable match among families of roughly equivalent social status. Of course, when a **dowry**—the money, goods, or property brought to the marriage by the bride—is involved, the parents may try to marry their daughter into a family of higher social status. Such an exchange of money or property for higher social status is considered a good deal by both families.

Similarly, in our own society it is usually considered appropriate for a younger woman to exchange her youth and beauty for the financial security and higher social status of an older man. However, it has been considered inappropriate for an older woman of high economic and social status to marry a much younger man. With increasing equality of the sexes, however, this pattern is gaining greater social acceptance.

Social exchanges are not guaranteed to be equitable. As we noted in Chapter 2, people in inequitable relationships usually feel uneasy. As a result, they try to convince themselves and others that the relationship really is equitable. If they fail in this attempt, they are likely to terminate the relationship. However, there are exceptions. Persons with low self-esteem, for example, tend to underestimate their market value and to "settle" for a mate, whereas people with high self-esteem tend to "choose" their mate. In addition, persons—especially males—who feel over-benefited are more likely to accept an inequitable relationship than persons who feel underbenefited.

Here it may be emphasized that we are dealing with the marriage market in terms of selecting a mate. The qualities that are important in casual dating may be quite different from those important in serious dating and pairing off (Berg & McQuinn, 1986). In addition, qualities that lead to pairing off and marriage—which Jeanne Whitehead (1981) refers to as "virtues"—may lose their appeal over time and become "vices" (Buss & Barnes, 1986). As a result, many people would not marry the same person if they had it to do over again. In fact, political scientist Ethel Klein (1986) found that only half of a large sample of wives would marry the same husband if they had it to do over again.

PAIRING OFF

To ensure the survival of marriage as an institution for the production, protection, and socialization of the young, each society makes provisions for young adult males and females to meet and pair off into permanent unions. Although the United States allows more personal freedom in choosing a mate than most other societies do, pairing off in this country is not a random matter. The courtship process usually guides mate selection in an orderly way, with a sequence that begins with casual dating and then moves to serious dating, engagement and/or cohabitation, and marriage.

Traditional Dating: Functions and Problems

Traditional dating—in which the male takes the initiative and plays the dominant role—has been a key part of the courtship process in the United States and has served a number of useful functions, ranging from recreation and companionship to learning social skills and selecting a mate. In recent years, however, traditional dating practices have undergone severe criticism and marked changes.

Smithsonian Institution Archive Center/Business Americana Collection

Smithsonian Institution Archive Center/Business Americana Collection

Functions of Traditional Dating.   During early adolescence, the emphasis in traditional dating is on recreation, companionship, and having fun, but with time, dating becomes more oriented toward learning, sex, and mate selection.

The following are among the main functions of dating for older adolescents:

1. Learning about members of the opposite sex and how to get along with them.
2. Improving communications and other social skills that enhance social attractiveness and intimate interactions.
3. Learning about ourselves and our market value and establishing standards for the later selection of a marriage partner.
4. Engaging in sexual exploration and gratification, if the partners so wish, and learning about our own sexuality.
5. Determining compatibility with different partners and eventually selecting a mate.

As we shall see, dating—whether traditional or contemporary—still performs these basic socialization functions in guiding young people toward marriage.

Criticisms of Traditional Dating.   Although traditional dating patterns do provide a framework for learning about members of the opposite sex and eventual mate selection, several major criticisms have been leveled against this approach to courtship. One major criticism is that traditional dating is a sexist bargaining arrangement in which the spending of money by the male is supposed to be rewarded with the acceptance of sex by the female. Because the male plays the dominant role in making the date and the female strives to please so that she will be invited out again, the dating situation is well suited for perpetuating the double standard and the exploitation of women (and of men as well, at least in financial terms).

A second major criticism of traditional dating is its superficiality and market orientation, in which each person puts up a good front to try to impress the other—at least on the first date—and to sell his or her assets in terms of physical appearance, desirable personality characteristics, and career prospects. In such an insincere setting, neither person has a chance to get to know the other as a real person.

Dating has also been criticized as being a deceitful game in which men are primarily concerned with obtaining sex while women are more concerned with commitment and finding a mate. This creates a game-playing situation in which the woman tries to sell her charms without revealing her true intent and the male tries to sell his assets for the purpose of sex, while avoiding getting "trapped" into marriage. In short, the dating partners are seen as having contradictory goals that lead each to behave in devious and insincere ways. Dating games may be played in terms of socially agreed-on "rules," but they are deadly serious and often destructive.

A fourth criticism of traditional dating is that it arouses anxiety; each partner tries hard to impress and exploit the other, all the while risking rejection. Even though the male is supposed to take the initiative and play the dominant role, the maneuvering and game playing of both partners tend to produce anxiety before, during, and after the date. For some, this anxiety involves a negative self-image. If the date goes badly, each automatically assumes he or she was at fault, not the partner. If turned down on a date, he or she takes the attitude of "No one ever wants to go out with me."

A number of related problems connected with the traditional dating script include the following:

1. *Difficulty in getting dates.*   Because the initiative in traditional dating is presumably up to the male and males tend to emphasize physical attractiveness in their choices of dates, it is often difficult for less-attractive women to get dates. However, the problem is by no means confined to women, for many men find that the most attractive females are already taken or that their invitations are rejected.

   A number of social scientists have argued that the problem of getting dates among many teenagers and young adults is due to lack of social skills, resulting in conditioned heterosexual social anxiety, a negative self-image, and the expectation of negative consequences from dating experiences (Curran, 1977). After a review of research studies of social-skills training approaches, Curran concluded that they were indeed effective in helping trainees get dates. However, in a more-recent study Lois Timmick (1982) suggested that such training may lead either to increased confidence in social interactions and a greater likelihood of "connecting" or to a race of robots flashing superficial smiles and saying all the "right" things.

2. *Aversive dating experiences.*   Even for those getting dates, dating experiences may not turn out to be pleasant. In an early study of "dates that failed," Albrecht (1972) found that a number of behaviors contributed to

the failure, including one partner being neglected or not introduced to others, one partner being unable to dance or otherwise engage in social activities, and a partner drinking too much. Other common offenses that make for uncomfortable dates are talking too much about ourselves, inability to carry on an intelligent conversation, and offensive eating habits or similar behaviors. For example, one woman complained that her date "spent the entire evening talking about himself and ended up thinking he knew all about me."

Unfortunately, it is unlikely that the person who is offended will tell his or her date about the offending behavior. Instead, he or she will simply avoid this person in the future. Without such feedback, the offender is likely to repeat the negative behavior, continue to have unsuccessful dating experiences, and suffer further rejection.

3. *Violence.*   One form of aversive dating experience that deserves special mention is interpersonal violence. In our review of singlehood and dating in Chapter 6, we noted that date rape as well as other forms of violence are relatively common. We need not review the research here, but it is useful to note that Bonnie Carlson (1987) has summarized the available findings on dating violence among high-school and college students. She found that the overall violence rates varied from 12–36 percent and that women were the initiators about as often as men. In a study of 6,000 women on 32 campuses, Mary Moss (1987) specifically focused on date rape. She found that one in eight female students was the victim of actual or attempted date rape, but 90 percent of these students never reported the incident.

Thus, as Carlson concluded, it would appear "that for some young people violence in intimate relationships is becoming an established pattern of behavior that is likely to repeat itself later in more permanent relationships" (p. 22).

"Getting Together" and Casual Dating

In recent years, traditional dating patterns in our society have undergone marked changes designed to counteract their sexist, hypocritical, and anxiety-producing nature. Bernard Murstein (1980) has summarized it this way:

> There is little doubt that the traditional "date" in which the male picked up the female at her home at an arranged time, wined and dined her at his expense, and returned her to her residence at an arranged time is disappearing. In high schools and colleges, according to informal reports by students, they tend to congregate in groups from which the majority gradually evolve into pairs, although retaining some allegiance to the group. There is less structure as to appropriate male-female behavior, expenses are often "dutch treat," and highly structured dating protocol has largely disappeared. (p. 780)

In short, the more-informal practices of getting together and casual dating have replaced the more-formal pattern of traditional dating for many young people. **Getting together** may involve joining informally with a group to listen to music, play volleyball, rollerskate, have a party, or whatever. Such groups tend to develop spontaneously, and the male is no longer responsible for planning the dating activity or picking up the tab. The emphasis is on meeting people in an informal setting and getting to know them as persons. If a specific couple find that they are attracted to each other, they may pair off.

Casual dating typically involves informally arranged meetings, such as getting together during a coffee break or for lunch. Such dates do not involve the commitment of more than a small amount of time, and neither party feels rejected if the other loses interest. In more-formal dating patterns, the female may feel hurt and rejected if the male does not ask her out again, and the male may feel rejected if he cannot arrange for a second date. Casual dating basically serves as a screening device for people who are attracted to each other but wish to get better acquainted before deciding whether to continue or terminate the encounter, as we saw in Chapter 2.

From Casual to Serious Dating

Braiker and Kelley (1979) have found that the transition from casual to **serious dating** is accompanied by a number of important changes:

> The relationship during serious dating is characterized by increasing reports of love feelings, the sense of belonging with the partner, and public recognition of the pair as constituting a definite unit. Moreover, the transition to serious dating is marked by an increase in conflict and negativity between partners. In this stage, couples also recognize the seriousness or depth of their feelings toward each other, are sexually intimate, discuss the possibility of marriage, and begin to plan their future together. The attraction to the partner now derives from need satisfactions as well as from the attractions of the previous stage. (pp. 148–149)

During serious dating, the partners become increasingly interdependent and the emerging exclusivity—with respect to what activities, including sex, will be shared with the partner only—tends to become a source of conflict. During this stage, jealousy sharply increases and tends to be resolved as conflicts concerning exclusivity become resolved. Conflicts also arise over differences in goals, values, and personality characteristics. This is also a period when each partner tends to make attributions about the self, such as "I'm in love," "I care about things that happen to my partner," "Our relationship is special," "My partner is someone I'd like to spend the rest of my life with," and "We can face the world together."

Braiker and Kelley have found several different styles of courtship among the couples they studied. For example, one couple might follow the typical progression from encounter to casual dating to serious dating, while another might go directly to serious dating after their first encounter. Some moved from one step to another with little or no conflict, while others reached transitional decision-making points where considerable conflict occurred before they proceeded with the relationship. Braiker and Kelley have suggested that conflict is a common accompaniment to feelings of love in close relationships, especially as the partners become increasingly knowledgeable about each other and as incompatibilities surface. Such conflicts, or "lovers' quarrels," function to force either a compromise and resolution of the conflict or a termination of the relationship. Thus, lovers' quarrels need not be destructive but may actually help the couple work out misunderstandings, disagreements, and differences. However, open and serious conflicts during the stage of serious dating do not augur well for the relationship.

Assuming that a relationship survives and leads to increasing interdependence, closeness, and commitment during the serious-dating stage, the next step usually involves engagement, cohabitation, or perhaps both. Of course, the couple may elope and short-circuit the usual courtship progression, but this is not typical and occurs most commonly among couples who have each been married before.

Engagement and/or Cohabitation

Traditionally, **engagement** represents the final stage in a couple's movement toward marriage. Essentially, it is a ritual symbolizing exclusive commitment to our partner in terms of a public announcement of our intent to marry. Interest-

Smithsonian Institution Archive Center/Business Americana Collection

ingly enough, Braiker and Kelley (1979) have found the transition from serious dating to engagement to be less pronounced than that from casual to serious dating.

As the final step before marriage, engagement serves a number of functions that may overlap with, but are somewhat different from, those in the serious-dating stage. Among its many functions, engagement

1. Provides a time to agree on and work out fundamental living arrangements. Where and how will the couple live? Will both work? How do they plan to spend their income?
2. Provides a time to re-examine and agree on both short-term and long-term goals and the methods they plan to use for achieving these goals.
3. Provides a time to get better acquainted with each other's families and to agree on how they will relate to in-laws and to each other's friends.
4. Provides a time to make a final check of each other in terms of common interests, values, goals, comfort in each other's company, and compatibility in general. As Box 7–6 indicates, premarital counseling may be helpful in pointing out potential problems.
5. Provides a time for working out final details of the wedding plans. Will they have a church wedding? Will the wedding be formal or informal? Who will be invited? Who will give the bride away? Who will serve as best man? What about rehearsals? What sort of honeymoon, if any, will they have?

While the engagement period is often thought of as a happy one in which each partner looks forward to the coming marriage, Braiker and Kelley have found that the "feelings reported to occur during engagement span the range from love, belonging, extreme happiness, and excitement to ambivalence, conflict, negativity, and anxiety, therefore suggesting that this stage of courtship may be a rather turbulent and traumatic period" (p. 149). Not only do the partners experience conflict in themselves and between each other, but they may encounter conflict with each other's families, who may disapprove of the marriage. On the other hand, as Thomas Kando (1978) has pointed out, engagement is "an expression of love, commitment, and joyful anticipation of marriage. It may be very meaningful not only to the engaged couple, but also to their parents, friends, and relatives, who are brought into contact with each other" (p. 141).

However, an increasing number of young people believe that cohabitation provides a better test of compatibility than engagement (Kotkin, 1985). But, as we noted in Chapter 6, available research findings fail to support this view. There is no evidence that those who cohabit prior to marriage have happier and more-durable marriages than those who have followed the more-conventional sequence from dating through engagement to marriage. Of course, happily married couples who cohabited prior to marriage may attribute their success to cohabitation. But this is an "after the fact" assessment that may or may not be accurate.

Although engagement today does tend to be more informal than in the past—possibly because many of the functions formerly reserved for the engagement period are now carried out during the stage of serious dating—it does involve a sense of mutual commitment that is lacking in cohabitation. When one of the cohabitors tires of the arrangement, he or she simply moves on (even though it is

Motusow/Monkmeyer Press Photo Service

often as hurtful to the other party as a broken engagement). If we were to criticize traditional engagement, it might be on the grounds of too much commitment and too little experience to ensure the couple are really compatible and ready for marriage. On the other hand, if we were to criticize cohabitation, it could well be on the ground that it leads to too much experience of a rather superficial type and too little commitment.

One special type of engagement is the long separated engagement, such as occurs when one partner is in the military service. These engagements may serve the function of maintaining commitment when the couple cannot be together. It also tests the relationship in terms of whether "absence makes the heart grow fonder" or "out of sight, out of mind." In addition, where uncertainty arises during the engagement period, it may be prolonged until the couple are in a better position to decide whether to get married or to terminate the engagement and possibly the relationship.

GETTING MARRIED

Americans are marrying in record numbers. There was an all-time high of almost 2.5 million marriages each year from 1980–1984. The number of marriages dropped slightly in 1985, but still reached a respectable 2,425,000 (National Center of Health Statistics, 1986). Apparently, the decrease in marriages resulted from more people marrying at a later age. The median age for first marriage was about 23.1 for women and 25.5 for men. Thus, each year more than 2 million married couples are added to the 50 million or more in the United States, while more than one million are subtracted by divorce. Of the marriages in 1985, almost 45 percent were remarriages in which one or both partners had been previously married and divorced. Thus, Americans appear to believe in marriage, even

BOX 7-3 / TWELVE QUESTIONS TO ASK BEFORE YOU MARRY

Some experts believe that only a minority of marriages (about 25 percent) function satisfactorily. The remainder continue as unhappy marriages or terminate in divorce. The questions that follow were developed during years of working with troubled marriages. Most of the difficulties that arose appeared to be derived from a few critical but avoidable trouble spots. These questions are designed to focus your attention on these critical areas:

1. Can I accept and live with his or her faults and shortcomings? (This question is based on the fact that too many people think they will be able to change their spouses after marriage.)

2. Can I visualize and accept his or her performance in the various roles called for during marriage—for example, mate, mother or father, companion, friend, provider, lover, and so on?

3. Am I willing to commit myself to the relationship and make sacrifices—if called for—in order to meet his or her needs?

4. Do I feel that my partner truly accepts me, is interested in meeting my needs, and can be relied on for emotional support in times of crisis?

5. Is there a mutual feeling of deep and enduring friendship?

6. Is he or she physically and sexually attractive to me?

7. Do we share similar interests and compatible goals?

8. Do I like who I am or the way I feel when I am with him or her?

9. Have we worked through emotional hurts and "hangovers" from past relationships?

10. Do we share common values and feel that the relationship is an equitable and egalitarian one?

11. Do I have a realistic view of myself, my proposed spouse, and the relationship I hope to achieve?

12. Have we compared goals and expectations for the marriage and resolved differences to our mutual satisfaction?

Negative answers to such questions do not necessarily doom your marriage, although they may give you cause to stop and think about the potential trouble spots that may arise. What you do about these potential sources of trouble will likely be important in determining the quality of your marriage, assuming your decision is to get married.

though they may lose faith in the desirability of specific marriages. Unlike the transition from serious dating to engagement, the transition from engagement and/or cohabitation to marriage is a major one. It represents a crucial commitment and a major change in legal and social status (see Box 7–3).

The Wedding

The processes of mate selection and courtship are largely private matters between the persons involved. But the **wedding** is a public act involving a legal-contractual agreement that marks a rite of passage from singlehood to the new social status of marriage. After the wedding, the individuals can never again return to the status of "single, never married."

Requirements.   In the interests of social stability and child-rearing, the state sets certain minimal requirements for the wedding. In our society, this involves:

1. A marriage license, which in most states requires blood tests to rule out the possibility that either partner has a sexually transmitted disease.
2. A wedding ceremony performed by a person legally permitted to do so, with each person signifying his or her consent to the marriage.
3. Two witnesses of legal age to verify the event.
4. Signatures on the license of the couple, the witnesses, and the official presiding at the ceremony.
5. Sending the completed license to the state capital for recording and filing.

There are, of course, prior restrictions on marriage. For example, marriages between close blood relatives are forbidden, as are marriages involving females or males who are underage (in most states men may marry at 18 and women at 16).

→✳B. A. MINK ✳←

715 S. HALSTED STREET,
CHICAGO

Smithsonian Institution Archive Center/Business Americana Collection

Tina Paul/Archive Pictures, Inc.

Many states also prohibit marriage of persons who are mentally retarded or who have been judged legally insane. Most states also require a waiting period of several days between issuance of the license and the actual wedding. Finally, a marriage in one state is legal in all other states.

The Ceremony.   Seven out of ten couples getting married for the first time choose a religious wedding—they are married in a church, synagogue, or temple. Such weddings are heavily infused with pageantry and ritual. Even weddings performed in the bride's home or other settings usually retain many of the traditional observances.

As Barbara Jo Chesser (1980) has pointed out, analyzing wedding rituals helps us to understand their meaning, both historically and sociologically. For example, "giving the bride away" by the father presumably goes back to a time when women were transferable property, although it has now come to signify parental approval of the wedding. Analyzing wedding rituals enables a young couple to select those that have special significance for their own ceremony. In addition, as the great French sociologist Emile Durkheim noted, traditions and rituals are the stuff that bind generations, people, and society together. Rituals tend to provide consistency between past and present as well as greater meaning and a sense of stability. Thus many social scientists consider today's young people as both healthily old-fashioned and realistically modern.

Of course, traditions and rituals do not come cheap, at least not in marriage. The average cost of a wedding in 1985 was $6,350, and even a $50,000 wedding was not considered to be an expensive one (Reed, 1986). A breakdown of wedding costs—based on the $6,350 average—is shown in Fig. 7–1. It is not unusual for couples to choose wedding ceremonies that are not traditional. They may write their own vows and involve friends and family in the ceremony. Some couples may modify the traditional wedding vows suggested in the *Book of Common Prayer* to reflect a more-egalitarian approach to the marriage. Nontraditional

Finally, we can't overlook the practical value of a wedding ring. It tells others something about our relationship potential. . . . The wedding ring has something to say to the wearer and the rest of the world.

Ralph Ranieri

Figure 7–1. Cost of the Average Wedding in 1986. (Source: Reed, Julia. "Wedding Bells—and Bills— Are Ringing." U.S. News & World Report, June 16, 1986 pp. 44–45.)

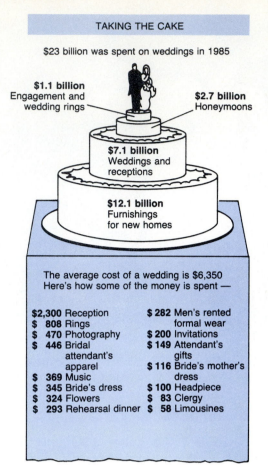

TAKING THE CAKE

$23 billion was spent on weddings in 1985

$1.1 billion
Engagement and
wedding rings

$2.7 billion
Honeymoons

$7.1 billion
Weddings and
receptions

$12.1 billion
Furnishings
for new homes

The average cost of a wedding is $6,350
Here's how some of the money is spent —

$2,300	Reception	**$ 282**	Men's rented formal wear
$ 808	Rings	**$ 200**	Invitations
$ 470	Photography	**$ 149**	Attendant's gifts
$ 446	Bridal attendant's apparel	**$ 116**	Bride's mother's dress
$ 369	Music	**$ 100**	Headpiece
$ 345	Bride's dress	**$ 83**	Clergy
$ 324	Flowers	**$ 58**	Limousines
$ 293	Rehearsal dinner		

weddings, such as simple civil ceremonies before a justice of the peace, seem to be more common among people who have been married before, but they also appeal to a sizable segment of young people embarking on their first marriage. It is interesting to note that an increasing number career-oriented women who marry choose not to wear their wedding rings. For example, Mary Rourke (1986) cites the case of a young woman who took off her wedding ring 4 hours after the ceremony and wears it only—if at all—when she is at home alone with her husband. Her reason? " 'Marriage is very personal, and it's not the first thing I want people to know about me' " (p. 1).

However, the prevailing trend in the 1980s seems to be toward more-traditional weddings for the previously unmarried and married alike.

The Honeymoon

Honeymoons as well as traditional marriages seem to be making a comeback— about 85 percent of all couples who marry plan and take honeymoons. In general, the **honeymoon** is considered a transition period that serves a number of useful functions. The period of privacy for the married couple helps them to make the adjustment from being separate individuals to being a couple who spend "their"

Smithsonian Institution Archive Center/Business Americana Collection

money, dress and undress in each other's presence, and share a common bedroom and bathroom. If they have had sex prior to marriage, the honeymoon provides a period for achieving sexual harmony. If they have not had previous intercourse, it provides a period for making the needed adjustment to marital sex. Because the traditional wedding is usually a rather hectic and tiring event, the "time out" of the honeymoon provides for needed recuperation. Finally, the honeymoon enables the couple to get better acquainted under favorable circumstances. Soon enough the mundane problems of everyday life will be imposing themselves on the marriage, leading to disagreements and other problems. In a sense, the honeymoon helps to build a reservoir of pleasant memories that will help to smooth the inevitable transition to the realities of marriage in day-to-day living.

Is the honeymoon a good idea? Is it worth the expense and time? Those questions can best be answered by individual couples. Nevertheless, the honeymoon is an event they will remember all their lives, and while they may take subsequent trips together, there is really only one honeymoon.

People do not marry people, not real ones anyway: they marry illusions and images . . . The exciting adventure of marriage is finding out who the partner really is.
James Framo

Marriage Contracts

Marriage is a legal contract that is entered into by three parties: the husband, the wife, and the state. As J. Gipson Wells (1976) has pointed out, the state attempts to regulate only the most basic aspects of the marital relationship:

> Its major concerns are first, that only capable persons be allowed to marry; thus, the laws on minimum age and mental competence. Second, it is concerned with basic human rights, so that family members are protected from cruelty and neglect. And

BOX 7-4 / PERSONAL MARRIAGE CONTRACTS

A personal marriage contract is an agreement negotiated by the couple prior to marriage. It is designed to spell out more clearly their mutual expectations, rights, and obligations. The topics covered in the contract may vary considerably, reflecting the particular concerns a couple bring to their marriage. Among the items the contract may deal with are sex-role expectations, sharing of financial resources, division of household tasks, responsibility in decision making, career commitments, religious beliefs and practices, exclusivity in sex and other activities, and possible contingencies that may arise (divorce, division of property, alimony, and child custody and support).

The contract is written in formal style, often with the assistance of an attorney, and signed by both parties. Of course, the laws of the state governing marriage take precedence over personal marriage contracts. Thus, even if a couple agree in their contract that in the event of divorce neither will pay alimony, the court may determine that alimony should be provided.

The intent of personal marriage contracts is to develop a clear and comfortable agreement that helps the couple understand the "fine print" of their relationship and that helps resolve certain issues *before* marriage that might have arisen after. To accommodate unforeseen problems and to provide flexibility, many contracts include a clause setting up periodic review and renegotiation of the agreement.

Some investigators suggest that such a contract reflects a pessimistic view of our proposed mate that may doom the marriage from the start. However, many others see marriage contracts as a way of placing the marriage on a solid footing from the start by getting the couple to address issues that they may otherwise avoid. Whether or not a couple choose to draw up a personal marriage contract, a discussion of the topics usually covered by such a contract can help both partners to understand better their impending marital relationship and to deal with conflicts that arise at this point rather than later in their marriage.

If their marriage does end in divorce, such a contract can save both partners a great deal of misunderstanding and grief, both emotional and financial.

third, it is concerned with the welfare of family members should the marriage break up; thus the existence of laws dealing with alimony and child support. (p. 35)

Within these basic guidelines, plus some specific details such as a marriage license, the legal contract imposed by the state on those wishing to marry is a highly flexible agreement that leaves considerable room for the couple to work out the details of their marriage.

In addition to the legal contract, couples may also negotiate a **personal marriage contract** prior to their wedding. The nature and functions of personal marital contracts are summarized in Boxes 7-4 and 7-5. It may be emphasized, however, that such contracts are designed to deal with various expectations and concerns that a couple may bring to their marriage—such as differences with respect to sex-roles, sharing financial resources, and exclusivity in sex. In addition, personal contracts usually deal with various problems that may arise in the event of divorce, such as division of property and child custody.

A major advantage of personal marriage contracts is that they force the couple to face issues that may arise in their marriage and to consider how to deal with

BOX 7–5   /   A MARRIAGE CONTRACT: 1855

The concept of marriage contracts is by no means a new one. In 1855, Lucy Stone and Henry B. Blackwell made the following formal commitment as a protest against conditions that still prevail in many states:

While acknowledging our mutual affection by publicly assuming the relationship of husband and wife, yet in justice to ourselves and a great principle, we deem it a duty to declare that this act on our part implies no sanction of, nor promise of voluntary obedience to such of the present laws on marriage as refuse to recognize the wife as an independent, rational being, while they confer upon the husband an injurious and unnatural superiority, investing him with legal powers which no honorable man would exercise, and which no man should possess. We protest, especially against the laws which give to the husband:

1. the custody of the wife's person;
2. the exclusive control and guardianship of their children;
3. the sole ownership of her personal property, and use of her real estate, unless previously settled upon her, or placed in the hands of trustees, as in the case of minors, lunatics, and idiots;

4. the absolute right to the product of her industry;
5. also against laws which give to the widower so much larger and more permanent an interest in the property of his deceased wife, than give to the widow in that of the deceased husband;
6. finally, against the whole system by which "the legal existence of the wife is suspended during the marriage," so that in most States, she neither has a legal part in the choice of her residence, nor can she make a will, nor sue or be sued in her own name, nor inherit property.

We believe that personal independence and equal human rights can never be forfeited, except for crime; that marriage should be an equal and permanent partnership, and so recognized by law; that until it is so recognized, married partners should provide against the radical injustice of present laws, by every means in their power. . . .

Most men and women in our society today —almost a century and a half later—would probably support the views expressed in this early marriage contract.

them, rather than to rely on the smug assumption that "Love will conquer all." A second major advantage is that such contracts reduce the likelihood of later accusations to the effect that "Before we were married, you led me to believe that. . . ." On the other hand, as Sharon Brehm (1985) has noted, if the couple are continually evaluating their relationship in contractual terms—for example, is the partner doing his or her share of housework, and so on—they may focus so hard on what's wrong that they forget to keep track of what's right in the relationship. In essence, trust and commitment can be jeopardized by legalism.

Marriage as a Commitment and a Transition

Marriage represents one of the most important commitments a person will ever make. The happiness of both partners will depend on the outcome of this commitment as well as on their readiness for, and ability to cope with, their new status.

Commitment to Whom?   In the marriage ceremony, the individual states his or her intent to maintain the marriage relationship with such words as "I will" and "I do." This publicly stated intent becomes a personal commitment to our marital partner, our family and our partner's family, society (or, more specifically, the state), and, if the ceremony is a religious one, God. Lest the commitment seem coercive, the wedding ceremony usually makes provision for a last chance to scrutinize the relationship before making the final commitment. This provision is contained in such phrases of the traditional ceremony as "Will you take this woman . . . ?" Although it would certainly be unconventional to say no at this point, the option is open to each partner.

Commitment to What?   In taking marital vows to what are we committing ourselves? In essence, the commitment is to the continuation or permanence of the marriage, usually to sexual exclusivity in the marriage, and to meeting certain needs of our partners. We, of course, expect to have our needs met in return. These needs include the following:

1. *Psychological needs*—the need for caring, affection, love, emotional support, security and stability, and romantic fulfillment as well as companionship and friendship; the need for a secure "home base."
2. *Sexual needs*—the need for emotional closeness and sexual gratification within a socially sanctioned setting.
3. *Material needs*—the need for economic necessities essential to survival and to live with some semblance of comfort and dignity.

Failure to meet any of these needs—in the form of lack of support, denial of sex, incompatibility, or mental cruelty—is grounds for divorce in most states.

Transition to New Social Status.   Aside from background differences, each couple must deal with a new social status as well as with meeting minimal standards of satisfaction as set both by the state and by the partners themselves. While the honeymoon may serve as a temporary shock absorber, the realities of being married—both positive and negative—soon strike home. Friends suddenly treat the couple differently. Social activities become geared to get-togethers with other married couples. Old activities and behaviors must give way to new because of adjustments not only to living with another person but also to filling roles

All people who marry enter into a very definite contract of needs and expectations. Whether they put it down on paper or not, they should realize that such a contract exists.

U.S. News & World Report

ELOPEMENT.—Whereas my wife Betsey has left my bed and board without any just cause or provocation, all persons are forbid harboring or trusting her on my account, as I shall pay no debts of her contracting after this date.
                                                JOHN GOVE.
Sempronius, August 25th, 1828.   30p

Smithsonian Institution Archive Center/Business Americana Collection

established by society. Social scientists have, in fact, delineated specific stages that couples go through in adjusting to marriage and have identified various types of marital patterns. We shall deal with these stages and types in Chapter 8. But, first, let us conclude this chapter by considering some of the enduring questions that are directly relevant to mate selection and marriage.

SOME ENDURING QUESTIONS AND ISSUES

There are a great many questions that remain unanswered and issues that remained unsolved in the area of mate selection and marriage. Here we shall deal with four that seem particularly pertinent: Is there a "one and only" mate for whom we are destined? Can marital success be predicted? How effective is premarital counseling? Is marriage for a lifetime obsolete?

Is There a "One and Only"?

Often when people have difficulties in their marriage and are unhappy, they feel they have picked the wrong person. If only they had picked "Mr. Right" or "Ms. Right," everything would have worked out with a fairy-tale ending. But the belief that there is only one person in the world who is just right for you is a myth. As psychologists Zev Wanderer and Erika Fabian state in their book *Making Love Work* (1979):

> Sure you will never love another person the same way as your present Beloved, simply because every person is different and you love each one for different reasons and in different ways. But you can definitely find more than one person to love. If this weren't so, why would people divorce? Why would they remarry? So take heart and be as objective as you can, *before* going into that long-term commitment. (p. 44)

The fact that there is no "one and only" in no way mitigates against careful screening of prospective spouses. Rather, it means that if one person doesn't measure up, assuming that our standards are realistic in terms of our own assets, there are many other persons who will. Robert Ringer, in his popular best-seller *Looking Out for Number One* (1977), underscores this idea:

> While it's true that you only need to find one person, that doesn't mean there's only one person available. There's no such thing as looking for the right man or woman. Anyone old enough to have graduated from the Diaper Corps knows all about the number of fish in the sea. Since no two are exactly alike, you're absolutely right if you think you'll never find another love like the last one. You won't, but what you will find is a different love, one which can bring you happiness in many new ways. The old and the new can't be compared, so don't try. . . . The plain truth is that there are many people with whom you can fall genuinely in love. (p. 287)

But when you are lonely and seem never to meet any eligible persons, it can be frustrating and discouraging. This point has been well illustrated by the findings of psychologists Connell Cowan and Melvyn Kinder (1985) in their book *Smart*

Women/Foolish Choices. These therapists reported the comments of some of their women patients to the effect that "In a room full of nice men, if there's one **rat,** I'll find him" and "The men I meet are either crazy, married, gay, or plain boring." The present author can cite similar examples from never-married and divorced singles—both men and women—as well as from unhappily married people doing a little "comparison shopping." Of course, such discouragement can lead to bad compromises and decisions.

However, if you know for what you are looking, if your demands are realistic, and if you make a systematic search, the results are likely to be favorable. In this world of over four billion people, there are undoubtedly many members of the opposite sex with whom you could fall in love and be happy. The trick is to continue the search until you meet someone who not only fills the bill but also responds favorably to you in return.

Can Marital Success Be Predicted?

It was Shakespeare who wrote, "The course of true love never did run smooth." Certainly the course of an intimate relationship as intense as marriage is rarely a smooth one. Yet, some people manage to surmount the difficulties and build stable and happy marriages, while others get involved in conflict-ridden and unhappy relationships that usually terminate. How can we account for the difference? We can't. Even the most careful consideration of the compatibility of proposed mates will not ensure that the marriage will be a happy one in 5 or 10 years. Although we can't as yet predict marital outcomes, there are a number of factors that correlate with marital adjustment, or at least with lower divorce rates. Here we shall briefly mention some of the more important ones.

. . . when two people are under the influence of the most violent, most insane, most delusive, and most transient of passions, they are required to swear that they will remain in that excited, abnormal, and exhausting condition continuously until death do them part.
Bernard Shaw

1. *Having happily married parents and being a happy person.* A number of investigators have found that happy as well as unhappy marriages tend to run in the family (Greenberg & Nay, 1982). People whose parents were happily married are more likely to achieve happy marriages than those whose parents were unhappily married or divorced. Apparently, children acquire warm, loving interpersonal styles through experiencing and observing the behavior of their parents. Similarly, happy people tend to make happy marital partners and happy marriages. Why? Perhaps because they are easier to live with. Perhaps they tend to emphasize the positive, even in a difficult marriage. In any event, coming from a happy home and being a happy person are significantly correlated with happiness in one's own marriage.

2. *Long courtship and late marriage.* There is an old saying, "Marry in haste and repent at leisure." Persons in short courtships are not really likely to know each other. As a result, each person may believe he or she has found the ideal mate, only to find that both the mate and the relationship are flawed. Persons who marry in their teens have about twice the divorce rate of those who marry later—at least age 19 for women and 22 for men (Spanier & Glick, 1981). Why? For one thing, teenage marriages are more likely to be between persons of lower educational and socioeconomic status and to be precipitated by pregnancy.

Ulrike Welsch

Thus, the individuals are ill-prepared for the financial responsibilities of marriage and yet are often faced immediately with the challenges of child-rearing—all of which add stress to the relationship.

3. *Personal maturity, adjustment, and competence.*   Personal maturity and adjustment appear to play important roles in fostering realistic expectations, tolerance of stress, and marital commitment. Conversely, there are many personality traits, such as irresponsibility and deceit, that are likely to lead to marital difficulties. Those who bring their "brokenness"—as Mandelbaum (1979) has referred to the damage inflicted by prior relationships—to a marriage may have difficulty relating effectively to a spouse and others. Individuals who are competent—who are skillful in communication, problem solving, and decision making—are much more likely to have happy marriages than individuals who lack competence.

4. *Religious affiliation and education.*   Most organized religions have discouraged divorce, and divorce rates are considerably lower for Catholics, Jews, and such Protestant groups as the Mormons. Even interfaith marriages, which are on the increase—today more than 50 percent of all Catholic marriages are interfaith (Levad, 1982)—do not appear to be associated with a higher divorce rate. The probability of divorce is also lower for men and women who have completed college than for those

who have completed only high school or have dropped out of school. However, we do not really know what role education plays in contributing to marital success.

5. *Age differences.*   Traditionally in America, age differences in marriage, roughly 5–10 years or more, involved an older husband and younger wife (Atkinson & Glass, 1985). Marriages involving an older woman and younger man were socially disapproved and considered taboo. Conventional wisdom had it that marriage across generations was almost certain to lead to unhappiness. Recent studies, however—such as that of Vera and others (1985)—have reported no significant differences in marital quality between groups of age-similar and age-dissimilar couples. In addition, an increasing number of women are marrying younger husbands (LeShan, 1986). Thus, love and marriage between generations, which has long been looked down on, are being re-examined and old taboos are giving way.

In addition to these factors, such correlates of marital adjustment as similarity and complementarity appear to be critical because their absence greatly reduces the probability of achieving a happy and enduring marriage. However, some marriages defy the odds and appear happy and stable despite a variety of negative factors. Perhaps these couples expect less of marriage and work harder at it. In general, however, a combination of factors—including environmental conditions and change—work together to determine the progress and outcome of marriage. But, as yet, we cannot predict what this outcome will be.

How Effective Is Premarital Counseling?

In theory, **premarital counseling** should be helpful in contributing to marital success by

1. Correcting unrealistic expectations and assumptions.
2. Helping couples improve their communication and conflict-resolving skills.
3. Pinpointing differences in goals, values, and other potential sources of disagreement and conflict.
4. Resolving problems that are causing sexual dissatisfaction in their present relationship.
5. Improving the overall quality of the premarital relationship with the hope that it will positively influence their marital relationship.

So far, however, results have been controversial and less impressive than most professional personnel had anticipated. David Mace (1985) has criticized premarital counseling on the basis of what he has called the "before-and-after" principle. By this he means that we try to teach a young couple everything they need to know about marriage and then drop out of the picture. As a consequence, the couple receives no assistance during the first crucial year of marriage, when difficult problems are likely to arise. Until premarital counseling programs follow

BOX 7–6 / PREMARITAL COUNSELING

We have noted the objectives of premarital counseling and the concerns expressed concerning its effectiveness, particularly without follow-up counseling during the first year of marriage. Here we shall briefly mention three systematic programs that have been developed and used in premarital counseling.

1. *Couples Communication Program (CCP).* Based on the assumptions that communication skills are essential in preventing later marital problems, this program focuses on four major aspects of the communication process:
   (a) Achieving better communication by clarifying the sender–receiver sequence.
   (b) Fostering awareness and expression of thoughts, feelings, and motives.
   (c) Promoting awareness of different kinds of communication—for example, verbal and nonverbal—and the impacts of each.
   (d) Training in the use of communication to enhance our own and our partners self-esteem.
2. *Premarital Relationship Improvement by Maximizing Empathy and Self-Disclosure (PRIMES).* This program also focuses on better communication by the following means.
   (a) Training in the expressive mode of communication with emphasis on feelings. For example, "You make me feel . . ."

   (b) Fostering empathic responding—for example, putting yourself in our partner's shoes, trying to feel the way he or she does.
   (c) Training in when and how to switch from the expressor to the responding mode—for example, from expressing our own feelings to responding to our partner's feelings.
   (d) Promoting better communication with other people.
3. *Premarital Relationship Enhancement Program (PREP).* This approach attempts to apply the principles of behavioral marital therapy to premarital relationships. In addition to stressing communication skills, PREP also focuses on some essential features of the behavioral approach.
   (a) Learning to monitor our own and our partner's behavior.
   (b) Ascertaining what behaviors please or displease our partner and emphasizing the positive.
   (c) Learning to negotiate changes in behavior.

The preceding programs take an educational approach to premarital counseling and utilize a trainer or cotrainers working with a group of couples. A variety of techniques, including role-playing, are utilized in the learning process. All three programs are highly structured; intensive; and time limited, for example, 6–8 weeks.

through during the first year of marriage, Mace does not anticipate very successful results. However, three programs which have reported positive results are summarized in Box 7–6. In addition, the problems couples deal with in premarital relationships may be quite different in type and severity from those they will have to deal with in marriage. Thus, it would appear that periodic "marital checkups"

Alan Carey/The Image Works

during the first critical year of marriage would help to ensure the effectiveness of premarital programs and reduce our staggering divorce rate.

Is Marriage for a Lifetime Obsolete?

"Till death us do part" has been an indisputable element of marriage vows in our society. The Western marriage has traditionally included the assumption of permanence, consistent with emphasis on marriage as providing security for the couple and their children and contributing to the stability of society as a whole. In recent years, however, our marital values have undergone a major change. Couples believe in permanence as long as they meet each other's needs and their marriage is a happy one.

Admittedly, our American ideal of a happy and enduring marriage is difficult to achieve. Alvin Toffler (1970) commented emphatically on this problem some two decades ago:

> Even in a relatively stagnant society, the mathematical odds are heavily stacked against a couple achieving . . . the ideal of parallel growth. The odds for success positively plummet, however, when the rate of change in society is accelerated, as it

is now doing. In a fast-moving society, in which many things change, not once, but repeatedly, in which the husband moves up and down a variety of economic and social scales, in which the family is again and again torn loose from home and community, in which individuals move further from the religion of origin, and further from traditional values, it is almost miraculous if two people develop at anything like comparable rates.

If, at the same time, average life expectancy rises from, say, fifty to seventy years, thereby lengthening the term during which this acrobatic feat of matched development is supposed to be maintained, the odds against success become absolutely astronomical. (p. 222)

Although we may not take as gloomy a view of the effects of long-term change on marriage as Toffler does, a widespread problem in contemporary marriages is that many marital partners do grow apart in interests, goals, and values, until they have almost nothing left in common. They may still like and respect each other, but the companionship and romance may have long since dwindled and died. This problem has led some social scientists to suggest that people should engage in **serial marriage;** that is, if a couple grow apart and fail to meet each other's needs, they should divorce and find new partners who do.

Commenting rather sarcastically on this suggestion, futurist Edward Cornish (1979) observed:

Today many people believe the purpose of marriage is simply to increase the happiness of the individuals involved. The marriage should, therefore, be maintained only so long as it makes both partners happy. If either partner ceases to "dig it," he or she has the right—almost the obligation—to end the marriage and move to a new relationship that will, hopefully, "double one's pleasure, double one's fun." (p. 49)

By taking such a dim view of serial marriage, Cornish is expressing the concern of many in our society over the astonishingly high divorce rate, the excessive amount of hurt and instability caused to families that come apart, and the cavalier attitudes of those who would don and doff mates as often as they change wardrobes. In fact, the prediction of George Masnick and Mary Jo Bane (1980) that long before the year 2000, reconstituted families—those involving remarriages—will outnumber those in which children live with both of their biological parents is rapidly becoming a reality. The problem of impermanence is a very real one.

Today, most young people have probably accepted the idea of serial marriage, even though they realize that the price is living their marriage in the shadow of divorce. Of course, few people marry with the clear expectation that their marriage will *not* be permanent. Although they consider permanence desirable and hope to achieve it in their own marriage, they nevertheless consider it unrealistic. Unless they feel that they have found the right person and consider themselves happy, they see divorce as an acceptable alternative. However, as marriage expert Jesse Bernard (1973) has pointed out, there should be "no illusion that breaking up a marriage is any easier because its possibility was anticipated. There is always heartache in the breakdown of a human relationship as intense as that of marriage. . . . Divorce or renewal, call it whatever you like, will be as painful in the future under one name as under any other" (p. 109).

Nevertheless, the great majority of divorced persons will remarry and strive again to achieve their ideal, which is a happy and enduring marriage. Peering into the future, Robert Francoeur (1984) has predicted that, even in the year 2020, most people will "have found it important to put their energies and time into developing some kind of a long-term commitment with another person, on a one-to-one basis" (p. 193).

In short, permanence in marriage may be both idealistic and difficult to achieve in today's world, but it is not obsolete.

SUMMARY—Chapter 7

1. Traditionally, marriage has served to regulate sexual behavior, to provide a social framework for child rearing, and to serve as a basic economic unit. Now marriage is more egalitarian, and people marry primarily for love, companionship, and self-fulfillment.

2. In today's mobile society, people are less like to marry the boy or girl next door than they are to meet their future mates at college or work. Simply waiting for someone to appear is less productive than becoming active in organized social activities, although many couples meet accidentally and without previous introduction. Some arrange to meet through computer and videotape matchmaking services.

3. People tend to select their mates on the bases of similarity, need complementarity, and compatibility. Most people have a mental list of attributes they seek in a mate and another list of disqualifiers. Unfortunately, many people make foolish choices in the marriage market.

4. Courtship in the United States is usually an orderly process that begins with casual dating, and then moves to serious dating, engagement and/or cohabitation, and marriage.

5. Traditional dating allows individuals to: learn more about themselves and members of the opposite sex; to improve their social skills; to engage in sexual exploration; and to assess their compatibility with different potential partners.

6. However, traditional dating has been criticized for being a sexist bargaining arrangement, for being superficial and insincere, for creating a deceitful game-playing situation, and for being anxiety producing. Among other problems related to traditional dating are difficulty in getting dates.

7. More informal practices of getting together and casual dating have replaced the traditional dating pattern for many young people. If such informal practices work out, the couple progress to pairing off and serious dating.

8. As interdependence and exclusivity increase in serious dating, so does conflict—lovers' quarrels—which can lead to a deepening relationship if they are resolved in a positive manner or to termination of the relationship if they are not.

9. The number of marriages and remarriages in the United States has reached an all-time high. Most are religious and expensive. Also making a comeback is the honeymoon which helps the couple adjust to the reality of being married and to recuperate from the rigors of the wedding.

10. Marriage is a basic legal contract imposed by the state, and many couples supplement it with a personal contract prior to the wedding. Legal agreements aside, the partners commit themselves to each other, to the continua-

tion of the marriage, and usually to sexual exclusivity. They expect each other to fulfill their psychological, sexual, and material needs. Failure to do any of these three is grounds for divorce in most states.

11. There is no "one and only" for each person. Undoubtedly there are many people with whom each of us could fall in love and marry. Whether a marriage will succeed is difficult or impossible to predict. However, research indicates that happy marriages tend to run in families, that a long courtship and late marriage make for more stability, and religious commitment tends to discourage divorce. Premarital counseling may or may not be of help.

12. We live in a fast-changing society within which marital partners develop and change at different rates. In addition, we are living longer—thus increasing the probability of growing apart as marital partners. But despite our high divorce rate and the emotional suffering involved, people usually remarry and try again. While people may be disillusioned by a given marriage, they still cling to the ideal of a happy and enduring marriage. In short, marriage for a lifetime is not obsolete.

8

MARRIAGE RELATIONSHIPS

For the first time in human history, our society provides men and women with the opportunity to choose mates and build marital relationships uniquely suited to their desires and needs. And if their first marriage fails, they have the freedom to try again.
—A. C. Chenault (1987), Unpublished Manuscript

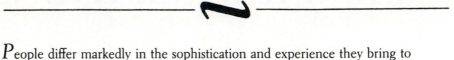

People differ markedly in the sophistication and experience they bring to marriage. Some have had an array of love affairs, some have lived with their present and other partners, and some have divorced one or more times. Still others have had little experience with members of the opposite sex. In addition, people may differ markedly in their goals and expectations for marriage as well as in the type of marital relationship they hope to achieve.

Nevertheless, there are certain aspects of marriage that all couples encounter to some extent. In this chapter, we shall examine the stages that occur in the transition from singlehood to marriage; the unique nature of marital sex; the types of marital relationships; marital happiness and enrichment; and alternative marital patterns, such as open marriage. Then in the following chapter we shall deal with dual-career marriages.

TRANSITION TO MARRIAGE

Although each partner and each couple experience the transition to marriage in a unique way, there do appear to be three typical stages that characterize the transition from single to married life.

Stage 1: The "Happy Honeymoon"

In the continuing romantic glow and excitement that accompanies the wedding and honeymoon, the couple are likely to experience optimism about any future problems and to expect the dramatic and tingling qualities of the relationship to continue evermore. The couple tend to tell themselves that, despite minor irritations and problems that may arise on the honeymoon, their own relationship is uniquely blessed. Regardless of the past experiences of others, they expect their romantic high to continue indefinitely. It is this romantic bliss, coupled with a time out from life, that helps the couple through the early days of marriage. Thus, stage 1 is often referred to as the "happy honeymoon" period.

Although a marriage cannot endure on fun alone, the "happy honeymoon" phase appears to be an important one in helping to establish a stable foundation for marriage. The couple's knowledge that they can enjoy their time alone together helps them weather the difficult times ahead and maintain their relationship as a source of satisfaction to them both.

Stratford/Monkmeyer Press Photo Service

Stage 2: Disillusionment and Regrets

Stage 2, disillusionment and regret, is often referred to as the "honeymoon is over" syndrome. It is characterized by conflicts, regrets, and ambivalence about the marriage. Now one or other partners feel they have made a grievous mistake, that they are trapped in an impossible marriage. Even though sexual and other aspects of the marriage may be satisfying, the hopes and fantasies of the courtship and honeymoon periods are replaced by disillusionment and disappointment (see Box 8–1). As Sander Breiner (1980) has described it:

> Sooner or later, however, reality asserts itself and the storm hits. This usually comes as a great shock to the young couple. The first misunderstanding, the initial fight, and the unexpected disappointment lead the couple quickly to the realization that after all, each partner is only a human being, with foibles and deficiencies. (pp. 247–248)

Unfortunately, the intimacy of marriage tends to exaggerate the partners' real or alleged faults. Now the previously inseparable lovebirds get on each other's nerves, and they seem to be continually arguing about something. The tendency is to blame each other for not living up to what was promised or for not even behaving the way the partner did during courtship. Often the partners experience a mounting sense of frustration and anger at being trapped in such a "stupid" situation, a marriage that obviously isn't working. The combination of emotional turmoil and fighting leads them to say, and sometimes do, things that make the continuation of the relationship even more difficult.

Daniel Goldstine and his associates (1977) have found that, whereas in stage 1 the couple has the pleasurable task of discovering their similarities, in stage 2 they must come to grips with their differences. Stage 2 also involves mutual disap-

---

BOX 8-1 / TEN BOOBY TRAPS THAT CAN DESTROY YOUR MARRIAGE

1. Unrealistic expectations and demands.
2. Incompatible sex-roles.
3. Lack of common goals, interests, and values.
4. Inadequate or aversive time together.
5. "Emotional leftovers" from prior relationships.
6. Wearing masks and playing games.
7. Misdiagnosing your marital problems; fighting the wrong wars.
8. Inadequate conflict-resolving skills.
9. Failure to keep channels of communication open.
10. Lack of awareness.

Marriage is to me apostasy, profanation of the sanctuary of my soul, violation of my manhood, sale of my birthright, shameful surrender, ignominious capitulation, acceptance of defeat. I shall decay like a thing that has served its purpose and is done with; I shall change from a man with a future to a man with a past. . . .

Bernard Shaw *Man and Superman*

proval, which is the more painful because it is unexpected. When people are falling in love, they usually get a concentrated dose of approval, often expressed in such statements as, "I really enjoy being around you because you make me feel good about myself." Now the appreciation turns to criticism, and the characteristic complaint becomes, "You make me feel so bad." It is during this phase that the couple learn to appreciate both their positive and their negative impact on each other—especially their vulnerability to hurt.

Unfortunately, some couples never recover from the hurt or the shock of discovering that their marriage will never be what they assumed, expected, or hoped it would be. When the feeling of having been deceived and betrayed by the partner is added to the picture, there may be little likelihood of the relationship surviving. The disillusionment and hurt may simply be too great to overcome.

Yet, for the marriage to survive, the couple must surmount stage 2. They must work through their **disillusionment,** their resentment at being trapped, their differences in goals and values, and their temptation to blame and hurt each other. Only then will they be free to accept each other as persons and to perceive and appreciate each other's good qualities.

The fact that many couples do not make it past this hurdle is attested to by the high incidence of divorce during the first year of marriage. Happily, however, most couples do succeed in weathering stage 2 and get on with their marriage.

Stage 3: Accommodation

Stage 3, **accommodation,** involves adjusting expectations for the relationship to realistic levels and rekindling the biochemical spark that originally brought the couple together. It means building a realistic and durable foundation based on the romantic love and positive qualities of the early days of the relationship.

Of course, this is much easier said than done, for the task requires mastery of the basic ingredients of intimate relationships described in Chapter 3, including effective communication, mutual self-disclosure, agreed-on ground rules, and skillful conflict resolution. It also requires a combination of awareness, caring, and commitment as well as just plain hard work.

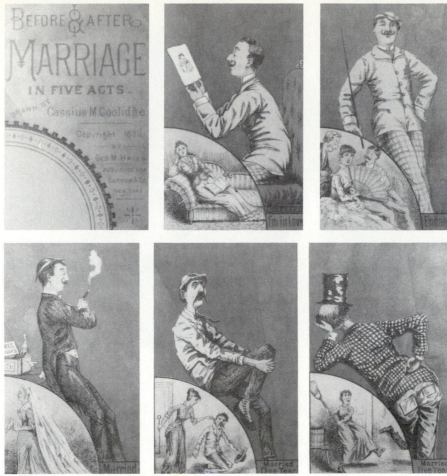

Smithsonian Institution Archive Center/Business Americana Collection

By this time it is probably apparent that the transition from singlehood to marriage is by no means easy for most people. We have not even mentioned the personal problems of adjusting to a changed identity, new roles and responsibilities, less freedom in relating to members of the opposite sex, and the many other demands that accompany the marital union. In short, *being married is different.*

THE UNIQUE ROLE OF SEX IN MARRIAGE

Marital sex tends to be more complicated than nonmarital sex because the degree of emotional involvement and commitment is usually greater for the marital partners, particularly during the early part of the marriage.

As we noted in Chapter 5, an important characteristic of romantic love is the desire for a sexual as well as a psychological union with the loved one. Thus, a unique aspect of marital sex is that it represents the ultimate fulfillment of sexual desires in a romantic and loving union of two people. Even though romantic love

Joel Gordon

often accompanies sex in nonmarital relationships, the "sexual bonding" in marriage probably contributes more to the intimacy of the relationship.

In their analysis of the role of sex in the development of close relationships, Judith and Anthony D'Augelli (1979) concluded that the more intimate the relationship, the more pleasurable and satisfying the sex. In essence, sexual enjoyment and fulfillment appear to parallel the degree of emotional closeness, and it is difficult to imagine a closer relationship than that of a truly happy marital union.

Another unique aspect of sex in marriage is that it represents the most basic form of marital communication. The messages sent and received can vary greatly. But in a truly happy marriage, sex communicates more on a simple nonverbal level than words alone could probably ever convey.

For many in our society, marriage continues to be the only context in which sex is expected and both morally and legally sanctioned. Thus, despite more-permissive attitudes about sex, marriage does provide relief for those persons who feel some measure of confusion and guilt about their nonmarital sexual behavior. In addition, of course, marital sex greatly reduces the possibility of exposure to sexually transmitted diseases, which are often a very real danger for sexually active singles.

Prerequisites for Sexual Compatibility

The importance attached to sex varies from couple to couple, and so do their ideas about what constitutes a satisfying and fulfilling sex life. What may be appropriate for one couple may be inappropriate for another. Yet there are certain conditions that marital counselors and sex therapists have delineated as being essential for most couples who wish to achieve and maintain a satisfying sex life. Because we dealt with this topic in Chapter 4, we need only summarize and re-emphasize a few points here. The following are among the prerequisites for sexual compatibility in marriage:

1. *Coming to grips with our own sexuality.*   Sexuality is a part of our humanness, and integrating it into our self-concept is essential for personal maturity and wholeness. This is particularly important for persons who have been raised in the moralistic tradition, who tend to repress or deny their sexual desires. Until they come to grips with the conflict between their sexual feelings and their upbringing, they will have difficulty achieving a satisfactory sex life.

2. *Communicating about sex.*   Not only is it essential that marital partners understand and feel comfortable with their own sexuality, but also it is of key importance that they communicate their sexual desires and expectations to each other. As pointed out in Box 8–2, one of the great myths of the so-called sexual revolution is that most people have suddenly opened up and are able to discuss sex in informed, rational, and objective ways. Sex remains, for most people, something to engage in but not to talk about. As Zev Wanderer and Erika Fabian (1979) have observed, the result is that "Many people . . . keep their desires to themselves and hope that their mate will read their mind. When he or she fails to do so, the silent partner feels angry and disappointed. They frequently blame their mate for being an unsatisfactory and insensitive lover" (p. 292).

   For sex to be mutually satisfying in marriage, the partners must communicate openly with each other and provide feedback during or after sexual encounters. Such communication—on a continuing basis—helps to ensure that sex will be an enjoyable part of the marriage for both partners (Banmen & Vogel, 1985). Some pointers for improving sexual communication are provided in Box 8–3.

3. *Realistic expectations.*   Unrealistic expectations extend to sex as well as to other aspects of marriage. If the couple have had premarital sex, the aura of romantic love surrounding it may have amplified the excitement of the sexual relationship, and it may be difficult or impossible to maintain this level of excitement over the long run.

   Realistic expectations also include the avoidance of conditions likely to "turn off" our marital partner. If one partner constantly limits the time, place, and conditions of sexual encounters, it is not likely to enhance the quality of their sex life. Nor is their sex life likely to be enhanced if one partner habitually waits passively for the other to take the initiative. In fact, the partner who is expected to take the initiative may well find sex to be more work than play and far from a romantic encounter.

4. *Sexual sensitivity.*   The term **sexual sensitivity** refers to being aware of our partner's desires, making needed adjustments when feasible and desirable, and planning our sex life rather than depending on spontaneous sexual encounters. Like most worthwhile endeavors, sexual satisfaction in marriage requires thought, time, and effort. Once we have banished the myth that the only really good encounters are spontaneous

BOX 8–2 / MYTHS ABOUT MARITAL SEX

The following myths about marital sex are common; those who take them to heart often experience impaired sexual desire, functioning, and pleasure.

1. *Men shouldn't express sensual feelings.* While it is considered appropriate for men to express sexual desire, it has traditionally been considered inappropriate for men to express more-tender and intimate feelings of a sensual nature.

2. *Sex is a command performance for husbands.* It is erroneously believed that men are expected to be performance machines, going through a specified set of motions to achieve a performance goal. This performance orientation is counterproductive in sex.

3. *Husbands are turned off by wives who take the initiative.* Traditionally, men have felt that sex is their responsibility; today, wives are becoming more assertive in the bedroom, and their husbands are, for the most part, welcoming this change.

4. *A man is always ready for sex.* According to this myth, tied to the idea of men as performance machines, a man is always ready for sex if the right button is pushed. The truth is, men get "headaches" too.

5. *Husbands don't need or want foreplay.* According to this myth, sex is intercourse, and anything before or after is "frills." We now know, of course, that foreplay can greatly enhance the quality of the sexual experience for both partners.

6. *Simultaneous orgasm is the ultimate sexual experience.* This myth has ruined many a sexual encounter, as each partner is so busy trying to satisfy the other that neither can fully enjoy his or her own orgasm.

7. *Intercourse during menstruation is harmful.* Although a woman may prefer not to have intercourse during her period, there is no basis for this myth; in fact, sexual intercourse may help alleviate some of the discomforts of menstruation.

8. *Happily married persons do not masturbate.* For many married men and women, masturbation continues to play a role in their sex lives, with no ill effects.

9. *Extramarital sex usually strengthens weak marriages.* To the contrary, extramarital sex may be a sign of a deteriorating marriage, or it may break the marriage if it is a weak one.

10. *The larger the husband's penis, the greater the sexual satisfaction for the wife.* Masters and Johnson discredited this myth. The vagina accommodates to the size of the penis.

11. *Sexual intercourse is much more satisfying when it is spontaneous.* The truth is, some of the best sexual encounters are planned, because the couple are able to set aside a time and place where they can totally devote themselves to each other, without interruption.

12. *Most married couples are able to discuss openly their sexual needs and desires with each other.* This is perhaps the biggest myth of all, perpetuated by the so-called sexual revolution. Unfortunately, most couples continue to be reluctant to discuss their sexual needs and desires.

BOX 8–3 / DISCOVERING YOUR MATE'S SEXUAL PREFERENCES

Despite more-permissive attitudes toward sex in our society, sex talk between marital partners continues to be difficult. Thus, discovering our partner's sexual preferences is not an easy task. In addressing this problem, Robert Crooks and Karla Baur (1980) have suggested the following procedures:

1. *Asking questions.* One way of discovering our partner's sexual preferences is simply to ask. However, certain types of questions are more likely to yield information than others. Simple yes or no questions—such as "Did you have an orgasm?" or "Do you like oral sex?"—may prove useful, but they provide little opportunity for expressing thoughts and feelings or for discussion. Open-ended questions—such as "What do you find most pleasurable when we are making love?" and "What could I do to add to your enjoyment?"—have the advantage of encouraging our partner to express feelings, thoughts, and ideas that he or she may have been reluctant to offer spontaneously. Finally, either/or questions—such as "Do you prefer the light on or off when we make love?" and "Am I being gentle enough or too rough?"—may prove effective if our partner is hesitant about discussing sexual matters. Such questions provide alternatives but do not pressure your partner into detailed answers.

2. *Self-disclosure.* When asking our partner questions that have strong emotional overtones, such as questions about oral sex, it may help to disclose some of our own feelings about the topic. If our partner reciprocates with a disclosure of his or her own, the mutual give-and-take may prove highly informative. Self-disclosure may thus pave the way for eliciting information from a partner who may feel uncomfortable about talking about sex or making initial disclosures. In some instances, self-disclosure may take the form of confiding sexual fantasies that help to desensitize our partner to sexual discussion.

3. *Comparing notes.* This may involve exchanging various kinds of information about sexual feelings and preferences, such as our views on the importance of foreplay, the way we achieve the most satisfying orgasms, and the area of our body most responsive to sensual stimulation. We may also find it helpful to provide feedback after having sex—discussing what we enjoyed most, what might have been better, and what we are looking forward to next time. Such discussions not only provide information but also foster intimacy.

4. *Giving permission.* This involves providing verbal encouragement and reassurance. We tell our partner that it is OK to talk about specific needs and preferences, to ask questions about our feelings on the subject, and so on. In short, it opens channels of communication and makes it easier for each partner to share feelings—both positive and negative—with the other.

5. *Learning to make requests.* Perhaps the most difficult part of sex talk for many individuals is to express their desires. One partner may assume that the other is a mindreader and is then disappointed and resentful when the partner does not fulfill this expectation. Learning to make requests is an important step, for it involves assuming responsibility for our own sexual satisfaction; it also opens up the same freedom for our partner. In general, such requests are more effective if they are

(continued)

BOX 8–3 (continued)

specific and clear. For example, saying "I do not enjoy the way you touch me —would you try something different?" is not very informative. It would be better to take our partner's hand and say, "I would like you to touch me here, like this."

It can readily be seen that discovering our mate's sexual preferences is not a one-way street. It is a reciprocal exchange of information intended to make marital sex more satisfying. However, discovering our mate's desires does not obligate us to accede to them if we find them unacceptable or distasteful. Usually such differences can be worked out. If not, we may simply have to accept an impasse, in which we respect each other's convictions even if we don't agree with them.

ones, it makes sense to devote needed time and energy to our sex life. This means setting aside time for lovemaking, without feeling upset if it doesn't occur as planned.

Sexual sensitivity also includes awareness of our partner's emotional and physical state. Expecting or demanding sex when the partner is under severe emotional stress or is fatigued or ill is not showing much sensitivity. Finally, sexual sensitivity means willingness to work out differences in attitudes toward sexual frequency, methods, special devices, birth-control methods, and other such concerns.

Most people see the problem of love primarily as that of being loved, rather than that of loving, of one's capacity to love.

Erich Fromm, p. 1

5. *Love and intimacy.* For a fulfilling sex life, it is not orgasms, but intimacy, that really counts. Many husbands and wives have frequent sex and have no difficulty achieving orgasms, but they still feel unfulfilled after sex because their relationship lacks love and intimacy. In essence, the quality of the marital relationship usually determines the quality of the couple's sex life, and not the other way around.

Finally, it should be emphasized that neither marital intimacy nor a fulfilling sex life are achieved once and for all. Both are lifetime undertakings.

Sexual Stages in Marriage

It has generally been assumed that the longer a couple has been married, the less satisfying their sex life is—presumably as a result of familiarity, routineness, and boredom. This assumption has been strongly supported by Carol Botwin (1985) in her book *Is There Sex After Marriage?* She reported that sex in marriage is decreasing and pointed to the preceding factors, as well as to dual-career marriages (which deprive couples of needed time together), the arrival of children (which limit their privacy), and to the erosion of channels of communication due to disuse. In short, the marital relationship deteriorates to a point where it has a negative influence on the couple's sex life. She concluded that until the relationship is repaired, sexual frequency and satisfaction are likely to suffer.

Other investigators have found what may be called a curvilinear relationship— in which sexual satisfaction tends to be high during the early years of marriage, to drop off during the middle years, and to improve again in the later years (Gove &

Peterson, 1980; Starr & Weiner, 1980; Ade-Ridder, 1985). However, some researchers—including Masters and Johnson (1974, 1985)—believe that a satisfying sex life can continue throughout an intimate and happy marriage even though some factors, such as frequency of sex, may change.

In a study of 100 couples who indicated that their marriages were "working," Ellen Frank and Carol Anderson (1980) found three distinctive sexual stages of marriage that they describe approximately as follows:

1. *Early marriage—years of satisfaction.*   Almost all the couples found sex pleasurable and satisfying in the beginning. Of the couples married less than 5 years, 91 percent of the women and 95 percent of the men indicated that their sex lives were either satisfying or very satisfying. None of the men in this early marriage group reported difficulty with erections, but about 25 percent had problems with premature ejaculation. About 18 percent of the couples in this group had sex four or five times a week, and more than 33 percent reported a frequency of two or three times a week.

2. *The middle years—the era of distractions.*   During the middle years of marriage—from about 5 to 20 years—the stresses and crises of adult life apparently had a negative impact on the couples' sex lives: "Things seem to fall apart a bit in the middle years, when more husbands and wives report that they are distracted from their sexual relationship" (p. 146).

   Interestingly, men and women tended to express this distraction in different ways. Men still maintained their interest in sex but were "troubled by attractions to women other than their wives." On the other hand, wives seemed to lose interest in sex itself and reported that it was "more difficult to relax prior to intercourse." During the middle and later years,

Randy Matusow/Archive Pictures, Inc.

40 percent of the men reported difficulty with premature ejaculation and 50 percent of the women—about the same as in early marriages—reported trouble having orgasm.

Because the middle years were found to be a period when nonsexual priorities were likely to be higher, the researchers considered foreplay to be more important at this time than during the early years of marriage. Yet more than 30 percent of the husbands and 40 percent of the wives reported too little foreplay in their sex lives. Nevertheless, more couples reported satisfaction than dissatisfaction in describing their married sex lives.

3. *The later years—a time for tenderness.*   For couples married more than 20 years, the husbands tended to be settled in their careers, and 79 percent of wives worked outside the home (as compared with 39 percent of the wives in the middle period). These couples rated their marriages high in satisfaction and compatibility, although they had a less than glowing view of their sex lives. Sexual frequency was less than for younger couples, and the men reported more difficulty getting and maintaining erections. The men seemed to accept this situation and rated

Mimi Forsyth/Monkmeyer Press Photo Service

their sex lives as satisfactory, but the women reported more dissatisfaction, describing themselves as less excited, less confident, and more resigned: "In fact, over half of the women in their forties use the word 'resignation' to describe their feelings about their sexual relationship" (p. 148). However, happily married couples who had been together 20 years or more were not too upset by the decrease in frequency—and, for women, satisfaction—of their sexual activities.

In analyzing their findings, Frank and Anderson concluded that what counts is not so much the quality of sexual performance as the quality of the feelings that go along with the sex. They pointed out that marriages go through some phases in which sex is extremely important and other periods when it doesn't matter as much. But if couples can weather the middle years, their sexual intimacy has the potential to improve in the later years of marriage, after children are gone and outside stresses are reduced.

How Important Is Sex in Marriage?

Is sexual satisfaction as important in achieving marital intimacy and happiness as marital intimacy is in achieving sexual satisfaction? One factor we must keep in mind in answering this question is that people vary greatly in the importance they attach to sex. Some couples consider themselves happily married even though they rarely engage in intercourse; others take what might be called a "sex-is-everything" approach and consider sexual satisfaction absolutely essential to marriage. As might be surmised, the majority of people fall between these two extremes; most consider sexual satisfaction to be important but not essential to marital happiness.

In studies of marital happiness, it has been found that most couples do not rate sex as high as other aspects of the marriage. For example, middle-class women asked to list the most important things in their marriage usually place love, companionship, and the ability to share their feelings with each other at the top of the list. Sexual satisfaction is usually considered less important. Furthermore, many couples who have "unsatisfactory" sex lives still consider their marriages happy or believe that a better sex life would not make their marriages much, or any, happier. As David Mace (1985) has noted, "A couple sharing a warm, loving attachment for each other and exercising open communication skills will find that it matters little how often they have sexual intercourse or how they perform it" (p. 31).

To answer our question, then, it seems that sexual satisfaction is desirable and important but not essential in a happy marriage. But as Dauw (1981) has noted, although a marriage can be happy despite a poor sex life, it would not be considered an ideal situation.

STYLES OF MARRIAGE

Social scientists use two broad categories in distinguishing types of marriages: traditional and egalitarian. **Traditional marriage** is based on the "male breadwinner/female homemaker" model, while **egalitarian marriage** is based on contemporary views of sex-role equality and changes in marital expectations. These

BOX 8–4 / TRADITIONAL VERSUS EGALITARIAN MARITAL SCRIPTS

Traditional marriage is based on the male breadwinner/female homemaker model; egalitarian marriage is based on contemporary views of sex-role equality and changes in marital expectations. These two different scripts can be compared and contrasted as follows:

Traditional Script	Egalitarian Script
Husband as provider, wife as homemaker and child-rearer	Sharing of provider, homemaker, and child-rearing roles
Fixed sex-roles following traditional masculine and feminine models	Flexible sex-roles determined in part by experience and by choice
Husband as primary decision maker	Decisions made jointly by marital partners
Sex is initiated by husband; the wife submits	Sex is initiated by either partner, with emphasis on mutual enjoyment
The husband is strong and silent; the wife is nurturant	Both partners share feelings and provide mutual emotional support
Conflict resolution is dominated by the husband	Conflicts are negotiated by the partners
Residence is determined by the husband's occupation	Residence takes into account for work of both partners
Personal growth is important for the husband, not the wife	Personal growth is important for both partners

two marital scripts are summarized in Box 8–4. Most marriages fall on a continuum somewhere between the pure versions of each type.

A number of other classifications of marital relationships have been developed. Many of these have been summarized by Douglas Synder and Gregory Smith (1986), who have also developed a useful classification of their own. However, the best-known and most widely used classification of marriages is based on an early study by John Cuber and Peggy Harroff (1968) of more than 400 couples who had been married for more than 10 years and had never seriously considered divorce. These researchers classified the couples into one of the following types: (1) conflict-habituated, (2) devitalized, (3) passive-congenial, (4) vital, and (5) total. Let us look briefly at each of these styles of marriage.

Conflict-Habituated

The **conflict-habituated marriage** is characterized by constant disagreement and quarreling. Although most of us would probably find such a marital relationship intolerable, these couples apparently thrive on the conflict and verbal skirmishes. In fact, it is the stimulation provided by the continual conflict—often aided by a satisfactory sex life—that presumably holds the marriage together. In short, the couple constantly fight, yet do not break up. They remain together because they somehow find the conflict and fighting rewarding.

Often these discordant marital patterns are based on **provocation,** in which both partners do or say things that they know will annoy the other, as if they receive satisfaction from keeping things stirred up. In any event, for better or for worse, they create their own unique pattern of interaction, as well as the climate and quality of their marriage.

Devitalized

In the **devitalized marriage** the couple once had a close and loving relationship —including a fulfilling sex life—but have drifted into an "emotional divorce" and empty marriage.

Even though the couple feel little more than indifference toward each other and have an unsatisfactory sex life, they somehow get along and maintain the marriage. Many undoubtedly consider it natural for marriage to become dull and routine after the romantic excitement and unrealistic highs of the earlier months and years of marriage have passed.

Cuber and Marroff concluded that the devitalized marriage is probably the most common type in our society. With time and perhaps a chance encounter with an exciting person, however, it is highly vulnerable to dissolution.

Passive-Congenial

The **passive-congenial marriage** differs from the devitalized in that the partners never had anything but an empty relationship to begin with and, hence, experience no sense of having lost an exciting and satisfying relationship. Often the marriage is one of convenience, and the couple remain together because of inertia, children, community standing, or financial considerations.

Many enter such marriages in a calculating and unemotional way. The lack of emotional involvement may typically result in less conflict, but the marriage is also less satisfying. The partners are resigned, rather than committed, to each other.

Vital

The **vital marriage** is a relatively ideal type of warm, loving relationship in which the partners are intensely interested in, and committed to, their relationship. They are not locked into restrictive togetherness; each is given room for autonomy and personal growth. At the same time, they engage in a great deal of mutuality and sharing. They place a premium on open communication and the quick resolution of conflicts. Chronic conflicts are rare. Most couples in vital marriages consider sex important and pleasurable, and the partners work at achieving sexual compatibility.

R. Hamilton/f/STOP

Paul Ammons and Nick Stinnett (1980) have found that partners in vital marriages tend to possess personality traits that foster (1) "otherness" rather than "selfness"; (2) sexual expressiveness; (3) determination; and (4) high ego strength, or stress tolerance. Ammons and Stinnett consider the greatest danger to vital marriages to stem from failure to balance individuality and mutuality (separateness and togetherness); either extreme represents a serious danger to the relationship.

Cuber and Harroff consider vital marriage to be the most satisfying and happy type but also the least common.

Total

The **total marriage** is similar to the vital but has more facets. Not only is the relationship a close and loving one, characterized by open communication and effective conflict resolution, but also the process of sharing is even more strongly emphasized. There is a minimum of conflict and private experience. Even business deals and professional activities are worked out together. Couples in such marriages may operate a store together, write books together, or otherwise intertwine their professional and personal lives.

Because marriage is subject to change over time, marriages may shift from one style to another. Furthermore, each type of marriage may be based on a traditional- or egalitarian-marriage script. Understanding the differences between marriage types may be helpful in planning the type of relationship you want and in working toward its achievement. It can also help those who are already married better understand the type of relationship they have established. In developing a marriage, partners can create their own heaven or hell, or perhaps their own purgatory.

MARITAL HAPPINESS AND ENRICHMENT

Most people marry with the hope and expectation of being happy. But what does "marital happiness" mean? Can it be assessed? Does it tend to decrease over time? If so, why? These are some of the questions we shall tackle initially. Then we shall explore the relatively new field of marital enrichment.

Marital Happiness Is . . .

Before proceeding, we may note that the terms **marital happiness, marital satisfaction,** and **marital adjustment** are used more or less interchangeably in the research literature. However, marital adjustment tends to focus more on how effectively the partners function as a team in coping with their problems. **Marital quality,** a less commonly used term, encompasses all of the prior terms (Johnson et al., 1986). Finally, **marital stability** refers to the probable continuation of the marriage.

Marital happiness is a difficult term to define. There are three main ways of attempting a definition: cultural norms, subjective evaluation, and specific indices.

BOX 8–5 / ANNIVERSARY THOUGHTS

ANNIVERSARY

I'm grateful
We still talk into the night,
Still caring
What the other thinks.
I'm grateful
You still laugh at my jokes,
Still hold me when I weep
    at two AM—

Your love, a warm coat
That hasn't worn out yet.
I'm grateful
You still share
Every song, every thought—
Still need
The sound of my voice, the warmth
    of my smile.
I'm grateful
The years of service
Have not worn away
Our partnership.

—*Marianne Jones*

Poem "Anniversary" by Marianne Jones, in Herbert J. Miles, "Two Become One," v. 41 #7, *Home Life*, April 1987, p. 35.

1. *Cultural norms.*   A person's evaluation of the happiness of his or her marriage is heavily dependent on learning and on his or her cultural background—including the influence of the mass media, schools, observation of parental and other adult models, religious concepts, peer-group standards, and personal experiences with members of the opposite sex.

   Such learning may lead to quite different standards for marital happiness or satisfaction, depending on the cultural norms to which the individual is exposed; that is, what constitutes appropriate marital roles and expectations, equitable relationships, and even marital satisfaction may vary greatly from one society to another, one subculture to another, and one person to another.

2. *Subjective evaluation.*   To a great extent, marital satisfaction—like sexual satisfaction—depends on the point of view of the person involved. It is a subjective evaluation because what might be considered a happy marriage to one person might be completely unacceptable to another. One woman's subjective evaluation of her marriage is described in Box 8–5.

   Although marital partners do tend to agree on the happiness of their marriage, this is by no means always true (Jacobson & Moore, 1981; Snyder & Smith, 1986). When the partners do report a marked difference in marital happiness, it is almost always the wife who is less satisfied (Schumm et al., 1985). Thus, these researchers refer to **his marriage** and **her marriage.** For this reason, marital counselors consider it important to understand not only what is happening in a distressed marriage but also how each partner perceives the situation. Often it is difficult to believe the partners are talking about the same marriage.

3. *Specific indices.*   The specific-indices approach involves the delineation of conditions that appear to be associated with marital happiness. Early studies, for example, found that the single most important predictor of

marital happiness was the person's background (Burgess & Wallin, 1953). A background characterized by a happy childhood, parents who were happily married, and parental discipline that was firm but not harsh was considered indicative of marital success.

Today, the emphasis seems to have shifted from the past—although it is by no means ignored—to the present. Love, companionship, open communication, emotional maturity, and compatible sex-roles tend to be associated with marital satisfaction; lack of common interests and goals, unmet expectations, incompatibility, and faulty communication tend to be associated with marital dissatisfaction. The delineation of such specific factors makes a more-objective assessment of marital happiness possible. But again there are problems. The indices that define happiness for one couple may not apply to another.

The three basic approaches to defining marital happiness—cultural norms, subjective evaluation, and specific indices—tend to complement each other. These basic approaches can also be implemented by theoretical perspectives— such as the social exchange theory, as illustrated in Box 8–6—but it is apparent that an adequate definition of marital happiness remains to be formulated.

Assessing Marital Happiness

Because we do not have an adequate definition of marital happiness, it would be unrealistic to assume that we can devise an accurate means of assessing it. Nevertheless, we may try in order to answer a number of important questions. How many people consider themselves happily married? Does marital happiness increase or decrease over time? Is marital happiness related to marital stability? What are some of the key factors in marital happiness? Is it possible to help people who consider themselves unhappily married achieve marital happiness?

Getting the answers to such questions is a difficult task. Researchers attempting this job must not only deal with the subjectivity of the marital couples being studied but also must devise research methods that will yield reliable and useful information on marital happiness. Here we will look at some of the methods that have been developed and the problems encountered in using these methods.

Methods and Problems of Measurement.

One popular approach to assessing marital happiness is the **global measure.** Here people are asked whether they consider their marriage to be happy or unhappy; or, perhaps they are asked, "How happy do you consider your marriage to be on a scale of 1–10—with 1 representing the perfect marriage?"

This is a favorite method of pollsters who rely on phone calls to collect their data. Of course, they try to get replies from a "representative" sampling of people in a given region or area of the country, or perhaps to compare people living in small communities with those living in large urban centers. One problem with this method, however, is that people are reluctant to give negative answers on the phone. For example, Vernon Edmonds (1967) found that respondents replied "True" to statements that were so idealized as to make their answers unbelievable—for example, "My marriage is a perfect success" or "If my mate has any faults, I am unaware of them."

BOX 8–6 / A SOCIAL EXCHANGE APPROACH TO MARRIAGE ENRICHMENT

Rodney Cate (1981) has described what he calls "an interpersonal resource exchange" program for couples. This program represents an application of social exchange concepts to marriage enrichment. Basic to the program is the idea that there are six types of resources that couples exchange—love, information, money, goods, services, and status—and that these resources may be seen as rewards. This approach is based on a "bank account" model of social exchange involving "deposits" and "withdrawals." Initially, the focus is on helping the partners become aware of the resources each possesses. "The couple are then helped to develop the skills needed to increase the exchange of valued resources, that is, how to increase their 'deposits'" (p. 212).

The program is designed for three to five couples at a time and consists of a 6-week program of one 2-hour session each week. Here's what happens in each of the six sessions:

1. The couples are helped to become more aware of what they can contribute to and derive from their relationship—as well as to improve the quality of their relationship—through the exchange of valued resources.

2. The participants are taught to become aware of the unused or underused resources they possess that are valuable in a relationship. By using these resources more fully, they can achieve more satisfying and rewarding exchanges with their partners. Various exercises, combined with the use of an "Inventory of Personal Strengths," help the participants become aware of previously known strengths and share them with their partners.

3. The focus in the third meeting is on (a) helping participants determine what they value in interpersonal resources; (b) understanding what their partner has to offer in terms of these value resources; and (c) understanding what resources their partner values. This information paves the way for a better exchange of resources.

4. This session emphasizes learning more-effective ways of communicating with each other, both verbally and nonverbally. Various exercises are used to help participants ascertain whether they have correctly received the messages their partners have sent. The couples are taught to use reflecting techniques in order to make sure that they heard the messages correctly and to give their partners feedback.

5. The participants are taught to formulate "resource exchange agreements," which specify the interpersonal resources that the partners wish to exchange to a greater extent in their relationship. To facilitate matters, each partner selects six resources that he or she would like to receive more of and shares them with the partner. In turn, the partner selects three of the six that he or she is willing to increase. These items are recorded in a written agreement, which is displayed in the couple's home. In some instances, the selected behaviors may involve emotion-laden areas, so emphasis is also placed on helping each partner acquire the skills essential for increasing the resources that are agreed on.

6. The concluding session is designed to allow participants to review and consolidate what they have learned in the program. Group members are made aware

(continued)

BOX 8–6 (*continued*)

that developmental changes and life events may alter needs and values in terms of the exchange of interpersonal resources. It is emphasized that the skills the couples have acquired can be used during such transition periods to assess the new situation and negotiate a modified and more appropriate exchange agreement.

In a preliminary evaluation of the program, it was found that significant positive changes were achieved in several areas of the couples' relationships: intimacy, warmth, satisfaction, sensitivity, trust, and communication. Equally important, the couples became more congruent in the value they placed on specific interpersonal resources over the program period.

A second popular survey approach is designed to describe a given population in great detail. For example, **questionnaires** might ask how many people in their 30s consider themselves happily married, whether a person would marry the same man or woman if given the opportunity to do it all over again, whether couples feel children have enriched or diminished their marriage, and so on. When magazines, such as *Redbook* and *Psychology Today*, include these questionnaires in a particular issue, they garner thousands of replies from readers. Of course, not all readers respond to the questionnaires, and those who do may tend to present themselves and their marriages in a favorable light. Nevertheless, these surveys have yielded a great deal of useful information about marital satisfaction and the conditions that appear to be related to it.

A third approach to measuring marital happiness involves using **marital-adjustment scales** that focus on various aspects of the relationship that are presumed to be associated with marital happiness, and stability (Roach et al., 1981; Snyder et al., 1981; Wampler et al., 1982). For example, the Dyadic Adjustment Scale developed by Graham Spanier (1976, 1979) focuses on four key aspects of marital or cohabiting relationships: (1) consensus—agreeing on goals, values, and decisions; (2) affection—being warm and affectionate with each other; (3) satisfaction—feeling good about the relationship and having no regrets; and (4) cohesion—working together on goals and projects. Answers to the questions on this scale are informative but are also subject to problems in interpretation. If, for example, a couple disagree on a variety of issues yet agree on those issues that are most important to them, they may score low on consensus yet have a happy marriage. Again, there is the risk that respondents may give socially acceptable answers that present them in a good light. With further refinement, however, such scales appear capable of identifying conditions that are good indicators of the quality of marital relationships.

Marital Happiness and Marital Stability

Many marriages that are considered "happy" by the partners end in divorce. Conversely, many marriages that are considered unhappy somehow endure. Thus, just being happy is not sufficient to ensure the stability or continuance of the marriage.

Here again the application of theoretical views have proven helpful. According to social exchange theory, for example, marital stability is defined in terms of a person's present marriage and the best available alternative. If you or your partner perceive an alternative mate who would provide a more-favorable cost/reward ratio and comparison level, the marriage would be considered unstable. Otherwise, your marriage would be considered stable, at least for the time being. To put it simply, if you think your present mate is as good a "deal" as the person you perceive to be the best possible alternative, your relationship is likely to be stable. If not, it is likely to be unstable. As we have noted, equitable relationships tend to be stable and inequitable relationships tend to be fragile and unstable.

From a more-comprehensive viewpoint, George Levinger (1979, 1980) based his evaluation of marital stability on three factors: (1) current marital satisfaction, (2) attractiveness of existing alternatives, and (3) barriers to marital dissolution. The role of barriers to dissolution is an idea of considerable merit, for indeed there are many possible barriers that tend to keep a marriage together, including economic considerations, children, religious convictions, and social pressures. Although marriage affords easy entry, there are many obstacles blocking the exit.

Marital happiness and stability are not constant—they may vary considerably over time. Many couples face the problem of growing apart in interests, goals, and values, so that they no longer meet each other's needs. In our complex and rapidly changing world, marital stability is not something that, once achieved, can be counted on to continue. Rather, it is a condition that couples must strive to maintain.

The Importance of Communication

The couple were seated at the window table eating their dinners. She was looking at him. He was looking at his plate.

"What are you thinking about?" she asked finally, engaging him with a half-smile, cocking her head flirtatiously, her fork poised in the air.

He returned her smile for a minute and said, "Oh, nothing," and went back to his dinner. His wife, with a glimmer of disappointment, a hint of hurt, pierced a heart of lettuce and joined him in a somewhat silent meal.

—*Earl Goodman (1982)*

Why didn't her husband answer her question? Why did he refuse to share his thoughts? Assuming the couple had formerly shared thoughts and feelings with each other, what changed, and why? We can probably think of a number of possible answers, but we really don't know why. We do know, however, that open and effective communication is extremely important in achieving marital satisfaction (Larsen, 1982; Montgomery, 1981; Noller, 1980, 1986).

In Chapter 3, we emphasized the importance of **metacommunication**—how the partners typically communicate with each other. Here we shall elaborate on this concept by considering several communication styles in marriage and how these styles may affect marital happiness and adjustment. The following are the **basic styles of communication:**

1. *Complementary.*   In this style, each partner serves as a counterpoint for the other. For example, one may do all the talking while the other does

all the listening. If both partners were to speak at the same time, they would be competing with each other for center stage. This form of communication is also referred to as **flexible**.

2. *Conventional.*   The couple maintains a casual, light, friendly, chatty conversation to avoid the real issues: "Cocktail party banter, the weather, etc. serve to maintain relationships while maintaining ignorance of the unique and private views of the speakers" (Hawkins, Weisberg, & Ray, 1980). This form of communication reduces self-disclosure to a minimum, often as a result of divergent interests (Mace, 1986).

3. *Speculative.*   This style is directed toward exploring the facets of an issue or problem. The speaker expresses tentative beliefs and ideas about the topic and waits respectfully to hear the opinions of his or her partner. This is an analytical style that emphasizes facts and problem solving rather than disclosure of feelings.

4. *Controlling.*   In this style, the intent is to persuade or to issue directions, thereby modifying or controlling the partner's behavior. The person's speech is usually sprinkled liberally with "You should," "You ought," and unsolicited pieces of advice. This style is high in self-disclosure of beliefs and feelings and tends to suppress contradictory beliefs and feelings in the partner.

5. *Contactful.*   Here, the intent is to share feelings and ideas. It is characterized by the speaker's willingness to express thoughts and feelings openly and to solicit and respectfully listen to those of the partner. Contactful communication is explicit, responsive, and accepting and involves a high degree of self-disclosure.

Communications can also be categorized as (1) **rewarding**—conveying acceptance, appreciation, and support; and (2) **negative** or **aversive**—conveying criticism of the partner and other negative personal messages. Patricia Noller (1985) found that the preferred mode for sending negative messages was with a smile, regardless of sex or level of marital adjustment.

What effect do these various styles and types of communication have on marital happiness? Unfortunately, we lack adequate research to answer this question. We do know that rewarding communication patterns create a much better marital climate than aversive ones. We also know that open channels of communication foster the sharing of feelings and concerns, in essence, getting problems out in the open where they can be dealt with (Noller & Venardos, 1986; Schumm et al., 1986). Finally, we do know that happily married couples—in contrast to unhappily married ones—talk more to each other, make more use of nonverbal communication, and are more sensitive to each other's needs and feelings. Beyond this, we can only conclude that the effects of given styles of communication depend on the persons involved, the nature of the relationship, and the environmental context of the marriage.

The characteristics of depressed marriages . . . are lack of energy in the partners, lack of intimacy—they are distant and not sharing; the partners not talking individually about their own needs; because they are starving each other and their relationship, impulsive behavior develops, including overeating, buying sprees, affairs; children getting more attention than the spouse; a noticeable lack of playfulness between the partners; both spouses getting very busy with such things as work, local politics, home, etc. What has happened is that the couple has gotten disillusioned . . . and such disappointments are normal because of the high expectations that the couple has about marriage.

Charles Jaekle

Marriage Enrichment

What is marriage enrichment? . . . Many programs have now emerged. Different in detail, they are based on the same concept—bringing groups of couples together, usually for a weekend, to examine their relationships in depth—not to look for problems but to achieve further growth and development.

—*David Mace (1986, p. 31)*

Unlike marital therapy programs, which involve marriages that are encountering serious difficulties, **marriage-enrichment** programs are primarily for couples with happy marriages who want to keep them that way and even improve on them. Thus, marriage enrichment provides a **preventive,** as well as a **growth,** function.

The marriage-enrichment movement was initiated by Father Gabriel Calvo, who held a retreat for married couples in Barcelona, Spain, in January of 1962. The same year, David and Vera Mace led a weekend retreat for married couples in the eastern Pennsylvania mountains. From these early beginnings, some 25 different marriage-enrichment programs have developed worldwide (L'Abate, 1985; Mace, 1986). These programs are loosely organized under the Council of Affiliated Marriage Enrichment Organizations (CAMEO).

Despite the diversity of approaches, marriage-enrichment programs are directed primarily toward three objectives: (1) building marital strengths, (2) uncovering and correcting potential marital weakness, and (3) developing untapped marriage potentials. Most marriage-enrichment programs are sponsored by religious groups and community-service agencies.

The most popular approach has been the marriage-encounter program established by the Roman Catholic Church in the late 1960s. (This program has also been adopted by a number of Protestant and Jewish groups.) Despite its religious orientation, it is open to non-Catholic couples who wish to attend. Programs are usually held on weekends, are attended by about six to fifteen couples, and are conducted by a team of one to three couples and a priest. One type of church-sponsored enrichment group is described in Box 8–7.

Most marriage-encounter or marriage-enrichment programs have the following elements in common:

1. Emphasis on the concept of a contemporary egalitarian marriage.
2. Encouragement of pleasurable feelings of attraction, desire, and friendship between the partners.
3. Emphasis on mutuality and responsibility.
4. Emphasis on the communication of feelings of affirmation, appreciation, love, and commitment.
5. Improvement in communications, self-disclosure, conflict-resolution skills, and other needed abilities.

Although it is not expected that all these goals will be achieved, marriage-enrichment programs do offer married couples an opportunity to build on their strengths and anticipate and prevent conflicts rather than to try to deal with them after the fact. Even if these five goals are achieved to only a limited degree, marriage-encounter programs can contribute to the happiness and stability of those couples who participate in a responsible and continuing way (Davis et al., 1982; Milholland & Avery, 1982; Lester & Doherty, 1983; Nickols et al., 1986).

This is not to say that *all* couples who attend marriage-encounter programs benefit from them, although *most* do. In a study comparing couples who benefited and couples who did not benefit from marriage-encounter weekends, William

BOX 8-7 / MARRIAGE ENRICHMENT AS A "MARITAL CHECKUP"

After spending countless hours counseling couples in marriages that had deteriorated beyond reconciliation, Father Edmund S. Nadolny (1981) concluded that a new approach was needed to emphasize regular "marital checkups" for married couples—similar to regular medical checkups.

This led to the establishment of regular monthly retreats for married couples at the Mercy Center in Madison, Connecticut. At a typical retreat, the session began with a film—at that time *The Weekend*, which depicted a married couple "trapped" together in a motel on a rainy day. Following the presentation, the couples evaluated the strengths and weaknesses of the marriage depicted in the film, and the assets and liabilities that each partner brought to the marriage. This discussion served as a springboard for questions directed to the couples attending the retreat. Why do you want to stay married? What is the principal defect of my partner as a person and as a spouse? What are his or her good qualities? What things do I like most about married life? What things least?

Following the discussion, the couples have time alone together to share their thoughts and relax. In essence, the retreat is designed to help the partners become more aware and to clarify what they want in their marriage and how they can achieve it. If difficulties come to light, they can be dealt with before they become major problems. In essence, these retreats function as regular marital checkups.

Dougherty and his associates (1986) found that couples who benefited the most as well as couples who became "marriage-encounter casualties" were likely to report serious marital distress prior to the weekend. Apparently, marriage-encounter weekends can have the impact to "kill or cure" when it comes to distressed marriages; it may be recalled that they are designed for good marriages and not seriously maladjusted ones. But all is not lost, because the "casualties" can be referred for marital therapy.

One component of most marriage enrichment programs is supplying basic "guidelines" for a happy marriage. While there are no simple "do's" and "don'ts" or easy steps to marital happiness, there do appear to be some tentative guidelines:

1. *Maintain awareness.*   Gain a realistic view of yourself, your partner, and your relationship—and keep it updated. For over time, change in these components is inevitable.

2. *Improve interpersonal skills.*   Develop effective communication, conflict-resolving, and other interpersonal skills—and use them. Emphasize nonverbal as well as verbal communication.

3. *Participate in mutual self-disclosure.*   Share more of your inner life with your partner than you would with anyone else—thoughts, feelings, hopes, dreams, failures, triumphs.

4. *Affirm your partner as a person.*   Express appreciation for your partner's good qualities. Don't torment your partner with his or her shortcomings. Don't try to make your partner over.

5. *Foster common interests, goals, and values.* Cultivate interests you can share together. Clarify and emphasize your common goals and values. Work together as a team in achieving your goals.

6. *Plan for time together.* Set aside time to be alone with each other. Make these occasions enjoyable ones that nuture your relationship. Remember that love requires time and attention.

7. *Establish a satisfying sex life.* Use your sex life not only as a source of pleasure but as a means of maintaining "contact," expressing love, and increasing intimacy.

8. *Be your partner's best friend.* "Be there" and provide support in times of illness, difficulty, and hardship. Remember love relationships are more likely to endure when the partner's like each other and are best friends as well as lovers.

9. *Communicate love and commitment.* Express your love and commitment verbally, physically, and materially. Don't hesitate to say "I love you" and to touch, hug, and kiss your mate. Do considerate things that ease your partner's burdens. Use gifts to express love.

10. *Don't operate in the red.* Keep the cost-reward ratio and comparison level favorable. You and your partner may "fall in love," but it takes skill and effort to develop and maintain a loving and enduring relationship.

We could add further suggestions such as making sure that sex roles and responsibilities are mutually agreed upon, clearly understood, and followed. It is also important for married couples to make the most effective use of environmental resources—such as marriage enrichment programs. And of key importance is applying the preceding guidelines in ways that best meet the needs of a particular couple.

ALTERNATIVE MARRIAGE PATTERNS

Will the transition taking place in marriage and family be confined largely to the change from traditional to egalitarian marriage and family patterns? Or will the current transition lead to nontraditional marriage and family forms, to alternative life styles? We shall attempt to answer this question—at least in a tentative way—in Chapter 14.

Here we shall comment briefly on three alternative marriage patterns—open marriage, gay marriage, and communal arrangements. Unfortunately, a lack of research data places severe restrictions on our comments, and, quite possibly, on the information.

Open Marriage

Anthropologists Nena and George O'Neill (1972) introduced the term **open marriage** to describe a marriage in which the partners are strongly committed to their own and their partner's growth. "Closed marriage," in their view, is a product of the expectation that each partner will be able to fulfill all of the other's needs—emotional, social, economic, intellectual, and sexual. Open marriage, on the other hand, recognizes that no one relationship can be expected to fill all these needs and is thus based on more-realistic expectations, such as encouragement of role flexibility, deep companionship with others, open and honest communications, and the option of nonexclusivity in sex. It is left to the individual couple to produce the freest, most egalitarian, and most growth-producing partnership possible for them.

The O'Neills (1972) have expressed the difference between open and closed marriage this way:

> A comparison of the two kinds of marriage points up the matter of choice: closed marriage offers no options, while open marriage is full of them. Closed marriage may offer a phantom security, a measure of static and stable contentment, but it will inevitably stunt growth. Open marriage offers to all of us, to the degree that we want to use it, the ability to continually expand our horizons. Knowing and fulfilling yourself along with your partner in open marriage instead of through your partner, as in closed marriage, becomes a voyage of discovery. Not only is it challenging, but it prepares us to flow with change. It offers you the possibility of elation as opposed to mere contentment. (pp. 264–265)

The O'Neills did not recommend extramarital sex as an essential part of open marriage. They only mentioned it as an option. Nevertheless, open marriage soon came to mean sexually open.

The issue of sexually open marriage created a great deal of controversy in the 1970s and proved to be an explosive one for married couples, families, and society. Although young people today may view fidelity as a choice rather than as a mandate, the trend has been away from sexual experimentation in marriage and toward achieving enduring romantic love. When the latter is not achieved, the marital partners have the options of divorce and remarriage. Perhaps serial marriage—together, in part, with the threat of AIDS—has outmoded open marriage.

Gay Marriage

It has been estimated that as many as one-fifth of homosexual men and a larger portion of homosexual women live in pairs and consider themselves married (Masters & Johnson, 1979; 1985).

A number of studies, such as that of Letitia Ann Peplau (1981), have delineated the nature and stability of such relationships. Her findings indicate that many gay men and women, like their heterosexual peers, desire a close and enduring relationship with one other person. Despite the fact that many pressures and obstacles confront such relationships, many **gay marriages** do endure and provide gratification for the partners. Although the unions are not legally sanctioned, many formal ceremonies have been performed by clergymen who believe that marriage is a sacred bond that may exist between persons committed to each other, regardless of biological gender (Dudley, 1979; Kurdek & Schmitt, 1987).

Interestingly enough, Peplau has found that gay marriages, while influenced by traditional marriage rules, tend to reject traditional husband–wife roles and are more like "best friendships" with flexible, shared roles and responsibilities plus the component of romantic and erotic attraction. In addition, Peplau found that sexually open marriages or infidelity were more a function of the quality of the relationship than of any need by homosexuals for sexual novelty, excitement, and variety. Peplau concluded that, although many people cling to the idea that gays are utterly different from the rest of humanity in terms of needing sexual variety, they are actually just as concerned with the issues of intimacy, commitment, and personal freedom as heterosexuals.

Furthermore, the same pitfalls that plague heterosexual marriages—poor communication, unrealistic expectations, and divergent goals and values—may undermine gay marriages as well.

Gays may not be "utterly different" from heterosexuals in needing sexual variety, but Peter Salovey and Judith Rodin (1985)—in a report on *Psychology Today's* Jealousy and Envy Survey—found that gay men and lesbians were somewhat more likely than heterosexuals to report affairs. In addition, they were less likely to report jealous reactions in such situations. These researchers speculate that gays do not attach the same importance to exclusivity in a committed relationship that heterosexuals do. However, with the tremendous toll being taking by AIDS in the gay community, sexual exclusivity in committed relationships appears to be taking on greater importance. AIDS is also subjecting the gay life style to severe social pressures.

Notably, about a third of women in lesbian relationships, and a smaller percentage of gay men, have been involved in heterosexual marriages at one time. Many—particularly lesbians—have children from prior marriages. This, of course, raises a number of issues, such as what to tell the children about the relationship and what kinds of affectionate behavior are appropriate in front of them.

Enrico Ferorelli/DOT

BOX 8–8 / A COMMUNE FOUNDED IN 1839

In the history of communes in our society, one of the most famous was the Oneida community founded in 1839. It was based in part on the concept of group marriage, and each male member was considered to be married to each female member. If a man wanted to have sex with a woman, he appeared before the central committee of the commune and made his request. If she consented, they were permitted to spend an hour or two in her room prior to returning to his own room for the night.

To avoid impregnating the woman, the man practiced coitus reservatus (intercourse without ejaculation). Young men who had not yet mastered this technique were only permitted to have sex with women beyond the age of menopause.

The commune disintegrated with the resignation in 1877 of its founder John Humphrey Noyes, who was a lawyer who had turned to the ministry. In large part, his resignation was apparently due to pressure brought on the Oneida community by Anthony Comstock, who appointed himself as the defender of American morals. After the disbandment of the community, many of the members were formally married. While the Oneida community endured for a considerable period of time, it also fell prey to the problem of handling sex in communes—in terms of internal and external pressures.

Communal Arrangements

A **commune** consists of three or more persons who associate voluntarily to establish a way of life. Some communes are religious—such as those of the Amish and Hutterites—and others are based on secular philosophies—such as behavioral psychology or Marxism—and represent attempts to build a society that could serve as a model or alternative for society as a whole. Still others are oriented toward mystical experiences and rely heavily on the use of drugs and other mind-expanding techniques. Another type of communal arrangement is group marriage, in which the members share sexual relations, economic responsibilities, and household duties. Group marriages usually consist of three to five persons and are relatively rare. Although group marriage is illegal in the United States, there are two small communities on the Arizona–Utah border in which polygamy is practiced and considered a religious rather than a legal problem (Japenga, 1986).

In recent times, we have seen the emergence of communes based on interpersonal and economic considerations. Many of these have been, or are, urban communes clustering around large colleges and universities. Others are so-called middle-class communes—including "cooperative families" for older people—based on economic needs and the desire to form a kind of family and community environment (Streib & Hilker, 1980; Fitzgerald, 1986).

In short, communes may vary greatly in guiding principles, relationships between members, and freedom of sexual expression. Box 8–8 describes a commune founded in 1839 which apparently fell prey to the problem of handling sex in communes. It would appear that surviving communes—either in the 19th century or in contemporary times—tended to forbid sex between members or to foster

Marriage isn't obsolete. The thing that's obsolete is the way we've been managing the nuclear family. Two people can't be all things to each other all the time. Our only hope for successful marriages is to build stronger collectives—groups of people living together with many mutual interests. We need cohesive, three-generational communities where each person, though married, can draw on a great number of people around him, rather than just on his spouse. This will filter down to the kids as well.

Margaret Mead

communal sex (Zablocki, 1977, 1980). Apparently, loving couples who "pair off" tend to break down communal bonds.

Zablocki estimated that during the late 1960s and early 1970s, there were some 250,000 persons—mostly single men and women—living in communes in the United States. However, members tend to come and go, and most communes are relatively short-lived, primarily because of economic problems, lack of organization, disillusionment, overidealism, poor planning, and interpersonal conflicts (Shey, 1977; Jansen, 1980). Nevertheless, a number of communes have endured over time. Communal arrangements may be one way of dealing with economic and other pressures on the nuclear family and on the widowed elderly. However, the communal experience can be destructive in some cases, as evidenced by the tragedy in Guyana with Jim Jones' commune.

For young people, communal involvement may provide varied forms of intimacy in a social setting that is a bit different from what they may be used to. This experience may contribute to their self-understanding, ability to relate to others, and personal maturity. On the other hand, joining certain types of communes—those that impose strict norms, standards, and roles, for example—may not only alienate friends and family but also may interfere with the individual's psychological growth, education, and career and in the long run be destructive rather than growth producing.

In our discussion of marriage relationships, including alternative marriage patterns, recurring themes have emerged: (1) the transition from singlehood to marriage occurs in stages; (2) marital sex is unique and plays an important role in marital satisfaction; (3) over time, a marital relationship can fall into specific types or patterns; (4) marital happiness is difficult to pinpoint and assess; and (5) enduring marriage requires a long-term commitment to maintaining the intimate relationship through communication, conflict-resolving skills, and similar efforts. All of these themes are interrelated and form a part of the total picture that provides us with a needed perspective on our marriage relationships.

SUMMARY—Chapter 8

1. The transition from single to married life typically involves three stages: "happy honeymoon," disillusionment and regrets, and accommodation—adjusting expectations for the marriage to realistic levels.

2. Among the prerequisites for sexual compatibility in marriage are: (a) coming to grips with one's own sexuality, (b) communicating openly about sex, (c) having realistic expectations, (d) being sensitive to one's partner's sexuality, and (e) love and intimacy.

3. Sexual satisfaction tends to be high during the early years of marriage, to drop off during the middle years, and to improve again in later years. While sexual satisfaction is an important and desirable part of marriage, it is not essential to a happy marriage.

4. The extreme forms of marriage are the traditional, in which the male is the breadwinner and the female the homemaker, and the egalitarian, in which both share responsibility and power. Today the trend in our society is strongly toward egalitarian marriages.

5. John Cuber and Peggy Haroff have identified five types of marriage: (a)

conflict-habituated, (b) devitalized, (c) passive-congenial, (d) vital, and (e) total. They concluded that the devitalized marriage—once close but now empty—is the most common and most vulnerable, and that vital marriage— warm, sharing, and loving—is the least common but happiest.

6. Three approaches to defining marital happiness are based on cultural norms, subjective evaluation, and specific indices. They tend to supplement each other and can be implemented by social exchange theory and general systems theory.

7. Researchers assessing marital happiness tend to use: (a) the global approach —asking whether a person feels happily married, perhaps on a scale of 1 to 10, (b) questionnaires, (c) marital adjustment scales, and (d) theoretical approaches, such as social exchange theory.

8. Marital partners typically communicate with each other according to a basic pattern. Five styles of communication in marriage are: (a) complementary, (b) conventional, (c) speculative, (d) controlling, and (e) contactful.

9. Marital happiness and marital stability are not identical. Unhappy marriages may endure while happy marriages may end in divorce. Stability depends on such factors as equity in the relationship, lack of interest in available alternatives, and barriers to marital dissolution.

10. An "open marriage" was originally defined as one in which the marital partners were strongly committed to their own and their partner's growth. However, it came to mean a sexually open marriage or intimate network. Open marriage has been outmoded by serial marriage as well as by the threat of AIDS. Group or communal marriages are rare.

11. Marriage enrichment programs are designed for happily married couples who wish to maintain and even improve their marriage. Such programs usually provide guidelines for achieving a happy marriage. Most are sponsored by religious groups and community service agencies.

12. Gay marriages are similar to heterosexual marriages in terms of benefits and pitfalls. Formerly, extramarital affairs appeared to be higher in gay marriages. With the threat of AIDS, both gay marriages and the gay life style are subject to severe social pressures.

13. At one time the concept of "open marriage"—which came to mean sexually open marriage—was a controversial issue. But serial marriage and AIDS have relegated it to the past. Communal arrangements offer an alternative to traditional marriage but are extremely rare.

DUAL-CAREER MARRIAGES

Many women are discovering that their once supportive husbands turn on them when their career aspirations threaten the imbalance of power in the home. Why is equality such a difficult concept for men to embrace?
  —Bebe Moore Cambpell (1987, p. 88)

In 1938, a national survey found that three-fourths of Americans disapproved of a married woman earning money if she had a husband capable of supporting her. Forty years later, another survey found a complete reversal of opinion: three-fourths of the population approved of employed wives. This dramatic shift of opinion reflected the increasing number of wives in the labor force: from 22 percent in 1950 to 41 percent in 1970 to 60 percent in 1985 (U.S. Department of Labor, 1981; U.S. Census Bureau, 1987).

As might be expected, this increase in employed wives has had profound effects on the lives of millions of American men and women—on their personal lives, on their marital relationships, on family planning and child rearing, on the workplace, and on our society. In fact, the traditional family portrait of breadwinner husband, homemaker wife, and 2 to 4 children now accounts for less than 10 percent of husband-wife families.

Our focus in this chapter will be on the phenomenal rise of dual-worker and dual-career marriages. First, we shall attempt to gain a perspective on working wives in our society. Next we shall note the distinction that is commonly made between dual-worker or dual-earner and dual-career marriages. Then we shall examine the consequences of dual-career marriages for wives, husbands, and marital relationships. Finally, we shall deal with the special problems of dual-career couples.

WORKING MARRIED WOMEN: A PERSPECTIVE

Women have always worked. The employment of married women, particularly mothers, outside the home has, however, been typically viewed as an unfortunate necessity at best and often as a tragedy.

—Moore and Hofferth (1979, p. 1)

The latter view, however, was confined largely to middle-class marriages and families. It was not characteristic of low-income, black, immigrant, and farm families (Aldous, 1981). For example, during most of the 19th century, it was not uncommon for the whole family—including the children—to work outside the home. Before the age of industrialization, all members usually had to work simply to assure family subsistence.

Traditional Employment of Married Women

The end of slavery did not enable most black married women to assume the traditional role of "homemaker." Discrimination and poverty forced more than half of them to work for wages—for example, as maids or in other low-paying jobs. Even women who worked on farms—and about half of them did in the 1800s—

Henley & Savage/Click—Chicago

earned money by the sale of butter, eggs, garden produce, and homemade products.

Until the turn of this century, it was also common for poorer families to take in lodgers. In the early 1900s, a survey of working-class households in New York showed that about one-half contained lodgers or boarders (Smuts, 1959). Married women were primarily responsible for maintaining rooms, supplying meals, and contributing to the marital or family income. Other married women took in laundry and served as seamstresses, using their residences as their place of work.

In the late 1800s, the Industrial Revolution was becoming well established, and a sizeable number of married women worked in textile mills and other industrial plants. These factory workers, mostly immigrants, usually wore easily washed blue-denim overalls and workshirts, which led to the label "blue-collar workers" (Schrank, 1981).

By the turn of this century, however, the Industrial Revolution led to an unusual change in the work roles of married men and women. Factory life now came to be viewed as incompatible with family life, and over time the two split apart. Men went off to work and assumed the role of "breadwinner," and women stayed home and assumed the role of "homemaker." Now a working wife reflected unfavorably on her husband as a "good provider." To be a "real man," the husband had to provide well for his family.

During World War I and World War II, women were brought into the work force in record numbers, but this situation was seen as exceptional and did not reflect on their spouses' masculinity. As soon as the wars were over, women returned to their role of taking care of the home and rearing children—perhaps, in part, to avoid the threat of women taking available jobs from men.

As we have noted, however, in the last 40 years the percentage of working wives has more than doubled and the cultural meaning of such employment has also changed. Now an employed married woman enhances her status without reflecting unfavorably on the status of her husband.

A summary review of the traditional employment of married women in our society is contained in Box 9–1.

BOX 9-1 / HISTORY OF WOMEN WORKING OUTSIDE THE HOME IN AMERICA: A SUMMARY

Dual-worker or dual-career marriages are not a new phenomenon in the United States. In varying numbers, women have always worked outside the home.

1. In colonial times, many women were active in business and professional pursuits.

2. In the 18th century and part of the 19th century, it was not uncommon for the whole family—including wives and children—to work outside the home to ensure family subsistence.

3. By the late-19th century, the Industrial Revolution was well established in the United States, and factory work for women was viewed as incompatible with family life. Thus, the "good-provider" role became established for men, and a working wife reflected unfavorably on the husband.

4. Women, in turn, assumed the "good-homemaker" role and handled household chores and rearing children. Because their duties were not outside the home and not paid for, these duties were not called work.

5. In many poorer families, however, economic necessity forced women to "work"—either outside the home in menial jobs or by taking in lodgers or doing similar activities. The picture was different on the "frontiers," where women often worked and fought alongside their men.

6. During World War I and World War II, women were brought into the labor force in record numbers. After the wars were over, most women returned to their "good-homemaker" roles.

7. During the last 30 years, however, there has been a steady increase in the number of women in the labor force. The cultural meaning of such employment has changed. Now it reflects favorably on the woman without damaging the man's role as a "good provider."

Today, dual-worker marriages are the norm and the career oriented educations and aspirations of today's college women are making dual-career marriages a reality as well as a rapidly developing trend.

Why Married Women Work Today

The answer varies. For many women—such as artists and writers—work is an important means of self-expression. For others, it is a source of self-identity and self-esteem. In reply to the question "Who are you?" most people reply with their occupation—for example, "I am a lawyer" or "I am a nurse." In a sense, we are what we do. In terms of self-esteem, many people's self-evaluation is based largely on the value society places on their type of work (see Fig. 9–1).

In addition, there are a number of specific and very good reasons why married women work today.

1. *Economic independence.* Some women do not want to be financially dependent on their husbands. Often they view such dependence as putting them in an inferior and vulnerable position.

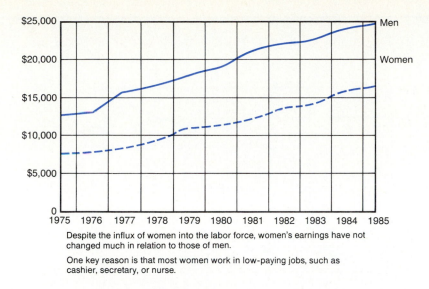

Figure 9–1. Median Income of Full-Time Male and Female Workers. (Source: U.S. Bureau of the Census, 1986.)

Despite the influx of women into the labor force, women's earnings have not changed much in relation to those of men.

One key reason is that most women work in low-paying jobs, such as cashier, secretary, or nurse.

2. *Achievement and personal growth.*   Many women work because they feel that a career offers them an opportunity for achievement and personal growth that they would not have as housewives.

3. *To avoid isolation and boredom.*   The workplace provides opportunities to meet and associate with interesting people rather than confinement to household chores in the relatively isolated setting of their homes.

4. *To afford material luxuries.*   A sizable number of women work to attain material luxuries—such as homes, new cars, travel, and other "finer things" that make life more enjoyable.

5. *Financial necessity.*   Many married women don't have the luxury of choice. The additional income is essential to ensure that their families have the basic necessities of life. Unless the husband's income is considerably above average, traditional single worker families with children are likely to have a difficult time making ends meet.

As a result, the number of wives working full time—many with young children—continues to increase (see Box 9–2). In fact, working women are expected to contribute about 40 percent of family income in 1990 as compared with 25 percent in 1980 (see Box 9–2).

Dual-Career Couples: An Emerging Form

Since the 1960s and 1970s, an increasing number of women are extending their educations; about half of all college graduates are now women. Many of these women are entering career-oriented professional fields. As a result, a relatively new form of marriage has emerged—**dual-career marriage.** Here, both husband and wife are committed to pursuing careers as well as marriage.

Unfortunately, this has led to considerable confusion in use of the terms **dual-earner marriage, dual-worker marriage,** and **dual-career marriages.** Susan Basow (1984), for example, considers clerical and service jobs as work and technical and professional jobs—such as teacher, nurse, and engineer—as careers. Thus, she distinguishes between dual-worker and dual-career marriages. Following a similar approach, Lucia Gilbert (1986) stresses the difference between

BOX 9–2 / PERCENTAGE OF MOTHERS IN LABOR FORCE, 1950–1990*

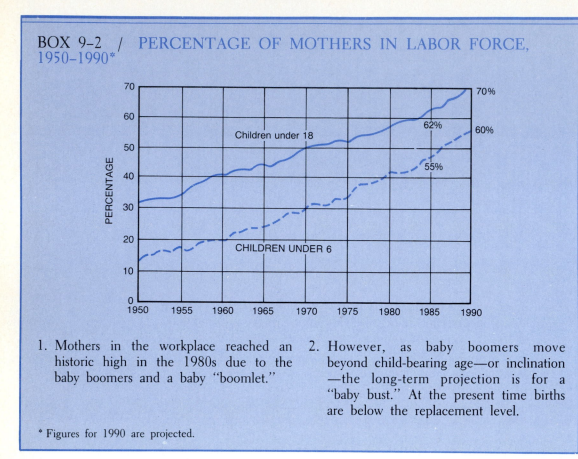

1. Mothers in the workplace reached an historic high in the 1980s due to the baby boomers and a baby "boomlet."

2. However, as baby boomers move beyond child-bearing age—or inclination—the long-term projection is for a "baby bust." At the present time births are below the replacement level.

* Figures for 1990 are projected.

dual-earner and dual-career marriages. In the former, the wife works solely out of economic necessity; in the latter, the wife pursues a career that she considers personally important. Although such distinctions are useful to keep in mind, dual-career marriages are too new to fit into any particular mold. Thus, for our purposes, we shall use the term **dual-career** to encompass marriages in which each partner is committed to, and consistently pursues, a given occupation. This, of course, does not preclude a change in occupations, should this become desirable or necessary. Box 9–3 lists some facts about women and the world of work.

In any event, our focus in this chapter will be on dual-career marriages, and how middle-class couples are managing to cope with this relatively new and novel—for them—form of marital arrangement. A useful starting point for our present discussion is with the research findings of Lucia Gilbert (1986). She studied 85 dual-career marriages in the Austin–San Antonio area of Texas. The partners were between 28 and 45, and most fit the label of "white middle-class." All couples had been married at least 2 years, and some had children. In each marriage, the husband and wife pursued his or her own full-time careers. Gilbert found that these marriages tended to fit into one of three categories.

1. *"Traditional" dual-career marriage.*   Here, each partner pursued a full-time career, but the wife also took responsibility for home and children. This left the husband free to pursue his career without the burden of household chores or child-rearing. The husbands were proud of their

BOX 9–3 / FACTS ABOUT WOMEN AND THE WORLD OF WORK

1. Number of workers in U.S. labor force	Over 115 million
2. Number of women in U.S. labor force	Over 50 million
3. Number of mothers of school age children in the labor force	Over 60 percent
4. Number of jobs that require a college degree and advanced skills	About 15 percent
5. Number of women college graduates who work	Over 70 percent
6. Number of women who work in households with incomes over $40,000 per year	Over 70 percent
7. Number of women in college who plan a career in business, engineering, law, or medicine	About 1 in 6
8. Number of women in prestige jobs, such as business executive, lawyer, or doctor	About 1 in 6
9. Number of women massed in low-paying, "pink-collar," service jobs, such as nurse, secretary, and receptionist	About 80 percent
10. Number of employed women who are single parents, usually as a result of divorce and court awarded custody of children	About 1 in 5

(Centron, 1986; Coleman et al., 1987; Robertson, 1987; U.S. Bureau of the Census, 1986; U.S. Bureau of the Census, 1987)

wives and encouraged them in their careers. Both partners wanted children. Both felt that their relationship was an equitable one; their relationship made sense in the social context in which they lived.

2. *"Role-sharing" dual-career marriages.*   These couples were at the other extreme from the traditional dual-career marriages. Here, both partners fully expected to pursue career and family roles. The husbands were considered "modern men" because they did not think it right to overload their wives with household and child-rearing, as well as career, demands. In terms of feminist ideals, Gilbert refers to these men as "successfully reconstructed." Unlike many so-called modern men who talk big but offer little actual help—except maybe in child-rearing—these husbands were shopping for groceries, washing dishes, changing diapers, and participating in other household and child-rearing tasks.

3. *"Transition" dual-career marriages.*   This group consisted of "participant fathers" in the sense that they were interested in being involved as fathers. They did not want their children to have the kind of mother-dominated parenting to which they had been subjected as children. These fathers wanted to spend time with their children, get to know them, and play active parental roles. Beyond this, however, these husbands were not of much use around the house. For them, "women's work was women's work."

In addition to the three types described by Gilbert, there are also less common forms of dual-career marriage. One form is the so-called **commuter marriage.**

BOX 9–4 / MYTHS ABOUT WOMEN WORKERS

Myth: Women work just for "pin money."
Fact: Most women work because of economic need.

Myth: Women don't really want to work. *Fact:* Most women would still work even if they did not have to.

Myth: Women are less-reliable employees. *Fact:* The difference in absences is small (5.1 days a year for women, 4.8 days a year for men) and disappears for women without children. Women workers actually waste less time on the job than men do.

Myth: Women have a higher job-turnover rate than men. *Fact:* When job-related variables (such as skill level and length of service) are controlled, no significant differences appear. Most women take some time off for child-rearing, but the number who do and the length of absence is decreasing. Most women are in the work force for more than 30 years; men for about 43.

Myth: Women cannot handle positions of power. *Fact:* Leadership ability is more related to sex-typing, specifically instrumental attributes, than to sex. Women supervisors typically are evaluated favorably. The most important factor in a woman manager's success is the attitude toward women held by her co-workers and subordinates.

Myth: Women cannot do men's jobs. *Fact:* The division of jobs by sex, except those related to procreative activities, is based on prejudice, tradition, and status. Because all sex differences that exist are distributed normally, individual differences outweigh any sex differences in determining a person's suitability for a particular job.

Myth: Women are not as concerned as men with getting ahead on the job. *Fact:* There are more women than men in menial and dead-end jobs, but men and women appear about equally concerned with getting ahead on the job.

Myth: Women with equal education and work qualifications earn as much as men for doing the same type and quality of work. *Fact:* As a group, women still earn about two-thirds of what men are paid for the same work. However, the gap has been gradually closing during the 1980s, but there remains a considerable way to go.

Here the couples only see each other on weekends or perhaps monthly. The commuter marriage is usually chosen reluctantly, when an important job opportunity becomes available for one spouse that is geographically distant from the workplace of the other. Such marriages have a number of disadvantages, including loneliness, and are usually temporary until the partners can find suitable positions in the same area (see Box 9–4).

Finally, it may be reemphasized that it is the career-oriented education and aspirations of today's college women that are making dual-career marriages a reality. With this brief introduction, let us examine some of the major consequences of dual-career marriages—for the wife, for the husband, and for the marital relationship.

CONSEQUENCES FOR MARRIED WOMEN

Dual-career marriages have both costs and rewards depending on the partners involved and their marital relationship. Nevertheless, there do seem to be certain

Erika Stone

consequences for employed married women that differ from those for unemployed married women.

When compared with housewives, for example, dual-career wives appear to be physically and emotionally healthier, to have higher self-esteem, to feel less socially isolated, and to be happier in general (Maracek & Ballou, 1981; Verbuge & Madans, 1985: National Center for Health Statistics, 1985). In addition, employed mothers tend to see child-rearing more in terms of self-fulfillment than in terms of self-sacrifice.

With this information in mind, let us consider some other important consequences for dual-career wives. Box 9–4 lists some common myths about employed married women.

Independence and Self-Esteem

Traditionally in our society, a woman's feelings of financial security and worth were largely based on the occupational success of her husband. Because few women had direct access to occupational success, it was assumed that they experienced their husband's success as their own. As a result, wives of high-status men typically reported contributing to the men's success by means of interest in their work, attention to their needs, emotional support in tackling their difficult challenges. In effect, the result—as Papanek (1973) described it—was a "two person career" in which the wife supplied guidance and emotional support and the husband took the "bows." In fact, there is an old saying to the effect that "Behind every successful man, there is a good woman."

This saying is by no means dead even today—as can be readily observed in the marriages of some of our state governors and prominent national politicians; It would appear that the husband's success reflects favorably on his "loyal and devoted" wife and enhances her feelings of personal identity and worth. "Not so," concluded researchers Anne Macke and her associates (1979). Thus, they referred to "The myth of vicarious involvement," and suggested that

> apart from her enhanced social standing as a successfully married woman, the husband's income is the only reward that a woman personally enjoys. Thus, a wife's vicarious success—the experience of her husband's success as her own—seems more myth than reality. (p. 56)

In addition, these researchers concluded that their findings supported "earlier assertions that women are harmed when they cannot acquire social rewards by their own efforts" (p. 58).

It would also appear that the woman who helps her husband "reach the top" is particularly vulnerable if her husband then opts for a younger woman, signaling the failure of the marriage and a divorce. Being emotionally as well as economically dependent on her husband, her loss of personal identity and self-esteem—along with some measure of financial security—is usually a highly traumatic experience.

Thus, it is not surprising that many married women pursue careers. Not only do they derive satisfaction from their work, but also they acquire economic independence and a sense of identity and worth that cannot be attained by simply being an appendage to their husband's career goals. Box 9–5 contains a list of questions commonly asked about career-oriented women.

BOX 9–5 / QUESTIONS COMMONLY ASKED ABOUT CAREER-ORIENTED WOMEN

1. Do career-oriented women have to work harder than similarly career-oriented men to succeed? In general, yes. To achieve acceptance and recognition they have to work as hard and then some.

2. In dual-career marriages, do the husbands share household and child-rearing responsibilities? Very few husbands do. Most are willing to "help out" but not to do "their share."

3. Are career-oriented women faced with upgrading their career skills or changing career fields every few years? Yes. Fifty percent of what an engineer knows is obsolete in 5 years; and 90 percent is obsolete in 10 years.

4. Would most dual-career wives prefer to take maternity leave to spend time with their young children? Yes. However, the workplace has been slow in making such leave available. And paid maternity leaves are almost unheard of in our society but not in some others, such as Sweden.

5. About half of all college graduates today are women. How many are committed to pursuing careers in traditionally male-dominated career fields, such as commercial airline pilot, engineer, or military officer? Very few, but their number is increasing. About 7 percent of engineers are women.

6. Is there a trend for high status, high paid, career-oriented young men and women to marry? Yes. And it appears to be creating a new form of upper class—at least in terms of income.

7. Why do many successful career women stop just short of the top, especially in business management? In our society, top level executive positions tend to be controlled by an "old-boy" network, and there is no "old-girl" network to counter it. As a result, many successful career women face both overt and covert discrimination, if they advance "too far."

8. Have our scientific and technological breakthroughs created new career fields and opportunities? Yes, but not many. Only about 15 percent of high level professional jobs are considered new, such as atomic physicist and computer science engineer.

Costs and Rewards Outside the Home

Many people take the view that housework is monotonous and dull and offers little in the way of challenge or rewards for the married woman who stays home. With her husband gone all day and the children in school, housework is a solo activity. Thus, many housewives do apparently feel isolated, restricted to boring household chores, and reduced to watching TV soaps a good portion of the day. Some of these women describe the situation as "like being in jail" or "like being in solitary confinement." Here, we are reminded of sociologist Jesse Bernard's famous dictum that "being a housewife makes women sick" (1973).

On the other hand, many people take the view that housework tends to be a naturally gratifying activity. They point out that there are now many labor-saving devices to take the drudgery out of housework and that the modern middle-class home is a high-technology center—a far cry from the home of the past. The modern housewife is supposed to be an expert on nutrition, exercise, child-rearing, and to have the extensive knowledge and skills required to operate the myriad new gadgets found in the contemporary home. If her husband appreciates her role and rewards her with approval and praise, she may find her work quite rewarding.

Of course, only a minority of housewives live and function in the somewhat idyllic home setting we have described. Far more live in decrepit homes or small apartments that could hardly be described in this manner. It is hardly surprising, then, that researchers have found full-time housewives to be less happy than wives who are employed full time. And this finding applies to low-status and low-paying jobs as well as to high-status and high-paying jobs. We are then confronted with the question of what the workplace has to offer that is more rewarding than the home for most married women.

Aside from the rewarding nature of work itself, the workplace provides a clearinghouse for social contacts, camaraderie, and friendships. As Joyce Brothers (1982) has described it:

> Women are escaping from the solitary confinement of the home into the office and laboratory, the sales territory and the stock exchange. They dress better and feel more attractive than when they stayed at home. They meet people. They face different challenges. Life becomes more exciting. And they get paid for it. (p. 48)

Whereas Joyce Brothers may be describing career women with relatively high-status jobs, even low-status and low-paying jobs can add to women's self-esteem. These women are doing something useful for which they receive recognition and get paid. If circumstances permit, many return to school on a part-time basis to upgrade their employment skills and increase their earning power.

However, the circumstances surrounding the job may make it aversive rather than rewarding; this statement also applies to high-status, high-paying positions. Many employed married women feel they are overqualified for the jobs they hold. Others feel discriminated against in terms of pay and advancement because they are women. And still others find "office politics" and the pettiness of the people with whom they work aversive rather than rewarding. On the other hand, many working women put up with boring work and other unfavorable conditions because they work with "such a great bunch of people." Of course, under ideal conditions they enjoy their work, feel fairly treated, and like the people with whom they work.

In general, it would appear that housework in and of itself doesn't make women happy or unhappy. Nor does employment outside the home. Rather, the difference seems to lie in the circumstances surrounding such work, the women involved, and their overall life situations.

Danger of "Overloading" and "Burnout"

The advantages of employment for dual-career wives can be offset by some very real disadvantages. Chief among these are overloading or **role strain** and burnout. Many dual-career wives try to combine the roles of wife, homemaker, parent, and career woman. In essence, they face a double day—one at work and one at home—and each makes its own considerable demands. This is particularly true for women who accept traditional sex-roles in their marriage. The result is overloading and burnout.

By overloading, we are referring to a combination of adjustive demands that add up to more stress than the person can comfortably cope with. In essence, the person is approaching or exceeding her stress tolerance (Coleman et al., 1987). The costs of overloading include a reduction in efficiency, lowered ability to cope with new adjustive demands, and a state of physical, emotional, and mental exhaustion. The latter symptoms are commonly referred to as burnout (Freudenberger, 1985; Coleman et al., 1987).

Overloading may also involve more subtle considerations. For example, there is a lack of specific standards for homemakers. Thus a dual-career wife may feel that she is neglecting her home responsibilities when in fact she is not. Another subtle factor is career success. This usually involves being promoted, taking on new and more difficult responsibilities, and putting in longer hours at work. These, in turn, take their toll in terms of worry, fatigue, less interest in sex, and less emotional support for her husband and his career problems. And as Nancy Josephson (1981) has pointed out, many career wives respond to these demands by trying to be Superwoman—holding down a high-paying career position, managing a home, being a good wife, and raising one or more children. Her advice is "Don't try to be one."

Since overloading and burnout are relatively common problems among dual-career wives, the following suggestions may prove useful.

Step 1. Admit you have a problem involving excessive stress that merits immediate attention.

Step 2. Pinpoint the nature and causes of the problem.

Step 3. Consider alternatives, such as setting more realistic goals and delegating authority to reduce the load.

Step 4. Schedule some non-work time and make a concerted effort to "recharge your batteries" during this time.

Step 5. Assess your intimate relationships. They are usually early casualties in overload and burnout. Improve them.

Two other suggestions are worthy of mention. **Think positively:** count your blessings and not your frustrations; and focus on your accomplishments and not your failures. Finally, **stay aware:** watch for early signs of overload in yourself and your mate; and take immediate remedial action. Remember the old saying that "an ounce of prevention is worth a pound of cure."

Today, more career wives are aware of the danger of overloading and burnout, and have learned to avoid them. Other career wives, however, are still trying "To have it all." A few succeed, but most don't. And the price in terms of overloading and burnout is high.

CONSEQUENCES FOR MARRIED MEN

What about the men in dual-career marriages? How do they fare compared to their wives? Although studies of employed married women are consistent in finding that the advantages usually outweigh the disadvantages, the picture is more confusing when it comes to married men. Aside from the economic advantages, however, married men commonly take a less-positive view toward dual-worker marriages than married women do.

"No Wife at Home"

In a dual-career marriage, the services and satisfactions that husbands have traditionally come to expect from their wives—when they function as combinations of homemakers, emotional-support systems, sex objects, and mothers—are inevitably reduced. In fact, husbands' positions as authority figures and decision makers are eroded. The result, as Joyce Brothers (1982) has pointed out, is that

> The husband in a dual-career marriage tends to feel cheated. He is not getting the care and attention that his friends and colleagues with nonworking wives enjoy. . . . Dinner is not on the table when he gets home. He has to rummage through the laundry basket for his socks. The bed is never made. He misses the rapt attention his wife used to pay to his stories of what went on at the office. Now she wants equal time to talk about what went on at her office. And she expects him to do the dishes while she puts the children to bed.
>
> Even the men, and I am thinking of the young men especially, who claim to support the women's movement still expect marriage to revolve around them and their interests. (p. 46)

Of course, for men who hold high-level managerial and professional positions, "no wife at home" can be a distinct disadvantage. Such positions are geared to the traditional male life style, which assumes minimal household and maximal work responsibilities. With "no wife at home" to lend accustomed and expected sup-

Ulrike Welsch

port, the career-oriented male may be subjected to additional stress. Of course, the same problem confronts working married women in high-status and high-paying positions—especially when the husband is reluctant or unwilling to do his share of household chores.

Decline of the "Good-Provider" Role

Traditionally, the man in our society bore the primary responsibility as provider and the woman centered her efforts on winning a "good provider" who could take care of her and the children she expected to have. Even if the man was not kind or loving, the woman viewed this as the price she had to pay for a good provider. If he had desirable qualities as well as being a good provider, it was considered a bonus.

The good-provider role has both its costs and its rewards. As Jesse Bernard (1981) has summarized it:

> Success in the good-provider role came . . . to define masculinity itself. The good provider had to achieve, to win, to succeed, to dominate. He was a *breadwinner*. He had to show strength, cunning, inventiveness, endurance—a whole range of traits henceforth defined as exclusively 'masculine.'. . . Men were judged as men by the level of living they provided. They were judged by the myth 'that endows a moneymaking man with sexiness and virility, and is based on man's dominance, strength, and ability to provide for and care for 'his' woman.' . . . The good provider became a player in the male competitive macho game. (p. 4)

Although the decline of the good-provider role has costs or disadvantages, it also has rewards or disadvantages. Even married men who see themselves as the main breadwinner in the family benefit from the additional income; with a second income in the marriage, these men can feel freer to choose or change jobs and accept or turn down promotions. Many can even afford to take time off for more-advanced training or perhaps for retraining in a different occupation. In addition, the married man has a buffer against unemployment in an uncertain marketplace. In short, dual-career marriages provide men with more flexibility and security in their careers than traditional marital roles do.

Change in Sex-Role Expectations

The decline in the good-provider role has resulted in two major changes for men in dual-career marriages. First, the man's central position of power and dominance in the family has inevitably eroded. He is no longer the "head man" around which the marriage and family revolve. Second, he is expected, and often pressured, to take over various domestic chores that he may consider "woman's work," and for which, as in the case of preparing meals, he may be poorly prepared. In essence, the emerging picture is one in which the man experiences a reduction in comforts and satisfactions, an eroding of his privileged status in the family, and an increase in domestic responsibilities.

Since Joyce Brothers wrote her vivid description of the typical dual-career marriage, men have changed considerably in their behavior. While they are slow about actually helping their wives with household chores, they have taken an active interest in helping to raise the children, and this has proven rewarding for all concerned. Despite their "bad press," an increasing number of these men are helping their wives with household chores—such as grocery shopping, house cleaning, and even meal preparing. But, admittedly, husbands still have a way to go before they achieve parity with their wives in doing household chores.

Perhaps more surprising, but less welcome, some of these men have discovered the Superman role. The results are similar to those accompanying the Superwoman syndrome—anxiety, fatigue, lowered efficiency, reduced interest in sex, and other symptoms of overload and burnout (Harrell & Baack, 1986). These researchers suggest that men are experiencing the same problems as their wives in trying to cope with careers, marriage, home, and children, but with less preparation. They also note that men do not have the range of magazines available to women; these magazines help women to cope with excessive stress in dual-career marriages. Nor do men have the social-support networks that women often have in dealing with problems in child-rearing. As a consequence, Harrell and Baack conclude that men may have much to gain in the long run from dual-career marriages. But, in the short run—with no wife at home—they may lose the supportive structure that enabled them to cope with severe career demands. Seemingly anticipating the future, Jesse Bernard (1981) pointed out almost a decade ago that, for these husbands,

> The good provider role may be on its way out, but its legitimate successor has not yet appeared on the scene. (p. 12)

CONSEQUENCES FOR THE MARITAL RELATIONSHIP

Traditionally, marriage has been thought of as the bringing together of the "instrumental" role of a man with the "expressive" role of a woman to create a family unit. Any other role arrangement was viewed as a threat to the stability of the family. Thus, dual-career marriages—in which the wife also assumed an instrumental role as an employed person outside the home—were initially viewed as a threat to the marital relationship and family stability. As we shall see, however, this is not necessarily true.

Here we shall examine the consequences of dual careers for marital relationships in four key areas: standard of living, sex-roles and power structure, family planning and child care, and marital satisfaction and stability.

Standard of Living

Money influences not only our lifestyle but also our feelings of control over events, self-esteem, security, and many other personal and environmental considerations. In our highly competitive society, this tends to put a good deal of stress on the man who tries to play the role of good provider. Unless his income is considerably above average, he is not likely to be considered a good provider or to enable his family to enjoy an average standard of living. Increasingly, it is becoming necessary for both marital partners to work if they are to maintain an average or superior standard of living.

Movie Still Archives, Santa Fe, New Mexico

Lack of sufficient money in the marriage can be a source of continuing anxiety and conflict, which tend to rob the marital relationship of vitality and warmth. When a couple lack the money they need to achieve an acceptable standard of living, it not only is demoralizing but also tends to give rise to continual conflicts over how the money that is available should be spent. If either partner is not a prudent money manager, the situation is likely to be even worse. One persistent source of frustration in the 1980s has been the financial inability of young married couples—including many dual-career couples—to achieve the "American dream" of owning their own home.

Unfortunately, the net economic gain in dual-career marriages is not as great as it might appear. Even though dual-career incomes average about 35–40 percent higher than single-career incomes, there are various costs incurred because both people work—such as transportation, day care for young children, eating out more often, and taking more-expensive vacations—that tend to erode the net gain. In addition, dual-career couples tend to live up to their income; they spend more money because they have more money.

Another thorny question in dealing with the income of dual-career couples is how to handle the finances. In traditional marriages, money is mutual income regardless of whether the husband or wife earns it. But in dual-career marriages, each partner may want to keep control of part or all of his or her income. This may work out, providing a substantial percentage of each partner's income is put into the marital pot. But, when the partners start playing financial games—for example, when she pays for vacations and he pays the everyday expenses—it can lead to misunderstandings and conflict.

Finally, an interesting trend that markedly affects the financial status of some dual-career couples seems to be emerging (Koepp et al., 1986). This is the trend for higher-income, career-oriented men and women to marry, thus creating marriages with combined incomes far in excess of the average family and of most other dual-career couples.

Sex-Roles and Power Structure

Does a dual-career marriage affect the sex-roles and power structure of the couple? Not as much as might be expected. Although the U.S. Bureau of the Census stopped automatically defining the male as head of the household in 1980, most people still view the man in that role. And, although some studies indicate that employed married women have achieved greater sex-role equality than their unemployed counterparts, the traditional division of labor and power still tends to predominate (Rachlin & Hansen, 1985; Yogev & Brett, 1985). In a series of studies of the perceived social status of dual-career couples, Richardson and Mahoney (1981) found that both high-school and college students evaluated a couple's social status solely as a function of the husband's occupational status; the wife's occupation had no effect on her general social status and little effect on her husband's.

Although a gap still exists between the ideal of egalitarian sex-roles and reality in most dual-career marriages, traditional sex-roles continue to be challenged. In the meantime, Vicki Rachlin and James Hansen (1985) have concluded that "equity may prove a more useful and workable concept than egalitarianism in understanding the marital dynamics of dual-career couples" (p. 160). In short, employed married women may not expect sex role equality, but they do expect equity—sex-roles that are fair in terms of the contributions of each partner to the marriage.

In terms of power, the situation is somewhat similar. Traditionally, the husband has contributed the most valuable resources to the marriage—at least in terms of money—and, consequently, has dominated decision making. Because women are often discriminated against in terms of pay and promotions, the husband often brings home more money than his wife. With more egalitarian sex-roles and marriages, however, this traditional male perogative is giving way to the new norm of interdependence in which both spouses share in decision making. That is, neither spouse holds the dominant power position in the marriage at all times; rather, both rely on or support each other as personal, professional, and family needs require. Usually this works out so that the spouse with the greatest expertise or knowledge in a given area is the one who exercises the greatest decision-making power in that area. In turn, this spouse defers to his or her partner in areas where the other partner has greater expertise.

The concept of interdependence also permits greater flexibility in meeting each others needs and dealing with crisis situations. For example, when career demands are particularly stressful for the husband, the wife may assume most, or all, of the household tasks. Conversely, when her career demands increase markedly—for example, following a promotion—the husband may relieve her of household chores. Similar temporary measures may be taken in dealing with child-rearing and other marital concerns.

In short, the picture that emerges is one in which the woman's career and role as co-provider contribute an overall thrust toward greater sex-role equality and flexible sharing of power and decision making.

Family Planning and Child Care

Most research studies of dual-career families find that the presence of children dramatically affects the nature of the marital relationship. The critical factor seems to be lack of time. As we have noted, women find it particularly stressful to meet the demands of simultaneously being a wife and mother and pursuing a career. The time during which at least one child is preschool appears to be particularly difficult for many working women. When Houseknecht and Macke (1981) compared marital adjustment among highly educated women with no children, with young children, or with grown children, they found the most effective overall adjustment in women whose children were 18 or older. Family size is also an important factor. As family size increases in dual-career arrangements, so does dissatisfaction with the amount of time available, the lack of time to pursue long-term career goals, and the limited time the partners have to share with each other. However, employed married women express more dissatisfaction with both their jobs and their domestic activities than do men, perhaps because they still bear the primary responsibilities for household chores.

One way that dual-career couples have attempted to minimize the stresses involved in combining professional, spousal, and parental roles is not to have children or to have only one child. Of course, family planning is becoming more common among married couples in general, and—like the decision not to have children—is not limited to dual-career couples. Another option is for the woman to establish herself professionally before having children, and then to take a relatively brief maternity leave, for example, 12–16 weeks (Catalyst, 1982). Some companies also provide for paternity, as well as maternity, leave so that the husband can help during the early weeks after the birth of the baby.

Dual-career couples with preschool children are likely to experience three key sources of stress: (1) trying to juggle three roles simultaneously, (2) worrying over the affects of both parents' employment on their child's development, and (3)

Martha Stewart/The Picture Cube

finding quality child care (Goldenberg, 1986). As we have mentioned, there are ways of coping with role strain, and many worries about the effects of working parents can be dismissed as unfounded. There is no evidence that child care by persons other than the mother or father is in itself damaging to the child. Indeed, in most societies, people other than the parents typically care for the children. The former concern with finding quality day-care facilities is being rapidly corrected because our society has become aware of this problem and is taking effective measures to remedy it (Kennedy, 1986).

In Chapter 10, we shall deal with the challenge of children in more detail. Here, our purpose was simply to point up some special problems often associated with having children in dual-career marriages.

Marital Satisfaction and Stability

The problems of who earns the livelihood, how each partner spends the work day, and who does the housework carry over and influence evenings and weekends. Thus, dual-career, as well as dual-earner and dual-worker, marriages are inevitably different from those in which the woman is a full-time homemaker. But does this difference make a difference in terms of marital satisfaction? Marital stability?

The answer would appear to be a qualified "Yes" to both questions. As a group, dual-career marriages do appear somewhat less satisfying and less stable. Why? In evaluating the perils of dual-career marriages, Anastasia Touflexis (1985) has suggested:

In part the difficulties stem from the complexity of working couples' lives. There are only so much energy, emotion, and especially time to go around. When the

Tom Ballard/EKM-Nepenthe

career-minded pair finally meet at home, they are usually exhausted. Often their conversation is confined to work. Intimacy erodes; boredom sets in. (p. 67)

For fatigued marital partners, even sex can become more of a duty than an emotionally gratifying experience. This may account in part for the findings of Constance Avery-Clark (1985) who studied over 200 married couples at the Masters and Johnson Institute. She found that married career women were more likely to experience inhibited sexual desire than their counterparts in ordinary jobs. She also found that 22 percent of men married to career women were impotent. This is about twice the rate of impotence for married men in general.

Perhaps the key point here is that dual-career marriages—at least when both partners are committed to high-level career positions—are inherently stressful. They require a high degree of skill in time management, communication, setting priorities, decision making, and coping with stress—both career and marital stress. If employed women are dissatisfied with their marriages, they appear more likely than unemployed women to divorce—possibly because their superior financial position provides them with more options.

In this context, Mary Regan and Helen Roland (1985) have found that contemporary college women aspire to high-status professional careers and have the commitment and career values necessary to achieve them. These researchers also found that contemporary college men are more career oriented than ever before. When two highly career-oriented college graduates get married and decide to have children, there is "a built-in potential for role conflict as individuals attempt to combine family and career roles" (p. 990).

To defuse this potentially explosive situation, these researchers suggest that one partner should lower his or her career aspirations. They anticipate that it will most likely be the woman who makes the compromise. "Alternative resolutions include divorce, conscious rejection of parenthood . . . as well as both spouses lowering their career aspirations" (p. 990).

In some cases, one partner may be dissatisfied with the marriage although the other may be satisfied. For example, when a woman's occupational prestige is higher than her husband's, she may express satisfaction with the marriage but he may not (Hornung & McCullough, 1981; Campbell, 1987). The effects of unconventional dual-career patterns also appear to be more negative for the husband than for the wife. It is likely that, as traditional sex role stereotypes are changed, the effects of status inequities between partners will change as well. Perhaps equally, or more, important—as Alice Rossi (1977) pointed out over a decade ago—is a change in the workplace to make it more responsive to, and appreciative of, women's reproductive functions. A step in this direction was taken in January 1987, when the U.S. Supreme Court upheld a California law that provides 4 months unpaid maternity leave for pregnant mothers and guarantees them their jobs back.

In sum, the effects of dual careers on marital satisfaction and stability appear to depend on the sex-role expectations, the level of career aspiration and commitment by each partner, essential time-management and related skills, the decision to have or not to have children, the marital relationship and persons involved, and their overall life situation.

In the final section of this chapter, we shall discuss ways of making dual-career marriages less stressful and more satisfying.

BOX 9-6 / SUMMARY OF COMMON PROBLEMS IN DUAL CAREER MARRIAGES

The problems in dual-career marriages do not differ markedly from those in single-earner marriages, but they are intensified by time pressures and other stresses characteristic of this marital form. As in single-earner marriages, the specific problems may vary considerably from one dual-career couple to another.

However, the following problems tend to be common to most dual-career marriages. For our present purposes, we shall deal with them in summary form.

1. *Communication.* This involves developing effective patterns of communication and using them to coordinate problems solving, decision making, and related activities. Of particular importance is listening to each other.

2. *Budgeting time.* Because time is very limited—in terms of being alone together, discussing problems, handling finances and household chores, and child-rearing—it is essential to use available time effectively.

3. *Household chores.* This involves taking inventory of what is required and working out an equitable distribution of duties, making allowance for times when one partner may need to assume more of the load.

4. *Mobility.* This involves the changing occupational picture, job transfers, and even career changes. In some cases, one partner may continue working while the other retrains for a different occupation.

5. *Sex life.* Despite pressures, fatigue, and limited time alone together, this involves planning time and ensuring conditions conducive to maintaining a satisfactory sex life, which is not an easy achievement.

6. *Careers.* When one partner gives his or her career first priority, the marriage is likely to suffer. Ambitious workalcoholics and dual-career marriages do not mix.

7. *Stress and overloading.* A high level of stress is characteristic of the dual-career life style. Thus, the partners must learn to cope with it. The alternative is overloading and burnout.

There are many other problems that tend to be intensified in dual-career marriages—including handling finances, providing each other with needed emotional support, and having children. In addition, there are estimated to be over one million "commuter dual-career marriages," in which the partners live in different geographical areas and see each other only on weekends or even less often. Here, the preceding problems not only are intensified but also take on a somewhat unique quality.

In essence, as the marital therapist Herbert Goldenberg (1986) has pointed out, "Each dual-career couple must develop its own unique, non-traditional structure for systematically attending to their complex lives" (p. 3).

SOLVING THE PROBLEMS OF DUAL-CAREER COUPLES

Dual-career marriage is a relatively new form of marriage, and there are few models or guidelines to help ensure its success. At the same time, this type of marriage is faced with a host of unique problems (Box 9–6). Prominent among these are avoiding career competition, juggling roles and responsibilities, establishing a social support structure, and working toward institutional and societal changes that will reduce the stress on dual-worker and dual-career couples.

Avoiding Career Competition.   Although a dual-career couple may insist that each approves of and supports the other's career aspirations, a below-the-surface competition may exist and intrude on the relationship. For example, if one partner is faced with severe career demands, or perhaps a career setback, the other may offer little in the way of emotional or practical support. Conversely, if one partner receives a high-level promotion, the other may feel envious, rather than joyful, at their partner's achievement.

Another type of career competition is probably more common, as well as less subtle. This is the husband's assumption that, because he has the higher income (which he usually does), his career is more important and should take precedence over his wife's. As a consequence, he may feel "entitled" to various privileges—such as not sharing in household chores—that can lead to resentment on the part of his wife. However, if she feels that their arrangement is an equitable one, as we noted in Lucia Gilbert's study, the arrangement may be acceptable, although by no means ideal.

Juggling Roles and Responsibilities.   The dual-career couple are also faced with the decision of whether or not to have children. If children do enter the picture, the partners have to make adjustments at work, at home, and in their marital relationship. These adjustments mean juggling roles for both spouses, and coping with the additional role of parent can be highly stressful. We have observed the futility of either partner trying to be a Superperson and the resulting overload and burnout when they try.

To minimize the stress involved in trying to juggle career, homemaker, and child-rearing roles, the wife needs backup from her husband. Although husbands have adapted well to child-rearing, they have been notably reluctant to participate in household chores. As a result, they place unnecessary stress on their wives, as well as on their marital relationship. If dual-career marriages are to prove compatible with having children, it would appear essential that the partners think through established sex-roles and social norms and work out an agreement that is equitable and has a high degree of flexibility.

Establishing a Social-Support Structure.   Obtaining support from a spouse absorbed in his or her own career may be difficult, but finding support from people outside the relationship and from the workplace is often more difficult. Often dual-career couples are so preoccupied with their own problems that they have little time to participate in, or perhaps build, a social-support network of other dual-career couples with whom they can share common problems and solutions. Such a support structure can offer a great deal of emotional support and help marital partners to deal with specific problems in their marriage. In lieu of these support networks, many dual-career couples are participating in marital workshops (See Box 9–7). Other couples are going to marital therapists who specialize in helping dual-career couples resolve their problems.

Working Toward Institutional and Social Change.   As we have noted, the workplace is geared for typical career-oriented married men and makes few provi-

BOX 9-7 / EXAMPLES OF WORKSHOP ACTIVITIES FOR DUAL-CAREER COUPLES

GROUP EXERCISES

Complete the Phrase. (Each person responds to the phrases by jotting down his or her initial thoughts.)

"Three wishes I have . . . ," "My career is . . . ," "Love is . . . ," "I am afraid of . . . ," "Three words my partner would use to describe me. . . ."

Role Scenarios. (Each person responds as though the situation is happening to him or her.)

Your spouse receives an offer of a better position that would require you to quit your job if you are to continue to live together.

You feel. . . . You say. . . .

Partner-of-the-Year Contest. Write a want ad describing traits you look for in a mate. Then identify those traits that would be beneficial in maintaining a healthy dual-career relationship and family.

SKILL CHECKLIST

Dual-Career Couple Survival Skill Inventory.
1. I am willing to negotiate and renegotiate my expectations.
   (Circle one.)   1   2   3   4   5
   Strongly disagree   Strongly agree
2. I am flexible—that is, I am willing to change myself and to accept change in my spouse or in our relationship.
   (Circle one.)   1   2   3   4   5
   Strongly disagree   Strongly agree

The Dual-Career Couple Job Readiness Inventory.
1. a. _____ I know where I would like to be 5 years from now in my career.

   b. _____ My mate knows where she or he would like to be five years from now in her or his career.

2. a. _____ I have researched (talked to someone in the organization, visited, read brochures and reports, and so forth) the organizations in which I wish to be employed.

   b. _____ My mate has researched (talked to someone in the organization, visited, read brochures and reports, and so forth) the organizations in which she or he wishes to be employed.

3. a. _____ I am aware of what kind of compromises I am willing to make now and 5 years from now.

   b. _____ My mate is aware of what kind of compromises she or he is willing to make now and 5 years from now.

Workshop activities such as these are commonly used by marital therapists who deal mainly with dual-career couples. Typically, such therapists rely heavily on general systems theory—focusing on communication patterns, roles and responsibilities, and similar areas. However, attention is also paid to feelings and frustrations that are often intense in dual-career marriages. Essentially, the objective of therapy is to clarify the career ambitions of each partner and to coordinate their careers and marital relationship in a way that nourishes both.

sions for assisting dual-career wives—particularly those who wish to have children. However, conditions are gradually and painfully changing so that maternity leave, flextime, job sharing, and quality child-care facilities are becoming more available.

It definitely appears that many of the problems confronting dual-career couples can be alleviated through changes in the workplace and society that provide a more congenial environment for this rapidly growing form of marriage.

Given all the problems, the potential rewards of dual-career marriages still appear to outweigh the costs. If the partners are able to resolve their personal, role, and marital problems, they can achieve a high level of personal fulfillment through their career achievements and family interactions.

SUMMARY—Chapter 9

1. About 60 percent of married women—including mothers with young children—are in the labor force, and the number continues to increase. Less than 10 percent of American families now consist of the traditional breadwinner husband, homemaker wife, and 2 to 4 children.

2. Married women are employed for one or more reasons: for economic independence from their husbands, for achievement and personal growth, to avoid isolation and boredom, to afford material luxuries, and because of financial necessity.

3. Dual-career marriages are those in which both partners pursue full-time careers. Some are "traditional" in that the wife assumes the additional responsibility for the home and children. Others are "role-sharing," in which those responsibilities are shared. Some are "transitional": the husbands help to care for the children but do not share the housework.

4. Employed wives are physically and emotionally healthier, are happier, and view child care more as fulfilling than as self-sacrificing. But when they add responsibility for the home and children to their career demands, they risk the danger of overload and burnout.

5. Husbands in dual-career marriages experience an erosion of their traditional status as authority figure, decision maker, and good provider; receive fewer services from their wives; and may resent being expected to help with "women's work." On the other hand, they benefit from the additional income; are freer to make advantageous professional or career decisions; and to some extent are learning to accept a share of household responsibility.

6. Two-career marriages affect a couple's standard of living as well as their sex roles and power relationship. The couple's standard of living rises but there are extra expenses attendant on the wife's employment and there may be conflict about dividing the income. Since the husband usually earns more, he retains more power; however, a new norm—"interdependence," or shared decision making—is emerging.

7. Family planning and child care are also affected. A preschool child is especially stressful to the employed wife, and many couples choose to have no children or only one, or to defer having children until the wife's career has been established and she can take a brief maternity leave. Couples also worry about having others care for the child, but there is no evidence that this harms the child and it is the accepted pattern in most societies.

8. Marital satisfaction and stability are adversely affected. Spouses with careers are often too tired for sex, more likely to be impotent or frigid, and quicker to divorce.

9. The problems of dual-career couples can be ameliorated by avoiding competition, juggling roles and responsibilities, and building a network of social support. Needed changes in the workplace—maternity and paternity leave, flextime, and job sharing—are being made, and child-care facilities are becoming more available. In general, the rewards of a dual-career marriage appear to outweigh its costs.

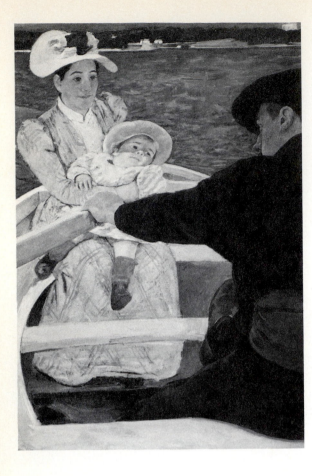

THE CHALLENGE OF CHILDREN

A baby is a statement of hope in an uncertain world.
—Keith Madson (1986, p. 20)

In the 1950s, two key reasons for getting married were to have sex and to have babies. There were other reasons—such as the division of labor between a good provider and a good homemaker—but the most popular incentives were the legalization of sexual activity and the creation of a family. Of course, many people did have sex and babies without getting married, but that was not usually intentional nor was it acceptable.

Although families differed in size, most couples hoped for at least four children. The family, in turn, was entrusted by society with providing physical care, love, and training essential for each child to mature into a responsible and productive citizen. In essence, society depended on the institutions of marriage and family to maintain and perpetuate the basic values of our culture and to ensure the future of our country.

This picture has undergone a marked change. Today, couples still have sex and babies when they marry, but they do so in a quite different context. The women's movement, a sexual revolution, better methods of contraception, planned parenthood, dual-career marriages and other changes have ushered in a new era of choice. Now it is common to have sex without marriage, sex without children, marriage without children, and even children without marriage. People who marry are more likely to plan their families to fit their careers, life styles, and other considerations; as a result, they will have fewer children and will have them at a later age. About 20 percent will opt for the child-free alternative. In addition, dual-career couples will spend less time with their children and have a reduced role in child-rearing.

In this chapter, we shall explore the choices that confront both individuals and couples with respect to having and rearing children. Specifically, we shall examine the reasons for having or not having children, the transition to becoming a parent, the psychological conditions that foster healthy child development, the common problems in child rearing, and the effects of children on marital satisfaction.

HAVING CHILDREN: A MATTER OF CHOICE

Should we have children? If so, when? How many? If not, why not? These are the kinds of questions that many couples ask—some before marriage, some after. These questions are applicable to divorced people who remarry as well as to never-married people.

Reasons for Having Children

This year, about 3 million American couples will experience an event with far-reaching consequences for them, for their marriage, and for our society: They

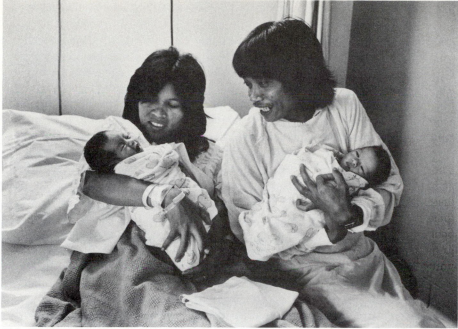

Ulrike Welsch

will have a baby. For over 40 percent, it will be their first child, and, for many, it will be their last. What are their reasons for having the baby?

People have children for a variety of reasons. Some of these arise out of the individual's own upbringing; some are related to our traditional cultural norms; and some are the result of inadvertent pregnancy.

1. *Cultural norms.*   Traditionally, there have been strong cultural pressures—including religious ones—to bear children, to be fruitful, and to contribute to the future of the group. The fact that most married couples do have children establishes a model for newlyweds to follow. When the members of our peer group are getting married and starting families, it is likely that we will follow their example.

   While cultural pressures to have children have decreased markedly in contemporary America, they are by no means extinct. Our own parents, our peers, and the mass media all tend to perpetuate the concepts of marriage and family. Sometimes these pressures are very subtle, as when parents tell their children, "When you grow up and have children of your own. . . ."

2. *To have a family of our own and to experience the rewards of rearing healthy, happy, and well-adjusted children whom we love and who love us in return.*   Unfortunately, this reason is far more complicated than is commonly assumed. A common belief, for example, is that children are a constant source of joy and happiness; but, even under the most favorable conditions, parenthood has costs as well as rewards.

   These costs can include a less-happy marriage during the child-rearing years, as well as personal costs in terms of time and energy. In addition, the financial costs of child-rearing in today's world are enormous. Nevertheless, most married couples are willing, and often eager, to accept the challenge of children.

3. *To provide support in old age.*   In many Third World countries, Social Security and pension plans are nonexistent. Thus, a married couple has to depend on their children to take care of them in old age when they are no longer able to support themselves. In our own society, this reason for having children may seem unwarranted. But observing older people among us can lead to thoughts about finding ourselves alone, sick, and poor in later years without anyone to care about us or to help us.

   Although most parents insist they will never be a burden to their children, independence in later years is not always possible. In essence, children are a form of insurance against the unexpected.

4. *Accidental pregnancies.*   For many people—particularly those who do not believe in abortion—an accidental pregnancy may lead to the decision to go ahead and have the baby. Often such pregnancies are not so "accidental." For example, a wife who realizes that she and her husband are bored with each other and growing apart may get pregnant in an effort to give their relationship new meaning and direction. In other cases, an "accidental" pregnancy may represent an attempt by one partner to force the other into an unwanted marriage. Most of us have probably heard the expression "shotgun wedding" used to describe this type of situation.

   By far, the greatest number of accidental pregnancies occur among teenagers in the United States. In 1985, more than one million teenage pregnancies occurred before marriage; unmarried teenagers accounted for over half of all teen births—births by women under 18 years of age (Stark, 1986; Smith, 1986). As we have noted, teenage pregnancies have become a major social problem. Ironically, we can send astronauts to the moon, but we seem unable to prevent more than one million unmarried teenage pregnancies each year.

5. *To give another human being the precious gift of life and assure our own immortality.*   To give another human being the gift of life and to care for him or her during the difficult years of childhood is one of the greatest of all human accomplishments.

   At the same time, it is also a way of being remembered, of saying, "I existed," "I was here," "I left my footprints in the sands of time." For families who can trace their lineage back several centuries—such as the royal family in England—having children is of great importance in passing on the family line. For the rest of us, having children is still an important way of being remembered, of establishing our place in the long line of generations, and—in a general sense—of establishing our own immortality.

To sum up, the decision to have children may be motivated by one or several of the preceding reasons, as well as by less-common ones. In view of the far-reaching and long-term consequences of this decision, it is important that married couples examine their motivation for having children and are in agreement on the decision.

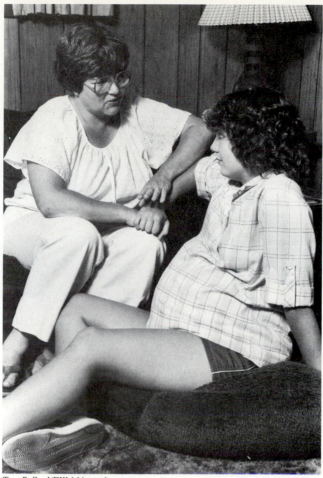

Tom Ballard/EKM-Nepenthe

Postponing Child-Bearing

As Janet Reading and Ellen Amatea (1986) have pointed out, "The modal pattern for today's American woman is that she is employed outside the home as well as married. Even women with children are expected to work, and in fact, a majority are employed" (pp. 255–256). As a result, many women who would have had children in their 20s a generation ago are now postponing child-bearing until they are well established in their careers.

Not only are these women waiting to have children, but also they will have fewer children than if they had started earlier. Particularly, if the woman likes her career and wishes to pursue it, her earlier dreams of perhaps having four children are likely to be modified; now one or two children may seem sufficient. Also, it is not easy to maintain the same standard of living when children come along. Thus, careers and financial considerations may enter into the decision to postpone having children or to have fewer children.

In addition, an old barrier to postponing child-bearing has given way. Formerly, it was thought that women over 35 represented a "high-risk" group in terms of fertility and having a healthy baby. But the marked increase in women 35

Hazel Hankin

and older having babies—coupled with medical advances—has made this traditional age barrier irrelevant (Parachini, 1986). In essence, a healthy 35-year-old or older woman "can look forward to as safe a pregnancy and as healthy an infant as a woman in her early 20s" (p. 1). Thus, a woman in her 30s—or even 40s—need not fear that the time for having a baby has passed her by, and dual-career couples have greater freedom of choice in terms of planning when to have children.

Remaining Child-Free

Some couples drift into a permanent state of deferred child-bearing, some choose to be child-free, and still others have it chosen for them. The drifters are often people who thought they would have children eventually but find that they like their lives the way they are. They never seem to be ready. Such people, single or married, often find that they prefer their child-free life even though they may not be entirely satisfied with it. In any event, they think children would make things worse rather than better.

There is a substantial number of people in our society who do not want children. Modern contraception, abortion, career orientation, and changing values have made the child-free alternative both possible and socially acceptable. But aside from couples who drift into a permanent state of deferred child-bearing, what are the reasons for choosing not to have children?

Some persons feel they would not make good parents, or at least not the kind of parents they think they should be. One young woman put it this way, "The best thing I can do for my children, in my opinion, is not to have any. I'm simply not cut out to be a mother." Other young people observe the confusion and frustration of their friends who married and started families without really understanding what parenting involved. As a consequence, they may be uncertain about having children, at least until they are more mature and ready to accept the responsibili-

BOX 10-1 / ADOPTION

Adoption is another way of becoming a parent. It is particularly useful for married couples who cannot conceive or who are at risk of having a child with serious genetic defects. It is also used by single adults who want children.

Adoption may pose a number of problems for would-be parents. For one thing, there has been a reduction in the number of available infants in recent years. In 1985, only one baby was available in the United States for each 40 couples wishing to adopt a baby. A second problem centers around the preadoption legal procedure. Adoption agencies are often biased when screening applicants and tend to rule out single persons and people with unorthodox life styles. Such rulings may be made even though the persons would make loving and competent parents. Of course, babies may be available in other countries, but international adoptions are often both expensive and risky. Still a third problem concerns new medical advances—for example, in vitro fertilization (IVF) and the use of surrogate mothers—that provide infertile couples with a range of options in addition to adoption.

Compared to biological children and stepchildren, adopted children may have several advantages. Prominent among these are really being wanted by their adoptive parents, being adopted by couples who have a higher than average income, and having a greater likelihood of two parents in the home.

Despite careful screening and adoption procedures, however, some adoptions do fail, resulting in the removal of the child from the adoptive home. This is usually a painful experience for both the parents and the child. One factor indicative of higher risk in adoption is the age of the child. The younger the infant, the greater the rate of success. Also, couples who have been married only a short time before adoption and those who are overloaded by the stresses of life are more likely to fail in their adoptive parenthood.

One problem that haunts many adoptive parents is whether to tell the child that he or she is adopted. A related problem is the desire of many children to learn more about their biological parents and the circumstances that led to their being put up for adoption. In general, however, it appears that these problems are taken in stride by adoptive parents and children who have established loving emotional bonds and a desirable family climate.

---

ties and stresses of parenthood. And, as we have noted, delaying child-bearing can lead to a permanent state of childlessness. In general, voluntarily childless women rate the costs of a child higher and the satisfactions lower than women who want children (Callan, 1986). Probably the same can be said about men who choose the child-free alternative.

Finally, there are those couples—one of every six couples in the United States—who are child-free because of inability to have children (Salazar, 1986). In view of changing values and life styles, this may not seem a great tragedy, but—as Lyn Harris (1985) has pointed out—most "couples facing infertility feel denied, cheated, punished, and left out" (p. 6). To add to their problem, the possibility of adopting a child has become increasingly remote (Box 10-1). Thus Marilyn Larkin (1985) has concluded that "To make it through the emotional

BOX 10-2 / INFERTILITY

"Why can't I have a baby?"

This is one of the most painful questions that a woman, and often her husband, can ask. Couples who are infertile tend to feel cheated, denied, and often punished. In many cases, sex becomes a chore, and there is a dangerous tendency to blame each other until medical analysis clarifies the problem.

In 1986, one out of six couples who wished to conceive were infertile. In about 50 percent of these cases, the wife was infertile as a result of diseased fallopian tubes. In most of the other cases, the husband was infertile; about 25 percent of American men suffer impaired fertility for reasons that may vary but are often unclear. In a minority of cases, both husband and wife were infertile. By means of a **fertility workup test,** which is time consuming and expensive, a medical clinic can usually pinpoint the source of the difficulty.

It has been estimated that over 60 percent of infertile couples can be helped, and the chances of reversing infertility by means of new medical procedures are increasing. But what about couples who can't be helped? Are they willing to consider unconventional approaches to having children? Some are and some aren't.

About half of infertile couples indicate they would accept in vitro fertilization. Here, the doctor surgically extracts an egg from the mother and places it in a laboratory dish with the father's sperm. If the conception "takes," the fertilized egg is then implanted in the mother. The chances are estimated to be about one in ten of having a baby on the first try, but the procedure can be repeated. About 200 medical clinics in the United States offer in vitro fertilization.

There are several other new approaches to dealing with infertility, including the use of surrogate mothers. However, the latter is not popular among infertile couples—in large part because they fear the surrogate mother will want to keep the baby, which is not an unrealistic fear.

For infertile couples, there are a number of resources to which they can turn. Prominent among these is RESOLVE, Inc., which provides a national information network for infertile couples and has local chapters in most states.

straits of infertility, couples need courage, endurance, and a commitment to each other" (p. 49). Although the transition to parenthood has received a great deal of research attention, the "transition to nonparenthood" has received very little (Matthews & Matthews, 1986).

Fortunately, some types of infertility can be medically corrected, and recent medical advances now make it possible for most couples to circumvent infertility and be the biological parents of a baby (see Box 10–2).

BECOMING PARENTS

One of the most important roles that a person can assume is becoming a parent. Unfortunately, it is also a role for which most people receive little, if any, preparation. True, there are a myriad of books on parenthood, but these are usually far from adequate when the real event occurs. Both the pregnancy and the arrival of the baby have profound effects on the woman, the man, and their relationship.

The choices that must be made, the nature of pregnancy and childbirth, and the effects on the marital couple are dealt with in Appendix B. Here, our focus is on assuming the role of parent.

When a Woman Becomes a Mother

> Women don't have "built-in" instincts that automatically make them good mothers when they give birth. The new baby must endure many of the "student" mother's mistakes.
>
> —A. C. Chenault (1987, unpublished work)

Many changes take place in a woman during pregnancy, from the obvious physical differences that anyone can see to the internal changes only she knows about. Physically, women have to adjust to their bodies, which are growing and changing to feed and care for a developing fetus. That means eating habits change. It also means dressing, walking, and sleeping in different ways to accommodate the growing, moving baby. These new routines may cause stress or the disruption of old patterns, which can be disconcerting to both partners. In addition, couples have to begin making room physically for a child long before he or she arrives.

Making room for the child mentally and emotionally is another matter. Many women experience a sense of completion as the baby nears delivery; they undergo a rise in self-esteem as the miracle of creation becomes more and more a fact of life. Even women who do not consider having children to be a primary goal of life derive feelings of wonder and pride from the knowledge that they can give birth to another human. Throughout pregnancy, women prepare for a new role—that of mother—and they often reflect about their own mother as well as about other mothers they have known.

When the baby does finally arrive, the mother usually finds that she has more to do than she ever imagined. Not only is there a baby to care for and the child's father to worry about, but also there may be new grandparents and other relatives and friends who want to see, hold, and do something for the baby. All this is likely to leave the mother feeling very tired. In addition, women who have had Caesareans, who have had complications during delivery, or whose babies have had complications need time to recuperate. A few women—about 1 in 400—experience emotional depression following the birth (Coleman et al., 1984). These depressive episodes, technically called postpartum depression, are commonly referred to as the "maternity blues" and usually clear up in a matter of days or at most a few weeks.

The new role of mother is a very exacting one. A baby is so helpless, so dependent, and so demanding of time and energy that the mother may feel incapable of coping with the combined demands of the baby plus those of the husband and the usual household chores she is expected to resume. Thus, it is often a good idea for a first-time mother to work out a support network prior to the birth so that she can get help if she needs it. Some women need more help becoming mothers than others. But, over time, these women usually feel increasingly competent in their new role as mother.

When a Man Becomes a Father

> A woman feels more vulnerable as well as more special when she is pregnant. There is a new life inside her. Her hormones are acting in novel ways. She clearly needs and deserves substantial support. But what of her spouse? He shows no physical signs of pregnancy, but in some ways, emotionally and psychologically, he is as pregnant as she is.
>
> —*Jerrold Lee Shapiro (1987, p. 36)*

Men often have more trouble adjusting to the role of father than women do to the role of mother. The husband is expected to play an increasingly active role during pregnancy and delivery as well as after the baby is born, but at the same time, he's caught in a double bind. Although his presence is requested, his feelings are not (Shapiro, 1987). Despite changes in the traditional male role, his feelings of fear, uncertainty, jealousy, and often anger are strictly taboo. They are incompatible with his male role in becoming a father. In a minority of cases, men may express these feelings indirectly by having an affair or other "acting-out" behavior.

Of course, some men react quite differently than others to the role changes, the increased responsibilities, and the changed relationships with their wives. Some feel quite comfortable about the pregnancy, the delivery, and the introduction of a third person into their marriage. Others are fearful that something may go wrong

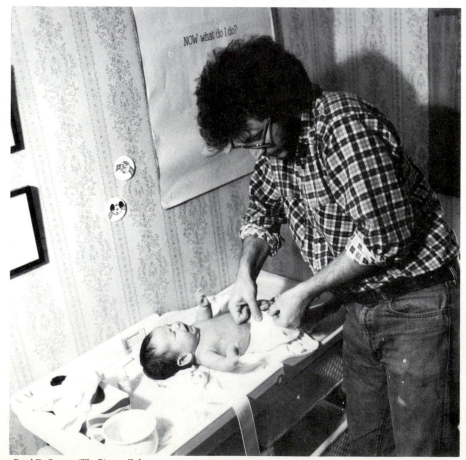

Read D. Brugger/The Picture Cube

during delivery; feel jealous of the baby who is getting all the attention; feel anxious about the baby replacing them as "number one" in their wife's affections; are angered by their wife's lack of availability—physically, emotionally, and sexually; and feel overburdened by additional financial and other responsibilities. As one frustrated father expressed it, "I don't even have the right to die anymore unless I can manage a large insurance policy, which I can't."

Jerrold Shapiro (1987) has concluded from his studies that, if fathers are to get a solid start on the role of parent, they must share their feelings and concerns with their wives. He also found that fathers who did so reported improved relationships with their wives, a more-positive feeling toward taking on the role of parent, and increased pride in having a family of their own.

When a Couple Becomes a Family

When the baby arrives, the husband and wife are no longer simply a couple—they are now part of a family. All family decisions must take the baby into consideration. As a consequence, there are inevitable changes in the marital relationship. The ways in which husband, wife, and baby work out these changes will become the **family system.**

With three people in the family, there are possibilities for alliances, partnerships, and secrets that were not there before. For one thing, no twosome can know everything that goes on between another twosome. The alliance between mother and child is different from that between father and child; and these alliances are different from the one between mother and father.

According to Cowan and others (1978), who followed couples from early in first pregnancies to when the babies were about 6 months old, decisions concerning the family undergo constant change. This means that

> In order for a couple to decide what kind of parents they want to be, they must take into account what kind of family they want to have, and begin to try some things consistent with the kind of people they are and the kind of baby they have. Parenting attitudes, then, provide links between individual identities, family practices, and societal norms. (p. 30)

In a more-recent study, Hilary Lips and Anne Morrison (1986) found that the transition to family by couples having their first child also involved a focus on family issues—including the problems encountered by mothers trying to return to their careers after having the baby.

In the remainder of this chapter, we shall examine the kinds of parenting roles that mothers and fathers assume and the kinds of decisions that arise for parents as their children grow. How couples see their roles and resolve the issues that arise determines the kind of family they will have and can profoundly affect the mental health and personalities of their children.

PSYCHOLOGICAL CONDITIONS FOSTERING HEALTHY DEVELOPMENT

The current generation of mothers and fathers represents a new breed. In most cases, they have chosen to become parents. Despite living in a world of social unrest and change, they accept the challenge of trying to rear healthy and well-

BOX 10–3 / A BILL OF RIGHTS FOR CHILDREN

The Joint Commission on Mental Health of Children (1970) formulated a *Bill of Rights for Children*. The following are among those rights:

1. The right to be wanted.
2. The right to be born healthy.
3. The right to live in a favorable environment.
4. The right to loving care.
5. The right to acquire the intellectual, emotional, and social skills for coping effectively in our society.

Although this Bill of Rights was published some two decades ago, it appears equally applicable today.

adjusted children. Unfortunately, however, many of today's parents receive little in the way of preparation for child-rearing other than "on-the-job" training. While they may have rather definite ideas about the "right" and "wrong" ways to bring up children, they often lack the needed information for coping with the challenge confronting them. Some rights for children are listed in Box 10–3. On the other hand, some parents may have too much information—they may be overwhelmed with child-rearing advice from experts of all types, from best-selling authors to their own parents.

Even before the baby is born, parents may begin to wonder about how they should deal with problems that may arise. How much and what kind of discipline should we use? Should we entrust our child to day care? What sort of school will be best? How much television should we let our child watch?

How parents deal with these questions as the child grows up depends on many factors, and the nature, course, and outcome of child-rearing are heavily influenced by the interplay between the child, the family, and their environment. The child brings into the family his or her own unique characteristics, and most parents quickly come to realize that the child is an active participant in his or her own development and not merely a passive object shaped by parents and environmental forces. Furthermore, the parents themselves have different personalities, family backgrounds, and beliefs concerning child-rearing that influence their interactions in the family. In the family itself, the number of children, the ordinal position of the child, the family climate, and the family situation (single-parent, reconstituted, and so on) all affect child development.

Each child is exposed to a unique interpersonal and family subculture, made up of interactions with significant others, including parents, siblings, and kinfolk. However, the child is also exposed to a more-general environment in which the entire family lives and functions. As Arlene Skolnick (1981) has pointed out, "Family life is bound up with social, economic, and ideological circumstances of particular times and places" (p. 43). One major consequence, notes Henry Ricciuti (1979), is that "attention is being directed not only to the child's experience within the family but also to the characteristics of the neighborhood, peer group, school, and larger society that may have an impact on children directly or indirectly through the effects of families" (p. 842).

Because of this broader environmental context in which the family lives and functions, parents must take into account a number of outside influences on their offspring. Paul Insel and Rudolf Moos (1974) stressed that some environments are supportive but that others can be destructive in a number of ways. Being able to do something about the destructive environmental elements is a major concern of many parents and of such social scientists as Urie Bronfenbrenner (1979). What are the effects on child development of working mothers, day care, peers, and slum environments? While generalizations are often made about these factors, research data—as Bronfenbrenner has noted—are hard to come by. However, parents can gain some comfort in knowing that psychologists and sociologists have identified a number of conditions within the family that can foster healthy development of children. Let us look at some of these factors.

Providing Love and Acceptance

Providing an atmosphere of love and acceptance has been demonstrated to be of key importance in healthy child development—especially in terms of self-esteem and worth. In one of the first comprehensive studies of child-rearing practices, Sears, Maccoby, and Levin (1957) concluded that the most crucial and pervasive of all the influences exerted in the home was the love and warmth expressed by parents. Later studies have supported this conclusion, demonstrating a close relationship between parental affection and the development of such traits as self-esteem, self-reliance, independence, and self-control. In addition, love and acceptance help children develop a basic sense of trust toward their parents and the world around them. This sense of trust becomes a major safeguard against fear and anxiety, giving the child the feeling of security needed to actively explore his or her environment and to master needed competencies (Erikson, 1968). Furthermore, many conditions that might otherwise impair development—physical handicaps, poverty—may be largely neutralized for the child who feels love and acceptance.

Love and acceptance usually form part of a broader pattern of positive family interaction and relationships. For example, parents who show acceptance also tend to show interest in the child and what he or she is doing, to respect the child as a person, and to display warmth and affection. Such parents typically encourage their children to interact with the world—within limits essential for their protection—and tend to provide firm, but not coercive, controls.

Conversely, parental rejection is likely to have negative consequences. Such rejection may be shown in a number of ways, such as physical neglect, denial of affection, lack of interest in the child's activities and achievements, harsh or inconsistent punishment, and lack of respect for the child's rights and feelings. In a few families, it also involves cruel and abusive treatment (see Box 10–4). For the child, the negative effects associated with such rejection include low self-esteem, feelings of insecurity and inadequacy, retarded intellectual development, increased aggression, loneliness, generalized fear or anxiety, guilt, depression, and later difficulties in giving and receiving love (Evoy, 1982; Coleman et al., 1987).

Supplying Structure and Discipline

A clearly structured environment—one that is orderly and consistent and in which the child knows what is expected and acceptable and what will be disapproved or punished—appears to foster healthy development. Three elements of structuring

BOX 10-4 / CHILD ABUSE

It has only been since the 1960s that child abuse has received much scientific and public attention. Michael Martin and James Walters (1982) have identified five types of child abuse:

1. Abandonment—temporary or permanent abandonment of child by parent or caregiver.
2. Neglect—deliberate acts on part of parent or caregiver that avoid meeting the child's basic needs.
3. Emotional abuse—deliberate devaluation of the child, which leads to psychological injury and failure to thrive.
4. Physical abuse—intentional physical injury of child, whether or not such injury is related to disciplinary action.
5. Sexual abuse—sexual contact between adult and child, whether the contact is initiated by the adult or child.

The incidence of physical abuse of children in the United States is estimated at about 2 million. In 1974, the Congress of the United States passed the Child Abuse Prevention and Treatment Act. This led to laws in all states requiring that persons knowing of such abuse report it. Nevertheless, many, if not most, cases go unreported.

Physical abuse may involve beatings leading to severe bruises and welts, abrasions and lacerations, puncture wounds, and burns and scalds. More than 2,000 children die each year as a result of such abuse and another 40,000 or more suffer serious injury—including over 5,000 cases of brain damage resulting in mental retardation.

Comparable figures for child sexual abuse are not available, although Sebold (1987) has estimated that up to 96,000 boys are sexually abused each year. And the comparable figures for girls is considered to be several times higher. (*Newsweek*, 1982; Sebold, 1987). The nature of the sexual abuse varies. However, fondling of the child's genitals, attempted vaginal intercourse, and oral–genital sex appear to be most common; forced masturbation and anal intercourse are much less common. The offender—even in the case of boys— is usually male. In the case of girls, the offender is usually the father or stepfather. Typically, the offender tries to maintain the relationship by telling the child that revealing the "secret" would break up the family or hurt the mother. Almost all children are fearful about revealing sexual abuse.

The effects of sexual abuse on the child depend on the child's age, the child's perception of the situation, and whether or not the child was traumatized by the incident or incidents (Elwell & Ephross, 1987). For girls, sexual abuse may lead to severe guilt feelings and long-term difficulties in relating to men on a sexual level.

seem particularly important: (1) clearly defined standards and limits, so that children understand what goals, means, and conduct are approved; (2) adequately defined roles for both older and younger members of the family, so that children know what is expected of both themselves and others; and (3) established methods of discipline that encourage desired behavior, discourage misbehavior, and deal with infractions as they occur. The limits, roles, and methods of dealing with a specific child should be realistic and appropriate to his or her age, needs, and abilities. Disciplinary approaches that help one child to develop and maintain desirable behaviors may make another child rebellious and still another child insecure and withdrawn.

Barclay Martin (1975) reviewed 27 different studies on the effects of harsh punishment. Although the definition of "harsh" varied somewhat from one study to another, it typically referred to punishment more severe than that used by most other parents in the same community. He concluded that harsh punishment in childhood was significantly correlated with aggression toward teachers, other children, and society. Boys who were harshly punished in childhood were more likely to become delinquents in adolescence than were boys who were not subjected to harsh discipline. Similarly, Brent Miller and others (1986) found that sexual permissiveness and behavior were highest among adolescents who viewed their parents as not being strict at all, intermediate among adolescents whose parents were overly strict, and lowest among adolescents with parents who were moderately strict.

In recent years, educators, psychologists, and sociologists have argued the case for "permissiveness" in child-rearing rather than old-fashioned discipline involving punishment. It has become apparent, however, that a child can be just as handicapped—albeit in a different way—by lack of structure. Too much permissiveness can produce spoiled, demanding, and inconsiderate children. Overly severe restraints and punishment, on the other hand, tend to foster fear of the punisher, reduced initiative and spontaneity, and a lack of trust in authority figures.

Diana Baumrind (1966, 1971), in a classic study, found that parents could be categorized into three groups, based on the degree of control they maintained over their children. **Authoritarian parents** were those who considered obedience a virtue, restricted their child's freedom, and used forceful methods of discipline. **Permissive parents** were those who allowed their child a good deal of leeway in regulating his or her own behavior. A middle ground was achieved by **authoritative parents,** who attempted to direct their child's behavior but involved the child in the decision-making process and allowed him or her a certain degree of independence. As might be expected, Baumrind found that permissive parents tended to raise children who lacked self-control and self-reliance and tended to be afraid of new experiences—perhaps because of lack of guidelines for dealing with such situations. Authoritarian parents tended to raise children who were obedient at home but overly aggressive or passive and dependent in other situations. Finally, the children of authoritative parents tended to be the most responsible, self-reliant, and competent.

In general, it would appear that freedom should be commensurate with maturity—with the child's ability to use freedom wisely—and that parents need to love their children enough to discipline them. When discipline involves punishment, it usually tells the child emphatically, "You've failed." Consequently, in punishing a child, it is important to

1. Ensure that the rules, the reasons for them, and the consequences of breaking them are explained in advance to the child.
2. Administer the punishment as soon after the disapproved behavior as possible, making the connection clear to the child.
3. Make clear what the child should have done—an alternative behavior—rather than just saying, in effect, "You misbehaved."

4. Ensure that it is the child's *behavior* and not the child that is rejected as unacceptable.

It is also important to exercise consistency in discipline. When the child is punished one time and ignored or rewarded the next for the same behavior, it is difficult to establish stable values for guiding his or her behavior. Punishment should also fit the crime in the sense of being appropriate to the behavior in question. It is also important to ensure that the desired behavior is within the physical, mental, emotional, and social capacity of the child. Otherwise, failure, frustration, and self-devaluation are likely to follow. In the long run, rewarding for good behavior is much more effective than punishing for bad behavior.

Encouraging Competence and Self-Confidence

The encouragement of competence often requires *guidance*. Usually we take it for granted that a child needs help in learning to read or write, but we may not realize that he or she also needs guidance in learning nonacademic skills. Today, children tend to be exposed to many ideas, situations, and points of view before they are mature enough to evaluate them critically. Thus, they need guidance in understanding and anticipating the consequences of given actions and in establishing appropriate values. At the same time, they also need guidance in developing the physical, intellectual, emotional, and social competencies needed to anticipate and meet the demands that will be made of them.

Children also need to succeed and to have their successes recognized. We need only observe a child's eager request to "Watch me, Mommy" or "Watch me, Daddy" as he or she demonstrates some newly acquired skill to understand the importance of success and recognition in the development of competence and self-confidence.

Although it would be imprudent, as well as impossible, to protect a child from every failure and misfortune, healthy development requires that the balance be kept on the side of success and positive experiences. All children experience setbacks, rejections, disappointments—experiences that challenge their feelings of capability and worth. But if, on balance, a child has more experiences adding to self-esteem rather than detracting from it, he or she can continue to grow in self-confidence. When a child does experience setbacks or failures in important situations, it is important to help him or her react constructively. This usually involves listening to the child's feelings, helping the child see the lesson to be gained from failure, and encouraging him or her to develop needed competencies so that this failure becomes a stepping stone to later successes.

Unfortunately, some parents place excessive pressures on their children to live up to unrealistically high standards. Where the child has the capacity for such high-level achievement, whether in school, sports, or other endeavors, things may work out. But, even in such cases, the child may be under such sustained pressure that little room is left for spontaneity or development as an integrated and independent person. More commonly, excessive demands promote failure, discouragement, and self-devaluation. Almost invariably, the child comes to feel, "I can't do it, so why try."

Presenting Appropriate Role Models

Research has shown that much of our learning occurs by observing and imitating models (Bandura, 1977). In their efforts to offer explicit instruction and guidance, parents often fail to realize how much they influence or teach their children through example. This applies not only to simple skills, such as table manners, but also to more important behaviors, such as coping with a crisis.

The presence of a parent-model who is a satisfactory example of appropriate, adaptive behavior can make a positive contribution to the child's healthy development. Unfortunately, children may also acquire the behaviors of parents who are seriously maladjusted (Coleman et al., 1987). For example, young people who become alcoholics have often grown up with at least one parent who drinks excessively. Similarly, studies of delinquent youths reveal a disproportionate number of parents who have committed antisocial or criminal acts. Box 10–7 describes several maladaptive family patterns and models that can have an undesirable effect on children.

We should note, however, that there is nothing inevitable in the effects of poor parental models on a child's development. The bad example of one parent may be made up for by the wisdom and concern of the other. Or the child may see the parent's behavior as a negative model, showing what not to do or be like. In their book *Cradles of Eminence* (1962), Victor and Mildred Goertzel looked back on the lives of 400 famous people and found that only 58 had come from warm, supportive, and relatively untroubled homes. The remainder had grown up in families that demonstrated "considerable pathology." In an attempt to understand children who seem to thrive despite pathogenic family and environmental conditions, Norman Garmezy and his associates (1976) studied a group of children he called the "invulnerables." Their findings indicated that such invulnerable children tended to find solutions rather than blaming others, to make the best of very little, and to show an unusual capacity for bouncing back after severe setbacks and traumas. In addition, these investigators suspected that the children had desirable role models somewhere in their lives.

Creating a Stimulating and Responsive Environment

Infants and young children do not have to learn to be curious. They are constantly exploring—touching, tasting, listening, looking. As their nerves and muscles mature and their mental capacities develop, the scope of their exploration widens. Soon they learn to talk and ask questions. Responsive parents provide an environment conducive to new, but not overwhelming, experiences, making learning pleasurable. On the other hand, a child's tendencies toward curiosity, exploration, and learning can be blocked by lack of opportunity and stimulation or by early experiences that teach him or her that curiosity is dangerous or unrewarding.

Children require feedback. Their inevitable questions of *who*, *what*, *where*, and *why* deserve to be answered and indeed should be encouraged. Children need to acquire a vast amount of information about themselves and their world—information that will enable them to assess problems accurately, to understand that actions have consequences, and to predict the probable outcome of their actions. Like adults, children experience feelings and conflicts that they need to talk about and explore. They need parents who are willing to listen and communicate in meaningful ways, rather than parents who answer questions with "Can't you see that I'm busy?" Parents who are willing and able to communicate serve as models for using language to acquire and convey information and to label both internal and external events accurately.

Of course, even parents with the best intentions and greatest efforts cannot guarantee that their children will be "perfect." Nor can they completely prevent unhealthy development because many other factors besides the parents influence the child's behavior and attitudes. An important factor in prevention, however, is the early detection and correction of undesirable trends, such as apathy, lying, and a negative self-concept. In the next sections, we will focus on some of these problems and how parents can deal with them.

PROBLEMS IN CHILD-REARING

> The nation's children are adjusting to change in the traditional family structure brought about by more working mothers and a rising divorce rate.
>
> —*American Chicle Youth Poll (1987, p. 1)*

There are three main areas in which child-rearing problems can arise: problems at the social level, problems with the parents and their relationship, and problems with the children themselves. It may also be pointed out that American parents are adjusting to major changes in life styles—such as divorce and remarriage—which inevitably affect child-rearing procedures and outcomes. Unfortunately, there are few guidelines to help single-parents and stepparents in child-rearing. Often TV and the mass media make it appear that children are "cute" and "enjoyable," and that child-rearing comes naturally. Actually, child-rearing skills have to be learned, and rearing healthy and well-adjusted children in today's world is anything but a simple task. Often parents enjoy their children after they are grown, rather than during the demanding process of rearing them.

In the preceding section, we described some of the conditions—such as love and acceptance—which foster healthy personal development. With our rapidly changing lifestyles, however, the question arises as to how effectively we can apply these conditions in actual practice. Thus, at the risk of some repetition, we shall open this chapter with a brief consideration of healthy and faulty personal development. This will help us to better understand the nature of problems in child-rearing.

Then we shall deal with three main areas in which child-rearing problems can arise: problems at the social level, distressed marital relationships, and problems with the children themselves. Finally, we shall comment on the question of whether parent training can be of help.

Healthy and Faulty Psychological Development

> Through his coping experiences the child discovers and measures himself, and develops his own perception of who and what he is and in time may become."
> (1962, p. 374).
>
> —*Lois Murphy*

In our brief review of healthy and faulty development, we shall focus on three considerations: (a) distinguishing between these two evaluations of development, (b) listing certain "built-in" trends toward personal maturity, and (c) noting three common types of faulty development. Throughout, our emphasis will be on psychological rather than physical development.

Defining Healthy Development.   There are two approaches that researchers have used in defining healthy and faulty development.

1. *"Normal" as healthy.*   This view considers development as normal when there is no apparent psychological **pathology** and no marked deviation from the group average. This is essentially an extension of the medical view that physical health is a lack of disease. Since the human system tends toward normality and health—on both biological and psychological levels—health is viewed as a universal phenomenon under favorable environmental conditions.

   This approach is not always adequate, however, in dealing with psychological development. Take the case of an adolescent who is making passing grades at school, getting along well with classmates and teachers, avoiding illegal drugs and delinquency, and overall considered a typical American youth. But he is just drifting along using only a fraction of his superior intellectual ability. This may not be "sick," but is it healthy?

2. *"Optimal" as healthy.*   This is a more positive view of healthy development. An absence of psychological pathology and adherence to the group average is not sufficient. Here healthy development goes beyond the group average in the direction of optimal development. This involves the maximal realization of capacities and the fulfillment of the individual's unique potential.

   Although this view of healthy development is a meaningful one that expands our perspective on development, social scientists are a long way from agreeing on the traits and behaviors that constitute optimal development. What people regard as desirable and optimal inevitably reflects the demands, beliefs, values, and customs of the larger society. Thus optimal development is a general principle and not something we are in a position to define and measure precisely and universally.

   This view seems to be gaining adherents, however, as new research enables us to eliminate many conditions long assumed to be an inevitable part of healthy development and to specify and create conditions conducive to the fuller development of psychological potentials.

Trends Toward Personal Maturity.   As we progress through the developmental stages from infancy to adulthood, there are certain trends toward personal maturity that appear to be uniquely characteristic of human beings. Although the details may vary from one society and one person to another, these trends involve the progression from a relatively helpless infant to a competent and contributing member of society.

1. *Dependence to self-direction.* One obvious progression toward maturity is from the dependency of infant and child to the independence and self-direction of adulthood. Associated with self-direction is: (a) the development of a clear sense of self-identity which enables us to answer the question "Who am I?" (b) the acquisition of information, competencies, and values, (c) the mastery of our immediate impulses and the exercise of self-control, (d) the ability to cope effectively with the inevitable disappointments, hurts, and frustrations of living, and (e) enough freedom from family and other social groups to be individuals in our own right.

2. *Ignorance to knowledge.* Although human beings are born in a state of relative ignorance, we rapidly acquire information about ourselves and our world. With time, this information is organized into a stable frame of reference which we use in guiding our behavior. To be adequate, this cognitive map must be realistic, relative to the kinds of problems we face or will face, and one in which we have faith.

3. *Incompetence to competence.* Our entire pre-adult period from infancy through adolescence is directed toward the mastery of intellectual, emotional, and social competencies needed for adulthood. We acquire skills in problem-solving and decision-making, learn to control and use our emotions, and learn to deal with other people and establish satisfying relationships. These competencies help to prepare us for the occupational, marital, sexual, and parental roles of adulthood.

4. *Amoral to moral.* The newborn infant is amoral, in the sense that he or she has no concept of "right" or "wrong." Very early, however, we learn that certain behaviors are approved or "good," while others are disapproved or "bad." With time, we learn a pattern of value assumptions that operate as inner guides of our behavior. These values are commonly referred to as our conscience. Initially, we tend to accept these values blindly. But with increasing maturity, we learn to appraise our values and to work out a personalized pattern of values.

5. *Self-centered to other-centered.* As infants, we are concerned almost exclusively with our own needs and desires. But with time, we develop an expanding understanding and concern for the needs and desires of others. This concern for the well-being of others as well as ourselves includes the ability to love significant others and to be concerned about and involved with people in our community and society as well as with people in other countries.

Of course, most or even all of these trends toward personal maturity may fail to reach their goals. We probably all know people who are deficient in one or more of them. Many children and adolescents in other societies—and to some extent even in our own—live in such aversive environments that it would be unrealistic to expect these trends to progress in usual ways.

Forms of Faulty Development. Although the human system tends toward health and normality, it is all too evident that this does not guarantee healthy development. Three common types of faulty psychological development have been delineated: arrested development, special vulnerability, and distorted development. These may occur singly or in combination. In one way or another, each impairs the individual's coping ability and adaptation.

1. *Arrested development.*   Here we are concerned with immaturies that may seriously impair our coping resources and adaptation. For example, adolescents who are overly dependent on their parents and avoid interaction with their peers are likely to encounter difficulties later in choosing a mate and establishing a happy marriage. Similarly, people whose behavior is dominated by their immediate desires lack a prerequisite for mature planning and decision making. On a more restrictive level, we could cite the case of young adults who throw temper tantrums when they don't get their way.

   Sometimes development in a given area may be arrested at a very immature level of functioning. More commonly, we move ahead but carry a residue of immature attitudes and behavior patterns into later developmental stages.

2. *Special vulnerabilities.*   Adverse life experiences, especially during early stages of development, may lower our resistance to certain types of stress. On a biological level, a severe case of influenza may result in lowered resistance to other types of respiratory disorders. On a psychological level, early traumatic experiences may create "psychic wounds" that never completely heal.

   A young girl who has shared a parent's intense feelings of self-devaluation and hurt during a bitter divorce may later find it extremely difficult or even impossible to cope with the threat of a divorce in her own marriage. Her early psychic wound is reopened, and she may suffer a "nervous breakdown." Similarly, many people are exposed to highly traumatic events in the course of our daily lives—such as being assaulted and raped, severe earthquakes, terrorist attacks, bombings, serious airline accidents, and prolonged military combat. As a consequence, those of us so traumatized may experience **post-traumatic stress disorder.** The symptoms may vary, but a common core is increased vulnerability to events that reactivate prior memories and feelings.

3. *Distorted development.*   Sometimes development proceeds in grossly undesirable forms or directions. Such distortions are readily apparent on biological as well as psychological levels. Children born without lower limbs or who suffer severe and prolonged malnutrition are examples of distortions on a biological level. On a psychological level, distorted development can be seen in the case of young people who murder for "kicks," teenagers who turn to prostitution to support their illegal drug habits, and adults who sexually abuse children.

   Although society allows for considerable variation, it usually draws the line when distorted development leads to behavior that is detrimental to the individual, to other people, and to the well-being of society.

In sum, healthy psychological development leads to adaptive behavior which is conducive to the well-being of the individual and group. On the other hand, faulty psychological development leads to maladaptive behavior which is detrimental to both the individual and the group.

BOX 10–5 / SOME FACTS ABOUT TELEVISION AND CHILD DEVELOPMENT

1. By the age of 18, the average child will have witnessed more than 18,000 murders and been subjected to more than 650,000 commercials.

2. The average high-school graduate in the United States will have spent more than 15,000 hours watching TV as compared with 11,000 hours in the classroom.

3. A child who sees a commercial over and over often persistently asks his or her mother or father for that brand of breakfast cereal or whatever the ad portrays that the child now wants.

4. Children who watch a great deal of TV perceive the world as more dangerous and frightening than those who watch very little.

5. Children spend more time watching TV than in any other activity except sleeping.

6. Preschoolers typically spend more time watching TV than it takes to earn a college degree.

7. Most television programs that children watch were intended for adults.

8. Children tend to believe what they see on TV, because they have no experiential basis for distinguishing fact from fantasy.

9. Television has as much or more impact on children than what they learn in school.

10. TV violence has been shown to be linked to more-aggressive and violent behavior on the part of child viewers.

A 2-year study by the National Institute of Mental Health, entitled "Television and Behavior: Ten Years of Scientific Progress and Implications for the Eighties" (1982), concluded that there is "overwhelming" evidence that "excessive" violence on TV leads to aggressive behavior in children. In short, violence on television is considered harmful to children. Studies made in Finland, Poland, and Australia have reached the same conclusion.

General Social Concerns

An early study dealing with child-rearing problems in a changing society was conducted by General Mills (1977). Most of the parents in this study pointed to problems in society as a whole as being of key importance. For example, 72 percent of the parents expressed concern about the standards of our society. More specifically, they were worried about drug use, street crime, economic problems, day-care facilities, the shortcomings of the public-education system, and broken marriages.

Parents today still share these problems, as well as others. Thus, we can add to the preceding list such issues as (1) sex education in the schools specifically aimed at preventing the spread of AIDS and other STDs among teenagers; (2) the amount of sex and violence to which children are exposed on television (Box 10–5 summarizes some of this data with respect to violence); and (3) raising children in the shadow of possible thermonuclear annihilation. The last concern is a threat many children and teenagers are acutely aware of and tend to deal with in terms of denial and fatalistic attitudes—for example, "If it happens, it happens. There's nothing I can do about it." Interestingly, parents still rate drug abuse as their primary concern, followed by street crime, sex, and economic problems.

Many parents and researchers are also dismayed at the decreasing influence of the family on children and teenagers and the increasing influence of peers and other outside influences. In 1960, for example, young people rated the top four influences in their lives as parents, teachers, friends/peers, and the clergy. The mass media ran a lowly eighth. But, by 1980, the order had changed to friends/peers first, followed by parents, the mass media, and teachers (Junior Achievement, 1981). With the increasing dependence on television and video games, it seems likely that peers and the mass media will occupy the top spots by 1990.

However, some researchers are predicting an increase in parental influence over time, at least in terms of nonsocial activities (Sebald, 1986). In essence, different issues will activate different reference groups. For example, social activities will remain peer oriented, whereas career concerns will tend to be parent oriented.

Probably the question asked by Keith Madsen (1985) summarizes the social concerns of parents in our society about having children as well as anyone can: "Do you really want to bring a child into this kind of world?" (p. 20).

Distressed Marital Relationships

A number of child-rearing problems center around the parents as persons and their marital relationship. For example, Ellen Galinsky (1980) found that couples with new infants often have an image of themselves as perfect parents and strive to achieve this image. However, as the infant progresses to childhood and begins to test new powers, to widen his or her social world, and to say "No," the parents start to find flaws in themselves. Now they face the challenge of making needed adjustments to adapt their parenting style to the changing needs of the child.

The advent of adolescence also tends to be a difficult time for parents. As the child's peers become ever more important, demands are made for more freedom from parental restraints, and questions are raised concerning the values and behaviors of the parents. Indeed, many parents find particular stages of their child's development more difficult to cope with than others. Some parents relate much more readily to babies and young children, whereas others get along better with older children and adolescents (Weinberg & Richards, 1981). In general, however, the role of parenting is considered a stressful one. Common problems of new parents are summarized in Box 10–6.

One indication of the stress of parenting is the attention paid to **parent burnout.** Joseph Procaccini (1983), for example, has suggested that as many as 50 percent of parents—particularly middle-class parents who strive to be Supermoms and Superdads—suffer from at least the beginnings of burnout. He has delineated five stages of burnout, all associated with excessive demands being made on the parent's time and energy resources:

1. Physiological burnout—feeling physically drained.
2. Social burnout—being irritable and difficult to deal with.
3. Intellectual burnout—having problems concentrating and thinking coherently about problems.

BOX 10-6 / COMMON PROBLEMS OF NEW PARENTS

There are many aspects of parenting with which new parents are inadequately prepared to deal. Commonly, the child requires far more time than they had anticipated, and the number of problems in the family increases as the marriage grows from a couple to a three-person family. Some of the common problems encountered include the following:

1. Difficulty in balancing personal needs and responsibilities as parents.
2. The wife's expectation that the husband will be more helpful in child care than he is actually capable of being or is willing to be.
3. Differences in ideas about child-rearing, leading to continual conflict.
4. The tendency of the parents to focus on how the child will enrich their lives and the lack of preparation for how the child will actually affect the marriage.
5. Realization for the first time of the amount of responsibility one has undertaken: another person's life for the next 18 years or more.

6. The tendency of the mother to focus on the needs of the child at the expense of meeting the emotional and sexual needs of the father, causing the father to feel jealous and neglected.
7. The problem of balancing the roles of spouse, worker, and parent.

To deal with such problems, child experts have proposed a number of guidelines. These include planning ahead for changes in routine; exploring and agreeing ahead of time on appropriate methods of child-rearing; discussing the type of family the couple wants to build; and preparing for the typical problems and changes over time that are inherent in parenthood. The couple also need to pay special attention to their relationship and to plan time together so that they can maintain the intimacy built prior to the pregnancy.

4. Psychoemotional burnout—resorting to tranquilizers or alcohol as a means of coping with demands.
5. Introspective burnout—questioning our own value system and becoming less willing to fulfill parental and other responsibilities.

Can parent burnout be avoided? Yes, says Procaccini, if parents can make a "time and energy audit" and adopt goals that are realistic in terms of the child's needs and their own limitations as parents. This means they must learn to accept themselves as less than perfect and to realize that many things are beyond their control.

If parents are to provide a favorable climate for their children, they must also maintain their marital bond as something apart from parenting. In essence, the couple's marriage sustains their role as parents. As Avner Barcai (1981) has pointed out:

As soon as the order of justification is reversed and parenting becomes the rationale for being a couple, the child is invested with an undue and disproportionate degree of power. . . .

BOX 10–7 / MALADAPTIVE FAMILY PATTERNS

Recent research on families as group systems has revealed that maladaptive behavior on the part of the child may be fostered by the general family environment as well as by the child's relationships with one or both parents. Although we have no models of the "ideal" family, five family patterns have been identified that typically have a detrimental effect on child development:

1. *The inadequate family.* This type of family is characterized by an inability to cope with the ordinary problems of living. It lacks the resources—physical or psychological—for meeting the demands on it. Such a family cannot provide children with needed feelings of safety or security, nor can it guide the children in the development of essential competencies.

2. *The disturbed family.* Disturbed homes may involve many pathological patterns, but some families appear to have certain characteristics in common: (a) the presence of parents who are fighting to maintain their own equilibrium and who are unable to give the child needed love and guidance; (b) enmeshment of the child in the emotional problems of the parents, to the detriment of his or her own development; and (c) exposure of the child to constant emotional turmoil, irrationality, and poor parental models.

3. *The antisocial family.* This type of family espouses values not accepted by the wider community. The parents may overtly or covertly engage in behavior that violates the standards of society, and they may be chronically in trouble with the law. Such antisocial characteristics as dishonesty and lack of concern for others provide undesirable role models for children.

4. *The abusive family.* These families are characterized by child abuse and lack of caring. This abuse may take the form of (a) abandonment; (b) physical abuse; (c) emotional abuse, such as severe rejection and devaluation of the child; (d) neglect, or the failure to provide for the child's basic needs; and (e) sexual abuse of the child by either parents or older siblings.

5. *The disrupted family.* The most common cause of a disrupted family is desertion by the father. This desertion leaves remaining family members with feelings of rejection in addition to financial and other problems. If the family is unable to reorganize effectively, the children are likely to suffer in their development.

These patterns are not mutually exclusive, and long-range effects of maladaptive family patterns may vary greatly (Coleman et al. (1987).

If there is no healthy couple system functioning concurrently with the parental system, there will be pathology regardless of verbalized intent to the contrary. (p. 335)

Unfortunately, young couples may have children before their marriage is well established, or they may neglect their marriage when children arrive. In many instances, the family pattern that is established is a maladaptive one—as in the case of abusive families. Several maladaptive family patterns are summarized in Box 10–7. In addition, one or both parents may evidence serious personal problems—for example, alcoholism and drug abuse. Such personal problems have a negative effect on the marital relationship and do not foster a family climate suitable for child-rearing.

Problems Presented by Children

The problems presented by children may vary considerably depending on the child, the family setting, and the child's stage of development. Parental complaints about young children commonly include irresponsibility, crying and whining, having temper tantrums, lying, stealing, and disobedience (General Mills, 1977; Bailey, 1982; Reiss et al., 1986). As children get older and enter the teen years, some earlier problems may drop out and some new ones may appear—such as sex and drug abuse.

The child-rearing problems reported by parents depend heavily on the parents' own education and training and on their expectations and goals. Thus, a middle-class parent whose child is not doing well in school may report a serious learning problem, whereas a blue-collar parent who feels isolated or alienated from education may not see this as a problem. Similarly, Chess and Thomas (1980) found that a number of middle-class parents reported that their children had sleeping problems, but working-class parents did not report this. These researchers suggested that this difference was not due to any differences in the children's actual sleep patterns but rather to differing life styles and expectations.

Disobedience often poses a difficult problem for parents who are inexperienced in child-rearing and uncertain about appropriate methods for discipline (Reiss et al., 1986). Some common approaches to discipline are summarized in Box 10–8. A related problem is the difficulty many young fathers experience in taking a more-active role in child-rearing. Often fathers are not adequately prepared for parenting responsibilities and are confused and ill at ease in their attempts to meet these demands (Kohl, 1981; Nannarone, 1983; Hanson & Bozett, 1985).

Fortunately, parents who are experiencing difficulties in child-rearing have two major resources: parent training and family counseling or therapy. Here, we shall comment briefly on parent training, and in the following chapter we shall describe family therapy.

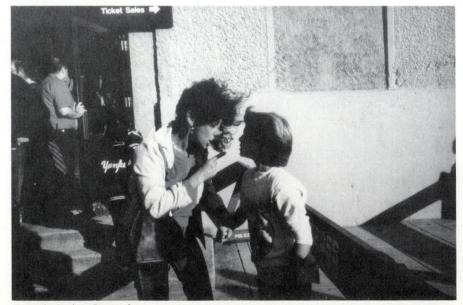

Joan Liftin/Archives Pictures, Inc.

BOX 10–8 / METHODS OF DISCIPLINE

In the past, discipline was thought of primarily as a method of punishment for undesirable behavior and preventing its recurrence. More recently, discipline has been thought of in more-positive terms as a means of behavior control for promoting healthy development—that is, for fostering desirable behavior, setting limits, and developing inner controls on the part of the child.

Physical Punishment.   Research studies have shown that harsh physical punishment provides a model of aggressive behavior that the child tends to emulate—often in his or her dealings with other children. In addition, such punishment can engender fear and hatred of the punishing person, a reduction in spontaneity and initiative, and lowered self-esteem. Often, too, it engenders a lack of trust in and friendliness toward authority figures.

Although mild physical punishment may be appropriate in some instances—particularly in families in which there is a great deal of love and emotional support—physical punishment is no longer viewed in terms of the old adage "Spare the rod and spoil the child."

Instead, psychological methods of discipline are now viewed as much more effective. But, whether physical or psychological, punishment must be consistent if the child is to develop a clear map of acceptable and unacceptable behaviors.

Psychological Techniques.   Psychological methods of discipline include reasoning; demonstrating confidence and trust; and rewarding responsible behavior with praise, recognition, and other reinforcement whenever it occurs. It helps when such discipline is based on goals, ground rules, and expectations that the child has helped establish.

Some parents use psychological techniques primarily for correcting or preventing infractions of rules. The most common techniques used for this purpose are withdrawal of love or privileges and eliciting feelings of guilt. However, both rewards and withdrawal of privileges may have inconsistent results as means of controlling and shaping a child's behavior, although in some cases these techniques may be highly effective. The nature of the reward given or the privilege withdrawn and the prior relationship with the parent are among the determinants of the outcome. In cases in which the parent has a warm relationship with the child, expressions of disapproval and suggestions of alternative behaviors often appear to be effective in helping the child to develop inner controls.

Reasoning has also proven generally effective in fostering desirable behaviors and preventing undesirable ones. Reasoning may include delineating the probable consequences of a given action before it occurs or tying consequences and actions together after the behavior. In essence, the use of logic in explaining the natural consequences of a given course of action helps the child to develop responsibility, self-discipline, and values.

Finally, it should be emphasized that a warm, loving family in which the dignity of each member is respected provides a climate for shaping the child's development, and this climate is more important than the particular methods of discipline used. In addition, children who come from such families typically try to conform to their parents' wishes and to use their parents as models for their own behavior. Consequently, they are less likely to need frequent or severe discipline. Thus, what matters most in child-rearing is the quality of parent–child relations, rather than specific techniques.

BOX 10–9 / COMMUNICATION FAILURE IN PARENT–CHILD INTERACTIONS

Parents can discourage children from asking questions and in other ways can fail to foster the "information exchange" essential for healthy development.

Inadequate communication patterns may take a number of forms. Some parents are too busy with their own concerns to listen to their children's problems. As a consequence, these parents often fail to give needed support and assistance during crisis periods. Other parents may have forgotten that the world often looks different to a child or adolescent or that rapid social change can lead to a real communications gap between generations.

In other cases, faulty communication takes more deviant forms. One such pattern that conveys contradictory messages has been termed the **double bind** by psychiatrist R. D. Laing. For example, a mother may complain of her son's lack of affection toward her but then freeze up and show strong disapproval whenever he tries to be demonstrative. Similarly, parents may convey one message by their words and another by their actions. A father may deplore lying and admonish his son never to tell a lie, but he himself may frequently lie.

An even more-subtle and damaging communication pattern is to contradict or undermine the child's statements and conclusions, so that he or she is left confused and unsure of his or her own mental processes. The effects of this pattern have been vividly described by R. Laing and A. Esterson (1964):

The ultimate of this is . . . when no matter how [a person] feels or how he acts, no matter what meaning he gives his situation, his feelings are denuded of validity, his acts are stripped of their motives, intentions, and consequences, the situation is robbed of meaning for him, so that he is totally mystified and alienated. (pp. 135–136)

Interestingly, the latter approach has commonly been a key part of "brainwashing" programs used on American prisoners of war—for example, American POWs in Vietnam. Hence, it is not surprising that this approach, together with other faulty communication patterns, is often found in the background of children and adolescents experiencing serious adjustment difficulties.

Can Parent Training Help?

Parent training is based on the assumption that parents have a major and predictable impact on the lives of their children. This may sound rather obvious, but, as Arlene Skolnick (1973) observed:

Researchers as well as parents have been frustrated in the search for clear or simple cause-and-effect relationships between things parents do or don't do and the way children turn out. There are no cookbook recipes for producing a particular kind of child. (p. 302)

Skolnick went on to point out that each child is unique, and the parenting methods that work with one child may not work with another—even in the same family. As we noted, however, there are certain conditions that tend to foster healthy psychological development in most children.

There has been a proliferation of approaches to parent training in recent years that has emphasized these and other relevant conditions. One approach that has received widespread acceptance is Parent Effectiveness Training (PET). Here, the focus is on improving the communication between parents and children, reducing family conflict, and increasing family cohesion. (See Box 10–9). One concept that is strongly emphasized is avoiding the use of authority and power in resolving parent–child conflicts. Advocates of PET point out that using power to win conflicts tends to impair parent–child relationships—especially with adolescents, who are likely to rebel against the use of parental authority. Thus, PET fosters "no-loser" conflict resolution, in which each person's needs are taken into consideration and each participates in final decision making concerning the issue in question.

The answer to our question "Can parent training help"? is "Probably yes." As Boggs (1983) has pointed out, however, it is important that parents familiarize themselves with several parent-training approaches and select the one that seems appropriate to them. See Box 10–10 for a summary of faulty parent–child relationships.

We have emphasized that having and rearing children consists of a series of decisions. Because there are no infallible guidelines to child-rearing and because parents are human, it is inevitable that they will make some mistakes. Many parents tend to blame themselves when things go wrong and may suffer from needless feelings of guilt and self-recrimination: "How did we let him down?" "What did I do wrong?" While there are no guarantees in child-rearing, one way to minimize bad decisions and poor choices is to follow this basic guideline: Gain a realistic view of your child, of yourself and your partner as parents, of your marriage and family life, and of the social environment as it affects your child. As

American Psychological Association

BOX 10–10 / SUMMARY OF FAULTY PARENT–CHILD RELATIONSHIPS

Undesirable Condition	Typical Effect on Child's Personality Development
Rejection	Feelings of anxiety, insecurity, low self-esteem, negativism, hostility, attention-seeking, loneliness, jealousy, and slowness in conscience development.
Overprotection—Domination	Submissiveness, lack of self-reliance, dependence in relations with others, low self-evaluation, some dulling of intellectual striving.
Overpermissiveness—Overindulgence	Selfishness, demanding attitude, inability to tolerate frustration, rebelliousness toward authority, excessive need of attention, lack of responsibility, inconsiderateness, exploitativeness in interpersonal relationships.
Perfectionism, With Unrealistic Demands	Lack of spontaneity, rigid conscience development, severe conflicts, tendency toward guilt and self-condemnation if there is failure to live up to parental demands.
Faulty Discipline: Lack of discipline	Inconsiderateness, aggressiveness, and antisocial tendencies.
Harsh, overly severe discipline	Fear, hatred of parent, little initiative or spontaneity, lack of friendly feelings toward others.
Inconsistent discipline	Difficulty in establishing stable values for guiding behavior; tendency toward highly aggressive behavior.
Contradictory Demands and Communications	As in case of "double bind" communications, the tendency toward confusion, lack of an integrated frame of reference, unclear self-identity, lack of initiative, self-devaluation.
Undesirable Parental Models	The learning of faulty values, formulation of unrealistic goals, development of maladaptive coping patterns.

we have emphasized throughout this book, being realistic is fundamental to successful relationships at all levels.

CHILDREN AND MARITAL SATISFACTION

Among the common beliefs about modern marriage are the views that children will enhance a marriage, that child-rearing comes naturally, and that children are a constant source of pride and joy. Unfortunately, research findings do not support these views. Sharon Brehm (1985) has summarized the situation this way:

That having children could have a negative effect on the way a couple feels about each other flies in the face of many cherished beliefs about home and family.

Certainly, it contradicts the expectations of most couples who are thinking about having children. (p. 286)

In essence, we are confronted with a conflict between belief and reality. In the final section of this chapter, we shall examine the research evidence bearing on this conflict.

Do Children Decrease Marital Satisfaction?

In our earlier discussion, we noted that marital satisfaction tends to follow a U-shaped curve—high initially, gradually decreasing until the 40s or 50s, and then increasing again. Curiously, this pattern of satisfaction tends to follow quite closely the arrival and departure of children.

This finding suggests that there may be something about having and rearing children that makes for a less-satisfying marital relationship. To test this possibility, researchers have compared the marital happiness of couples with and without children. The results are consistent in showing that childless couples *as a group* report greater marital satisfaction than couples with children (Harriman, 1986; Belsky et al., 1985; Belsky et al., 1986; Worthington & Buston, 1987).

Next, researchers attempted to determine at what age the child is most likely to be associated with a reduction in marital satisfaction. No clear pattern has emerged—perhaps because of a lack of longitudinal studies of marital couples during the child-rearing years. For some couples, the most difficult period appears to be the first year; for others, the elementary-school years; and, for others, the teen years. In general, however, the decrease in marital satisfaction continues until the children leave home to build lives of their own.

Ironically, the departure of the last child may trigger the so-called "empty-nest syndrome," particularly on the part of mothers whose lives have been centered around their children. These mothers may feel that they no longer have a meaningful role to play and go through a period of depression and readjustment. Even more ironic perhaps is the increase in the "cluttered-nest" syndrome—for example, when a son or daughter is divorced and moves back in with his or her parents. Often, too, the daughter has custody of children that she brings with her. In referring to the return of adult children to the "family nest," Lois Duncan (1981) has described the situation from a parent's point of view: "They may be 'yours' for eighteen years, but you are 'theirs' till you die" (p. 6).

More typically, with the departure of the last child, the parents have time to get reacquainted and assess their marital relationship. Some parents find that they have grown apart and have little in common. The result may be a continuing, but unsatisfactory, marriage, or a divorce. But, for most parents, marital satisfaction shows a marked increase.

The answer to our question "Do children decrease marital satisfaction?" is "Yes" for most couples. This decrease in marital satisfaction usually occurs when starting as well as expanding a family, whether the couple has one child or several. Finally, once the children leave home, marital satisfaction increases for most couples. In essence, it appears less rewarding to raise a family than to have it done—at least in terms of marital relationships.

It may be emphasized, however, that many couples find having children is rewarding personally, as well as in terms of their marital relationship. The follow-

Joan Liftin/Archives Pictures, Inc.

ing quote from Charlotte Fisher (1987) reveals how rewarding it may be to raise a healthy and well-adjusted child.

> With all my mistakes, you managed to survive—admirably. In fact, somewhere along the line I must've done a few things right because I couldn't ask for a more lovable daughter nor a more likable friend. You're a neat lady, Beth, and I'm proud of you. (p. 19)

SUMMARY—Chapter 10

1. In the 1950s, most people married to have sex and children, usually four. Today it is common to have sex without marriage and marriage without children. Having children, within or outside of marriage, is much more a matter of choice.

2. Couples have children for a variety of reasons: cultural pressure, the rewards of a loving family, to support them in old age, accidentally, or to perpetuate the family line.

3. Employed married women, now the norm, are having children later and fewer of them. Children may interfere with a career and create financial problems. In addition, later pregnancies are now considered safe. Many couples do not want children, believing that the disadvantages outweigh the advantages. And many couples, one out of every six in our society, are infertile. Often the latter problem can be solved, but it is costly both emotionally and financially.

4. Pregnancy and parenthood require numerous adjustments by the mother, the father, and in the relationship. Women have to adjust to bodily changes, to their new role as mother, and to the stresses of caring for a baby. Men must adjust to the new role of father, provide extra assistance, and often to deal with feelings of jealousy as the baby becomes the focus of attention.

5. The course of child development is influenced by the unique characteristics of the child, the personalities of the parents, the marital relationship, the family climate, and the environment in which the family lives.

6. Among actions that parents can take to foster healthy child development are (a) providing love and acceptance, (b) supplying structure and discipline of an authoritative rather than permissive or authoritarian nature, (c) encourage competence and self-confidence by providing needed guidance, serve as appropriate role models, and create a stimulating and responsive environment.

7. In child-rearing, problems usually occur in three main areas: (a) social concerns—such as crime and violence, drug abuse, and the high incidence of divorce, (b) parental difficulties—such as financial difficulties, overloading, and unhappy marriages, and (c) problems presented by the child—such as being disobedient, lying, stealing, and experimenting with drugs. Specific problems depend to a large extent on parental resources, standards, and expectations.

8. Children tend to decrease marital satisfaction and continue to do so until they leave home and build a life of their own. Many parents can be helped by parent effectiveness training (PET), which is designed to improve communication, reduce conflict, and increase cohesion within the family. In general, parents derive great satisfaction from having reared children successfully.

11

MARITAL CONFLICT, COPING, AND CHANGE

Why do marriages go wrong? The answer, of course, is that, for one reason or another, they don't go right. And why don't they go right? Because, when the couple settle down together, things don't turn out as they had expected. The reality doesn't measure up to the expectation.

—David Mace (1986, p. 30)

Although few, if any, writers have claimed that marriage is a bed of roses, many young people assume that their marriage will somehow be different—that it will be conflict-free, harmonious, and happy. However, in light of the intensity of marital relationships and the likelihood that the partners will not agree on everything, conflict seems to be an inevitable part of marriage.

In this chapter, we shall deal with the nature and sources of marital conflict; with effective and ineffective ways of coping with marital conflict, including the use of marital therapy; and with change in marital relationships over time.

THE NATURE OF MARITAL CONFLICT

Marital conflicts are disagreements that arise between partners as a result of incompatible needs, goals, and expectations. For example, if one partner wants sex more often than the other, a disagreement or conflict has arisen. Conflict represents an adjustive demand that the partners must resolve to maintain the harmony of their marriage.

A broader term—**marital stress**—is often used to encompass not only conflicts but also other adjustive demands, such as serious illness, loss of employment, and career pressures that require coping behavior on the part of one or both partners. Although our focus in this chapter shall be on marital conflicts, it is useful to keep this broader perspective of marital problems in mind.

Types of Marital Conflict

Marital conflicts may be rational or irrational, overt or covert, and acute or chronic, and personal or interpersonal.

Rational and Irrational Conflicts.   **Rational conflicts** are based on realistic differences of opinion about some issue. For example, a couple may disagree on their spending priorities. Should they buy a new car or try to accumulate savings for a down payment on a condominium? Although the husband may feel strongly about the car and the wife about the savings, this type of conflict can usually be dealt with logically by means of reasoning, negotiating, and compromise.

Irrational conflicts, on the other hand, are usually based on the eccentric personal characteristics of one or both partners. For example, one partner may be overly sensitive, quick-tempered, critical, argumentative, or prone to blaming the other when things go wrong. Extreme jealousy can also lead to irrational conflicts,

Roy Roper/EKM-Nepenthe

as when the husband is convinced that his wife is trying to seduce other men, and nothing she can say or do seems to appease him.

Overt and Covert Conflicts.

Overt conflict is open disagreement between the marital partners. The disagreement is usually brought up by one partner as an issue to be resolved. Of course, bringing the conflict out into the open where the partners can deal with it is no guarantee that it will be resolved, but it seems to offer the best hope.

Covert conflict, in contrast, is concealed or hidden. As sociologist Gerald Leslie (1979) has pointed out, covert conflict is one of the most significant and devastating ways in which marital partners struggle against each other. Because covert conflict is not out in the open, its existence is usually inferred from various "symptoms"—withholding of affection; reduction of sharing, lack of communication; and development of psychosomatic reactions such as headaches, chronic muscle tension, or depression. Even when the partners are aware that a conflict exists, they may perceive it as being so potentially devastating to the marriage that they purposely relegate it to covert status. It is simply "too hot to handle."

Acute and Chronic Conflict.

Acute conflicts are short-lived "lovers' quarrels" that tend to occur in the early stages of marriage as the couple try to resolve various differences that arise and to work out the ground rules for their marriage. Once such conflicts are resolved, they tend to disappear from the marital relationship.

Chronic conflicts, on the other hand, are those that are never satisfactorily resolved and constitute a continuing burden on the marriage. For example, even after a couple has worked out a budget, one partner may impulsively buy things that the couple doesn't need and can't afford. Chronic conflicts may also center around differences in sex-role expectations to which one or both partners cannot adjust. Even in a dual-career marriage, for example, the husband may be unwilling

Quite obviously, few—if any— marriages live up to the ideals contained in some of the classic marriage manuals or popular mythology. Those who accept these ideas about what a marital relationship should "really" be are likely to see their marriage as problematic and to start working toward its solution until divorce do them part. Their concrete problem is not their marriage, but their

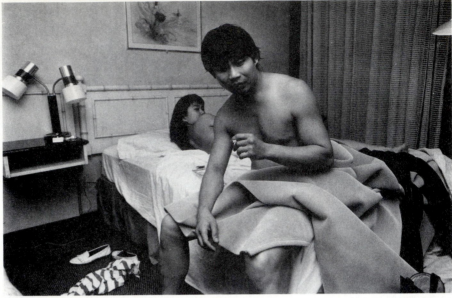

Corky Lee

attempts at finding the solution to a problem which in the first place is not a problem and which, even if it were one, could not be solved on the level on which they attempt to change it.

Watzlawick, Weakland, and Fisch

to do his share of household chores. Other sources of chronic conflict include disagreements about the frequency of sex and the appropriateness of specific techniques of sexual gratification.

Personal and Interpersonal.   We usually think of marital conflict as being between the two partners, or **interpersonal.** However, conflict can also occur on a **personal** level. Suppose, for example, that Jeannie and Tom discuss the possibility of having children. Tom is strongly opposed, and Jeannie agrees to go along with his wishes. Tom assumes the issue has been resolved, but Jeannie still wants to have children. In her mind, the conflict is not resolved but continues to trouble her. Thus, a conflict may be tearing one partner apart emotionally although the other partner may not even be aware of it. In essence, the conflict has been transferred from the interpersonal level to the personal level. Marital therapists often ask, "Who owns the problem?" to get at this type of situation.

Severity of Marital Conflict

The severity of marital conflict refers to the degree of disruption in the relationship that will result if the conflict is not resolved. Some unresolved conflicts may cause only minor annoyance and are said to be **nonbasic;** others may threaten the continuation of the marriage and are said to be **basic.**

Of course, the wear and tear of minor, or nonbasic, conflicts can accumulate over time and threaten the marriage. In fact, Lazarus (1981) has contended that seemingly trivial everyday hassles can be more destructive over time than occasional crucial disagreements. In essence, they seem to drain the enjoyment and love out of the marital relationship.

In general, the severity of marital conflict is determined by three factors: (1) the number, importance, and duration of conflicts; (2) the characteristics of the partners; and (3) the external resources and supports available to them.

1. Number, Importance, and Duration of Conflicts.   Conflicts can vary in the number, importance, and duration of disagreements. As the number of disagreements increases, so does the stress faced by the marital partners. For example, a couple trying to deal simultaneously with disagreements about sex, household chores, and spending money are faced with a more-severe conflict situation than a couple confronted with only one of these disagreements. Unfortunately, conflicts do not usually stand in line and wait their turn to be resolved; each seems to demand immediate attention.

The importance of the disagreement is also a key factor in the severity of the conflict. The partners may agree on practically everything, but one basic disagreement—such as one centering on infidelity—may threaten the continuation of the marriage. Of course, when important disagreements or problems accumulate, the severity of the adjustive demands escalates accordingly. Similarly, the longer a conflict continues, the more severe it is likely to become. Much as a chronic illness usually requires greater adjustment than an acute or temporary one, so chronic conflicts are likely to be more severe than acute ones that are quickly resolved and put to rest.

2. Characteristics of the Partners.   One factor that is often crucial in determining the severity of conflict is the way each partner perceives the disagreement. The fact that a husband comes home from work and leaves his clothes strewn all

Tom Ballard/EKM-Nepenthe

over the house as he prepares for a shower may not seem like a big deal to him, but to his wife—who comes home from work tired and is expected to pick up after him—it may be perceived as a lack of caring or consideration for her needs and feelings. Similarly, if one partner feels that the other is making demands that are beyond his or her power to meet or that are in violation of his or her moral convictions, that partner is likely to find the conflict more stressful.

Another key characteristic of marital partners that can influence the severity of conflict is stress tolerance, or the ability to cope with adjustive demands. For a person who feels inadequate, has a negative self-image, and is only marginally adjusted, even minor disagreements may be too much to handle. Or one partner may have serious career or other problems outside marriage that make marital conflicts even more stressful. Our coping resources are limited, and if they are already mobilized for dealing with other sources of stress, we may be hard pressed to deal with marital conflicts as well.

3. External Resources.   Material resources can intensify or weaken the severity of marital conflict. Affluent people, for example, can talk things over with a qualified marital counselor or even remove themselves from the stressful marital situation and spend a few days at some pleasant resort while sorting things out. People with little money, on the other hand, have fewer options available to them in their efforts to resolve marital conflicts. Thus, what may be a minor conflict for an affluent couple might be a major conflict for a poorer couple.

Effects of Marital Conflict

Although it may be tempting to believe that our marriage has been made in heaven, the reality is that marital partners build their own cozy little heaven or hell right here on earth. To a large extent, the outcome depends on the type and severity of conflicts and the effectiveness with which they are resolved. Conflicts will arise—that's a fact of marital life.

Possible Positive Effects.   Some conflicts can be desirable, in that they help the couple develop skills in resolving problems. Conflicts are often a constructive part of early marriage as the partners work out their modus operandi for living together. Often, too, conflicts help the partners to understand themselves and each other, as well as their relationship, and to avoid unnecessary future conflicts. Openly communicating about and resolving conflicts in effective ways can promote a spirit of mutuality and trust that fosters increased intimacy and commitment. In fact, marital partners often report that they feel closer and happier after they have resolved a serious conflict. Some couples say that having conflicts is worth it just for the fun they have "making up" afterward.

Possible Negative Effects.   In a pioneering study, Lewis Terman (1938) found that the one factor that clearly differentiated unhappy from happy married couples was the extent of conflict in the marriage. For example, a common complaint in unhappy marriages was that one partner was quick tempered, overly sensitive, argumentative, and nagging. In a later study—based on diaries of conflicts and arguments—Birchler, Weiss, and Vincent (1975) found that couples experiencing marital distress reported an average of 3.4 conflicts during a 5-day period, whereas couples considered happily married only reported 1 conflict on the average over this same time period.

As we noted in Chapter 3, Harriet Braiker and Harold Kelley (1979) concluded that conflicts tend to have negative effects over the long run unless the following conditions are met: (1) the frequency and intensity of conflicts is low, (2) there is a background of positive interaction between the partners, and (3) the couple is superior in conflict-coping capabilities. In addition, these investigators noted that continual conflicts may in and of themselves become a source of conflict.

The disagreements that lead to quarrels during early marriage are not likely to be the same disagreements that lead the couple to quarrel 10 or 20 years later. As the partners and their relationship change over time, so do many of the problems that they confront. Often, too, the couple's conflict-resolving skills improve over time, so that disagreements that might once have created serious difficulties can now be taken in stride. However, in marriages that are deteriorating, the ability of the partners to solve even relatively minor conflicts may be seriously impaired. It is useful to recall here that couples tend to focus on cost/reward ratio and comparison level most often during the formative stages of marriage and during times when serious conflicts arise.

COMMON SOURCES OF MARITAL CONFLICT

Once two people have made a commitment to each other in marriage, many factors come to bear on the outcome of their relationship. What they make of their marriage depends heavily on their daily pattern of living and on their adjustment to each other's needs, habits, and personalities. It also depends on their ability to cope with the conflicts, both major and minor, that inevitably arise as they build their marital relationship.

There are, of course, many potential sources of conflict, which vary according to the partner's personalities, the social context of their marriage, and the stage of their marital relationship. In general, however, the most important sources of conflict in marriage are unmet needs and expectations, money, roles and responsibilities, power struggles, sexual difficulties, jealousy and possessiveness, anger and violence, and extramarital affairs (Fig. 11–1).

Unmet Needs and Expectations

During the so-called "happy honeymoon" phase of marriage, most marital partners present themselves in a favorable light. They usually give extra attention to their appearance and behavior in order to delight, please, or impress each other, while they tend to mask their undesirable qualities in the glow of love and romance. But, as the couple get to know each other better, it becomes impossible to maintain a false self. The wife soon discovers that her husband acts like an adolescent when he's with his friends or that he really hates her favorite actor; the husband discovers that his wife is cranky in the mornings or that she is bored by his favorite hobby. It is also likely that one or both partners will fail to meet the unrealistic expectations of the other. This process tends to be exaggerated when the marital partners view marriage in terms of an exchange of material and emotional goods. When the first "delivery" isn't made, difficulties begin.

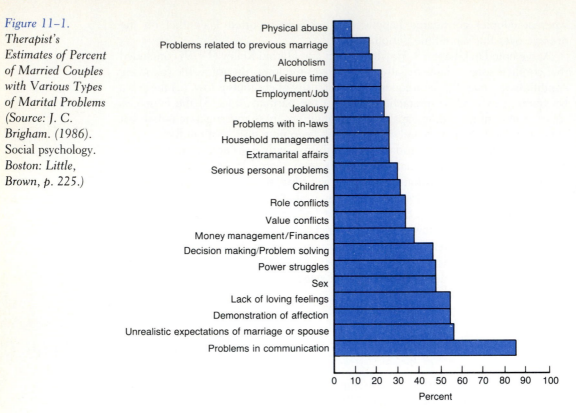

Figure 11–1. Therapist's Estimates of Percent of Married Couples with Various Types of Marital Problems (Source: J. C. Brigham. (1986). Social psychology. Boston: Little, Brown, p. 225.)

These difficulties may be followed by a variety of possible reactions. One partner may reduce the amount of praise or attention given to the other, which is taken as a sign of loss of love by the deprived partner. Disagreements and quarrels may also ensue, and the partners may resent each other for being different from what they had expected. One or both partners may tend to withdraw their emotional involvement. Both are now likely to re-examine the situation in terms of cost/reward ratio and comparison level.

As we saw in Chapter 8, this phase of the relationship is critical. If the conflict of interests—the apparent lack of common motives, goals, and values—continues, the relationship may be severely limited in terms of intimacy or commitment or it may terminate. On the other hand, if the partners make needed adjustments, the process of building a close and loving relationship moves ahead.

Money

Money ranks as the single most common cause of conflict in marriage. Conflicts arise over who earns the money; who spends how much on what; and who manages the money in terms of paying bills, borrowing, and investing. In their study of husbands and wives, Pietropinto and Siminauer (1979) found not only that money is a major source of conflict in marriage, but also that debts are the greatest crises in most marriages.

Although it has been said that "Americans know the cost of everything and the value of nothing," there are several reasons why money is so important in our society. First, money is essential for obtaining the necessities of life as well as some of the luxury items that many think make life worth living. Of course, a vast advertising medium constantly exposes us to the many desirable things we would like to have but can't afford—from new cars and beautiful homes to dream vacations. In addition, we need financial resources to meet emergencies, such as hospitalization. Second, money influences not only a couple's life style but also their security, feeling of control over events, acceptance by others, self-esteem, and many other personal and environmental considerations. Whether we like it or not, in our highly competitive and materialistic society, "Money talks."

Roles and Responsibilities

It would seem that, with today's "enlightened" views, few conflicts would stem from sex-roles, but such is not the case. For one thing, men seem to be slower than women in understanding, accepting, and adjusting to changed sex-roles. Although an increasing number of wives have accepted the new, more-egalitarian sex-roles and are trying to shape their marriages accordingly, a sizable number of husbands are suffering from "liberation shock." Many seem willing to change, but they don't know how to go about it, nor do they feel comfortable with that change. Many new fathers, for example, feel that the signals have been switched on them in the middle of their marital relationship—especially when they are expected to assume their share of household and child-care responsibilities. We have commented on this problem before and need not pursue it here.

It may be noted, however, that the role expectations with which each partner enters the marriage have to do not only with who does *what* but also with *how* it should be done. The couple may agree that the wife will prepare the meals, for example, but they may disagree on the kind of meals she should prepare. Thus,

Frank Siteman/The Picture Cube

difficulties may arise with respect to roles and in terms of the behaviors involved in enacting these roles. Such difficulties can be a potent source of conflict.

Finally, roles and responsibilities may change markedly over time for one or both marital partners, which can be an additional source of conflict. This is particularly true when the role change has a major impact on the marriage—for example, when the wife receives a high-level executive appointment or is elected to political office.

Power Struggles

In 1963, Jay Haley, a marriage therapist and researcher, concluded that the major conflict in marriage centers around the control of power—who tells whom what to do and under what circumstances. Today, researchers still consider power to be a key issue to be worked out in marriage, but now the emphasis is on decision-making power—that is, who decides where to go on vacation, what car to buy, and so on—rather than on "control" power (Scanzoni, 1979; Gray-Little & Burks, 1983; Podsakoff & Schriesheim, 1985).

The power of each spouse is primarily based on the value of his or her resources—both marital and personal—in the interpersonal marketplace. Thus, if one partner perceives the power relationship as inequitable, he or she may attempt to negotiate a distribution of power that is more "fair." However, if there is a major discrepancy in resources between husband and wife, the partner with the greatest resources has the greatest power, and if these resources are considered both valuable and irreplaceable, the less-endowed spouse may feel compelled to accept the status quo even though he or she may resent it.

Partners who come from diverse cultural backgrounds are particularly likely to experience differing role expectations and difficulties in resolving power conflicts. Although some couples seem to have few difficulties in the allocation of power, many others seem to be in a constant power struggle—sometimes overt and sometimes hidden. The couple who argue about whose turn it is to empty the trash may actually be battling about a more-fundamental and unresolved issue in their relationship. They may use a variety of strategies in this underlying struggle, some of which are likely to prove damaging in the long run (Falbo & Peplau, 1980).

As we have noted, the trend in recent years has been toward more-egalitarian marriages, in which the partners share in making important decisions but have autonomy in making others, depending on the knowledge and expertise of the partner in a given area. But, no matter what the power setup in a marriage, there are likely to be conflicts over who makes decisions about what.

Sexual Difficulties

Intercourse in marriage is the chief mode of sexual expression for most adults, and today it is usually assumed that both partners will find satisfaction in their sexual relationship.

Even when the couple agree on the desirability of sex, however, they may disagree on various details, such as appropriate or desired frequency, methods to be used, length of foreplay, willingness to experiment with new techniques or positions, time of day, setting, and who takes the initiative. Some of these details may continue to be a source of irritation to one or both partners.

Perhaps the most common problem among marital partners is unequal levels of desire, followed closely by differences of opinion about methods and who should take the initiative (Masters & Johnson, 1985). As we noted earlier, sexual dysfunctions and lack of desire can be a source of distress to both partners. To further complicate matters, people differ markedly in their knowledge about sexual behavior, in their background of sexual experience, and in their sexual skills and preferences.

In any event, marital conflict and lack of closeness in the marital relationship take their toll in the sexual area. Sexual dissatisfaction, in turn, tends to intensify conflicts in other areas as well as to increase the likelihood of extramarital affairs (Masters & Johnson, 1985; Moultrup, 1986).

Jealousy and Possessiveness

> In a world where we are so at the mercy of rapid change and capricious chance, it is little wonder that we seek stability and certainty in intimate relationships, especially with the one we love most. Anything that seems to upset or interfere with that becomes a threat. Jealousy . . . is one understandable response to this situation.
>
> —*N. R. Lobsenz (1975, p. 77)*

Nancy Friday (1985) has presented the same problem in the form of a question —"When we are jealous, what are we afraid of?" In short, the related problems of jealousy and possessiveness are common sources of conflict in marriage. Whatever draws the partner's attention away—whether it is work, another person, an absorbing hobby, or even children—may arouse jealousy. Because jealousy and possessiveness are commonly based on feelings of insecurity and inadequacy, they may both indicate and complicate an already troubled marriage.

Persons who have experienced hurtful rejection in prior intimate relationships, or who, for other reasons, lack feelings of adequacy or worth, often depend heavily on their marital partners for bolstering their self-concept. Thus, Robert Bringle (1981) has pointed out that talking about jealous feelings and analyzing their origins can be helpful. He also notes that being sensitive to the partner's need for social support when he or she is jealous can reduce the ill effects of jealousy when it does occur.

It also helps to be aware that males who tend to play a traditional sex-role in marriage are particularly prone to difficulties with both possessiveness and jealousy. These men tend to view their wives as "property" and expect them to play the role delineated and approved for them. If a wife plays a more-liberated or contemporary role, the potential for marital conflict is readily apparent.

To avoid such unnecessary conflicts, it seems essential that we give our marital partner a little "breathing space." Whether male or female, our partner is an independent person who demands and requires a considerable amount of autonomy and freedom. When one partner tries to "build a fence around" and possess the other, the result is needless jealousy and conflict. As Maxine Schnall (1979) has succinctly expressed it, "Out here in the adult world, we have to understand that there is only so much we can or should get from another person, and only so much we ourselves can give" (p. 6).

Anger and Violence

In dealing with the problem of **anger** in marriage, David Mace (1985) has commented as follows:

> This is what makes marriage so complicated. We marry because we want love. But we often fail to recognize that the closeness of marriage will inevitably bring us plenty of anger as well. Sooner or later, we learn that the quest for intimacy inevitably leads to conflict. . . . The anger, then, drives us apart, and the love and intimacy temporarily disappear. If this happens too often or too violently, the result is alienation. The marriage then either breaks up or becomes an empty shell. (p. 31)

Anger is a common reaction to interference with our needs, and in a relationship as close as marriage, such interference almost inevitably occurs. When we are angry, we tend to retaliate. And curiously enough, when we are angry, our feelings of love tend to be submerged. During an initial session with a wife in marital therapy, for example, she may vent her anger in highly derogatory statements about her husband. An inexperienced therapist might respond with a suggestion such as, "If you're husband is as you describe him, perhaps you should consider divorce." She is likely to reply, "You don't understand at all, Doctor. He has many good qualities. Why do you think I married him?" Having vented her anger, her underlying feelings of love and caring are then free to surface. But while she feels intense anger and resentment, her positive emotions are effectively blocked.

Thus, it is important that feelings of anger be dealt with constructively in the marital relationship if the partners are to avoid unnecessary conflict and distancing. Suggestions for dealing with anger are summarized in Box 11–1.

Violence seems to occur among families in most countries. Historically, it has been associated with the dominant status of the husband; the subordinate status of the wife has often been accompanied by physical abuse, and even rape, by the husband.

Joel Gordon

BOX 11-1 / DEALING WITH ANGER IN MARITAL RELATIONSHIPS

In dealing constructively with anger in marriage, three steps appear essential:

1. Helping our partner to understand that it is all right for him or her to be angry with us.
2. Listening to our partner's feelings without interrupting or becoming defensive or resentful.
3. Clearing a time when the partners can examine the situation calmly and rationally.

The overall objective here is to get the anger out in the open where it can be dealt with.

However, achieving these steps may be far from an easy task. For example, when feelings of hurt and anger are "too hot to handle," it may be necessary to give the situation time to cool down, but the anger should be cleared up without unnecessary delay. Anger has the peculiar power to suppress positive feelings toward our partner; the longer the anger festers, the more damage it is likely to do to the relationship. Also, many people have difficulty accepting anger from others because they already feel inadequate and insecure. Still others feel that everyone should love and appreciate them at all times, especially their mate. It is necessary to give up this erroneous notion and muster sufficient resources to accept the partner's anger without getting emotionally upset in return. Of course, there may be some satisfaction in reacting angrily to the seemingly unjustified anger of our mate, but such self-indulgence rarely pays off.

Ironically, once the partner has vented his or her anger—"has gotten the problem off his or her chest"—more-positive feelings are free to surface. It is usually a rather simple matter to work things out from there. Often a conciliatory statement —such as "What can I do to make things up to you?"—can be helpful, if it is made after the hurt and anger have been fully expressed.

The preceding approach to coping with anger has been strongly recommended by a group of researchers at the University of Michigan (Julius et al., 1986). Aside from the psychological damage that suppressed anger can do to a relationship—especially over time—these researchers note that it can lead to high blood pressure and other undesirable physical symptoms on the part of the partner experiencing the anger. It would seem that the old saying "Marriage can make you sick" should not be taken lightly.

Despite laws in our society to protect women from physical abuse by husbands, a great deal of violence still "goes on behind the closed doors of millions of American homes" (Straus & Gelles, 1986, p. 466). In their study of a nationally representative sample of over 3,500 families, these researchers estimated that over one and a half million wives were beaten by their husbands in 1985. Although wife beating appears to be decreasing, it is still a rather common "American pastime" (see Box 11-2). This is not entirely a one-way street; a sizable number of women also resort to violence in interactions with their husbands.

The causes, effects, and treatment of spousal violence is beyond the scope of our present discussion. But it is apparent that the conflicts and complexities introduced into marital relationships by spousal violence are tremendous in scope.

BOX 11–2 / IS WIFE BEATING AN AMERICAN PASTIME?

The following statistics reveal a far-from-pleasant picture of domestic tranquility in American homes.

1. The FBI estimates that 3 to 4 million women are assaulted in their homes each year by their husbands or other intimates.
2. About one woman in ten will be assaulted by her husband at some time in her marriage.
3. The average wife who presses charges against her husband has been beaten more than 35 times.
4. A sizable number of police officers are killed or injured each year while trying to cope with domestic violence.
5. Spouse abuse resulting in absenteeism on the job results in an economic loss of several billion dollars each year.

At present, the causal factors in spouse abuse are not entirely clear, and the picture may differ considerably from one case to another. However, the following factors have been related to spousal violence.

1. *The cycle of violence.* Persons who have experienced violent and abusive childhoods are more likely to become spouse abusers when they grow up than are individuals who have experienced little or no violence during their childhood years. In essence, "violence begets violence."
2. *Socioeconomic status.* Family violence is more prevalent in low socioeconomic families. Of course, this finding does not mean that spousal violence or child abuse is confined to lower-class households. In fact, spouse and child abuse can be found in families across the socioeconomic spectrum.
3. *Stress.* The incidence of domestic violence is directly related to social and environmental stress. For example, unemployment, financial problems, job dissatisfaction, poverty, and pregnancy are related to family violence.

4. *Social isolation.* Social isolation raises the risk of both spouse abuse and child abuse. Such social isolation apparently makes it more difficult for the victims of abuse to see their situation objectively and also to use social-support systems that might otherwise help the person to deal with his or her plight.

Other conditions have also been implicated in wife beating. Initially, the assaults are mild and infrequent, and the husband is usually contrite and swears he will make it up to his wife and it will never happen again. By the time the wife realizes that the beatings have become a dangerous and permanent aspect of her marriage, she is often emotionally attached to, and feels dependent on, her husband. This is true even in dual-career marriages in which the wife is not economically dependent on her husband. Staying in the relationship appears to be a testimonial to the old saying that "Hope springs eternal" or to the power of emotional bonding and denial of reality.

The establishment of "safe houses" and shelters—staffed by trained personnel—now provide abused wives with an alternative. But few women seem to take advantage of this alternative until they are convinced that their own lives—and possibly their children's lives—are endangered. Later, many of these wives return home, apparently enticed by the rosy promises of their husbands, and the beatings begin again.

Here, it may be pointed out that men are not the only offenders in spouse abuse. A sizable number of women apparently beat their husbands; however, there is little research data on husband beating. Finally, Is wife beating decreasing? The answer is a tentative "Yes." After some 10 years of treatment and prevention efforts, the trend appears to be toward reduction. Based on Walter (1984), Hanneke & Shields (1985), Straus & Gelles (1986), Weidman (1986), and Uniform Crime Reports, (1987).

Extramarital Affairs

Extramarital sex (EMS) is considered the Bermuda Triangle of the matrimonial seas. Certainly, affairs have accounted for a sizable number of "lost marriages." Yet, like the Bermuda Triangle, EMS is still pretty much a mystery. Despite the reported frequency of extramarital affairs—40–60 percent of marriages presumably experience them, at least they did prior to AIDS becoming such a prominent feature of the sexual scene—the amount and severity of conflict generated by such affairs have not been adequately researched.

Laura Singer (1981) has pointed out that, during the early years of marriage, the specter of the "other woman" or "other man" often arises. At this point, the couple may stop and ask, "Okay, what meaning does it have for us and our marriage?" Singer suggests that if the EMS is related to problems in the marriage and is approached as such, the problem can often be worked out. But jealousy, resentment, and feeling put down may rule out this approach, and, even if it is used, the EMS still may exact a high toll in conflict and hurt.

One basic problem in dealing with an extramarital affair is whether or not to tell the spouse. Many people feel that the spouse should not be told and that, in fact, the spouse would have to be blind not to discover the situation himself or herself. For example, the husband may start staying "late at the office" one or more evenings a week. He may look at his wife in certain ways or not look at her at all, his way of touching her may change, and he may be constantly fatigued or preoccupied, mouthing excuses like, "Sorry, dear, but I have a lot on my mind these days."

We have emphasized the importance of open communication, honesty, and trust in marital relationships throughout this book. But the problem of whether to admit to extramarital affairs is a complex one. For one thing, a breach of communication, honesty, and trust has already occurred. In addition, the partner engaging in the EMS may feel guilty and be tempted to confess the affair without fully realizing that he or she may irreparably damage the marriage. Of course, from the viewpoint of the spouse, such an admission may be the only way to find out that there is a serious problem in the marriage and to attempt changes that would make EMS unnecessary.

Unfortunately, however, once the mate is informed, his or her response may not be a rational discussion of the problem but rather a torrent of recrimination and resentment that may severely hamper any further communication (Moultrup, 1986). The outraged mate may feel that not only have the wedding vows been violated but also that he or she has been betrayed and devalued as a person. In short, revealing an extramarital affair may be terribly traumatic to the partner on the receiving end.

In a specific marriage, the outcome will depend in large part on the sexual values of the marital partners, the nature of their relationship, and whether or not the EMS poses a threat to the continuation of their marriage. In addition, with the appearance of AIDS on the sexual scene, an extramarital affair takes on a new and potentially deadly dimension. In 1987, there were a sizable number of documented cases in which wives had been infected with the AIDS virus by their husbands. What effect AIDS will have in reducing EMS remains to be seen, but EMS has become a very special type of marital problem.

In this section, we have touched on several sources of marital conflict and stress. But there are many others, including different "kinds of loving" and the

BOX 11-3 / ALCOHOLISM AND THE FAMILY

The commonly used problem drugs in our society are alcohol, barbiturates, tranquilizers, amphetamines, marijuana, cocaine, and heroin. Of these drugs, alcohol is by far the most widely used and abused. There are more than 100 million users of alcohol over the age of 15 in our society. Most of the users rarely, if ever, cause trouble for themselves or others. Unfortunately, however, some 10 million or more are alcohol abusers or alcoholics, and there are some 200,000 or more new cases each year.

The potential detrimental effects of alcoholism—for the individual, his or her loved ones, and society—are legion. Bengelsdorf (1970) has pointed out that abuse of alcohol "has killed more people, sent more victims to hospitals, generated more police arrests, broken up more marriages and homes, and cost industry more money than has the abuse of heroin, amphetamines, barbiturates, and marijuana combined" (p. 7). He could also have included cocaine in this list.

Alcoholism in the United States cuts across all educational, occupational, and socioeconomic boundaries. It is considered a serious problem in industry, in the professions, and in the military; it is found among such seemingly unlikely candidates as surgeons, police officers, and airline pilots. However, the great majority of alcoholics are men and women who are married and living with their families, who still hold jobs—often important ones—and are accepted members of their communities. Although alcoholism has traditionally been considered to be more prevalent among males than females, this distinction seems to be disappearing in our society.

Some investigators prefer to think of alcohol abuse as a "learned behavior disorder" and prefer to use the term **problem drinking** rather than **alcoholism.**

Presumably, some problem drinkers can learn to use alcohol in a moderate and controlled way for social purposes. Other investigators, however, view alcoholism as a disease and consider the only cure to be total abstinence. Many assume that this disease results from an hereditary predisposition that leads to the loss of control over alcohol intake.

Although a vast amount of research has been done on alcoholism, it has focused mainly on the pathology of the individual alcoholic. The bulk of this research has failed to deal with the profound influence of alcohol abuse on married and family life. Millions of American marriages and families are adversely affected by the drinking of one or both spouses. This includes more than 25 million children of alcoholics in this country.

Often a person married to an alcoholic is unaware of the extent to which—gradually and inevitably—many of the decisions he or she makes each day are based on the expectation that the mate will be drinking. In such cases, the wife is becoming "drinking-husband oriented" or the husband is becoming "drinking-wife oriented." Eventually, the entire marriage, including social life and sexual behavior, may be dominated by the drinking of the alcoholic spouse. As might be expected, the probability of divorce in such marriages is several times greater than among married couples who do not drink excessively.

Probably the best-known and most successful treatment for alcoholism is that of Alcoholics Anonymous (AA), which was founded in 1935 by two recovered alcoholics. Since then, AA has grown to over 10,000 groups in the United States, and many other countries have also established groups. In addition, AA has affiliated organizations for the spouses and children of alcoholics. The phone number of the AA group in your area can be obtained by simply dialing local information.

havoc created by inadequate communication. Alcoholism is a source of stress in a sizable number of marriages (Box 11–3). Also career pressures and other problems outside the marriage can take their toll both mentally and physically—often making the partner irritable, depressed, and unpleasant to be around. The existence of this pattern has led to the observation that "When your marital partner seems to deserve love least, he or she may need it most."

RESOLVING MARITAL CONFLICT

Although there is no mandate that says marital conflicts have to be resolved or marital relationships have to be continued, there are strong motives for most married couples to resolve their difficulties. For one thing, a couple in love will want to keep conflicts from threatening their relationship. Second, if the cost/reward ratio and comparison level are still favorable, each partner will want to continue a rewarding relationship. Third, the couple may wish to avoid the emotional, financial, moral, and other traumas of separation and divorce.

In this section, we shall first examine some basic guidelines for resolving marital conflicts through negotiation. Then, we shall note some of the barriers that can make conflict resolution difficult or impossible. Finally, we shall comment on marital therapy as a possible source of help.

Negotiation: Some Guidelines

> Successful collaborative negotiation lies in finding out what the other side really wants and showing them how to get it, while you get what you want.
>
> —*Herb Cohen (1980 p. 161)*

While Cohen's statement may seem unduly cynical, it does represent the core of successful negotiation in resolving most conflicts. But achieving this result may be far from simple. However, the following guidelines may be of help.

1. Pinpointing the Problem.   "What are we fighting about?" is a question marital partners commonly ask. In some instances the question is easy to answer; in others, it isn't.

Pinpointing the problem often starts on the most fundamental level: recognizing that a problem exists. This awareness may come through such symptoms as frequent quarreling over seemingly trivial issues. What the couple quarrel about may not be the actual problem. For example, when a couple argue about whose turn it is to do the laundry or the grocery shopping, the actual conflict may involve differing sex-role concepts and expectations.

Because of the intense emotional climate in marriage, it is difficult for the couple to view themselves and their relationship objectively. Yet, until they pinpoint the actual problem, it is not likely to be resolved. This process is commonly referred to as **redefining,** or **reframing,** the problem (Coyne, 1985). Often the process of empathic listening is helpful here. The essential objective of empathic listening is for each partner to understand the other's point of view. This requires really listening and asking for clarification when it is needed. Empathic listening may also involve reflecting in your own words what your partner has said. This shows that you are really listening and whether or not you understand what your partner is trying to convey.

Finally, in pinpointing the problem it is important to keep the focus on needs, feelings, and concerns—not on solutions (Rogers, 1987). This helps the partners to arrive at a mutual understanding of what the problem is.

2. Exploring Options.   The second step in negotiating is exploring options—possible alternative solutions to resolving the conflict. Here, it is important to consider alternative solutions even though some of them may appear impractical. One of the quickest ways to kill creativity in exploring options is to belittle our partner's ideas.

After a list of options has been drawn up, it is time to evaluate each option in terms of its probable consequences for the partners and their relationship. The objective here is to decide on an option that seems to offer the best solution to the problem in terms of costs and rewards. After this evaluation process is completed, the partners usually end up with a list of several possible options; that is, options that merit consideration in making a decision. For an example of one couple's negotiating see Box 11–4.

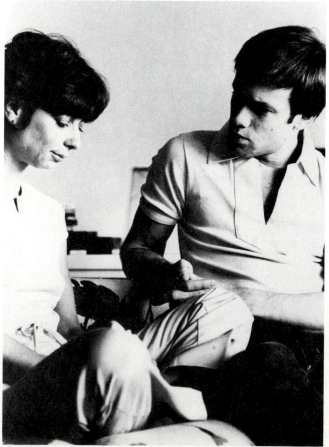

Joel Gordon

BOX 11-4 / NEGOTIATING A CONFLICT OVER HOUSEWORK

Paula Luckadoo (1981) reports a good example of negotiating a satisfactory solution to a marital conflict. The situation involved a couple in a dual-career marriage. The husband had agreed to do his share of housework but simply didn't know how to do what his wife considered routine housekeeping chores. After several months of bickering about who would do what and when, the couple arrived at a pragmatic solution to their problem.

They began by discussing what each expected of the other in the way of housekeeping chores. Then they talked about specific chores, indicating how often each task should be done, as well as their feelings about doing a given task. Their system started with an evaluation of specific household chores.

They listed all the "must do" tasks, from buying groceries to taking out the garbage. To each task they assigned numerical scores. One score indicated how frequently the task required doing; the other score indicated the difficulty of the task and how much skill was required to accomplish it. The tasks were then scored on the basis of a frequency scale and a difficulty scale:

Frequency Scale

2 = less than once per month
4 = monthly
6 = bimonthly (twice a month)
8 = weekly
10 = once or more daily

Difficulty Scale

2 = no skill required
4 = task requires some skill or training
6 = actual experience required
8 = considerable prior experience required

They assigned a difficulty value and a frequency value to each task, and using the above scales added them up for a total score. For example, vacuum cleaning was given a difficulty value of two and a frequency value of eight—for a total score of ten points. Cooking was given a difficulty score of eight and a frequency value of ten—for a total of eighteen points.

Next, they accepted tasks which they preferred or were required to do because of required skills. For example, the husband was good at vacuuming but couldn't cook. Then the couple divided the remaining tasks between them. In essence, there was an attempt to achieve a 50–50 split of chores. The outcome was a prescribed list of responsibilities for each partner, together with a schedule for doing them.

The couple considered another advantage of this system to be its flexibility. For example, they moved from a small apartment to a big house which was in dire need of repair. As a result, they were faced with yard work and home-repair tasks. Because the husband had the necessary skills for handling those tasks and the wife didn't, she ended up assuming some of the tasks for which he had formerly been responsible. And when her job at a bank required weekend and late night work, the tasks were temporarily redistributed on a 75–25 basis, rather than the originally agreed-upon 50–50 split. (pp. 60–61)

At the time this report was published, the couple's negotiated arrangement had been in operation for about 3 years and was considered an unqualified success. One feature that appears to have contributed to its success was its flexibility. As changes occur in a marriage, agreements have to be renegotiated and updated to meet changed demands, a factor built into the couple's system. In addition, their negotiation was based on commitment to the marriage and was done in a spirit of care and cooperation. Because each partner felt the final agreement was something in which he or she had fully participated, their method helped create an atmosphere of harmony and mutuality, both in household chores and in the marriage as a whole.

3. Deciding on an Alternative and Specifying the Behavior to Be Changed. The objective here is to decide on an alternative that seems to offer the best solution all the way around. After this alternative has been chosen, it is time to negotiate the actual behavior change required to put this proposed solution into operation.

The actual process of negotiating may take a variety of forms. In a relationship in which one partner has a dominant role and the other a submissive role, there is often a concession by the partner in the subordinate position. Typically, however, negotiating involves trade-offs from both sides. Suppose, for example, that the husband fumes about the fact that his wife rarely cooks dinner, requiring him to eat fast food more often than he would like. The wife, on the other hand, is aggravated by the fact that her husband leaves dirty clothes around the house and never picks them up. As a result of negotiating the problem, the wife agrees to cook dinner four nights a week, and the husband agrees to pick up his clothes. The negotiating terminates when the partners agree on a solution to their problems or when one partner refuses to make any further concessions, saying, "That's it. I won't go beyond this point." For example, the wife may say that four nights of cooking is her maximum and if her husband wants home-cooked food on the other days, he can make it himself. The husband may say, in turn, that he will pick up his things, but he draws the line on helping with the laundry. If the negotiating is successful, the final outcome is a compromise that neither may consider an ideal solution but with which both can live.

One trend that is becoming more popular these days is to say, "Let's do it together," rather than, "I'll do this if you'll do that." For example, the husband and wife may find that they enjoy preparing meals together and that clothes get picked up faster when they both do the work.

4. Evaluating Change—Using Feedback. Conflict resolution has occurred when the behavior changes agreed on in the negotiations have been put into action and they work—when the changes in roles, obligations, or resources have established a more-equitable social exchange or have resolved the issue at hand.

But what if the feedback is unfavorable? What if the husband doesn't like the meals his wife grudgingly throws together four nights a week, and what if the wife is annoyed by the fact that the husband seems to create more messes while picking up his clothes? Sometimes, minor adjustments or corrections can be made to salvage the situation. If the couple has pinpointed the wrong problem, it is necessary to go back to the drawing board and start over.

As feedback becomes available, it becomes an important part of the overall process of conflict resolution. In fact, such feedback may be as important as the original negotiated change in shaping the later aspects of thought and action. When we have sufficient feedback and use it to correct behavior in progress, it becomes a key part of the overall conflict-resolving sequence.

In concluding our brief review of negotiation, several additional points merit consideration. Although negotiating is a basic method of resolving disagreements and conflicts, other patterns may also be involved. Often, for example, one partner may have to adjust to conditions that he or she dislikes but that come as part of the "package deal." For example, a woman whose husband is in the military service may not like the fact that his work keeps him away from home, but she may simply have to adjust to this situation. Similarly, a person who marries someone with children will have to adjust to sharing the spouse's time with the children, as well as taking some responsibility for them.

In some instances, pinpointing the problem may lead the partners to agree that the issue is one on which they can afford to disagree, such as differing political opinions. Such differences are not a problem that has to be resolved in order for the partners to respect each other, to get along well together, and to achieve mutual goals.

In some cases, negotiating may also depend heavily on whether the issue is one of fact or opinion. If the couple are in disagreement about one partner's excessive smoking or drinking, they are dealing with objective facts. However, if their disagreement is about child-rearing methods, they are in the realm of opinion, which makes the conflict more difficult to solve.

Finally, negotiating is by no means always a matter of objectivity and reason. One or both partners may resort to all manner of persuasive techniques, including crying, appealing to fairness, making threats, calling names, using sex as a reward, withholding sex as punishment, and even using violence. Making use of such techniques in order to try to come out on top in the situation crosses the boundary line from negotiation to manipulation. In dealing with such difficult situations, the words of former President of the United States John F. Kennedy come to mind:

> Let us begin anew, remembering on both sides that civility is not a sign of weakness, that sincerity is always subject to proof. Let us never negotiate out of fear. But let us never fear to negotiate.

This statement was made in the context of negotiations among nations, but it also seems to apply directly to negotiations on the level of intimate relationships.

Barriers to Conflict Resolution

A variety of conditions and behaviors may act as barriers to resolving conflicts. Leading the parade are incorrectly identifying the problem, manipulation, and faulty communication. Other barriers include the following:

1. Denying that there is a problem.
2. Refusing to talk about the problem, or not sticking to the issue.
3. Taking a fighting stance, giving in, or withdrawing.
4. Putting the partner down—attacking your partner instead of the problem.
5. Becoming emotional, defensive, and irrational.
6. Demanding that the partner be the one to make any changes.
7. Competing with the partner so that the situation becomes a matter of "one-upmanship."
8. Perceiving the marriage differently from the partner so that essentially there are two marriages: *his* and *hers*.
9. Carrying over "unfinished business" from a prior intimate relationship.
10. Coming up with a solution that becomes a new problem so that the cure is worse than the disease.

Many of these barriers to resolving conflicts involve personal immaturity or maladjustment, as well as inaccurate perceptions and undesirable behaviors, on the part of one or both partners. For example, in a 9-year study of 487 couples, John Gottman (1979) found that taking a defensive stance—being more concerned with defending our viewpoint than with resolving the conflict—is a major source of bitterness and marital unhappiness. He discovered that happily married couples tended to be task-oriented instead of defense-oriented in dealing with their conflicts and, thus, managed to resolve their differences rapidly and effectively without leaving any "emotional scars."

Finally, in dealing with barriers to conflict resolution, it is useful to remember that some behaviors are highly resistant to change. Hence, it is important not to expect "too much too soon" or to become discouraged and give up. As the old Chinese proverb goes, "A journey of a thousand miles starts with a single step."

Can Marital Therapy Help?

Marital counseling or marital therapy (the terms are used interchangeably) began in the 1920s. However, it was not until the climbing divorce rate in the 1970s that client demand for marital therapy led to a rapid expansion of the field.

Although the primary intent of **marital therapy** is to assist couples in coping with their marital problems, it is not aimed at preserving marital bonds at all costs. In some marriages, the relationship has deteriorated to the point where it cannot be salvaged; in others, one partner wants out. In such instances, as Arnold Lazarus (1981) has pointed out, the marriage therapist becomes a "divorce therapist."

When Do You Need Marital Therapy?

There is no simple formula to tell you when marital therapy might be of help in your marriage. There is agreement, however, that waiting too long to get help—when you need it—can make your marital problems more difficult or impossible to resolve.

In an effort to increase awareness of danger signs in marriage, John Engel and others (1985) have suggested asking such questions as

1. Do you frequently find fault with your partner?
2. Are there many ways in which you would like to change your partner?
3. Do you argue continually over minor issues?
4. Do you feel that serious disagreements never get resolved?
5. Do you feel free to express your feelings to your partner?
6. Do you feel discouraged and depressed about your marriage?
7. Do you wish you had not married this person?

"Yes" answers to one or more of these questions are warning signs of distress in your marriage.

Reluctance to Seek Marital Therapy.

Many marital couples are reluctant to seek professional assistance with their problems. If one partner wants out of the marriage, he or she may see marriage therapy as a waste of time and money and refuse to see a therapist. In such cases, the spouse who is still emotionally invested in the marriage often goes for marital therapy on an individual basis. Although the therapy experience may be constructive, it is not likely to salvage the marriage.

Another common cause of reluctance to see a marriage therapist is the partners' view that their marriage is nobody's business but their own. They usually feel that they should be able to handle the problems that do arise without baring their private lives to a stranger. So who does go to see marital therapists? Veroff (1981) found that men and women who seek professional help have (1) positive expectations about the efficacy of such help, (2) an orientation toward attributing difficulties to inadequacies in themselves, and (3) a sense of self-integrity that is not violated by admitting the need for professional assistance.

Finally, marital therapy can be relatively expensive, which may deter some couples from seeking assistance. Community service agencies may provide marital counseling free or on an ability-to-pay basis, but such services are not always available or may require a long waiting period.

Approaches to Marital Therapy.   Typically, the marital partners are seen together or in a group with several other couples. The number and length of counseling sessions may vary but usually consist of about six 50-minute sessions —commonly referred to as 50-minute hours. The overall therapy program focuses on resolving conflicts and improving the couple's marital relationship.

Many marital therapists rely heavily on the use of psychological tests and rating scales in assessing the characteristics of the marital partners and their relationship. Marital therapists also make extensive use of videotaping and playing back portions of the couple's session for them. One young wife shared the following information with her husband after viewing a playback of their first therapy session:

> See! There it is—loud and clear! As usual, you didn't let me express my feelings or opinions but interrupted me with your own. You're always *telling* me what I *think*, without asking me what I think or feel. And I can see what I have been doing in response—withdrawing into silence. I feel like . . . well . . . what's the use? (Coleman, 1979, p. 421)

The husband agreed with her assessment of the replay, and the videotaping proved helpful in improving the marital relationship.

Although marital therapists may use a variety of techniques—depending on the needs of the couple or couples involved—they often differ in their overall orientation. Here, we shall limit our discussion to three rather distinctive approaches to marital therapy: transactional analysis, rational-emotive therapy, and behaviorial marital therapy.

1. *Transactional Analysis (TA).*   Eric Berne (1964, 1972) developed an innovative form of marital therapy based on the notion that each of us is part parent, part child, and part adult.

   Parent: The part of us stemming from use of our parents as models. "Put on a sweater if you are going out in the cold" or "You shouldn't eat so much" are examples of our parent speaking.

   Child: The part of us carried over from childhood feelings. "I don't want to wear a sweater, and don't always yell at me" is an example of our child speaking.

Adult: The part of us that is grown up and responds rationally and appropriately to the situation. "I don't think it is really cold enough for a sweater" is an example of our adult speaking.

In TA, the therapist analyzes the interactions among group members (that is, married couples) and helps the participants understand the "ego state" in which they are communicating with each other. As long as each marital partner responds to the other in the way that he or she is being addressed—for example, as a child to a parent—the transactions may continue indefinitely. However, when one partner decides to stop playing his or her usual role, conflicts develop that must be worked out. For example, a couple may discover that one partner has been playing a child role to the spouse's parent role and that this is the primary basis of their marital difficulties. The counseling or therapy process thus becomes one of helping the couple to interact as one adult to another.

2. *Rational-Emotive Therapy (RET).* This is a form of cognitive therapy aimed at changing the individual's irrational and self-defeating thought processes (Ellis & Harper, 1961; Ellis, 1973, 1987). Applied to marital therapy, it assumes that many marital conflicts are a result of, and maintained by, irrational beliefs that the partners have about themselves and their relationship. For example, the wife may believe that the husband should always take the initiative in sex, creating a continuing conflict between the marital partners.

Often such irrational beliefs take more-subtle forms. Suppose that in a dual-career marriage the husband procrastinates and otherwise manages to avoid helping his wife with household responsibilities. As a result, his wife is overloaded and resentful, and their once harmonious relationship has become conflict-ridden. Is the husband aware of the beliefs on which his behavior is based? For example, his beliefs may include

A real man doesn't do woman's work.
Housework is woman's work.
If she can't handle her work, that is her problem.
After all, I earn far more money than she does.

The husband may be unaware of these self-defeating beliefs and the damage they are doing to his marriage. In RET, he would have to face these beliefs and deal with them.

3. *Behavioral Marital Therapy.* Here, the basic assumption is usually made that marital conflicts are the result of one or both partners engaging in behavior that is aversive to the other. Because the marital partners presumably lack competence in dealing with such problem behaviors, the therapist focuses on helping the partners reduce aversive, and increase rewarding, behaviors by means of well-established principles of learning. Although it is seemingly simple, behaviorial marital therapy can involve complex therapeutic procedures that need not concern us here.

Despite differences in orientation and techniques of these and other systematic approaches to marital therapy, the following steps are usually involved:

1. Assessing the marital conflict and the resources of the partners.
2. Exploring and evaluating the available options for resolving the problem.

3. Negotiating change—deciding on a course of action designed to resolve the marital conflicts or problems.

4. Taking action and evaluating feedback.

5. Introducing strategies to help maintain positive change.

In this process, a good deal of effort is usually directed toward helping the marital partners improve their communication and conflict-resolving skills so that they will be better able to deal with conflicts on their own.

Family Therapy.   Often this question is asked: What is the difference between marital therapy and family therapy?

> All of the ingredients in a family that count are changeable and correctible— individual self-worth, communication system, and rules. There is hope, then, that anything can change.
>
> —*Virginia Satir (1972)*

Perhaps the most widely used approach to **family therapy** is the conjoint family therapy of Virginia Satir (1967, 1972). Satir emphasizes improving faulty communication, interactions, and relationships and fostering a family system that better meets the needs of family members.

Although rising from different roots, family therapy and marital therapy have become increasingly fused into an overall therapy approach. In fact, conjoint family therapy—as indicated by the above quote—is applicable to marital, as well as family, therapy. Thus, there seems to be very little difference between marital therapy and family therapy.

We could add other approaches to our review of marital therapy, but we cannot hope to encompass the huge scope of this field in the present chapter. However, Box 11–5 briefly describes the nature of **crisis intervention.** In the following chapter, we shall comment briefly on **divorce therapy.**

PASSAGES: CHANGES IN MARITAL RELATIONSHIPS OVER TIME

> Although we seldom notice the effects of the passage of time on a relationship while time is passing, we can often look back and realize how important a role time played in what happened"
>
> —*Sharon Brehm (1985, p. 283)*

Adults are well aware that "They lived happily ever after" is not the end of the story. Growing up, getting married, and raising a family take up about 40 years of the average person's life span. What happens to people and their marriages during the 35 years or more that remain?

The attempt to answer this question has led to the concepts of **life-span development** and **life flow**—the systematic study of the tasks, conflicts, and themes that characterize early, middle, and later adulthood (Neugarten & Neugarten, 1987). An early milestone here was Gail Sheehy's (1974) book *Passages:*

BOX 11–5 / CRISIS INTERVENTION

Most people are familiar with the term **crisis centers.** These centers provide immediate and specialized medical intervention for life-threatening conditions—for example, burn centers.

Crisis intervention has also emerged as a response to the need for immediate help by individuals, marital partners, and families confronted with highly stressful situations—often with situations that exceed their coping resources. To meet this need, two modes of intervention have been developed: (1) the telephone "hot line" and (2) facilities providing for face-to-face discussion. Often a person uses the "hot line" to arrange for a crisis interview. In recent years, "hot lines" and related facilities have become available for people undergoing a wide range of crises, including persons contemplating suicide and victims of rape.

An illustration of how such crisis intervention works might involve the emotional turmoil of one marital partner who comes home unexpectedly and finds his or her mate having an affair with a mutual friend. Here, the person can call a crisis "hot line" and talk to a qualified person who listens and tries to be of help. In addition, an immediate appointment may be arranged with a qualified marriage and divorce therapist who is "on call." The primary concern of such crisis intervention is the current situation with which the individual is trying to cope. Admittedly, such intervention may do little more than provide an "emotional Band-Aid," but the important point is that the person needs and receives immediate help.

Predictable Crises of Adult Life, which led to public awareness that there is life after adolescence, school, and marriage; she points to some of the changes and crises that typically occur in the course of our adult lives and the marital life cycle.

Here, we shall briefly outline three transition periods and their general impact on people and marriage: midlife, retirement and the later years, and widowhood.

Marriage and the Midlife Crisis

Is there a **midlife crisis?** Some people would probably answer "Yes," others "No." In her book *Passages,* Gail Sheehy presents men and women in midcareer trying to recapture bits and pieces of their lost inner selves and to break out of the confines of rigid sex-roles. On the other hand, Nancy Schlossberg (1987) considers it a creation of the mass media. As she has pointed out, "Crisis, transition and change occur all through life" (p. 74). The author of this book is inclined to think that for some people the midlife crisis is very real, indeed; for others, it may represent a mild transition; and for still others, it may be a nonevent—an expected event that fails to occur.

But, assuming that the midlife crisis is real—at least for many people—when does it occur? This question is difficult to answer because it is somewhat unclear when midlife begins and ends. In general, however, midlife encompasses the period from the late 30s to the early 60s.

This is a period when a number of stressful events are likely to occur—such as the last child leaving home (see Box 11–6), experiencing a nagging sense of

BOX 11–6 / THE EMPTY-NEST SYNDROME: REALITY OR ILLUSION?

This is a large lie, a myth that a shattered and depressed woman lives inside the shell of an empty nest. . . . It is a distorted view of womanhood.

—Joel Greenberg (1978, p. 74)

Is it really a distorted view of womanhood? The answer appears to depend on the attitudes and life situation of the woman involved. Some women do view the departure of their children with a sigh of relief, but others do not. To complicate matters, the children may never "really" depart. As Lois Duncan (1981) has expressed it, "They may be 'yours' for eighteen years, but you are 'theirs' till you die" (p. 6). After the children leave the nest, they often come back for help and to have their wounds soothed. Whatever their ages, the woman is still their mother. Thus, Duncan refers to "the myth" of the empty nest.

It appears that while the empty-nest syndrome is a reality for some couples, it is largely an illusion for most. In fact, Norval Glenn (1975) analyzed six national surveys and concluded that, despite individual differences, raising a family "is less fun to be doing than to have done" (p. 2).

In any event, once the children leave home, the couple face the problem of assessing their marital relationship and the changes that may be in order. Couples who have remained together "for the children's sake" may find that they have grown apart and that their relationship is untenable. They may terminate their marriage. Here, the children leaving the home is complicated by the dissolution of the marriage. On the other hand, for some couples this reassessment enables them to rediscover the reasons for which they married. They may find that they still share many common interests, enjoy each other's companionship, and look forward to many exciting times together. As Avner Barcai (1981) summarized it, "Family lost—couple regained" (p. 358).

Ulrike Welsch

BOX 11-7 / GRANDPARENTS: A FAMILY RESOURCE

Another major event in the midlife period is becoming a grandparent. Interestingly enough, conflicts between grandparents and grandchildren are usually minor compared to those between parents and children. In fact, grandparents often serve as mediators between parents and children. They may also be a valuable resource as custodians of family history. In stepfamilies, the latter may be particularly valuable in helping children to understand their "roots" and feel part of a respected broader family.

Of course, grandparents may not be interested in helping to raise grandchildren. "I've raised my kids and that is enough" is not an uncommon attitude. In other cases, grandparents may lose contact with their grandchildren when their married son or daughter is divorced and child custody goes to the other spouse. In fact, the latter has become so common that most states now have laws permitting grandparents to sue for visitation rights in order to stay in touch with their grandchildren. On the other hand, divorce may unify the generations when a couple's daughter is divorced and moves back home with her children.

In essence, the grandparent role can be a rewarding one for both grandparents and grandchildren. Thus, social scientists generally accept the view that "Grandparents and grandchildren need each other."

meaningless in our work, and feeling trapped in a marriage that is worn out. It is also a time when the couple may become grandparents, and when both partners realize that they are getting "older" and that time is running out (Box 11–7). Often it is a shock to realize that we have more years behind us than ahead.

Such life experiences are likely to trigger some very basic feelings and questions:

- Did I make the right choices in the past?
- What kind of a future is there for me?
- There's so much that I want to accomplish but I need more time.
- Is this all there is?
- Have I accomplished anything that people will remember me by?

For both husband and wife, midlife is a time to get reacquainted and to examine their marriage. By the time their last child leaves home, they may be relative strangers. Often the husband evidences "sexual burnout," stemming from boredom and satiation with the same sexual partner and practices (Masters & Johnson, 1985). On the other hand, female sexuality in midlife tends to bloom rather than to diminish. Lillian Rubin (1979) found that many of the women she interviewed were just discovering their sexual selves in middle age after having been trapped by traditional female roles in early marriage. After the children left home, the wives learned to enjoy sex and to take the initiative rather than just to submit passively. This period, when the partners get reacquainted, is often a crisis point in their marriage; the departure of children does not automatically bring magic back into their relationship. At this time, the partners usually realize how much they have grown apart and that their marriage will never be what they had always assumed it would be.

For both men and women, midlife is a time when extramarital affairs may develop. In fact, Levinson (1986) considers such affairs more common than most people realize. The husband may meet a younger woman who finds him mature, distinguished looking, and sexy and who is not hesitant about making overtures even though she may know he is married. This, in turn, often elicits a sense of adequacy, youthfulness, and adventure on his part. In trying to recapture his youth, he may divorce his wife. Or it may work the other way around. If the wife is an attractive career woman, she may meet a younger man who intrigues her and who is far better able to meet her new-found sexual desires. Both of the preceding patterns have become relatively common events. And when they involve motion-picture and television stars, they usually receive interesting writeups in the news media.

On the other hand, many middleaged couples still find each other physically attractive and use their new-found insights and time together to revitalize their marriage. Because both are different people from the ones they married, getting acquainted again can be an exciting experience. With their children gone, they may have the time and money to enjoy travel and other interesting activities together, to become close companions again, and to rebuild their feelings of friendship and sexuality.

We shall end our review of midlife with an overall view of this period which has been well captured by Kathleen Mogul (1979):

> In essence, midlife is seen as the time when previous choices in important life areas and the ensuing successes, failures, satisfactions, and disappointments are reviewed and reworked in the context of old aspirations and wishes, the current recognition of limitations in oneself, and the finiteness of opportunities and of time itself. Midlife combines the sense of "another chance" with that of a "final chance." (p. 1139)

In sum, the midlife crisis can play havoc with careers and marriages, or it can be a period of renewal and planning for the future. The outcome appears to depend on the individual, the quality of his or her marriage, and environmental resources and limitations. Although it can be a rewarding experience, it can also be an extremely painful one.

Middlehood as a stage in the family life cycle—a period when the tasks and responsibilities of earlier phases of adulthood are done—is a relatively recent part of human experience, the product of . . . a steadily increasing life expectancy, changes in fertility patterns due to more effective contraception, a declining number of children per family, an earlier end to the childbearing and child-rearing phases of women's lives, and a growing concern for more egalitarian relationships between women and men both inside and outside the family.

Lillian Rubin

Retirement and the Later Years

Grow old along with me!
The best is yet to be
The last of life,
for which the first was made.

—Robert Browning

People who give every appearance of being 55 or older show up steadily in decent restaurants, at sports events, on pleasure cruises, and in vacation spots, and in almost all respects act like ordinary human beings.

Sid Bernstein

It has been said that, next to dying, the realization that we are getting old is probably the most profound shock of our life time. Each day, this shock is brought home to over 5,000 Americans who cross the invisible barrier of age 65—the age the Bureau of the Census still uses as the demarcation line between middle age and old age (Fig. 11–2). And at age 70—the mandatory age of retirement for most employees—the senior citizen is "benched" for the remainder of the game.

Individuals respond to retirement in different ways. For those whose personal definition is heavily dependent on what they do, there tends to be a loss of identity

Fig. 11–2. The Greying of America (Senior citizens— age 65 and older). (Source: U.S. Census Bureau.)

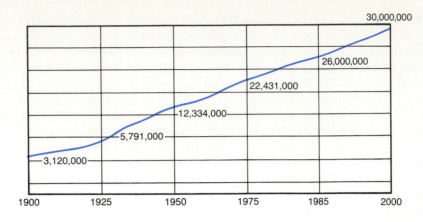

The projected figure for 2030 is approximately 50 million.

and self-esteem. In addition, there is usually a loss of friends with whom we have worked. And, of course, retirement often brings a reduction in income.

It is useful to view aging in terms of three dimensions—biological, psychological, and social. *Biological* aging may be retarded by healthful behavior, but it is still an inevitable part of the human life cycle. Contrary to popular belief, however, the great majority of older Americans—some 24 million—are able to manage quite well on their own. And older Americans are not devoid of sex. In a study of 800 men and women over 60, Starr and Weiner (1980) found that almost 90 percent still had sexual relations, albeit less frequently. In a study of couples living in a retirement community—with an average age of 74.8 years—Linda Ade-Ridder (1985) found over 60 percent to be sexually active (see Box 11–8). Interestingly, 35 percent of these couples had celebrated their 50th wedding anniversary.

Smithsonian Institution Archive Center/Business Americana Collection

BOX 11-8 / AGING AND SEX

A 78-year-old man expresses his attitude toward sex:

I think my wife and I have sex oftener than our two married children. It seems to get better every month. Perhaps because we are so close to each other and realize that we have so little time left. When you are over 75, you can't count beyond today or even all of today. So we try to make the most of the time God has allotted to us. We have never compared notes with our children, because they don't like to talk about sex openly—at least not with us. I think they have difficulty accepting the fact that their older parents still have sexual needs and desires and still find great pleasure in being sexually intimate with each other. Perhaps it is shocking to them for their aging parents to be sexual creatures. But we love each other and feel good, not ashamed, about fulfilling our sexual desires and being so close. For we know that each time is to be treasured. It may be the last we shall ever have together in this world.

Sociological aging is largely a matter of the social roles assigned to older people in a given society. In some societies, aging is accompanied by increased social status and respect. Among the Navajo, for example, a tribal elder is a revered leader, respected by the younger members for his or her experience and wisdom (Huyck, 1974). Similarly, in countries such as Pakistan and China, older people are expected to continue to play a productive role, and they do. But, in our society, the marked increase in older people—from some 3 million in 1900 to over 30 million in 1990—has caught us largely unprepared. As a result, we have failed to provide roles or social status for older people that help to provide meaning and dignity to their lives. In fact, the term **role obsolence** has been used to describe society's attitude toward the older person having outlived his or her usefulness. In *psychological* aging, many older people come to accept this attitude and behave accordingly—as old people.

Marriage during the retirement years tends to continue along pretty much as it has been. Those couples who have warm and loving relationships usually continue to be warm and loving, and those partners who have drifted apart usually remain that way. However, there is a difference during the retirement years between traditional marriages and dual-career marriages. Wives who have been home-makers often find it difficult to adjust to having the husband around all day and may even resent it (Hill & Dorfman, 1982). On the other hand, dual-career couples may retire at the same time, so they can spend more time together and enjoy the years that remain (Tryban, 1985).

Morris Medley (1987) has suggested that postretirement marriages can be fitted into one of three categories:

1. *The husband-wife.*   Here, the marital partners stress the intimate nature of their relationship, for example, dual-career couples who coordinate their retirements in order to spend more time together.
2. *The parent-child.*   Here, one spouse assumes the nurturant and protec-

On the first day of your life the government records your presence. On the last day of your life the government records your departure. On the 23,741st day of your life the government declares you are officially old. Oh, they don't put it quite that way. They give you two little cards and start paying part of your medical bills and sending you spending money every month.

Jack Mabley

Mark Godfrey/Archive Pictures, Inc.

People talk about what 'senior citizens' want as if those over 65 were a homogeneous group. People do not suddenly become alike when they reach 65. In reality, they are a group of

tive role of parent, while the other assumes a submissive, dependent child–type role. This pattern may occur when one spouse is incapacitated.

3. *The associates.* Here, the couple remain friends but find their most rewarding moments outside the marriage.

As Medley has concluded, each category may best fit a given marital situation and provide the couple with a feeling of well-being and sense of fulfillment. Of course, for many marriages, some combination of these three categories may prove most rewarding.

"And a Time to . . .": Widowhood

great diversity with needs, wants, and desires that vary widely depending on income, age, education, health status, and geographic location.

Jain Malkin

To every thing there is a season, a time to every purpose under the heaven:
A time to be born and a time to die. . . .

—*Ecclesiastes 3:1–9*

"He's gone and the world is a strange, lonely place." The marriages of most elderly couples are not terminated by separation or divorce, but by the death of one spouse, usually the husband. Statistics reveal that three-fourths of married women will someday experience the loss of their spouse. On the average, women live about 8 years longer than men, and, because men tend to marry women somewhat younger than themselves, most women can expect to be widows for about 10 years. In isolated cases, however, matters may be altered somewhat by "target dates" for death (see Box 11–9).

As we noted in Chapter 6, there were more than 13 million widowed persons in the United States in 1986, forced into singlehood by the death of a spouse. Of

BOX 11-9 / ARE THERE TARGET DATES FOR DEATH?

Many older persons seem determined to live until a given target date. In fact, the available evidence indicates that older persons are more likely to die after a holiday or birthday rather than before. Cases have also been recorded of terminally ill patients who managed to stay alive until an important event took place—such as the birth of a grandchild or a wedding anniversary.

Apparently, the setting of such "target dates" is relatively common. Many persons in late middle age, for example, will state that they want to live until New Years Day of the year 2000, to see the dawning of the 21st century. In other cases, happily married couples state that they want to die when their mates do. So traumatic is the loss of the mate in such cases that the bereavement may actually precipitate the surviving spouse's own death. This has been called the "broken-heart syndrome."

A number of cases have also been recorded of persons in seemingly good health who actually died on the target dates for death that they set for themselves. Sigmund Freud, George Bernard Shaw, and Carl Sandberg have been cited as examples of persons whose specific target dates became "emotionally invested deadlines" for living.

One of the most interesting cases with respect to target dates for death is that of Samuel Clemens (Mark Twain). He was born on November 30, 1835, when Halley's comet made its spectacular appearance in the sky; and he died—as he had predicted—on April 21, 1910, when Halley's comet returned. Death was attributed to a heart attack, but the question still remains as to the underlying cause. Was it the excitement surrounding the fiery comet's return, or the conviction that the incontrovertible date for death had arrived?

(Fisher & Dlin, 1972; Parkes, Benjamin & Fitzgerald, 1969; Rawitch, 1973).

these widowed persons, women outnumbered men by more than 5 to 1—approximately 11.3 million to 2.1 million.

Adjustment to Widowhood.   The death of one's mate is a highly stressful event for most people. As Carolyn Balkwell (1981) has noted, it is "an event which leads the individual through the transition from married person to a widowed person. And this requires the formation of a new self-identity and the taking-on of new social roles" (p. 117). Unfortunately, there are no guidelines or support systems in our society that come into operation automatically. Thus, widowhood among older people in our society has been described as a "roleless role."

1. *The common problem of griefwork.*   C. Murray Parkes (1972) found that widows generally go through three stages in their mourning or grief work. And these stages apply to widowers as well.

   a. An initial stage of shock or numbness accompanied by a strong tendency to deny or screen out the reality of what has happened.

   b. A second stage involving depression, anxiety, and the so-called pangs of grief. The surviving spouse may also experience anger at their mate for leaving them all alone and guilt for not having done enough. "If I had only done this or that, maybe my beloved mate would not have died."

BOX 11–10 / DEALING WITH THE IMPENDING DEATH OF ONE'S MATE

The death of one's mate is ordinarily the most stressful event in a person's life. It can be particularly stressful when death follows a long illness with which the surviving spouse has to deal. The following information may be of help.

1. Treat your mate as a person, not a disease. Often terminally ill patients have little control over their treatment or lives in a hospital setting.

2. Communicate openly with your dying mate. Your mate has a right to know what is happening. "Protecting" your mate from the knowledge of his or her condition is not helpful.

3. Ask your mate what he or she needs. Often dying people are concerned about their affairs being in order, or perhaps wish to see a friend or family member.

4. Understand the stages that terminally ill patients commonly go through as they try to cope with their impending death as delineated by Elisabeth Kübler-Ross (1969).

Stage 1: Denial. "No, not me—it can't be true!"
Stage 2: Anger. "It is me. It wasn't a mistake. . . . Why me?"
Stage 3: Bargaining. "If I do this or that, maybe my life will be prolonged."
Stage 4: Depression: "What's the use?"
Stage 5: Acceptance: "I am ready now for the long journey."

5. Accept and work through your feelings of grief. It is part of the healing process in dealing with your mate's death.

c. The stage of recovery in which the person gives up hope of recovering what they have lost and begins to make the necessary readjustment to life.

The process of grief work may vary considerably in duration and intensity. In general, it usually lasts from a few weeks to several months. In some cases, however, it may last for several years; and for some persons, it is never completed (Caplan, 1981). Often, too, the widow or widower may experience "anniversary reactions"—poignant memories of the lost husband or wife—on special occasions, such as anniversaries, birthdays, and holidays. It is also common for the surviving spouse to feel a strong sense of the presence of the dead husband or wife from time to time.

Such grief work seems to be a "built-in" coping reaction that operates with a minimum of learning, and is characteristic of most people going through such personal tragedies. Box 11–10 summarizes certain measures one can take to deal with the impending death of one's spouse.

2. *Adjustment of widows.*   The widow must not only fend for herself in becoming whole again and establishing new relationships, but she is likely to be faced with several other difficult problems.

One major problem is usually a lack of financial resources. For many widows, the death of the husband means the loss of the main source of financial support and a lowering of living standards. Even if the wife works, the income of both partners may have been needed to maintain an adequate standard of living. This problem is likely to be particularly acute for couples in lower income categories.

Another problem is loneliness. The word "widow" comes from the Sanskrit for "empty," and many widows feel that this is an apt description of their changed lives. Friendships that had been maintained by the couple seem to drift away. Because older women greatly outnumber men in their age group, attempts to cope with loneliness may be largely confined to friendships with other women. But as Carolyn Balkwell (1981) found, many older widows do not find interactions in a "society of widows" adequate protection from loneliness. This type of friendship does not meet the woman's need for a deep compassionate relationship, it does not kill the feeling that she is no longer a love object and no longer has anyone to love, and it does not reduce her "homesickness" for her past married life. Balkwell found that intense feelings of loneliness characterized over half of the widowed population.

3. *Adjustment of widowers.*   Both sexes face essentially the same problems of adjusting to a new social role, to becoming single again, and to loneliness and isolation. However, widowers are more prone to a deterioration in physical health and to dying; and they have a relatively high suicide rate. Parkes, Benjamin, and Fitzgerald (1969) reported that the death rate during the six months following loss of a spouse was 40 percent higher for widowers than might otherwise have been expected. The incidence of deaths from heart disorders was so high that these researchers referred to this finding as the "broken heart syndrome." More recent research findings support this finding of greater physical stress for widowers (Clayton, 1979; Clark, Siviski, and Weiner, 1986; Schwartz-Borden, 1986).

In some ways, however, widowhood seems to be less stressful for men. Men who are still working have a way to provide some measure of identity and financial support. Many men remarry. However, many widowers withdraw from social contacts into a self-imposed isolation. The common belief that widowhood is easier for men seems to depend on the person involved.

Widowhood and Remarriage.   Widowed singles are much less likely to remarry than divorced singles. Even in the 45–54 age range, the divorced were almost twice as likely to remarry as the widowed (Glick, 1980, 1985). In part, this is the result of age and the decreased pool of eligible males. But, in part, it is also the result of the length of bereavement. Some people manage to complete the period of bereavement in a few weeks or months, but for many others it is a matter of years. For some, it is never completed (Caplan, 1981).

For persons widowed before age 55, the remarriage rate for men is about 70 percent and for women about 45 percent. After age 55, however, the remarriage rate decreases rapidly—especially for women. After age 65, the chances of a widow remarrying are slim. In general, older men tend to marry women younger than themselves—usually 7 to 10 years younger. In addition, women's longer life span is another reason why older widows are unlikely to remarry.

Loneliness is a common problem for older widowed persons, and many remarry to meet their need for intimate companionship and to avoid loneliness. How happy are such marriages? Although data are hard to come by, McKain

(1969) studied 100 couples who married after the bride was sixty. The factors that seemed to correlate with a happy marriage were:

1. The bride and groom were well-acquainted before marriage and frequently had known each other for a long time.
2. They had the approval of friends and of their children.
3. They lived in a home or apartment that had not belonged to either partner prior to the marriage.
4. They had an income adequate to live without economic hardship.
5. Both partners were well adjusted to retirement.

McKain found that about three-fourths of the marriages were judged as happy or successful in terms of the couple showing respect and affection for each other, finding enjoyment in each other's company, and having no serious complaints about their marital relationship. Later research studies support these early findings (Teachman & Heckert, 1985).

In our brief discussion of "passages," one theme that stands out is the inevitable change in marital and family relationships over time. These changes occur on physiological, psychological, interpersonal, and social levels. Charlotte Buhler (1968) found that when older persons were asked to summarize their lives, their statements usually fell into one of three categories: "All in all it was a good life," "There were so many disappointments," and "It all came to nothing" (p. 185). Of course, the quality of our lives is determined by many factors. But our marital and intimate relationships are usually of crucial importance. And to successfully navigate the passages of the marital or family life cycle is not an easy task.

SUMMARY—Chapter 11

1. Marital conflicts result from incompatible needs, goals, and expectations. They may be rational or irrational, overt or covert, acute or chronic, personal or impersonal. Marital stress, a broader term, also includes conflict resulting from serious illness, unemployment, and career pressures.
2. The severity of marital conflicts depends on their number, importance, and duration; the characteristics of the partners; and the external resources and support available to them.
3. Conflict can be constructive, helping the couple to increase their mutual understanding and to work out their problems, or it can be destructive.
4. The most important sources of conflict in marriage are: unmet needs and expectations; money; roles and responsibilities; power struggles; sexual difficulties; jealousy and possessiveness; anger and violence; and extramarital affairs. Of these, money—who earns it, who spends it and on what, and who manages it—is the most common source of conflict.
5. Perhaps the most common sexual problem is unequal levels of desire, followed closely by differences about methods and who should take the initiative. Jealousy is more closely related to possessiveness, to which men who view their wives as their "property" are particularly prone. Whatever draws the partner away—work, another person, a hobby, even children—can arouse jealousy.

6. Anger, a reaction to interference with our needs, is usually inevitable in marriage. In some cases, anger may lead to physical abuse and even rape of wives by their husbands.

7. Extramarital affairs occur in some 40–60 percent of marriages and may or may not reflect a serious problem. Despite the value of open communication, telling one's partner about it may destroy the marriage. The threat of AIDS is expected to reduce the incidence of extramarital affairs.

8. Negotiation is a basic approach to resolving marital as well as other problems. It involves: (a) pinpointing or defining the problem, (b) exploring options or alternatives, (c) deciding on a given alternative and specifying the behavior to be changed, and (d) evaluating the change. Successful negotiation may require acceptance of an unpleasant but unavoidable fact of life, or it may acknowledging the partner's right to disagree on something.

9. The chief barriers to the resolution of conflicts are misidentifying the problem, manipulation, and faulty communication.

10. Marital counseling, also called marital therapy, focuses on clarifying and resolving conflicts and improving the couple's marital relationship. Many couples are reluctant to seek therapy. One partner may want out of the marriage, or the couple may feel that their problems are a private matter.

11. The midlife crisis, which is not a universal experience, is a period of re-evaluation of one's marriage, career, and identity. Whether it creates havoc or renewal appears to depend on the individual, the quality of the marriage, and available resources. It can be rewarding or very painful.

12. Retirement can affect marriage in a number of ways. Some wives resent having their husbands at home all the time, but others welcome the companionship. Some couples find that they have little in common anymore and find it difficult to communicate. In some marriages, a role reversal occurs in which the husband becomes more dependent and the wife becomes more achievement oriented.

13. The death of a spouse, which ends long term marriage, is one of the most stressful events in a person's life. The death rate of older men, for example, rises 40 percent within the first six months of widowhood, and the widowed of both sexes suffer from loneliness and isolation.

14. About half of the people who are widowed in midlife remarry, but only a small percentage of those over age sixty-five do. In later life, widowed persons often remarry to avoid loneliness. Nevertheless, such marriages are often considered to be happy ones.

TERMINATING
RELATIONSHIPS
AND
STARTING
OVER

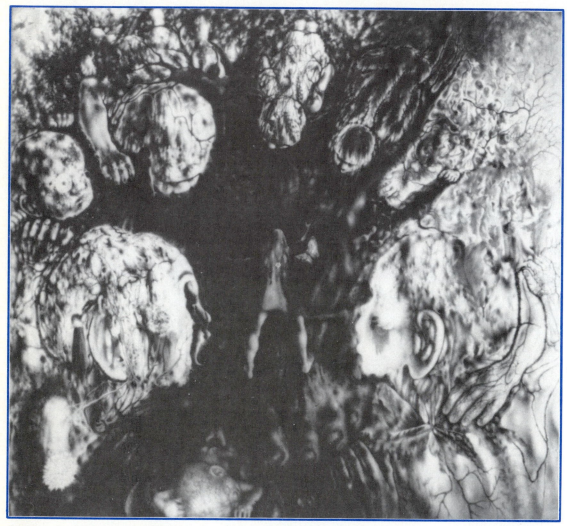

Tchelitchew, Pavel: Hide and Seek (1940–42) *Collection, The Museum of Modern Art, New York.*

SEPARATION, DIVORCE, AND SINGLE-PARENT FAMILIES

Love the quest
Marriage the conquest,
Divorce the inquest.

—Helen Rowland (1980, p. 117)

Divorce is an old problem. The ancient Hebrews, Greeks, and Romans made provisions for divorce and speculated on its causes and effects. But nothing in world history compares to the dramatic increase in divorce that has occurred in the United States in this century. In 1920, only one in seven marriages ended in divorce. In 1960, the ratio had increased to one in four, and, by 1980, it was one in two, when some 2.4 million marriages were performed and about 1.2 million divorces were obtained. With slight variations, the latter rate has continued through 1985, when 1,187,000 divorces were obtained (National Center for Health Statistics, 1986). An additional 300,000 or more marriages are terminated each year as a result of annulment, legal separation, or desertion. Indeed, the current American rate of marital dissolution, which is the highest the world has ever known, is predicted to continue and possibly rise. However, unless an effective method of prevention or treatment for AIDS is found, the divorce rate may be slowed slightly. Whatever the incidence in the future, however, divorce has had, and is having, a tremendous impact on our values and way of life.

In this chapter, we shall begin with a brief description of the legalities of divorce in America including "no-fault" divorce and divorce mediation. Included in this first section will be a brief look at patterns of divorce in our society. Then, we shall consider the major causes and effects of divorce. Finally, we shall deal with the increasing problem of single-parent families. Throughout, we shall emphasize the consequences of divorce for those involved, including children.

DIVORCE, AMERICAN STYLE

I used to feel that when you said "I do," you kept the marriage together come hell or high water. I switched when my readers described in detail what hell was like and how frightening high water can be. When a marriage goes sour and there's no love, respect, or loyalty left, I believe it's a mockery to try to hold it together with chicken wire and glue.

—Ann Landers

We can hardly argue with Ann Landers' sentiments. On the other hand, we must keep in mind that divorce is no painless cure-all for matrimonial ills. Although it may be more painful for some people than for others, it is considered one of the most traumatic experiences most people will ever have to face. Even though the patients recover, they will never be quite the same.

In the United States, the trauma of divorce has often been compounded by the workings of the legal system and the procedures required to dissolve a marriage.

BOX 12-1 / SOME SELECTED TERMS CONCERNING DIVORCE

Legal Divorce	Constitutes a public declaration that the marriage has ended.
Separation	May be a trial period to determine whether divorce is desirable or a period of waiting for the divorce decree.
Mediation	Trying to work out an agreement concerning the terms of divorce —for example, division of resources—without going to court with attorneys in adversarial proceedings.
Divorce Therapists	Marital therapists who work extensively with divorcing couples.
Lawyers	Lawyers referred to as **advocates** try to remove obstacles to negotiation. Others, referred to as **counselors**, focus on their client's emotional state in an effort to produce a lasting settlement. Still other lawyers represent their client in an adversarial role.
Annulment	Dissolution by the court of an invalid marriage. A valid marriage cannot be annulled.
Custody	Custody of children usually goes to the mother but is sometimes contested by the father, who wants custody himself. Although joint custody can lead to myriad problems, it has become increasingly popular. Legislated joint custody involves the passing of laws that require consideration of joint custody first in divorce cases.
Mediators	Trained persons—including lawyers—who try to help the divorcing parties negotiate a settlement of the major issues.
Reconciliation	The use of conflict-resolution techniques in an attempt to save a valued marital relationship. Reconciliation cannot happen unless and until one party makes the first move.

Furthermore, some types, or patterns, of divorce are more traumatizing than others. In this section, we shall examine the evolution of the American legal approach to divorce and then we shall look at three common patterns found in divorcing couples (for some divorce terms see Box 12–1).

Divorce Law: The Legalities

Divorce as it was practiced among the ancient Greeks, Romans, and Hebrews was a private affair usually worked out between spouses and their relatives. With the advent of Christianity, marriage was sanctioned by the church and could only be dissolved by death—although with time the ecclesiastical courts did on occasion grant annulments that enabled the spouses to live separately (but not to remarry). With the Christian Reformation, the power to grant annulments and divorces was transferred from the Church to the State. But divorce was still not easily obtained: A divorce could only be granted when one spouse had seriously wronged the other, as in adultery, desertion, or extreme cruelty. This approach gave rise to the adversary process of divorce.

STATE OF NEW YORK.

No. 17.

IN SENATE,

January 3, 1861.

Introduced on notice by Mr. RAMSEY---read twice and referred to the committee on the judiciary---reported from said committee for the consideration of the Senate, and committed to the committee of the whole.

AN ACT

In regard to divorces dissolving the marriage contract.

The People of the State of New-York, represented in Senate and Assembly, do enact as follows:

1   SECTION 1. In addition to the cases in which a divorce, dissolving the
2   the marriage contract, may now be decreed by the supreme court, such a
3   divorce may be decreed by said court in either of the cases following:
4   1. Where either party to the marriage shall, for the period of three
5   years next preceding the application for such divorce, have willfully
6   deserted the other party to the marriage, and neglected to perform to such
7   party the duties imposed by their relation.
8   2. Where there is, and shall have been, for the period of one year
9   next preceding the application for such divorce, continuous and repeated
10   instances of cruel and inhuman treatment by either party, so as greatly to
11   impair the health or endanger the life of the other party, thereby render-
12   ing it unsafe to live with the party guilty of such cruelty or inhumanity.

1   § 2. The foregoing sections shall not apply to any person who shall not
2   have been an actual resident of this state for the period of five years next
3   preceding such application for such divorce.

[Senate, No. 17.]   1   (I. 11, G. 0. 15.)

Smithsonian Institution Archive Center/Business Americana Collection

Traditional Divorce: The Adversary Process.   The traditional approach to divorce in the United States required that one partner publicly prove the other guilty of adultery, cruelty, or some other offense recognized as a legal grounds for divorce. This approach, called the "fault doctrine," had a number of interesting consequences:

1. It made the divorce process an adversary procedure that pitted one spouse against the other in legal combat—the victim versus the offender.
2. It influenced the division of property and awarding of alimony—property and support were given to the innocent victim as a reward and were extracted from the offender as punishment.
3. It often led to hypocrisy and collusion. For example, because adultery was the only grounds for divorce in New York State until 1966, many couples used trumped up adultery charges to obtain a divorce.

4. It tended not only to make each spouse suspicious and distrustful of the other but also to breed anger, resentment, and even hatred.

In his book *My Life in Court*, Louis Nizer (1972) pointed out that, although many legal cases involve extreme emotion, "none of them, even in their most aggravated form, can equal the sheer unadulterated venom of the matrimonial contest" (p. 153).

Under the traditional system, the legal grounds for divorce varied from one state to another, although certain offenses—adultery, willful desertion, and cruelty—were considered legal grounds in most states. Conforming to these legal requirements often involved bringing false charges against our spouse. In addition, these divorces were often quite expensive. In short, the traditional adversary system was considered ethically, emotionally, and financially undesirable.

No-Fault Divorce. In 1970, the State of California passed a revolutionary piece of legislation, the Family Law Act, which was the first in the United States to abolish the concept of fault in divorce proceedings. It replaced the fault-linked grounds with a neutral substitute: "irreconcilable differences leading to the irremediable breakdown of the marriage."

With a speed few experts foresaw, "no-fault" became the American way of divorce. In fact, by 1977, it had been adopted by all but three states and, by 1986, all but one—South Dakota. However, some states adopting no-fault have also retained traditional fault grounds, such as cruelty and desertion.

Because the formerly tough divorce laws had presumably acted as constraints on marital dissolution, it was feared that no-fault divorce—in making divorce easier and less unpleasant—would lead to a flood of divorces. In fact, the adoption of no-fault laws did coincide with a dramatic increase in the U.S. divorce rate in the 1970s. A number of studies have shown, however, that no-fault divorce had little if anything to do with the increase in divorce in most states (Wright & Stetson, 1978; Maher, 1979; Dixon & Weitzman, 1980); that is, the increase in divorce would have occurred with or without no-fault.

Because there are no "offender and no victim" to punish, the dissolution of marriage without blame has raised some problems with respect to property and income settlements (Weitzman, 1985; McGrath, 1986). But there is little doubt that no-fault divorce has reduced the hypocrisy and collusion, as well as the hatred and acrimony, elicited by the traditional adversary system.

Divorce Mediation. Although no-fault divorce represented a major advance over the adversary system, its appearance did not alter the adversarial way in which divorces were processed; that is, each spouse usually hired a lawyer to represent him or her in obtaining the best possible property settlement and so on. In this sense, then, the bitterness and anger generated by the adversary system continued. However, things began to change in the mid-1970s with the advent of **divorce mediation.**

Instead of making the husband and wife legal adversaries, divorce mediation uses principles of cooperation and conflict resolution (Coogler et al., 1979; Von Jares, 1986). The mediator cannot impose a settlement but rather listens impartially to both parties and tries to help them work out an equitable separation agreement. The major responsibility for working out the agreement rests with the spouses, not the mediator. The agreement deals with the division of property, alimony, child support, child custody, visitation privileges, and the myriad other details that must be covered in the final divorce settlement. The mediation agreement is worked out in everyday language and is signed by the parties involved. It is then presented to the court for approval. Box 12–2 shows a sample separation agreement.

The American Arbitration Association, court systems in various states, and private groups—for example, the American Association for Marriage and Family Therapy (AAMFT)—have established mediation services. However, such services are still not available throughout the country. In addition, many couples fail to use these services, either because they are not aware of them or because they prefer to hire lawyers to sort out their conflicting interests. Of course, by becoming legal adversaries, they run the risk of escalating anger and distrust as well as the financial costs of the divorce. Fortunately, less than 10 percent of divorce cases end up as economic battles in court. Most divorcing couples are able to work out agreements without getting involved in legal and financial hassles.

Trends in Family Law.   Although no-fault divorce is probably the most conspicuous new trend in family law, other recent changes regarding alimony and child custody are also worthy of note. For example, most courts now view married couples as economic and social equals and try to see that each partner gets his or her fair share of property acquired during the marriage. Alimony has for the most part been de-emphasized and desexed. Increasingly the ex-partners are sharing both child custody and support, which helps reduce parental conflict after the divorce.

Another notable trend has been the simplification of filing procedures, thereby facilitating the "do-it-yourself" divorce. California and a number of other states also have a process called "summary dissolution," which is a simple procedure for couples who have been married less than 2 years, have no children from the marriage, and own no real estate. Although there is a waiting period—usually 6 months—before the divorce becomes final, the whole thing can be handled by mail.

There are three major problems with current divorce law. For couples with property, the expenses of preparing a separation agreement are usually high. Some procedure is needed for reducing them. Second, current divorce laws are designed to deal with property rather than with income (Blair, 1986). As a result, women with children who have been homemakers or earn relatively low incomes compared to their husbands are often at a disadvantage. Finally, although the husband and wife may each retain an attorney to represent their interests, their children have no legal representation. Unfortunately, no-fault divorce has not been particularly successful in dealing with child-custody problems.

Patterns of Divorce

- Gabriella and Ramon have been unhappy in their marriage for a long time. Gabriella likes to go camping, go to shows, take in football and basketball games. Ramon is a homebody and would rather read or work on his coin collection. They constantly talk of getting a divorce, but they fight over who should handle the legal aspects and who will have custody of their son, Julio.

BOX 12–2 / A SAMPLE SEPARATION AGREEMENT

The following agreement is a fairly simple one. It shows the kinds of issues that must be considered, but it shouldn't be used as a model for writing your own agreement. Each case is unique and each agreement must be constructed to deal with a different set of problems.

This agreement is between a man and a woman who have been married nearly 11 years and who have an 8-year-old son.

They've agreed that the wife will have custody of the son and that the husband will contribute $6,000 a year for the son's support. The husband will also pay for the son's college education and will record the son as a dependent for tax purposes. The wife will receive $6,000 a year for 3 years for maintenance while she goes back to college. They've agreed to sell their house and split the proceeds equally.

We, Ann Jones and Paul Jones, made this agreement on March 30, 1981.

We were married on June 1, 1970, and our only child, Robert, was born September 27, 1972. Because our marriage is seriously damaged beyond repair, we have separated and intend to live apart for the rest of our lives. We want to divide our property and make whatever legal and financial arrangements are necessary under the circumstances. The purpose of this document is to record the terms we have agreed on:

1. *Independence.* Except as noted below, each of us will live completely independent of the other, as if we were unmarried. We will not interfere with each other in any way.

2. *Custody of our child.* Ann will have custody of our child as long as he is a minor, and he will live with her.

3. *The child's visits.* The child will visit Paul at these times: every other weekend, from 6 P.M. Friday to 6 P.M. Sunday; during the Christmas and Easter school holidays, from 6 P.M. the last day of school before the holiday to 6 P.M. the day before school starts again; and at least 30 days during the summer recess. Paul will pick the child up at home at the beginning of the visiting period and take him home at the end of the period. If we agree to do so, this schedule may be changed for any particular visit.

During the child's visits, Paul will pay for the child's food, transportation, housing, and any other expenses connected with the visit. If Paul and Ann ever live permanently or temporarily at places more than 50 miles apart, the schedule for the child's visits with his father will be rearranged so it is equivalent to the present schedule.

4. *Payments for child support.* As basic child support, Paul will pay Ann $6,000 a year in $500 installments payable on the first day of each month. The last installment will be due on the first month after the date of this agreement. These payments will terminate under any of these conditions: if either parent or the child dies; if the child marries; if the child becomes fully self-supporting; if the child reaches his 21st birthday; if the child stops living permanently with his mother (excluding periods away at school or college); or if the father assumes custody by written agreement or by court order.

5. *Payments for college.* If the child goes to college and if he remains a student in good standing, Paul will pay for room and board, textbooks, tuition, laboratory fees, and any other charges billed by the college. These college payments will be in addition to the support payments described in section 4.

(continued)

BOX 12-2 (continued)

Paul's obligation to make these payments will terminate under any of these conditions: if either parent dies; if the child receives his bachelor's degree; or if the child reaches his 23rd birthday.

6. *Payments for maintenance.* Paul will pay Ann $6,000 a year in $500 installments payable on the first day of each month. The first installment will be due the first month after the date of this agreement. These payments will terminate under any of these conditions: after the thirty-sixth monthly payment; if either Paul or Ann dies; if Ann remarries; or if Ann chooses to live with another male not related by blood or marriage.

7. *Personal property.* We have divided all the property acquired during our marriage. The list appended to this agreement shows the items each of us will own separately from now on. We are satisfied with this division, and neither will later ask the other for any of the property divided according to this agreement.

8. *Real estate.* We jointly own the house and land at 100 Ridge Road, Saltmine, Ohio. We will try to sell this property as soon as possible. After the sale, we will pay off the mortgage and divide the net proceeds equally. In the interim, Paul will pay 70 percent of the carrying costs (mortgage payments, property taxes, and homeowners insurance premiums) and Ann will pay 30 percent.

9. *Taxes.* The maintenance payments described in section 6 will be considered part of Ann's taxable income. If those payments are affected by a subsequent change in the tax laws, the payments will be adjusted so Ann will end up with an after-tax maintenance income equal to the amount resulting from the present arrangement.

As in the past, we will file a joint income-tax return this year. If there are any refunds, we will share them equally. If there are any taxes, assessments, or penalties due, each of us will pay half. Next year, the child will be listed as a dependent on Paul's tax returns.

10. *Debts.* A list of debts is appended to this agreement, indicating which debts will be paid by Paul and which by Ann. Our understanding is that there are no other debts for which we are jointly liable, and we agree not to incur any such debts in the future.

11. *Cooperation in handling documents.* We will promptly sign and deliver any papers necessary to carry out the terms of this agreement.

12. *Entire agreement.* We have made no agreements about separation other than those detailed in this document. If we choose to make any changes later on, the changes must be in writing and signed and dated by both of us.

13. *Governing laws.* We made this agreement in Ohio, and it is covered by the laws of that state.

14. *Partial invalidity.* If we find that part of this agreement isn't valid for some reason, the rest of the agreement will remain in effect.

15. *Subsequent divorce.* If we are divorced later, we will ask the court to append this agreement to the divorce decree.

16. *Waiver of estate claims.* Except with respect to the terms already stated in this agreement, each of us agrees not to make any claims against the other's estate. We also waive all such rights that exist in the future.

17. *Release from other obligations.* Except as noted in this agreement, and except

(continued)

> ## BOX 12–2 *(continued)*
>
> for any obligations in connection with a subsequent divorce decree, each of us releases the other from all past, present, and future obligations.
>
> 18. *Change of status or address.* If one of us remarries, he or she will notify the other of the date and the name of the new spouse. Also, each will notify the other of any change of address.
>
> 19. *Binding effect.* This agreement will be binding on our heirs, representatives, and assignees.
>
> Signed: _____
> Ann Jones
> 100 Ridge Road
> Saltmine, Ohio
>
> Signed: _____
> Paul Jones
> 4 Valley Road
> Saltmine, Ohio
>
> Notarized: On _____, 1981, Ann and Paul Jones signed this document in my presence.
> Signed: _____, Notary Public

- Joe was shocked to come home from work one day to find Dorothea with her bags packed, heading out the door. She nervously told him that she had been seeing another man and had decided to get a divorce—then she climbed into her car and drove off.
- It was on their tenth anniversary that Shirley and Randolph decided to take a closer look at their marriage. They didn't like what they saw. They rarely spoke; they both had jobs that kept them busy; and they had separate, active social lives. The idea of trying to revive the marriage appealed to neither of them. "Shall we call it quits?" Shirley asked.

As these three vignettes show, the decision to seek a divorce does not follow a single pattern. In fact, investigators have identified several distinct **patterns of divorce** decision making (Kressel et al., 1980; Vaughn, 1986; Lloyd & Zick, 1986). Here, we shall focus on three categories of divorcing couples worked out by Kressel and others (1980). These categories are based on the partners feelings about ending their relationship and on the way they go about it. Each of these patterns has consequences for the constructive or destructive nature of the termination (see Table 12–1 for a Divorce Proneness Questionaire).

The Enmeshed Pattern. The **enmeshed pattern** is characterized by ambivalence on the part of both partners. Kressel and others (1980) described a couple exemplifying this pattern:

> The parties debated the pros and cons of divorce, often bitterly; agreed to divorce and then changed their minds; and once a "final" decision was made proved unable to implement it. They maintained a common residence after the decision and they may have continued sleeping in the same bed and having sexual relations. (p. 107)

Couples in this pattern tend to squabble over the smallest details and appear to use the negotiating process for continuing rather than ending the relationship. After the divorce is finally obtained, the parties are bitter toward each other, blame the other for the divorce, and are dissatisfied with the terms of the settlement.

Table 12–1.   ASSESSING DIVORCE PRONENESS

ASK THE QUESTION FOR EACH INDICATOR AND CIRCLE THE ANSWER GIVEN:

Indicators of marital instability	Not divorce prone	Divorce prone
Sometimes married people think they would enjoy living apart from their spouse. How often do you feel this way? Would you say very often, often, occasionally, or never?	Occasionally or never	Very often or often
Even people who get along quite well with their spouse sometimes wonder whether their marriage is working out. Have you thought your marriage might be in trouble within the last 3 years?	No	Yes
As far as you know, has your spouse ever thought your marriage was in trouble?	No	Yes
Have you talked with family members, friends, clergy, counselors, or social workers about problems in your marriage within the last 3 years?	No	Yes
As far as you know, has your (husband/wife) talked with relatives, friends, or a counselor about problems either of you were having with your marriage?	No	Yes
Has the thought of getting a divorce or separation crossed your mind in the last 3 years?	No	Yes
As far as you know, has the thought of divorce or separation crossed your (husband's/wife's) mind in the last 3 years?	No	Yes
Have you or your spouse seriously suggested the idea of divorce in the last 3 years?	No	Yes
Have you talked about dividing up the property?	No	Yes
Have you talked about consulting an attorney?	No	Yes
Have you or your spouse consulted an attorney about a divorce or separation?	No	Yes
Because of problems people are having with their marriage, they sometimes leave home either for a short time or as a trial separation. Has this happened in your marriage within the last 3 years?	No	Yes
Have you talked with your spouse about filing for divorce or separation?	No	Yes
Have you or your (husband/wife) filed for a divorce or separation petition?	No	Yes

COUNT THE NUMBER OF DIVORCE PRONE ANSWERS (include "don't know" as a "yes") AND RECORD HERE: _____
CIRCLE THE CHANCES OF DIVORCE IN THE NEXT 3 YEARS AS FOLLOWS:

Proneness to divorce score	Chance of divorce
0–2	22
3–4	26
5–6	31
7–9	38
10+	43

Attractions and barriers to divorce

ASK THE QUESTIONS BELOW AND ADD OR SUBTRACT POINTS FROM THE CHANCE OF DIVORCE SCORE ACCORDING TO THE ANSWERS.

I'm going to mention some of the things couples sometimes do together. For each one, I would like you to tell me how often you and your spouse do this together.

Number of answer

How often do you eat your main meal together—almost always, usually, occasionally, or never?

1 never   2 occasionally   3 usually   4 almost always   _____

Table 12–1.   (*continued*)

How often do you visit friends together?

    1 never   2 occasionally   3 usually   4 almost always   _____

Work together on projects around the house?

    1 never   2 occasionally   3 usually   4 almost always   _____

When you go out—say, to play cards, bowling, or a movie—how often do you do this together?

    1 never   2 occasionally   3 usually   4 almost always   _____

ADD THE NUMBERS FOR FREQUENCY OF DOING THINGS TOGETHER. IF THE TOTAL IS BETWEEN 13 AND 16, SUBTRACT 12 FROM DIVORCE CHANCE SCORE AND IF TOTAL IS BETWEEN 9 AND 12, SUBTRACT 10.

               NEW DIVORCE CHANCE SCORE   _____

If you had to do it all over again, would you (a) marry the same person, (b) marry someone else, or (c) not marry at all?

IF ANSWER IS NOT MARRY AT ALL (c), ADD 11 TO THE LAST DIVORCE CHANCE SCORE. IF (a) OR (b), PROCEED TO THE NEXT ITEM.

               NEW DIVORCE CHANCE SCORE   _____

Do you own or rent your home?

IF HOME IS OWNED, SUBTRACT 6 FROM LAST DIVORCE CHANCE SCORE.

               NEW DIVORCE CHANCE SCORE   _____

In general, how much would you say your religious beliefs influence your daily life— very much, quite a bit, some, a little, or none?

IF SOME, QUITE A BIT, OR VERY MUCH, SUBTRACT 4 FROM LAST DIVORCE CHANCE SCORE.

               NEW DIVORCE CHANCE SCORE   _____

How many years have you been married to your spouse?

IF COUPLE HAS BEEN MARRIED LESS THAN FIVE YEARS, ADD 3 TO LAST DIVORCE CHANCE SCORE.

               FINAL DIVORCE CHANCE SCORE   _____

Example: A person who scores 1 on the divorce proneness scale would start with a 22% chance of getting a divorce within 3 years. But if a person does a lot of things with their spouse (for example, scores 14 on frequency of doing things together), the probability is lowered by 12 points to 10%. If the couple is buying their home, subtract another 6 points, lowering their divorce proneness to 4%. Finally, if religion has at least some importance in their lives, the score would be reduced to 0. (Edwards, Johnson, and Booth, 1987)

Laurel Richardson (1979) has referred to this type of termination as the "drag-out" pattern, which draws out over a period of months or years: "In such endings, the ambivalence of one partner and the desire of the other seem to mesh in such a way as to keep both of them hooked" (p. 408). But eventually the relationship does end.

The Nonmutual Pattern.   Unfortunately, the decision to end a marriage is usually **nonmutual**—that is, one partner wants out, but the other wants to

Joel Gordon

continue the marriage. This pattern is the most common observed by Kressel and his associates, and it accounted for about 60 percent of the divorcing couples.

The eagerness of one partner to end the marriage and the often desperate measures taken by the other partner to maintain it make for a difficult divorce; that is, the divorce is characterized by unnecessary emotional and legal complications and by severe hurt or trauma for the person who is still emotionally involved and wants to continue the relationship.

In many cases, such as the example of Joe and Dorothea, the relationship ends without warning, leaving the unsuspecting partner in a state of shock. Paschal Baute (1980) refers to this as the "Pearl Harbor–type attack," in which someone you assumed loves you suddenly informs you that he or she is no longer in love with you and may even have found someone new. As we might expect, the consequences can be devastating and long-lasting.

The Disengaged Pattern.   Kressel and his associates describe the **disengaged pattern** as follows:

> This pattern is distinguished by the notably low level of ambivalence about ending the marriage that characterized the entire period of divorce decision making. Of all

BOX 12–3 / SUMMARY OF BACKGROUND FACTORS RELATED TO DIVORCES

Family Background	Higher divorce rate among persons raised in unhappy homes and/or by divorced parents.
Educational Level	The lower the educational level, the higher the divorce rate; an exception is, women with graduate degrees.
Occupational Status	Higher divorce rate for those in low-income and low-status occupations. Different divorce rates among professionals depending on area—but, in general, lower.
Racial Background	Marriages among blacks more divorce prone than marriages among whites.
Religion	Higher divorce rates among non–church goers and protestants than among Catholics, Jews, and Mormons.
Length of Courtship	Divorce rates higher for those with brief courtships.
Age at Time of Marriage	Divorce rates higher for those marrying in their teens, but not for older people.
People Who Have Been Divorced Before	Higher divorce rates among people who remarry after divorce—especially if remarriage involves stepchildren.
Factors Not Related to Divorce Rate	Interracial, mixed religion, sexual experience prior to marriage, cohabitation prior to marriage, age differences between spouses.

(Kitson, Barbri, & Roach, 1985)

our couples, these were the ones in which the flame of intimacy had come to burn the least brightly—and so, too, the heat of conflict. . . . The overall impression was of two people who were no longer interested enough in each other to work any further in saving their marriage. (p. 112)

Typically, the relationship terminates slowly, through a gradual process of deterioration and decreasing involvement that Richardson (1979) has referred to as the "peter-out" pattern. The partners just drift apart until there is nothing left to sustain the relationship. As might be expected, Kressel and others found that couples exhibiting the disengaged pattern showed the most successful post-divorce adjustment of the three groups.

Although these three patterns are perhaps the most common, there are others as well, and some divorces may represent a blending of patterns. For example, a couple may agree to divorce in a decision that seems to follow the disengaged pattern, yet one partner may have a greater emotional investment in the marriage than he or she is willing to admit and may suffer a great deal as a result.

Studying patterns of divorce allows researchers to evaluate constructive and destructive decision-making processes and post-divorce outcomes. The overall objective is to help develop guidelines for "uncoupling" marriage partners with minimal damage to the partners and to their children. (For a summary of other factors related to divorce see Box 12–3.)

BOX 12–4 / REASONS GIVEN FOR FAILURE OF FIRST MARRIAGE

When 500 remarried people were asked why their first marriages failed, the following reasons were cited (Albrecht, 1979, p. 862).

	Listed First (N)	(Order)	Total Number of Times Listed	(Order)
Infidelity	168	(1)	255	(1)
No longer loved each other	103	(2)	188	(2)
Emotional problems	53	(3)	185	(3)
Financial problems	30	(4)	135	(4)
Physical abuse	29	(5)	72	(8)
Alcohol	25	(6)	47	(9)
Sexual problems	22	(7)	115	(5)
Problems with in-laws	16	(8)	81	(6)
Neglect of children	11	(9)	74	(7)
Communication problems	10	(10)	18	(11)
Married too young	9	(11)	14	(12)
Job conflicts	7	(12)	20	(10)
Other	7		19	

Typically, there is a constellation of causes, rather than a single problem, that precipitates divorce (Cleek & Pearson, 1985). In general, middle-class couples tended to be more concerned with emotional satisfactions and lower-class couples with financial problems. However, economic reverses may also lead to the dissolution of middle-class marriages (South, 1985). Also, the causes listed by wives tended to differ somewhat from those listed by husbands. In addition to a "his" and "her" marriage, there would also appear to be a "his" and "her" divorce.

THE CAUSES OF DIVORCE

The question of why a couple decide to get a divorce at a given time is a difficult and often impossible one to answer. Each marriage has its conflicts that must be successfully resolved if the marriage is to survive. If they cannot be, the long period of disagreement, indecision, and growing bitterness that occurs before the couple finally decide to separate may be more traumatic than the actual break itself (Vaughan, 1986). An examination of any divorce story will reveal that there are always two versions (his and hers) and that the breakup had no single cause—that many things came together to dissolve the marriage. These causes involve not only the personal characteristics of the partners and the nature of the relationship but also numerous aspects of the society and the specific life situation in which the partners live (see Box 12–4).

Marriage takes place in a social context. In the United States, a number of factors have contributed to the high and still-rising divorce rate. These include societal attitudes, the changing nature of marriage and the family, and economic considerations. As might be expected, the reasons for divorce today differ from the reasons offered a generation ago (Kitson & Sussman, 1982; Poor, 1986; Booth et al., 1986).

Social Acceptance of Divorce.   Less than 50 years ago, divorce was considered immoral, disgraceful, and (for the wealthy) scandalous. The stigma of divorce could even ruin political careers. Yet, today divorce has become a socially acceptable solution to an unhappy marital situation. Divorced men and women are no longer stigmatized in their personal lives or their careers. In fact, most communities now have divorce-support groups for singles and single parents. Although divorce is not contagious, its ready availability at low social cost may make it an easy out when things don't go well in a marriage.

Changing Demands on Marriage and the Family.   Today, the demands placed on marriage and the family are different in many ways from those placed on it in the past. Traditionally, marriage in American society was relatively pragmatic, and the roles of husband and wife were clearly delineated. In the new egalitarian marriage, however, roles and responsibilities have to be worked out. In addition, tremendous demands are placed on the marital relationship for love, companionship, intimacy, and social support. Marriage is expected to serve as a haven in a heartless world, as a refuge from loneliness, and as a supplier of all emotional needs. Unfortunately, the more people expect from marriage—especially in terms of unrealistic expectations—the more likely they are to be disappointed.

Dual-Worker Marriages.   The educational orientation of young women today tends to be toward self-development and acquiring job skills rather than toward the traditional role of wife and homemaker. Often the demands of a career tend to pull partners in different directions and force them to pursue different, and sometimes incompatible, goals. As we noted in Chapter 9, a common complaint in dual-career marriages is lack of interaction time together—especially pleasant interaction time. Career demands may leave one or both partners so preoccupied and fatigued that their time alone rarely involves intimate sharing and sex. Rather, they tend to live under the same roof as separate but caring individuals. Over time, they are likely to grow apart unless they are aware of the problem and make the necessary time for maintaining and enriching their marriage.

Economic Considerations.   In traditional marriage, the woman was usually financially dependent on her husband as the breadwinner of the family. Although she might have dreamed about divorce or separation, she could ill afford it.

With the explosive increase in dual-worker marriages, well over half of married women are employed outside the home. Most do not make as much money as their husbands, but the gap is gradually being closed. In any event, they now have the economic means to dissolve the marriage if it is an unhappy one.

Of course, some couples who have geared their life style to the two-paycheck income may find divorce financially impractical. In general, however, both marital partners are now more economically free to choose divorce. Ann Goetting (1979) suggested that affluence in our society better enables people to "afford" divorce and thus considered such affluence to be a major social factor contributing to divorce. Certainly, in modern dual-career marriages, either partner would likely have the financial means to afford a divorce if he or she perceived the marriage to be unsatisfactory.

Changing Role of Divorce.   During the last decade, divorce seems to have become a *stage* in married life rather than the end of it. Because divorce no longer carries much social stigma, most divorced people remarry within a relatively short time and continue with married life. Today, one marriage in four involves a divorced man, and the proportion is even higher for women. Young people in particular tend to remarry almost without exception. Many sociologists now think of divorce not as eroding the institution of marriage but as a necessary adaptation of marriage to social change—an adaptation from "lifelong monogamy" to serial marriage or "serial monogamy." In short, divorce has now seemingly become a part of married life—perhaps an indispensable part. The AIDS epidemic might slow the divorce process temporarily, but it is not likely to do so once an effective method of prevention or treatment has been developed.

Three other social factors that contribute to the high divorce rate merit mentioning at this point. First is the lack of preparation by young people for coping with the problems of marriage. Many enter marriage with little thought about what it actually involves. In fact, it is easier to get a marriage license than a driver's license. Second—and really a theme underlying all the other social factors—is the general decline in moral, religious, economic, and social barriers to divorce that has occurred over the past 50 years. Without these barriers, divorce has become a relatively easy solution to both simple and complex marital problems. Finally, with the longer life expectations currently enjoyed by American men and women, couples are forced into the prospect of spending more years with their partners than most couples in the past. After 10 or 15 years of marriage, a person may look at his or her spouse and wonder, "Do I really want to spend the next 30 or 40 years with this person?"

Personal Factors

What leads individuals to become dissatisfied with their marriage? Although there are many personal factors that can lead to such dissatisfaction, here we shall comment on three that commonly lead to trouble.

Unrealistic Expectations and Evaluations.   Many persons become disappointed and disenchanted when they find marriage does not live up to their expectations that their partner is not the idealized person originally seen through the eyes of love. As we have pointed out, resentment and disagreement may arise over differences between expectations and realities, leading one or both partners to withdraw emotional involvement and to re-examine the relationship.

Not only do young couples often have unrealistic expectations about their marriage, but they tend to overestimate the interests, goals, and values that they share. They may find themselves bored and lonely in each other's company, or they may disagree about where to go in the evening, how to spend money, which goals to pursue, what's right and what's wrong, and so on. In other instances, they may feel they are in fundamental agreement concerning ground rules when in actuality they aren't—often as a result of taking things for granted rather than discussing and clarifying them, particularly in the areas of sex-roles and infidelity. Thus, the couple may find they are "incompatible." The term **incompatibility** may cover a multitude of characteristics that lead to marital conflict and unhappiness, such as sexual incompatibility, differences in temperament, and a general lack of personality "fit."

Fading of Romantic Love.   Another personal factor in marital dissatisfaction is the fading of romantic love. As the heady joys and excitement of the new relationship give way beneath the dull and demanding routines of everyday life, from doing dishes to paying bills, the partners may feel that the love has gone out of their marriage. Although they may still care for each other and enjoy being together, they are not socialized to appreciate fully these essential aspects of love. They believe that without romance and excitement their marriage is a failure, and they may as well terminate the relationship and look elsewhere for the missing ingredient they consider so essential.

Some couples are able to maintain the romance and excitement of their marriage over the years, but most long-standing marriages are marked by a decline of various factors associated with marital satisfaction and happiness, such as expressions of affection, sex, interaction time together, intimate communication, and expressions of emotional support and commitment. A problem that all marriage partners face is long-term change in each other and its effect on the relationship. This is particularly true for couples whose differing career demands and other personal changes lead them not only in different directions but also in incompatible ones. Thus, one of the most common personal factors is growing and drifting apart, as evidenced by loss of emotional intensity; boredom; decreased sexual activity; and divergence of interests, goals, and values.

"Leftovers" from Prior Relationships.   Another factor is the personal problems people bring into a marriage. Because over 40 percent of marriages involve a man or woman who has been divorced at least once, there are millions of marriages in which one or both spouses have brought along "leftovers" from another marriage (Glick, 1980; Glick & Lin, 1986). Such leftovers include habits, possessions, friendships, financial obligations, and often children that must either be cared for or visited regularly. These leftovers are also likely to include "emotional debris" with which the new spouse must deal, as well as some hard-earned wisdom. Even if the partners have never been married before, the "dowry" they bring to the marriage may include personal immaturities and hangups, annoying habits, or unpleasant personality characteristics. In essence, people bring their problems with them into marriage; when these problems are serious ones, they are likely to damage or destroy the marital relationship. This also holds true for personal problems that develop during the marriage, such as drug abuse, alcoholism, or violent behavior.

Of course, there are many other personal factors that may enter into the decision to terminate a marriage. Some of these factors are mentioned in Box 12–5, which describes some of the "danger signals" that indicate a marriage is in trouble. Other factors are discussed in Box 12–6, "How to Tell When It's Over."

BOX 12–5 / HOW TO TELL WHEN A MARRIAGE IS IN TROUBLE

How can people tell when their marriage is "on the rocks"? Before the marital relationship deteriorates to the point of no return, there are usually danger signals warning that the marriage is in trouble. Such signals include:

1. *Frequent and unproductive arguments.* Some marriages are conflict-habituated —bickering has been incorporated into the couple's pattern of living together and seems to be an accepted part of the marriage. In other marriages, however, serious and continued conflicts occur that can hurt the marital partners as well as the quality of their relationship.

2. *Little pleasure in each other's company.* Although a decline in romantic love seems characteristic of most marriages over time, a chronic loss of pleasure in each other's company is more serious, because it signals a dangerous growing apart. The couple may sit in a restaurant with nothing to say to each other, unsmiling, staring into space, wondering what they are doing there with each other.

3. *Feelings of loneliness and isolation.* Even in marital relationships, feeling isolated and lonely from time to time is not uncommon. But chronic feelings of loneliness and isolation in marriage indicate that certain basic needs for companionship and intimacy are not being met.

4. *Lack of sexual satisfaction.* In Chapter 8, we noted the importance of sexual satisfaction—particularly during the early years of marriage—as a barometer of the closeness and quality of the marital relationship. Because it is possible to have a happy marriage despite an unsatisfactory sex life, we must exercise caution in drawing any conclusions here. On the other hand, because unhappy marital relationships are almost always accompanied by a lack of sexual satisfaction, it may well serve as a warning sign of a deteriorating relationship, especially if the initial sexual adjustment in the marriage was satisfactory.

5. *Inability to communicate.* Failing communication takes many forms. The couple may be unable to discuss even the simplest problem in a coherent and rational way, they may have little if anything to say to each other, or they may speak only negatively to each other. In general, meaningful sharing is replaced by ritual exchange or by silence.

Other possible danger signals include turning against each other when things don't go well, viewing marital conflicts as the result of a bad choice of partner, persistent thinking about divorce, and consistent operating "in the red" in terms of cost/reward ratio or comparison level.

All these warning signs are indicative of a seriously troubled or deteriorating marital relationship, but they may not yet signal its imminent termination. They are ominous, however, especially when several are present.

Relationship Factors

There are certain types of marital relationships that may be considered maladaptive or destructive in that they are seriously detrimental to one or both partners. As we shall see, such relationships contain the seeds of their own destruction.

BOX 12–6 / HOW TO TELL WHEN IT'S OVER

Although there is no simple answer to telling when a marriage has run its course, Fredelle Maynard (1978) has found that certain feelings and states of mind seem common to those who decide it's over: "Whether you're approaching the end of a marriage, a very close relationship, or a love affair, the signs of rigor mortis are much the same. When the signs appear, the damage is usually irreparable" (p. 84). What are these signs of "rigor mortis"?

1. *You no longer care or feel anything.* As long as the partners can quarrel, feel angry and hurt, and even attack each other verbally, there would appear to be some life left in the relationship. But once one partner ceases to care or feel, the relationship is likely to end. "My husband and I battled constantly throughout our marriage," one divorced woman told Maynard. "As long as the fights continued—as long as he had the power to hurt or enrage me—I felt life in the relationship. Then one evening at dinner he said, 'In case you're wondering, I spent last night with another woman—a lovely, warm, *responsive* woman. I'm sick to death of your moping.' And you know, I didn't feel

jealous or rejected or angry or even curious. All I said was, 'Please pass the salt.' A moment like that and you suddenly realize it's final" (p. 84).

2. *You have grown apart and you have nothing left in common.* Far less tragic than the loss of feeling is growing apart. Even though it may be equally lethal as far as the relationship is concerned, the partners can still respect and care about each other—and perhaps even remain good friends.

3. *"I love you but I'm not* in love *with you."* Of the many paradoxes of romantic love, this is probably the most devastating when it happens. What can you do? What can you say? In a sense, you are a recipient of love but also a victim, for you have somehow lost the romantic love that the partner feels is essential for maintaining the relationship. In essence, your partner is telling you in a loving way that the marriage is over and he or she wants out. There's nothing you can do about it.

4. *"I'm in love with someone else."* Usually things have gone wrong in the marriage long before a third party appears on the scene—it is well-nigh impossible for a third party to break up a truly close and happy marriage. On the other hand, in a marriage that is already in trouble, it may be relatively easy.

Fraudulent Agreements. The marriage contract—whether or not it is discussed or put in writing—stipulates the type of relationship a couple hopes to achieve and what each partner hopes to contribute to, and receive from, the relationship. In a fraudulent contract, the terms are violated by a partner who never intended to abide by them in the first place. He or she simply agreed to whatever seemed necessary to ensure the marriage. Such fraudulent patterns may take a variety of forms, but a simple example may suffice. Let us assume that during the period of courtship the partners agree to an egalitarian relationship in their marriage. Prior to the marriage, the relationship is indeed egalitarian—each partner enacts the

"That was a line from your first marriage, wasn't it?"
Drawing by William Hamilton, © 1987 The New Yorker Magazine, Inc.

appropriate role behavior. But, once married, the husband reverts to a traditional and authoritarian role, perhaps justifying it on the grounds that his wife is too immature to handle an egalitarian relationship. Of course, many fraudulent relationships continue, but if the defrauded partner feels deceived and used, he or she may act to terminate the marriage. Ironically, if the husband in our example really loves his wife but wants her on his terms, his behavior is ultimately self-defeating and destructive to him as well.

Discordant Relationships.   Some degree of friction seems inevitable in marriage, and in some marriages bickering seems to be an accepted way of life. However, chronic and serious conflict is usually destructive to both the partners and the relationship. Discordant relationships may result from a variety of factors, including unrealistic expectations, personal maladjustment, and marital agreements that turn out to be unsatisfactory. The conflict may center on a number of issues so that it seems that the partners can't agree on anything, or it may focus on some enduring issue, such as sex or money, that can't seem to be resolved. In any event, the unfavorable climate produced by continual conflict is likely to result in reduced interaction time, less open communication, less pleasure in each other's company, and less marital sex. Of course, a combination of such factors may lead to both marital dissatisfaction and dissolution.

Disqualifying Relationships.   In disqualifying relationships, the integrity of one partner is under sustained attack. A common theme is the "double bind," in which the partner is "damned if he does and damned if he doesn't." For example, a husband may complain that his wife never takes the initiative in sex, but when she does he finds some excuse to reject her advances. In short, she can't win in either situation and is likely to feel confused, devalued, and discouraged. Another disconcerting and devaluing tactic is to use disqualifying communications; that is, whenever one person makes a serious comment on some topic, the partner points out that the comment is in error, is only partially true, or is certainly open to serious question. The potentially damaging effects of such disqualifying communications have been vividly described by Laing and Esterson (1964): "When no matter how [a person] feels or how he acts, no matter what meaning he gives his situation, his feelings are denuded of validity, his acts are stripped of their motives, intentions, and consequences, the situation is robbed of its meaning for him, so that he is totally mystified and alienated" (pp. 135–136). Unless one partner manages to "break" the other, such a disqualifying relationship is likely to prove intolerable.

Collusion.   In collusion, a marital relationship is established based on "deviant" terms insisted on by one partner. Typically, such terms call for the partners to ignore or deny jointly some aspect of reality. For example, a man who drinks excessively or who has several girlfriends may agree to enter a marriage if his wife-to-be agrees to accept his drinking or promiscuous behavior. His partner may not wish to agree to these deviant terms, but she is forced to if she wants to marry this particular man. The ensuing marriage is maladaptive because, over time, the husband's behavior may interfere with other aspects of the couple's life. For example, excessive drinking may lead to problems at work and may even lead to hospitalization, and philandering may hamper the couple's sex and social lives as well as expose them to the possibility of contacting AIDS. Either way, tremendous stress is put on the wife and the marital relationship.

Collusion is also maladaptive if both partners behave in a deviant manner, as when both are alcoholics. The terms of the deviant contract may be acceptable to both partners, but the results are likely to make a satisfying marriage impossible.

Violent Marriages.   In Chapter 11, we dealt in some detail with the problem of spouse abuse, and we need not repeat that material here.

However, two comments do appear relevant. First, marital and family violence is considered the most common unreported form of violence in our society. As we noted, children who witness, and are the victims of, such violence in the home may be oriented toward violence in their own later marriage and family life.

Second, we live in an unduly violent culture, and the violence portrayed in the mass media is considered by many social scientists to contribute materially to the high incidence of violence in the home as well as in our society at large (Mace, 1986; Coleman et al., 1987).

Family relations pertain to a plane where the ordinary rules of judgment and conduct do not apply. They are a labyrinth of tensions, quarrels, and reconciliations, whose logic is self-contradictory, whose ethics step from a cozy jungle, and whose values and criteria are distorted like the curved space of a self-contained universe. It is a universe saturated with memories from which no lessons are drawn; saturated with a past which provides no guidance to the future. For in this universe, after each crisis and reconciliation, time always starts afresh and history is always in the year zero.

Arthur Koestler

Environmental Factors

There are many sources of environmental stress that can affect the mental and physical health of the marital partners and the quality of their relationship. One of the most significant factors is financial problems. In Chapter 11, we noted that money ranks as the single most common source of conflict and that financial problems in the form of debts constitute a major crisis for many married couples.

A related source of stress is unemployment, which brings with it both economic hardship and self-devaluation. It is often particularly difficult for the out-of-work husband, who feels that he has failed in the role of "breadwinner." Few things are more anxiety arousing or degrading than constant concern over the livelihood of our family or over our ability to make a living. The consequence for marriage may be flare-ups over minor irritations, feelings of failure and depression, and tension created by pent-up frustration. In fact, unemployment can be as debilitating psychologically as it is financially.

For many people who *are* employed, a major source of stress is job dissatisfaction and "burnout." A common cause of job dissatisfaction is feeling that we are overeducated or overqualified for the type of work we are doing. Job burnout refers to performing the same occupational tasks day after day until one more day of the same becomes intolerable. Whatever the source of occupational problems, they place stress on the individual and on his or her marital relationship.

Perhaps the bottom line is that marriage is not lived in a vacuum. Environmental conditions may tend either to support and strengthen marriage and family life or to undermine their happiness and stability.

THE EFFECTS OF DIVORCE

> For the person who goes through a divorce, an entire life is often turned topsy-turvy. Intimate bonds with another person are broken; relationships with children are changed; friendship patterns are disrupted; different living arrangements must be established; employment must often be obtained. . . .
>
> —*Stan Albrecht (1980, p. 59)*

A legal divorce constitutes a public declaration that the marriage has ended. The wedding vows have been repealed. Thus, divorce can have far-reaching effects on the marital partners, depending on their personalities, their emotional involvement in the marriage, the duration and happiness of the marriage, whether or not the couple have children, and the way in which the relationship is terminated.

Here, we shall focus on the emotional, economic, social, and sexual effects of divorce. Then we shall review the effects on children and the topic of single-parent families.

Emotional Effects

One lesson many people learn from divorce is that even an unhappy marital relationship is still a relationship and that ending a once-close relationship is far from painless—especially for a partner who is still emotionally involved. But even for the person seeking the divorce, the resulting emotional stress may be far greater than he or she had bargained for.

Divorce as an Emotional Crisis.   The feelings and emotions accompanying divorce vary from person to person and are difficult to capture in words. But they commonly include some of the following:

- Feelings of having failed in one of life's most important tasks.
- Feelings of grief and depression.
- Feelings of anger, frustration, inadequacy.
- Feelings of self-recrimination and guilt.
- Feelings of rejection and being unlovable.
- Feelings of intense loneliness and having lost our identity as a marital partner.
- Feelings of regret and thoughts of "what might have been."
- Irrational thoughts and behavior—such as uncontrollable crying spells, suicidal thoughts, excessive drinking and drug abuse, and in some cases "reunion fantasies."

Often the overall emotional reaction is referred to as **grief work.** It is a necessary period of mourning that enables the person to gradually assimilate the loss into his or her self-structure and view it as an event of the past. It is difficult for us to understand how distressing the emotional impact of divorce can be unless we have been there, unless we have been on the receiving end of a divorce. We shall deal further with grief work in our discussion of rebuilding in Chapter 13.

Sex Differences in Emotional Effects.   In a study of 500 divorced persons from eight Rocky Mountain states, Albrecht (1980) found that divorce was perceived as more traumatic by women than by men. This was true whether the divorce had occurred within the last year or some time before that. A similar pattern was noted by sociologist Maureen Baker (1980) among 150 divorced or separated men and women she interviewed in Toronto, Canada. The subjects were between ages 15 and 45 and had been divorced or separated for not more than 2 years. Baker found that although a majority of wives had initiated the divorce, they also reported greater suffering from loneliness, depression, and anxiety about the future than did the men.

In a study of 60 divorced couples in Marin County, California, Judith Wallerstein and Joan Kelly (1980a) found that most of the men reported that they had regained a sense of stability and coherence within the second year following the divorce whereas the women tended to be well into the third postseparation year before reaching that point. Further, when Chiriboga, Roberts, and Stein (1978) studied the psychological well-being of 309 recently separated men and women ages 20 to 79 in California, they found that the women were significantly less happy than the men. It is also of interest to note that Janice Kiecolt-Glaser (1986) found that the stress of divorce lowered women's stress tolerance, making them more vulnerable to illness. It also seems probable that divorced men show a reduction in stress tolerance and vulnerability to illness—especially when they did not initiate the divorce.

Kenneth Kressel's (1980) in-depth interviews with divorced persons revealed that men appeared to be more cut off from the emotional aspects of divorce and more prone to deny that they had any difficulty adjusting psychologically. Thus, men may be at a disadvantage because they appear to have more difficulty understanding and expressing their emotions and seeking emotional support than women. Kressel concluded that the men seemed "far more bewildered by the entire experience" (p. 237).

Finally, Judith Wallerstein (1985) followed 52 middle-class couples—mostly white—for a period of 10 years following their breakup. The couples lived in

California and had been married for an average of 11 years prior to their divorce. She found that in 63 percent of the families, one partner reported an improvement in their lives. Younger women were much more likely to report such an improvement than men—55 percent to 32 percent. But for older women—who were 40 or over at the time of the breakup—life was much grimmer after their divorce.

In general, then, it would appear that, although women experience the greater emotional impact during the initial period after the divorce, they make a better adjustment than men over the long haul—except for women who are older when the divorce occurs. The latter category also includes women who have played traditional homemaker and child-rearing roles and lack the occupational skills that would enable them to make a decent living. As one newly divorced woman who entered the job market expressed it, "It's as if all the roles were changed while you were somewhere else."

Economic Effects

The economic consequences of divorce include dividing common possessions and property and working out financial obligations such as alimony and child support.

Division of Common Possessions and Property.

Over time, a married couple accumulates various cherished possessions, such as furniture, a stereo system, silverware, knickknacks, collectibles, a car, and so on. The couple usually attempt to divide things 50–50 because even in dual-career marriages, the things purchased by one spouse are usually considered to be the property of both. This division of possessions involves a good deal of bargaining: "I'll give up this if you'll give up that." Albrecht (1980) found that the majority of marital partners were satisfied with the result, about 30 percent of the males and 20 percent of the females expressed dissatisfaction with the division of common possessions. About 4 percent were so glad to get the situation over with that they didn't care what arrangements were made.

When it comes to a home the couple own in common, the situation is often more difficult to resolve, as there are usually mortgage payments, taxes, maintenance, and other costs to be considered—not to mention the cost involved in finding acceptable living accommodations for the spouse who moves out. In some instances, financial considerations make it necessary for the couple to sell their home—with little hope of either partner acquiring a new one. In general, property settlements involving homes are emotionally and financially painful to the couple.

Division of Income—Alimony and Child Support.

In the 1950s and 1960s, it was not uncommon to hear of women maintaining a high standard of living based on alimony from their ex-husbands. But there were never many, and there are fewer today, because the introduction of no-fault divorce has reduced the leverage that women formerly exerted over their husbands as "victims" in the divorce proceedings. Even in the late 1970s, only about one in seven women obtaining divorces were awarded alimony or "maintenance," and the amount of money was usually insufficient in terms of the cost of living. In addition, the alimony was usually awarded for fixed, and often short-term, periods. The 1980 Census revealed that only one-third of the women awarded alimony payments actually received them.

Stephen Shames/Visions

The same is generally true in the 1980s. Wives who are awarded custody of the children usually receive alimony and child support, but often the husband is unable to maintain payments or manages to evade them. However, court rulings have been more strictly enforced in recent years. But even for those fathers who do make child support payments, it is often difficult to maintain a reasonable standard of living themselves.

Nevertheless, it is usually the mother who suffers the most (Blair, 1986; McGrath, 1986; Weitzman, 1985). Even in dual-worker marriages, the wife usually earns considerably less than her husband, and—without the help of child-support payments—she may find it difficult to make ends meet. But, as we have emphasized, the mother who has played the role of homemaker and lacks market-able skills is at the greatest economic disadvantage. Such women usually have to develop some kind of useful work skills and obtain whatever employment they can find—often at minimum wages. Thus, the divorced woman has not only to play the roles of mother and worker—and often father as well—but also to shoulder the main financial responsibilities on a very limited budget.

Social Effects

The effects of getting a divorce tend to be generally disruptive on the social lives of the marital partners. Kando (1978) has summarized the situation this way:

> It results in a rearrangement of one's circle of friends, of the relatives with whom one associates, and of one's other social and occupational relationships. To one's married friends, one often becomes persona non grata. You are a threat, a potential homewrecker. One of the more painful learning experiences most divorced people have had is to discover not only a lack of compassion on the part of their friends, but, in fact, suddenly being dropped and avoided at the time of greatest need and vulnerability. (p. 390)

Most of the person's usual social activities were likely to be couple oriented prior to the divorce. Now, he or she has become the "extra" person—an uncomfortable and sometimes embarrassing role that cannot usually be maintained. In short, as divorced persons, they no longer fit in. Consequently, they lose relationships that have been both emotionally and socially important. This has been called the "ripple effect" of divorce.

Many married friends are lost not only because they do not want to take sides but also because they tend to think of divorce as contagious. Having a divorced friend around may be a continual reminder that divorce can be a solution to marital problems. Divorced persons may also be seen as a potential threat to our marriage, competing for our mate. Take the case of Carlos and Cheryl. When Carlos' best friend, Brad, came to them for sympathy after the breakup of his marriage, Cheryl let him cry on her shoulder and spent long hours listening to his woes. Before Carlos knew it, Cheryl and Brad had fallen in love and he was left out in the cold.

Finally, it may be emphasized that we have not discussed the "psychic divorce" as Bohannan (1972) has labeled it. This refers to the separation of the self from the marital relationship and becoming a single person once again. We shall deal with this difficult and important task in Chapter 13 in our discussion of rebuilding.

Sexual Effects

While divorce unquestionably has a major impact on a person's sex life, this area suffers—as do so many others in marriage and intimate relationships—from a dearth of research data.

In many cases, a couple's sex life is affected months or even years before the divorce takes place. An uncorrected problem of premature ejaculation, lack of desire, or other sexual inadequacy may have characterized the couple's sex life. In other instances, a once-satisfying sex life has deteriorated along with the marriage. Either way, the couple may consider the sexual problem to be a major factor in their breakup.

But what about the person's sex life after the divorce? In some cases, one or both partners may have established a sexual relationship outside the marriage prior to the divorce, thus minimizing the problem. But, for many, the problem is not so simple. The individual's sex life, such as it was, is now disrupted and he or she is faced with a choice between getting along without sex, masturbating, engaging in a series of casual affairs, or trying to establish a meaningful sexual relationship. If a woman has custody of children, she may hesitate to get involved in dating and sex for fear of upsetting the children. And, compared to her ex-husband—unless she is very young—she has a more-limited range of eligible men from whom to choose, because divorced men tend to date and to marry women who are younger than their ex-wives. In our discussion of singlehood in Chapter 6, we also noted the tendency of predatory males to consider it open season on divorcées on the sexual hunting ground. However, with the increasing fear of AIDS, these predatory males may find the hunting very limited.

To complicate matters, a person whose sole sex partner has been his or her spouse—at least for a number of years—may feel inadequately prepared for sexual experiences with new partners. Philip and Lorna Sarrel (1980) have noted that, although some divorced persons are able to move rapidly into a commitment with a new partner, others must go through a long transition phase before they attempt to build another intimate relationship.

Finally, a sizable number of divorced persons continue to have sex with their ex-spouses. Melvin Burke and Joanne Grant (1982) estimated that 90 percent of divorced persons have thought about it, 75 percent have discussed it, and 30 percent have actually engaged in sex with their ex-partner.

Children of Divorce

> Children and adolescents whose parents separate and divorce often suffer a great deal of short-term emotional trauma, as a result of the separation itself or of the parental conflict before and after it.
>
> *—Norval Glenn (1985, p. 68)*

Not many years ago, unhappily married couples usually stayed together "for the good of the children." With the increase in divorce beginning in the 1960s came the development of a more-optimistic view that divorce is actually better for the children than a conflict-ridden family. A good deal of early research did support this view (Landis, 1962; Thomas, 1976). However, more-recent research is much more neutral regarding the merits of divorce versus living in an embattled home. As Wallerstein and Kelly (1980a) pointed out, it would appear that divorce is neither more nor less beneficial to children than a home filled with parent conflict.

These divergent viewpoints are worthy of consideration. "Children of divorce" represent a large and increasing segment of our child population. Each year, for example, over one million children experience the divorce of their parents. Although 8 percent of our children lived in single-parent families in 1960, the number had increased to 40 percent by the early 1980s. As we noted in Chapter 1, it has been estimated that over 50 percent of children born in the middle to late 1980s will live in a single parent family at some time before they are 18 years of age. Thus the effects of divorce on children in our society poses a very real question.

Available research studies indicate that the impact of divorce on children varies with their age, sex, and personality as well as with the circumstances of their family and relationment in the research literature on the following points:

1. It takes 1 to 5 years for children to adjust to the impact of their parent's divorce.
2. During this period, children commonly need help in dealing with feelings of rejection, anger, and guilt—as well as fear of abandonment.
3. Mothers are the custodial parents in about 90 percent of divorce cases involving children. Seventy-five percent of single parent mothers work —usually at low status and low paying jobs.
4. About 1 child in 4 in our society lives below the government mandated poverty line, and the majority of these children are from single parent families headed by mothers. Thirty-five percent of these mothers are from minority groups.
5. As adults, children of divorce are not as happy and are more divorce prone than children from intact families—perhaps due to fear of failure and less commitment.

Joel Gordon

There also appears to be general agreement among researchers that predictions and conclusions about the long term effects of divorce on children—positive, negative, or neutral—should be viewed with both caution and skepticism. As Glynnis Walker (1986) has pointed out, it would also appear that we need to change our outmoded view of "normal family life," and to study its affects on the increasing number of children of divorce.

Perhaps Box 12–7—which contains summary data from one of the rare longitudinal studies in this field—will help to broaden our perspective.

SINGLE-PARENT FAMILIES

The rising incidence of divorce in our society has led to a marked increase in single-parent families. In 1986, for example, there were over 5 million separated or divorced mothers heading families that included children under 18 years of age. In addition, there were about 1,500,000 divorced fathers who headed single-parent families. These single-parent families included about 12 million children of divorce (see Figure 12–1).

In addition, the number of single parents in our society is augmented by those resulting from the death of a spouse, unwed parenthood, and temporary absence of one parent. Overall, about 70 percent of single parents are the result of divorce, 14 percent the result of the death of a parent, and 10 percent or more the result of unwed mothers. An additional 5–6 percent are listed as due to the temporary absence of one parent—for example, one parent is in prison.

Despite the growing prevalence of this family type, however, relatively little research exists on the topic, few practical guidelines are available, and social-support systems are in short supply. In short, these "new families"—together with step-parent families—are the pioneers of new life styles.

BOX 12–7 / CHILDREN OF DIVORCE: A LONGITUDINAL STUDY

Wallerstein and Kelly (1980) conducted a five year longitudinal study of the effects of divorce on children. Their subjects were 60 families with 113 children living in Marin County, California. These families were mainly from higher socioeconomic levels, and the findings cannot be generalized to families for whom the financial consequences of divorce may be far more devastating. Interestingly, all but two families who began the study were able to complete their interviews at the 5-year mark in 1980.

1. *Initial impact of the separation.* Some 80 percent of the children had not been prepared for the parent's separation. Suddenly their world collapsed. As might be expected, their initial reaction was shock and denial, followed by a mixture of anger, fear, and depression depending in part on the age of the child. Toddlers tended to regress and become more dependent. Older children varied. Some blamed themselves somehow for their parent's separation; others expressed anger at the parent whom they felt caused the breakup; and others dreamed up fanciful reasons for the separation, apparently in an attempt to make some sense out of it. Teenagers tended to have a different problem, the "loyalty dilemma." Here one parent tried to get the teenager to side with him or her and to disapprove of the other parent.

   Girls tended to be harder hit than boys, perhaps because they did not receive as much emotional support from their mothers and more was expected of them. Two factors, however, tended to cut across sex and age boundaries—a "slippage" in school and an obsessive desire to reunite the parents. This obsessive desire was dramatically illustrated by a 2½-year-old who "spent fretful hours trying to place his father's hand in his mother's hand" (Franke et al., 1980, p. 74).

   Interestingly, despite their superior socioeconomic status, most of these parents were having financial, as well as emotional, difficulties with the separation.

2. *Eighteen months after the divorce.* At the 18 month mark, conditions had improved considerably, although both parents and children showed signs of stress. Among the children, preadolescent boys were having the most difficult time adjusting to their new life situation. About 90 percent preferred their family situation prior to the divorce.

3. *Five years after the divorce.* By this time, things had improved markedly. About 34 percent of the children appeared to be doing especially well psychologically, in terms of high self-esteem, coping at school and home, and having a sense of self-sufficiency. Roughly 29 percent were in the middle range of psychological health. Their school performance and interactions with peers and adults were appropriate. However, underlying feelings of diminished self-esteem—and sometimes anger—hampered their full development. The final 30 percent of the children were intensely unhappy and dissatisfied with their lives. However, they had moved ahead in school.

   These researchers were also struck by the intense loneliness evidenced by about 27 percent of the overall group of children. Overall, however, these children seemed to be adjusting well to their parent's earlier divorce. Nevertheless, Wallerstein and Kelly found that all of the children in their study

had the sense of having sustained a difficult and unhappy time in their lives . . . that a significant part of their childhood had been a sad or frightening time. (p. 34)

Figure 12–1. A
Profile of
Households of
American Youth
Aged 8–17 Years.
(Source: American
Chicle Youth Poll,
1987.)

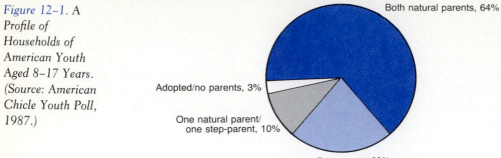

Both natural parents, 64%

Adopted/no parents, 3%

One natural parent/
one step-parent, 10%

One parent, 23%

Arlene Collins/Monkmeyer Press Photo Service

In this final section of the chapter, we shall examine some of the experiences, problems, and adjustments of people in single-parent households. We shall also draw on the available research to dispel some common misconceptions and suggest a few tentative guidelines for coping in this family setting.

The Single-Parent Family System

Divorce is a disorganizing and reorganizing process in a family with children. The process extends over time, often several years. Although it has, like most life events and crises, the potential for growth and new integrations, the road is often rocky and tortuous and many people underestimate the vicissitudes and difficulties of the transition.

—*Wallerstein and Kelly (1977, p. 5)*

If divorces did not involve children, it would simplify matters considerably; but they do. In about three out of four divorces, children are involved (Furstenberg & Nord, 1985; Norton & Glick, 1986). Because the court usually awards child custody to the mother, the great majority—about 90 percent—of single-parent families are headed by women.

Although most people are well aware that separation and divorce are traumatic events, they tend to believe that, once these steps are taken, everything will fall into place. But with children involved, it is a far different matter. Regardless of whether the mother or father is responsible for establishing the new family system, it cannot be done overnight. Rarely is the custodial parent prepared for the difficult path that lies ahead (see Box 12–8).

Following separation of the parents, there is a period of disequilibrium in the family system that usually lasts for most of the first year and often much longer. This is a period of both disorganization and reorganization. Roles and responsibilities have to be modified, new priorities and ground rules have to be agreed on, and effective methods of discipline have to be worked out. Because money is usually a serious problem, a realistic budget has to be developed and adhered to. The family home may have to be sold, and less-expensive living quarters found. Often children who had their own room have to "double up." More-supportive relationships among family members are required. In short, a new family system has to be established to meet the needs of members—as well as possible—and enable the family to cope with the problems of living.

While this reorganization of the family system is going on, each member has to come to terms with his or her emotional reactions to the separation and its meaning for their lives. In a very real sense, required changes in the family system may have to be made by members who are still in a state of shock.

Unlike all other major shifts in family composition, there exist virtually no rituals or rites of passage to assist families with the difficulties inherent in the process of divorce.

Edward Beal

Mothers and Fathers as Single Parents

Separation and divorce are highly stressful for parents and children alike. Parents have to learn to function not only as single parents but also as single persons. This combination often places parents, particularly custodial mothers, under severe overload.

BOX 12–8 / HELPING CHILDREN OF DIVORCE

What can parents and children do to minimize the negative effects of divorce? There are a few tried-and-true dos and don'ts that apply to this situation. The following suggestions may not be appropriate for very young children or for older teenagers; rather, they are aimed at children in the 4–12 age range. In some instances, a specific do or don't may be more relevant for boys or for girls.

In applying these dos and don'ts, it is useful to remember that children have strong feelings about their parents' divorce and are trying to make sense out of a hurtful and perplexing situation.

DOS

1. Help the child to understand that although the parents may no longer love each other and want to live together, they still love the child; reassure the child that he or she will not be abandoned.

2. Make it clear that the child is not responsible for the parents' separation—that he or she has done nothing wrong. Emphasize that the decision to separate was made—perhaps reluctantly—by the parents.

3. Help the child work through his or her feelings of anger toward the parent who initiated the separation or who the child perceives as being at fault. Help the child to appreciate visits from the absent parent.

4. If the father–son relationship is a close one, take precautions to ensure that it remains that way; father–son relationships are twice as likely to deteriorate after divorce as are father–daughter relationships.

5. Consider the possibility of joint custody or another arrangement that keeps both parents actively involved in the care of the children, and try to agree on and maintain consistent disciplinary rules.

DON'TS

1. Don't get involved in custody battles that force the child to make a choice. This can be highly stressful for the child.

2. Don't overburden the child with taking on too many roles and responsibilities—particularly the role of the absent parent. Avoid using the child as an emotional crutch.

3. Avoid blaming the other parent and forming parent–child coalitions against the absent parent. Don't use the child as a pawn in a war game between the parents.

4. Don't neglect the child during the stressful period when the mother or father starts dating or remarries. This is particularly important because the period is highly stressful for both parents and children.

5. Don't require the child to renounce a biological parent as the price for winning the support of a step-parent.

Many families find it useful to seek professional counseling. The counselor can help the parents cope with the difficult task of building separate social and sexual lives while cooperating in the care and raising of the children. If both parents are able to give the child attention and care, the child will make a better adjustment to the divorce.

In general, there appear to be four key levels of possible overload for the single parent.

1. *Responsibility overload.* The parent has to make the important decisions regarding the children's behavior and family life. From financial details to domestic duties, there is no one else to turn to for direction. Children can assume many responsibilities, but they look to the parent for decisions regarding key issues in their lives. In addition, the parent has to function as referee and judge.

   It is in this area of increased responsibility that the single parent may feel the greatest effects of having lost a system of interaction in which many decisions are shared. Instead of feeling free to make decisions without interference, the single parent may feel unsure, tense, and under pressure.

2. *Task overload.* This particularly affects the mother as custodial parent. Barbara Goldfarb and Roger Libby (1984) studied 36 single-parent mothers in a university community. The women were well educated but lacked occupational skills. As a result, these mothers were faced with the tasks of trying to find and maintain work, go to school in order to upgrade their occupational skills, handle budgeting and household chores, and maintain a minimum social life for themselves and their children.

   Most single parents have little time for friends, which leads to a social isolation that makes their new life seem very confining. Although they are now free from the problems that accompanied their marriage, most are not free enough to find themselves as social, sexual, and interesting adults—at least not as soon as many would like.

3. *Emotional overload.* The single parent has to be available to his or her children emotionally, even when exhausted and drained of energy reserves. Even when the parent is so stressed as to feel irrational and unresponsive, there is no partner to help. In some instances, an emotionally overloaded parent may lash out verbally, or even physically, at the child simply because the child is there and making additional demands. Most parents realize their mistakes and feel bad about themselves when such incidents occur because now they have not only failed at marriage but also seem in danger of failing at child-rearing.

4. *Financial overload.* Perhaps the bottom line for the single parent is money. Few couples with children have the financial resources to maintain two households after the divorce, but it is the single-parent mother who is at the greatest disadvantage. In the Goldfarb and Libby (1985) study, 98 percent of the mothers stated that financial support was a major problem. Only a minority received child-support payments and an even smaller minority received alimony; in neither case was the amount of money sufficient. As Lenore Weitzman (1985) has pointed out, the result has been that most single-parent mothers are forced into the role of good provider. Unfortunately, most lack the occupational skills necessary to assume this role. In 1981, the U.S. Census reported that over half of all female-headed households—including divorced, bereaved, and never-married mothers—faced severe economic hardship. During the

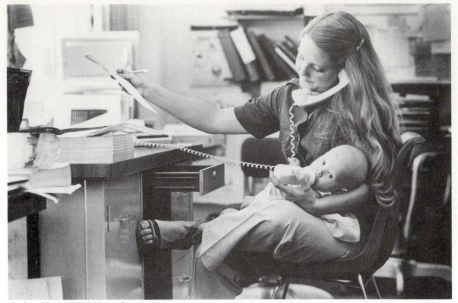

Cathey Cheney/EKM-Nepenthe

Ulrike Welsch

mid-1980s, this problem was intensified as the social-support net provided by the government for single-parent mothers was subjected to increasingly restrictive guidelines. This general situation has been referred to as "**the feminization of poverty** in America."

Addressing themselves to this situation, Sharyn Crossman and Jean Edmondson (1985) have suggested that career counselors for students incorporate four elements into their program:

a. Make it clear that career training is just as important for women as it is for men.

b. Counsel the delay of marriage until after necessary training and job experience have been obtained.

c. Help young women realize that divorce or bereavement can happen to them.

d. Help young women understand that being a homemaker who moves in and out of dead-end jobs to earn extra money does not prepare them for the good-provider role.

The importance of these points is underscored by the comment of a widowed mother of four children, "The shock of realizing you have children to support and no skills to do it with is a worse shock than learning your husband is dead" (p. 473).

Despite all the stress and heartache, many single parents—both mothers and fathers—think of the experience as a constructive one (Goldfarb & Libby, 1984; Meredith, 1985; Risman, 1986). Although they may not function well initially, they learn rapidly as they go along. In the process of dealing with new problems, balancing their own needs against those of their children, and coping with severe overload, they learn to rely on their own inner strength and potential. With success comes increased confidence and self-esteem. In addition, many feel that they have developed a special relationship with their children that was not there before. Overall, they are determined to make a better life for themselves and their children (see Boxes 12–9 and 12–10).

Most research has viewed the one-parent family as [sick] rather than focusing on how positive family functioning and support systems facilitate development of social, emotional, and intellectual competence in children of one-parent families.
E. Mavis Hetherington

The "Other Parent"

One of the main differences between single-parent families today and those in times past is that the parent is not dead but probably lives in the same city or area. Even if he or she does not live nearby, the fact that the parent is alive means that they play a continuing role in the new family system. It is up to the custodial parent to work out visitations.

An amicable separation and divorce make it possible to work out visiting and other rights without great difficulty, but often the pain and bitterness remaining from the divorce make matters difficult. Many painful memories, buried hurts, and smoldering angers tend to come to the surface when **divorced parents** have to see each other or talk to each other about their children. In an interesting study, Constance Ahrons (1985) followed 98 divorced couples for 5 years and found that they related in four different ways:

1. *Perfect Pals.* These couples enjoyed spending time together and sharing activities with their children. None of the ex-marital partners had remarried. This type accounted for 12 percent of the couples.

BOX 12-9 / FATHERS AS CUSTODIAL PARENTS: SOME FACTS

1. About 10 percent of single-parent families are headed by custodial fathers. Ordinarily, the father gains custody of children in divorce cases only when the mother doesn't want custody or is considered incompetent as a mother, for example, if she is an alcoholic, a prostitute, or some other undesirable parental model.

2. About 1.5 million men have custody of over 3.5 million children in the United States.

3. Most single-parent fathers are not adequately prepared for raising children on their own. However, they can learn rapidly and be loving and effective parents.

4. Resources to help single-parent fathers include workshops, classes, self-help groups, social workers, family therapists, and other trained personnel.

5. Available research indicates that most fathers feel competent and comfortable as custodial parents—sometimes after a rather "shaky" start.

Thus, as Barbara Risman (1986) has pointed out, "specialists who work with single parents need to be aware that 'mothering' is not an exclusively female skill" (p. 95).

---

2. *Cooperative Colleagues.* These couples also got along well together but spent less time with each other. Their interactions focused on their children. Many had remarried. This type accounted for 38 percent of the couples.

3. *Angry Associates.* These couples would only communicate about issues involving the children; they were quick to argue and fight. This type accounted for 25 percent of the couples.

4. *Fiery Foes.* These couples went to considerable lengths to avoid seeing, or even talking to, each other. Often they tried to force the children to choose sides. This type accounted for 24 percent of the couples.

Which of these groups was the happiest? Cooperative Colleagues came in first, followed by Perfect Pals; these encompassed about half the couples. Ahrons pointed out that because families do continue after divorce, we need to develop some guidelines or rules of etiquette to deal with this common situation in our society.

The latter point seems particularly well taken because it is a tremendous asset to have parents who put aside their own feelings and spend time with their children (Lowery & Settle, 1985). When an aversive relationship exists between the parents, the noncustodial parent tends to spend less and less time with the children. The pain is too great; the rewards are too few. Because it is often the situation, rather than the children, that drives the noncustodial parent away, it would appear possible to help matters by developing guidelines that receive widespread social acceptance. In addition, such guidelines might help to deal with long-lasting negative feelings between former marital partners. For example, Wallerstein (1985) found that 40 percent of the women and almost 30 percent of the men in her study remained intensely angry toward, and felt exploited and rejected by, their ex-spouses 10 years after their divorce.

BOX 12–10 / MOTHERS AS CUSTODIAL PARENTS: SOME FACTS

1. About 8 percent of single-parent families are headed by women.
2. About 90 percent of single-parent families are headed by mothers.
3. By 1990, it is estimated that one child in four will spend some time in a single-parent family—usually headed by the mother. By the year 2000, the estimate is one in two.
4. Single-parent families headed by mothers typically suffer markedly lower income and living standards. The median income of single-parent mothers is just above the government-set poverty line.
5. Because they have to do it together, the family tone is usually more loving and cooperative.
6. Despite low income and overloading, single-parent mothers learn that they can manage, take charge of their lives, and take care of their children. With time, they gain in competence and confidence.

Although these families do cope remarkably well, they receive little help from our society, which has not yet adjusted to the national trend toward a continued high incidence of divorce and single-parent families—mostly headed by mothers.

What About Joint Custody?

Traditionally, the mother has usually been granted custody of the children in divorce cases, unless she was considered unfit by the court. Recently, however, the concept of **joint custody** has received a good deal of professional attention as a means of maintaining continuity between parents and children in cases of divorce.

Because there is practically no research to clarify the advantages and disadvantages, perhaps the simplist way to gain an initial impression of this form of child custody is in terms of a series of questions.

1. *What is joint custody?* It is a form of custody in which both parents share in caring for and raising the children. Contrary to popular opinion, the sharing need not be equal. For example, the time spent by the children with each of their parents may be little or no different than under present custody arrangements; nor need the parent's financial contributions be equal. The basic idea is that both parents—particularly the father—maintain active, if limited, roles in helping to rear their children.

2. *Is joint custody in the best interest of the children?* The presumption is that the maximum involvement of the parents is in the best interest of the children. Of course, an underlying assumption is that joint custody is likely to ensure greater parental involvement than either maternal custody or paternal custody.

3. *Does joint custody shuttle the children between two different homes and disrupt the stability of their environment?* Because the custodial parent —usually the mother—has to work to make ends meet, the children are

Being a father means being asked, without knowing how, to explain the world. He was twelve when I left home. You can't explain divorce to a twelve-year-old. He learns to accept it. You hope, you constantly pray, that he'll understand in time that a man can stop loving his wife but never his son.

Anthony Brandt

presently shuttled back and forth from day-care centers, baby sitters, relatives, and so on. Thus, shuttling the children between two households should not present a new problem.

4. *If the parents are hostile toward each other—or if one is hostile toward the other—is joint custody a good idea?*   The presumption is that children need both parents following the divorce, and that the children can handle the marital conflict more readily than the loss of a parent who stops coming to see them.

5. *Does joint custody work?*   According to a review of available literature by Beverly Ferreiro (1985), it does. For example, in one study, none of the joint custody fathers had "split the scene." In fact, they spent considerably more time with their children than did noncustodial fathers. Because joint-custody fathers do not feel deprived of their rights as parents, they also appear much more likely to maintain child-custody payments.

There are conditions, of course, that may make joint custody impractical. Parents may agree on their custody preference, distance apart may make joint custody pretty much out of the question, or spouses who are undesirable parents (for example, those who beat their mate and children) may make joint custody undesirable. If the custody arrangements are left up to the parents, the choice usually favors mother custody over joint custody (Lowery, 1985). However, in 1985, Illinois signed a new joint-custody law that makes it possible for the court to mandate joint custody if it is considered in the best interest of the children (Goldman, 1985). In addition, California and a number of other states have changed their divorce laws to favor joint custody.

The jury is still out on the long-term merits of joint custody, but it is becoming the preferred custody arrangement in more and more divorce cases.

DIVORCE THERAPY

As a consequence of the high incidence of divorce and the desperate need of many couples for assistance during this critical period, a new mental health specialty of **divorce therapy** has emerged in the last decade. If a marriage can be salvaged, fine; but, if it is beyond repair, the aim of the divorce therapist is to help the couple end their marriage with a minimum of damage to themselves and their children. Thus, divorce therapy may be considered "recoupling" therapy as well as "uncoupling" therapy.

Divorce therapy does not tell the couple what to do. Rather, divorce therapy focuses on understanding the marital relationship and the feelings and motives of the partners. During this period, it is suggested that no final decision to divorce be made or steps taken to contact lawyers. Rather, the time is devoted to facing reality concerning the strengths and weaknesses of the marriage and the real feelings the partners have about maintaining it. Marital partners are often unreliable sources of information about themselves and their marriage. For example, a man who loudly asserts that he wants a divorce may actually be trying to frighten his wife into changing her sexual behavior or some other attitude or behavior. Were the marriage to break up, he might be completely shattered. Another husband might feel that his marriage is hopeless and really wants out but can't handle the guilt of telling his dependent wife that he is leaving her. He is perpetuating a pretense and postponing the inevitable termination of a bad marriage—which is unfair to both partners.

At some point, of course, some decision concerning the marriage has to be made: Can it be salvaged, or is it terminal? If, for example, the couple and the therapist agree that the marriage is not salvageable, the focus may then shift to helping the more-dependent and emotionally involved partner to withstand and prepare for the stress that lies ahead.

Does divorce therapy help? Most clients and professionals seem to think that it does (Lazarus, 1981; Ellis & Bernard, 1985; Sprenkle, 1985). Clients usually indicate that they have been helped in such areas as expression of feelings, ability to communicate with their partner, emotional support, and understanding of themselves and their relationship. In addition, they obtain useful information—for example, information about Parents Without Partners (PWP) and other self-help and social-support groups. Professionals usually consider divorce therapy helpful if it promotes personal growth and enables the marital partners to "recouple" if it is feasible. If the decision is to divorce, then success is gauged not only on the personal growth of one or both partners but also on enabling them to "uncouple" with a minimum of emotional and financial damage to all concerned.

SUMMARY—Chapter 12

1. One in two marriages in the United States ends in divorce, the highest rate the world has ever known. Until recently, the trauma of divorce was increased by making it an adversarial proceeding in which one of the partners had to be proved at serious fault.

2. In the 1970s, no-fault divorce became the primary legal procedure. It has reduced the hypocrisy and acrimony inherent in the previous method, but it is still an adversarial procedure requiring two attorneys. Divorce mediation, based on cooperation and conflict resolution, is further lessening the adversarial nature of many divorces.

3. Most courts now view married couples as economic and social equals; alimony has been de-emphasized and desexed; and filing procedures have been simplified. But there are still problems. Couples with property find separation agreements expensive. Property, rather than income, is divided, so that homemakers, women with children, or those who earn less than their husbands are often at a disadvantage. No one represents the children, although decisions about custody have not been particularly successful.

4. Common patterns of divorce include the enmeshed pattern, in which the decision is prolonged and bitter; the nonmutual pattern, in which only one of the partners wants a divorce (60 percent of divorces are of this type); and the disengaged pattern, in which the partners slowly drift apart.

5. Among the social factors that contribute to divorce are its social acceptability, the excessive demands people make of marriage, the stresses of dual-career marriage, greater economic independence of the partners, and serial monogamy.

6. Personal factors that contribute to divorce are unrealistic expectations and evaluations of the spouses, the fading of romantic love, and leftovers—

including children—from previous marriages. A marriage may contain the seeds of its own destruction by being based on a fraudulent agreement; by involving the disqualification, or devaluing of a partner; by being collusive; or by being violent.

7. Among the environmental factors that contribute to divorce are financial problems, unemployment, and job problems.

8. Divorce is an emotional crisis and recovering from it requires grief work, a period of mourning that enables the person to come to terms with a traumatic event. Although women initiate most divorces, they appear to suffer greater ensuing loneliness, depression, and anxiety. Younger women who are able to earn their own living seem to benefit more from divorce than any other group.

9. The economic consequences of divorce include division of property (usually 50–50) and of income, usually in the form of alimony and child-support payments by the man. In the 1970s, only one in seven women were awarded alimony, usually too little and mostly unremitted. Fewer receive alimony now. Payments for child support are usually inadequate and evaded. As a result, the woman often suffers great economic hardship.

10. The social and sexual lives of divorced people are disrupted. They are often viewed as threats by their married friends; at the least, they no longer "fit in." Finding new sexual partners requires self-confidence, which has ebbed, and finding eligible partners, which may be difficult and which has become dangerous because of AIDS. About one third of divorced couples have engaged in sex with their ex-spouses.

11. More than 40 percent of the children in the United States live in single-parent households. In general, they do not appear to be better or worse off than they were in conflict-filled homes: the effect of a divorce varies with the child's age, sex, personality, the family's circumstances, and the child's relationships with the parents. Although the short-term effects on most children are damaging, most are able to adjust and function successfully in the long run.

12. Three-fourths of divorces involve children. Since custody is usually awarded to the mother, 90 percent of single-parent families are headed by women. This single parent is overloaded by too much responsibility, too much emotional stress, and has too much to do. The bottom line is that there is not enough money. Most single mothers are poor, a situation known as "the feminization of poverty."

13. Divorced parents relate to each other as perfect pals; as cooperative colleagues (the largest group); as angry associates; and as fiery foes.

14. Joint custody allows both parents to share, not necessarily equally, in caring for and raising the children. Although not always possible or desirable, joint custody arrangements are increasing and research indicates that they may be advantageous to the children.

15. Divorce therapy seems to help people to decide whether divorce is necessary and, if so, to help them end the marriage with a minimum of damage to themselves and their children.

REBUILDING, REMARRIAGE, AND STEPFAMILIES

The great love of your life has left you, and you are feeling terrible. They used to call it a "broken heart." But that was before the psychologists took over. Now it's known as the loss-distress syndrome. It means the same thing, of course. And it hurts just as much even if it doesn't sound quite so dramatic.
—William Overend (L.A. Times, July 10, 1977, Part V, p. 1)

A divorce does not wipe out the past and leave us with a clean slate. Rather, we are saddled with emotional, economic, social, and other excess baggage from our marriage that makes it necessary to do a lot of sorting out, reorganizing, and discarding before we are ready to "start over" in the sense of falling in love again and remarrying. In fact, simply surviving and coping with reality demands during the first year after divorce is a Herculean task for most people. The popularity of "advice to the lovelorn" columns and magazine articles on surviving divorce attest to the desire of millions of people to find ways for coping with the trauma of divorce. As we noted in Chapter 12, each year more than 2 million adults and 1 million children are involved in this highly stressful situation.

In this chapter, we shall explore some of the basic tasks people must accomplish in the rebuilding process. We will also be looking at the problems involved in re-entering the "dating and mating" marketplace and in learning to love again. Finally, we shall examine the special characteristics and problems of remarriage and stepfamilies and suggest some tentative guidelines.

SURVIVING DIVORCE: SOME BASIC TASKS

Despite the tremendous personal impact of divorce, there is little research on the subject of surviving divorce and rebuilding our shattered life. But there do seem to be certain tasks that must be accomplished if the transition from marriage to "divorcehood" is to be managed effectively. These tasks include griefwork; dealing with depression, anger, and guilt; re-evaluating the marriage; avoiding loneliness traps; and coping with reality demands.

Perhaps the most fundamental task is seeking out and using a **self-help group** —that is, a volunteer community or church-backed workshop made up of persons who "have been there," can understand your situation, and can help you deal with it (see Box 13–1). As George Albee (1986) has emphasized:

> Research has made it very clear that people who have the support of self-help organizations are much better off emotionally than those who face their problems alone. (p. 64)

Such a source of social support can help the individual cope with the difficult problems created by divorce, problems to which we shall now turn.

BOX 13–1 / WOULD A DIVORCE CEREMONY HELP?

Unlike all other major shifts in family composition, there exists virtually no rituals or rites of passage to assist families with the difficulties inherent in the process of divorce.
—*Edward Beal (1982, p. 3)*

Marriage is an act consummated in an atmosphere of gaiety and happiness supported by social ritual and ceremony. Divorce, on the other hand, is an act often consummated in an atmosphere of intense anger and bitterness, with attention focused on disputes over property, money, and children rather than on motives and feelings. As a consequence, some clergymen and marriage and divorce therapists have suggested a "divorce ceremony" as a helpful way of dealing with anger, guilt, and other negative emotions and of gaining a sense of psychological closure.

Phyllis L. Clay (1980), an ordained minister with the Disciples of Christ, joined with her husband in writing and performing such a divorce ceremony to end their 13-year marriage. It was a difficult task, and tears came more than once. "We remembered our beautiful beginning and mourned the passing of our dreams of the perfect couple" (p. 2). She reported that the ceremony had a healing effect and helped her to say "good-bye" on both the emotional and intellectual levels.

Grollman and Sams (1978) put the need for such a ceremony into poetry (pp. 9–10):

Divorce is a kind of death
In many ways it is worse.
With death, there is a funeral.
There are
flowers,
words of sympathy,
hugs,
talk of happy memories.
Friends and family come together
They grieve with the survivor.
In divorce, one mourns alone.
For divorce there is no public ceremony
No crowd of comforting friends.
There was just a day in court
All business
Legal jargon,
lawyers,
uninvolved strangers.
No comfort
No sympathy
No real feelings allowed.
You want to laugh or scream.

Although a divorce ceremony might help some couples through the emotional trauma of divorce, it is doubtful that such a ceremony will gain widespread popularity. However, the needs described by those who advocate such ceremonies are indeed real, and too few people are equipped to deal with those needs.

From Living Through Your Divorce *by Earl A. Grollman and Marjorie L. Sams. Copyright © 1978 by Earl A. Grollman and Marjorie Sams. Reprinted by permission of Beacon Press.*

Griefwork: Coping with Loss

Right now your major role is to stop the pain. Unfortunately, your mind isn't working too well these days. You can't focus on your job, yourself, or other people. You aren't the fascinating person you used to be. You are, in fact, getting to be a drag. And you know it. . . . So what are you going to do?

—*William Overend (1977, p. 1)*

Unfortunately, there isn't much you can do, for the loss of a loved one or of a relationship sets in motion a train of negative emotions and psychological distress called **grief.** Although the pain of grief is inevitable, it usually follows a prescribed course and diminishes over time. Perhaps there is some consolation in knowing that one is not alone in such pain—there are many other people going through the same experience and being just as devastated. The agony may seem unbearable at first, but with time the pain eases.

The period of mourning required for a person to adjust psychologically to loss is called **griefwork.** In a sense, it is an adjustment to the realization that an important part of ourselves is missing. When a marriage breaks up, the partners no longer think of themselves as "whole." They have identified with their role as husband or wife, as part of a married couple. Without this identity, they do not feel complete. In marital dissolution, the partners lose far more than part of themselves. They also lose the companionship, intimacy, and emotional support of the spouse, and they lose a way of life, the pleasure of the spouse's company, and the dream of a happy marriage. As Dory Beatrice (1979) has expressed it, "Newly single people often need to say good-bye not only to their former spouse but to an entire past" (p. 160).

Through griefwork, the person can try to come to terms with what he or she is actually mourning. It is essentially a healing process that helps the individual to become whole again and to be able to pursue a new life free of the hurts inflicted by loss. Grief can vary greatly in intensity and duration. The key factors appear to be the closeness of the marital relationship and the perceived preventability of the divorce.

Intensity of Grief.   Intense grief involves a mixture of psychological and physiological symptoms that typically include anxiety, depression, anger, guilt, self-recrimination, confusion, inadequacy, loneliness, and hopelessness. The person may experience uncontrollable crying spells, loss of appetite and sexual desire, difficulty in sleeping, and health problems. The person's problem-solving and coping abilities tend to be seriously impaired, and he or she is likely to have difficulty handling everyday decisions. Often the person tends to become dependent, suggestible, compliant, and preoccupied with thoughts of the lost mate.

Individuals who did not feel close to their spouses or who greatly desired divorce are more likely to have a mild grief reaction. They may experience some measure of sadness, loneliness, and irritability, but they do not have the feelings of despair, hopelessness, and severe depression that characterize the intense grief reaction. Such mild grief reactions are also likely to occur with couples whose marriage has deteriorated over a long period. Such couples are "emotionally divorced" long before the actual separation and may have undergone some degree of "anticipatory mourning" while still married.

Duration of Grief.   According to some researchers, grief reactions to divorce usually run their course in a matter of months—typically about 3 months to a year (Caplan, 1981). Other researchers consider such grief reactions to require a minimum of 2 years (Hansen & Shireman, 1986).

In addition, a number of conditions can prolong the grief reaction:

1. More-intense grief reactions tend to last longer.
2. Past losses of a similar nature may prolong the grief reaction. For example, a woman who was severely traumatized by the divorce of her parents when she was a child may have difficulty dealing with her own divorce. Similarly, Hansen and Shireman (1986) cite the case of a woman whose

Joel Gordon

unresolved emotions about a prior divorce were effectively blocking her present grief reaction.

3. Age and length of marriage—particularly for women in their 40s and 50s who have been married for many years—may prolong grief reactions to divorce (Wallerstein, 1985).

4. Efforts to abort the grief reaction—such as denying our feelings, minimizing the importance of the loss, trying to find someone to replace the lost person, or relying heavily on alcohol or drugs—may also prolong the mourning period.

Further complicating matters are reunion fantasies and anniversary reactions, which can continue even after the griefwork is presumably over. **Reunion fantasies** may take various forms. For example, they may occur in dreams of being happily married to the former spouse. Or, we may mistake someone in the supermarket checkout line for our ex-spouse, thus arousing long buried feelings. **Anniversary reactions** are usually inexplicable feelings of depression that tend to occur on an ex-spouse's birthday, on wedding anniversaries, or on holidays such as Christmas and New Year's. In some instances, they may be accompanied by memories of happy events and by feelings of sadness about what "might have been."

Can Griefwork Be Facilitated?   The answer is a guarded Yes. A social-support system such as a postdivorce workshop can help remove feelings of isolation and reassure individuals that their feelings are normal, that they are not going "crazy." The workshop environment may also enable them to express feelings of anger, guilt, depression, and having been betrayed by their loved ones. If griefwork is to be successfully completed, the divorced person must work through such feelings toward the lost spouse. Perhaps of more immediate importance, individuals can, with the help of social supports, gain a perspective on what lies ahead and can realize that despite the terrible pain and distress they will survive and gradually become "whole" persons once again.

Social-support systems can also be helpful in counteracting the advice of well-meaning friends who offer such platitudes as "You're lucky to get out of the marriage," "You were too good for him," "Forget the past and get on with your life," or "The best way to get over one woman is in the arms of another." Hearing these words simply evades the real issues and prolongs the griefwork.

Finally, griefwork can be facilitated if the person is able to deal with the feelings of depression, anger, and guilt that usually complicate the trauma of divorce, to re-evaluate the marriage, and to cope with everyday reality demands. As we shall see, doing so helps the person gain a feeling of laying the past to rest.

Dealing with Depression, Anger, and Guilt

Three interrelated emotions—depression, anger, and guilt—are an inevitable part of personal loss and griefwork. Such feelings reflect the way we perceive our loss and its effect on us. They need to be expressed and worked through if the process of griefwork and rebuilding is to follow its normal course. A fourth emotion that commonly accompanies griefwork is anxiety. Let us focus on the role of each of these emotions in the reconstruction process following divorce.

Depression.   The initial reaction to a serious personal loss is often shock and denial, during which the individual tends to screen out the reality of what has happened. This reaction serves an important function in protecting the person from the full impact of his or her loss. In the face of reality, however, this initial defensive reaction gradually gives way and is typically followed by depression.

Depression is a complex emotion characterized by sadness, self-blame, and repetitive thoughts about the lost relationship and what might have been. Because no way is perceived for regaining the lost mate, the person tends to withdraw into an "emotional cave" to lick his or her wounds. In this sense, depression may have a healing function. However, depression can also be camouflaged by fatigue, insomnia, and lack of zest in living. Such a reaction may be harmful because the depression is not permitted to perform its healing function.

Fortunately, over a period of weeks or months, the depression gradually decreases in intensity—although there may be occasional flare-ups accompanied by uncontrollable crying jags. A social-support group can be particularly helpful in counteracting feelings of hopelessness and providing understanding and reassurance.

Anger.   As Bertha Simos (1979) has noted, "Most people think that grief is primarily sorrow. It comes as a surprise to many, therefore, to find that anger is a prominent aspect of grief" (p. 103). **Anger** is a common response to frustration —to being interfered with. The anger may stem from frustrating or hurtful behavior by the mate during the marriage, or it may be inspired by the divorce— anger at being rejected, at being left alone and deprived, or at having our trust and love betrayed. Intense anger can also be directed at a third person who is perceived as having "stolen" our mate.

Anger directed outward—primarily at the ex-spouse—is considered an essential and healthy part of the mourning process. But some people have difficulty accepting their anger and try to repress it. They may consider such intense feelings of anger toward a loved one to be wrong, or their anger may be so intense they are afraid to express it. Instead, they try to deny its existence, or they turn it against themselves. Either way, the results can be harmful. Anger turned inward produces self-blame and guilt, intensifies depression, and may even lead to suicidal feelings. Repressed anger can produce severe psychological and physiological stress. In short, unexpressed anger can seriously interfere with the successful completion of griefwork—until such anger is expressed and worked through, one is not truly free of the ex-spouse.

Although it is important to express feelings of anger, it is also vitally important not to carry them out in overt action. Fortunately, we come equipped with a built-in "safety valve"—fantasy. Most of us have rich fantasy lives in which we act out our anger and hostility toward those we view as treating us unfairly, including our lost mate as well as anyone standing in the way of reunion. We may imagine shooting, poisoning, drowning, or maiming the person, or just giving him or her a good tongue-lashing. Repeated fantasies of this type tend to reduce our feelings of anger to a point where we can cope with them without getting unduly upset. Eventually, the feelings dissipate as griefwork progresses.

Guilt.   People experience a sense of **guilt** when they violate ethical or moral principles in which they believe—either by doing something they consider wrong or by failing to do something they consider required. **Guilt** is characterized by a feeling of being bad, evil, and unworthy, and is usually intermixed with remorse, self-recrimination, and anxiety. As Gelven (1973) has noted, "Of all the forms of mental suffering, perhaps none is as pervasive or as intense as the ache of guilt" (p. 69).

Guilt may stem from a number of sources related to marriage and divorce, including the following:

1. Knowing that we have hurt another person by taking the initiative in divorce
2. Pinpointing things that we did wrong or things we should have done that might have saved the marriage
3. Knowing that we have caused suffering and unhappiness to our children. The pleas of children for the family to get back together often add to the burden of guilt
4. Realizing that we have not lived up to the vows and commitment to the marriage and thus may be seen as selfish, irresponsible, and a deserter
5. Realizing that we have been deceitful and greedy in the division of property and related matters

Most of us postpone face-to-face confrontations with ourselves until our proverbial backs are against the wall. It is usually a brush with death or a divorce that precipitates life-changing revelations about our needs, or dreams, and our acceptance of mortality. When the rug has been pulled out from under your feet, you can't help but forget the mundane concerns that normally dominate your existence, thoughts about raises and vacations and weekend activities. Only when a major upheaval occurs do the real issues surface: what do you want out of life? What do you need from a partner? What do you intend to do about your shortcomings?
Marilyn Murray Willison

Feelings of guilt are often augmented by feelings of shame. Although these terms are often used interchangeably, guilt refers to self-blame and self-recrimination and shame refers to feelings of humiliation and inferiority. For example, breaking your wedding vows and insisting on a divorce that is deeply hurtful to your partner would elicit guilt; feeling that you could not "hold-on" to your partner would elicit shame.

Some people try to deal with the guilt often associated with divorce by severe self-blame and recrimination; others project the blame on their partners—the divorce is now all "their" fault. However, neither approach is constructive. An honest confession of our guilt concerning the divorce is the most important step in dealing with it. This may take place in a postdivorce workshop in which the person can express his or her feelings in an understanding and nonjudgmental atmosphere.

Important too in overcoming the guilt associated with divorce is the realization that we are all human and sometimes make mistakes. With this understanding, the person is better equipped to realize that the past is now history and that all he or she can really do is to learn and not make the same mistake again.

Anxiety.   Another emotion that commonly complicates griefwork is **anxiety**—a vague feeling of apprehension about possible failures, setbacks, losses, and other poorly defined potential difficulties. Unlike fear, which is a response to a clearly defined danger, anxiety is a reaction to a threat or danger that is not clearly perceived—and may lie in the future rather than the present (Fishman & Sheehan, 1985; Coleman et al., 1987).

A certain amount of anxiety and worry is probably an inevitable by-product of modern living. In divorce, however, such normal anxiety and worry tend to be intensified by feelings of insecurity and inadequacy. These feelings of inadequacy may be augmented by feelings of worthlessness and "unlovableness"—a highly aversive combination.

Fortunately, being a good worrier—anticipating and preparing ourself for problems that lie ahead—can help restore feelings of competence and alleviate anxiety. In a study of constructive worrying, Janis and Mann (1977) concluded that "In order for the work of worrying to be complete, it seems that *each source of stress* must be anticipated and 'worked through' in advance" (p. 394).

Here again, a social-support group can be of service in preparing the individual for the types of problems that are likely to lie ahead and in devising ways of coping with these problems. In this way, at least some of the anxiety can be reduced.

Re-evaluating One's Marriage

Another important component of rebuilding after divorce is re-evaluating the marriage. In essence, we try to sort out what happened in the marriage and to find answers to such questions as:

> How did it come to be dissolved? What were the strengths and weaknesses of the relationship? What was each partner's contribution to the problems? What led him or her to choose this person as a mate originally? What vestiges of their relationships with their parents were brought into the marriage; how did these affect the marriage? What have they learned from this experience? What will they do differently in the future? (Beatrice, 1979, p. 162)

This process of sorting out helps divorced persons become more aware of themselves, their ex-mates, and their marital relationships. For example, they can become more understanding of the beliefs and values—and possible emotional hang-ups—that led them to choose that particular mate. They may realize for the first time how their own wishful thinking, personal immaturity, or lack of needed skills played a role in the failure of the marriage. And, for the first time, they may gain a realistic view of the person they married. In fact, there is a saying to the effect that "To know a person you have to marry him. But to *really* know him, you have to divorce him."

Although exploring the prior marriage relationship is often intensely painful, it can help us to understand the relationship, its strengths and weaknesses, the reasons for its failure, and the ways in which it enriched as well as saddened our life. Such understanding can help us to achieve a feeling of psychological **closure** —of closing the book on this page of our life.

At the same time, such feedback can serve as a basis for reducing the likelihood of making similar mistakes in a future relationship (see Box 13–2).

Unless a person's prior marriage is sorted out and better understood, he or she is quite likely to continue to make the same mistakes in subsequent relationships. As Dory Beatrice (1979) has pointed out, "Therapists are all familiar with the person who leaves an unhappy marriage, only to quickly enter another relationship with similar dysfunctional patterns. . . . The reevaluation process is designed to break up this sort of pattern, and to get people moving in a more satisfying direction" (p. 162). Beatrice cites the example of Mrs. S., a woman seeking therapy after the breakup of her second marriage:

> In both her first and second marriages she had become a battered wife, yet had wanted both marriages to continue, and blamed herself completely for their dissolution. Her history revealed, predictably, a childhood in which she had been frequently beaten by her father. She grew up assuming that she must have done *something* to deserve this treatment, and that it was all her fault. She also had learned to associate affection and attention with abuse. Thus, she sought the same type of relationship in her marriages, highly motivated by crippling guilt and a need for punishment. When one husband left her, she again felt it was her fault and she proceeded, unconsciously, to seek and find exactly the same situation in a second marriage. (p. 162)

Here again, members of a postdivorce workshop, who have been there themselves and have learned from the experience, are able to empathize with newer group members and to help them sort out and work through blocks to exploring and re-evaluating their former marriage.

Avoiding Loneliness Traps

Lonely times can be used for strengthening internal resources and building up resilience.

—*Jeff Meer (1985, p. 32)*

Among the divorced, **loneliness** is a major problem (see Box 13–3). Although most of us have experienced loneliness, it is difficult to describe. According to

BOX 13–2 / IS CREATIVE DIVORCE A MYTH?

Most of us postpone face-to-face confrontations with ourselves until our proverbial backs are against the wall. It is usually a brush with death or a divorce that precipitates life-changing revelations about our needs, or dreams, and our acceptance of mortality. When the rug has been pulled out from under your feet, you can't help but forget the mundane concerns that normally dominate your existence, thoughts about raises and vacations and weekend activities. Only when a major upheaval occurs do the real issues surface: what do you want out of life? What do you need from a partner? What do you intend to do about your shortcomings?
—*Marilyn Murray Willison (1979, p. 6)*

In the mid-1970s, a new concept emerged called "creative divorce." In his popular book of that title, Mel Krantzler (1975) told of his own emotional devastation when, at age 50, after 24 years of marriage, he and his wife divorced. But, despite intense feelings of guilt, loneliness, and helplessness, this self-described "boring, bored, male chauvinist workaholic" was able to survive the experience and use it for personal growth.

In the late 1970s, this theme was popularly pursued with vigor—as reflected in the statement by Marilyn Willison—and presumably reflected a shift from "for better or for worse" to the new ethic of personal growth and self-fulfillment. As Blood and Blood (1979) expressed it, "Marriage should not continue once it turns out to be 'for worse' " (p. 488). Rather than being trapped in the prolonged agony of a bad marriage, the individual was encouraged to terminate the relationship when it appeared that life together was worse than it would be apart. According to this approach, the marital commitment is conditional and continues only so long as the partners' journeys take them in the same direction and they find happiness together. As soon as either partner finds that his or her self-fulfillment and growth lead in a different direction, it is appropriate for the couple to divorce.

Because neither partner is really at "fault" in such a situation, presumably the partners should remain on amicable terms. They may remain friends with each other, with their old friends, and even with new partners. Thus, Ann Juhasz (1979) made a persuasive case for a "severed strand" rather than a "busted bond" view of divorce. Instead of discarding the entire relationship, the partners simply discard the strands that fail to withstand the strain and retain the intact strands of the relationship. According to Juhasz, "This approach is sound from a mental health point of view since it leads to enhancement of self-esteem. In addition, it moves away from the concept of people as things, as disposable objects, easily discarded when out of style or slightly worn. Rather than a mosaic of battered bonds and shattered fragments, strong unsevered strands from past relationships become woven into the fiber of the present, providing hope for the future and the courage to plan and face it" (p. 481). In short, the individual tries to minimize the loss by maintaining a network of relationships from the past that provides for a greater continuity in his or her life, as well as emotional support for coping with present and future problems.

This optimistic view of divorce as a potential growth experience was quite popular in the "Me Decade" of the 1970s. For some persons—usually the initiator who wanted out of the marriage—it may have been growth producing; but for the partner who wanted to maintain the marriage, it was usually a terribly hurtful experience. In any event, it gradually became apparent that there is no "easy" and "creative" way out of divorce for either partner. Even Mel Krantzler (1978) admitted that creative divorce represented an earlier phase of his thinking about the subject. The consequences of divorce are often more traumatic than either partner had bargained for, and they last far longer. In a relationship as intense as marriage, the emotional bonds run deep, and breaking them is neither easy nor painless.

BOX 13-3 / THE NYU LONELINESS SCALE*

For each question below, circle the most appropriate answer. Then add up the numbers that correspond to the answers you chose. Your total scores should fall between 80 (not at all lonely) and 320 (very lonely).

1. When I am completely alone, I feel lonely:
   Almost never (10)
   Occasionally (16)
   About half the time (24)
   Often (32)
   Most of the time (40)

2. How often do you feel lonely?
   Never, or almost never (10)
   Rarely (11)
   Occasionally (17)
   About half the time (23)
   Quite often (29)
   Most of the time (34)
   All the time, or almost all the time (40)

3. When you feel lonely, do you usually feel:
   I never feel lonely (10)
   Slightly lonely (13)
   Somewhat lonely (20)
   Fairly lonely (27)
   Very lonely (33)
   Extremely lonely (40)

4. Compared to people your own age, how lonely do you think you are?
   Much less lonely (10)
   Somewhat less lonely (16)
   About average (24)
   Somewhat lonelier (32)
   Much lonelier (40)

5. I am a lonely person
   Strongly disagree (10)
   Disagree (20)
   Agree (30)
   Strongly agree (40)

6. I always was a lonely person
   Strongly disagree (10)
   Disagree (20)
   Agree (30)
   Strongly agree (40)

7. I always will be a lonely person
   Strongly disagree (10)
   Disagree (20)
   Agree (30)
   Strongly agree (40)

8. Other people think of me as a lonely person
   Strongly disagree (10)
   Disagree (20)
   Agree (30)
   Strongly agree (40)

Loneliness scores on this scale:
Average loneliness among respondents to newspaper surveys was about 170. Rubenstein and Shaver suggest that

   80–132 = least lonely
   133–170 = less lonely than average

   171–206 = more lonely than average
   207–320 = most lonely

* Rubenstein and Shaver, 1982.

psychiatrist Allan Fromme (1965), "True loneliness is a basic sense of unconnectedness with people. It is in essence the denial of satisfaction of a deep need that we all share, the need to form relationships, to become attached, to love and be loved in some way" (p. 448).

BOX 13-4 / ONE WOMAN'S EXPERIENCE OF LONELINESS AFTER DIVORCE

After the divorce was over, I found myself devastated. It wasn't so much being alone, because I had anticipated that. It was the quality of the aloneness that I hadn't expected.

What is this quality like? It's a cold big bed and a diary instead of a friend and lover. I miss the expectance when someone you care about is going to call or come home.
I can spend much time alone—but somehow it's lonelier when I know there'll be no phone ring or knock on the door."

—*Alice Kosner (1979, p. 22)*

A distinction is often made between chronic and situational loneliness. **Chronic loneliness** appears to be common among people who lack the communicative and other interpersonal skills needed to form warm and meaningful relationships with others. **Situational loneliness,** on the other hand, is imposed on the individual—for example, by divorce. The latter form of loneliness is part of the grieving process that the divorced person goes through before he or she is ready for a new relationship (see Box 13-4). Trying to hasten this process by a premature affair or hasty marriage is likely to make matters worse rather than better.

The magnitude of the problem of loneliness among the divorced is indicated by the findings of Hetherington and others (1978), who reported that both the men and women in their study expressed "excruciating" feelings of loneliness, and, in every case, things got steadily worse during the first year following divorce. In his book *The Broken Heart: The Medical Consequences of Loneliness*, James Lynch (1977) describes how the loneliness accompanying divorce—with its ripple effect that extends from the loss of our mate to the loss of friends as well—can be highly stressful and even endanger the person's health.

Unfortunately, there are many people in our society who have never learned to be alone. When loneliness is suddenly thrust on them through loss of a mate, they often react with desperation, depression, and a variety of self-defeating behaviors. Some of these behaviors are both common and well-defined and may be referred to as **loneliness traps.** They include the following:

1. *Viewing loneliness as a weakness.*   Individuals who attribute their loneliness to deficiencies in themselves tend to fall into a state of isolation, inaction, and depression. Our society strongly emphasizes the notions of autonomy and independence, which in turn foster the view that to admit dependence on another person and to feel lonely is a sign of weakness. This view, together with lack of preparation for being alone, tends to be incapacitating (Jones et al., 1982).

2. *"Clinging" and "hanging on."*   Many newly divorced persons, especially those who were highly dependent on their marriages to provide meaning and fulfillment in their lives, seem unable to accept the reality that their marriages are over. As a result, they tend to deny the termination of the relationship and to engage in various maneuvers—such as

pleading, getting sick, or threatening suicide—designed to keep a hold on the partner.

3. *Meaningless sexual episodes.*   Sexual promiscuity could be considered a form of escape behavior, but it also represents a desperate but futile attempt to bolster self-esteem and to find intimacy again as an antidote to pain, distress, and loneliness. But promiscuity is an inadequate cure for a broken heart. In fact, meaningless sexual behavior can be self-destructive and can significantly prolong the period of mourning.

4. *Love and marriage on the rebound.*   Of all the loneliness traps, this is probably the most seductive and least avoided. Until the person has done the required griefwork and is whole again, he or she is in no position to form a meaningful and fulfilling relationship with someone else. Yet, in their desperate efforts to ease the pain, some individuals may convince themselves that they really are in love and may enter into premature and unfortunate love relationships or marriages. As we have noted, the new relationships are likely to duplicate the dysfunctional aspects of the previous ones. In addition, because their self-esteem has usually been eroded by feelings of failure and rejection, they are quite likely to settle for partners who are not up to their usual standards.

How can a divorced person cope with loneliness? Divorce and the loss of our loved partner are likely to precipitate what might be called a "loneliness crisis." So what, if anything, can be done? The first step is to accept the fact that intense feelings of loneliness are to be expected and that they are not a sign of weakness or inferiority. Second is to realize that to have a friend, we must be a friend—to get love, we must give love. As Lynch (1980) pointed out, this idea may sound very elementary, but its validity has been known for thousands of years. The third step is to realize that the pain will decrease in the months ahead; having hope for the future can make it easier to endure the present loneliness. Finally, as we have emphasized repeatedly, there is no substitute for a social-support system. In the supportive atmosphere of a divorce workshop or similar group, we can learn to understand, express, accept, and endure our loneliness.

Realizing that there are some positive steps that can be taken to deal with loneliness not only can help one endure but also can contribute to a sense of personal accomplishment, knowing that we can accept and live with ourself— alone at times if necessary. Thus, loneliness can ultimately prove to be a self-affirming experience.

> *When asked what they fear most, a great majority of single persons answer "loneliness." It is not unusual to feel this way because society as a whole stresses that you seek outside of yourself for entertainment, and totally fails to teach you how to nourish yourself. Being alone is viewed as unacceptable and a fearful situation. Unfortunately, we have become so accustomed to defining ourselves as others see us that many of us have forgotten or never knew that to establish relationships you have to first be an individual in your own right.*
> Betsy Nicholson Callahan

Coping with Reality Demands

Life goes on despite divorce. While doing griefwork and mastering the other basic tasks required to survive divorce, a person must also cope with reality demands— such as new roles and responsibilities, financial problems, and work—and adapt to a changed way of life that usually involves a lower standard of living.

Lack of money poses a major problem for most divorced husbands and wives. Many wives who have not worked before or who are not working at the time of divorce must find employment. They often face low-paying, low-status jobs until they can develop more-marketable skills. As one 42-year-old displaced home-worker expressed it:

Although I once had a part-time job in a cafeteria, I have never worked before outside my home. Now I feel like a helpless animal in a hostile jungle. I simply don't know how to cope. I have no job skills and who would want me anyway at my age? I guess I will have to learn to survive in that jungle out there or face annihilation—at least as a person. But it's discouraging. I don't even know where to start.

For mothers who have functioned primarily as homemakers, divorce introduces a particularly difficult change in roles and responsibilities. As Janet Kohne (1981) has pointed out, "Their role as wife ends and their role as mother is disrupted. . . . In turn they become heads of their families, a role discontinuous with their socialization and marital experience" (p. 230). Such socially unsupported role transitions often pose difficult adjustive demands for the divorced mother, much as they do for the newly unemployed or for older persons forced to retire and live on greatly reduced incomes. In essence, the newly divorced mother is faced with juggling a variety of roles, ranging from employee and single parent to decision maker and authority wielder. And her responsibilities for child-rearing are greatly increased as shared parenting is decreased.

Divorced men also have their share of problems. Because the mother is usually granted custody of the children, the father is confronted with the fact that he will not see them often and that, over time, they will play a less-important role in his life, and he in theirs. Men who think of themselves as self-reliant and competent may find it difficult to adjust to the realization of how dependent they were on their wives for such physical comforts as food, sex, and pleasant living quarters. Often seemingly simple household chores—grocery shopping, cooking, doing the laundry, and housecleaning—prove to be major problems for men who have depended on their wives to perform all these tasks.

A problem that plagues both husbands and wives is change in their social relationships. As we saw in Chapter 12, friends and relatives see the divorced person in a new light, and relationships can change dramatically. And, of course, contact with our in-laws—some of whom may have been our closest friends— usually ceases. In short, divorce results in alienation not only from our spouse but also from many other people we have known socially.

In addition, the ex-partners have to work out a new relationship with each other, deal with the problems of visitation rights, and cope with the feelings aroused by the ex-spouse dating, having sex, and possibly remarrying. As might be expected, anger as well as emotional hurt often complicate the picture. Often, too, it is particularly frightening for people who have been married for some time to face returning to the single world—especially during a period when reality demands are highly stressful, self-esteem is at a low ebb, and uncertainty and fear of failure are intense. The affect that joint custody, rather than maternal or paternal custody, will have on these various problems remains to be determined. But it appears likely that it will intensify some problems and alleviate others.

In the meantime, utilizing available social-support systems can make a difference. If either or both ex-partners are overwhelmed by reality problems, they may have little or no energy available for griefwork, re-evaluation, or identity development. Thus, coping effectively with reality demands is essential for the process of rebuilding to proceed in a normal and healthy way.

In dealing with the basic tasks in surviving divorce, we have taken an active, rather than a passive, role in adjusting to divorce. This approach is based on the assumption that by understanding and actively dealing with these basic tasks, we can influence the course of our recovery. Now, as we turn to the second phase of adjusting to divorce—"becoming whole again"—we shall continue with our active approach.

BECOMING "WHOLE" AGAIN

In her address as the keynote speaker of the ninth annual North American Conference of Separated/Divorced Catholics, Patricia Livingston (1980) described her divorce as "a time of great darkness—a time of alienation. I felt as if I was in a thicket with a marshy undergrowth where everything was in shadow. Behind me was the city . . . but I knew that I couldn't go back, that I was in exile . . ." (p. 1). Despite all the pain and loneliness that a person experiences in divorce, however, Livingston felt that one finds a new meaning that she calls the "gift": "Out of this experience of pain, one has a challenge to grow, to redefine oneself, to come out with more than before" (p. 1). It is in meeting this challenge of growing and establishing a new identity that one is able to become a "whole" person again.

Establishing a New Identity as a Single Person

Establishing a new identity means learning to be a single person again. With divorce, we lose our identity as a husband or wife, as a partner in a marriage relationship, and as a married person. Married friends may have difficulty knowing how to relate to the divorced person, further adding to the loss of identity. As Livingston described it, "You are no longer what you were, but at the same time you're not yet who you will become" (p. 1).

Although part of building a new identity is adjusting to the role of single person, a more-important part is re-evaluating ourself in terms of values, goals, assets, liabilities, and priorities. Even though divorce is an extremely disorganizing process, it also forces considerable reorganization on both individual and family levels. As Betsy Callahan (1979) has put it:

> Divorce is an emotional crisis triggered by a sudden and unexpected loss. The ending of a marriage may jolt you out of the self-defeating "maturity myth" and force you to look at yourself and to analyze where you were and how you got there. Crisis puts you in a position from which you cannot return to what used to be. At the point where one emotionally grasps that the marriage is dead, one has no option but to change. . . . You realize that you are not "home safe" and must develop values and assumptions to live by. (p. 15)

Despite some potential advantages, however, the period of identity building is a time of sadness about the past and anxiety about the future; it is a time when the person feels a pervasive sense of vulnerability. Often the person feels as if he or she is in a sort of void—no longer meaningfully connected with another person, yet not ready for or comfortable with independence.

Facing ourself in terms of what we have been, who we are now, and what we want to make of the future is a scary task for many people, especially if they have been married for several years. Judith Finlayson (1980), in describing her own feelings of initial panic following her unexpected divorce, put it this way: "I was a typical middle-class housewife with a degree in helplessness" (p. 65). She points out that most women are taught to believe that safety and satisfaction lie in dependence on their husbands and on their marriages. The necessity of becoming autonomous and self-directing tends to carry the threat of having to pay the price of giving up close relationships—because many women view the two as incompatible. For Finlayson, the realization that modern marriages are based on mutual respect, the fostering of each other's growth, and a balance between autonomy and togetherness came as a startling but welcome revelation and made her transition to a new identity as a single person easier.

The realization that our marriage is really over and that we may have to establish a new identity and new way of life can be an exciting adventure as well as a traumatic and painful experience. In time, the wounds of divorce heal for most people. Meanwhile, it takes courage to re-evaluate the past, cope with the present, and plan and prepare for the future. As one woman surveyed for *McCalls* magazine said, "The best thing that's happened is that someone I knew only slightly emerged as a good and true friend, a strong but compassionate, funny, articulate

Joel Gordon

person whom I am beginning to enjoy thoroughly. That person is me!" (Kosner, 1979, p. 160).

Repairing Damaged Self-Esteem

I've been married twice, and both times the same thing happened. The relationship started out really romantic, candlelight and roses and great sex to go with our promises of everlasting love. But once we got married and caught up in the day-to-day routine, the romance faded. The marriage became dull. We lost interest in each other. We each began to go our own way, and finally—both times—agreed to divorce. Part of me is now really cynical about romance, but part of me still wants to believe. And part of me is wondering if there is something wrong with me, if maybe I can't make love last because I am just not lovable.

—Nathaniel Brandon (1987, p. 12)

For many people divorce is damaging to self-esteem—particularly if the partner wanted the divorce. Persons who are basically self-confident and have high self-esteem may be shaken but usually regain their self-esteem without undue damage. But for persons whose self-esteem was low to begin with, the divorce may be convincing proof that they are inferior, unworthy, and unlovable.

One result of such damaged self-esteem is that it blocks the person's efforts to become a "whole" person again. For mastering the tasks of dating, sexual encounters, and learning to love again still lie ahead. Unfortunately, the person is likely to idealize and become overly dependent on the first date who bolsters their self-esteem—and thus becomes an easy prey to sexual advances. And in some cases the result is a marriage on the rebound based on the desperate need to feel good about oneself rather than on a love relationship between equals.

As we noted in Chapter 2, enhancing self-esteem is not an easy task. One basic approach, however, is to recognize and correct irrational and self-defeating assumptions about oneself. In his formulation of Rational-Emotive-Therapy, Albert Ellis (1973, 1987) has described a number of such **irrational beliefs** which are common in our society. Among the most important are:

1. A worthy person should be loved and approved by everyone.
2. A worthy person should be competent in everything he or she does.
3. A person fails in an important venture—such as marriage, because of inadequacies on his or her part.

To correct such irrational and self-defeating beliefs, it is essential to realize that beliefs—like actions—have consequences. Until such beliefs are corrected, the consequences are likely to be aversive. In this general context, Ellis also emphasizes the importance of learning what you can from your prior marriage, and then relegating it to the past—to stop blaming yourself, feeling rejected, and dwelling on "what might have been."

If you feel unworthy, undeserving, and unlovable, you are likely to end up with a new partner who confirms your worst suspicions about yourself. On the other hand, if you feel you are a worthy person deserving of respect, love, and happiness, you are much more likely to find a partner who respects and loves you and whom you can respect and love in return.

Dating

They are the dazed and staggering, the newly divorced, returning to a world different from the one they left when they got married.

—*Laura Green (1981, p. 1, Part III)*

Part of establishing a new life and an identity as a single person is attempting to establish new interpersonal relationships. Learning to date again and relate to members of the opposite sex is often a difficult task, especially for persons who have been married for several years and are re-entering a changed world with new rules and routines.

Dating has much to offer the divorced person who is in the process of becoming autonomous and establishing a new identity: (1) Dating provides companionship and helps overcome loneliness; (2) enables the person to meet and compare a variety of people and to explore different ways of relating; (3) gives the opportunity to see how the person feels about sex, intimacy, and different life styles; and (4) gives the person a chance to test and improve social skills and to learn more about himself or herself. If the person is able to relate effectively to others, he or she is provided with needed encouragement and self-affirmation.

In earlier chapters, we explored the nature of encounters and noted that never-married and divorced singles face many of the same problems in meeting people, dating, and sex. But some problems are different for newly divorced persons who are trying to get back "in circulation."

Meeting People.   The newly divorced person often has trouble meeting people, or at least meeting people he or she considers attractive and possibly eligible as potential mates. There are a number of formalized ways available for people to meet. For example, there are many organized groups for singles, such as Parents Without Partners and singles clubs for professional people. Some people use newspaper or magazine ads to contact potential dates, and some avail themselves of computer videotape-dating services.

People usually have some idea of the type of person they want to meet. Unfortunately, their mental images or fantasies tend to be based on high standards—much as they were in their premarital days. They want someone who is attractive, intelligent, dependable, affectionate, supportive, productive, and financially well-off. Such expectations often pose a problem for the person whose previous spouse had many of these qualities because such spouses are often difficult to replace. In short, really good "merchandise" is often hard to find in the interpersonal marketplace and usually doesn't remain available very long.

In addition, the competition for attractive mates is often stiff. Take the example of George. He had been dating and having sex with Laura—an attractive 30-year-old divorcée with two children—for more than 6 months but told her he "wasn't the marrying type." One weekend, he went to a convention in Las Vegas, and while he was gone Laura accepted a date from another man. At the convention, George had a chance to do some thinking and realized that he was in love with Laura and wanted to marry her. But, when he returned, it was too late. The other man proved to be more competition than George could handle, even though he pleaded his case and asked for another chance. Thus, timing and decisiveness can be important considerations in the marriage market.

Fear of Dating.   Many newly divorced persons suffer from damaged self-esteem and uncertainty and retreat into a self-imposed exile. After a few months, however, loneliness—often combined with pressure from well-meaning friends—usually drives them into fearful and often panic-stricken dating. They are so afraid because dating carries with it the possibility of further rejection. In fact, fear of rejection is considered to be the greatest barrier to successful dating (Callahan, 1979). Furthermore, the person often feels old and not attractive enough to interest anyone really desirable. He or she worries about somehow mismanaging the evening, looking foolish, or being exploited for money or sex.

For the person who has been married several years, dating is a particularly difficult problem. As Maxine Schnall (1979) has reported, "Over and over again I hear women and men in the postdivorce and widowhood period describing themselves as wretchedly awkward and self-conscious in dating situations, confused about their values and disturbed by a lot of the same old sexual conflicts they experienced in their premarital dating days" (p. 60). Admittedly, the rules of the dating game have undergone considerable changes in the 7–10 years since the person previously dated. Individuals who have been married for several years simply don't relate to the opposite sex the same way they did in their youth. Some men, for example, find it difficult to cope with women who aggressively ask them for dates or sex.

It is helpful to realize, however, that most divorced people are insecure about the dating game; it is also reassuring to discover how many other people in the singles world are also newly divorced. Except for the very young, most people they meet will have been married and may still be experiencing the pain of marital dissolution. They often find that they share a common bond that makes for mutual understanding and compassion. It also helps them to see dating partners as unique people like themselves, rather than as sex objects or as potential adversaries in the dating game.

Hazards in Dating Too Soon.   In the wake of divorce, many men and women try too soon and too desperately to fill the void left by their departed spouses. Regardless of who initiated the divorce, both partners usually experience a sense of failure in an important enterprise, a lowering of self-esteem, and a feeling of being incomplete. Unfortunately, however, as Terry Levy and Wendy Joffe (1978) have noted, "There is a tendency to impulsively seek intimate relationships in order to avoid the pain of mourning the dead relationship and the anxiety of being alone" (p. 269). Such premature dating—seeing others while still feeling like half of a team that has broken up—is considered the most anxiety-arousing aspect of dating. The person may feel he or she has very little to offer and may wonder, "What am I doing here?"

Although time is needed for mourning the death of a relationship and rebuilding self-esteem and a new identity, this fact often goes unrecognized by the newly divorced individual. This is especially true for people who feel abandoned and devalued and have a desperate need to find another partner to fill the void *now*. But, until they have worked through their emotional ties to their former spouses, evaluated the former marriage, and worked on establishing a new identity as a single person, they are likely to find dating confusing, anxiety arousing, and destructive.

How much time does this take? It depends on the person, the closeness of the former relationship, who took the initiative in the divorce, whether a third person

People supposedly go places and try and broaden their social contacts . . . but they're stuck in their old patterns. They wait to be approached and then are disappointed in those who approach them. Or they do the approaching but approach only those whom they don't really want—the "safe" ones who won't reject them.

Eunice Miller

BOX 13–5 / WHAT WENT WRONG?

The pitfalls of the sexual scene for divorced persons are illustrated by the following story:

Barbara is 28 and had been married for 8 years. A month after her divorce, several women friends persuaded her to go out on the town to celebrate her new freedom. A man named Michael asked her to dance.

"We had so much in common. He'd been divorced three years and had a six-year-old son with almost the same name as my daughter," she writes. "He was charming, attractive and said all the right things. He had been in a car accident the night before and was hurting both physically and emotionally, and my nurturing side really took over.

"I wanted to hold him and take all his pain away and at the same time have his touch take some of my pain away. The way he held my face when we kissed the first time, the gentleness and feeling in his hands overwhelmed me. Was it all an act, a game to get me to his apartment?

"All night he reached out to make sure I was still there; I had never felt such tenderness from a man. Morning came. We talked, he asked for my phone number and got it. I asked for nothing—and got that. It's been two weeks, and still no word from my shining knight."

Barbara feels destroyed. "Wasn't I good enough, smart enough, attractive enough to rate a phone call and a second try? You can't imagine the number of sleepless nights I've spent wondering why. Maybe after eight years of being grounded, my first flight was bound to be a little shaky, but now I find that most single women have had experiences like this" (Sanderson, 1980, p. 12).

was involved, and the severity of reality demands. It also depends, in part, on the understanding and support of the person we date. The latter is particularly important for persons with children because they become part of the dating equation. Despite such complications, however, many men and women re-enter the singles scene within 3–6 months after their separation. Others require a year or perhaps considerably longer.

Dealing with Sexual Encounters

As we noted in our discussion of the singles life, many men look on divorced women as easy sexual marks; (see Box 13–5) and, in an effort to ward off feelings of rejection and depression, many divorced women may behave in ways that encourage this viewpoint (Scarf, 1980; Wallerstein, 1985). On the other hand, many divorced women complain of difficulty in having a pleasant evening with a date without a later hassle over going to bed with him.

However, this picture is not entirely one-sided. Many women on the singles hunting ground are quite aggressive in their sexual behavior. This may prove to be a difficult problem for a newly divorced man whose last sexual encounter was with his ex-wife. Often such men are uncertain as to how to proceed and are anxious about impotence and failure to perform satisfactorily. Although they may have had fantasies about how exciting it will be when they are single again—especially if they took the initiative in obtaining the divorce—reality may not be as comfortable or appealing as their fantasies.

In addition, divorced parents who start an active dating and sex life shortly after their separation may disturb the children. This appears to be particularly true for women in our society. The children may see the new man as a threat if they perceive him as displacing the departed parent; they may feel that their mother is being disloyal to their father; or they may feel jealous of the newcomer's place in their mother's affections (Franke et al., 1980; Rothstein, 1986). In divorce therapy involving a woman and her children, the question often arises "How are we supposed to act when Mom brings her bed-partner home?"

However, most children adjust well over a period of time, especially if they feel included in the relationship. Lynda Bird Franke (1980) quoted one 9-year-old girl who told her mother, "I'd be furious with you if you had a secret lover we didn't know about. But Larry is a friend to all of us" (p. 62). Often the children seem to be less disturbed by their mother's sexual activity than the parent is. "I caught one guy sneaking out of the house at 5 A.M.," said one 12-year old boy in disgust. "Why didn't he want to have breakfast with me?" (p. 62). In fact, many children feel abandoned by the noncustodial parent and hope even for the appearance of a normal family. Perhaps the greatest danger to the children is the temporary neglect when parents start dating and get enmeshed in the social whirl.

In summary, there are no well-established rules for divorced persons to follow in their sexual behavior. Rather, it is a matter of clarifying sexual needs, feelings, and values—and developing a sexual policy that is right for the individual. Of course, the sexual policy must address the problem of casual sex and not be dictated by fear of rejection if one chooses to say "No." Lurking in the background is the ever-present shadow of AIDS.

Learning to Love Again

Learning to love again is the final task in surviving divorce and rebuilding. While this sounds like an easy task, it isn't. For one thing, the person must be free of the influence of the ex-partner in terms of romantic attraction or resentment and hate. This does not preclude a positive but "non-involved" relationship. Bohannan (1971) has referred to this distancing from one's ex-mate as a "psychic divorce."

A second factor is having an accurate view of one's role in the breakup of the prior marriage. Putting the blame on your partner or yourself and having an inaccurate view of your respective roles in the dissolution of the marriage can prevent a new relationship from getting off the ground—or to crash if it does. A third factor is having sufficient self-esteem to feel worthy of love, respect, and happiness. For in this way the person is likely to choose someone whom they can love, admire, and respect in return. Here our early discussion of rebuilding damaged self-esteem is directly applicable.

Finally, the person must learn to trust someone again; after being hurt, this requires courage. In fact, some people are so scorched by divorce that they find it difficult or impossible to trust a member of the opposite sex ever again. Although they may not want to be alone, they may limit involvements to superficial relationships. If a relationship appears to be getting too close, they may remove the threat and anxiety by doing or saying something that sabotages the relationship.

In persons suffering less-severe damage, an intimate relationship may be permitted to become only so close and no closer. This relationship might even extend to cohabitation but not to marriage, which is still too threatening. In a sense, such people seem to be experimenting with intimacy once again but are afraid to let things go too far. Cohabitation probably contributes greatly to reducing fears and preparing the person for remarriage. Hanna and Knaub (1981) found, for example, that remarried couples who had cohabitated judged their remarriages to be more successful than those who had not.

Again, we are confronted with a key paradox of love—that of needing and wanting a loving relationship but at the same time being terribly vulnerable to emotional hurt. Perhaps the point to realize is that failure in one marriage does not make the dream of a happy marriage less valued or necessarily less attainable. Having survived a divorce and completed the tasks of rebuilding, the person is now much better equipped to make the dream of romantic love come true. The task in "starting over" is to move from dependence through independence to *inter*dependence—the highest form of intimate relationship.

REMARRIAGE

Arrival at the state of remarriage involves a number of successive transitions, which may have progressed from first marriage, to separation, to one-parent household, a courting period, living together without marriage, and finally to remarriage and the structuring of a new family. This process requires a redefinition of individual identity and involves major changes in family structure and function.

Messinger, Walker, and Freeman

But one lives and loves, suffers and forgets, and begins again—perhaps even thinking that this time, this new time, is to be permanent.

—*Clark E. Moustakas (1961, p. 264)*

During the emotional turmoil of divorce, remarriage may not seem a realistic possibility. But, as we noted in Chapter 1, five out of six divorced men and four out of five divorced women do remarry. About 80 percent of divorced people remarry within 4 years—the average time elapsing between divorce and remarriage being about 2 years and decreasing (Norton & Moorman, 1987). However, about one in five divorced persons remarry within the first year following divorce, often to someone with whom they had established a relationship prior to their divorce. About 60 percent or more of divorced people have children.

Remarriage is not a new event in our society. But, in the early 1900s, almost all remarriages were of widowed persons. As the divorce rate climbed during the 1950s and beyond, so has the incidence of remarriages. By 1985, over 40 percent of all remarriages involved a "repeat performance" by one or both partners (Norton & Moorman, 1987). If the remarriage doesn't work—and unfortunately over half do not—the partners will divorce and probably try again and perhaps again. In 1986, an estimated 3 million people in the United States had been divorced at least twice.

Do these statistics indicate that remarriage is a high-risk venture compared to first marriages? Do they indicate that people remarry for the wrong reasons? Do they mean that people who have been divorced are "trigger happy" and get divorced again at the first sign of trouble? Do they indicate that remarriages are less happy than first marriages? In this section, we shall attempt to answer these and other questions about remarriage, which is a topic that is sadly neglected in social-science research but affects the lives of millions of Americans.

Why and When People Remarry

How is it that individuals so recently liberated from the bonds of matrimonial misfortune become willing recruits for another try?

—*Frank Furstenberg (1980, p. 443)*

Samuel Johnson, 18th century English writer and critic, once referred to remarriage as the "triumph of hope over experience." In fact, one of the great paradoxes of remarriage is that men and women who experienced a painful and traumatic divorce see no inconsistency in remarrying to reduce the loneliness and distress of their single status. Indeed, they often remarry before the wounds of the prior marriage are fully healed.

Both personal needs and societal pressures tend to steer divorced persons toward remarriage. A young divorced mother of three with a lack of job skills may desire to remarry for a variety of reasons—to alleviate her financial situation; to provide her children with a father; and to receive companionship, sexual intimacy, and emotional support. Often, too, divorced persons feel awkward around their married friends. In addition, divorced men, as well as women, may find themselves "struggling" to combine homemaking, child-rearing, and good-provider roles. Factors such as these—combined with many of the reasons they married in the first place—lead most divorced persons to remarry.

Thus, it is not surprising that the majority of divorced men and women find new mates they consider right for them and remarry. Most divorced men remarry in their late 30s; most divorced women remarry in their early 30s. However, there are divorced people who remarry in their early 20s or even before and also those who remarry in the 60s and later. For widowed persons, the average age of remarriage is considerably higher than for divorced persons. This is to be expected because widowhood usually takes place at a later age than divorce.

Well-educated women with good incomes are more likely to delay remarriage or not to remarry at all. Apparently, career satisfaction and independence, supplemented in some cases by cohabitation or love affairs, seem to meet their needs. On the other hand, women with less education and income often hasten to remarry —possibly because they are less employable as well as economically disadvantaged and remarriage is more of a financial necessity for them (Spanier & Glick, 1980; Glick & Lin, 1986).

Although the interval from divorce to remarriage may vary considerably, only a minority of individuals voluntarily substitute cohabitation, love affairs, or a singles life style for remarriage. In short, divorced persons belong in the ranks of those who believe in marriage. Although their prior marriage relationship may not have worked out, few people become disillusioned with the ideal of love and marriage.

Factors in Selecting a New Mate

For many, marriage has provided a sort of training school that has enabled them to gain experience and understanding they did not get in formal schooling or in real life prior to marriage. Particularly important is the improved understanding—of ourself, of other people, and of close relationships—that in turn influences the selection of a new mate.

People for whom divorce has been highly traumatic usually emerge from emotional isolation hesitantly, step by step. As they gradually make contact and get reinvolved with others, their desire to remarry eventually surfaces. Although their view of marriage may still be idealistic, they now realize that romantic love does not "conquer all." In short, individuals are more realistic the second time around and definitely do not want to become "two-time losers." Here, as we discussed in Chapter 3, the concept of **awareness**—of seeing things the way they are—appears of definite value: As a divorced person, you must gain a realistic view of yourself, of your proposed mate, and of the potential relationship.

A Realistic View of Yourself.   Included here are an evaluation of your goals and motives, your assets and liabilities, and your "market value." It also includes answers to many questions. "Have the wounds from your divorce healed?" "Do you really understand your own contribution to the failure of your previous marriage?" "Are you actually 'ready' to make a second attempt at marriage?" As one young man told Hunt and Hunt (1977):

> I'm working very hard on my own contributions to the failure of my marriage. It's not easy to grow up, at my age, but I'm trying to—and succeeding. I'll get married again when I'm more mature and emotionally skillful. I wanted and expected too much from my wife. Now I believe that if I can take full responsibility for myself and be more realistic about what I expect another can do for me, my relationships will be happier. (p. 106)

Often there are certain questions that divorced persons may ask themselves, such as:

1. Do I continually make comparisons between a prospective mate and my previous spouse?
2. Do I feel in a rush to get into this marriage in order to get the other one completely out of my mind?
3. Do I feel that marrying this person will prove to my ex-spouse that I can attract someone better?
4. Do I lack enthusiasm about getting married but feel the children need a mother or father and a complete family?
5. Do I feel reluctant to talk freely with this person about sex, money, values, goals, and things he or she does that upset me?

If the answer to any of the questions is Yes, the best advice is: Don't repeat "I do."

Checking Out the Other Person.   Often in first marriages, people tend to marry illusions rather than real people. Their vision is distorted by romantically tinted lenses. It is hoped that the second time around they will be more realistic.

What does being more realistic involve? It means checking out the person's background, beliefs, goals, values, interests, habits, emotional hangups, problem behaviors (excessive drinking, drug abuse, or violence), sex-role behavior, and expectations about marriage. It also involves, as Jean Baer (1972) has pointed out in her book on how to live happily with a man who has been married before, observing his behavior in a variety of situations, observing how he handles himself under tension and when things don't go quite the way he wants them to, and observing the kind of people he associates with, admires, or uses as role models. It means being alert to deceit or manipulation in his dealings with other people and with yourself. And it involves noting any discrepancy between what he says and what he does—in the final analysis, actions speak louder than words. If the person has been married before, it is wise to check out—insofar as possible—the nature of the marriage relationship, the reasons for its failure, who initiated the divorce, how much the person was emotionally damaged by the divorce, the way he now perceives his previous marriage, and whether he has recovered from the emotional trauma.

Finally, being realistic involves checking out the personality "fit" between yourself and the potential partner. Are there sufficient interests, values, and goals in common? Is he easy to communicate with? Is he willing to negotiate and make compromises in resolving disagreements and conflicts? Is he supportive of your personal growth as well as his own? In short, would he rate as a low-, medium-, or high-risk person in relation to marriage? (For a man, this same evaluation would apply to a previously married woman.)

Evaluating the Potential Relationship.   What kind of marriage relationship is realistically possible with this other person? What are each partner's needs, desires, and expectations with respect to the relationship? Are both partners' expectations realistic? Are both willing and able to make a deep commitment to the new marriage and to make every effort to maintain and enrich it?

Often a key consideration is the tendency for a woman who played the traditional dependent wife role in her former marriage to want a more-egalitarian relationship than she had before. Fortunately, more and more men who had played a traditional male role in their former marriages also want a more-egalitarian marriage with more maturity, sharing, and companionship. As one middle-aged accountant said, "I don't really need a housekeeper. I need a companion and friend." In their study of the transition from divorce to remarriage in Centre County, Pennsylvania, Graham Spanier and Frank Furstenberg (1982) have found that remarried couples reported greater flexibility in handling household tasks, more shared decision making, and less adherence to strictly defined sex-roles.

The second-time-around marital expectations may vary greatly, depending on the age, economic situation, previous marriage, and so on of the persons involved. For example, a woman with children who is desperately struggling to get by may yearn for a strong, loving man who will cope with the financial problems and be a good stepfather. Similarly, an older woman faced with a restricted marriage market may be interested in and accepting of men who are quite different from her in terms of education, cultural background, and economic status. She may also consider a man who is much younger than she is. In earlier years, she probably would not have considered such men as possible mates. But, faced with reality, her expectations may change. (Seskin, 1985).

Most of the same factors that influenced the choice of your first mate also operate with your second, but there appear to be other factors involved as well, in terms of increased awareness and understanding and more-realistic expectations. Although some people do make the same mistake again and again, following a pattern of "I take thee . . . and thee . . . and thee . . . ," many other people do

'You're kidding!'
'Have you lost your mind?'
Those were my friends' reactions when I announced my plans to remarry. The fact that my fiancée had five kids still at home must have concerned them. . . . I wondered if they knew something I didn't know.
Allan Schwartz
(1986, p. 22)

learn from experience and make wiser and more-realistic decisions the second time around.

Is Remarriage Really Different?

In our discussion of evaluating the potential relationship in a new marriage, we have in part answered this question. But remarriage is different in other ways, too.

For one thing, a divorced person not only is older and more experienced but also is likely to be quite different in many respects than he or she was when first married. The experience of marriage and the trauma of divorce inevitably change a person in many ways—some minor and some major. Among these changes are likely to be somewhat different goals and expectations with respect to marriage. Furthermore, the person is likely to be changed by the emotional scars carried over from the marriage and divorce. Second, the new spouse is inevitably different in many ways from the first spouse. Third, the marriage relationship built with this new person will inevitably be different from the first marriage relationship. The differences may be desirable or undesirable, and they lead to new experiences and adjustive demands. As Frank Furstenberg (1980) has expressed it, "To some degree, the clock is reset when the second marriage begins" (p. 450).

There are many other differences that make remarriage different from the prior marriage. Couples who are remarrying are somewhat less likely to have a formal engagement and more likely to cohabit as a means of testing their compatibility. Some, but not all, are likely to have a less-formal wedding. If children are involved, a whole new host of adjustive demands is created. If both partners have children, there is the problem of "blending" the two single-parent families. This says nothing of problems concerning visitation privileges of ex-spouses, relating to both

"Please go away, dear. I know we had some good years, but I'm married to Number Two now."
Drawing by Weber; © 1982 The New Yorker Magazine, Inc.

BOX 13–6 / THE TRANSITION FROM MARRIAGE TO REMARRIAGE

Essentially, there are five stages in the transition from marriage to remarriage. A successful transition depends on the mastery of key tasks at each stage as well as the person's ability to deal with new, and perhaps unexpected, conflicts and challenges.

1. *Surviving divorce and becoming a whole person again.* For the majority of divorced women, this also involves establishing a single-parent family.
2. *"Getting back into circulation."* This involves dating and dealing with sexual encounters, and eventually learning to love again.
3. A *period of courting.* This involves establishing an intimate relationship with a new partner. Often it also involves a period of cohabitation.
4. *Making plans for remarriage.* This involves decisions concerning the wedding, a possible honeymoon, agreeing on a place to live, and related problems.
5. *Remarriage.* This requires a change in identity from a divorced single to a remarried person, adjusting to a new mate, and often structuring a stepfamily system.

As Mary Whiteside (1982) has pointed out, each stage can be difficult and contains the potential for conflict, disorganization, and failure. Success depends not only on mastering the tasks associated with each stage but also on "the continued evolution of the family structure in the face of new developmental challenges" (p. 68).

ex-spouses, or functioning as a step-parent. Finally, there is the problem of adjusting to new in-laws and to the friends of the new spouse.

How Difficult Is the Transition to Remarriage?

If we view being a divorced single person as a way station rather than a final destination, then the question arises as to why so little attention has been given to the tasks essential for making the transition from being a divorced single person to being a remarried one (see Box 13–6). Ann Goetting (1982) has identified six stations of remarriage:

1. *Emotional remarriage*—establishing a bond of attraction, trust, and commitment with a new partner.
2. *Psychic remarriage*—resuming a life style in which each partner is again viewed as a member of a partnership.
3. *Community remarriage*—re-entering the world of couples from the world of divorced singles.
4. *Parental remarriage*—relating to the children of the new spouse.
5. *Economic remarriage*—re-establishing a marital household as an economic unit.

6. *Legal remarriage*—dealing with legal implications of remarriage for alimony, child support, and other legal arrangements made in connection with divorce.

The difficulty of these tasks depends on the persons involved and on their life situations. For example, if one partner is still struggling with the emotional trauma of the prior divorce, the task of emotional remarriage may be more difficult. In addition, economic remarriage may be complicated by children. The important thing is to anticipate these tasks and be prepared to deal with them.

A successful remarriage inevitably involves undoing or refashioning many of the patterns and notions developed during the previous marriage. This in turn raises a number of questions. What kinds of experiences in the first marriage are more likely to influence the second one for better or for worse? What are the effects of age and experience on the divorced person's attitudes toward remarriage? How can changes in marital and parental roles best be accomplished? What influences do emotional scars exert on the remarriage, and what is the best way to deal with such negative influences? Unfortunately, we do not yet have adequate answers to these questions. But a partial answer might include being sure that you are not marrying on the rebound, that you are free of emotional entanglement with your ex-spouse, and that you have learned some constructive lessons from your prior marriage—including how to avoid the common pitfalls in marriage. If your proposed mate has been married before, these conditions would also apply to him or her.

Although remarriage is different from first marriage in many ways, it is far from being an alien experience for someone who has been married before.

How Happy and How Stable Are Remarriages?

Do divorced persons choose better the second time around? Have they learned valuable lessons from their prior marriage? Are they likely to resort to divorce again as a solution to marital problems?

Here, again, research is scanty and often contradictory. Using data from a national survey, Helen Weingarten (1980) concluded that the remarried appear similar to first-marrieds in current well-being and marital adjustment. Using similar data, Norval Glenn (1981) stated, "These findings indicate remarkably small long-term negative effects of marital failure on the well-being of persons who remarry after divorce" (p. 61). On the other hand, the "global," or overall life, happiness of remarried women appears to be less than that of either first-married women or remarried men (Cherlin, 1981). In remarriages that involve children, the happiness of the step-parent—whether husband or wife—tends to be impaired (White & Booth, 1985). Later in this section, we shall comment on the role of children in remarriages and on their effect on marital happiness.

We cannot conclude much about the happiness of remarriages. Some are happy; some are unhappy. But, in general, it would appear that there are no marked differences in the happiness of first marriages and remarriages—with the possible exception of remarriages in which stepchildren are involved. This brings us to the matter of the stability of remarriages. Here, the findings are less positive. About 60 percent of all remarriages fail, and the average length of remarriages is only 5 years. When children are involved, as many as 75 percent end in divorce (White & Booth, 1985; *U.S. News & World Report*, 1986/1987; Lagoni & Cook, 1985; Stone, 1986). As Glick (1980) has suggested, perhaps a first divorce provides information about how to get a second one, and, hence, makes a second divorce more likely. As he notes, however, this may apply to women in remarriages rather than to men.

Finally, marriages in which one or both spouses have had multiple prior divorces are probably considerably less stable than intact first marriages or remarriages in which one or both spouses have only had one prior marriage. But there are many exceptions, and each remarriage—in terms of happiness and stability—has to be evaluated on its own merits.

PROBLEMS IN REMARRIAGES AND STEPFAMILIES

Most of the problems we dealt with in marriage—such as money, sex, and emotional leftovers—also play key roles in remarriage. Other problems in marriage—such as extramarital affairs and ineffective communication—tend to be replaced in remarriage by problems involving step-parent–stepchild relationships and the structure of the stepfamily system.

At the risk of some repetition, we shall briefly review several problems common to marriage and remarriage, but in the context of remarriage. Then we shall focus on problems associated with step-parents, stepchildren, and stepfamilies.

Money and Sex

Although money and sex are common and important problems in both marriage and remarriage, they take on a somewhat "different look" in remarriage.

Money.   In remarriage, financial problems often stem from first marriages. For example, the husband may have to make child-support payments to his ex-wife, or the new wife's ex-husband may have stopped making alimony and child-support payments when she remarried. Such problems can create an acute financial situation for the couple and considerably reduce their standard of living. In their detailed study of remarried persons in eight Western states, Albrecht and others (1983) found financial difficulties to be an overwhelming problem in many remarriage situations.

Money problems can also take more-subtle forms. The wife may feel guilty about the financial burden her children place on her new husband, or she may resent his paying out so much of his income to his ex-wife. Similarly, the new husband may feel guilty because he is a "poor provider" for his new family, or he may resent supporting "someone else's" children. As the children grow older and need more money for education and other matters, the allocation of limited funds can pose a major problem. For example, the stepfather may be primarily concerned about his own children, while the stepmother is primarily concerned about hers.

Another potential money problem arises if both partners have lived independently for a while and don't like the idea of pooling their resources with another person. Such couples may need to work out an agreement for paying mutual bills, keeping bank accounts, and dealing with other financial matters.

It is interesting to note that divorce and remarriage have different effects on the financial status of both men and women. Randal Day and Stephan Bahr (1986) undertook an intensive 10-year study of couples who (1) remained married, (2) divorced and did not remarry, or (3) divorced and remarried during this period. These researchers found that women had a substantial decrease in income following divorce and men had a substantial increase. On the other hand, remarriage increased the per-capita family income of women and reduced the per-capita income of men.

Sex.   In his survey of divorced and remarried persons, Albrecht (1979, 1983) found that sex ranked third among the problems in remarriages, whereas it ranked seventh among problems in first marriages terminated by divorce.

Sex problems often occur in remarriages, because the marital partners bring quite different backgrounds and expectations about sexual activities to their remarriage. For partners whose previous marriage lasted for several years, sexual convictions and practices may have become largely habitual; in essence, their sexual practices have become for them the "right way" to do things. If this "right way" conflicts with the partner's views and prior experiences, it may create a serious problem—especially if the partners have not learned to communicate about sexual matters.

As with money problems, sex problems can take a more-subtle form in remarriage. For example, in dealing with the rivalry between her children and new spouse for attention and affection, the wife may reduce the frequency of sex; or she may be angry because her husband is lavishing too much time and attention on his children and not on her. Reducing sex is one way of showing her anger and punishing him. Similarly, a father may feel guilty about the pain he has caused his children—particularly a teenage daughter—by remarrying. As a result, he may expend a disproportionate amount of time and affection on his children at the expense of his wife—including a reduction in sex.

Interestingly enough, infidelity—a key problem in the breakup of first marriages—is usually not a problem in remarriages. Albrecht found that only 5 out of 369 persons mentioned it as a problem in their remarriage.

Emotional Leftovers—Unfinished Business

Remarriage does not end or, "bury," the first marriage. Inevitably, elements of the previous marriage and divorce carry over into the remarriage, as we noted in the case of sexual patterns. Although such "leftovers" are usually thought of as being negative, there may also be positive "ghosts" from the past that influence the present. For example, the husband may remember unnecessary miscommunications that helped to destroy his first marriage and may resolve to maintain open and effective channels of communication in the new marriage; or the wife may have learned that her extravagance played a major role in the failure of her first marriage and may make a concerted effort to avoid this problem in her second marriage.

On the other hand, if the divorced person has not completed his or her griefwork, places the entire blame for the breakup of the marriage on the ex-spouse, and carries over feelings of resentment and hate, the "ghosts" that haunt the new marriage will be negative ones. In Chapter 12, we noted that in her followup of the California Children of Divorce Project, Judith Wallerstein (1985) found that about 40 percent of the women and a smaller but significant number of men remained intensely angry at their former mates 10 years after the divorce. How these feelings affected their remarriages—most of the men and women had remarried during this time—is not known. But it seems unlikely that the influence was a constructive one. In fact, under such conditions the new spouse is often used to "dump" feelings on.

Of course, most remarried persons bring some unfinished business to their new marriage, and part of building the new marital relationship involves working through these emotional leftovers. However, if this unfinished business dominates the new marriage, it will prove destructive. Here, an old saying seems particularly applicable, "For a good second marriage, end the first."

Step-parent–Stepchild Relationships

To be a success at stepparenting—as in any major career—one needs knowledge, preparation, and dedication. With all that, success with a second family is a game of craps at best. There simply are no guarantees.

—*Allan Schwartz (1986, p. 23)*

We often think of remarriage as simply a matter of getting out of one marriage and into another. For some young divorced persons, this picture may be essentially accurate; but for the great majority of persons who remarry, it is not (see Box 13–7). In more than 60 percent of all remarriages, one partner has custody of one or more children under 18, and another 20 percent are noncustodial parents (Glick, 1980; Glick & Lin, 1986; Norton & Moorman, 1987). Thus, a distinct minority of remarriages are child-free.

As a result, the partners in remarriage are confronted not only with the usual adjustive problems of marriage and parenthood but also with some additional problems that are unique to stepfamilies. Prominent among the latter is the problem of step-parent–stepchild relationships. This problem may vary somewhat in nature and difficulty, depending on the age and sex of the persons involved. A young woman who marries a much older man, for example, may have to relate to live-in stepchildren who are almost as old—or perhaps older—than she is. In some cases, it is easier for the stepfather than the stepmother, particularly if the children view him as a knight in armor who has come to rescue a struggling family. But as Allan Schwartz (1986) has pointed out, he is much more likely to be viewed as the "resident intruder." In fact, parenting stepchildren has been called "one of the most difficult of all human assignments" (White & Booth, 1985).

Step-parenting is not only a difficult but also a highly complex task about which we know very little (see Box 13–8). In short, there are no adequate guidelines for being a good step-parent. Consequently, it would seem most useful here to focus on some of the problems that seem inherent to step-parent–stepchild relationships. From the child's viewpoint, for example, the parent's marriage creates some very real problems. To summarize a few of them:

BOX 13-7 / DOES HAVING CHILDREN AFFECT THE CHANCES FOR REMARRIAGE?

What effect do children have on a divorcée's chances for remarriage? Helen Koo and C. M. Suchindran (1980) found that for women under 25, being childless increased the chances of remarriage; For women aged 25–34, children had no effect on the incidence of remarriage; and for women over 35, being childless actually decreased the prospects for remarriage.

As the investigators point out, these statistics need to be interpreted with caution. For example, childless women over 35 may have careers that are personally and financially rewarding and, thus, feel less need to remarry or may be highly selective in remarrying. In contrast, a young woman who works and is a single parent may find that her children place such heavy demands on her time that it is difficult for her to re-enter the marriage market. This may account for the finding that among women who were divorced before age 30, there was a tendency for the chances of remarriage to decrease as the number of children increased (Glick, 1980; Glick & Lin, 1986).

In any event, for women divorced before age 30, the presence of young children tended to affect both the rate and the timing of remarriage. However, it may be emphasized that there are several factors—including a woman's attractiveness—that may be more important than the presence of children in determining the rate and timing of remarriage.

1. The child is confronted with sharing his or her parent with the new spouse. For the boy who has taken a highly protective and possessive attitude toward his divorced mother, this problem may be particularly difficult.

2. The child may fear putting down roots in the new family for fear it, too, will end in divorce—which is a realistic consideration.

3. The child is likely to have to adjust to different ways of doing things from those to which he or she is accustomed. The child is also likely to resent being disciplined by the step-parent for behavior that his or her own parent had tolerated.

4. The child may feel guilty if he or she likes the step-parent because of feeling disloyal to the noncustodial parent who may still be in the picture via visitation rights.

5. The child has to give up the dream of his or her parents getting back together—and this may not be easy to do. In addition, this tends to breed hostility toward the step-parent.

If both parents bring children into the remarriage, the situation becomes even more complicated and difficult. Now the child has to adjust to unwanted stepsiblings. Another possibility that may complicate the situation is the remarried couple wanting to have children of their own.

From the standpoint of the step-parent, a number of difficulties also appear to be "built-in" to the situation:

REBUILDING, REMARRIAGE, AND STEPFAMILIES **451**

BOX 13–8 / SOME QUESTIONS ABOUT STEP-PARENT–STEPCHILD RELATIONSHIPS

1. How can "ground rules" be best established in step-parent–stepchild relationships?

2. If stepchildren experience loyalty conflicts, how can they be best resolved?

3. How can establishing boundaries between the new marital partners and stepchildren be best accomplished?

4. When the stepchild requires discipline, what is the most effective approach for the step-parent to take?

5. If step-parent–stepchild relationships get off to a bad start, what is the best way to correct the situation?

6. How does the decision of the new marital partners to have a child of their own affect step-parent–stepchild relationships?

7. When both partners bring children into the remarriage, how does this affect step-parent–stepchild relationships?

8. What is the most effective way of dealing with a stepchild who tries to "sabotage" the remarriage?

9. If a teenage stepchild develops a "crush" on the step-parent—which is not unusual among teenage daughters and distinguished-looking stepfathers or teenage stepsons and young, attractive stepmothers—what is the best way to deal with the situation?

10. If a stepchild and step-parent establish a close and constructive relationship but the remarriage breaks up, how can the situation be best handled?

Unfortunately, there are no simple answers to these questions. We have mentioned some general guidelines in our discussion, but each step-parent–stepchild relationship differs and problems that arise may have to be dealt with on their own merits and the overall stepfamily situation. However, step-parents who are "aware" and have developed communication, conflict-resolving, and other interpersonal skills are likely to be most effective.

(Based in part on Ganong & Coleman, 1986).

---

1. It is difficult to love someone else's children—especially if the child is resentful and difficult. As a step-parent, you may have to adjust to the realization that the stepchildren will never love you nor you them.

2. Stepchildren appear adept at using the technique of "divide and conquer," which may create unnecessary conflicts and tensions between the spouses. Often the stepchild sabotages the new marriage by "carrying tales" about the step-parent that are negative in nature and often greatly exaggerated.

3. Your new spouse may not want, or permit, you to discipline his or her children. This leads to an angry step-parent and a spoiled child.

4. It is difficult for a step-parent to feel that he or she is number one in the life of the new spouse. When "the chips are down," the step-parent is expendable, the children aren't.

5. Few people want to raise someone else's children—especially when finances are limited and the money required by the child deprives the step-parent of things he or she needs or wants.

Although many people maintain that marriage is lovelier the second time around, stepchildren are likely to make it trickier. Many step-parents are unable to overcome the obstacles, but others develop close relationships with their stepchildren, relationships that contribute to the happiness of the new marriage and to the structuring of the new family system.

Relating to the Ex-Spouse

> If the coping process has been successful, the relationship between the former partners will be marked by a balanced view of the good as well as the bad aspects of the marriage and an objective view of the former spouse. The co-parenting relationship will be handled smoothly and tactfully on both sides.
>
> —*Kenneth Kressel (1980, p. 238)*

How many formerly married couples are able to work out such a balanced relationship? Probably many do, but we don't know how many. Most of the limited research on this subject has focused on the disputes—and often continuing "guerilla warfare"—between the ex-spouses over child support, visitation rights, and related matters. Such continuing warfare can be highly destructive not only to the ex-partners but also to the children and the new marriage. Betsy Callahan (1979), for example, describes the havoc that can be created in a remarriage by an ex-spouse who won't let go of their former relationship:

> Often [the person] is obsessed with feelings of having been mistreated during the marriage and can't bear the fact that an ex-spouse would leave them. Hassling over how the ex-spouse is dealing with the children, denying visitation rights or support keeps them involved in the old relationship and becomes a vehicle for their anger. Making the ex-spouse's second marriage as uncomfortable as possible by constant interference seems to be the goal. . . . (p. 106)

In our discussion of divorce and single-parent families, we commented on the various ways in which ex-mates relate to each other—ranging from Perfect Pals to Fiery Foes (Ahrons, 1986). Our intent was to show how amicable separation and divorce are helpful in working out custody and visitation rights as well as in establishing an environment that encourages the noncustodial parent to see his or her children on a regular basis.

Here, we are also concerned with how the interaction between the ex-spouses affects the new marriage. It seems highly probable that the new spouse would not welcome the Perfect Pals relationship, and the Fiery Foes relationship seems to create no end of trouble. It may be recalled, however, that Constance Ahrons found two additional types of relationships between ex-spouses that she labeled Angry Associates and Cooperative Colleagues. In the latter type of relationship, interaction between the ex-spouses focused on the children, and it enabled the ex-spouses to work out most problems involving the children in a constructive way. Although they spent little time with each other, the ex-spouses did get along well together.

In short, the Cooperative Colleagues relationship involved mutual respect and tact and appeared to work in the best interests of all concerned—including the 38 percent of ex-spouses who had remarried. Because Ahrons' study covered a time span of 5 years, it would seem to be the best guideline we have to follow in terms of ex-spouse relationships in the context of remarriage.

Structuring the Stepfamily System

A stepfamily is a family born out of the losses endured by each family member: the child has lost a parent, at least one parent has lost a partner and even a previously unmarried stepparent has lost the dream of a nuclear family.

—*Greta Stanton (1987, p. 2)*

As in the case of the single-parent family, there are no social norms or guidelines to help in structuring the stepfamily system. Largely for this reason, the stepfamily has been called "an incomplete institution." In addition, stepfamilies are likely to be far more complex than single-parent families, which further complicates the problem of structure.

In terms of complexity, there are simple stepfather families, simple stepmother families, and complex stepfamilies in which both spouses bring children into the new marriage. Also, one or both step-parents may have been married more than once before and are custodial or noncustodial parents of children from several prior marriages. To cite a rather extreme but not necessarily atypical example:

Johnny's mother has recently remarried. He now lives with his mother, new stepfather, two halfsiblings from his mother's earlier marriage, and four stepsiblings from his stepfather's previous marriages. In addition, he visits his father every other weekend where he is in contact with his father's new wife and her two children from a prior marriage. When time permits he visits with his four grandparents and several aunts and uncles.

Essentially, structuring a stepfamily involves the same ingredients as structuring a nuclear or single-parent family. All are concerned with family goals, roles and responsibilities, power and decision making, ground rules and discipline, boundaries, methods for coping with conflicts and other family problems, and channels of communication. However, structuring a stepfamily, especially a complex one, may be far more difficult.

In single-family systems, for example, a system of roles and rules tends to develop over time. These family systems tend to be rather democratic in that the children usually have "voting rights" and are accustomed to sharing. In some single-parent families, however, the children—especially the oldest male—may take over and become the controlling force. Now, let us suppose that the new remarriage involves a father with children who is accustomed to power and decision making—who, in essence is accustomed to running and controlling the family. To blend these two different family systems in a remarriage becomes an extremely difficult, if not impossible, task. This is especially true if either parent refuses to cooperate in establishing a new system to deal with the present situation.

In addition, structuring a stepfamily may take rather unusual twists and turns. Elinor Rosenberg and Fady Hajal (1985) cite an interesting illustration:

. . . a ten-year-old girl and an eleven-year-old boy were sweethearts. In fact, it was through their relationship that their divorced parents met and later married. As the boy described it several years later: 'That was really weird—one day she was my girl friend, and the next day, she was my sister.' When these two children reached puberty, the family went into a crisis. (p. 291)

As these researchers point out, the task of maintaining sexual boundaries in the nuclear family, as well as in the single-parent family, is supported by clear incest taboos. However, sexual relations between stepsiblings are not incestuous. Yet, families and family therapists often deal with them as if they were, thus creating intense conflict and guilt on the part of many stepsiblings. Of course, their behavior may be illegal, but that is another issue. As Rosenberg and Hajal concluded, "Once again we see the lack of guidelines that make life in remarried families full of uncomfortable ambiguities" (p. 291).

Finally, it may be emphasized that establishing boundaries is a key task in the structuring process for stepfamilies. Boundaries function essentially as "distance-regulating mechanisms," and it is essential that a strong boundary be established around the new marital partners that doesn't exclude the children but does provide the couple with needed privacy.

Although we could mention other problem areas in stepfamilies—such as myriad legal issues—it is hoped that the preceding discussion provides a glimpse of the difficulties that may be involved in this increasingly common family form.

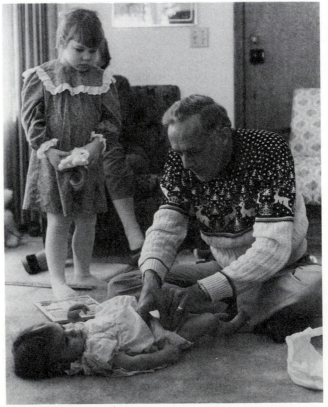

Michael Siluk/EKM-Nepenthe

GUIDELINES FOR A HAPPY REMARRIAGE AND STEPFAMILY

After reviewing some of the problems in remarriage and stepfamilies, it may seem that the problems are insurmountable, but they need not be.

The guidelines that we outlined in Chapter 8 for building a happy marriage also apply to building a happy remarriage. However, there are some additional guidelines that apply specifically to remarriage.

1. *Clear up as much "unfinished business" and "emotional garbage" as possible from your previous marriage and divorce.* Even hostile remarks about your previous spouse and how terrible he or she was can make your mate realize that there is still an emotional attachment—that you have not fully worked through your feelings. In addition, your spouse may ask himself or herself whether you really evaluated your prior marriage—its strengths and weaknesses—and your role in its failure or whether you are bringing the same problem behaviors to the present relationship. Even bad habits that you developed during your first marriage can carry over and impede development in the new one.

2. *Don't make comparisons between your present partner and your ex-spouse.* You are married to a different person who has his or her own way of doing things—not to mention different interests, beliefs, goals, and values. Even mentally dwelling on negative comparisons can be destructive. The comparisons should have been worked through before the remarriage. Blurting out a statement such as "Well at least my ex was a good businessperson" can be highly damaging to your new relationship. Implicit in points 1 and 2 is the admonition, "Don't use your present spouse as a 'dumping ground' for emotional leftovers from your prior marriage."

3. *Avoid "guerilla warfare" with your ex-spouse.* As we noted, ex-spouses may deliberately use harassing tactics—for example, over visitation rights, how you are treating the children, and so on—to keep you involved in the prior relationship. In addition, they may try to gain some control over your present marriage by making it as unpleasant as possible. Consulting a divorce therapist may be helpful in clarifying your rights and taking appropriate action.

4. *Don't try to forget.* Your past marriage is never truly dead and buried. There will be moments when little things—an old photograph, a song, or perhaps a minor triumph of your children—remind you of your ex-partner and happy times. These memories and feelings are natural and will gradually diminish in intensity but perhaps not in importance if you do not deny your inner feelings. Although your past marriage in many ways provides a baseline against which you can compare your present one, remember that similar events and behaviors are occurring in a new context and may not have the same meaning or significance. Because your first spouse used business trips for having affairs, don't assume that your present spouse uses them for the same purpose. In short, don't try to forget the past, but don't live in it either.

5. *Don't neglect the children but . . .* don't make your spouse feel that he

or she ranks after the children in your affection. Although your children do require love and attention, they will, in a few short years, be building lives of their own. You may still be important to them, but their primary responsibility is to their spouse and family. Remember that children are the primary cause of divorce in remarriage. The most important person in your life is your new mate. Make him or her feel that way. A useful procedure is to establish around you and your mate a boundary that does not exclude the children but provides needed privacy and time to be alone for you and your new spouse.

6. *Allow time.*   As the saying goes, "Rome wasn't built in a day." Building a new and happy marriage will not take place overnight. You are different people coming from different backgrounds of marital experience, and it will take time to work problems out. In addition, allow time for your stepchildren to accept you at their own pace. Remember that they may never come to love you, or you them. However, one matter that can't wait is making clear "Who's in charge—the parents or the children." Children who get their way by going to their parent for permission—by-passing the step-parent—are in control. The newly married couple are the ones who should be.

7. *Make effective use of what you have learned from your previous marriage and divorce.*   Re-evaluating your previous marriage and your role in its failure should help you avoid making the same mistakes again. Making effective use of what you have learned and the ways in which you have changed should prove invaluable in building, maintaining, and enriching a loving and fulfilling marriage. Workshops can also help you prepare for remarriage by alerting you to the kinds of problems that you will likely be confronting. If indicated, don't hesitate to utilize remarriage counseling or therapy.

Two additional points merit consideration. In establishing an effective step-family system, some remarried persons find it helpful to utilize a general systems viewpoint. Here the focus is on such factors as patterns of communication, ground rules, roles and responsibilities, conflict resolution, decision making, and methods of discipline. The overall objective is to blend these components into an effective stepfamily system. Finally, it is important to have a realistic view of yourself, your partner, your remarriage, and the stepfamily system—and to be aware of changes over time.

While the preceding guidelines do not guarantee the success of remarriage, they can make the adjustment less difficult for parents and children alike.

In the opening to our section on remarriage, we quoted the dour view of Samuel Johnson that remarriage is the "triumph of hope over experience." In many cases, this statement appears to be true. However, we live in a new social setting, with changed values and opportunities. Today, divorced persons have the opportunity to learn a great deal more about marriage and divorce than those in previous generations. They have the opportunity to build new relationships that combine romantic love with companionship and shared goals. Perhaps the majority of persons who remarry can change Johnson's statement to "Remarriage is the triumph of experience over damaged hope." In the long run, most of us need intimacy, and we can only achieve it through committing ourselves to building truly close relationships. Remarriage, like marriage, can be seen as a starting line, not a finishing line—for much of your marital script remains to be written.

SUMMARY—Chapter 13

1. The grief experienced after divorce varies in duration and intensity, depending on the former relationship, but it generally lasts three months to a year; some think at least two years. Grief can be prolonged by its intensity, by past losses, by age, by the duration of the marriage, and by denial or resorting to drugs.

2. Depression, anger, guilt, shame, and anxiety are normal components of grief. Social support groups can help; they can also facilitate the necessary task of re-evaluating the marriage.

3. Loneliness is a major component of the grief process but it can be strengthening. Trying to avert it or shorten its duration can trap one—into, for example, viewing it as weakness, clinging to one's ex-partner, engaging in meaningless affairs, or falling in love and marrying on the rebound. Here the cure may be worse than the disease.

4. Becoming whole again means establishing a new identity as a single person. Becoming self-directing and autonomous requires a re-evaluation of oneself and one's goals. Often a daunting task, it can become an exciting adventure.

5. Dating has as much to offer the divorced as the never-married young person, but it is more problematic. Meeting potential mates is more difficult and, while many newly divorced persons are afraid to date at all, others date too soon. Many men view divorced women as easy prey and, on the other hand, aggressive women often frighten newly divorced men. Nevertheless, many divorced persons begin dating within 3–6 months of their separation, although others wait a year or more.

6. Parents who have custody of a child may worry about upsetting the child by introducing a new partner, and the child may indeed feel threatened. After a time, however, children adjust better to a parent's sexual affairs than the parent does and often want to be acknowledged rather than avoided by a lover. Perhaps the greatest danger children face is neglect when the parent becomes part of a new social whirl.

7. Learning to love again is moving from independence to interdependence. Many interpose a period of cohabitation, an intermediate step that they report increases their chances of successful remarriage.

8. Four of five divorced women and five of six divorced men remarry, and 60 percent have had one or more children. They remarry because of personal and social pressures. Mothers may remarry for financial support and to provide a father for the children; men may feel lonely, awkward, and incompetent; both may want companionship, sexual intimacy, and emotional support. Most people remarry in their thirties.

9. People are more realistic about remarriage. They attempt to gain a more realistic view of themselves, of the other person, and of the potential relationship. Many have learned from experience and make wiser decisions the

second time. They are also less likely to have formal engagements and weddings, and more likely to live together before marrying.

10. Remarriage has six aspects: emotional, psychic, community, parental, economic, and legal. All of these can be thought of as tasks whose difficulty depends on the individuals and their situations.

11. Research into the success of second marriages is scanty and contradictory. Some find little difference between first and second marriages, yet remarried women report less happiness than women in first marriages or remarried men and the happiness of a step-parent is doubtful. About 60 percent of all remarriages fail, and their average length is only five years; when there are children, 75 percent end in divorce. When one or both spouses have been divorced more than once, the odds fall even further.

12. Remarriage alters problems common to all marriages and adds new ones. Financial problems, complicated by divorce agreements, become overwhelming. Sexual problems loom larger although infidelity is less frequent. Emotional leftovers from a previous marriage are damaging. Stepchildren create conflict and ex-spouses foment trouble. Finally, structuring a step-family system is very complicated, especially when the original families were organized differently.

13. Among the guidelines for a successful marriage are: (1) clear up emotional leftovers from the first marriage; (2) don't compare the new spouse with the ex-spouse; (3) avoid guerilla warfare with the ex-spouse; (4) don't forget the past, but don't live in it either; (5) avoid placing your children ahead of your spouse; (6) allow time to work problems out but make it clear that the parents, not the children, are in charge; (7) make good use of past experience; (8) be aware of change in yourself, your spouse, and the children; and (9) do not hesitate to seek remarriage counseling or therapy.

V

HORIZONS

The Bridge. by Joseph Stella, Collection of the Newark Museum

MARRIAGE AND FAMILY IN THE EARLY 21ST CENTURY

For better or for worse, we are developing into a world that moves at electronic speeds. Technology is giving us the means to simulate environments of any space or time. It is likely that we will spend increasing amounts of time in these artificial realities. . . . They will allow us to interact with the past, the present, and the future; to role-play different cultures and value systems; and even to attempt survival in a world with different laws of physics and nature.

—Gareth Branwyn (1986, p. 35)

---

*I*n recent years a growing number of people and organizations have become directly involved in delineating possible futures for our society and for our planet as a whole. Interdisciplinary teams of scientists, historians, and specialists from other fields have been established—by the federal government, major universities, and private foundations—to devote their energies to considering alternative futures open to us and the probable consequences of given alternatives in planning a good future.

One of the chief messages of the futurists is that rapid and accelerating technological and social change have reached a point of no return. This change is leading us from an industrial society to a new and uncertain information society; the transformation is proving highly stressful for institutions and individuals alike.

A second key message of the futurists is that, throughout history, those organisms that have been unable to adapt to the demands of a changing environment have perished. Curiously enough, the dinosaur—which was not noted for its superior intelligence—survived some 150 million years, and humans are an endangered species after only 2 or 3 million years on this planet.

Unlike the dinosaur, however, humans have options. We are not trapped in some absurd fate (like the dinosaurs were) but can simulate alternative futures, make choices, and actively participate in shaping our future—including the type of marriage and family life best suited for us. Thus, it becomes essential to explore and evaluate our available options carefully.

In this concluding chapter, we shall consider some possible "scenarios" for marriage and family in the early 21st century. Although there are variations— for example, Branwyn (1986) and Renfro (1987)—the scenario technique involves imagining and thinking through various possibilities while keeping them within the bounds of reality.

THE FUTURE OF MARRIAGE AND FAMILY: SOME CONFLICTING SCENARIOS

The following scenarios are largely based on the conditions we mentioned in Chapter 1 as essential for understanding the changes taking place in contemporary marriage and family: (1) that America is going through a wrenching transforma- tion from an industrial age to an information age; (2) that, when environments change, institutions and people also change as they attempt to adapt; and (3) that

BOX 14-1 / A LONG DAY'S JOURNEY INTO TOMORROW

The sociologist Featherstone (1979) describes the last scene in Eugene O'Neill's great family drama, *Long Day's Journey into Night*, as follows:

> Sitting together in a dwindling pool of light, the darkness growing, the family talks on. Fathers, mothers, brothers, sisters are trying to explain: not understanding, not comprehending; loving one another, but hating and hurting each other; tangling and untangling like badly cast fishing lines, a group of inviolate, wounded selves. O'Neill's characters, like the rest of us, are speaking about the family in order to explain their attitudes toward life itself (p. 52).

If we reflect on this description for a moment, we can see how deeply our beliefs, values, and attitudes toward life are enmeshed with our intimate relationships. The former inevitably shapes the type of relationships we establish. Thus, in the future, marriage and other intimate relationships will reflect our social structures, value systems, and attitudes toward individuals and life itself.

these changes—in the environment, institutions, and people—interact in shaping the future. For these scenarios, the author is also indebted to Edward Cornish (1979, 1987), president of the World Future Society.

Scenario 1: Revitalize Marriage and Family

In a period when technological and social changes are testing the resilience of our political, educational, and other institutions, it seems like a good idea to many people to try and shore up marriage and family as a source of stability and strength.

Such a program would probably include three key components:

1. *More-effective methods of mate selection.* Computers and other technological advances—such as videotapes and videophones—help people not only to meet a far larger number of eligible mates but also to choose more-compatible ones. For example, a computer could keep track of the interests, goals, values, education, skills, appearance, and health status of millions of people. Thus, the "computer matchmaker" could offer the individual a virtual "cafeteria" of choices in mate selection—potentially eligible partners from our society and from all over the world. By means of modern air travel, meetings could be arranged in a matter of hours or, at most, a few days.

   But to use this approach effectively requires far greater knowledge of intimate relationships than is now available. Through research, such knowledge could become available within a few years. In the meantime, we do know enough to improve on our present batting average.

2. *Education for marriage.*   As we have noted, few enterprises in our society start with such high hopes and expectations as contemporary marriage—and so regularly end in disappointment, hurt, and failure. Certainly, our educational system could provide young people with more courses and more information on marriage and intimate relationships. This information could also be designed to help young people improve communication, problem-solving, and other interpersonal skills. These are essential ingredients in building, maintaining, and enriching marriage and family relationships.

Again, however, for such an approach to achieve a high level of effectiveness would require the expenditure of far more time and money on research and education—both in our society and on a cross-cultural level.

3. *Providing social-support systems.*   Our society has traditionally provided marriage and family with a great deal of privacy and independence from outside governmental or other interference. Only under extreme conditions, such as child abuse, do outside agencies intervene. Many people feel strongly that this is the way matters should remain.

Increasingly, however, voluntary support systems focus on helping troubled marriages and families. In addition, **social-support systems** are available to help families cope with unexpected crises—such as illness, disasters, and death in the family. The missing ingredient here seems to be clearly defined policies for implementing such coping resources in times of crisis; missing also seems to be an agreed-on family policy to

"*I guess I'm fortunate. All of my marriages have been happy.*"
Drawing by Weber; © 1982 *The New Yorker Magazine, Inc.*

which religious and other institutions, as well as governmental agencies, can subscribe.

How realistic is the idea that marriage and family can undergo such a revitalization? We do not know, but one distinct danger is that—in our efforts to revitalize marriage and family—we would attempt to implement, and perhaps even enforce, roles and relationships that are no longer suitable in our changing world (Melton, 1987).

Scenario 2: Return to Traditional Patterns

> The present is uninviting, the future uncertain—long live the past.
>
> —Amatai Etzioni (1980, p. 12)

In times of turmoil, uncertainty, and change, people often turn to the past for a sense of identity, meaning, and guidance. Instead of pursuing new patterns, they turn back to old ones. Thus, the turbulent and rebellious 1960s led to the nostalgia for previous decades during the 1970s. For example, there was a return to traditional rituals, such as formal church marriages, wedding gowns, and all the wedding trimmings.

People who adopt a return-to-tradition scenario for the future tend to feel that the continuation of present trends will lead to unworkable absurdities, such as more divorces than marriages each year. They view social trends as basically cyclic in nature and point to the tendency of the pendulum to swing from one extreme to the other and then to reach a point of semi-equilibrium somewhere in between. The pendulum may shift from child-free marriages toward large families and then settle at about two children per family in the future. In essence, changes that are extreme by historical standards tend to be reversed, so that the marriage and family patterns of the future may well return to less-extreme forms. Certainly the couple and family have always been the basic unit of human society. While wars and other social upheavals have temporarily disrupted marriage and family patterns, these patterns regain their equilibrium once events have run their course.

But it seems unlikely that people can return successfully to the past, partly because their nostalgic and selective views of the past are unrealistic and depict a past that never existed in the first place (Skolnick, 1981). More important, almost all phases of human life have been revolutionized, and it seems unlikely that marriage and family patterns can remain unaffected. As Cornish (1979) has expressed it:

Though certain trends in the family may seem to lead to absurdities, and therefore some reversion to previous lifestyles may be expected, the status quo scenario may be challenged on the grounds that lifestyles are not likely to remain unchanged if almost every other aspect of human life is revolutionized. (p. 54)

Among the many changes that seem unlikely to revert to previous patterns are greater sex-role equality, dual-worker marriages, and family planning using effective methods of contraception.

Of course, instead of returning to the past, we may see a "freezing" of the present, so that present trends are not permitted to continue to further extremes.

But, in view of the accelerating and relatively uncontrolled nature of technological and social changes today, such a freeze seems both unrealistic and unlikely in the near future.

Scenario 3: Continue Present Trends

Another way of looking at marriage and family in the early 21st century is to anticipate that present trends will continue. The divorce rate will remain high and become the normal way to end marriage. Already more marriages are terminated each year by divorce than by death. Although divorce is still not viewed as the most desirable way to deal with marital problems, it is now socially acceptable and, at some point, it may become the appropriate way to end unhappy marriages.

At the same time, serial marriages—which are also socially acceptable—will increase as divorced persons remarry. The time span between divorce and remarriage may decrease from the present 3-year average to 2 years or even one. If present trends continue, marriages in which one or both partners have been married before will soon become more common than marriages of single never-marrieds. Remarriage may well become the normal pattern for marriage. In fact, long-term marriages in which neither partner has been married before may become exceedingly rare. More commonly, couples will remain married so long as each partner finds the relationship rewarding, but as soon as the relationship is perceived as unsatisfactory, the couple will seek a no-fault divorce and each will look for a new partner. They will probably cohabit with these partners before remarrying. However, cohabitation will probably be a precursor to marriage rather than an alternative.

What effect will the increasing incidence of serial marriage have on the family? For one thing, the high divorce rate will lead directly to more single-parent families; joint custody following divorce will become more common; and, as divorced parents remarry, there will be more stepfamilies. Before the year 2000, it is probable that stepfamilies will come to outnumber those in which children live with both biological parents.

The continuation of present trends may lead to some rather extreme scenarios. For example, one scenario envisions a form of **free-enterprise relationship** in which no marriage license is required. A couple would be free to make any sexual or living arrangement they choose and to terminate the relationship without need for a divorce. In the event of dissolution of the relationship, the division of property and other matters would be the sole responsibility of the partners; neither lawyers nor representatives of the state would be involved. Where children are involved, matters might be more complicated, but again it would be up to the partners to work things out. Government would get out of the marriage and family business and let the principles of the interpersonal marketplace serve as regulators of what actually happens.

In any event, the continuation of present trends would provide individuals with a wide range of options regarding marriage and family—whether and when to marry, whether and when to have children, whether to continue a marriage, and so on. Commitment would exist only insofar as people felt that their mates are enhancing their lives. Here, it may be emphasized that Scenario 3 is based on the assumption that modern medicine will conquer AIDS.

Scenario 4: Apply Strict Government Control

At the present time, government plays a minimal role in marriage and family. Aside from issuing marriage licenses and divorces, it actually controls little of what goes on in marriage and family. Most people probably feel that this is the way things should be; however, a fourth scenario for the future is one in which an authoritarian government takes full control over these institutions.

In terms of marriage, this could involve meeting strict requirements in order to be granted permission to marry. The individual might have to supply proof of freedom from sexually transmitted diseases, genetic disorders, and other serious diseases or handicapping conditions. He or she might also have to show evidence of an acceptable level of intelligence and emotional maturity and have no background of nonconformist ideas or actions that might be viewed as a threat to the State.

The government might decide not only whether a person can marry, but *whom.* A person might be barred from marrying someone of a different race, ethnic background, or economic status. Or the government might act as a marriage broker, deciding who will marry whom and when. Because divorce would reflect on the wisdom of the government's choices, divorces would probably not be granted—or granted only under the most unusual conditions to privileged members of society.

In terms of family, the government would play an equally dominant role. It would decide who could have children, how many, and when. To ensure control, it might require persons wishing to have children to obtain a license for parent-

Michael Siluk/EKM-Nepenthe

BOX 14–2 / "THE SHAPE OF THINGS TO COME?"

In terms of social programs, Sweden has been referred to as a "trendsetter" and one of the most "modernized" nations in the world. Pursuing this concept, David Popenoe (1987) has suggested that a study of the changing marital and family patterns in Sweden may shed some light on the probable changes that lie in store for us.

With this suggestion in mind, we shall briefly review some of Popenoe's findings in contemporary Sweden and contrast them with changing marital and family patterns in our own society. All figures are approximate and most are based on 1985 data (Popenoe, 1987; Ringen, 1986; Blanc, 1987; Ministry of Labor, 1985).

	Sweden	United States
1. Age at marriage	27 for women; 30 for men.	23 for women; 25.5 for men.
2. Marriage rate	75 percent and dropping. Lowest rate in industrial world; out of fashion. Marriage ceremony—out of fashion.	90 percent.
3. Cohabitation (a) Prior to marriage (b) In place of marriage	98 percent 25 percent—highest in industrial world. Gradually replacing marriage.	25–35 percent. 5 percent.
4. Family dissolution (a) Divorce rate (b) Dyads who cohabit instead of marrying	 Over 40 percent and increasing. Over 75 percent. Overall rate highest in industrial world—of family dissolution.	 About 50 percent and holding steady.
5. Single-parent families— usually headed by mothers	About 35 percent of families.	Over 20 percent of families.
6. Children born to unmarried parents	50 percent of all births. Same legal rights—no stigma.	About 21 percent.
7. Remarriage	60 percent women; 65 percent men.	75 percent women; 80 percent men.
8. Mothers in labor force with children under 7 years of age	85 percent; highest in industrial world.	About 60 percent.

(continued)

> ## BOX 14–2 (continued)
>
> Although cohabitation is gradually replacing marriage and Sweden has a high rate of family dissolution, 90 percent of men and women plan on forming a monogamous dyad at some time in their lives. Most also want children—two being the ideal. Sweden also has "parental insurance," which provides up to 9 months leave from employment with nearly full pay.
>
> Sweden has moved farther from the traditional nuclear family than any other industrial nation, but Popenoe concluded from his findings that the family as an institution in Sweden is "not on the verge of disappearance." However, Popenoe also concluded that changing marital and family forms will have far-reaching social consequences. But he feels that it would be premature to predict what these consequences may be.

hood. This scenario would restrict present freedom, and only those approved by the State would be permitted to bear children. The State would also probably play an active role in child-rearing—perhaps removing the children from the natural parents and rearing them in a state-approved facility, or instituting other measures (Box 14–2).

How likely is this scenario? Again, we do not know. But various aspects, such as requiring the completion of a marriage and family course in high school in order to obtain a marriage license, may well be put into effect. If the existing government perceives marital and family instability to be a threat to our society, it may well try to institute more-radical measures along the lines we have mentioned.

Scenario 5: Abolish Marriage and Family

In 1949, George Orwell wrote a powerful and prophetic book called *1984*, which foretold the destruction of free Western society, including such basic institutions as marriage and family. In Orwell's vision, this destruction would come about through the control of science and technology by particular political groups. Our society would become completely bureaucratized and highly stratified. Freedom and choice would become relics of the past. The State would take over the functions of the family by controlling child-bearing, and close personal relationships, as well as enduring commitments, would be made impossible by the new social environment.

As Cornish (1979) has pointed out, one form of the "abolition of marriage and family" scenario similar to Orwell's *1984* would have the government officially outlawing marriage and family and taking over the functions once provided by these institutions:

For example, government agencies might collect sperm and ova from suitable donors, combine them in test-tubes, and then allow the fertilized ova to gestate under careful supervision in artificial wombs that would nourish and protect the baby until it was ready to breathe air and consume through its mouth. While the baby was developing into a child and later an adolescent and adult, he would be cared for by professionals rather than kinfolk. The child would have no family, at least not in the traditional sense. Possibly he might be trained to think of mankind as his family, but possibly the word *family* would have such an archaic, unpleasant, and primitive connotation that it would not be used—except in discussing the bad days of the past. (p. 54)

New methods of preserving sperm and ova would make it possible for the State to select biological parents from people no longer living. For example, the biological father of a child might be a Nobel Prize winner in physics who died in 1984, while the mother might be a 27-year-old Ph.D. in astrophysics who teaches at M.I.T. Or both parents might be already gone from this life. Such approaches would probably be experimental, as government scientists strive to produce a superior breed of humans. As methods of genetic engineering undergo further advances, even more-sophisticated techniques that would revolutionize reproductive engineering might be introduced. Although such techniques are being developed for beneficial use in our democratic society, their potential for misuse indicates that we should "proceed with caution."

SCENARIOS MOST LIKELY TO OCCUR

> The future is not some place we are going to, but one we are creating. The paths to it are not found but made, and the activity of making them changes both the maker and the destination.
>
> —*Schaar (1974, p. 1)*

Contrary to popular opinion, it is not the primary goal of the futurists to predict the future; rather, their primary objective is to stimulate our thinking about "alternative futures" and to help us make decisions that will lead to a better future.

Most of us do speculate, however, about what the future will be like in our lifetime and perhaps beyond (some probable short-term trends in marriage and family are summarized in Box 14–3). So, based on the scenarios we have described, let us attempt some tentative predictions about marriage and family in the years ahead—into the early 21st century.

It seems probable that some combination of Scenarios 1 and 3—revitalization of marriage and family and continuation of present trends—may describe the future in the 1990s. But, by the year 2010, a combination of Scenarios 3 and 4—continuation of present trends and application of strict government control—may be closer to the mark. Beyond this point, Scenario 4—application of strict government control—would appear to have the edge.

But let us re-emphasize that the couple and the family have endured as basic structures of society from the Stone Age to the Space Age. If romantic love proves to be an idea whose time has come, the resilience and durability of marriage and family may be far greater than many social scientists realize. Admittedly, of course, implementing enduring romantic love may not be easy—and, for many people, it may be impossible. But if people increasingly succeed in this endeavor, we may as human beings enter a new and higher realm of human existence.

BOX 14-3 / SHORT-TERM TRENDS IN MARRIAGE AND FAMILY

The following trends appear likely to continue in marriage and family through the 1990s.

1. Equality between the sexes in occupational, political, marital, and other areas will increase—based on the theme of "equal but different."
2. Cohabitation will increase—especially for persons considering remarriage.
3. Marriage rate—will remain steady or show slight decrease.
4. Age at marriage—will gradually increase, probably to about 25 for women and 27 for men (first marriages).
5. Dual-career marriages—will gradually increase as two salaries become essential to maintain standard of living.
6. Children—couples will have fewer children and at a later age. Many dual-career couples, in particular, will opt for no children.

7. Working mothers—will gradually increase as mothers receive paid maternity leave and better child-care facilities become available.
8. Divorce rate—will remain relatively stable.
9. Remarriage rate—will remain high.
10. Single-parent and stepfamilies—will remain high but the economic plight of single-parent mothers will be improved.

In addition, an increasing number of people are expected to divorce and remarry more than once, thus perpetuating "serial monogamy." Other factors—such as number of sexual partners prior to marriage, extramarital affairs, and the number of persons who divorce and remarry several times—will be strongly influenced by whether or not preventive measures and/or effective treatment for AIDS are developed.

We have now concluded our journey together in exploring marriage and intimate relationships. From here on, your author-guide can accompany you no farther. At the close of his journeys, Tennyson's Ulysses says, "I am a part of all that I have met." It is the author's sincere hope that the readers of this book will remember the concepts and people they have met in their journey, and that what they have learned will become a meaningful part of their lives.

SUMMARY—Chapter 14

1. Futurists have suggested several scenarios depicting marriage and family in the early 21st Century. In the first scenario, marriage and family would be revitalized through improved methods of selecting mates, better education for marriage, and social support systems.
2. A second suggestion is that there will be a return to traditional patterns as the pendulum of change reverses. This seems unlikely because nostalgic views of the past are unrealistic and depict a past that never existed. Even a freezing of the present situation seems unlikely in view of the acceleration of social change.

3. The third scenario is a continuation of current trends. Divorce, remarriage, and cohabitation as a precursor to remarriage will become even more prevalent. Joint custody, single-parent families, and step-families will become the norm. Another possibility is that free-enterprise relationships, without benefit of marriage licenses and separation without legal assistance, will become widespread.

4. In the fourth scenario, an authoritarian government will take full control over marriage and family, deciding who will marry whom and when, and who can have children and how many. Divorce would be permitted rarely and children would be reared under state supervision.

5. In a fifth scenario, marriage and family would be outlawed. The state would control childbirth by genetic engineering and artificial gestation, and close relationships and enduring commitments would be made impossible.

6. The primary goal of the futurists is not to predict the future accurately. Rather it is to stimulate our thinking about "alternative futures" and to help us make decisions that will create a better future.

7. A combination of some of the scenarios seems most likely within the next or the next few decades. Yet the couple and the family have been basic to society since the Stone Age and their resilience may be far greater than many social scientists realize. Together with romantic love more fully realized, they may enable us to enter a new and higher realm of existence.

A

ANATOMY AND PHYSIOLOGY OF SEXUAL RESPONSE

*T*he organs of the female and male reproductive systems are designed to ensure the continuity of the human species. On the basis of function, reproductive organs may be grouped into two general categories: (1) gonads and (2) accessory sex organs.

The *gonads* or *primary sex organs* are the ovaries in the female and the testes in the male. Their function in reproduction is to produce sex cells called *gametes*. Whereas the ovaries produce ova, the testes produce spermatozoa (sperm cells). The union of an ovum and a spermatozoon is called fertilization, and the product is a fertilized ovum or zygote. Under normal conditions, the zygote will develop into an embryo and later a fetus in the mother's body. In addition to producing gametes, the gonads also secrete hormones that influence the development of secondary sex characteristics and reproductive cycles. The ovaries secrete estrogens and progesterone, and the testes secrete androgens, the most important of which is testosterone.

Accessory sex organs function in the transportation, protection, and nourishment of gametes once they leave the gonads. Female accessory sex organs include the uterine tubes, uterus, vagina, and external genitals. Male accessory sex organs include the scrotum, testes, epididymis, ductus deferens, ejaculatory duct, seminal vesicles, prostate gland, bulbourethral glands, urethra, and penis.

FEMALE REPRODUCTIVE ORGANS

Primary Sex Organs

The *ovaries* or female gonads are paired glands that resemble almonds in size and shape. They are located in the upper pelvic cavity, one on each side of the uterus, and are held in position by a series of ligaments. When an ovary is sectioned, its components can be seen. The outer covering is a single layer of cells, the germinal epithelium, that serves as a source of ovarian follicles. The core of an ovary consists of an outer dense layer of connective tissue (cortex) and an inner loose layer of connective tissue (medulla). The cortex contains the ovarian follicles, which are ova and their surrounding tissues.

Starting at puberty and continuing throughout the reproductive years of a female, a follicle matures and ruptures about every twenty-eight days. Discharge of the ovum (ovulation) makes it available for fertilization. Maturation and discharge of an ovum are under the influence of a follicle-stimulating hormone (FSH) and a luteinizing hormone (LH) secreted by the anterior pituitary gland. Functionally, then, the ovaries produce ova, discharge ova, and secrete estrogens and progesterone.

Accessory Sex Organs

The two *uterine (fallopian) tubes* extend from the vicinity of the ovaries to the uterus, where they connect with the upper portion of the uterus. Each tube is about four inches long. The part of the uterine tube near the ovary is funnel-shaped and is fringed by a series of finger-like projections. Movement of the projections plus muscular contractions of the wall of the uterine tube help sweep a discharged ovum through the tube into the uterus. Fertilization of an ovum takes place in the uterine tube, usually within twenty-four hours following ovulation. Once the fertilized ovum descends into the uterus, it attaches to the uterine wall where development continues. At times, fertilization occurs outside the uterine

Figure A-1.
Organs of the female reproductive system.

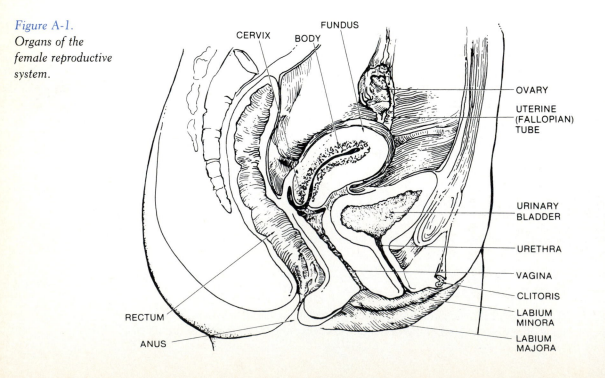

tube, and the ovum may develop on one of the pelvic organs. Such a phenomenon is called an ectopic pregnancy.

The *uterus* is an inverted pear-shaped organ between the urinary bladder and rectum. Its upper portion, or fundus, is connected to the uterine tubes. The major central portion is called the body, and the bottom is a constricted region called the cervix. The cervix joins with the vagina. Like the ovaries, the uterus is held in position by a series of ligaments. Most of the uterine wall consists of muscle called the myometrium. Contractions of the myometrium are important in expelling the fetus during labor.

The lining of the uterus is a mucous membrane called the endometrium. The superficial layer of the endometrium undergoes a series of changes each month in preparation for receiving a fertilized ovum. The attachment of a fertilized ovum to the lining of the uterus is known as implantation. Through the attachment, the developing ovum derives its nutrients from the mother and eliminates its wastes. If an ovum is not fertilized, it disintegrates, and the superficial portion of the endometrium is shed as part of the menstrual flow. Estrogens and progesterone regulate the menstrual cycle. The uterus, therefore, functions in labor, implantation, and menstruation.

The *vagina* is a muscular canal that extends from the uterine cervix to the exterior. Its opening to the exterior is known as the vaginal orifice and is surrounded by a fold of mucous membrane, the hymen. Although the lining of the vagina is acid and thus injurious to spermatozoa, semen contains an alkaline substance that neutralizes the acid to ensure survival of the spermatozoa. Functionally, the vagina serves as a passageway for the menstrual flow, the receptacle organ for the penis during sexual intercourse, and the lower portion of the birth canal during delivery.

The *female external genital organs* are collectively referred to as the *vulva*. Its principal subdivisions are as follows:

1. *Mons pubis*. An elevation of adipose tissue covered by coarse pubic hair. Its development is brought about by estrogens.

2. *Labia majora*. These are two folds of skin that extend back from the mons pubis. Externally, they are covered by pubic hair.

3. *Labia minora*. These are two smaller folds of mucous membrane between the labia majora. The labia minora do not bear pubic hair.

4. *Vestibule*. A cleft between the labia minora that contains the vaginal orifice and urethral orifice, the external opening of the urethra. The urethra conveys urine from the urinary bladder to the exterior.

5. *Greater vestibular (Bartholin's) glands*. Small, paired glands that open by ducts into a groove between the hymen and labia minora. The glands produce a secretion that lubricates the vestibule during sexual intercourse.

6. *Paraurethral (Skene's) glands*. Numerous glands whose ducts open on either side of the urethral orifice. Secretions from these glands also lubricate the vestibule.

7. *Clitoris*. Small, cylindrical mass of erectile tissue and nerves at the front junction of the labia minora. Most of it is covered by a prepuce (foreskin) formed by the labia minora; the exposed portion is called the glans. The clitoris is capable of enlargement, due to engorgement with blood when stimulated by touch.

Menstrual Cycle

The *menstrual cycle* refers to a series of changes in the endometrium of a nonpregnant female, approximately every twenty-eight days. Its purpose is to prepare the endometrium to receive a fertilized ovum for implantation. The menstrual cycle is closely coordinated with the ovarian cycle in which an ovum develops, matures, and is discharged.

The menstrual cycle is divided into three principal phases: (1) menstrual, (2) preovulatory, and (3) postovulatory. The menstrual phase is the periodic discharge of the superficial layer of the endometrium, an indication that pregnancy has not occurred. During this phase, an ovarian follicle is beginning its development. It is characterized by regrowth of the endometrium in anticipation of fertilization and implantation. In the ovary, follicle development continues as an ovum progresses toward ovulation. The postovulatory phase is the period of time following ovulation but before the beginning of the next menstrual phase. It is characterized by the continued thickening of the endometrium. If fertilization and implantation do not occur, another menstrual cycle begins. If they do occur, a structure in the ovary, the corpus luteum, secretes hormones that support the early stages of pregnancy.

MALE REPRODUCTIVE ORGANS

Primary Sex Organs

The *scrotum* is an extension of the skin of the abdomen that supports the testes. Externally, it looks like a single pouch of loose skin with a midline ridge, the raphe. Internally, the scrotum is divided by a septum into two sacs, each containing a testis. Under the skin of the scrotum is a layer of muscle, the dartos, whose contraction produces the wrinkled appearance of the scrotum.

The *testes* or male gonads are paired glands within the scrotum. Each is covered by a connective tissue and divided into smaller compartments called lobules. Each lobule contains tightly coiled seminiferous tubules that produce spermatozoa. Between the tubules are cells known as interstitial endocrinocytes (cells of Lydig) that secrete the male hormone testosterone. When spermatozoa mature, they are moved from the seminiferous tubules into a network of ducts in the testis called the rete testis. From here the spermatozoa are transported outside of the testis into a series of ducts called efferent ducts.

Accessory Sex Organs

The *epididymis* is a comma-shaped organ that lies along the back of each testis. Within it is a duct, the ductus epididymis, that receives spermatozoa from the efferent ducts. Functionally, the ductus epididymis is the place where maturation of spermatozoa occurs. The ductus epididymis also stores spermatozoa and propels them toward the exterior during ejaculation. Spermatozoa may remain in

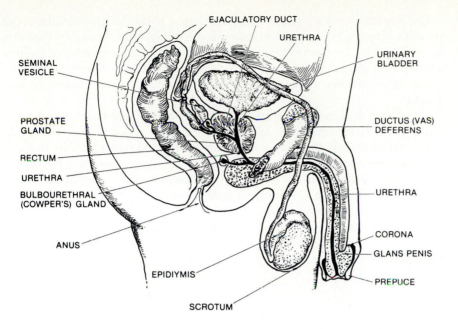

storage for up to four weeks in the ductus epididymis. After that, they are reabsorbed by the body.

The *ductus (vas) deferens* is a continuation of the ductus epididymis. It ascends along the back surface of each testis, passes through the body wall through the inguinal canal, enters the pelvic cavity, and loops over the side and down the back surface of the urinary bladder. The inguinal canal is a slit-like passageway in the abdominal wall. Functionally, the ductus deferens stores spermatozoa for up to several months and propels them toward the exterior during ejaculation. One method of sterilization in males is called vasectomy and consists of removal of a portion of each ductus deferens.

Traveling along with the ductus deferens as it moves out of the testis are a testicular artery, testicular vein, lymphatic vessels, nerves, and the cremaster muscle. The structures are wrapped in a sheath and make up the *spermatic cord*, which passes through the inguinal canal. The cremaster muscle elevates the testes during sexual stimulation and exposure to cold. The production and survival of spermatozoa require a temperature about $3\,^\circ F$ less than normal body temperature. During exposure to cold, the cremaster muscle contracts and draws the testes closer to the body to absorb body heat. Exposure to warmth reverses the process.

Behind the urinary bladder are the *ejaculatory ducts*. They are formed by the union of the ductus deferens and a duct from a gland called the seminal vesicle. The ejaculatory duct propels spermatozoa into the urethra.

The *urethra* is the terminal duct of the male reproductive system and is a common passageway for both spermatozoa and urine. It passes through the prostate gland and penis.

The paired *seminal vesicles* are glands on the back surface of the urinary bladder. They secrete an alkaline, viscous substance into the ejaculatory duct that contributes to the viability of spermatozoa. The seminal vesicles contribute about 60 percent of the volume of semen, a mixture of spermatozoa and secretions of several glands.

The *prostate gland* is a single, doughnut-shaped gland that encircles the upper part of the urethra, just below the urinary bladder. It secretes an alkaline fluid into the urethra. The secretion of the prostate gland contributes to motility of spermatozoa and constitutes about 13 to 33 percent of the volume of semen. In older males, the prostate may enlarge and press on the urethra, thus obstructing the flow of urine.

The paired *bulbourethral (Cowper's) glands* are located below the prostate gland. They secrete mucus for lubrication during sexual intercourse and a substance that neutralizes the acid in urine. Their secretion passes into the urethra.

The *penis* is the organ of copulation, used to introduce semen into the vagina. It consists of a shaft and an expanded tip, the glans. The raised ridge of the glans is referred to as the corona. Covering the glans is a loosely fitting prepuce (foreskin). Removal of the prepuce is known as circumcision. Internally, the penis consists of the cylindrical masses of erectile tissue, which contain numerous spaces that fill with blood when sexually stimulated. This causes the penis to enlarge and become firm and is referred to as an erection.

SEXUAL INTERCOURSE

Sexual intercourse is the process by which spermatozoa are deposited in the vagina. The male sex act consists of erection, lubrication, and orgasm. Under the influence of nerve impulses from the lower part of the spinal cord in response to sexual arousal, erection occurs. Lubrication is supplied by mucus from the bulbourethral glands. Orgasm consists of a series of sensory and motor responses, such as rapid heart rate, elevated blood pressure, increased respirations, and pleasurable sensations. In addition, male orgasm includes ejaculation. The first stage of ejaculation is called emission, the movement of spermatozoa and secretions from the prostate gland and seminal vesicles into the urethra. This movement is brought about by muscular contractions of the various ducts and glands of the male reproductive system. The second stage of ejaculation is called expulsion, the forceful propulsion of semen from the urethra to the exterior.

The female sex act also consists of erection, lubrication, and orgasm. As with erection in males, sexual arousal in females results in impulses from the lower part of the spinal cord that stimulate the female genitals, especially erection of the clitoris. Lubrication for the female is supplied by secretion from the greater vestibular and paraurethral glands. Female orgasm, like that of the male, includes widespread sensory and motor responses. It does not, however, include an ejaculation component.

PRENATAL DEVELOPMENT AND CHILDBIRTH

*P*renatal development begins at the time of conception, when an ovum (or egg cell) is fertilized by a sperm. The union of the ovum and the sperm normally takes place in the oviduct (uterine tube) as the ovum is being conducted from the ovary to the uterus. After ovulation, the ovum is viable for approximately twenty-four hours. If it is not fertilized within the first day, it loses its ability to unite with a sperm. To reach and fertilize the ovum, the sperm must propel themselves from the vagina, through the uterus, and along the oviduct. Of the nearly 300 million sperm that are deposited in the vagina, only 1,000 to 2,000 sperm survive the fifteen- to eighteen-hour journey to meet the ovum, and only a single sperm succeeds in fertilizing the ovum. Sperm remain viable (able to fertilize an ovum) for about forty-eight hours after deposition within the female reproductive tract.

THE STAGES OF PRENATAL DEVELOPMENT

Prenatal growth (Figure B-1) occurs in three stages:

1. The *preembryonic stage* extends from the fertilization of the ovum to the formation of the three-layered embryonic disc. This stage encompasses the first three weeks.
2. The *embryonic stage* is a time of rapid growth and differentiation. All of the major organs of the body are formed during this stage. The stage extends from the fourth to the eighth week, inclusive.
3. The *fetal stage* is characterized by rapid growth of the body and further development of the organs and systems that appeared during the embryonic stage. The fetal stage extends from the ninth to the thirty-eighth week.

Traditionally, prenatal development is divided into three three-month periods, or *trimesters*.

Figure B-1.
Prenatal
development. These
12- to 38-week
fetuses are about
half actual size.

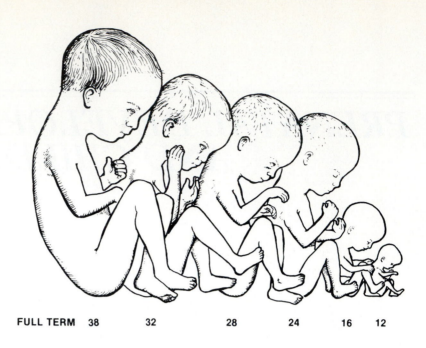

FULL TERM   38   32   28   24   16   12

The First Trimester of Pregnancy

The first trimester (three months) of pregnancy encompasses the preembryonic stage, the embryonic stage, and the first four weeks of the fetal stage. During these first twelve weeks, the developing child grows from a single-celled fertilized zygote to a fetus, complete with all of the major organ systems.

Within the first two days after fertilization, the zygote begins the first phase of development, which is termed *cleavage*. The single-celled zygote divides into two cells about thirty hours after fertilization. Ten to twenty hours later, these two cells divide into four cells. Thereafter, cellular division continues at a fairly regular pace. At about the sixteen-cell stage (five to eight days after ovulation), the morula enters the uterine cavity. At this stage, the morula consists of a centrally placed group of cells, the inner cell mass, which is surrounded by a layer of cells, the outer cell mass. The inner cell mass of the morula is destined to become the embryo; the outer cell mass is destined to help form the fetal membranes.

At about six days after ovulation, the developing mass of cells implants in the uterine lining. Implantation normally takes place in the upper part of the posterior wall of the uterus near the midline. The inner cell mass flattens and is now called the *embryonic disc*. By the twelfth day after fertilization, the embryonic disc divides into two cell layers, the ectoderm and the endoderm. The embryonic endoderm is in contact with the *yolk sac*, an embryonic cavity from which the digestive system will develop. The embryonic ectoderm is in contact with the amniotic cavity, which will, in time, expand to encircle the entire embryo. By the sixteenth day a third cell layer, the mesoderm, has formed. The mesoderm takes up an intermediate position between the ectoderm and endoderm. The embryonic disc is now a three-layered structure.

All of the tissues of the body are derived from these three cell layers. The ectoderm gives rise to the outer layer of the skin (epidermis), nervous system, eyes, hair, nails, and some glands. The mesoderm gives rise to all types of muscle (including the heart), bones and cartilage, blood vessels and blood, connective tissue, ovaries or testes, kidneys, the inner layer of the skin (dermis), and some glands. The endoderm develops into the lungs, digestive system, thymus, liver, thyroid and parathyroid glands, pancreas, spleen and urinary bladder.

During the seventeenth through twenty-first days, the embryonic disc grows in length and width. The embryo folds ventrally in the head and tail regions, causing the embryonic disc to become C-shaped. By the end of the third week, the first major systems, the cardiovascular system and central nervous system, are beginning to appear. Patches of mesoderm coalesce near the presumptive spinal cord to form the first *somites*, the precursors of the skeletal muscles. At this point, the developing child is called an *embryo*. This point marks the transition from the preembryonic period to the embryonic period.

Fetal membranes protect the embryo and provide for its respiration, nourishment, and excretion. These membranes include the yolk sac, the allantois, the amnion, and the chorion. The *yolk sac* plays a role in the transfer of nutrients and forms the *allantois*, from which part of the intestinal tract develops. The yolk sac and allantois combine with the body stalk to form the umbilical cord. The blood vessels of the allantois eventually enlarge and become the blood vessels of the umbilical cord. The *amnion* forms the wall of the amniotic cavity. It is initially attached to the periphery of the embryonic disc. Later in development, the amnion surrounds the embryo and forms an outer coating for the umbilical cord, attaching to the edge of the placenta. The amniotic cavity is filled with a pale, straw-colored watery fluid, the amniotic fluid. This fluid is initially produced by the cells of the amnion. Later, when the kidneys of the embryo are functioning, urine from the embryo supplements the amniotic fluid. After the ninth week, the amniotic fluid is swallowed and absorbed through the digestive tract. The fluid serves as water for the fetus to drink, keeps the fetus at an even temperature and protects the fetus from injury while allowing freedom of movement. At full term, the amniotic cavity contains about one liter of amniotic fluid. The fluid is shed just prior to delivery, following the rupture of the amnion.

The *chorion* is the outermost of the fetal membranes. The outer surface of the chorion possesses thin processes (villi), which are directed toward the endometrium. This portion of the chorion is the fetal contribution to the placenta. The *placenta*, which forms during the fourth month of pregnancy, functions as a respiratory, nutritive, and excretory organ for the fetus. It supplies oxygen and removes carbon dioxide; it supplies nutrients and removes wastes. The placenta also serves as a filter, protecting the fetus from bacteria and viruses. The placenta produces hormones (estrogen and progesterone) that are responsible for maintaining the integrity of the uterine endometrium throughout the rest of pregnancy.

By the fourth week, most of the body systems are present in rudimentary form. The neural tube and lung buds, the precursors of the central nervous system and respiratory system, respectively, are present. Eyes, inner ears, and nose appear in primitive form. The three major processes of the face (forehead process, upper jaw process and lower jaw process) are apparent. The number of somites increases greatly. The yolk sac begins to form the intestine; the esophagus, stomach, liver, and pancreas differentiate. The thyroid gland and thymus begin to develop. The limb buds are apparent. The heart is beating and the primitive circulatory system is connected to the blood vessels of the chorion. The embryo measures about 5 mm ($\frac{1}{5}$ in) in crown-to-rump (C.R.) length.

During the fifth week, the rate of growth of the head exceeds that of the other regions. The rapid development of the brain is responsible for the extensive growth of the head. The limbs begin to differentiate. The arms develop slightly earlier than the legs. The precursors of the hands and feet appear. The parathyroid glands and the spleen begin to form. The external genitalia are apparent in primitive form (too primitive, however, to distinguish the sex of the embryo by visual inspection). The stomach and intestinal tract continue to develop. The embryo measures about 8 mm ($\frac{1}{3}$ in) in C.R. length.

In the sixth week, the embryo continues to assume an increasingly human appearance. The facial processes merge toward the midline to form the face. The external ears begin to appear. The eyes become more obvious as pigment begins to appear in the retina. Early indications of fingers and toes appear as the arms and legs continue to develop. The trunk and neck begin to straighten. The embryo attains a C.R. length of 13 mm ($\frac{1}{2}$ in).

The developing intestine herniates into the umbilical cord during the seventh week. This umbilical herniation is a normal phase of the development of the intestine because the rapidly growing intestine exceeds the capacity of the abdomen and pushes into the umbilical cord. Later in development (during the twelfth week), the intestine will return to the abdomen. The arms and legs undergo extensive change. Notches form that demarcate the fingers. The embryo grows to 18 mm ($\frac{3}{4}$ in) in C.R. length.

At the beginning of the final (eighth) week of the embryonic period, the fingers are short and noticeably webbed. The toes begin to appear. By the end of the eighth week, the fingers and toes are lengthened and more distinct. The tail bud completely disappears. The embryo is distinctly human in appearance. The body is covered with a thin skin. There is no subcutaneous layer of fat. The head is round, but it is still disproportionately large. The nose is more prominent. The eyes are more forwardly directed. The eyelids are apparent, and the eyes are usually open. Toward the end of the week, the eyelids begin to fuse closed. The neck region is evident. The abdomen is less protuberant. The intestinal tract is still within the proximal portion of the umbilical cord. The bones begin to ossify. Although the external genitalia have developed further, determination of the sex of the embryo is still not possible. The embryo weighs about 1 gm ($\frac{1}{30}$ oz) and measures 23 mm (about 1 in) in C.R. length.

At the beginning of the ninth week, the head constitutes nearly half of what is now called the fetus. Throughout the ninth through twelfth weeks, the body grows rapidly, while growth of the head slows somewhat. The neck is well defined. The face is broad, and the forehead is high and prominent. The ears are low-set. The eyelids are fused and will not reopen until the sixth month. During the third month, the arms attain their final form and proportions. Nails are present on the tips of the fingers. The legs are still somewhat shorter than their final relative lengths. The lungs adopt their final form, although they are collapsed. The intestinal tract returns to the abdomen from its herniation into the umbilical cord. The kidney begins to secrete urine into the amniotic cavity. The fetus now actively swallows amniotic fluid. The external genitalia adopt their final form. It is now possible to identify the sex of the fetus by visual inspection. The fetus attains a C.R. length of 87 mm (3½ in) and weighs 45 gm (1½ oz).

The Second Trimester of Pregnancy

Growth is very rapid during the fourth month. The body continues to grow faster than the head. The head is quite erect at this time. The legs lengthen. The lower jaw grows forward, forming a chin. Scalp hair develops. The external ears rise to a higher level on the sides of the head. The skeleton is ossifying rapidly. Joint capsules develop. Blood cells are produced by the liver, spleen, and bone marrow. The fetus reaches a C.R. length of 140 mm (5½ in) and a weight of 200 gm (6⅔ oz).

Growth slows somewhat between the seventeenth and twentieth weeks. The body is covered with fine hair. Oil glands (sebaceous glands) of the skin secrete an oily substance, called the *vernix*, which covers the skin until birth. The thick layer of vernix protects the delicate skin of the fetus from abrasions and from chapping due to its being constantly bathed in amniotic fluid. Fetal movements (known as "quickening") are strong enough to be felt by the mother during this period. The fetal heartbeat can be heard through a stethoscope placed on the mother's abdomen. Toenails have developed. The fetus grows to a C.R. length of about 190 mm (7½ in) and a weight of about 460 gm (15⅓ oz).

There is substantial weight gain throughout the sixth month. The skin is very wrinkled and red. There is little subcutaneous fat at this time, which accounts for the wrinkled appearance of the skin. The head is still relatively large. The eyelids now reopen. Eyebrows and eyelashes are present. Although all organs are well developed, the respiratory and vascular systems are still quite immature. As a result, few infants born at twenty-four weeks are able to survive. At this stage, the fetus weighs 820 gm (27 oz) and has reached a C.R. length of 230 mm (9½ in).

The Third Trimester of Pregnancy

Subcutaneous fat is deposited from the twenty-fifth week through the twenty-eighth week. The deposition of fat gives the fetus a more rounded, less wrinkled appearance. The hair on the head is longer. If born at this stage, the infant will probably survive, if carefully attended. At birth, babies of this age cry and move vigorously. The fetus reaches about 270 mm (11 in) in C.R. length and weighs about 1300 gm (2 lb, 9 oz).

During the eighth month, the skin becomes quite smooth with further deposition of subcutaneous fat. The arms and legs may appear quite chubby. The fingernails reach the ends of the fingers, but the toenails do not yet reach the ends of the toes. The embryo attains a C.R. length of 300 mm (12 in) and a weight of about 2,100 gm (4 lb, 6 oz). If born at this stage, the fetus has an excellent chance of survival.

Most fetuses are quite plump from the thirty-third through the thirty-eighth weeks. Nails project beyond the ends of the fingers and toes. The bones of the skull are firm. The chest is prominent. The breasts protrude in both sexes. By the end of the thirty-eighth week, the fetus normally measures about 360 mm (14½ in) in C.R. length and weighs from 2,500 to 5,000 gm, with an average weight of 3,500 gm (from 5 lb, 3 oz to 10 lb, 6 oz; average weight, 7 lb, 4 oz).

Congenital Defects

During prenatal development, the embryo or the fetus is sensitive to a great variety of potentially harmful environmental agents. The environment of the fetus consists of the interior of the mother's uterus and the placental connection with the mother's bloodstream. Any agent that affects the mother's body or enters her bloodstream could affect the fetus by interfering with the normal course of its development. The earlier in the prenatal developmental period that exposure to a harmful agent occurs, the more severe will be the congenital effect. The developing infant is especially sensitive to harmful environmental agents during the first trimester, when the major organs and systems of the body are being established.

One of the most widely recognized, potentially harmful environmental agents is X-rays. Intense X-irradiation can cause very severe congenital malformations of the fetus. While there is little proof that diagnostic X-rays (e.g., dental X-rays, chest X-rays) cause congenital malformations, extreme caution should be exercised in exposing a pregnant woman to X-rays, particularly during the first trimester. Actively dividing cells, such as those of the central nervous system during the first trimester of pregnancy, seem to be particularly susceptible to damage by X-rays. Interference with the normal development of the cells of the central nervous system may lead to mental retardation.

Infectious agents are a class of potentially harmful environmental agents. The Rubella virus, which causes German measles, is a well-known example. About 15 to 20 percent of the infants who are born to women who had German measles during the first trimester of pregnancy are congenitally malformed. The most common malformations are cataracts, cardiac malformations, and deafness. As with all environmental agents, the earlier in the pregnancy the exposure occurs, the more severe will be the malformations. A less well-known infectious agent that can adversely affect the fetus is *Toxoplasma gondii*, a parasitic protozoan that causes the disease toxoplasmosis. The protozoan is contracted in two ways: by eating raw meat (e.g., steak tartare) or by coming into contact with infected animals (usually cats). The disease in adults is extremely mild and is characterized by flu-like symptoms. However, the protozoan may cross the placental membrane and infect the fetus, causing severe destructive changes in the brain and eyes.

Drugs taken by the mother may have powerful effects on the fetus and may produce serious congenital malformations. Two drugs that are known to affect the fetus are thalidomide and diethylstilbestrol (DES). Thalidomide was used in Europe (and less widely in the United States) during the late 1950s and early 1960s as an anti-nausea medication and sleeping pill. By the mid-1960s, it became apparent that thalidomide caused severe congenital malformations of the limbs (including the total absence of arms and legs). DES was commonly used in the 1940s and 1950s to treat women with histories of miscarriages. In the mid-1970s, it was determined that young women whose mothers had taken DES during their pregnancies had much higher incidences of cancer of the cervix and vagina than women whose mothers did not take DES during their pregnancies. Thus, DES affects the fetus in a way that is not detected until fifteen to twenty-five years after birth. Other drugs that are suspected of producing congenital malformations are anticonvulsant drugs (diphenylhydantoin, trimethadione), antipsychotic drugs (phenothiazine, lithium), antianxiety drugs (Valium [diazepam], meprobamate) and antitumor drugs (aminopterin, methotrexate). Lastly, there is increasing evidence that aspirin, which is the drug most commonly taken during pregnancy, is potentially harmful to the developing fetus. All of these drugs with suspected harmful effects should be avoided during pregnancy, unless absolutely necessary.

Although they are not commonly thought of as drugs, alcohol and nicotine can affect the developing fetus. Maternal alcoholism is often associated with severe congenital malformations. Fetal alcohol syndrome is characterized by mental retardation, growth deficiency, limb deformities, cardiac abnormalities, and craniofacial abnormalities. Even moderate alcohol consumption during pregnancy may be detrimental to fetal development. Smoking during pregnancy is also harmful to the developing fetus. While nicotine does not seem to cause congenital malformations, it does retard fetal growth. Nicotine causes a decrease in the flow of blood to the uterus, thereby lowering the supply of oxygen to the fetus. The resulting oxygen deficiency impairs cell growth and may have a detrimental effect on mental development. In addition, women who are heavy smokers are twice as likely to deliver their babies prematurely as are women who do not smoke.

Maternal nutritional deficiency does not seem to cause congenital abnormalities, with the exception of maternal iodine deficiency, which can cause cretinism. The most common effect of maternal poor nutrition is the retardation of fetal growth (and, possibly, of fetal mental development). Poorly nourished mothers tend to have infants of much lower birth weights than do women with proper nutrition.

Methods of Monitoring the Fetus Within the Uterus

The obstetrician has several methods for monitoring the progress of fetal development. Frequent examinations of the expanding uterus and determination of the date of the first appearance of fetal movements are of great value in estimating the maturity of the fetus. Repeated determinations of the maternal urinary excretion of the hormone estradiol has been found to be a rapid and accurate method for following the growth rate of the fetus. In addition, several methods are now available for directly assessing the status of the fetus before birth. These techniques include amniocentesis, fetoscopy, and ultrasonography.

Amniocentesis is the sampling of amniotic fluid. A needle is inserted through the mother's abdominal wall and through the wall of the uterus into the amniotic cavity. Amniotic fluid is withdrawn with a syringe. Amniocentesis is difficult to perform before the end of the first trimester. Following amniocentesis, the amniotic fluid can be tested for the presence of chemical components that are known to leak into the amniotic fluid from the circulation of fetuses that have neural tube defects (spina bifida, anencephaly). Amniotic fluid examination is also important in assessing the severity of erythroblastosis fetalis (blue-baby syndrome). This condition, which is caused by a mismatching of fetal and maternal Rh blood groups (mother, Rh−; fetus, Rh+, like its father), results in the destruction of fetal red blood cells by antibodies from the mother's bloodstream. Monitoring of the degree of anemia exhibited by the fetus (due to the destruction of red blood cells) will determine when an intrauterine transfusion of the fetus becomes necessary. The sex of the fetus can be determined by examination of the fetal cells that are normally shed into the amniotic fluid. These fetal cells can be grown in cell cultures and studied to reveal chromosomal abnormalities (such as those that cause Down's syndrome) or metabolic disorders (such as those that cause Tay-Sachs disease).

Fetoscopy is the direct visualization of the fetus by means of a flexible, illuminated fiber-optical lighting instrument. The fetoscope is introduced through a hollow tube (or trochar), which is inserted through the mother's abdominal wall and uterine wall. Using the fetoscope, the fetus can be examined, and biopsies of skin and blood samples can be obtained. Fetoscopy is most easily (and most safely) performed at the end of the fourth month of pregnancy, when the amniotic cavity is large enough to accommodate the trochar.

Ultrasonography, or ultrasound (sonar) techniques, can be used to study the fetus in the uterus. The size of the fetal head and the C.R. length can be measured with accuracy and reliability. Fetal abnormalities, uterine tumors, multiple pregnancies, and the location of the placenta can be detected by this technique. Ultrasonography is routinely used to locate the fetus prior to insertion of the needle used for amniocentesis or the trochar used for fetoscopy.

LABOR AND DELIVERY

Since the late 1960s, fetal heart monitoring has become a routine procedure for assessing the status of the fetus during labor. Electronic sensors are attached to the mother's abdomen (and, during the second stage of labor, to the baby's scalp). These sensors record the fetal electrocardiogram (EKG) as well as an indication of the contractions of the uterus. The monitoring system provides the obstetrician with instantaneous information about the welfare of the fetus. It provides a means of very quickly recognizing fetal distress during labor. Extreme fetal distress may necessitate the delivery of the infant by Caesarean section.

Labor (or childbirth or parturition) is the process by which the fetus, placenta, and fetal membranes are forcibly expelled from the mother's reproductive tract. The factors that initiate labor are not clearly understood.

Three to four weeks before birth, the fetus assumes a slightly lower position in the uterus (the change in position of the fetus is called "lightening"). The fetus is usually in a head-downward position, facing backward. In about 5 percent of births, delivery is difficult because the baby's buttocks (breech presentation), shoulder (shoulder presentation), foot (incomplete breech), or face (brow presentation) emerges first from the vagina.

Labor (Figure B-2) can be divided into three stages: The *first stage* begins when the cervix of the uterus begins to dilate in response to the onset of regular contractions of the uterus. This stage lasts about twelve hours for first pregnancies and about seven hours for subsequent pregnancies. There are, however, wide variations.

The *second stage* of labor begins when the cervix is completely dilated and ends with the birth of the infant. The second stage lasts about fifty minutes for first pregnancies and about twenty minutes for subsequent pregnancies.

The *third stage* begins when the infant is delivered and ends when the afterbirth (placenta and fetal membranes) is delivered. This stage usually lasts less than

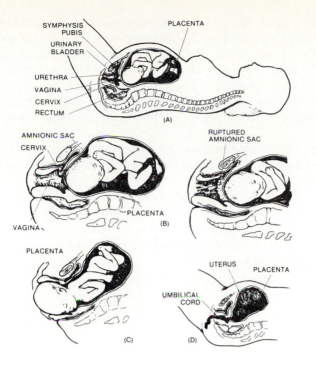

SYMPHYSIS PUBIS
PLACENTA
URINARY BLADDER
URETHRA
VAGINA
CERVIX
RECTUM
(A)

AMNIONIC SAC
CERVIX
RUPTURED AMNIONIC SAC
PLACENTA
VAGINA
(B)

PLACENTA
(C)

UTERUS   PLACENTA
UMBILICAL CORD
(D)

Figure B-2.
The birth process.
(a) Fetal position prior to birth. (b) Dilation. Protrusion of amnionic sac through partly dilated cervix. Amnionic sac ruptured and complete dilation of cervix. (c) Expulsion stage. (d) Placental stage.

thirty minutes. After delivery of the afterbirth, the uterus continues to contract. These contractions constrict the arteries that formerly supplied the placenta, thereby preventing excessive bleeding from the placental site.

With the expulsion of the placenta, there is a sudden decline in the levels of the hormones (estrogen and progesterone) that the placenta had been secreting. The greatly thickened and richly vascularized endometrium of the uterus becomes unstable and is shed piecemeal, along with a small amount of blood. This loss of blood and endometrium is the first menstruation following pregnancy.

Changes in the Infant at Birth

At the moment of birth, the infant must undergo extreme physiological adjustments for the change from intrauterine to extrauterine existence. Many of these adjustments occur during the first day of life. Other adjustments occur over the first four weeks of life. The first four weeks of life, which comprise the *neonatal period*, are a critical time for the infant. The highest mortality rate in childhood occurs during this period.

One of the earliest and most obvious neonatal adjustments is the initiation of respiratory activity. Very soon after delivery, the infant begins to gasp strongly. The gasping serves to expand and inflate the lungs. When the lungs have inflated, normal rhythmic breathing movements begin. Rhythmic breathing movements are normally established within one minute after birth. The average newborn breathes at a rate of approximately forty breaths per minute (nearly three times the adult rate).

A second neonatal adjustment is the redirection of blood through the heart and lungs. While the fetus was in the uterus, very little blood was circulated to its nonfunctioning lungs. With the initiation of respiration, the distribution of blood through the heart must change. The channels between the right and left atria of the heart (the foramen ovale) and the communication between the pulmonary artery and the aorta (the ductus arteriosus) close, establishing the adult circulatory pattern. These two changes serve to separate completely the pulmonary circulation to the lungs from the systemic circulation to the body. The pulse rate of the newborn is rapid, with an average of 130 beats per minute (nearly twice the adult rate).

Heat regulation mechanisms are rather immature in the newborn. After birth, body temperature drops by about three degrees. Body temperature stabilizes within eight hours.

A normal, full-term infant weighs between 2.5 and 5 kg (5½ and 11 lb), averaging 3.5 kg (7½ lb). Up to 10 percent of birth weight is lost during the first three to five days, primarily due to the loss of fluids. The lost weight is usually regained by the fourteenth day. During the next three months, the baby gains approximately 30 gm (1 oz) per day.

C

FINANCES AND THE FAMILY

*F*amily patterns of spending have undergone major changes in recent years. Almost all American families have had to face squarely the dilemma of limited financial resources in a nation that offers a staggering array of products and services for consumption. This trend toward a highly technical, multiple-option society that focuses on provision of services and information as opposed to industrial production appears to be the wave of the future (Naisbitt, 1982). While new directions and changes within society can generate concern, they also offer the opportunity to use resources in new and creative ways. Using money wisely to acquire those goods and services that are needed or highly desired and to increase personal or family worth is the challenge facing the modern American family in today's economy.

Many factors affect the financial decisions that families make. Internal factors such as values, goals, and personal preferences, and external forces such as norms, customs, social pressures, technology, and advertising all affect how families spend money. Monetary decisions concerning day-to-day purchases and long-range investments can be a point of agreement and harmony or major conflict within a family. Spending patterns constitute a source of marital compatibility or incompatibility. That is why money, a scarce but valued resource, must be managed well. Compatibility in goals, desires, and spending patterns can strengthen a marital relationship. Cooperative decision making by husband and wife as to how monies are to be spent also provides an excellent role model for children to emulate.

THE FAMILY BUDGET

A *budget* is one of the most important financial management tools. It is defined as the process of identifying income over a designated period of time, describing how those funds are to be spent for consumption and investment, keeping records of income and expenditures, and developing a plan of appropriate actions in the event of a change in income/expenditure patterns (Apilado and Morehart, 1980). A budget is a financial guide for spending and investment that allows a family to exercise control over their resources.

There is no magic formula for budgeting that fits all families' needs. Each family must develop a budget consistent with their unique values, goals, and priorities. However, some general rules for budgeting may be helpful (Wolf, 1981, pp. 29–30):

1. Set specific financial goals.
2. Identify fixed expenditures and provide for their payment.
3. Save for major expenses throughout several budget periods.
4. Develop priorities for general expenditures.
5. Maintain accurate records of income and expenditures.
6. Be realistic in differentiating between needs and wants.
7. Avoid a budget that is too restrictive.
8. Keep budgeting procedures simple.

A budget can be developed for varying lengths of time: weekly, monthly, bimonthly, or for any period of time that is a logical unit for the family. Regardless of the actual length of the budget period, budgets should be set up for a year at a time to allow flexibility and ample opportunity for revisions to enhance financial stability. A well-planned budget can help a family deal with inflation, maintain good credit, and maximize wealth. Budgeting in either a single-parent or two-parent family should be a team effort. That is, all family members who are old enough to comprehend simple principles of money management should be involved in discussion and planning of the family budget.

Budgeting has two major objectives that must be accomplished if the process is to be successful (Bailard, Biehl, and Kaiser, 1982). First, a system of disciplined spending must be sustained. Only monies allocated for particular goods and services should be spent on those expense categories. For example, money designated for rent cannot be spent on entertainment. Many problems in family financial management are the result of imbalance between income and spending. This imbalance frequently results from inefficient priorities. Thus, the second objective is to reduce the amount of money wasted through needless expenditures in each budgeted category.

Budgets are not "financial monsters" that control those families that develop them. Instead, budgets are meant to be *controlled by families* and to optimize chances for financial success. Budgets can help families get what they really want, prevent spending beyond income, maintain interpersonal harmony among family members, help keep track of expenditures, put the family in control of spending, and help them stay there (Leet and Driggers, 1983).

The U.S. Bureau of Labor and Statistics maintains updated survey data on how the typical American family spends its income. Almost 60 percent of income is spent in three major categories: housing, food, and taxes. Housing, which includes utilities, is a significant part of any budget. Adequate housing is essential for the health and well-being of families. While housing is a necessity, it is also a luxury: As income increases, a larger proportion is spent on housing. It is the largest

SYGMA, J. P. Laffont

Budgeting should involve the entire family.

category of spending. Quality food is important to maintain family energy levels and to prevent the occurrence of illness or debilitating health problems.

A significant part of family income goes for federal, state, or local taxes. While some of this money is returned to families in unemployment compensation and Social Security benefits, 12 percent of annual income is still spent—a significant amount (Miller, Power, and Meyer, 1983).

Ways of investing to reduce or delay taxes will be discussed later in this Appendix.

Twenty percent of family income is spent on transportation, clothing, and medical care. In our mobile society, frequent use of public or private transportation is essential for employment, shopping, and recreation. Economy in this area can be achieved by car pooling, finding housing close to work, and walking or biking when possible. Expenditures for clothing will be highest in areas with seasonal change. Needs for clothing are increased by the various seasons for which family members must dress. Medical care expenditures fluctuate according to the developmental stage of the family. During childbearing and child-rearing years as well as during retirement years, medical expenses tend to be higher than during middle adult years. The exception to this rule occurs when major chronic health problems occur prematurely, requiring high medical expenditures.

Developing a Goal Work-sheet

Since a budget should be tailored to the unique needs of each family, long-term and short-term financial goals must be identified. Long-term goals can be stated in general terms while short-term goals should be more specific. Both types of goals must be further classified as to whether they are essential or desired but nonessential. Goals must then be prioritized. An example of a long-term goal is to save money for a new home. A short-term goal might be to purchase tires for the family car. The contrast between essential goals and desirable goals is illustrated by the following example. The Olssons have been married for two years, are renting a one-bedroom apartment, and want to start a family within the next two or three years. They also would like to take a trip to Florida in the near future. They think that starting a family soon is essential. A trip to Florida would be nice but is not absolutely necessary. Therefore, in prioritizing their long-term financial goals, expenses related to starting a family would be given higher priority than expenses for a trip to Florida.

A goal work-sheet can be helpful in clarifying financial priorities. Goals may relate either to income or to expenditures. Tables C–1 and C–2 present examples of goal work-sheets addressing both long-term and short-term priorities of the Olsson family.

The Budgeting Process

Construction of a simple financial goal work-sheet as described in the previous section is the first step toward developing a successful budget. The second step in budgeting is to *estimate income*. A family must know how much money they make, how much is taken out for taxes and other benefits, and what actual take-home pay is. *Gross income* is the total amount that a family earns. *Net income* is what remains after taxes and is often referred to as disposable income. Income is usually best estimated by monthly intervals over a period of one year. All sources of income must be taken into consideration. These include salaries, commissions, interest, dividends, and bonuses.

Table C–1.   THE OLSSONS' (BILL AND MARY) LONG-RANGE FINANCIAL GOALS (JANUARY 1987 TO DECEMBER 1990)

Goals By Year	Essential/Desirable		Priority
1987			
Save money to buy home	E		3
Buy new bedroom furniture		D	5
Buy a car	E		1
Look for a two-bedroom apartment	E		2
Bill work on master's degree		D	4
1988			
Take a vacation in Florida		D	4
Have first child	E		1
Buy new living room furniture		D	2
Decorate nursery		D	3
1989			
Bill look for higher-paying job		D	4
Buy baby clothes	E		1
Provide for well-baby care	E		2
Mary resume nursing career part-time	E		3
1990			
Buy a new home		D	2
Invest in stocks		D	3
Mary look for full-time position	E		1
Take a trip to California		D	4

E = Essential goal; D = Desirable but nonessential goal.

Table C–2.   THE OLSSONS' (BILL AND MARY) SHORT-TERM
FINANCIAL GOALS (JANUARY 1987 to DECEMBER 1987)

Goal	Essential/Desirable		Priority
Bill finish bachelor of arts degree	E		1
Mary finish bachelor of science degree	E		1
Purchase new clothes for work	E		4
Save one-third of Mary's salary		D	5
Pay off student loans	E		2
Go skiing in Colorado		D	9
Go camping for two weeks in Canada		D	8
Purchase stereo equipment		D	7
Replace tires on second car	E		3
Buy golf clubs for Mary		D	6

E = Essential goal; D = Desirable but nonessential goal.

The third step in developing a budget is to *estimate expenses*. Estimating expenses for the coming year should take into account what expenses have been in previous years plus any new money outlays that will be required in the current year. Expenses can be classified as *fixed* or *variable*. Fixed expenses are those that you have committed your family to pay either by contract or agreement. Examples of fixed expenses are rent, house mortgage, utilities, insurance, car payments, and repayment of loans. Fixed expenses may be due on a monthly, quarterly, or semiannual basis. Regular savings may also be included in this category.

Variable expenses, such as food, clothing, and transportation, may recur each month but vary in amount. Other variable expenditures are encountered at irregular intervals, such as vacations or costs of entertainment. It is normal for households from time to time to have unexpected expenses, such as those for replacement of broken appliances, car repairs, illness, or accidents. Setting aside money for a financial crisis is an important part of the budgeting process. This may be a fixed or variable amount each month. This money should be kept in a savings account or placed in investments that are readily convertible into cash. While it is tempting to use this reserve money for recreation and other wants or needs, having a reserve may mean the difference between meeting financial commitments or failing to meet them in the event of an emergency.

The next step in the budgeting process is to *plan how the family will spend its money* for the coming months based on short-term and long-term goals and priorities. Income for the year and estimated fixed and variable expenses should be compared on both an annual and month-to-month basis. A balanced budget exists when total income for the year equals or exceeds expenses. It is possible to have a budget deficit some months and a budget surplus in others. Remedies for deficits include transferring expenditures from months in which budget deficits occur to months in which budget surpluses exist, transferring income to months where budget deficits occur, or using savings investments or loans to cover temporary deficits (Gitman, 1978).

An unbalanced annual budget is of much more concern than monthly variations. A preferred approach to avoiding this situation is to cut lower priority items out of the budget or defer them to other years. Much less desirable is liquidating enough savings and investments or borrowing to meet the total budget deficit for the year. The latter is not recommended as it defeats the purpose of a budget, which is to increase a family's financial security and net worth.

A suggested format for a family budget plan appears in Table C–3. It should be noted that all sources of income are identified and expenses are estimated. Grouping expenses into categories makes it easier to plan expenditures that balance with income.

Table C–3.   SUGGESTED FORMAT FOR A FAMILY BUDGET PLAN

Item	Jan.	Feb.	Nov.	Dec.	Total
Income: Husband, Job Wife, Job Other Income Total Income					
Housing Expense: Mortgage Rent Utilities Telephone Home Insurance Property Taxes Furniture Maintenance					
Automobile Expense: Car Payment Car Insurance License Gas and Oil Maintenance					
Food: Food and Beverages Personal Care Products Restaurants					
Clothing: Husband Wife Children					
Insurance: Health Premium Life Premium					
Miscellaneous: Gifts and Contributions Education Recreation Savings and Investments Emergency Fund					

Here are some basic spending rules identified by Freeman and Graf (1980) that will be helpful in setting maximums in various categories of budgeting:

1. Short-term borrowing (one year or less) should not exceed 20 percent of monthly income.
2. Life insurance coverage is at its optimum when premiums account for 10 percent of income, except for those with special needs, other sources of income, investments, or anticipated inheritance.
3. In periods of rapid inflation, a homebuyer may keep up with the cost of living by acquiring a mortgage for the smallest possible amount for the longest period of time.
4. Set aside six months' salary for emergencies.

These general rules, along with U.S. Bureau of Labor Statistics data on how families at three different levels of living allocate income can assist a family in establishing prudent spending patterns.

Evaluation of Budget Adherence

Good record-keeping is essential to determine adherence to estimated expenses in each budget category. A simple way to keep track of expenses is to organize a small notebook by category and record all expenditures immediately. Extent of budget adherence should be determined each month until the family is aware of adherence patterns. Categories in which greater or lesser amounts of money are spent than estimated should be examined. The rationale for constructing a budget plan is to come as close to estimated expenses in actual expenses as possible.

Surpluses in certain budget categories, if no deficits exist in other categories, can be accumulated to purchase extra items that the family wants. If possible, these items should be selected so that they are employed by all. This serves as a source of reward and reinforcement for budget adherence.

Several important guidelines for budget adherence should be kept in mind. First, adherence to budget should not put unnecessary strain on any family member. For instance, if the food budget is not adequate, actual expenses will exceed estimates, and the budget must be adjusted to a more realistic level. Second, do not pay for things such as life insurance on a monthly basis to avoid deficits since this will result in unnecessarily high service charges. If an insurance premium is due, it may be best to pay it out of reserve funds and run a temporary monthly deficit (Bailard, Biehl, and Kaiser, 1982). Third, any time a budget category has a negative balance at the end of the month, purchase of items in that category should, if possible, be held back until the balance is positive again. Fourth, the family should have enough self-constraint to avoid deliberately overspending in any category. A flippant or apathetic attitude about the family budget on the part of any family member can undermine careful financial planning.

Adjusting the Budget

Several months after instituting a new budget, the family should evaluate it. Is the family pleased with the results of expenditures? Are family members happy with what they are achieving, e.g., purchases, savings, investments? Even if a family is adhering to their budget and there are no monthly deficits, a budget must be flexible to allow changing needs and desires of the family to be met. Goals and values of the family change from month to month and throughout the life cycle. While recreational needs may be very important to a family during one month, the need for clothing may emerge as a priority during another month. As the family matures, income may change, such as going from one to two salaries or vice versa. It is obviously easier to upgrade than to downgrade lifestyle. Expenses may also change, such as when building a new home, returning to school for more education, or sending children to college. These cyclic family changes must be taken into consideration in flexible and realistic budget planning.

After careful evaluation, a few families will find that they have a special talent for keeping expenses within their income without a budget. They can function well with a mental budget and need to be less concerned about working out on paper all steps of the budget process. Even these families will still find it worthwhile to keep an accurate record of expenditures, especially those that are income tax deductible. Other families, probably the majority, will find that a budget is invaluable in allowing them to get the most out of the money that they earn. These families should continue budgeting, streamlining the process to make it as efficient as possible. In return, they will reap a great deal of satisfaction from thoughtful and responsible planning for use of financial resources.

TAXATION

Governments provide many goods and services to citizens. Among other things, they provide national defense, a court system, fire and police protection, public aid, health care, an educational system, and libraries. It takes a great deal of money just to provide those services that are mandated by Congress. In fact, federal, state, and local governments are currently attempting to cut back expenses after a long period of deficit spending. Such cuts will affect many of the important programs that government provides. For example, cuts in Medicare/Medicaid benefits have already taken place. This will adversely affect access to health care by the indigent and elderly.

Governments must be financed by the people that they serve. While some of the monies paid to government are returned to us in the form of benefits, such as Social Security and unemployment compensation, other dollars are spent for direct expenses incurred in administering government services. Monies returned to society in the form of benefits are called *transfer payments*. Transfer payments can take the form of money or in-kind subsidies, such as food stamps, public housing, or medical care, for which there is no charge to the recipient (Leet and Driggers, 1983). Mandated government programs composed exclusively of transfer payments are referred to as *entitlement programs*. These programs are intended by Congress to provide for truly needy citizens. Individuals in the United States have generally been in agreement with this use of tax monies, even though there is less agreement as to how much should be spent for this purpose and who the recipients should be.

Government is indeed big business. Individual income taxes constitute more than a third of government income.

Principles of Taxation

Two basic views exist concerning who should be taxed and how they should be taxed. One widely accepted belief is that taxes should be levied according to the *benefit principle*. That is, people should be taxed in proportion to the benefits that they receive from government services. For example, since government monies are used to maintain roads, families who operate automobiles and buy gasoline should pay for use of public highways. Property taxes are another example of this principle. The more property a family has, the more taxes they pay. It is assumed that the need for fire and police protection as well as other government services such as sanitation is increased the more property is owned. While the benefit principle appears equitable in some situations, it is impossible to apply in others. How could mothers who receive formula for their infants and food through the Women, Infants, and Children (WIC) Program pay for their benefits when all have low incomes and many are unemployed?

Another approach to taxation is called the *ability to pay principle*. The basic assumption is that the burden to support government services should fall most heavily on those with the greater income or wealth. An underlying assumption is that as income increases, less of each dollar is spent to meet essential needs and more is spent as discretionary income. That is, more of each dollar earned is spent on luxuries and nonessential items the higher the income. However, what would be the incentive to work if not for the added benefits that higher income brings?

Four approaches to taxation that reflect these principles in various ways will be discussed: proportional taxation, progressive taxation, regressive taxation, and flat-rate taxation.

Proportional Taxation.   With this approach to taxation, every wage earner pays a fixed percentage of tax on every dollar of income. When an income tax is proportional, more money is taken from higher income groups even though the percentage remains the same. For example, if the proportion is set at 22 percent, families earning $10,000 will pay $2,200 while families earning $50,000 will pay $11,000. Milton Friedman, a Nobel Prize-winning economist, has argued that proportional tax is more equitable than any other approach and could generate the same amount of money for government as the current system of tax if there were no deductions or loopholes (Lect and Driggers, 1983).

Progressive Taxation.   With progressive taxation, the more a family earns, the higher the percentage taken out of each dollar. Thus, taxes take a larger and larger fraction of a family's income as earnings rise. Federal income tax is the best example of a progressive tax. In the current tax system, both the absolute dollar amount and the percentage of tax increase across successive income brackets. A family can calculate their average tax rate by dividing total taxes withheld by total income earned. The highest percentage tax that a family can pay under current laws is 50 percent.

Regressive Taxation.   A regressive tax rate takes away a lower percentage of income as earnings rise. If one accepts the ability to pay principle, this tax is least equitable because it extracts a larger percentage of income as earnings decline. A good example of a regressive tax is state sales tax. While the percent of tax on a dollar is the same for all families, lower income families spend a larger proportion of their income on food than do families with higher incomes. Thus, a low income family may spend 24 percent of their income on sales-taxable food while a more affluent family may spend only 10 percent. In relation to income, the percent given to the state for sales tax is higher in the low income family.

Flat-Rate Taxation.   With a flat rate approach to taxation, a fixed percent of taxes is set for all families, but there are no deductions regardless of size of family or liabilities. With this approach, the tax code could no longer be used to promote such goals as home ownership and energy conservation. No longer being able to deduct charitable contributions would raise the cost of donating to churches, the poor, and other worthy causes. Most likely, this would decrease families' willingness to share their resources with others in need. Proponents of this system argue that such an approach would greatly simplify income tax returns. All that would be required is the return of a postcard. Milton Friedman has stated that with such a taxing system, families could use their assets in the most productive way rather than in the most tax-evasive way (Crickmer, 1982).

Tax Forms

Families should become familiar with various income tax forms so that they can select the one that best meets their needs. Form 1040A is the simplest form that can be filed by a family that does not wish to itemize deductions and that has a gross income consisting primarily of wages. To use the form, dividends and interest must total less than $400. Deductions are expenses that may be subtracted from one's gross income or adjusted gross income, thus decreasing the taxes paid. The only allowable deductions are those specified in tax laws or regulations. There is also a one page form, 1040EZ, for single individuals with no dependents. Both of the above can be completed very quickly and without professional assistance.

Form 1040 is much more complex, but it allows the most specificity in reporting income and deductions. All United States citizens, including minors, and all aliens residing in the country must file income tax returns on one of these forms by April 15 of each year if their gross income for the previous year exceeds specified limits. For example, married couples filing a joint return must file if their combined gross income exceeds $7560 in 1987 and $8900 in 1988.

The decision of couples to file joint or separate returns should be made after careful deliberation. In instances where one spouse has a low or negligible income, filing a joint return usually results in a lower tax.

An additional form that families should be familiar with is the W-2 Form, on which the total wages subject to withholding, the amount of income tax withheld by an employer, and the total amount withheld for Social Security taxes (FICA) are reported. Another form, W-4, is used by working family members to file with an employer the number of dependent exemptions.

Reducing Taxes

Families with higher than marginal incomes must pay taxes. However, there are legal means for reducing the amount of taxes paid. To lower taxes, a family must reduce their taxable income. They must also increase their tax credits by investing in certain kinds of equipment or real estate. Bailard, Biehl, and Kaiser (1982) have suggested several common methods for tax reduction. The first is to *keep good records*. Failure to take all legal deductions can increase the amount of taxes paid. Secondly, new homeowners can *deduct a portion of sales tax* paid for the year in which they are landscaping, remodeling, or furnishing a home. If all receipts are kept, generally more than the average sales tax is found to have been spent.

Another way to get maximum value from itemized deductions is to *prepay some of them or postpone payment*, clustering as many as possible in one year so that their aggregate value exceeds the zero bracket amount.

Still other suggestions for reducing taxes include: *charitable gifts of stocks* as opposed to cash, *investment in real estate*, and *making business your pleasure*. What is meant by the last item is that making a profit out of things you enjoy can result in deductible business expenses instead of nondeductible personal expenses. For example, if you like to travel, consider becoming a travel agent.

Professional Assistance

There are a number of sources of professional assistance available to families for income tax counseling and for filling out income tax returns. A list of individuals who may be helpful can be obtained from your local IRS office. Private income tax services are also available. Knowing a satisfied customer from one of the private agencies can be helpful in selecting such services wisely.

A family can also employ a tax accountant. Certified public accountants are generally quite expensive, but often they are the most reliable source of help. Tax accountants may not only assist in preparing the tax returns but they may also accompany the individual to the IRS office if he or she is later audited.

A final word of advice is in order. Good records make it much easier to file income tax returns and may increase deductions. Keep tax records in a fireproof file and label the files according to types of income, deductions and credits. Accurate records of medical expenses, interest payments, interest income, and charitable contributions can be invaluable in preparing the next year's income tax returns.

CREDIT

Credit is created whenever a seller transfers the possession of goods to a buyer in return for a money claim (Greene and Dince, 1983). Common kinds of credit include charge accounts and credit cards. Buying on credit allows families access to products and services before they actually have to pay for them. This has distinct advantages for it enhances the quality of a family's lifestyle. However, credit also has its disadvantages. Using credit creates liability. A *liability* is a debt owed to a creditor and an obligation to pay off the amount of the debt, usually with interest. Any user of credit should be aware of the fact that household liabilities account for the largest share of outstanding debt in the United States today (not counting the federal deficit). Incurring such debts should not be undertaken lightly.

Some general guidelines for using credit have been identified by Apilado and Morehart (1980):

1. Borrow only for high-priority needs (see your financial goal work-sheet).
2. Don't let debts exceed your ability to pay.
3. Be aware of what exact interest or finance charges are.
4. Minimize interest costs.
5. Protect your credit rating.
6. Be aware of the consequences of excessive debt.
7. Seek help from qualified personnel if excessive debt occurs.

Before incurring debt, a family should check their budget carefully to determine if such a debt is feasible. The budget must allow one to make the necessary payments on time.

Building a Credit History

Having a good record at a credit bureau is essential for obtaining credit. It is important for both husband and wife to establish a good credit history. Everyone has a right to know what is in his or her bureau report. The Fair Credit Reporting Act gives us the right to insist that a credit bureau recheck any wrong or incomplete information in our report (*Consumer Reports*, 1983). A good credit history can be established in the following ways: opening a checking and a savings account; taking out a small loan from a bank and paying it back promptly; not borrowing from small loan companies as it may prevent your obtaining other credit; accepting credit cards offered by a bank or a major department store; not applying for credit too often; and paying all bills promptly.

If a couple has joint credit accounts, they should be reported to the credit bureau in both names, that is, John White and Judy White rather than Mr. and Mrs. John White. It is also important to remember that if unanticipated expenses or loss of income prevents payment of debts, a family should immediately notify their creditors and, if possible, work out alternative arrangements. Debts not paid on time will be reported to the credit bureau as "late" and will be reflected in both spouses' credit ratings.

Types of Charge Accounts

To be knowledgeable consumers, families must be aware of the types of charge accounts available and the terms for payment. Use of charge accounts and credit cards should not be entered into without careful thought and planning. Some of the most common types of charge accounts are thirty-day accounts, open-end credit accounts, bank credit cards, and national credit cards.

A thirty-day account requires that a debt incurred be paid in thirty days with no interest charged for this convenience. Open-end credit accounts are another common type of account used by major department stores. If a family has such an account, they can continue to charge purchases up to a specific amount without paying off previous debts. Two kinds of open-end credit are budget charge accounts and option charge accounts. In a budget charge account, a family is required to pay only a specified portion of the bill within the first thirty days. The remaining balance is paid off within the next twelve months but can be paid off earlier. Interest charges on this type of account run 1.5 to 2 percent per month or 18 to 24 percent per year. Option charge accounts allow a family to pay part or all of the bill within thirty days with no interest charge. Any remaining amount must be paid over three to six months with generally the same interest charges on the unpaid balance as a budget charge account.

Bank credit charge cards are a third type of charge arrangement. Common examples of bank credit accounts are VISA and MasterCard. Purchases may be made at numerous locations, and a family will receive only one monthly statement for all purchases. Retail stores participating in this charge account system pay the bank a small percentage of the profits from merchandise sold in this way. In turn, the bank assumes the responsibility for debt collection, debt investigation, and the risk of bad debts. Often the charge to the department store for this service is passed on to the consumer in higher prices. If the account is paid off within twenty-five days of billing, there are no finance charges. Every family has a limit to the credit they can use depending on their credit rating. Purchases charged must never exceed this limit.

National credit cards are another type of charge account. They are issued by private credit organizations. The most common are American Express, Diners Club, and Carte Blanche. These cards generally are used for charging services such as airline tickets, hotel accommodations, restaurant bills, and entertainment expenses. Some stores also accept these cards for purchases, but they are less widely accepted for this purpose than bank credit cards. They also differ from bank programs in that their requirements for credit are more rigid. However, once you have been accepted as a card holder, credit limits imposed may be higher than with bank credit cards.

Advantages and Disadvantages of Credit Cards

The use of credit cards has distinct advantages, but it also has disadvantages. Certainly, when a family is short of cash and wishes to make a purchase, a credit card is handy. It is safer to carry than a large amount of cash. Credit cards also provide consumers with the opportunity to stop payment on items with which they are dissatisfied.

A major disadvantage is that the consumer is liable for unauthorized use of the card. The Electronic Fund Transfer Act of 1979 limits a cardholder's liability to $50 on a lost or stolen card if it is reported within two days. The liability increases to $500 if the two-day limit is passed and the bank or organization can prove that the card would not have been misused if the consumer had reported the loss (Freeman and Graf, 1980). Also, information on credit cards can be falsified. The consumer should always check to see that the correct amount has been entered for purchases made before signing the credit slip. In addition, monthly bills should be checked to see that salesclerks have not increased the amount of the charge after the credit slips have been signed.

The decision to use credit cards should be made after careful examination of credit options available. Families should gather information about the various credit cards and weigh the costs and benefits in light of their needs.

Installment Credit

Installment credit requires the consumer to assume a schedule of fixed payments over a period of time for items purchased. Installment credit rather than a charge account is generally used when large items are purchased. Unlike open-ended credit, installment credit involves a down payment; interest charges begin immediately; and if the debt is paid off ahead of schedule, a prepayment penalty may be charged. Installment credit involves a *purchase agreement* that may be written either by the creditor or by a major bank or finance company. Since there are several components of the purchase agreement, including a sales contract to protect the creditor against defaults in payment, a family should read and understand all terms of the agreement before signing it.

Sources of installment loans include commercial banks, credit unions, savings and loan associations, life insurance companies, consumer finance companies, loan sharks, and pawnbrokers. Each source has its advantages and disadvantages.

Commercial banks are stable institutions that generally have the lowest annual percentage rate (APR) of any formal lending institution. Having a good credit record on payment of a bank loan can make other sources of credit available for a family. Three types of cash loans are generally available from a bank: conventional installment loans, other types of installment loans, and single-payment loans. Disadvantages to consider are that banks generally lend money only to individuals with good credit records and small loans or short-term loans may be difficult to acquire.

Credit unions are often organized in a particular work setting or community by people who pool their savings to make loans to individuals within the group at cooperatively established interest rates. Credit unions may charge a maximum APR, but both small and large loans are available at short and long maturities. Frequently there is no prepayment penalty. The major disadvantage for a family is the threat to privacy in revealing their financial status and related problems to co-workers.

Savings and loan associations provide loans of various types: home improvement loans, mobile loans, and passbook loans. Passbook loans are the most common type and consist of a loan backed by a savings account, which involves installment payments of a prescribed amount over a specific time period. These loans generally have low APRs. However, a family must have a savings account to take advantage of this type of loan and can only borrow up to the amount that they have in savings.

Commercial finance companies provide loans of all sizes, and qualification for loans is easier than at other lending institutions. However, a major disadvantage is the APR, which may be 36 percent or higher.

Pawnbrokers and loan sharks should be strictly avoided. Both have extremely high APRs, as high as 120 percent and 1,200 percent respectively. While pawnbrokers operate legally, loan sharks operate illegally. Individuals who desperately need money should seek assistance from a qualified financial counselor. Illegal means of acquiring money can result in even greater financial problems.

Several suggestions should be heeded in shopping for credit. Be sure that existing credit accounts are up-to-date prior to seeking credit. Get an idea of what the rates are from different lenders and the requirements for credit. Be prepared to discuss your budget in detail and prepare a list of all your debts, amounts borrowed, current amounts owed, and the size of the monthly payments.

The lender wants to be assured that the risk in lending will pay off. The "Three C's" will help you keep in mind what creditors are looking for: *capacity*, *character*, and *collateral*. Creditors will ask many questions to ascertain a family's capacity to pay back the loan. These questions should be answered as accurately as possible. The creditor is also looking for character, that is, the willingness of the consumer to pay back the loan according to the established requirements. A credit history is often consulted to determine the character of the individual seeking a loan. Finally, the creditor wants to know if the individual has any collateral or assets of value. Assets are attached to pay a loan in the event of inability or unwillingness to do so. All this information is necessary to process a loan application.

Relief of Credit Obligations

If families overextend themselves financially, they should seek professional counseling. Signs of trouble include: not being able to make payments on time, getting delinquency notices, receiving letters from collection agencies, and seeking new loans to pay off old debts (Leet and Driggers, 1983). There are 276 credit counseling centers around the United States that provide free services to consumers. If you are unable to locate a local branch of the Consumer Credit Counseling Service, write to the National Foundation for Consumer Credit, Washington, DC 20006. Credit unions and family service agencies also offer financial counseling.

Consolidation of loans is another way to deal with credit obligations. A consolidation loan allows a family to put all of their debts into one loan on which they make one payment a month. However, the total cost of such a loan may be higher than the cumulative cost of the individual credit obligations.

Bankruptcy is a last resort to avoid financial insolvency. Bankruptcy is a court action that declares persons free of most of their debts because of inability to pay them. Husbands and wives must file separately. Declaring bankruptcy becomes a part of one's credit record for the next decade, severely limiting future ability to obtain credit. In full bankruptcy, all assets are sold to pay off debts except those protected under the law, e.g., $7,500 equity in a home and burial plot, interest up to $1,200 in a motor vehicle. The bankrupt individual is then cleared of the rest of the debt, except possibly mortgages, alimony, and child support. In Chapter 13 bankruptcy, the individual is provided the opportunity to pay off debts according to a court-supervised schedule of payments. The typical term of repayment is three years (Freeman and Graf, 1980). Chapter 13 bankruptcy does not appear on the individual's credit record.

In summary, credit should only be acquired by families who clearly understand the rules of the game and intend to play by them. Credit can be used wisely to increase buying power but should not be misused or abused.

SAVINGS AND INVESTMENTS

Identifying financial goals and the time frame in which the family expects to accomplish them is the first step in beginning a successful investment program.

There are many places to invest and save. The most common are banks, savings and loan associations, and credit unions. Most savings institutions offer two kinds of accounts: regular accounts and special accounts. Money can be deposited or withdrawn from regular accounts at any time. Money deposited in a special account usually must be left in for a certain period of time but draws higher interest than it would in a regular account.

Another form of savings is investing in government securities. However, the yield on such securities varies a great deal. U.S. savings bonds have a low yield while Treasury bills (T-bills) have a higher yield. Still another place to invest is a money-market mutual fund. These funds are run by investment companies and pool investors' money to buy large bank certificates of deposit, high-paying government securities, and the high-yield bonds of major corporations. The stock market is also a place for investment. By buying shares of stock, a family can invest in a corporation. Preferred stocks have a fixed annual dividend that remains the same. Dividends on preferred stock must be paid before dividends on common stock. A family interested in investing in the stock market should find a local, licensed broker whom they feel they can trust. Equity mutual funds are a way of letting experts in the stock market invest for you. Mutual funds are investment companies that sell shares to individual investors because they believe that they can make better investment decisions than individuals.

There are various types of investment income, the most common of which are interest, dividends, rent, and capital gains. Interest is money that the family receives for letting someone else use your money. Dividends are portions of company profits paid to stockholders. Rent is received from real estate or other property that the family owns but others are using. Capital gains are the profits received from sale of property or other investments.

The family considering a savings plan should check to see how interest is compounded and paid by the institution being considered. Over time, using various computation methods, differences in interest may be considerable.

Concerns of Investors

Families who decide to invest in the stock market or in real estate as opposed to placing their money in a savings account should be aware of the greater risks entailed even though in the long run they may make more money from such investments. Some stocks can increase or decrease in value within a relatively short period of time. Other stocks are more stable. Real estate can also fluctuate in value but is generally more stable than stocks. In addition, monies invested in either the stock market or real estate are not as liquid as they would be in a bank account. That is, money is not as readily available if needed for unanticipated expenses or an emergency.

Taking financial risks is necessary if maximum profits are to be realized. However, such risks should be undertaken only after careful thought and planning. A family might use the following check points to determine if their current financial status allows them to take such risks.

1. Has an adequate amount of money been set aside for emergencies?
2. Can family needs be supplied with current income?

3. Do we know an investment counselor or stockbroker whose judgment we trust?

4. Are we willing to risk losing money as well as making money?

5. Do we have adequate insurance coverage for life, property, and health?

6. Are the employed members of the family fairly secure in their present positions?

7. What is our time frame for return on investment—short-term, long-term, or both?

8. If the investment is in real estate, will the income cover the cost of monthly payments and operation expenses?

9. If investment is in stocks, how safe is the original amount invested? Will the investment actually increase in worth, and how large are dividends?

Other forms of investment are also available but generally require more expertise and knowledge of the investment field than savings or financial securities. Monies may be invested in antiques (e.g., furniture, dishes, cars), memorabilia (e.g., comics, political buttons), art, stamps, coins, precious metals, or precious stones. A family investing in any of these areas is most likely to experience long-term rather than short-term gain. In addition, the family should be aware of the projected annual increase in value of such investments.

INSURANCE

Insurance is designed to prevent financial calamity due to chance occurrences that decrease monetary worth. All families should carry insurance to decrease the risk of financial loss.

Insurance covers only fortuitous (chance) personal losses. If a family has not accumulated much financial worth, they may question why they need insurance. However, if the family car was damaged in an accident, the family would have the cost of buying another car or fixing the damaged one, as well as finding other means of transportation while the car was being fixed or a replacement being sought. Such a loss would probably mean a decrease in worth.

Risks can be minimized, transferred or personally assumed. One can minimize the risk of danger to his or her car by driving carefully, avoiding particularly heavy traffic, and not driving when intoxicated. The probability of damage to household and property is less if one makes sure all electrical appliances are safe, locks up securely when leaving the house, and does not smoke in bed. Both public and private organizations attempt to educate the public in order to decrease the occurrence of personal loss.

Risks are transferred to someone else, an insurance company, when insurance is purchased. A fee, or *premium*, is charged for insurance, with the amount depending on the size of the potential loss that could occur. The risks that should be transferred to insurance companies are those that involve a large loss but are unlikely to occur. Risks that have a high probability of occurrence but result in little loss will be too expensive to insure. The cost of insurance increases as the probability of loss goes up.

A third way to deal with risk is to personally take responsibility for the potential loss. While this is appropriate for small losses, most families do not have the financial assets to cover large losses.

Determining what a family should insure is important. The first step in making this decision is to sit down and identify all assets and their respective values. The cost of insurance can be high, so a family should decide what assets would cause the most severe financial setback if lost, and insure those items. Common assets insured include property, automobile, health, and life. Health and life are important to insure since they protect the family's net worth and future income. A family must also make a decision about what perils they will insure against. The more risks insured against, the higher the premium. Most insurance has deductible clauses; that is, if a loss occurs, the insured pays up to a particular amount before insurance coverage begins. A family should have an emergency fund out of which such deductibles can be paid.

Property Insurance

A homeowner's policy covers house and attached/adjacent structures up to replacement cost. Personal property coverage is based on actual value or depreciated replacement cost (Apilado and Morehart, 1980). Insurance should cover at least 80 percent of the replacement cost of a home. Most policies have coinsurance clauses to encourage the insurer to carry that amount. Otherwise, the insured may be financially penalized if a loss occurs because the insurance company will pay a much lower amount than actual replacement cost. For full protection against loss, a family needs to buy a policy with a face value equal to 100 percent of the value of their home. In today's economic climate, it is recommended that a family carry insurance for 100 percent of replacement cost for any property that they own.

The best investment is a homeowner's policy that provides the following four kinds of insurance: property insurance on house, personal property insurance on other possessions, liability insurance, and medical payment insurance. A homeowner's policy generally includes protection against loss through fire, wind, hail, smoke, theft, and breakage (windows, etc.). This also includes living expenses for motel accommodations for a number of days while the damaged property is being refurbished or replaced. Personal property insurance covers loss of property due to fire, theft, or mysterious disappearance. Homeowner's policies also include protection to cover injuries that occur on the property and medical payment insurance to cover the cost of treating the injuries. Renter's insurance is also available to cover personal property and liability should someone fall on the rented premises.

Three types of homeowner's policies are available: basic coverage, broad coverage, and comprehensive coverage. Comprehensive coverage is the most expensive and covers all perils except natural disasters such as floods, earthquakes, and war and nuclear attack. When buying homeowner's or other forms of property insurance, the family should be aware of the types of coverage that each policy offers and the amount of coverage.

Automobile Insurance

The four main types of automobile insurance are liability insurance, which protects the insured from lawsuits if he or she injures someone or damages their property with his or her car; collision insurance, which reimburses the insured if his or her car is damaged; comprehensive insurance, which protects against loss due to fire, theft, wind, hail, and falling objects; and medical payment insurance, which pays for medical expenses of all passengers injured while riding in the insured's car or of family members while riding in any car (Wolf, 1981).

In some states, no-fault insurance for bodily injuries is offered. Under this type of insurance, the insurance company of the injured individual pays regardless of who is at fault. The insurance company can then sue the other driver or his or her insurance company. It is thought that this type of coverage may prevent the costs of going to court for minor injuries. No-fault insurance offers a limited amount of coverage and does not offer any settlement for pain or severe mental anguish (Wolf, 1981).

Uninsured motorist endorsement is also available in most states, which is coverage for any accidents or injuries caused to the insured or the insured's family by an individual who does not have insurance. After his or her insurance company pay such claims, it may, in turn, sue the uninsured individual to recover the losses.

Health Insurance

Health insurance can protect a family against sickness, accident, and disability. Each family needs to decide what types of insurance it wishes to carry based on family health history, past personal history, and anticipated health problems in the future. Since many health problems cannot be anticipated, at least basic coverage and disability insurance are recommended. Expenses generally covered under a basic plan are hospital expenses, medical expenses, and surgical expenses.

Major medical coverage protects against financial loss from treatment of long-term illnesses or health problems for which the cost of treatment is very high. Most major medical policies also cover treatment for mental health problems. A comprehensive policy combines basic coverage with major medical coverage. Catastrophic insurance begins where major medical coverage leaves off; that is, it covers illnesses the treatment of which may cost up to $500,000. Because the cost of catastrophic insurance is so high, few people carry it. However, if a family has a history of serious medical problems, they may wish to consider purchasing catastrophic insurance coverage.

Dental insurance is another type of health insurance coverage that may be purchased. Most dental policies are deductibles and cover basic cost of fillings and extractions as well as more costly work, such as dentures, oral surgery, and orthodontia. The number of families carrying dental insurance in the United States has rapidly increased since the late 1960s.

One of the hazards that confronts everyone regardless of age is the loss of full earning potential through accident or injury. Some occupations carry higher risk of disability than others. The probability of partial or total disability is greater for young and middle-aged adults than the loss of life. Disability insurance generally has two features: payment for lost earnings as a result of an accident and payment for lost earnings as a result of illness. There is usually a waiting period before benefit payments begin. Disability insurance pays various percentages of income for varying periods depending on the specific policy. The rates for insurance also vary with the occupation of the individual.

Another type of medical expense protection that families should be aware of is the *health maintenance organization* (HMO). HMOs are prepaid health plans that provide care for a fixed amount per month. Membership is on a voluntary basis. The purpose of HMO is to promote health and prevent illness, thereby decreasing the incidence of acute or chronic illness expenses. A good HMO offers services from a variety of specialists, including physicians, nurse clinicians or practitioners, health educators, nutritionists, and psychologists. HMOs with only physician services cannot offer the comprehensive health care that such organizations were originally intended to provide.

A final type of health protection to be discussed in this chapter is national health insurance. The major coverage programs are Medicare and Medicaid. Medicare covers health care expenses after sixty-five years of age. In 1973, Medicare coverage was extended to disability payments for individuals under sixty-five with severe kidney disease.

Benefits are also available under certain conditions for spouses. Medicaid covers medical expenses for individuals who meet the income requirements, e.g., unemployed or low income. Because of the Tax Equity and Fiscal Responsibility Act (TEFRA) of 1982, expenses covered under both of these plans have been markedly decreased. However, you should be aware of what such plans provide and the eligibility requirements for each.

Life Insurance

Life insurance can be purchased individually or by a group of people who share a common employer or membership in the same association. Three types of life insurance that families should be aware of are term insurance, whole life insurance, and limited-pay insurance. Term insurance pays benefits to survivors in one lump sum in case of death during the period of the insurance policy. Term insurance usually runs for one to five years. When purchasing term insurance, make sure that it is renewable. However, a family should keep in mind that every time term insurance is renewed, the premium goes up as the insured person is older and the risk of death is higher. While term insurance is the least expensive type during a family's younger years, there is no accumulation of cash value as with the other types of policies.

Whole life insurance, sometimes called straight life or ordinary life insurance, pays benefits in the event of death to the survivors identified as beneficiaries. In addition, it provides a form of savings account. The premium on whole life for a young family is higher than term insurance, but part of the payment goes toward the cash value of the policy. Whole life covers an individual from the day the policy is written to 100 years of age. Neither the amount of the policy nor the premium paid changes over time. As the cash value of the policy increases, the amount that the insurance company has to pay in the event of death increases. If the insured stops paying premiums and wishes to receive the cash value of the policy at any time, that value can be calculated and paid to the policy holder. Policies that pay dividends on cash value can also be purchased. These dividends can be used to reduce the cost of the premium, received as cash, left with the company to earn interest, or used to purchase additional insurance (Freeman and Graf, 1980). Generally, such participating policies are a better investment than nonparticipating policies if the profit history of the insurance company is good.

Limited-pay insurance is similar to whole life in that the policy runs to age 100 and the face amount of the policy remains the same. It differs from whole life in that the policy is paid up in a specified number of years or by a certain age. At the time the policy is paid up, cash value does not equal face value. The cash value at that point continues to earn interest that may go toward increasing the cash value of the policy. The premiums for this kind of policy are higher than whole life since the policy is paid up in a shorter period of time.

When buying life insurance, each family must select the policy that best meets their needs. The face value of the policy that should be purchased can be determined by taking the estimated resources of a family and subtracting the obligations or expenses that would be incurred following the death of an insured family member. Expenses would include: funeral and burial costs, fee for settling the estate, estate and inheritance taxes, unpaid debts, cost of college education for family members who may desire it, and family living expenses for at least one year (Freeman and Graf, 1980).

Regardless of their resources, many families do not want to liquidate real estate and other assets to pay expenses following death of an insured family member. Calculation of resources should focus on those that are liquid, such as savings accounts, income of surviving spouse, pensions, survivor benefits, interest and dividends, and cash on hand. Selling stocks, real estate, or other property to cover expenses at the time of a family member's death may greatly decrease the financial worth or income of the family.

PLANNING FOR RETIREMENT

While many young couples give little thought to retirement, advance planning can increase the likelihood of greater comfort and satisfaction in later years. Active preparation for retirement should begin at least twenty years prior to the expected retirement date. While the total population of the United States has doubled since 1900, there has been a *sevenfold* increase in the number of persons over sixty-five years of age. In 1900, one in thirty Americans was over the age of sixty-five compared to an anticipated one in five in 2020. The population seventy-five years and older is the fastest-growing age group (Eisdorfer, 1983). While individuals over sixty-five hold about 30 percent of discretionary spending power, they also experience a higher incidence of chronic illnesses and mental health problems than younger populations. The high cost of health care and inflation challenge society's ability to support the elderly. Recent legislation that decreases benefits from Medicare and Social Security compounds the problem.

There are several steps in planning for retirement that will be discussed briefly here: setting retirement goals, establishing retirement needs, and developing specific financial strategies. First, you must be aware of the age at which you and your spouse plan to retire. Subtract your current age from that figure to get an idea of the number of years that you have to plan for retirement. In the current economic climate, families should plan to rely less on social programs, where benefits are diminishing, and more on their own resources. A statement of retirement goals should include not only when retirement is planned but whether the couple will continue to work part-time, plans for geographic relocation, or wishes to travel or engage in other costly recreational activities during the course of later years.

Anticipated expenses in retirement, including basic living expenses such as housing, food, clothing, transportation, taxes, and insurance, should be estimated. Total annual living expenses to maintain a satisfying lifestyle as well as recurrent extra expenses such as travel, entertainment, and recreation should be calculated and multiplied by the number of years that both spouses expect to live following retirement. Inflation should be included in the calculations. Some expenditures will be less than in earlier years, but older persons consume about three times as many dollars of medical care per capita as younger persons (Eisdorfer, 1983). While Americans are engaging increasingly in physical fitness activities and good nutritional practices to promote health, there is not enough data at this time to determine if such practices will decrease the incidence of chronic illness and related medical expenses among the aging.

Specific financial strategies should be developed to create or maintain sources of retirement income. Social Security is a source of retirement benefits, but in recent years there has been increasing concern about the ability of the federal government to pay retirement benefits out of current revenues. The problem will become more severe in the twenty-first century. Retirement plans such as IRAs and Keogh plans have been discussed in previous sections. Other sources of retirement income include employer-sponsored retirement plans, real estate investments, and investments in various types of financial securities. The major emphasis in retirement should be on maintaining an adequate income as opposed to generating capital appreciation.

Careful thought and planning for retirement is essential if a family is to maximize their productivity and enjoyment of later years. Investment strategies for retirement should be flexible, allowing adaptation from pre-retirement to post-retirement years.

IN CONCLUSION

The purpose of this Appendix has been to provide general guidelines for wise management of resources. Each family's financial needs are unique. Thus, no one approach to financial planning can be prescribed for all families. Planning for basic living expenses, taxes, credit, savings and investments, and insurance, as well as retirement, have all been discussed. Since many problems in marital and family relationships are the result of insufficient income or poor management of money, the wise couple will begin to plan thoughtfully, even prior to marriage. Avoiding the pitfalls that financial problems can pose increases the probability of a successful marriage and greater enjoyment of all phases of life, from young adult through retirement years.

REFERENCES—Appendix C

Apilado, V. P., and Morehart, T. B. *Personal Finance Management*. St. Paul, MN: West, 1980.

Bailard, T. E., Biehl, D. L., and Kaiser, R. W. *Personal Money Management*, 4th ed. Chicago: Science Research Associates, 1982.

Consumer Reports. "What Makes You a Good Credit Risk?" *Consumer Reports*, 48 (1983), 254–259.

Crickmer, B. "The Flat-rate Tax: What's Ahead?" *Nation's Business*, 70 (1982), 22–24.

Eisdorfer, C. "Conceptual Models of Aging: The Challenge of a New Frontier," *American Psychologist*, 38 (1983), 197–202.

Freeman, M. H., and Graf, D. *Money Management: A Guide to Saving, Spending, and Investing*. Indianapolis: Bobbs-Merrill, 1980.

Gitman, L. J. *Personal Finance*. Hinsdale, IL: The Dryden Press, 1978.

Greene, M. R., and Dince, R. R. *Personal Finance Management*. Cincinnati: South-Western, 1983.

Leet, D. R., and Driggers, J. *Economic Decisions for Consumers*. Belmont, CA: Wadsworth, 1983.

Miller, R. L., Power, F. B., and Meyer, R. L. *Personal Finance Today*, 2nd ed. St. Paul, MN: West, 1983.

Naisbitt, J. *Megatrends: Ten Directions Transforming Our Lives*. New York: Warner Books, 1982.

Wolf, H. A. *Personal Finance*, 6th ed. Boston: Allyn & Bacon, 1981.

BIBLIOGRAPHY

Chapter 1

Bem, S. L. (1985). Androgyny and general schema theory: A conceptual and empirical integration. In *Nebraska symposium on motivation. Psychology and gender* V. 32, ed. T. B. Sonderegger, 179–226. Lincoln: University of Nebraska Press.

————. (1976). Probing the promise of androgyny. In *Beyond sex role stereotypes: Readings toward a psychology of androgyny*, ed. A. G. Kaplan and J. P. Bean. Boston: Little, Brown.

Bohannan, P. (1971). The six stations of divorce. In *Divorce and after*, ed. P. Bohanan, 33–62. Garden City, NY: Doubleday.

Brehm, S. S. (1985). *Intimate relationships*. New York: Random House.

Connecticut Mutual Life Insurance Company. (1981). Connecticut Mutual Life report on American values in the 1980s. Summarized in *Marriage and Divorce Today*, 6 (June 1):1.

Cornish, E. (1979). The future of the family in an age of loneliness. *The Futurist* 13 (Feb.):45–58.

————. (1987). The great transformation. *The Futurist* 21 #2 (Mar.–Apr.):2, 58.

Farrell, W. (1984). The evolution of sex roles: The transformation of masculine and feminine values. In *Marriage and the family in the year 2020*, ed. L. A. Kirkendall and A. E. Gravatt, 134–160. Buffalo, NY: Prometheus Books.

The Futurist. (1986). Outlook '87 and beyond. 20 #6 (Nov.–Dec.):53–60.

Glick, P. C., and S.-L. Lin. (1986). Recent changes in divorce and remarriage. *Journal of Marriage and the Family* 48 #4 (Nov.):737–747.

Goldfarb, B., and R. W. Libby. (1984). Mothers and children alone: The stamp of poverty. *Alternate Lifestyles* 6 (Summer):243–258.

Harrison, D. F. (1986). Conceptual issues in measuring and assessing family problems. *Family Therapy* 13 #1:85–94.

Haveren, T. (1980). Quoted in WHCF hears the revisionist news: Families in the good old days had it worse. *Behavior Today* 11 (June 9):1–2.

Hawes, G. R. (1984). Second careers. *The encyclopedia of second careers*. New York: Commerce Clearing House.

Hoffman, L., and H. J. Hoffman. (1985). The lives and adventures of dual-career couples. *Family Therapy* 12 #2:124–148.

Hudson, W. W., and D. F. Harrison. (1986). Conceptual issues in measuring and assessing family problems. *Family Therapy* 13 #1:85–94.

Johnson, R. (1981). Mouth of 1980: Friends and peers more influential than parents. *Behavior Today* 12 (Feb.):2.

The Kiplinger Washington Letter. (1986). A special Kiplinger report. The next 10 years (Jan.):4.

Koop, C. E. (1987). People making news. *U.S. News and World Report* (May 4):13.

Landers, S. (1986). Latchkey kids. *The APA Monitor* 17 #12 (Dec.):1, 6–7.

Long, V. O. (1986). Relationship of masculinity to self-esteem and self-acceptance in female professionals, college students, clients, and victims of domestic violence. *Journal of Consulting and Clinical Psychology* 54 #3:323–327.

Mace, D. (1986). Should Christians divorce? *Journal of Marriage and Family Living* 68 #7 (July):31.

McBee, S. (1985). Morality. Survey by the Roper Organization for *U.S. News and World Report* (Dec. 9):52–58.

National Center for Health Statistics. (1986). Vital statistics summary, marriage and divorce statistics for 1985. 34 #12 (Mar. 24).

Norton, A. J., and J. E. Moorman. (1987). Current trends in marriage and divorce among American women. *Journal of Marriage and the Family* 49 (Feb.):3–14.

Porter, A. (1986). Work in the new information age. *The Futurist* 20 #5 (Sept.–Oct.):9–14.

Robertson, I. (1977). *Sociology*. New York: Worth.

Sennett, R. (1987). The age of self-control. *Vogue* (April):362–363, 398.

Skolnick, A. (1981). The family and its discontents. *Society* 18 (Jan.–Feb.):42–47.

Toffler, A. (1970). *Future shock*. New York: Random House.

———. (1980). *The third wave*. New York: Morrow.

U.S. Bureau of the Census. (1980). *Household and family characteristics, March 1979*. Current population reports, series P-20, no. 352. Washington, D.C.: U.S. Government Printing Office.

U.S. News and World Report. (1986–1987). Survival for stepparents (Dec. 29, 1986–Jan. 5, 1987):95.

Visher, J., and E. Visher. (1986). It is predicted that by 1990 less than one-third of all families will be traditional households. *Behavior Today Newsletter* 17 #17 (April 28):8–9.

Weitzman, L. (1985). *The divorce revolution*. New York: Free Press.

White House Task Force Report on the Family. (1986). Washington, D.C.: U.S. Government Printing Office.

Yankelovich, D. (1981). New rules in American life: Searching for self-fulfillment in a world turned upside down. *Psychology Today* (April):35*ff*.

Chapter 2

Aronson, E. (1980). *The social animal*. 3d. ed. San Francisco: W. H. Freeman.

Bandura, A. (1982). The psychology of chance encounters and life paths. *American Psychologist* 37 (July):747–755.

Basow, S. (1980). *Sex role stereotypes: Traditions and alternatives*. Monterey, CA: Brooks/Cole.

Berkowitz, L. (1980). *A survey of social psychology*. New York: Holt, Rinehart & Winston.

Berscheid, E., and W. Graziano. (1979). The initiation of social relationships and interpersonal attraction. In *Social exchange in developing relationships*, ed. R. L. Burgess and T. L. Huston, 31–60. New York: Academic Press.

Berscheid, E., and E. H. Walster. (1978). *Interpersonal attraction*. 2d. ed. Reading, MA: Addison-Wesley.

Bower, S. A., and G. H. Bower. (1976). *Asserting yourself: A practical guide for positive change*. Reading, MA: Addison-Wesley.

Braiker, H. B., and H. H. Kelley. (1979). Conflict in the development of close relationships. In *Social exchange in developing relationships*, ed. R. L. Burgess and T. L. Huston, 135–168. New York: Academic Press.

Brehm, S. S. (1985). *Intimate relationships*. New York: Random House.

Coleman, E., and B. Edwards. (1979). *Brief encounters*. Garden City, NY: Doubleday.

Cornish, E. (1987). Moonlight, violins, briefs, and bytes. *The Futurist* 21 #1 (Jan.–Feb.):2, 58.

Cunningham, M. R. (1986). Measuring the physical in physical attractiveness: Quasi-experiments on the sociobiology of female facial beauty. *Journal of Personality & Social Psychology* 50, 5:925–935.

Curtis, R. C., and K. Miller. (1986). Believing another likes or dislikes you: Behaviors making the beliefs come true. *Journal of Personality and Social Psychology* 51 #2:284–290.

Dion, K., E. Berscheid, and E. Walster. (1972). What is beautiful is good. *Journal of Personality and Social Psychology* 24:285–290.

Edelmann, R. J. (1985). Social embarrassment: An analysis of the process. *Journal of Social and Personal Relationships* 2:195–213.

Goffman, E. (1952). On cooling the mark out: Some aspects of adaptation to failure. *Psychiatry* 15:451–463.

————. (1959). *The presentation of self in everyday life*. Garden City, NY: Doubleday/Anchor.

Gollwitzer, P. M., and R. A. Wicklund. (1985). Self-symbolizing and the neglect of others' perspectives. *Journal of Personality and Social Psychology* 48 #3:702–715.

Grush, J. E., and J. G. Yehl. (1979). Marital roles, sex differences, and interpersonal attraction. *Journal of Personality and Social Psychology* 37:116–123.

Hall, E. T. (1979). Learning the Arabs' silent language. *Psychology Today* (August):18–23.

Hatfield, E., and S. Sprecher. (1986). *Mirror, mirror . . . The importance of looks in everyday life*. New York: SUNY Press.

Ian, J. (1977). "At seventeen." Quoted in R. Ringer, *Looking out for number one*. New York: Fawcett.

Jellison, J. M., and J. Greene. (1981). A self-presentation approach to the fundamental attribution error: The norm of internality. *Journal of Personality and Social Psychology* 40:643–649.

Jobin, J. (1979). Courtship: How the game is played today. *Redbook* (July):33*ff*.

Levinger, G. (1979). A social exchange view on the dissolution of pair relationships. In *Social exchange in developing relationships*, ed. R. L. Burgess and T. L. Huston, 169–193. New York: Academic Press.

Joyce, J. (1916). *Portrait of the artist as a young man*. New York: Viking Penguin.

Mall, J. (1986). Men send mixed signals on attitudes. Roper Poll. *Los Angeles Times* Part VI (Apr. 27):1, 20.

Mehlman, R. G. and G. R. Snyder. Excuse theory: A test of the protective role of attributions. *Journal of Personality and Social Psychology* 49 #4:994–1001.

Miller, L. C., J. H. Berg, and R. L. Archer. (1983). Openers: Individuals who elicit self-disclosure. *Journal of Personality and Social Psychology* 44 (June):1234–1244.

Murstein, B. I. (1980). Mate selection in the 1970s. *Journal of Marriage and the Family* 42 (Nov.):777–792.

Nevid, J. S. (1985). Choose me. *Psychology Today* 19 #8 (Aug.):66–67.

Nisbett, R. E., and T. D. Wilson. (1977). The halo effect: Evidence for unconscious alteration of judgments. *Journal of Personality and Social Psychology* 34:250–256.

Peterson, K. S. (1986). Single men say easy sex is unsafe. Special for *USA Today* (July 7):7–10.

Rogers, L. (1985). Self-esteem. *Journal of Marriage and Family Living* 67 #5 (June):6–8.

Roosevelt, E. (1971). Quoted in J. P. Lash, *Eleanor and Franklin*. New York: Norton.

Rother, D., C. R. Snyder, and L. M. Pace. (1986). Dimensions of favorable self-presentation. *Journal of Personality and Social Psychology* 51 #4:867–874.

Snyder, M. (1980). The many me's of the self-monitor. *Psychology Today* (March):23–30.

———, E. Berscheid, and P. Glick. (1985). Focusing on the exterior and the interior: Two investigations of the initiation of personal relationships. *Journal of Personality and Social Psychology* 48 #6:1427–1439.

Snyder, M., and S. Gangestad. (1982). Choosing social situations: Two investigations of self-monitoring processes. *Journal of Personality and Social Psychology* 43:123–135.

Snyder, M., and J. A. Simpson. (1984). Self-monitoring and dating relationships. *Journal of Personality and Social Psychology* 47 #6:1281–1291.

Walster, E., F. Aronson, D. Abrahams, and L. Rottman. (1966). Importance of physical attractiveness in dating behavior. *Journal of Personality and Social Psychology* 4:508–516.

Walster, E., and G. Walster. (1978). *A new look at love*. Reading, MA: Addison-Wesley.

Walster, E., G. W. Walster, and E. Berscheid. (1978). *Equity: Theory and research*. Boston: Allyn & Bacon.

Wills, C. (1981). I'll call you. *Cosmopolitan* (July):3*ff*.

Chapter 3

Archer, D., and R. Akert. (1977). How well do you read body language? *Psychology Today* (Oct.):68–72*ff*.

Baxter, L. A., and W. W. Wilmont. (1985). Taboo topics in close relationships. *Journal of Social and Personal Relationships* 2:253–269.

Bower, S. A., and G. Bower. (1976). *Asserting yourself*. Reading, MA: Addison-Wesley.

Braiker, H., and H. H. Kelley. (1979). Conflicts in the development of close relationships. In *Social exchange in developing relationships*, ed. R. L. Burgess and T. L. Huston, 135–168. New York: Academic Press.

Brehm, S. S. (1985). *Intimate relationships*. New York: Random House.

Burgess, E. W., P. Wallin, and G. D. Schultz. (1953). *Courtship, engagement, and marriage*. Philadelphia: Lippincott.

Clark, K. B. (1980). Empathy: A neglected topic in psychological research. *American Psychologist* 35 (Feb.):187–190.

Coleman, J. C., et al. (1987). *Contemporary psychology and effective behavior*. Glenview, IL: Scott, Foresman and Co.

Cozby, P. C. (1973). Self-disclosure: A literature review. *Psychology Bulletin* 75:73–91.

Dellinger, S., and B. Deane. (1980). *Communicating effectively*. New York: Chilton Books.

Duck, S. (1984). *Personal relationships 5: Repairing personal relationships*. New York: Academic Press.

————, and R. Gilmour (eds.). (1981). Personal relationships. In *Developing personal relationships*. London: Academic Press.

Gaelick, L., G. V. Bodenhausen, and R. S. Wyer, Jr. (1985). Emotional communication in close relationships. *Journal of Personality and Social Psychology* 51 #4:1246–1265.

Gallois, C., and V. J. Callan. (1986). Decoding emotional messages: Influence of ethnicity, sex, message type, and channel. *Journal of Personality and Social Psychology* 51 #4:755–762.

Gitter, A. C., and H. Black. (1976). Is self-disclosure self-revealing? *Journal of Counseling Psychology* 23:327–332.

Hall, J. A. (1978). Gender effects in decoding nonverbal clues. *Psychology Bulletin* 85:845–857.

Hammarskjöld, D. (1974). *Markings*. New York: Alfred A. Knopf.

Hatfield, E. (1985). Getting to know you isn't easy. *Honolulu Star Bulletin* (Sept. 17):B-1.

Huston, T. L., and R. L. Burgess. (1979). Social exchange in developing relationships: An overview. In *Social exchange in developing relationships*, ed. R. L. Burgess and T. L. Huston, 3–28. New York: Academic Press.

Johnson, J. A. (1981). The 'self-disclosure' and 'self-presentation' views of item response dynamics and personality scale validity. *Journal of Personality and Social Psychology* 40:761–769.

Johnson-George, C., and W. Swap. (1982). Measurement of specific interpersonal trust: Construction and validation of a scale to assess trust in a specific order. *Journal of Personality and Social Psychology* 43:1306–1317.

Kanter R. M. (1972). *Commitment and community: Communes and utopias in sociological perspective*. Cambridge, MA: Harvard University Press.

Kelley, H. H. (1979). *Personal relationships: Their structures and processes*. Hillsdale, NJ: Erlbaum.

Kern, M. M. (1981). Do you really listen to your spouse? *Marriage and Family Living* 63:9.

Kopp, S. (1972). *If you meet the Buddha on the road, kill him!* Palo Alto, CA: Science and Behavior Books.

Kudoh, T., and D. Matsumoto. (1985). Cross-cultural examination of the semantic dimensions of body postures. *Journal of Personality and Social Psychology* 48 #6:1440–1446.

Lasswell, M., and N. Lobsensz. (1980). *Styles of loving: Why you love the way you do*. Garden City, NY: Doubleday.

Levinger, G. (1979). A social exchange view on the dissolution of pair relationships. In *Social exchange in developing relationships*, ed. R. L. Burgess and T. L. Juston, 169–193. New York: Academic Press.

————, and H. L. Raush (eds.). (1977). *Close relationships: Perspectives on the meaning of intimacy*. Amherst: University of Massachusetts Press.

Losconcy, L. (1985). Mining intimacy for all its worth. *Journal of Marriage and the Family* 67 #9 (Sept.):22–24.

Ludwig, D., and J. N. Franco. (1986). Effects of reciprocity and self-monitoring on self-disclosure with a new acquaintance. *Journal of Personality and Social Psychology* 50 #6:1077–1082.

Lund, M. (1985). The development of investment and commitment scales for predicting continuity of personal relationships. *Journal of Social and Personal Relationships* 2:3–23.

Marietta, D. E. (1982). The ethics of using people. *The Humanist* V. 42:27–29.

Markus, H., and P. Nurius. (1986). Possible selves. *American Psychologist* 41 #9 (Sept.):954–969.

McGee, T. (1953). In John D. MacDonald, *The scarlet ruse and other great mysteries*. New York: John D. MacDonald Publishing.

Michaels, J. W., A. C. Acock, and J. N. Edwards. (1986). Social exchange and equity determinants of relationship commitment. *Journal of Social and Personal Relationships* 3:161–175.

Middlebrook, P. N. (1980). *Social psychology and modern life*. 2d. ed. New York: Alfred A. Knopf.

Miller, G. R., P. A. Mongeau, and C. Sleight. (1986). Fudging with friends and lying to lovers: Deceptive communication in personal relationships. *Journal of Social and Personal Relationships* 3:495–512.

Milholland, T. A., and A. W. Avery. (1982). Effects of marriage encounter on self-disclosure, trust, and marital satisfaction. *Journal of Marital and Family Therapy* 8 (April):87–89.

Neimeyer, G. J., and R. A. Neimeyer. (1985). Relational trajectories: A personal construct contribution. *Journal of Social and Personal Relationships* 2:325–349.

O'Neill, N., and G. O'Neill. (1974). *Shifting gears*. New York: M. Evans and Co.

Rempel, J. K., J. G. Holmes, and M. P. Zanna. (1985). Trust in close relationships. *Journal of Personality and Social Psychology* 49 #1:95–112.

Robertson, I. (1981). *Sociology*. 2d. ed. New York: Worth.

Rogers, C. R. (1969). *Freedom to learn: A view of what education might become*. Columbus OH: Charles E. Merrill.

Rosenblatt, P. C. (1977). Needed research on commitment in marriage. In *Close relationships*, ed. G. Levinger and H. L. Raush. Amherst: University of Massachusetts Press.

Scanzoni, J. (1979). Social exchange and behavioral independence. In *Social exchange in developing relationships*, ed. R. L. Burgess and T. L. Huston, 61–98. New York: Academic Press.

Schaefer, M. T., and D. H. Olson. (1981). Assessing intimacy: The PAIR inventory. *Journal of Marital and Family Therapy* 7:47–60.

Smith, G. W. (1975). *Hidding meaning*. New York: Wyden.

Strassberg, D., H. Robak, M. D'Antonio, and H. Gabel. (1977). Self-disclosure: A critical and selective review of the clinical literature. *Comprehensive Psychiatry* 18:21–30.

Wagner, H. L., C. J. MacDonald, and A. S. R. Manstead. (1986). Communication of individual emotions by spontaneous facial expressions. *Journal of Personality and Social Psychology* 50 #4:737–743.

Waller, W. (1951). *The family: A dynamic interpretation*. New York: Dryden.

Walters, L. H. (1982). Are families different from other groups? *Journal of Marriage and the Family* 44 (Nov.):841–850.

Chapter 4

Adams, V. (1980). Sex therapies in perspective. *Psychology Today* (Aug.):35–36.

The American College of Obstetricians and Gynecologists. (1986). Method and effectiveness of contraceptives. Reported by *News America Syndicate*.

American Psychiatric Association. (1980). *Diagnostic and statistical manual of mental disorders*. 3d. ed. Washington, D.C.: American Psychiatric Association.

Arndt, W. B., J. C. Foehl, and F. E. Good. (1985). Specific sexual fantasy themes: A multidimensional study. *Journal of Personality and Social Psychology* 48 #2:472–480.

Barlow, D. H. (1986). Causes of sexual dysfunction: The role of anxiety and cognitive interference. *Journal of Counseling and Clinical Psychology* 54 #2:91–96.

Bell, A., M. Weinberg, and S. K. Hammersmith. (1981). *Sexual preference*. Bloomington, IN: Indiana University Press.

Bezold, C., J. Peck, and R. Olson. (1987). Special section on AIDS: AIDS and the year 2000. *The Futurist* 21 (November–December):9.

Blinder, M. (1985). Counseling the sexually function but dissatisfied client. *Family Therapy* 12 #2:91–96.

Boston Women's Health Book Collective. (1976). *Our bodies, ourselves*. New York: Simon & Schuster.

California. (1986). College follies, '86. (Aug.):59–61, 63.

Christopher, F. S., and R. M. Cate. (1985). Anticipated influences on sexual decision-making for first intercourse. *Family Relations* 34 #2 (April):265–270.

Clayton, R. R., and J. Bokemeier. (1980). Premarital sex in the seventies. *Journal of Marriage and the Family* 42:759–775.

Coleman, J. C., C. G. Morris, and A. G. Glaros. (1987). *Contemporary psychology and effective behavior*. 6th ed. Glenview, IL: Scott, Foresman and Co.

Coppola, V., R. West, and J. Huck. (1983). The AIDS epidemic: The change in gay life-style. *Newsweek* (April 18):80.

Cornish, Edward. (1987). The social consequences of AIDS. *The Futurist* 21 (November–December):2, 46.

Cotroneo, M., and B. R. Krasner. (1977). A study of abortion and problems in decision-making. *Journal of Marriage and Family Counseling* 3 (Jan.):69–76.

Crooks, R., and K. Baur. (1980). *Our sexuality*. Menlo Park, CA: Benjamin/ Cummings.

DeLamater, J. D., and MacCorquodale, P. (1979). *Premarital sexuality: Attitudes, relationships, behavior*. Madison: University of Wisconsin Press.

Dicks, H. V. (1967). *Marital tensions*. London: Routledge & Kegan Paul.

Eisenman, R. (1982). Sexual behavior as related to sex fantasies and experimental manipulation of authoritarianism and creativity. *Journal of Personality and Social Psychology* 43:853–860.

Evans, M., and B. Zilbergeld. (1980). The inadequacy of Masters and Johnson. *Psychology Today* 14 (Aug.):29–34, 37–43.

Federal Centers for Disease Control. (1986–1987). Reported in *U.S. News and World Report* (Dec. 29, 1986–Jan. 5, 1987):20.

Finlay, B. A. (1981). Sexual differences in correlates of abortion attitudes among college students. *Journal of Marriage and the Family* 43 (Aug.):571–582.

Gagnon, J. (1977). *Human sexualities*. Glenview, IL: Scott, Foresman and Co.

Gelman, D., et al. (1980). The games teenagers play. *Newsweek* (Sept. 1):48–53.

Gest, T. (1983). Abortion in America: ABC's of a raging battle. *U.S. News and World Report* (Jan. 24):47–49.

Glen, N., and C. Weaver. Article in *Journal of Marriage and the Family* (In press, 1987).

Goldstein, M. J., B. L. Baker, and R. R. Jamison. (1980). *Abnormal psychology*. Boston: Little, Brown.

Guttmacher Institute. (1981). *Teenage pregnancy: The problem that hasn't gone away*. New York: Alan Guttmacher Institute.

Halpern, H. (1986). Herpes panic: Is less new good news? *Los Angeles Times* Part V (March 3):2.

Henriques, F. (1959). *Love in action: The sociology of sex*. New York: Dell.

Henshaw, S. K. (1986). *Induced abortion: A world review, 1986*. New York: Alan Guttmacher Institute.

Hite, S. (1976). *The Hite report*. New York: Macmillan.

———. (1981). *The Hite report on male sexuality*. New York: Alfred A. Knopf.

———. (1987). *Women and love, a cultural revolution in progress*. New York: Knopf.

Horn, M. C., and K. Tanfer. (1985). Virginity at marriage, a thing of the past: New report. *Marriage and Divorce Today Newsletter* 10 #31 (March 4):3–4.

Hunt, M. (1974). *Sexual behavior in the 1970s*. Chicago: Playboy Press.

The Impotence Information Center. (1986). *Impotence—Help in the USA*. Minneapolis, MN: Impotence Information Center, Department USA.

Isaacson, W., A. Constable, and D. S. Jackson. (1983). Holding firm on abortion. *Time* (June 27):14–15.

Istvan, J., and W. Griffitt. (1980). Effects of sexual desirability on dating desirability and marriage desirability: An experimental study. *Journal of Marriage and the Family* 42:377–385.

Jessor, R., F. Costa, L. Jessor, and J. E. Donovan. (1983). Time of first intercourse: A prospective study. *Journal of Personality and Social Psychology* 44:608–626.

Juhasz, A. M. (1975). A chain of sexual decision-making. *The Family Coordinator* 24 (Jan.):40–47.

Kagan, J. (1985). On love and violence. *Science* (March):28–29, 32.

Kando, T. M. (1978). *Sexual behavior and family life in transition*. New York: Elsevier.

Kantrowitz, B., et al. (1987). Kids and contraceptives. *Newsweek* (Feb. 16):54–58, 84–85.

Kaplan, H. S. (1975). *The illustrated manual of sex therapy*. New York: Quadrangle.

———. (1974). *The new sex therapy*. New York: Brunner/Mazel.

Kellog, J. H. (1979). *Plain facts for young and old*. Burlington, IA: Degner & Condit.

Kinsey, A. C., et al. (1948). *Sexual behavior in the human male*. Philadelphia: W. B. Saunders.

———. (1953). *Sexual behavior in the human female*. Philadelphia: W. B. Saunders.

Kraft-Ebing, R. von. (1950). *Psychopathica sexualis*. New York: Pioneer Publishers.

Koop, C. E. (1986). AIDS: The Surgeon General's report on acquired immune deficiency syndrome. Reprinted as a public service by *The Los Angeles Times* (Dec. 7):1–8.

Krannich, R. S. (1980). Abortion in the United States: Past, present, and future trends. *Family Relations* (July):365–374.

La Plante, M. N., N. B. McCormick, and G. G. Brannigan. (1980). Living the sexual script: College students' views of influence in sexual encounters. *Journal of Sex Research* (Nov.):12–20.

Levay, A. N., and A. Kagle. (1983). Interminable sex therapy: A report on ten cases of therapeutic gridlock. *Journal of Marital and Family Therapy* 9 (Jan.):1–9.

LoPiccolo, J., and W. E. Stock. (1986). Treatment of sexual dysfunction. *Journal of Counseling and Clinical Psychology* 54 #2:158–167.

Mall, J. (1986). Teen pregnancy and abortion studied. *Los Angeles Times* Part VI (Dec. 7):20.

Marin, P. (1983). A revolution's broken promises. *Psychology Today* 17 (July):50–57.

Marmos, J. (ed.). (1980). *Homosexual behavior: A modern appraisal*. New York: Basic Books.

Masters W., and V. Johnson. (1966). *Human sexual response*. Boston: Little, Brown.

———. (1970). *Human sexual inadequacy*. Boston: Little, Brown.

———. (1975). *The pleasure bond*. Boston: Little, Brown.

———. (1979). *Homosexuality in perspective*. Boston: Little, Brown.

Masters, W., V. Johnson, and R. C. Kolodny. (1985). *Sex and human loving*. Boston: Little, Brown.

McAuliffe, K., J. Carey, S. Wells, B. E. Quick, and M. Dobbin. (1987). AIDS: At the dawn of fear. *U.S. News and World Report* (Jan. 12):60–69.

Messenger, J. C. (1971). Sex and repression in an Irish folk community. In *Human sexual behavior*, ed. D. S. Marshall and R. S. Suggs, 3–37. New York: Basic Books.

Morganthau, T., V. Coppola, J. Carry, N. Cooper, G. Rain, J. McCormick, and B. Finlay. (1983). Gay America in transition. *Newsweek* (Aug. 8):30–36, 39–40.

The National Academy of Science. (1986). Report on AIDS in the United States. Reported in *U.S. News and World Report* (Jan. 12, 1987):60–69.

The National Research Council. (1986). *Special report on teen pregnancy*. Washington, D.C.: U.S. Government Printing Office.

Peplau, L. A. (1977). What homosexuals want. *Psychology Today* (March):28–38.

———, Z. Rubin, and C. T. Hill. (1977). Sexual intimacy in dating relationships. *Journal of Social Issues* 33:86–109.

Pietropinto, A., and J. Simenauer. (1979). *Husbands and wives: A nationwide survey*. New York: Time Books.

Planned Parenthood Affiliates of Southern California. (1986). *Sex education for parents*. Los Angeles, CA: Planned Parenthood Affiliates.

Planned Parenthood Federation of America, Inc. (1986). Louis Harris poll. Reported in *Behavior Today Newsletter* (Dec. 29):5.

Platt John. (1987). The future of AIDS. *The Futurist* 21 (November–December):10–17.

Playboy Survey. (1982). *Los Angeles Times* Part V (Nov. 19):1–3.

Population Crisis Committee. (1986). What America is missing. *U.S. News and World Report* (May 26):43.

Proctor, E. B., N. N. Wagner, and J. C. Butler. (1974). The differentiation of male and female orgasm: An experimental study. In *Perspectives in human sexuality*, ed. N. N. Wagner, 115–132. New York: Behavioral Publications.

Reiss, I. L. (1981). Some observations on ideology and sexuality in America. *Journal of Marriage and the Family* V. 43 (May):271–283.

Risman, B., C. T. Hill, Z. Rubin, and L. A. Peplau. (1981). Living together in college: Implications for courtship. *Journal of Marriage and the Family* 43 (Feb.):77–83.

Robinson, I. E., and D. Jedlicka. (1982). Changes in sexual attitudes and behaviors of college students, 1965–1980: A research note. *Journal of Marriage and the Family* 44:237–230.

Rosellini, L., and E. Goode. (1987). AIDS: When fear takes charge. *U.S. News & World Report* (October 12):60–70.

Rubenstein, C. (1983). The modern art of courtly love. *Psychology Today* 17 (July):40–49.

Rubenstein, C., and C. Tavris (1987). Special survey results: 26,000 women reveal the secrets of intimacy. *Redbook* (September):147–149.

Sarrel, P., and L. Sarrel. (1980). *The Redbook report on sexual relationships*. New York: Redbook Publishing.

Scarf, M. (1980). The promiscuous woman. *Psychology Today* (July):78–87.

Schumer, F. (1983). *Abnormal psychology*. Lexington, MA: D. C. Heath.

Seligman, J., M. Gosnell, V. Coppola, and M. Hager. (1983). The AIDS epidemic. *Newsweek* (April 18):74–80.

Skrzycki, C., and M. H. Gallagher. (1986). The risky business of birth control. *U.S. News and World Report* (May 26):42–43.

Sorensen, R. C. (1973). *Adolescent sexuality in contemporary America*. New York: World Publishing.

Spanier, G. B., and R. L. Margolis. (1983). Marital separation and extramarital sexual behavior. *Marriage and Divorce Today* 8 (May 30):4.

Tavris, C., and T. Jayaratne. (1976). How happy is your marriage? What 75,000 wives say about their most intimate relationship. *Redbook* (June):90–92*ff*.

Traupmann, J., E. Hatfield, and P. Wexler. (1983). Equity and sexual satisfaction in dating couples. *British Journal of Social Psychology* 22:33–40.

Turkington, C. (1986). Split Supreme Court rules sodomy illegal. APA *Monitor* 17 #6 (Aug.):34.

U.S. Food and Drug Administration. (1985). *New birth control chart*. Pueblo, CO: Consumer Information Center.

Vance, E. B., and N. N. Wagner. (1981). Written descriptions of orgasm: A study of sex differences. *Archives of Sexual Behavior* 5:87–98.

Waterman, C. D., and E. J. Chiauzzi. (1982). The role of orgasm in male and female sexual enjoyment. *Journal of Sex Research* 18:146–159.

Wiest, W. (1977). Semantic differential profiles of orgasm and other experiences among men and women. *Sex Roles* 3:399–403.

Wolfe, L. (1981). *The Cosmo report*. New York: Arbor House.

———. (1982). The next sexual hype. *New York* (April 19).

Zelnick, M., and J. Kanter. (1977). Sexual and contraceptive experiences of young, unmarried women in the United States, 1976 and 1971. *Family Planning Perspectives* 9:55–71.

Zilbergeld, B., and C. Ellison. (1979). Social skills training as an adjunct to sex therapy. *Journal of Sex and Marital Therapy* 5:340–350.

Chapter 5

Ainsworth, M. (1985). Patterns of love charted in studies. Reported in *New York Times* (Sept. 10):C-1, C-6.

Altman, I., and D. A. Taylor. (1973). *Social penetration: The development of interpersonal relationships*. New York: Holt, Rinehart & Winston.

Barlow, D. H. (1986). Causes of sexual dysfunction: The role of anxiety and cognitive interference. *Journal of Counseling and Clinical Psychology* 54 #2:140–148.

Berscheid, E. (1983). Emotion. In *Close relationships*, ed. H. H. Kelley et al., 110–168. New York: Freeman.

———, and E. H. Walster. (1978). *Interpersonal attraction*. 2d ed. (Reading, MA: Addison-Wesley.

Braiker, H., and H. Kelley. (1979). Conflict in the development of close relationships. In *Social exchange in developing relationships*, ed. R. L. Burgess and T. L. Huston, 135–168. New York: Academic Press.

Branden, N. (1987). Quoted in T. Gindick. The subject is romance. *Los Angeles Times* Part V (Sept. 27):1, 18.

Branden, N. (1987). Is there life after marriage? *Q* 1 #2 (Feb.):12–14, 43.

―――. (1980). *The psychology of romantic love*. Los Angeles, CA: J. P. Tarcher.

Brehm, S. S. (1985). *Intimate relationships*. New York: Random House.

Bulcroft, K., and M. O'Connor-Roden. (1987). Never too late. *Psychology Today* 20 #66 (June):66–69.

Buscaglia, L. and G. Welles. (1986). Love, growing in love, living in love. *USA Weekend*. (Feb. 7–9):5.

California. (1986). College follies, '86. (Aug.):59–61, 63.

Christopher, F. S., and R. M. Cate. (1985). Anticipated influences on sexual decision-making for first intercourse. *Family Relations* 34 #2 (April):265–270.

Coleman, J. C., et al. (1987). *Contemporary psychology and effective behavior*. Glenview, IL: Scott, Foresman and Co.

Cornish, E. (1987). Moonlight, violins, briefs, and bytes. *The Futurist* 21 #1 (Jan.–Feb.):2, 58.

Croft, R. (1952). Love. Reprinted from *The family book of best loved poems*. New York: Doubleday and Co.

Cummings, R. (1971). *Friendship*. Winona, MN: St. Mary's College Press.

Cunningham, M. R. (1986). Measuring the physical in physical attractiveness: Quasi-experiments on the sociobiology of female facial beauty. *Journal of Personality and Social Psychology* 50 #5:925–935.

Curtis, R. C., and K. Miller. (1986). Believing another likes or dislikes you: Behaviors making the beliefs come true. *Journal of Personality and Social Psychology* 51 #2:284–290.

Davis, K. E. (1985). Near and dear: Friendship and love compared. *Psychology Today* 19 #2 (Feb.):22–28, 30.

Duck, S. (1983). *Friends for life*. New York: St. Martins Press.

Edelmann, R. J. (1985). Social embarrassment: An analysis of the process. *Journal of Social and Personal Relationships* 2:195–213.

Federal Centers for Disease Control. (1986–1987). Reported in *U.S. News and World Report* (Dec. 29, 1986–Jan. 5, 1987):20.

Fromm, E. (1956). *The art of loving*. New York: Harper & Row.

Gathorne-Hardy, J. (1981). *Marriage, love, sex and divorce*. New York: Summit Books.

Gaylin, W. (1978). Being touched and being hurt. *Psychology Today* 12 (Dec.):117–120.

―――. (1986). *Rediscovering love*. New York: Viking.

Gollwitzer, P. M., and R. A. Wicklund. (1985). Self-symbolizing and the neglect of others' perspectives. *Journal of Personality and Social Psychology* 48 #3:702–715.

Halpern, H. (1986). Herpes panic: Is less new good news? *Los Angeles Times* Part V (March 3):2.

Harvey, J. H., R. Flanary, and M. Morgan. (1986). Vivid memories of vivid loves gone by. *Journal of Social and Personal Relationships* 3:359–373.

Hatfield, E., and G. W. Walster. (1978). A *new look at love*. Reading, MA: Addison-Wesley.

————, and S. Sprecher. (1986). *Mirror, mirror . . . The importance of looks in everyday life*. New York: SUNY Press.

Heller, D. (1987). A Meditation on lost love. *Psychology Today* 55 #3 (March):74–75.

Hendrick, C., and S. Hendrick. (1986). A theory and method of love. *Journal of Personality and Social Psychology* 50 #2:392–402.

Hinde, R. A. (1979). *Toward understanding relationships*. London: Academic Press.

Horn, J. (1976). Love: The most important ingredient is happiness. *Psychology Today* 10 (July):98–102.

Hunt, M. M. (1959). *The natural history of love*. New York: Alfred A. Knopf.

The Impotence Information Center. (1986). Impotence—Help in the USA. Reported in *U.S. News and World Report* (June 9):80.

Jacoby, A., and J. D. Williams. (1985). Effects of premarital sexual standards and behavior on dating and marriage desirability. *Journal of Marriage and the Family* (Nov.):1059–1065.

Horn, M. C., and K. Tanfer. (1985). Virginity at marriage, a thing of the past: New report. *Marriage and Divorce Today Newsletter* 10 #31 (March 4):3–4.

Kagan, J. (1985). On love and violence. *Science* (March):28–29, 32.

Kelley, H. H. (1983). Love and commitment. In *Close relationships*, ed. H. H. Kelley et al., 265–314. New York: Freeman.

Koop, C. E. (1986). AIDS: The Surgeon General's report on acquired immune deficiency syndrome. Reprinted as a public service by *The Los Angeles Times* (Dec. 7):1–8.

Kurland, M. (1953). Romantic love and economic considerations: A cultural comparison. *Journal of Educational Sociology* 27 (Oct.):72–79.

Larzelere, R. E., and T. L. Huston. (1980). The dyadic trust scale: Toward understanding interpersonal trust in close relationships. *Journal of Marriage and the Family* 42:595–604.

Lasswell, T. E., and M. E. Lasswell. (1976). I love you but I'm not in love with you. *Journal of Marriage and Family Counseling* 2:211–224.

Lasswell, M., and N. Lobsenz. (1980). *Styles of loving*. Garden City, NY: Doubleday, 1980.

Lee, J. A. (1973). *The colours of love*. Toronto, Canada: New Press.

————. (1974). The styles of loving. *Psychology Today* (Oct.):44–51.

————. (1977). A typology of styles of loving. *Personal and Social Psychology Bulletin* 3:173–182.

Levinger, G. (1983). Development and change. In *Close relationships*, ed. H. H. Kelley et al., 315–359. New York: Freeman.

————, M. Rands, and R. Talaber. (1977). *The assessment of involvement and rewardingness in close and casual pair relationships*. Amherst: University of Massachusetts.

Livingston, K. R. (1980). Love as a process of reducing uncertainty. In *On love and loving*, ed. K. S. Pope, 133–151. San Francisco: Jossey-Bass.

LoPiccolo, J., and W. E. Stock. (1986). Treatment of sexual dysfunction. *Journal of Counseling and Clinical Psychology* 54 #2:158–167.

Lund, M. (1985). The development of investment and commitment scales for predicting continuity of personal relationships. *Journal of Personality and Social Psychology* 2:3–23.

Mall, J. (1986). Men send mixed signals on attitudes. *Los Angeles Times* Part VI (April 27):1, 20.

Masters, W., V. Johnson, and R. C. Kolodny. (1985). *Sex and human loving.* Boston: Little, Brown.

Mead, M. (1960). Quoted in A. Drich, *The anatomy of love.* New York: Dell.

McAuliffe, K., J. Carey, S. Wells, B. E. Quick, and M. Dobbin. (1987). AIDS: At the dawn of fear. *U.S. News and World Report* (Jan. 12):60–69.

Mehlman, R. C., and C. R. Snyder. (1985). Excuse theory: A test of the protective role of attributions. *Journal of Personality and Social Psychology* 49 #4:994–1001.

Millay, E. St. V. (1956). What lips my lips have kissed. *Collected poems.* New York: Harper & Row.

Murstein, B. I. (1976). *Who will marry whom? Theories and research in marital choice.* New York: Springer.

Nevid, J. S. (1985). Choose me. *Psychology Today* 19 #8 (Aug.):66–67.

Peele, S., and A. Brodsky. (1976). *Love and addiction.* New York: New American Library.

Peterson, K. S. (1986). Single men say easy sex is unsafe. Special for *USA Today* (July 7):7–10.

Planned Parenthood Federation of America, Inc. (1986). Louis Harris poll. Reported in *Behavior Today Newsletter* (Dec. 29):5.

Rand, A. (1965). *The virtue of selfishness.* New York: New American Library.

Robertson, I. (1981). *Sociology.* New York: Worth Publishing Co.

Rogers, L. (1985). Self-esteem. *Journal of Marriage and Family Living* 67 #5 (June):6–8.

The Roper Organization. (1987). How enduring is love in marriage? Special survey.

Rother, D. L., C. R. Snyder, and L. M. Pace. (1986). Dimensions of favorable self-presentation. *Journal of Personality and Social Psychology* 51 #4:867–874.

Rubin, Z. (1970). Measurement of romantic love. *Journal of Personality and Social Psychology* 16:265–273.

———, L. A. Peplau, and C. T. Hill. (1978). Loving and leaving: Sex differences in romantic attachments. *Journal of Social Issues* 34:7–27.

Russell, B. (1951). *The autobiography of Bertrand Russell.* Vol. 1. New York: Simon & Schuster.

Salovey, P., and J. Rodin. (1985). The heart of jealousy. A report on *Psychology Today*'s jealousy and envy survey. *Psychology Today* 19 #9 (Sept.):22–25, 28–31.

———. (1986). The differentiation of social-comparison and romantic jealousy. *Journal of Personality and Social Psychology* 50 #6:1100–1112.

Solomon, R. C. (1981a). *Love: Emotion, myth, and metaphor*. Garden City, NY: Anchor Press/Doubleday.

———. (1981b). The love lost in clichés. *Psychology Today* 15 (Oct.):83–88*ff*.

Snyder, M., E. Bercheif, and P. Glick. (1985). Focusing on the exterior and the interior: Two investigations of the initiation of personal relationships. *Journal of Personality and Social Psychology* 48 #6:1427–1439.

Snyder, M., and J. A. Simpson. (1984). Self-monitoring and dating relationships. *Journal of Personality and Social Psychology* 47 #6:1281–1291.

Sternberg, R. J. (1986). A triangular theory of love. *Psychological Review* 93 #2:119–135.

———, and S. Grojek. (1984). The nature of love. *Journal of Personality and Social Psychology* 47:312–329.

Tennov, D. (1979). *Love and limerence*. New York: Stein & Day.

Traupmann, J., E. Hatfield, and P. Wexler. (1983). Equity and sexual satisfaction in dating couples. *British Journal of Social Psychology* 22:33–40.

Trotter, R. J. (1986). The three faces of love. *Psychology Today* (Sept.):46–50, 54.

Walster, E., et al. (1966). Importance of physical attraction in dating behavior. *Journal of Personality and Social Psychology* 4:508–516.

Walster, E., and G. W. Walster. (1978). *A new look at love*. Reading, MA: Addison-Wesley.

Waterman, C. D., and E. J. Chiauzzi. (1982). The role of orgasm in male and female sexual enjoyment. *Journal of Sex Research* 18:146–159.

Weiss, R. S. (1975). *Marital separation*. New York: Basic Books.

Wheelis, A. (1966). *The illusionless man: Some fantasies and meditations on disillusionment*. New York: Harper/Colophon.

Wilkinson, M. L. (1978). Romantic love and sexual expression. *The Family Coordinator* 27 (April): 141–148.

Chapter 6

Abernathy, T. J. (1981). Adolescent cohabitation: A form of courtship or marriage? *Adolescence* 16 (Winter):791–797.

Anderson, D., and R. Briato. (1981). The mental health of the never-married. *Alternative Lifestyles* 4:108–124.

Behrens, D. (1981). "Needed": Usable word for 'living together.' *Honolulu Star Bulletin and Advertiser* (Jan. 1):C-1.

Bernard, J. (1981). Facing the future. *Society* 18 (Jan.–Feb.):53–59.

Blanc, A. K. (1987). The formation and dissolution of second unions: Marriage and cohabitation in Sweden and Norway. *Journal of Marriage and the Family* 49 (May):391–400.

Cockrum, J., and P. White. (1985). Influences on the life satisfaction of never-married men and women. *Family Relations* 34 #4 (Oct.):551–556.

Eckclaar, J. M., and S. N. Katz (eds.). *Marriage and cohabitation in contemporary societies: Areas of legal, social and ethical change: An international and interdisciplinary study*. Toronto, Canada: Butterworth.

Furstenberg, F. K. (1980). Reflections on remarriage. *Journal of Family Issues* 1 (Dec.):433–453.

Gargan, L. (1981). Singles: An examination of two stereotypes. *Family Relations* 30 (July):377–385.

_____, and M. Melko. (1982). *Singles: Myths and realities*. Beverly Hills, CA: Sage.

Glick, P. C. (1980). Remarriage: Some recent changes and variations. *Journal of Family Issues* 1 (Dec.):455–478.

_____. (1981). Changing nature of American families. Reported in *Marriage and Divorce Today* 7 (Nov. 23):1.

_____. (1985). More Americans repeatedly remarrying. *Marriage and Divorce Today* 10 #33 (March 18):1.

Gwartney-Gibbs, P. A. (1986). The institutionalization of premarital cohabitation: Estimates from marriage license applications, 1970 and 1980. *Journal of Marriage and the Family* 48 (May):423–434.

Hite, S. (1981). *The Hite report on male sexuality*. New York: Alfred A. Knopf.

Jackson, T. (1985). New study indicates date rape common. *Behavior Today Newsletter* 16 #23 (June):7.

Jacques, J., and K. J. Chason. (1979). Cohabitation: Its impact on marital success. *Family Coordinator* 28 (Jan.):35–39.

Jong-Gierveld, J., and M. Aalberts. (1980). Singlehood: A creative or lonely experience. *Alternative Lifestyles* 3 (Aug.):350–368.

Kando, T. (1978). *Sexual behavior and family life in transition*. New York: Elsevier.

Kantrowitz, B., V. Quade, R. Ernsberger, Jr., and D. Shapiro. (1986). Fear of sex. *Newsweek* (Nov. 24):40, 42.

Khoo, S.-E. (1987). Living together as married: A profile of de facto couples in Australia. *Journal of Marriage and the Family* 49 (Feb.):185–191.

Kotkin, M. (1985). To marry or live together? *Lifestyles: A journal of changing patterns* 7 #3 (Spring):156–170.

Lane, K. E., and P. Gwartney-Gibbs. (1985). Violence in the context of dating and sex. *Journal of Family Issues* 6 #1 (March):45–59.

Lewin, B. (1982). Unmarried cohabitation: A marriage form in a changing society. *Journal of Marriage and the Family* 44 (Aug.):763–773.

Libby, R. W. (1977). Creative singlehood as a sexual life-style: Beyond marriage as a rite of passage. In *Marriage and alternatives*, ed. R. W. Libby and R. N. Whitehurst. Glenview, IL: Scott, Foresman.

Mace, D., and V. Mace. (1981). What is marriage beyond living together? Some Quaker reactions to cohabitation. *Family Relations* 30 (Jan.):10–17.

Macklin, E. D. (1974). Cohabitation in college: Going very steady. *Psychology Today* (Nov.):53–59.

_____. (1978a). Review of research on nonmarital cohabitation in the United States. In *Exploring intimate lifestyles*, ed. B. I. Murstein. New York: Springer.

_____. (1978b). Nonmarital heterosexual cohabitation. *Marriage and Family Review* 1 (March–April):2–10.

Masters, W., V. Johnson, and R. C. Kolodny. (1986). *Masters and Johnson on sex and human loving*. Boston: Little, Brown.

Nadelson, C. C., and M. T. Notman. (1981). To marry or not to marry: A choice. *American Journal of Psychiatry* 138:1352–1356.

Newcomb, M. D. (1986). Cohabitation, marriage and divorce among adolescents and young adults. *Journal of Social and Personal Relationships* 3:473–494.

———, and P. R. Bentler. (1980a). Cohabitation before marriage: A comparison of married couples who did not cohabit. *Alternative Lifestyles* 3 (Feb.):65–85.

———. (1980b). Assessment of personality and demographic aspects of cohabitation and marital success. *Journal of Personality Assessment* 44 (Feb.):11–24.

Newcomb, P. R. (1979). Cohabitation in America: An assessment of consequences. *Journal of Marriage and the Family* 41:597–602.

Papenoe, D. (1987). Beyond the nuclear family: A statistical portrait of the changing family in Sweden. *Journal of Marriage and the Family* 49 (Feb.):173–183.

Ridley, C. A., D. J. Peterman, and A. W. Avery. (1978). Cohabitation: Does it make for a better marriage? *Family Coordinator* 27 (April):129–136.

Risman, B. J., C. Hill, Z. Rubin, and L. A. Peplau. (1981). Living together in college: Implications for courtship. *Journal of Marriage and the Family* 43 (Feb.):77–83.

Rubenstein, C. (1981). Relationships: Practice marriages don't make perfect. *Psychology Today* (July):19.

Schnall, M. (1979). Learning to love again. *Woman's Day* (May 22):56–62.

Stein, P. J. (1976). *Single*. Englewood Cliffs, NJ: Prentice-Hall.

———. (1978). The lifestyles and life changes of the never married. *Marriage and Family Review* 3 (July–Aug.):1–11.

Trost, J. (1981). Cohabitation in the Nordic countries: From deviant phenomenon to social institution. *Alternative Lifestyles* 4 (Nov.):401–427.

U.S. Bureau of the Census. (1982). *Current population reports*. Washington, D.C.: U.S. Government Printing Office.

Vaughan, D. (1979). Uncoupling. *Alternative Lifestyles* 2 (Nov.):415–442.

Yllo, K., and M. Strauss. (1981). Interpersonal violence among married and cohabiting couples. *Family Relations* 30 (July):339–347.

Chapter 7

Albrecht, R. (1972). A study of dates that failed. In *Encounters: Love, marriage, and the family*, 57–63. Boston: Holbrook Press.

Atkinson, M. P., and B. L. Glass. (1985). Marital age heterogamy and homogamy, 1900–1980. *Journal of Marriage and the Family* 47 #3 (Aug.):685–691.

Berg, J. H., and R. D. McQuinn. (1986). Attraction and exchange in continuing and noncontinuing dating relationships. *Journal of Personality and Social Psychology* 50 #5:942–952.

Bernard, J. (1973). *The future of marriage*. New York: Bantam Books.

Braiker, H., and H. H. Kelley. (1979). Conflict in the development of close relationships. In *Social exchange in developing relationships*, ed. R. L. Burgess and T. L. Huston, 135–168. New York: Academic Press.

Brehm, S. S. (1985). *Intimate relationships*. New York: Random House.

Buss, D. M., and M. Barnes. (1986). Preferences in human mate selection. *Journal of Personality and Social Psychology* 50 #3:559–570.

Carlson, B. E. (1987). Dating violence: A research review and comparison with spouse abuse. *Social Casework* 68 #1 (Jan.):16–23.

Chesser, B. J. (1980). Analysis of wedding rituals: An attempt to make weddings more meaningful. *Family Relations* 29 (April):204–209.

Cornish, E. (1979). The future of the family: Intimacy in an age of loneliness. *The Futurist* 8 (Feb.):45–48.

Cowan, C., and M. Kinder. (1985). *Smart women, foolish choices: Finding the right man and avoiding the wrong ones.* New York: Clarkson N. Potter.

Curran, J. P. (1977). Skills training as an approach to the treatment of heterosexual-social anxiety: A review. *Psychological Bulletin* 84:140–157.

Erickson, J. (1981). Marital pickups replace Cupid. *Honolulu Advertiser* (May 26):C-1.

Framo, J. L. (1982). *Explorations in marital and family therapy.* New York: Springer Publishing Company.

Francoeur, R. T. (1985). Moral concepts in the year 2020: The individual, the family, and society. In *Marriage and the family in the year 2020,* ed. L. A. Kirkendall and A. E. Gravatt, 183–204. Buffalo, NY: Prometheus.

Gelman, D., N. Greenberg, T. A. Jackson, and D. Shirley. (1985). 'Unmarried' counseling. *Newsweek* (June 17):78.

Goode, W. J. (1964). *The family.* Englewood Cliffs, NJ: Prentice-Hall.

Greenberg, E. F., and R. Nay. (1982). The intergenerational transmission of marital instability. *Journal of Marriage and the Family* 44 (May):335–347.

Kando, T. M. (1978). *Sexual behavior and family life in transition.* New York: Elsevier.

Kelly, C., T. L. Huston, and R. M. Cate. (1985). Premarital relationship correlates of the erosion of satisfaction in marriage. *Journal of Social and Personal Relationships* 2:167–178.

Kelly, E. L., and J. J. Conley. (1987). Personality and compatibility: A perspective analysis of marital stability and marital satisfaction. *Journal of Personality and Social Psychology* 52 #1:27–40.

Klein, E. (1986). Only half of wives would rewed hubby. *The Arizona Republic* (June 20):D16.

Kotkin, M. (1985). To marry or live together? *Lifestyles: A journal of changing patterns* 7 #3 (Spring):156–170.

Labov, T., and J. A. Jacobs. (1986). Intermarriage in Hawaii, 1950–1983. *Journal of Marriage and the Family* 48 #1 (Feb.):79–88.

LeShan, E. (1986). Talking it over. *Woman's Day* (May 27):14.

Levad, K. (1982). Interfaith marriage. *Journal of Marriage and Family Living* 64 (April):10–11.

Mace, D. (1985). How to cut the divorce rate in half. *Journal of Marriage and Family Living* 68 #11 (Nov.):31.

———. (1986). Christian marriage as partnership. *Journal of Marriage and Family Living* 68 #11 (Nov.):31.

Mandelbaum, A. (1979). Parenting and marital love: When is it good enough? *Marriage and Family Living* 61 (June):8–15.

Masnick, G., and M. J. Bane. (1980). *The nation's families: 1960–1990*. Cambridge, MA: M.I.T.–Harvard Joint Center for Urban Studies.

Moss, M. (1987). One in 8 female students is a victim of date rape or a rape attempt. *Behavior Today Newsletter* 18 #7 (Feb.):8.

Murstein, B. (1980). Mate selection in the 1970s. *Journal of Marriage and the Family* 42 (Nov.):777–792.

National Center for Health Statistics. (1986). *Provision marriage statistics for 1985*. Hyattville, MD: U.S. Government.

Nevid, J. S. (1985). Choose me. *Psychology Today* (Aug.):66–67.

Olsen, D. (1987). Computerized premarital inventories reveal likelihood of future divorce. *Marriage and Divorce Today Newsletter* 12 #23 (Jan. 5):2–3.

Ranieri, R. (1987). Is the wearing of wedding bands a tradition to value? *Marriage and Family Living* 69, 11 (November):7.

Reed, J. (1986). Wedding bells—and bills—are ringing. *U.S. News and World Report* (June 16):44–45.

Ringer, R. (1977). *Looking out for number one*. New York: Fawcett.

Rourke, M. (1986). Customs, ideas about wedding bands have a new ring to them. *Los Angeles Times* Part V (Nov. 28):1, 12.

Shaw, B. (1954). *Getting married: Selected plays with prefaces*. New York: Dodd, Mead.

Seskin, J. (1985). When older women marry younger men. *Woman's Day* (April 30):82–83, 144.

Spanier, G. B., and P. C. Glick. (1981). Marital instability in the United States: Some correlates and recent changes. *Family Relations* 30 (July):329–338.

Tavris, C., and T. E. Jayaratne. (1976). How happy is your marriage? What 75,000 wives say about their most intimate relationship. *Redbook* (June):90–92ff.

Timmick, L. (1982). Now you can learn to be likable, confident, socially successful for only the cost of your present education. *Psychology Today* (Aug.):42–44, 46, 48.

Toffler, A. (1970). *Future shock*. New York: Random House.

Vera, H., D. H. Berardo, and F. M. Berardo. (1985). Age heterogamy in marriage. *Journal of Marriage and the Family* 47 #3 (Aug.):553–566.

Wanderer, Z., and E. Fabian. (1979). *Making love work*. New York: Putnam's.

Weingarten, H. R. (1985). Marital status and well-being: A national study comparing first married, currently divorced, and remarried adults. *Journal of Marriage and the Family* 47 #3 (Aug.):653–662.

Wells, J. G. (1976). A critical look at personal marriage contracts. *Family Coordinator* 25 (Jan.):33–37.

Winch, R. F. (1971). *The modern family*. 3d. ed. New York: Holt.

Chapter 8

Ade-Ritter, L. (1985). Quality of marriage: A comparison of golden wedding couples and couples married less than 50 years. *Lifestyles: A Journal of Changing Patterns* 7 #4:224–236.

Ammons, P., and N. Stinnett. (1980). The vital marriage: A closer look. *Family Relations* 29:37–42.

Banmen, J., and N. A. Vogel. (1985). The relationship between marital quality and interpersonal sexual communication. *Family Therapy* 12 #1:46–58.

Bohannan, P. (1972). The six stations of divorce. In *Readings in the psychology of women*. New York: Harper & Row.

Botwin, C. (1985). *Is there sex after marriage?* New York: Atcom.

Burgess, E. W., and P. Wallin. (1953). *Courtship, engagement, and marriage*. Philadelphia: Lippincott.

Cady, B. (1891). For God's sake, don't tell my wife! *Los Angeles Magazine* (Feb.):133–134.

Crooks, R., and K. Baur. (1980). *Our sexuality*. Menlo Park, CA: Benjamin Cummings.

Cuber, J. F., and P. B. Harroff. (1968). Five kinds of relationships. In *Sourcebook in marriage and the family*, ed. M. B. Sussman, 301–308. Boston: Houghton Mifflin.

D'Augelli, J. F., and A. R. D'Augelli. (1979). Sexual involvement and relationship development: A cognitive developmental approach. In *Social exchange in developing relationships*, ed. R. L. Burgess and T. L. Huston, 307–349. New York: Academic Press.

Davis, E. C., et al. (1982). Effects of weekend and weekly marriage enrichment program formats. *Family Relations* 31 (Jan.):85–90.

Doherty, W. J., M. E. Lester, and G. Leigh. (1986). Marriage encounter weekends: Couples who win and couples who lose. *Journal of Marriage and Family Therapy* 12 #1 (Jan.):49–61.

Dudley, E. (1979). Rainbows and realities: Current trends in marriage and its alternatives. *The Futurist* (Feb.):23–31.

Edmonsa, C. (1967). Marriage conventionalization: Definition and measurement. *Journal of Marriage and the Family* 29:681–688.

Francoeur, R. T. (1984). Moral concepts in the year 2020: The individual, the family, and society. In *Marriage and the family in the year 2020*, ed. L. A. Kirkendall and A. E. Gravett, 183–204. Buffalo, NY: Prometheus Books.

Fitzgerald, F. (1986). *Cities on a hill: A journey through contemporary American cultures*. New York: Simon & Schuster.

Frank, E., and C. Anderson. (1980). The sexual stages of marriage. *Family Circle* (Feb.):64*ff*.

Goldstine, D., L. Larner, S. Zuckerman, and H. Goldstine. (1977). *The dance-away lover*. New York: Morrow.

Goodman, E. (1982). Quoted in C. I. Notarius and J. S. Johnson. Emotional expression in husbands and wives. *Journal of Marriage and the Family* 42:483–489.

Hawkins, J., G. Weisberg, and D. Ray. (1980). Spouse differences in communication style: Preference, perception, and behavior. *Journal of Marriage and the Family* 42 (Aug.):479–490.

Hite, S. (1987). *Women and love, a cultural revolution in progress*. New York: Knopf.

Jackle, C. (1981). Quoted in *Marriage and Divorce Today* 6:3.

Jacobson, N. S., and D. Moore. (1981). Spouses as observers of the events in their relationship. *Journal of Counseling and Clinical Psychology* 49:269–277.

Jansen, H. (1980). Communes. *Alternative Lifestyles*. 3 (Aug.):255–276.

Japenga, A. (1986). Arizona town's uneasy marriage to polygamy. *Los Angeles Times* Part VI (April 13):1, 20–21.

Johnson, D., L. K. White, J. N. Edwards, and A. Booth. (1986). Dimensions of marital quality. Toward methodological and conceptual refinement. *Journal of Family Issues* 7 #1 (March):31–49.

Kanter, R. M. (1972). *Commitment and community: Communes and utopias in sociological perspective*. Cambridge, MA: Harvard University Press.

Kurdek, L. A., and J. P. Schmitt. (1986). Relationship quality of partners in heterosexual married, heterosexual cohabiting, and gay and lesbian relationships. *Journal of Personality and Social Psychology* 51 (April):711–720.

L'Abate, L. (1985). Structure enrichment (SE) with couples and families. *Family Relations* 34 (April):169–175.

Larsen, J. (1982). Remedying dysfunctional marital communication. *Social Casework* 63 (Jan.):15–25.

Lederer, W., and D. Jackson. (1968). *The mirages of marriage*. New York: W. W. Norton.

Lester, M. E., and W. J. Doherty. (1983). Couples' long-term evaluations of their marriage encounter experience. *Journal of Marital and Family Therapy* 9 (April):87–89.

Levinger, G. (1979). A social exchange view on the dissolution of pair relationships. In *Social exchange in developing relationships*, ed. R. L. Burgess and T. L. Huston, 169–193. New York: Academic Press.

_____, and L. R. Huesmann. (1980). An 'incremental exchange' perspective on the pair relationship. In *Social exchange: Advances in theory and research*, ed. K. K. Gergen, M. S. Greenberg, and R. H. Willis. New York: Plenum.

Losoncy, L. (1985). Mining intimacy for all its worth. *Journal of Marriage and Family Living* 67 #9 (Sept.):22–24.

Mace, D. (1985). Sex in modern marriage. *Journal of Marriage and Family Living* 67 #11 (Nov.):31.

_____. (1986a). What is marital enrichment? *Journal of Marriage and Family Living* 68 #1 (Jan.):31.

_____. (1986b). When you can't communicate. *Journal of Marriage and Family Living* 68 #9 (Sept.):31.

Masters, W., and V. Johnson. (1974). *The pleasure bond*. Boston: Little, Brown.

_____. (1979). *Homosexuality in perspective*. Boston: Little, Brown.

_____, and R. Kolodny. (1985). *On sex and human loving*. Boston: Little, Brown.

Mead, M. Quoted in Rainbows and realities. *The Futurist* 13 (1979):27.

Miles, H. J. (1987). Two become one. *Home Life* 41 #7 (April):34–35.

Milholland, T. A., and A. A. Avery. (1982). Effects of marriage encounter on self-disclosure, trust, and marital satisfaction. *Journal of Marital and Family Therapy* 8 (April):87–89.

Montgomery, B. M. (1981). The form and function of quality communication in marriage. *Family Relations* 30 (Jan.):21–20.

Nadolny, E. S. (1981). In Retreats that help marriages, ed. A. B. Haines. *Journal of Marriage and Family Living* 63 (Aug.):21–23.

Nickols, S. A., D. C. Fournier, and S. Y. Nickols. (1986). Evaluation of preparation for marriage workshop. *Family Relations* 35:563–571.

Noller, P. (1980). Misunderstanding in marital communication: A study of couples' nonverbal communication. *Journal of Personality and Social Psychology* 39:1135–1148.

———. (1985). Negative communication in marriage. *Journal of Social and Personal Relationships* 2:289–301.

———, and C. Venardos. (1986). Communication awareness in married couples. *Journal of Social and Personal Relationships* 3:31–42.

O'Neill, N., and G. O'Neill. (1972). *Open marriage*. New York: Avon Books.

Peplau, L. A. (1981). What homosexuals want. *Psychology Today* (March):28–34.

Pike, G. R., and A. L. Sillars. (1985). Reciprocity of marital communication. *Journal of Social and Personal Relationships* 2:303–434.

Roach, A. J., L. P. Frazier, and S. R. Bowden. (1981). The marital satisfaction scale: Development of a measure for intervention research. *Journal of Marriage and the Family* 43 (Aug.):537–546.

Roth, S. (1985). Psychotherapy with lesbian couples: Individual issues, female socialization, and the social context. *Journal of Marriage and Family Therapy* 11 #3 (July):273–286.

Salovey, P., and J. Rodin. (1985). The heart of jealousy. *Psychology Today* 19 #9 (Sept.):22–25, 28–29.

Schafer, R. N., and P. M. Keith. (1981). Equity in marital roles across the family life cycle. *Journal of Marriage and the Family* 43 (May):359–367.

Schumm, W. R., H. L. Barnes, S. R. Bollman, A. P. Jurich, and M. A. Bugaighis. (1986). Self-disclosure and marital satisfaction revisited. *Family Relations* 34 (April):241–247.

Schumm, W. R., A. P. Jurich, S. R. Bollmann, and M. A. Bugaighis. (1985). His and her marriage revisited. *Journal of Family Issues* 6 #2 (June):221–227.

Shaw, B. (1951). *Man and superman*. New York: Dodd, Mead.

Shey, T. H. (1977). Why communes fail: A comparative analysis of the viability of Danish and American communes. *Journal of Marriage and the Family* 39 (Aug.):605–613.

Snyder, D. K., and G. T. Smith. (1986). Classification of marital relationships: An empirical approach. *Journal of Marriage and the Family* 48 (Feb.):137–146.

Snyder, D. K., R. M. Wills, and T. W. Keiser. (1981). Empirical validation of the marital satisfaction inventory: An actuarial approach. *Journal of Counseling and Clinical Psychology* 49:262–268.

Spanier, G. (1976). Measuring dyadic adjustment: New scales for assessing the quality of marriage and similar dyads. *Journal of Marriage and the Family* 38 (Feb.):15–28.

———. (1979). The measurement if marital quality. *Journal of Sex and Marital Therapy* 5 (Fall):288–299.

———, and R. A. Lewis. (1980). Marital quality: A review of the seventies. *Journal of Marriage and the Family* 42 (Nov.):825–839.

Starr, B. D., and M. N. Weiner. (1980). *The Starr-Weiner report on sex and sexuality in the mature years*. New York: The Atlantic Institute.

Strieb, G. F., and M. A. Hilker. (1980). The cooperative 'family.' *Alternative Lifestyles* 3 (May):167–184.

Tavris, C., and T. Jayartne. (1976). How happy is your marriage? What 75,000 wives say about their most intimate relationship. *Redbook* (June):90–92.

Wampler, K. S., and G. S. Powell. (1982). The Barrett-Lennard relationship inventory as a measure of marital satisfaction. *Family Relations* 31 (Jan.):139–145.

Wanderer, Z., and E. Fabian. (1979). *Making love work*. New York: G. P. Putnam's Sons.

Watson, M. A. (1981). Sexual open marriages: Three perspectives. *Alternative Lifestyles* 4 (Feb.):3–21.

Zablocki, B. (1977). *Alienation and investment in the urban communes*. New York: Center for Policy Research.

————. (1980). *Alienation and charisma: A study of contemporary American communes*. New York: Free Press.

Chapter 9

Aldous, J. (1981). From dual-earner to dual-career families and back again. *Journal of Family Issues* 2 #2 (June):115–125.

Avery-Clark, C. (1985). Career women most likely to suffer from inhibited sexual desire. *Behavior Today Newsletter* 16 #34 (Aug.):4–6.

Basow, S. (1984). Dual-worker marriages. In J. C. Coleman, *Intimate relationships, marriage, and family*. 1st ed., 335–366. Indianapolis, IN: Bobbs-Merrill.

Bernard, J. (1981). The good provider role. *American Psychologist* 36 #1:1–12.

Bolles, R. (1981). The meaning of career. *The Sunday Star Bulletin and Advertiser* (Nov. 4):D-2.

Brothers, J. (1982). Men in love and marriage. *Woman's Day* (Jan. 12):43–47, 50, 92.

Catalyst. (1982). *Corporations and two-career families: Directions for the future*. New York: Catalyst.

Centron, M. (1986). Looking at the future of American business. *The Futurist* 20 #2 (March–April):25–27.

Consumer Research Center. (1986). *The conference board: The working woman: A progress report*. New York: Consumer Research Center.

Ferree, M. M. (1976). The confused American housewife. *Psychology Today* (Sept.):76, 78, 80.

Gerson, K. (1986). Briefcase, baby or both? *Psychology Today* 20 #1 (Nov.):30–35.

Gilbert, L. (1986). *Men in dual-career families: Current realities and future prospects*. Hillsdale, NJ: Lawrence Erlbaum.

Glick, P. C. (1975). A demographer looks at American families. *Journal of Marriage and the Family* 37 #2:15–28.

Goldenberg, H. (1986). Treating contemporary couples in dual-career relationships. *Family Therapy Today* 1 #1:1–4, 7.

Harrell, T. W., and J. Baack. (1986). In New problems in dual-career marriages, ed. J. Mall. *Los Angeles Times* Part VI (Aug. 10):7.

Hirsch, B. J., and B. D. Rapkin. (1986). Multiple roles, social networks, and women's well-being. *Journal of Personality and Social Psychology* 51 #6:1237–1247.

Hornung, C. A., and B. C. McCullough. (1981). Status relationships in dual-employment marriages: Consequences for psychological well-being. *Journal of Marriage and the Family* 43:125–141.

Houseknecht, S. K., and A. S. Macke. (1981). Combining marriage and career: The marital adjustment of professional women. *Journal of Marriage and the Family* 43:651–661.

Josephson, N. (1981). Superwomen. *House & Garden* (March):138, 197–198.

Kelly, R. F., and P. Voydanoff. (1985). Work/family role strain among employed parents. *Family Relations* 34 #3 (July):367–374.

Kennedy, J. M. (1986). Day care spreading in industry. *Los Angeles Times* Part I (Sept. 16):1, 18.

Koep, S., G. Bolte, J. D. Hull. (1986). Is the middle class shrinking? *Time* (Nov. 3):54–56.

Mace, J. (1985). Marriage and housework. *Journal of Marriage and Family Living* 67 #5 (May):31.

Macke, A. S., G. W. Bohrnstedt, and E. Bernstein. (1979). Housewives' self-esteem and their husbands' success: The myth of vicarious involvement. *Journal of Marriage and the Family* 41 #1 (Feb.):51–57.

Maracek, J., and D. J. Ballou. (1981). Family roles and women's mental health. *Professional Psychology* 12:39–46.

Moore, K. A., and S. L. Hofferth. (1979). Effect of women's employment on marriage: Formation, stability, and roles. *Marriage and Family Review* 2 #2:1, 27–36.

Newberry, P., M. Weissman, and J. K. Myers. (1979). Working wives and housewives: Do they differ in mental status and social adjustment? *American Journal of Orthopsychiatry* 49 #2 (April):282–291.

Papaneck, H. (1973). Men, women, and work: Reflection on the two-person career. In *Changing women in a changing society*, ed. J. Huber, 90–110. Chicago: University of Chicago Press.

Pleck, J. H. (1985). *Working wives, working husbands*. Beverly Hills, CA: Sage.

Rachlin, V. C., and J. C. Hansen. (1985). The impact of equity or egalitarianism on dual-career couples. *Family Therapy* 12 #2:123–149.

Regan, M. C., and H. E. Roland. (1985). Rearranging family and career priorities: Professional women and men of the eighties. *Journal of Marriage and the Family* 47 (Nov.):985–992.

Rubenstein, C. (1982). Real men don't earn less than their wives. *Psychology Today* (Jan.):36–41.

Russo, N. F. (1976). The motherhood mandate. *Journal of Social Issues* 32:143–153.

Scanzoni, J. (1972). *Sexual bargaining: Power politics in American marriage*. Englewood Cliffs, NJ: Prentice-Hall.

Schrank, R. (1981). Prestige and blue-collar workers. *The Sunday Star Bulletin and Advertiser* (Oct. 4):B-8.

Smith, A. D., and W. J. Reid. (1986). Role expectations and attitudes in dual-earner families. *Social Casework: The Journal of Contemporary Social Work* 67 #7:394–402.

Smuts, R. W. (1959). *Women and work in America*. New York: Columbia University Press.

Special Kiplinger Report. (1986). *The next 10 years*. Washington, D.C.: Kiplinger Editors.

Spitze, G. D., and L. J. Waite. (1981). Wives' employment: The role of husbands' perceived attitudes. *Journal of Marriage and the Family* 43 #1 (Feb.):117–124.

Thomas, E., et al. (1986). Growing pains at 40. *Time* (May 19):20–26, 35–38, 41.

Toufexis, A. (1985). The perils of dual careers. *Time* (May 13):67.

U.S. Department of Labor. (1981). *Perspectives on working women*. Washington, D.C.: U.S. Government Printing Office.

————. (1986). *Mothers in the work force*. Washington, D.C.: U.S. Government Printing Office.

Verbruge, L. M., and J. H. Madans. (1985). Women's roles and health. *Marriage and Divorce Today Newsletter* 10 #39 (April):3–4.

Weingarten, K. (1978). Employment patterns of professional couples and their distribution of involvement in the family. *Psychology of Women Quarterly* 3:43–52.

Yankelovich, D. (1981). *New rules in American life: Searching for self-fulfillment in a world turned upside down*. New York: Random House.

Yogev, S. (1981). Do professional women have egalitarian relationships? *Journal of Marriage and the Family* 43:865–871.

————, and J. Brett. (1985). Perceptions of the division of housework and child care and marital satisfaction. *Journal of Marriage and the Family* 47 #3:609–616.

Chapter 10

Bailey, J. (1982). Your child and stealing. *Marriage and Family Living* 64 (Oct.):10–11*ff*.

Bandura, A. (1977). *Social learning theory*. Englewood, NJ: Prentice-Hall.

Barcai, A. (1981). Normative family development. *Journal of Marital and Family Therapy* (July):353–359.

Baumrind, D. (1966). Effects of authoritarian parent control on child behavior. *Child Development* 37:887–907.

Belsky, J. (1985). Exploring individual differences in marital change across the transition to parenthood: The role of violated expectations. *Journal of Marriage and the Family* 47 (Nov.):1037–1044.

————, M. E. Lang, and M. Rovine. (1985). Stability and change in marriage across the transition to parenthood: A second study. *Journal of Marriage and the Family* 47 (Nov.):855–865.

Belsky, J., M. E. Lang, and T. L. Huston. (1986). Sex typing and division of labor as determinants of marital change across the transition to parenthood. *Journal of Personality and Social Psychology* 50 #3:517–522.

Boggs, C. L. (1983). An analysis of selected Christian child-rearing manuals. *Family Relations* 32 (Jan.):73–80.

Brehm, S. S. (1985). *Intimate relationships*. New York: Random House.

Bronfenbrenner, U. (1979). Contexts of child rearing: Problems and prospects. *American Psychologist* 34 (Oct.):844–850.

Callan, V. J. (1986). The impact of the first birth: Married and single women preferring childlessness, one child, or two children. *Journal of Marriage and the Family* 48 (May):261–269.

Coleman, J. C., et al. (1987). *Contemporary psychology and effective behavior*. 6th ed. Glenview, IL: Scott, Foresman.

Coleman, J. C., J. Butcher, and R. Carson. (1984). *Abnormal psychology and modern life*. Glenview, IL: Scott, Foresman.

Cowan, C., P. A. Cowan, L. Coie, and J. D. Coie. (1978). Becoming a family: The impact of the first child's birth on the couple's relationship. In *The first child and family formation*, ed. W. Miller and L. Norman. Chapel Hill, NC: Carolina Population Center.

Duncan, L. (1981). The myth of the empty nest. *Journal of Marriage and Family Living* 63 #4 (April):6–8.

Elwell, M. E., and P. H. Ephross. (1987). Initial reactions of sexually abused children. *Social Casework* 68 #2 (Feb.):109–116.

Erikson, E. H. (1968). *Identity, youth, and crisis*. New York: W. W. Norton.

Evoy, J. J. (1982). *The rejected: Psychological consequences of parental rejection*. University Park, PA: Pennsylvania State University Press.

Fine, M. A., B. W. Donnelly, and P. Voydanoff. (1986). Adjustment and satisfaction of parents. A comparison of intact, single-parent, and stepparent families. *Journal of Family Issues* 7 #4 (Dec.):391–404.

Fisher, C. L. (1987). From mother with love. *Journal of Marriage and Family Living* 69 #5 (May):18–19.

Galinsky, E. (1980). *Between generations: The six stages of parenthood*. New York: Times Books.

Garmezy, N. (1976). Vulnerable and invulnerable: Theory, research, and intervention. American Psychological Association MS 1337.

General Mills. (1977). *Raising children in a changing society*. The General Mills American family report. Minneapolis, MN: General Mills.

Goertzel, V., and M. Goertzel. (1962). *Cradles of eminence*. Boston: Little, Brown.

Hanson, S. M. H., and F. W. Bozett (eds.). (1985). *Dimensions of fatherhood*. Beverly Hills, CA: Sage.

Harriman, L. C. (1986). Marital adjustment as related to personal and marital changes accompanying parenthood. *Family Relations* 34 (April):233–239.

Harris, L. (1985). No choice: No children. *Journal of Marriage and Family Living* 67 #8 (Aug.):6–8.

Insel, P., and R. Moos. (1974). Psychological environments: Expanding the scope of human ecology. *American Psychologist* 29 (March):179–188.

Joint Commission on Mental Health of Children. (1970). *Crisis in child mental health: Challenge for the 1970s*. New York: Harper & Row.

Junior Achievement. (1981). Youth of 1980: Friends and peers more influential than parents. *Behavior Today* (Feb. 23):8.

Kohl, R. (1981). Research: A look at new fathers. *Confo Memo* 3 (Winter):6.

Laing, R. D., and A. Esterson. (1964). *Sanity, madness, and the family*. London: Tavistock.

Larkin, M. (1985). Wanting and waiting. *Health* (July):49–51.

Lips, H. M., and A. Morrison. (1986). Changes in the sense of family among couples having their first child. *Journal of Social and Personal Relationships* 3:393–400.

Mace, D. (1986). What is marriage for? *Journal of Marriage and Family Living* 68 #8 (Aug.):33.

Madsen, K. (1986). Do you really want to bring a child into this kind of world? *Journal of Marriage and Family Living* 68 #1 (Jan.):20–21.

Martin, B. (1975). *Review of child development research*, vol. 4, ed. F. D. Horowitz. Chicago, IL: University of Chicago Press.

Martin, M. J., and J. Walters. (1982). Familial correlates of selected types of child abuse and neglect. *Journal of Marriage and the Family* 44 (May):267–276.

Matthews, R., and A. M. Matthews. (1986). Infertility and involuntary childlessness: The transition to nonparenthood. *Journal of Marriage and the Family* 48 #3 (Aug.):641–649.

Merrill, P. H. (1985). RESOLVE. *Journal of Marriage and Family Living* 67 #8 (Aug.):10–11.

Miller, B. C., J. K. McCoy, T. D. Olson, and C. M. Wallace. (1986). Parental discipline and control attempts in relation to adolescent sexual attitudes and behavior. *Journal of Marriage and the Family* 48 (Aug.):503–512.

Murphy, L. (1962). *The widening world of childhood*, 374. New York: Basic Books.

Nannarone, N. (1983). Career father. *Journal of Marriage and Family Living* 65 (June):8–11.

National Institute of Mental Health. (1969). *The mental health of urban America*. Washington, D.C.: Public Health Service, Publication 1906.

Parachini, A. (1986). Over-35 pregnancy no longer termed 'risky.' *Los Angeles Times* Part VI (March 25):1, 4.

Procaccini, J. (1983). 'Parent burnout': Latest sign of today's stresses. *U.S. News and World Report* (March 7):76–77.

Reading, J., and E. S. Amatea. (1986). Role deviance or role diversification: Reassessing the psychological factors affecting the parenthood choice of career-oriented women. *Journal of Marriage and the Family* 48 (May):255–260.

Reis, J., L. Barbera-Stein, and S. Bennett. (1986). Ecological determinants of parenting. *Family Relations* 35 (Oct.):547–554.

Rempel, J. (1985). Childless elderly: What are they missing? *Journal of Marriage and the Family* 47 #2 (May):343–348.

Ricciuti, H. N. (1979). Identifying the problems and needs of our children. *American Psychologist* 34:842–843.

Salazar, L. P. (1986). *Infertility: How couples can cope*. Boston: Resolve, Inc.

Seabold, J. (1987). Indicators of child sexual abuse in males. *Social Casework* 68 #2 (Feb.):75–80.

Sears, R., E. Maccoby, and H. Levin. (1957). *Patterns of child rearing*. New York: Harper & Row.

Sebald, H. (1986). Adolescents' shifting orientation toward parents and peers: A curvilinear trend over recent decades. *Journal of Marriage and the Family* 48 (Feb.):5–13.

Shapiro, J. E. (1987). The expectant father. *Psychology Today* 21 #1 (Jan.):36–39, 42.

Skolnick, A. (1973). *The intimate environment*. Boston: Little, Brown.

———. (1981). The family and its discontents. *Society* 18 (Jan.–Feb.):42–47.

Smith, L. (1986). Teen-age pregnancies on the rise. *Los Angeles Times* Part I (July 29):1, 3, 14.

Stark, E. (1986). Young, innocent and pregnant. *Psychology Today* 20 #10 (Oct.):28–35.

Weinberg, S. L., and M. S. Richardson. (1981). Dimensions of stress in early parenting. *Journal of Counseling and Clinical Psychology* 49:686–693.

Worthington, Jr., E. L., and B. G. Buston. (1986). The marriage relationship during the transition to parenthood. *Journal of Family Issues* 7 #4 (Dec.):443–473.

Chapter 11

Ade-Ritter, L. (1985). Quality of marriage: A comparison of golden wedding couples and couples married less than 50 years. *Lifestyles: A Journal of Changing Patterns* 7 #4:224–236.

American Chicle Youth Poll. (1987). American children adjust to changes in traditional family structure. *Marriage and Divorce Today* 12 (March 29):1–2.

Barcai, A. (1981). Normative family development. *Journal of Marital and Family Therapy* 7 (July):353–359.

Beal, Edward. (1982). Divorce especially harmful to health of males. *Marriage and Divorce Today* 7 (May 31):3.

Bengelsdorf, I. S. (1970). Alcohol, morphine addictions believed chemically similar. *Los Angeles Times* (March 5):7.

Berne, E. (1964). *Games people play: The psychology of human relationships*. New York: Grove Press.

———. (1972). *What do you say after you say hello?* New York: Grove Press.

Bernstein, S. (1985). In other words. *Mature Outlook* 38 (March/April):48.

Braiker, H. B., and H. Kelley. (1979). Conflict in the development of close relationships. In *Social exchange in developing relationships*, ed. R. Burgess and T. Huston. New York: Academic Press.

Branden, N. (1987). Is there life after marriage? *Q* 1 #2:12–14, 43.

Brehm, S. S. (1985). *Intimate relationships*. New York: Random House.

Brigham, J. C. (1986). *Social psychology*. Boston: Little, Brown.

Bringle, R. G. (1981). Conceptualizing jealousy as a disposition. *Alternative Lifestyles* 4 (Aug.):274–290.

Buhler, C. (1968). The course of human life as a psychological problem. *Human Development* 11:184–200.

Caplan, G. (1981). Mastery of stress: Psychosocial aspects. *American Journal of Psychiatry* 134 (April):413–420.

Clark, P., R. Siviski, and R. Weiner. (1986). Coping strategies of widows in the first year. *Family Relations* 35:425–430.

Clayton, P. (1979). The sequelae and nonsequelae of conjugal bereavement. *American Journal of Psychiatry* 136:1520–1534.

Cohen, H. (1980). *You can negotiate anything*. New York: Lyle Stuart.

Coleman, J. C. (1979). *Contemporary psychology and effective behavior*. Glenview, IL: Scott, Foresman.

Coyne, J. C. (1985). Toward a theory of frames and reframing: The social nature of frames. *Journal of Marital and Family Therapy* 11 #4:377–344.

Duncan, L. (1981). The myth of the empty nest. *Journal of Marriage and Family Living* 63 #4 (April):6–8.

Ellis, A. (1973). Rational-emotive therapy. In *Current psychotherapies*, ed. R. J. Corsini. Itasca, IL: Peacock Publishers.

———, and R. Harper. (1961). *Creative marriage*. New York: Lyle Stuart.

Elwell, M., and P. Ephross. (1987). Initial reactions of sexually abused children. *Social Casework* 68 (Feb.):109–116.

Engel, J. W., L. J. Mathews, and V. Halverson. (1985). *Marriage and family counseling in Hawaii: A consumer guide*. Honolulu, HI: University of Hawaii Press.

Falbo, T., and L. Peplau. (1980). Power struggles in intimate relationships. *Journal of Personality and Social Psychology* 38:618–628.

Fischer, H. K., and B. M. Dlin. (1972). Psychogenic determinants of time of illness or death by anniversary reactions and emotional deadlines. *Psychomatics* 13 #3 (May–June):170–173.

Friday, N. (1985). *Jealousy*. New York: Morrow.

Galloway, J. L., and P. A. Avery. (1984). American's forgotten resources: Grandparents. *U.S. News and World Report* (April 30):76–77.

Glick, P. C. (1980). Remarriage: Some recent changes and variations. *Journal of Family Issues* 4 (Dec.):445–478.

———. (1985). More Americans repeatedly remarrying. *Marriage and Divorce Today Newsletter* 10 #33 (March 18):1.

Glenn, N., and C. Weaver. (1981). The contribution of marital happiness to global happiness. *Journal of Marriage and the Family* 43:161–168.

Gottman, J. (1979). *Marital interaction: Experimental investigations*. New York: Academic Press.

Greenberg, J. (1978). Adulthood comes of age. *Science News* 114:4.

Haley, J. (1963). *Strategies of psychotherapy*. New York: Grune and Stratton.

Hanneke, C. R., and N. A. Shields. (1985). Marital rape: Implications for the helping professions. *Social Casework* 68 #8:451–458.

Huyck, M. (1974). *Growing older*. Englewood Cliffs, NJ: Prentice-Hall.

Julius, M. (1986). Marital stress and suppressed anger linked to death of spouses. *Marriage and Divorce Today Newsletter* 11 #35 (March 31):1–2.

Kahn, J., and J. C. Coyne, and G. Margolin. (1985). Depression and marital disagreement: The social construction of despair. *Journal of Personal and Social Relationships* 2 #4 (Dec.):447–461.

Kolevzon, M. A., and R. G. Green. (1985). *Family therapy models*. New York: Springer-Verlag.

Kosner, A. (1979). Starting over: What divorced women discover. *McCalls* (March):22–28.

Kübler-Ross, E. (1969). *On death and dying*. New York: Macmillan.

———. (1975). *Death: The final stage of growth*. Englewood Cliffs, NJ: Prentice-Hall.

Lauer, J., and R. Lauer. (1987). *Till death do us part*. New York: Haworth Press.

Lazarus, A. (1981). Divorce counseling or marriage therapy? A therapeutic opinion. *Journal of Marital and Family Therapy* (Jan.):15–22.

Lazarus, R. (1981). Little hazards can be hazardous to health. *Psychology Today* (July):58–61.

Leighton, D., and C. Kluckhohn. (1948). *Children of the people*. Cambridge, MA: Harvard University Press.

Leslie, G. (1979). *The family in social context*, 4th ed. New York: Oxford University Press.

Levinson, D. J. (1982). Midlife crisis: Is it unavoidable? *U.S. News and World Report* (Oct. 25):72–74.

———. (1986). A conception of adult development. *American Psychologist* 41:3–13.

Lobenz, P. (1975). Taming the green-eyed monster. *Redbook* (March):74–77.

Luckadoo, P. How to stop fighting over housework. *Redbook* (April):60–61.

Mabley, J. (1985). In other words. *Mature Outlook* 38 (March/April):48.

Mace, D. (1985). Anger in marriage. *Journal of Marriage and Family Living* 67 #3 (March):30.

———. (1986). Marriage matters: Why do marriages go wrong? *Marriage and Family Living* 68:30.

———. (1987). As a couple, how do you deal with anger? *Journal of Marriage and Family Living* 69 #2 (Feb.):31.

Masters, W., V. Johnson, and R. Kolodny. (1985). *On sex and human loving*. Boston: Little, Brown.

McKain, J. (1987). Lifestyles and values of older Americans. *Designers West* 34 (July):104, 171–172.

Medley, M. L. (1977). Marital adjustment in the post-retirement years. *The Family Coordinator* (Jan.):5–11.

Mogul, K. M. (1979). Women in midlife: Decisions, rewards, and conflicts related to work and careers. *American Journal of Psychiatry* 136 #9 (Sept.):207–222.

Moultrup. D. (1986). How to treat couples involved in extramarital affairs. *Behavior Today* 17 #51 (Dec.):1–3.

Neugarten, B., and D. A. Neugarten. (1987). The changing meanings of age. *Psychology Today* 21 #5 (May):29–33.

Parkes, C. M., B. Benjamin, and B. G. Fitzgerald. (1969). Broken heart: A statistical study of increased mortality among widowers. *British Medical Journal* 1 (March 22):740–743.

Pietropinto, A., and J. Simenauer. (1979). *Husbands and wives: A nationwide survey of marriage*. New York: Times Books.

Podsakoff, P. M., and C. A. Schriesheim. (1985). Field studies of French and

Raven's bases of power: Critique, reanalysis, and suggestions for future research. *Psychological Bulletin* 97 #3:387–411.

Rawitch, R. (1973). Oscar winner dies on day he predicted. *Los Angeles Times* Part II (July 5):2.

Rogers, L. (1987). Negotiating. *Marriage and Family Living* 69 (March):18–20.

Rubenstein, C., and Shaver, P. (1982). *In search of intimacy*. New York: Delacorte Press.

Rubin, L. (1979). *Women of a certain age: The midlife search for self*. New York: Harper & Row.

Satir, V. (1967). *Conjoint family therapy*. Rev. ed. Palo Alto, CA: Science and Behavior Books.

_____. (1972). *Peoplemaking*. Palo Alto, CA: Science and Behavior Books.

_____, and M. Baldwin. (1983). *Satir step by step: A guide to creating change in families*. Palo Alto, CA: Science and Behavior Books.

Satir, V., J. Stachowiak, and H. Taskman (eds.). (1975). *Helping families to change*. New York: Aronson.

Schlossberg, N. C. (1987). Taking the mystery out of change. *Psychology Today* 21 #5 (May):74–75.

Sheehy, G. (1974). *Passages: Predictable crises of adult life*. New York: Dutton.

Starr, B. D., and M. N. Weiner. (1980). *The Starr-Weiner report on sex and sexuality in the mature years*. New York: The Atlantic Institute.

Straus, M. A., and R. J. Gelles. (1986). Societal change and change in family violence from 1975 to 1985 as revealed in two national surveys. *Journal of Marriage and the Family* 48 #3 (Aug.):465–479.

Teachman, J., and A. Heckert. (1985). The impact of age and children on remarriage. *Journal of Family Issues* 6 (June):185–203.

Terman, L. (1938). *Psychosocial factors in marital happiness*. New York: McGraw-Hill.

Tryban, G. M. (1985). Effects of work and retirement within long-term marital relationships. *Lifestyles: A Journal of Changing Patterns* 7 #4 (Summer):207–222.

Uniform Crime Reports. Federal Bureau of Investigation. U.S. Department of Justice. Washington, D.C.: U.S. Government Printing Office, 1987.

Walker, L. E. (1984). *The battered woman syndrome*. New York: Springer-Verlag.

Watzlawick, P., J. Weakland, and R. Fisch. (1974). *Change: Principles of problem formation and problem resolution*. New York: Norton.

Weidman, A. (1986). Family therapy with violent couples. *Social Casework: The Journal of Contemporary Social Work* 67 #4 (April):211–218.

Weisman, A. (1972). Psychosocial death. *Psychology Today* 6 #6 (Nov.):77–78, 83–84, 86.

Chapter 12

Ahrons, C. (1985). Research reveals many former spouse relationships positive. *Marriage and Divorce Today* 11 #4 (Nov. 4):3–4.

_____. (1986). Perfect Pals or Fiery Foes. *American Health* (March):80.

Albrecht, S. L. (1979). Correlates of marital happiness among the remarried. *Journal of Marriage and the Family* 41:857–867.

———. (1980). Reactions and adjustment to divorce: Differences in the experiences of males and females. *Family Relations* 29:59–68.

American Chicle Youth Poll. (1987). American Children adjust to changes in traditional family structure. Reported in *Marriage and Divorce Today Newsletter* 12:1–2.

Arendell, T. (1986). *Mothers and divorce*. Berkeley, CA: University of California Press.

Baker, M. (1980). Divorce harder on women. *Marriage and Divorce Today* 6 (Dec. 15):3–4.

Baute, P. (1980). Worst form of spouse abuse: The Pearl Harbor–type attack. *Marriage and Divorce* 6 (Dec. 15):2–3.

Beal, E. (1980). Separation, divorce, and single-parent families. In *The family life cycle*, ed. E. Carter and M. McGoldrick. New York: Gardner Press.

Blair, G. (1986). Women who divorce: Are they getting a fair deal? *Woman's Day* (May 27):36, 38, 40, 44.

Bohannon, P. (1971). The six stations of divorce. In *Divorce and after*, ed. P. Bohannon, 33–62. Garden City, NY: Doubleday.

Booth, A., D. R. Johnson, L. K. White, and J. N. Edwards. (1986). Divorce and marital instability over the life course. *Journal of Family Issues* 7 #4 (Dec.):421–442.

Brandt, A. (1982). Father love. *Esquire* (Jan.):81–89.

Burke, M., and J. B. Grant. (1982). *Games divorced people play*. Englewood Cliffs: NJ: Prentice-Hall.

Chiriboga, D. A., J. Roberts, and J. A. Stein. (1978). Psychological well-being during marital separation. *Journal of Divorce* 2 (Fall):21–36.

Clay, P. L. (1981). A personal divorce ceremony. *Marriage and Divorce Today Newsletter* 5 (July 21):2.

Cleek, M. G., and T. A. Pearson. (1985). Perceived causes of divorce: An analysis of interrelationships. *Journal of Marriage and the Family* 47 #1 (Feb.):179–183.

Coogler, O. J., R. E. Weber, and P. C. McKenry. (1979). Divorce mediation: A means of facilitating divorce and adjustment. *The Family Coordinator* 28 (April):255–259.

Crossman, S. M., and J. E. Edmondson. (1985). Personal and family resources supportive of displaced homemakers; financial adjustment. *Family Relations* 34 #4 (Oct.):465–474.

Dixon, R. B., and L. J. Weitzman. (1980). Evaluating the impact of no-fault divorce in California. *Family Relations* 29 (July):297–307.

Edwards, J. N., D. R. Johnson, and A. Booth. (1987). Coming apart: A prognostic instrument of marital breakup. *Family Relations* 36 #2 (April):168–170.

Ellis, A., and M. E. Bernard. (1985). *Clinical applications of ration-emotive therapy*. New York: Plenum Press.

Espenshade, T. J. (1979). The economic consequences of divorce. *Journal of Marriage and the Family* 39 (Aug.):615–625.

Ferreiro, B. W. (1985). Joint custody after divorce—It works. *Marriage and Divorce Today Newsletter* 10 #42 (May 20):2–3.

Franke, L., et al. (1980). The children of divorce. *Newsweek* (Feb. 11):58–63.

Furstenberg, F. F., and C. Nord. (1985). Parenting apart: Patterns of childbearing after marital disruption. *Journal of Marriage and the Family* (Nov.):393–904.

Galloway, J. L., and P. A. Avery. (1984). America's forgotten resources: Grandparents. *U.S. News and World Report* (April 30):76–77.

Glenn, N. D. (1985). Children of divorce. *Psychology Today* 19 #6 (June):68–69.

———, and K. B. Kramer. (1985). The psychological well-being of adult children of divorce. *Journal of Marriage and the Family* (Nov.):905–912.

Glick, P. C. (1979). The future of the American family. *Current Population Reports*. Special Studies Series P-23, No. 78.

———. (1980). Remarriage: Some recent changes and variations. *Journal of Family Issues* 1 (Dec.):455–478.

———. (1981). Revealing insights on remarriage. *Marriage and Divorce Today* 6 (March 16):3–4.

———, and S. L. Lin. (1986). Recent changes in divorce and remarriage. *Journal of Marriage and the Family* 48 #4 (Nov.):737–747.

Goetting, A. (1979). Some societal-level explanations for the rising divorce rate. *Family Therapy* 6:72–87.

Goldfarb, B., and R. W. Libby. (1985). Mothers and children alone: The stamp of poverty. *Alternative Lifestyles* 6 #4:242–258.

Goldman, K. I. (1985). Joint custody law addresses parental involvement. *Marriage and Divorce Today* 11 #11 (Oct. 14):1–2.

Hetherington, E. M. (1979). Children and divorce. In *Divorce and Separation: Context, Causes, and Consequences*, ed. G. Levinger and O. Moles. New York: Basic Books.

Hunt, B., and M. Hunt. (1979). *The divorce experiment*. New York: McGraw-Hill.

Kando, T. (1978). *Sexual behavior and family life in transition*. New York: Elsevier Science.

Kiecolt-Glaser, J. (1986). Depression, stress and divorce take a heavy toll on the body, making it vulnerable to illness. *Behavior Today* 17 #23 (June 9):8.

Kitson, G. C., K. B. Barbri, and M. J. Roach. (1985). Who divorces and why: A review. *Journal of Family Issues* 6 #1 (Sept.):255–293.

Kitson, G. C., and M. B. Sussman. (1982). Marital complaints, demographic characteristics, and symptoms of mental distress in divorce. *Journal of Marriage and the Family* 44 (Feb.):87–115.

Koestler, A. (1954). *The invisible writing*. New York: Macmillan.

Kressel, K. (1980). Patterns of coping in divorce and some implications for clinical practice. *Family Relations* 29 (April):234–240.

———, et al. (1980). A typology of divorcing couples: Implications for mediation and the divorce process. *Family Process* 19 (June):101–116.

Laing, R. D., and A. Esterson. (1964). *Sanity, madness, and the family*. London: Tavistock.

Landis, J. T. (1962). A comparison of children from divorced and nondivorced unhappy marriages. *The Family Life Coordinator* 11:61–65.

Lazarus, A. A. (1981). Divorce counseling or marriage therapy? A therapeutic option. *Journal of Marital and Family Therapy* 7 (Jan.):15–22.

Lloyd, S. A., and C. D. Zick. (1986). Divorce at mid and later life: Does the empirical evidence support the theory? *Journal of Divorce* 9 #3 (Spring):89–102.

Lowery, C. R. (1985). Child custody in divorce: Parents' decisions and perceptions. *Family Relations* 34 (April):241–249.

———, and S. A. Settle. (1985). Effects of divorce on children: Differential impact of custody and visitation patterns. *Family Relations* 34 #4 (Oct.):455–462.

Maher, C. (1979). No-fault divorce—No rush to end marriages. *Los Angeles Times* Part V (Jan. 16):1.

Maynard, F. (1978). How to tell when it's over. *Woman's Day* (April 24):84–87*ff.*

McGrath, A. (1986). Dividing the spoils of divorce. *U.S. News and World Report* (April 7):57–58.

Meredith, D. (1985). Mom, dad and the kids. *Psychology Today* 19 #6 (June):60, 62, 64–66.

Nizer, L. (1972). *My life in court.* Benwood, WV: Pyramid.

Norton, A. J., and P. C. Glick. (1986). One-parent families: A social and economic profile. *Family Relations* 35 (Jan.):9–17.

Poor, C. (1986). Evangelicals see divorce as a common occurrence. *Marriage and Divorce Today* 11 #50 (July 14):4.

Rasmussen, P. K., and K. J. Ferraro. (1979). The divorced process. *Alternative Lifestyles* 2 (Nov.):443–460.

Richardson, L. (1979). The 'other woman': The end of the long affair. *Alternative Lifestyles* 2 (Nov.):397–414.

Risman, B. J. (1986). Can men 'mother'? Life as a single father. *Family Relations* 35 #1 (Jan.):95–102.

Rowland, H. (1980). In J. Boles. Mass media column. *Alternative Lifestyles* (Feb.):117.

Sarrel, P., and L. Sarrel. (1980). Sexual passages: How divorce affects sexuality. *Redbook* (May):19*ff.*

South, S. J. (1985). Economic conditions and the divorce rate: A time-series analysis of the postwar United States. *Journal of Marriage and the Family* 47 #1 (Feb.):31–41.

Sprenkle, D. H. (ed.). (1985). *Divorce therapy.* New York: Haworth Press.

Stack, S. (1980). The effects of marital dissolution on suicide. *Journal of Marriage and the Family* 42 (Feb.):83–92.

Thomas, C. (1976). How good is the one-parent home? *The Single Parent* 19:5–6*ff.*

U.S. Bureau of the Census. (1984). *Household and family characteristics: March, 1984.* Current Population Reports P-20, No. 398. Washington, D.C.: U.S. Government Printing Office.

Vaughn, D. (1986). *Uncoupling: Turning points in intimate relationships*. London: Oxford University Press.

Von Jares, E. (1986). Meditation. *Journal of Marriage and Family Living* 68 #4 (April):10–13.

Walker, G. (1986). *Solomon's children*. New York: Arbor House.

Wallerstein, J. (1985). Women after divorce: A preliminary report from a 10 year follow up. *American Journal of Orthopsychiatry* 56 #1:65–71.

_____. (1985). Women and divorce: Ten years after, ed. J. Fischman. *Psychology Today* 20:21–24.

_____, and J. B. Kelly. (1980a). Effects of divorce on the visiting father-child relationship. *American Journal of Psychiatry* 137:1534–1539.

_____. (1980b). *Surviving the breakup: How children and parents cope with divorce*. New York: Basic Books.

Weiss, R. S. (1975). *Marital separation*. New York: Basic Books.

Weitzman, L. (1985). *The divorce revolution*. New York: The Free Press.

Williams, R. (1977). Alimony: The short goodbye. *Psychology Today* (July):71–77ff.

Wright, G. C., and D. M. Stetson. (1978). The impact of no-fault divorce law reform in American states. *Journal of Marriage and the Family* 40 (Aug.):575–580.

Chapter 13

Adamson, W. C. (1987). Questions and answers to use in helping parents and children through the divorce process. *Marriage and Divorce Today* 12 #42 (May 18):1.

Ahrons, C. (1980). The continuing relationship between divorced spouses: Positive impact. *Marriage and Divorce Today* 5 (June 9):2–3.

Albee, G. W. (1985). The answer is prevention. *Psychology Today* 19 #2 (Feb.):60–62, 64.

Albrecht, S. L. (1979). Correlates of marital happiness among the remarried. *Journal of Marriage and the Family* 41:857–867.

_____, H. M. Bahr, and K. L. Goodman. (1983). *Divorce and remarriage: Problems, adaptations, and adjustments*. Westport, CT: Greenwood Publishing Co.

Baer, J. (1972). *The second wife: How to live happily with a man who has been married before*. Garden City, NY: Doubleday.

Beal, E. (1982). Divorce especially harmful to health of males. *Marriage and Divorce Today Newsletter* 7 (May 31):3.

Beatrice, D. K. (1979). Divorce: Problems, goals, and growth facilitation. *Social Casework* 60 (March):157–165.

Berman, W. H. (1985). Continued attachment after legal divorce. *Journal of Family Issues* 6 #3 (Sept.):375–392.

Blood, R., and M. Blood. (1979). Amicable divorce. *Alternative Lifestyles* 2:483–498.

Bloom, B. L., and K. R. Kindle. (1985). Demographic factors in the continuing relationship between former spouses. *Family Relations* 34 (July):375–381.

Bohannon, P. (1971). Divorce chains, households of remarriage, and multiple divorces. In *Divorce and after*, ed. P. Bohannon. New York: Doubleday.

Branden, N. (1987). Is there life after marriage? *Q* 2:483–498.

Brown, P., B. J. Felton, V. Whiteman, and R. Manela. (1980). Attachment and distress following separation. *Journal of Divorce* 3 (Summer):303–317.

Buehler, C., M. J. Hogan, B. Johnson, and R. J. Levy. (1986). Remarriage following divorce. *Journal of Family Issues* 7 #4 (Dec.):405–420.

Burns, C. (1985). *Stepmotherhood*. New York: Time Books.

Callahan, B. N. (1979). *Separation and divorce*. New York: Family Services Association.

Caplan, G. (1981). Mastery of stress: Psychosocial aspects. *American Journal of Psychiatry* 134 (April):413–420.

Cherlin, A. (1981). *Marriage, divorce, and remarriage. Social trends in the United States*. Cambridge, MA: Harvard University Press.

Chirboga, D., L. Catron, and P. Weiler. (1987). Childhood stress and adult functioning during marital separation. *Family Relations* 36 (April):163–166.

Clay, P. L. (1980). A personal divorce ceremony. *Marriage and Divorce Today* 5 (July):2.

Coleman, J. C., C. G. Morris, and A. G. Glaros. (1987). *Contemporary psychology and effective behavior*. 6th ed. Glenview, IL: Scott, Foresman.

Coleman, M., and L. Ganong. (1987). An evaluation of the stepfamily self-help literature for children and adolescents. *Family Relations* 36 (Jan.):61–65.

Day, R. D., and S. J. Bahr. (1986). Income change following divorce and remarriage. *Journal of Divorce* 9 #3 (Spring):75–88.

Ellis, A. (1973). Rational-emotive therapy. In *Current psychotherapies*, ed. R. Corsini. Itasca, IL: Peacock Publishers.

———. (1987). The impossibility of achieving consistently good mental health. *American Psychologist* 42 (April):364–375.

Finlayson, J. (1980). How to make it through the night—and so on. . . . *New Woman* (July–Aug.):65–66.

Fishman, S. M., and D. V. Sheehan. (1985). Anxiety and panic: Their cause and treatment. *Psychology Today* 19 #4:26–32.

Franke, L. B., et al. (1980). The children of divorce. *Newsweek* (Feb. 11):58–63.

Fromme, A. (1965). *The ability to love*. New York: Farrar, Straus & Giroux.

Furstenberg, F. F. (1980). Reflections on marriage. *Journal of Family Issues* 1 (Dec.):443–453.

———, and G. Spanier. (1984). *Recycling the family: Remarriage after divorce*. Beverly Hills, CA: Sage.

Ganong, L. H., and M. Coleman. (1986). A comparison of clinical and empirical literature on children of stepfamilies. *Journal of Marriage and the Family* 48 (May):309–318.

Gelven, M. (1973). Guilt and human meaning. *Humanitas* 9:69–81.

Glenn, N. D. (1981). The well-being of persons remarried after divorce. *Journal of Family Issues* 2 (March):61–75.

Glick, P. C. (1980). Remarriage: Some recent changes and variations. *Journal of Family Issues* 1 (Dec.):455–478.

_____. (1981). Revealing insights on remarriage. *Marriage and Divorce Today* 1 (March 16):3–4.

_____. (1985). More Americans repeatedly remarrying. *Marriage and Family Today* 10 #33 (March 18):1.

_____, and S.-L. Lin. (1986). Recent changes in divorce and remarriage. *Journal of Marriage and the Family* 48 (Nov.):737–747.

Goetting, A. (1980). Former spouse–current spouse relationships. *Journal of Family Issues* 1:58–80.

_____. (1982). The six stations of remarriage: Developmental tasks of remarriage after divorce. *Family Relations* 31 (April):213–222.

Green, L. (1981). Guide to sex and sensibility for suddenly singles. *Honolulu Star Bulletin and Advertiser* (June 21):C1.

Grollman, E., and M. Sams. (1978). *Living through your divorce*. Boston: Beacon Press.

Hanna, S., and P. Knaub. (1981). Cohabitation before marriage. *Alternative Lifestyles* 4:507–522.

Hansen, L. B., and J. F. Shireman. (1986). The process of emotional divorce: Examination of theory. *Social Casework* 67 #6 (June):323–331.

Hunt, M., and B. Hunt. (1977). After divorce: Who gets married again—and when? *Redbook* (Oct.):106–114.

_____. (1979). *The divorce experiment*. New York: McGraw-Hill.

Janis, I. L., and I. Mann. (1977). *Decision making*. New York: Free Press.

Johnson, B. H. (1985). Single mothers following separation and divorce: Making it on your own. *Family Relations* 35 (Jan.):189–197.

Jones, W. H., S. A. Hobbs, and D. Hockenbury. (1982). Loneliness and social skill deficits. *Journal of Personality and Social Psychology* 42:682–689.

Juhasz, A. (1979). A concept of divorce. *Alternative Lifestyles* 2:471–482.

Khoo, H., and C. M. Suchindran. (1980). Effects of children on women's remarriage prospects. *Journal of Family Issues* 1:497–515.

Kitson, G. C. (1982). Attachment to the spouse in divorce: A scale and its application. *Journal of Marriage and the Family* 44 (May):379–393.

Kohne, J. A. (1981). From wife to family head: Transitions in self-identity. *Psychiatry* 44 (Aug.):230–240.

Kosner, A. (1979). Starting over: What divorced women discover. *McCalls* (March):22–28*ff*.

Krantzler, M. (1978). Demographic and attitude shifts are leveling divorce rates. *Behavior Today* 9 (July 10):2.

Kressel, K. (1980). Patterns on coping in divorce and some implications for clinical practice. *Family Relations* 29 (April):234–240.

Lagoni, L. S., and A. Skinner. (1985). Stepfamilies: A content analysis of the popular literature, 1961–1982. *Family Relations* 34 #4 (Oct.):521–525.

Levy, T., and W. Joffe. (1978). Counseling couples through separation: A developmental approach. *Family Therapy* 5:267–276.

Livingston, P. (1980). Divorce: The darkness and the gift. *Marriage and Divorce Today* 6 (Aug. 18):1–2.

Lynch, J. J. (1977). *The broken heart: The medical consequences of loneliness.* New York: Basic Books.

———. (1980). Warning: Living alone is dangerous to your health. *U.S. News and World Report* (June 30):47–48.

Meer, J. (1985). Loneliness. *Psychology Today* 19 #7 (July):28–33.

Mills, D. M. (1986). Fitting in: The challenge of stepparenting. *Marriage and Family Living* 68 #2 (Feb.):22–24.

Moustakas, C. (1961). *Loneliness.* Englewood Cliffs, NJ: Prentice-Hall.

Norton, A. J., and J. E. Moorman. (1987). Current trends in marriage and divorce among American women. *Journal of Marriage and the Family* 49 (Feb.):3–14.

Oh, S. (1986). Remarried men and remarried women: How are they different? *Journal of Divorce* 9 #4 (Summer):107–113.

Overend, W. (1977). What to do when it's over. *Los Angeles Times* Part V (July 10):1.

Petronio, S., and T. Endres. (1986). Dating issues: How single mothers and single fathers differ with full-time children in the household. *Journal of Divorce* 9 #4 (Summer):79–87.

Rosenberg, E., and F. Haja. (1985). Stepsibling relationships in remarried families. *Social Casework* 66 #5 (May):587–592.

Rothstein, R. (1986). My mom, the merry widow. *50 Plus* 26 #7 (July):66–67.

Rubenstein, C. M., and P. Shaver. (1982). *In search of intimacy.* New York: Delacorte Press.

———, and L. A. Peplau. (1979). Loneliness. *Human Nature* 2 (Feb.):58–65.

Sanderson, J. (1980). Liberated male: Disaster an instant affair. *Los Angeles Times* Part V (Sept. 21):12.

Scarf, M. (1980). The promiscuous woman. *Psychology Today* (July):78–87.

Schnall, M. (1979). Learning to love again. *Woman's Day* (May 22):56–62.

Schwartz, W. A. (1986). Fitting in: The challenge of stepparenting. *Marriage and Family Living* 68 #2 (Feb.):22–24.

Seskin, J. (1985). When older women marry younger men. *Woman's Day* (April 30):82–83.

Simos, B. (1979). *A time to grieve: Loss as a universal human experience.* New York: Family Services Association.

Spanier, G., and F. Furstenberg. (1982). Remarriage after divorce: A longitudinal analysis of well-being. *Journal of Marriage and the Family* 44:709–720.

Spanier, G., and P. Glick. (1980). Paths to remarriage. *Journal of Divorce* 3:283–298.

Stanton, G. W. (1987). The special plight of children in stepfamilies. *Marriage and Divorce Today Newsletter* 12 #25 (Jan. 19):2.

Stone, J. (1986). The marriage go-round. *Health* 18 #10 (Oct.):54–60.

USNWR. (1986–1987). For those with a stepchild. *U.S. News and World Report* (Dec. 29, 1986–Jan. 5, 1987):95.

Wald, E. (1981). *The remarried family.* New York: Family Service Association of America.

Wallenstein, J., and J. B. Kelly. (1980). *Surviving the breakup: How children and parents cope with divorce.* New York: Basic Books.

Weingarten, H. (1980). Remarriage and well-being. *Journal of Family Issues* 1:553–559.

White, L., and A. Booth. (1985). The quality and stability of remarriages: The role of stepchildren. *American Sociological Review* (Oct.):689–698.

Whiteside, M. (1982). Remarriage: A family developmental process. *Journal of Marriage and Family Therapy* 8 (April):59–68.

Willison, M. M. (1979). How to deal with an unhappy marriage. *Family Weekly* (Oct.):6–8.

Chapter 14

Berne, E. (1964). *Games people play: The psychology of human relationships.* New York: Grove Press.

Blanc, A. K. (1987). The formation and dissolution of second unions: Marriage and cohabitation in Sweden and Norway. *Journal of Marriage and the Family* 49 (May):391–400.

———. (1972). *What do you say after you say hello?* New York: Grove Press.

Branwyn, G. (1986). Gaming. Simulating future realities. *The Futurist* 20 #1 (Jan.–Feb.):29–35.

Cetron, M. (1983). Serial monogamy: The matrimonial pattern of the future. *Marriage and Divorce Today* 8 (March):3.

Cherlin, A., and F. Furstenberg. (1983). The American family in the year 2000. *The Futurist* (June):7–14.

Cornish, E. (1979). The future of the family: Intimacy in an age of loneliness. *The Futurist* (Feb.):45–58.

———. (1985). Outlook '86—and beyond. *The Futurist* 19 #6 (Dec.):51–60.

———. (1987). The great transformation. *The Futurist* 21 #2 (March–April):2, 58.

Ellis, A. (1973). Rational-emotive therapy. In *Current psychotherapies*, ed. R. J. Corsini. Itasca, IL: Peacock Publishers.

———. (1986). Mental health: Not predictable but possible. *APA Monitor* (Oct.):34.

———. (1987). The impossibility of achieving consistently good mental health. *American Psychologist* 42 #4 (April):364–375.

———, and R. Harper. (1961). *Creative marriage.* New York: Lyle Stuart.

Engel, J. W., L. J. Mathews, and V. Halverson. (1985). *Marriage and family counseling in Hawaii: A consumer's guide.* Honolulu, HI: University of Hawaii Press.

Etzioni, A. (1980). Rehashing the seventies. *Society* 17 (Jan.–Feb.):12–13.

Featherstone, J. (1979). Family matters. *Harvard Educational Review* 49 (Feb.):20–52.

Francoeur, R. T. (1984). Moral concepts in the year 2020: The individual, the family, and society. In *Marriage and the family in the year 2020*, ed. L. A. Kirkendall and A. E. Gravatt, 183–204. Buffalo, NY: Prometheus Books.

Melton, G. B. (1987). The clashing of symbols. Prelude to child and family policy. *American Psychologist* 42 #4 (April):345–354.

Ministry of Labor. (1985). *Side by side: A report on equality between men and women in Sweden, 1985*. Stockholm: Gotab.

Popenoe, D. (1987). Beyond the nuclear family: A statistical portrait of the changing family in Sweden. *Journal of Marriage and the Family* 49 (Feb.):173–183.

Renfro, W. L. (1987). Future histories: A new approach to scenarios. *The Futurist* 21 #2 (March–April):38–41.

Ringen, S. (1985). *Difference and similarity: Two studies in comparative income distribution*. Stockholm, Sweden: Instititet Forskning.

Schaar, J. (1974). *Footnotes to the future*. Washington, D.C.: Futuremics, Inc.

Skolnick, A. (1981). The family and its discontents. *Society* 18 (Jan.–Feb.):42–47.

Troust, J. (1985). Marriage and nonmarital cohabitation. In *The Noridic family: Perspective on family research*, ed. J. Rogers and H. Norman, 109–119. Upsalla: Upsalla University, Department of History.

Wagner, C. G. (1986). Future focus. A collective search for solution. *The Futurist* 20 #6 (Nov.–Dec.): 29–37.

GLOSSARY

Abstinence   Voluntarily doing without sex. *See also* Masturbation.

Acceptance   Not taking a judgmental attitude toward another person.

Accommodation   Adjusting your expectations of marriage to realistic levels following disillusionment.

Achilles' heel   Special vulnerability to a specific type of stress.

Adjustment   Outcome of an individual's efforts to meet personal needs and environmental demands.

Agape   *See* Styles of loving.

Alienation   Situation that results when people feel they can no longer influence their social world, and hence become "aliens" in a hostile environment.

Ambivalence   Simultaneous existence of contradictory emotional attitudes toward the same person; for example, love and hate.

Androgynous   Traditional masculine and feminine characteristics shown in an individual.

Anger   Common reaction to interference with our needs; often associated with marital violence.

Angry Associates   Way in which divorced parents relate, communicating only about the children and being quick to argue.

Anxiety   Vague feeling of apprehension about possible failures, setbacks, losses, and other poorly defined potential difficulties; often elicited by threat.

Assumed similarity   Assumption that other people are very much like ourselves. *See also* Implicit personality theory.

Attachment   Condition characterized by intense bonding. Attachment may continue after other aspects of love have faded.

Aversive conditioning   Learning that a given act has painful or socially disapproved consequences and is to be avoided.

Awareness   Seeing things the way they are; having a realistic view of yourself, your partner, and of the relationship.

Behavioral marital therapy   Form of marital therapy based on the assumption that marital conflicts result from one or both partners engaging in behavior that is aversive to the other.

Bisexuals   Persons sexually attracted to both males and females.

Body language   Posture, acting bored, speaking in a monotone, and other aspects of nonverbal communication that influence the other person whether you are receiving or sending a message.

Caring   Concern for the well-being of another person.

Casual dating   Stage in courtship that involves informal meetings, such as getting together during coffee breaks or for lunch. Expenses are usually shared by the male and female. *See also* Traditional dating.

Casual sex   Sexual intercourse that does not involve emotional closeness.

Cohabitation   Arrangement whereby couples live together without benefit of a marriage contract, sometimes as an alternative to marriage and sometimes as a trial marriage.

Commitment   Avowed or inferred intent of each partner to maintain a relationship.

Commune   Three or more persons who associate voluntarily to establish a way of life; communes and the marital arrangements they sanction are varied.

Communication   Sending or receiving information; may use verbal or nonverbal means.

Companionate love   Love involving deep attachment and friendly affection; commonly follows when romantic love fades.

Comparison level   In social-exchange theory, standards against which we evaluate our present encounters and relationships.

Compatibility   How two people get along, or fit in terms of personality.

Complementarity   Sometimes called the attraction of opposites: occurs when one person's resources compensate for the other's lack; also known as need complementarity.

Complete love   In Sternberg's Triangular Theory of Love, involves intense and relatively equal measures of passion, intimacy, and commitment.

Conflict   Simultaneous arousal of opposing impulses, desires, or motives.

Conscience   Functioning of an individual's system of moral values in the approval or disapproval of his or her own thoughts or actions; in essence, inner control of behavior.

Continuum   Measurement of a characteristic on a continuous scale from an extreme low point to an extreme high point—for example, height from extremely short to extremely tall.

Cooperative Colleagues   Way in which divorced parents relate, getting along well but focusing their interactions around the children.

Costs   Any negatively valued consequences incurred by a person in a relationship.

Courtship   Process of selecting a mate in our society; usually follows sequence from casual dating to serious dating, engagement or cohabitation, and marriage.

Crisis   Stress situation that approaches or exceeds the adaptive capacities of the individual or group.

Date rape   Use of physical force to obtain sexual intercourse; often alcohol or drugs are involved and may be used to assist or in place of physical force.

Denial   Self-protective reaction many people use to screen out the hurtful reality of past, present, or anticipated future events—such as impending death.

Depression   Complex emotion characterized by sadness, self-blame, and repetitive thoughts about what might have been.

Differential association   Seeing and interacting with a certain person or persons to a much greater extent than with other people.

Disengaged pattern of divorce   Couple has drifted apart until there is nothing left to sustain the relationship. *See also* Patterns of divorce.

Disillusionment   After the honeymoon, stage in which members of a marriage discover that their hopes and expectations are not going to be realized. *See also* Accommodation.

Disqualifiers   Characteristics in others that people avoid when looking for a mate; also called mate-selection filters.

Diversionary tactics   Subtle ways of changing or avoiding the topic of conversation.

Divorce mediation   Mediation by an arbitrator, resulting in a divorce settlement that is then presented to a court for approval. *See also* Traditional divorce.

Divorced parents   Found to relate in four different ways: Perfect Pals, Cooperative Colleagues, Angry Associates, and Fiery Foes.

Divorce therapy   Therapy designed to enable a couple to divorce with a minimum of emotional and financial damage but also to salvage their marriage if possible. *See also* Marital therapy.

Double bind   Situation in which an individual will be disapproved for performing a certain act and disapproved if he or she does not perform it.

Double standard   Allows men to enjoy sex and engage in premarital and extramarital affairs but does not permit women to do so.

Dual-career marriage   Marriage in which each partner is committed to the marriage but also to pursuing a career.

Dual-earner marriage   Marriage in which each partner is employed in the labor force; the wife usually works because of economic necessity.

Dual-worker marriage   Marriage in which each partner is employed in the labor force; many wives work part time, depending on financial need and other circumstances.

Ecology   Field of science that deals with the relationship between living organisms and their environment.

Egalitarian marriage   Marriage involving greater sex-role equality in decision making, with both partners sharing in financial support, home-making, and child-rearing.

Empty nest   Time in a relationship when the last child leaves home and the parents are confronted with the problem of readjusting to each other without the child or children.

Endogamy   Marriage within the same social category.

Ethnic group   Subgroup of people with their own shared cultural heritage who are regarded as socially distinct.

Extended family   Family in which more than two generations of the same kinship line live together.

Engagement   Final stage in courtship; usually involves the exclusive commitment to a partner by a public announcement of intention to marry.

Enmeshed pattern of divorce   Characterized by the ambivalence of both partners to obtaining a divorce; the decision drags out but is eventually resolved.

Equity theory   Concept that people are most comfortable in a relationship when they think it is a fair one in which they are getting what they deserve.

Eros   *See* Styles of loving.

Expressive characteristics   Traditionally feminine traits such as nurturance, compassion, and affection.

Family   Relatively permanent group of people who live together, function as an economic unit, and rear their children; members may be related by marriage or other bonds.

Family system   When a child is born, the marital relationship changes; the ways in which mother, father, and baby work out these changes is the family system.

Family therapy   Very similar to marital therapy (*see also*), but focused on improving the family system.

Feedback   Response you get from the person who has received your message.

Fellatio   *See* Oral–genital sex.

Feminization of poverty   About 90 percent of single-parent families are headed by mothers, most of whom lack the occupational skills to be good providers; as a result, the family faces severe financial hardship.

Fiery Foes   Way in which divorced parents relate, avoiding each other and often trying to force the children to choose sides.

Foreplay   Prelude to sexual intercourse rather than an end in itself; a common complaint of married women is that their husbands do not engage in sufficient foreplay.

Free-enterprise relationship   Futuristic view of marriage in which no license is required and the marriage can be terminated without divorce.

Frigidity   Inability of a woman to experience sexual pleasure and orgasm; older term that has been replaced by inhibited sexual excitement.

Fundamental attribution error   Attributing another person's behavior to his or her personality makeup rather than to the situation that may have elicited the behavior.

Future shock   Condition brought about when social change is so rapid that the individual cannot cope effectively; in essence, the future has arrived too soon.

Gay marriage   Commitment by two persons of the same sex to live together as a married couple; although not legal, a ceremony may be performed by a member of the clergy.

Gender identity   Person's subjective feeling of being male or female regardless of his or her actual sex.

Gender roles   Behaviors, obligations, and privileges that society considers appropriate for each sex; roughly synonymous with sex-roles.

General systems theory   Comprehensive approach to the behavior of living systems, from individuals to nations; the focus is on the structural, functional, and field properties of the system being studied.

Global measure   Way of assessing marital happiness; consists of asking one or both partners how happy he or she considers the marriage to be.

Grief   Psychological distress following a loss, may vary in intensity and duration; often includes feelings of depression, anger, and guilt; anxiety also common.

Griefwork   Period of mourning required for a person to adjust psychologically to his or her loss, for example, the death of a mate.

Ground rules   Structure of a relationship in terms of goals, roles and responsibilities, and standards of satisfaction.

Guilt   Intensely unpleasant emotion characterized by blaming yourself for an unfortunate event; usually intermixed with remorse and self-recrimination.

Halo effect   Distorts first impressions because you focus on a single characteristic that you particularly like or dislike; this reaction then affects your response to the person's other characteristics, without your awareness.

High-risk group   Group showing high vulnerability to a particular mental or physical disorder, or proneness to a given type of behavior, for example, divorce prone.

Homogamy   Marriage between two persons who share similar social characteristics.

Homosexuals   Persons who prefer to have sexual relations with members of the same sex. *See also* Bisexuals.

Honeymoon   Transitional period that enables a couple, in privacy, to make the transition from being single to being a married couple. *See also* Disillusionment.

Implicit personality theory   Based on your own experience and assumptions about human nature and used to evaluate new acquaintances; closely related to assumed similarity.

Impotence   *See* Inhibited sexual excitement.

Inhibited orgasm   Sexual dysfunction; in men, the inability to trigger an ejaculation or extreme difficulty in doing so; in women, the most common female dysfunction, called primary orgasmic dysfunction.

Incest taboo   Profound moral prohibition against sexual contact between parents and their children and other categories of relatives.

Infatuation   Intense romantic relationship, usually brief, and characterized by wishful thinking and disregard of realistic considerations.

Inhibited sexual excitement   Sexual dysfunction; in men, the inability to achieve or maintain an erection, formerly called impotence; in women, an absence or insufficiency of sexual response, formerly called frigidity.

Interactive disqualification   Situation that arises when two people have everything going for them but lack compatibility or personality fit.

Interdependence   Sharing of responsibilities and decision making in marriage; however, partner with greater expertise in a given area may make the decision in that area.

Institution   Stable cluster of norms, values, roles and statuses, and groups that develop around and focus on a basic social need.

Instrumental characteristics   Traditionally masculine traits such as competitiveness, aggressiveness, and courage. *See also* Expressive characteristics.

Jealousy   Feelings of being left out of some personal interest or activity in your partner's life; fear of losing love.

Joint custody   Form of child custody in which both parents share in caring for and raising the children, not necessarily in equal degrees.

Latchkey children   Children who arrive home after school before either parent returns from work.

Lesbian   Female homosexual.

Ludus   *See* Styles of loving.

Loneliness   Basic sense of unconnectedness with people; chronic loneliness results from the inability to form meaningful relationships with others; situational loneliness is usually temporary.

Maladaptive behavior   Behavior that is detrimental to the individual and/or the group.

Mania   *See* Styles of loving.

Marital conflicts   Disagreements that arise as a result of incompatible needs, goals, and expectations.

Marital counseling   *See* Marital therapy.

Marital happiness Somewhat intangible condition based on the subjective evaluation of each marital partner as to whether the marriage is or is not a happy one.

Marital stability Probability that the marriage will continue; in social exchange theory, the marriage is considered stable when neither partner perceives a better alternative.

Marital stress Encompasses marital conflicts and also adjustive demands such as serious illness, loss of employment, and career problems.

Marital therapy Primarily designed to assist couples in coping with their problems, but not to preserve the marriage at all costs; also called marital counseling.

Marriage Legal and socially approved mating arrangement between husband, wife, and state; marriage confers certain duties and privileges on the marital couple.

Marriage enrichment Programs designed for happily married couples to anticipate problems and take immediate corrective measures, and to promote growth of the marriage.

Marriage market In social-exchange theory, the marriage market consists of places and activities where eligible males and females can meet.

Market value According to social-exchange theory, what a person has to offer others in the interpersonal marketplace.

Mass media Television, newspapers, magazines, and other forms of communication that reach a large audience without any personal contact between sender and receiver.

Masturbation Self-stimulation for sexual gratification; a form of abstinence.

Mate selection filters Successive barriers that screen out potential mates until the field is narrowed to a few from which the person chooses.

Menopause Cessation of ovulation, menstruation, and fertility in the woman; menopause usually occurs between the ages of 45 and 50.

Metacommunication Typical ways in which two people communicate with each other.

Midlife crisis Occurring between the ages of the late thirties and early sixties, but not in everyone's life; a period of re-evaluation of marriage and career.

Models Analogies that help scientists order their findings and see important relationships.

Modern marriage Marriage in which the husband and wife share equally in decisions about power and responsibility.

Monogamy Marriage that involves one spouse of each sex.

Moralistic societies Societies that approve of sex for procreation only and forbid sex for pleasure, especially for women.

Mutual liking Our response to persons who like us; we tend to like them in return.

Naturalistic societies Societies that view sex as a normal activity to be cultivated and enjoyed, usually by women as well as men. *See also* Moralistic societies.

Need Biological or psychological condition that must be met to keep inner-body conditions within a range essential for normal development and functioning.

Need complementarity *See* Complementarity.

Negotiation Discussing or bargaining with the intent of reaching an agreement; common method of settling marital conflicts.

No-fault divorce Legal dissolution of a marriage without proof of fault by either partner. *See also* Traditional divorce.

Nonmutual pattern of divorce Divorce wanted by only one partner and usually harmful to the other; the most common pattern.

Nonverbal messages Facial expressions, gestures, vocal inflections, pauses, touches, and body language that convey affective information.

Norms Shared values or guidelines that specify the behavior appropriate in a given situation.

Open marriage Marriage in which the partners are committed to their own and each other's growth along with each other, rather than exclusively through each other, as in closed marriage.

Oral–genital sex   Oral stimulation of a partner's genitals; oral stimulation of the female is cunnilingus; of the male, fellatio.

Orgasm   Climax of the sex act, characterized in men by the ejaculation of sperm; in women, by rhythmic contractions of the lower body.

Overgeneralize   Form a global evaluation of another person based on inadequate information.

Overloading   When the adjustive demands confronting a person strain his or her coping resources; often used to refer to the role strain experienced by working married women.

Parent burnout   Result of the stress of parenting, particularly among middle-class parents who try to be Supermoms and Superdads.

Pathogenic families   Marital relationships that lead to faulty development and behavior on the part of their offspring.

Patterns of divorce   Three patterns of divorce have been identified: the enmeshed pattern, the nonmutual pattern, and the disengaged pattern.

Perfect Pals   Way in which divorced parents relate, enjoying spending time together and sharing activities with their children.

Performance anxiety   Worry over how or whether you will perform in a sexual situation; cause of sexual dysfunction.

Personal marriage contract   Separate legal agreement made by a couple before their wedding, setting forth their understanding of various arrangements about property, income, child custody, and so forth. *See also* Marriage.

Personality   Relatively stable pattern of thoughts, feelings, and actions characteristic of a given individual.

Petting   Erotic caressing of another person, sometimes to the point of orgasm.

Platonic love   Transcendental or spiritual form of love, usually involving two men, in which ecstasy is achieved by nonsexual adoration; ideal of the ancient Greeks.

Polygamy   Marriage involving a spouse of one sex and two or more legal spouses of the other sex.

Post-retirement marriage   Marital relationship following the retirement of one or both marital partners; often requires major adjustments by marital partners.

Power   Ability to control the behavior of others with or without their consent and to refuse to meet unacceptable demands of others.

Prejudice   Negative, irrational, and inflexible attitude toward members of a specific group or category of others.

Premarital counseling   Counseling of couples before marriage, usually to increase their ability to communicate with each other, explore possible areas of discord, or solve sexual problems.

Premature ejaculation   Inability of a man to control ejaculation long enough for his partner to achieve sexual satisfaction.

Pressure   Adjustive demand that requires the individual to speed up, intensify, or change the direction of goal-oriented behavior.

Profession   Occupation that requires extensive training in or systematic knowledge of an art or science.

Random sample   Sample selected so that each member of the population in question has the same chance of being selected; roughly equivalent to representative sample.

Rational-emotive therapy   Form of marital therapy aimed at revealing the irrational beliefs that partners have about themselves and each other.

Reciprocity   Mutual self-disclosure; when one person discloses personal information, the other responds in kind.

Resource theory   Offshoot of social-exchange theory that emphasizes the resources each person brings to the relationship—for example, money, attractiveness, or warmth.

Rewards   Any positively valued consequence that a person gains from an encounter or relationship; when the rewards outweigh the costs, the outcome is a profit. *See also* Social-exchange theory.

Role   Behavior patterns attached to a particular position and status in society; failure to conform to role expectations may result in loss of the position.

Role obsolescence   Term used to describe what happens when someone reaches retirement age, and in our society is usually considered to have outlived his or her usefulness.

Role performance   Actual behavior of a person playing a particular role; extent to which a person's behavior conforms to role expectations.

Role-sharing dual-career marriage   Dual-career marriage in which both partners share the work of home-making and child care.

Role strain   Excessive stress resulting from trying to play too many roles at once, such as women in dual-career marriages who accept traditional male–female sex-roles; also, attempting to play a role for which you are not qualified.

Romantic love   In Sternberg's Triangular Theory of Love, balance of passion, intimacy, and commitment in ample and about-equal measure.

Self   Individual's experience of having a distinct personal identity; central reference point around which experiences and actions are organized.

Self-concept   Individual's evaluation of his or her identity, capabilities, limitations, and worth; negative self-concept can be highly detrimental to the person.

Self-disclosure   Revealing personal information to another person.

Self-esteem   Value a person places on himself or herself; applying standards we use in evaluating others to assessing our own worth.

Self-fulfilling prophecy   Prediction leading to behavior that makes the prediction come true.

Self-fulfillment   Actualizing your potential and aspirations, and becoming the best that you are capable of becoming.

Self-help group   Volunteer community or church-backed workshop made up of persons who have been in your situation. *See also* Social support systems.

Self-identity   Individual's perception of who he or she is apart from all other people; clear sense of self-identity provides a feeling of continuity over time.

Self-monitoring scale   Device to gauge people's ability to monitor the impression they are making on others.

Serial marriage   Marriage followed by divorce and remarriage *ad seriatum*.

Serial monogamy   Practice of marrying more than once by divorcing and remarrying; roughly equivalent to serial polygamy.

Serious dating   *See* Courtship.

Sexual fantasy   Indulging in fantasies about sex when daydreaming or during actual sexual encounters; such fantasies are usually sexually stimulating.

Sexual intercourse   Vaginal intercourse between heterosexuals.

Sexual response sequence   Its four stages are excitement, which includes foreplay; the plateau phase; the orgasm; and resolution, a physiological return to normal.

Sexual revolution   Name given to the change in the United States in the 1960s and 1970s, which made it a more naturalistic society and led to greater permissiveness in sex.

Sexual script   Similar to the script for a play that contains the instructions for each actor; a person may write his or her own sexual script based on experience.

Sexual sensitivity   Being aware of your partner's desires, making needed adjustments, and planning your shared sex life.

Sex-roles   Society's expectations of how males and females should behave.

Sexually transmitted diseases (STDs)   Include AIDS, genital herpes, and *Chlamydia trachomatis*, the most common infection.

Sexual-values system   Sexual behavior that is approved or disapproved by society and by the individual.

Similarity   Accounts for our attraction to people who are like ourselves in physical, mental, and emotional characteristics and have similar backgrounds and values; this is called the theory of homogamy.

Singles   People who have never married or who are separated, divorced, or widowed.

Single-parent families   Composed of at least one child under 18 and only one parent, usually the mother. *See also* Feminization of poverty.

Social-exchange theory   Based on the idea that relationships are formed to meet individual needs and that they are trading situations in which costs are balanced against rewards. *See also* Equity theory and Resource theory.

Socialization   Process of a person's learning the skills, knowledge, and roles essential for competent and socially acceptable behavior in a given society.

Social-support system   Agencies, largely private or voluntary but also governmental, available to help individuals, couples, and families to cope with problems, and, especially, crises; also personal arrangements made by working mothers and others to provide help in time of trouble or difficulty. *See also* Self-help group.

Social sciences   Fields in science focusing on understanding, predicting, and, to some extent, controlling human behavior.

Social structure   Basic components and their interrelationships in a social system.

Sociology   Field of science devoted to the study of human society and social behavior.

Stepfamilies   Remarriages in which one or both spouses have offspring from a previous marriage; also known as blended, remarried, and reconstituted families.

Stereotypes   Oversimplified but widely shared beliefs about groups of people that are applied to all members of a group without considering the differences among them.

Storge   *See* Styles of loving.

Styles of communication   Basic styles of communication are thought to be complementary, or flexible; conventional, or small talk; speculative, or analytic; controlling, or persuasive and dictatorial; and contactful, or sharing.

Styles of loving   Classification advanced by John Lee and including six types: (1) eros, passionate love; (2) storge, companionate love; (3) ludus, playful sexuality; (4) mania, possessive love; (5) pragma, love that has a practical basis; and (6) agape, unselfish love. *See also* Romantic love.

Styles of marriage   Classified by Cuber and Harroff into conflict-habituated; devitalized; passive-congenial; vital; and total.

Symbolic-interaction theory   Emphasizes the interaction between people in terms of symbols, such as signs, gestures, language, shared rules, and social roles.

Stress   Any adjustive demand that requires coping behavior on the part of the individual; stress may vary in severity from mild to excessive.

Taboo   Powerful social belief that some specific act will have aversive consequences and is to be avoided; example is the incest taboo.

Technology   Practical application of scientific or other knowledge; usually based on scientific research findings.

Theories   More comprehensive than models, having a more clearly formulated and agreed-on structure.

Third Wave   Alvin Toffler's term for the transformation of our society from an industrial age to an information age.

Threat   Anticipation of harm that usually arouses anxiety; often the actual source of the threat is not clearly perceived.

Traditional dating   Social arrangement, part of courtship, in which the male plays the dominant role, inviting the female to join him and paying the expenses; part of traditional courtship.

Traditional divorce   In the United States, adversarial judicial procedure that required one partner to prove the other guilty of such transgressions as adultery, desertion, or cruelty.

Traditional dual-career marriage   Dual-career marriage in which the wife assumes responsibility for the home and children.

Traditional marriage   Marriage in which the husband is the breadwinner and the wife the homemaker.

Transactional analysis   Form of marital therapy designed to help the couple react as one adult to another.

Transitional dual-career marriage   Dual-career marriage in which the husband actively assists in child care but not in household chores.

Trauma   In the social sciences, an intensely painful emotional experience, often producing a lasting psychic effect or wound.

Trial marriage   Cohabitation entered into as a way of determining whether a marriage would be successful.

Wedding   Public act involving a legal contract that marks a rite of passage from singlehood to marriage.

INDEX